PEDIATRIC HOME CARE

A Comprehensive Approach

Edited by

Patricia A. McCoy, RN, MSN, MBA
Director of Quality Assurance
20th Tactical Fighter Wing Hospital
Upper Heyford, England

Wendy L. Votroubek, RN, MPH
Clinical Nurse Specialist, Pediatric Pulmonary
University Medical Center
Tucson, Arizona

AN ASPEN PUBLICATION®
Aspen Publishers, Inc.
Gaithersburg, Maryland
1990

Library of Congress Cataloging-in-Publication Data

Pediatric home care: a comprehensive approach/edited by
Patricia A. McCoy, Wendy L. Votroubek.
p. cm.
"An Aspen publication."
Includes bibliographical references.
ISBN: 0-8342-0096-1
1. Pediatric nursing. 2. Chronically ill children--Home care.
I. McCoy, Patricia A. II. Votroubek, Wendy L.
[DNLM: 1. Home Care Services--nurses' instruction.
2. Pediatric Nursing. WY 159 P3695]
RJ245.P384   1989   610.73'62--dc20   DNLM/DLC
for Library of Congress
89-17914
CIP

The authors have made every effort to ensure the accuracy of the information herein,
particularly with regard to drug selection and dose. However, appropriate information
sources should be consulted, especially for new or unfamiliar drugs or procedures. It is the
responsibility of every practitioner to evaluate the appropriateness of a particular
opinion in the context of actual clinical situations and with due consideration to new
developments. Authors, editors, and the publisher cannot be held responsible for any
typographical or other errors found in this book.

Editorial Services: Mary Beth Roesser
Lisa J. McCullough

Library of Congress Catalog Card Number: 89-17914
ISBN: 0-8342-0096-1

Printed in Canada

1 2 3 4 5

To all children in the homes who have touched our lives

Table of Contents

Foreword

Children with complex medical needs have the right to a home and all the attending love and support that come from being part of a family. Our society must strive toward assisting families of these children so that this is possible. Caring for children with complex medical needs at home is often a complex and difficult task and requires the coordinated efforts of many persons. Family members and professionals must work together as partners, at times developing new skills and attitudes, to care for these children.

The Surgeon General of the United States has highlighted the need for a family-centered approach to health care as part of a national agenda. In this call for action, there are seven important steps needed to achieve family-centered community-based care for children with special health care needs.

1. Pledge a national commitment to all children with special health care needs and to their families.
2. Encourage building community-based service systems.
3. Assist in ensuring adequate preparation of care providers.
4. Develop coalitions to improve the delivery of services.
5. Establish guidelines to control costs of services.
6. Encourage and support the development of adequate health care financing.
7. Continue to conduct research and to disseminate information.

The system is faced with a significant challenge in achieving this goal for children with complex health care needs. We must increase the capability of families, professionals, and the community to provide the needed services. We must increase our ability to develop realistic, functional, and coordinated home care plans for these children and their families. We must assure a comprehensive continuum of quality services that are uniformly available to families.

Significant training and service needs must be met to reach these objectives. Professionals must be trained to respect the role of families in the care of their children, to adapt their skills to fit the care of children in the home, and to provide advocacy for these services. Service systems must be improved to establish community-based, coordinated services. Care management represents a serious and important aspect of the service system that must be reviewed. Tertiary and community-based health services must develop adequate communication and service patterns. And most importantly, there must be adequate financing for these services so that families can maintain their usual standard of living and not become ''health poor'' because of a system that favors health care in the hospitals.

This book represents an outstanding resource in addressing some of these issues. Providing home care for children with complex medical needs requires an array of resources and new skills, which are presented in the chapters that follow. I commend the editors and the contributors for providing a comprehensive discussion of the theoretical and practical aspects of caring for these children. This extremely pertinent information will benefit all of us.

Phyllis R. Magrab, PhD
Professor, Pediatrics
Georgetown University, Washington, DC

Preface

This book was conceived as a method of filling a need we discovered in our efforts to provide quality pediatric home care. We searched for and could not find a single source document that provided not only technical guidance but also information on growth and development and the impacts of home care on the family. We needed a reference intended specifically for pediatric care in the home that was comprehensive, easy to use, and well organized.

This book provides the type of reference material we were searching for. It is a comprehensive reference for nurses specializing in pediatric care in the home. It is a valuable tool for discharge planners and social workers involved in the rapidly expanding field of home care. It also will be of interest to parents whose children are receiving care in the home for an illness that, until recently, would have required inpatient treatment. Agencies and hospitals developing home care programs will find the information presented valuable in discharge planning and in developing care plans for a wide range of pediatric patients.

This book is unique in several respects. It is the first reference for the home care nurse that provides technical guidance as well as information on growth and development and family considerations for children with chronic illnesses. It is intended for daily use and reference and is organized by clinical systems. The practitioner is provided with information on technology, social concerns, growth and development, and family interaction in addition to clinical guidance. The care plans, based on nursing diagnosis, provide concise guidelines for many home care issues. The contributors and the editors are experienced in home health care and thus the text is their expertise. Many persons on the leading edge of clinical and social developments for home care of pediatric patients have helped develop the first comprehensive pediatric home care reference. We hope it helps in your efforts to provide quality care.

Acknowledgments

A book of this scope could not have been completed without the assistance of many colleagues, friends, and family members. Specifically, we thank the contributing authors for producing chapters that help share their expertise with the nursing profession. We also thank Darlene Como, formerly editorial director at Aspen Publishers, Inc., for her patience and enthusiasm in helping us complete this manuscript.

We are grateful for the talents of Nora Voutas for her artistic work on the range of motion illustrations and of Anne Goldman for her invaluable secretarial assistance in preparing this manuscript. We also thank Robin Klaehn, regional director, and Faith Barry, branch manager, of Medical Personnel Pool, Inc. for their insight and encouragement.

Finally, we express very warm and special thanks to Cliff Massengill and Catharine Drozdowski, who consistently offered moral support and helped renew our enthusiasm for this project. They helped review various chapters and provided editorial comments. Without their support, we could not have completed this project.

Contributors

Lynn R. Anderson, RN, MS
Assistant Patient Care Manager—Nurseries
Tucson Medical Center
Tucson, AZ

Patricia A. Edwards, RN, MA, CNAA
Assistant Professor and Curriculum
  Coordinator
Department of Nursing
Simmons College
Boston, MA

Adele Lee Entz, RN, MN
Faculty
Arizona State University
College of Nursing
Tempe, AZ

Lynn M. Feenan, RN, MS
Pediatric Pulmonary Clinical Nurse Specialist
University of Wisconsin Hospital and Clinics
Madison, WI

**Loretta Forlaw, RN, MSN, CNSN, LTC,
  AN**
Doctoral Candidate
The Catholic University of America
Washington, DC

**Mary Lou Fragomeni-Nuttall, MS, CCC/
  SLP**
Supervisor, Speech/Language Pathology and
  Audiology
Restorative Services
Tucson Medical Center
Tucson, AZ

Sharon Frierdich, RNC, MS, PNP
Pediatric Oncology Clinical Nurse Specialist
University of Wisconsin Hospital and Clinics
Madison, WI

Linda M. Gaudet, MSW
Psychotherapist
Private Practice
Tucson, AZ

Janice A. Greer, RN, MS, CDE
Endocrine Clinical Nurse Specialist
Phoenix Children's Hospital
Phoenix, AZ

Nancy J. Harris, OTR
Supervisor
Occupational Therapy Department
Tucson Medical Center
Tucson, AZ

Joanne K. H. Howard, RN, PhD
Assistant Professor
Intercollegiate Center for Nursing Education
Spokane, WA

Belinda B. Martin, RN, MS, PNP
Home Coordinator
Children's Hospital of Los Angeles
Los Angeles, CA

Jill K. Martindale, PT
Pediatric Physical Therapist
Private Practice
Pueblo Pediatric Therapy
Tucson, AZ

Patricia A. McCoy, RN, MSN, MBA
Director of Quality Assurance
20th Tactical Fighter Wing Hospital
Upper Heyford, England

Cheree Matta Posch, RN, MSN, CPNP
Pediatric Clinical Nurse Specialist
Children's Specialized Hospital
Mountainside, NJ

Gail M. Powers, MSW
Psychotherapist
Private Practice
Tucson, AZ

Karen A. Shannon
President, Founder
Sick Kids [Need] Involved People
Severna Park, MD

Marilee Thompson Tollefson, RN, MSN
Nursing Consultant
Continuity of Care
Children's Hospital National Medical Center
Washington, DC

Karen C. Uzark, RN, PhD
Clinical Specialist in Pediatric Cardiology
C.S. Mott Children's Hospital
Ann Arbor, MI

Wendy L. Votroubek, RN, MPH
Clinical Nurse Specialist, Pediatric Pulmonary
University Medical Center
Tucson, Arizona

Deborah Klein Walker, EdD
Assistant Commission at Massachusetts
Commonwealth of Massachusetts
Executive Office of Human Services
Department of Public Health
Bureau of Parent Child and Adolescent Health
Boston, MA

Nancy Williams, MS, CCC/SLP
Pediatric Speech Therapist
Private Practice
Pueblo Pediatric Therapy
Tucson, AZ

Part I

Discharge Planning Issues

Chapter 1

Discharge Planning

Patricia A. McCoy

Home care is an attempt to normalize the life of a child with significant physical illness in a family and community context and setting to minimize the disruptive impact of the child's condition and to foster maximal growth and development (Stein 1984). The success of the home care experience is dependent on a thorough discharge plan initiated in the hospital by the primary care team and communicated in detail to the home care agency.

The American Nurses' Association (1975) has defined *discharge planning* as that "part of the continuity of care process which is designed to prepare the patient or client for the next phase of care, whether it be self-care, care by family members, or care by an organized provider." Discharge planning should be initiated as early as possible and must be tailored to meet the specific needs of the child and family. The discharge planning process incorporates the determination of the child's home care needs, the child's capacity for self-care, an assessment of the child's living conditions, the identification of health or social care resources needed to ensure high-quality home care, and counseling of the child and family to prepare them for home care (American Hospital Association 1984). While the goal of discharge planning is to ensure a smooth transition between hospital and home, it should be remembered that home care may not be feasible for every child and family. Alternatives should be discussed, and the parents should not be pressured into caring for their child

at home. Medical, social, or financial concerns may preclude home care as a realistic alternative.

In this chapter the process involved in discharge planning for the pediatric patient and family is discussed. The concept of case management as a method for coordinating services for the child and family requiring home care is detailed, and an outline is provided of the essential components of the discharge planning process. Incorporating these components into the discharge plan ensures that all critical aspects of home care are addressed.

CASE MANAGEMENT

Case management is an extremely important component of the discharge planning process because it offers service coordination to families. There is no generally accepted definition of "case management," but an amendment to the Title V Maternal and Child Health Services Block Grant defines *case management services* as "services to promote the effective and efficient organization and utilization of resources to assure access to necessary comprehensive services for children and their families" (Omnibus Budget Reconciliation Act 1986). Underlying the case management concept is the belief that some children and families have a variety of medical, psychosocial, educational, developmental, and environmental problems and that such families often may need assistance with service coordination (American Academy of Pediatrics 1984). The function of ensuring that the required services are delivered and paid for may be undertaken by the parents; shared between the parents and another entity; or delegated to a program, a vendor, a social service agency, or another organization. It has also been suggested that public health nurses be considered as case managers because of their capability to manage both medical and logistical factors. Regardless of who provides the professional component of case management, the services should be family centered and responsive to the varying needs of the child and family (Gittler and Colton 1986).

Professional case managers are responsible for coordinating the services of other providers. The functions of the case manager include (1) helping the family avoid duplication of services; (2) providing the family with information regarding alternatives in care choices, available services, and their rights as parents; (3) initiating referrals that are consistent with the care plan and acceptable to the needs of the family; and (4) acting as an advocate for the family in negotiations to obtain necessary services (Bilotti 1984). The case manager should also explain the recommendations of health care providers so as to help the family comply with these recommendations and, if possible, to remove any barriers to compliance, to coordinate services, to locate required services, to help the family secure funding, and to monitor activities to ensure the child has received the specified follow-up services (Gittler and Colton 1986).

A case manager must be identified before the discharge process begins. It is important that one person be responsible for organizing and coordinating the discharge planning process. This individual should be removed from the child's acute medical and nursing needs because persons providing acute care services do not have the time to perform effective discharge planning. This responsibility may rest with the social worker, discharge planner, or the primary nurse for the rehabilitation stage. Mechanisms for coordination include case conferences, telephone calls, chart notes, and informal staff discussions. Community-based case management programs are available in some states that can assist the health care professional or the family in undertaking case management for children with special health care needs (Gittler and Colton 1986).

The complexity of case management tasks varies from child to child. Complexity escalates rapidly with increases in the number of attendants and vendors, the variability of the child's condition, and the number of payment sources (*Brook Lodge Symposium* 1983). The importance of close coordination of financial management and clinical/social management cannot be overemphasized. The goal of case management should be to help the families gain skills and independence in problem solving, management of community resources, and self-advocacy. Most families find that the services of a case manager are extremely beneficial during the discharge planning process and the initial transition from hospital to home (Kaufman and Lichtenstein 1985). As the family becomes more comfortable and established with providing care for the child, the role of the professional case manager changes. The family is now ready to assume the role of case manager, relying on the professional case manager (either hospital or agency based) for advice, guidance, or as temporary coordinator support in cases of significant changes in the home setting.

Many areas have case management programs that are either independently operated, components of larger state programs for Children with Special Health Care Needs (formerly state Crippled Children's Services programs), or part of a statewide network of regional centers. These services either provide or arrange for provision of specialized health care services for chronically ill children and their families. Case management resources are listed in Appendix A.

DISCHARGE PLANNING PROCESS

The feasibility of home care depends on many factors. The American Academy of Pediatrics (1984) Task Force on Home Care has identified several factors that should be considered in selecting candidates for home care. These include patient factors (potential benefits and risks and care needs); family factors (the presence of involved family members and an appropriate home setting, including whenever possible at least two knowledgeable family members); and community factors (medical, social, and educational supports). In addition, the most

1. Medically stable child
2. Family willing and able to have child at home
3. Family motivated to gain skill for and knowledge of child's care
4. Adequate family support systems available
5. Financial support systems available
6. Residence structurally appropriate
7. Community resources available
8. Local medical supervision available
9. Trained home care providers available
10. Alternative method of care available should the home care experience prove unsatisfactory

Source: Adapted from "Tucson's First Homebound Ventilator Child: Kim Nichols" by P.A. McCoy and W.L. Votroubek, *Caring*, with permission of National Association for Home Care, © December 1986.

crucial factors in determining feasibility for home care are the child's disease process and medical stability. Criteria for home care are listed in Exhibit 1-1.

Medical Stability of the Child

The child must be medically stable prior to discharge. Medical stability can be defined in a number of ways; however, the general minimal guideline is lack of complications requiring in-house care for a 1-month period and that major diagnostic studies or therapeutic decisions are not anticipated prior to 1-month's time. Coexistent diseases should be well controlled, and the patient should not require frequent hospital admissions or emergency visits for treatment (American Academy of Chest Physicians 1986).

The child must be in close communication with the medical center capable of coordinating the required subspecialty. A local physician should be responsible for routine care and must understand the child's medical needs in order to carry out instructions. A copy of the child's medical plan, recommended follow-up care, and expected discharge date should be given to the local physician for review at least 2 weeks prior to discharge.

The Family's Role in Discharge Planning

Parents assume a variety of roles, including teacher, housekeeper, cook, chauffeur, and sub-stitute playmate, among many others. Additional roles emerge for parents of children requiring home care services. Parents must now become part-time nurses, case managers, and therapists. They must learn complicated new skills and procedures and a new vocabulary that includes medical, legal, and financial jargon. They find that assimilation can be very demanding and the roles difficult to balance (Kaufman and Lichtenstein 1985).

An alliance between parents and professionals is essential to quality home care for the child (Kirkhart 1984). All team members must realize that each family's circumstances are unique. Families must be involved in all aspects of care and decision making. Effective communication between parents and professionals will foster this relationship. Clear expectations should be discussed with the parents regarding the child's needs at home, evaluation of the residence, accessibility of transportation, evaluation of existing community resources, and educational offerings in the community. Parents must identify what is realistic and workable in their home.

The Hospital's Role in Discharge Planning

Hospital personnel have a responsibility to ensure that the discharge planning process maintains the family structure. It is important, therefore, to involve the family in all aspects of care and decision making. Families usually know what they need and whether the plan will work. It has been noted that involvement and commitment of families can make home care work despite other drawbacks.

It is essential that an interdisciplinary team approach be used when developing a discharge plan. The team's goal is to help the child and family master the tasks and competencies involved in the child's care. The areas of competency for the child include physical care, motor development, and affective and cognitive development. The areas of competency for the family include the ability to manage the demands of parenting, a household, social life, and job. Members of the team are listed in Exhibit 1-2.

Components of the Discharge Planning Process

Comprehensive planning for all aspects of home care is essential to minimize physical and

Exhibit 1-2 Interdisciplinary Team Members

1. Physician
2. Family
3. Primary nurse
4. Social worker or discharge planner
5. School teacher
6. Home care agency
7. Therapists (as determined as necessary)
   - Physical
   - Respiratory
   - Occupational
   - Dietary
   - Speech
8. Durable medical equipment company (once equipment and supplies have been identified)

Source: Adapted from "Tucson's First Homebound Ventilator Child: Kim Nichols" by P.A. McCoy and W.L. Votroubek, *Caring,* with permission of National Association for Home Care, © December 1986.

Exhibit 1-3 Discharge Planning Components

1. Evaluation of family support systems
2. Identification of funding sources
3. Identification of equipment and supplies
4. Securing of vendor contracts
5. Evaluation of the residential structure
6. Preparation of written care plan
7. Communication with community agencies
8. Discharge teaching
9. Development of discharge plan
10. Program evaluation

Source: Adapted from "Tucson's First Homebound Ventilator Child: Kim Nichols" by P.A. McCoy and W.L. Votroubek, *Caring,* with permission of National Association for Home Care, © December 1986.

emotional risk to the child, adverse effects on the family members, or unforeseen financial burdens (American Academy of Pediatrics 1984). Home care requires a well conceived, flexible plan that covers a wide array of contingencies (Stein 1984). The plan should include a system for managing emergencies, both medical and family, and a mechanism for providing continual social and emotional support to the family and child. It should also provide an appropriate alternative to home care, such as respite care or long-term placement, if home care does not appear to be the most effective method for the child and the family.

The variety of methods available for discharge planning is striking. Clearly, there is no one correct approach. However, the process of discharge planning can be made simpler by recognizing core components. With these components in mind, a strategy for tackling the individual complexities of discharge planning for the child and family exists. The components of the discharge planning process are listed in Exhibit 1-3.

Evaluation of Family Support Systems

The team should be aware of barriers that may affect successful discharge planning. An assessment should be done with the child and family to identify any problems pertaining to home care. This can be accomplished through psychosocial assessment designed to assist the home care team

in evaluating whether the decision for home care is appropriate. Psychosocial assessment for the child would typically include evaluation of developmental capability, anticipated ability to adapt to the home environment, relationship with parents, and desire to go home (*Brook Lodge Symposium* 1983). Evaluation from the family perspective usually addresses the parents' desire to take the child home, their motivation, their emotional stability and maturity, and their involvement with and commitment to the child (*Brook Lodge Symposium,* 1983).

Most families are eager to have their child at home. The complexities of daily care can be mastered by the family with time and appropriate teaching. No matter how comfortable the family may be with their roles, the development of stressors is inevitable once the child is at home. Therefore, families need to be given a clear and accurate description of the scope of the care needs, including physical, social, and psychological aspects (Giovannoni 1985). Many stressors are predictable; some are unique to the individual family. Examples of stressors include (1) the issue of privacy with nurses in the home 8 to 24 hours a day; (2) control, nurturing, and supporting the child while nurses provide hands-on care; and (3) turning the home into a hospital room with equipment, alarms, and supplies.

Home care has the potential for keeping families together and giving the child greater independence, but it can have a detrimental impact as well (Childress et al. 1984). The key to a successful outcome is the identification of support systems for the family. Each family should have an identified support system to share concerns about the impact of returning the child to the home. Initially, this will be the social worker, case coordinator, or discharge planner. Other sources of support need to be identified when the child is discharged home. Many families have found it helpful to share problems and concerns with parents who have experienced similar situations. Attention should be given to identifying temporary respite care services for families that do not have private-duty nurses available on a regular basis. This ensures that the family can obtain temporary relief from caregiving responsibilities. The reader is referred to Chapter 19 for information on interventions for the family dealing with stress. In addition, a variety of support services that the parent can contact for information regarding assistance are listed in Appendix A.

Home care is not for every child and family. All available alternatives must be explained to the parents, who must not be pressured into assuming responsibility for a child's care if they are unwilling or unable to do so. A psychosocial assessment can be extremely beneficial in determining the parents' ability to cope with a specialized home care program. A thorough psychosocial assessment should uncover and, it is hoped, prevent some of the more common problems faced by families.

Identification of Funding Sources

The cost of home care can be a significant burden to families. Although home care is cost effective (Cabin 1985), many insurance companies that pay 100 percent of inpatient costs will only pay a partial percentage of home care costs (Burr et al. 1983). Uninsured costs of home care can financially overwhelm a family already burdened with nonreimbursable deductions such as insurance deductibles, traveling expenses during hospitalization, home renovations for the child, and increased utility bills after discharge (McCarthy 1986). Home care generally costs less than hospital care, but it can still be expensive. It is essential to know if the child's insurance policy has a lifetime limit for reimbursement and the specific details of home care coverage under private and/or public funding.

The system for financing home care is a mix of federal and state programs and of private insurance companies. The complexity of the system can be particularly frustrating for parents with a child whose existence is dependent on both specialized medical procedures and equipment and on health care services. Most families have a large portion of their medical care supported by a third-party payer, but there are still large gaps in coverage that can cause severe financial burdens. Investigation of eligibility for federal, state, and local government funds should be conducted under the direction of the discharge planner or social worker. Applications will need to be submitted by the parent or guardian of the child after the funding sources have been identified. The processing of applications can take several weeks to several months. The reader is referred to Chapter 3 for a further discussion on the funding of pediatric home care.

Identification of Equipment and Supplies

There are several factors to consider when selecting equipment for home care. These include the child's safety needs, the availability and use of single items rather than kits to contain costs, comparison of cost with ease of use (e.g., need for additional knowledge and skills, parents' ability to learn, and portability of equipment), and cost to rent versus cost to purchase.

Early identification of equipment and supply needs is important in order to facilitate discharge. Preparation of equipment and supply lists must be completed before any type of funding package can be submitted. The cost and quality of items must be identified and should include (1) initial purchases, (2) monthly rental equipment, (3) monthly supplies, and (4) monthly supplies to be purchased by and reimbursement made to parents. Consider that most supplies for home care need to be clean but not sterile. Some items can be reused at home (i.e., tracheostomy tubes and straight catheters). These items should be identified to help decrease expenses.

The type of equipment and supplies to be used in the home should first be used in the hospital setting so that the family can become familiar and proficient in their use. Once choices of equipment and supplies are finalized, parents and caregivers may find it helpful to develop an inventory list for reordering purposes. This list should include the name of the supply or equipment, the standard minimum and maximum stock number, and an empty space for current stock and the number of an item ordered.

Securing of Vendor Contracts

Bids should be obtained from durable medical equipment (DME) vendors after equipment and supplies have been identified. These price quotations for equipment should include the cost of purchasing an item versus the cost of rental, service, and repurchase agreements. Price should not be the only criteria for selecting a DME vendor. Availability of service, reliability of the vendor, and ease of use are other important factors. Rental agreements should always include the option to purchase. In addition, a repurchase agreement should be included in the original contract. This will help reduce losses if the child requires new or different equipment.

Community suppliers must guarantee continuous availability, maintenance, and replacement of equipment. In addition, the DME vendor should have the ability to provide all DME and disposable supplies. This will help prevent multiple contracts and the difficulties associated with coordinating requests through many different vendors. In addition, it is important that the DME vendor be available to service equipment malfunctions on a 24-hour basis. Criteria for selecting DME vendors are listed in Exhibit 1-4.

Evaluation of the Residential Structure

An environmental assessment should be conducted early in the discharge planning process to determine if the child's requirements necessitate structural modifications. The house must meet local safety, sanitation, and building requirements and, depending on the child's condition, should be evaluated for the adequacy of space, outlets, wiring, and accessibility for emergencies. Changes in the home may be necessary to accommodate special medical equipment. These changes might include grounding all electrical outlets, building a ramp from the sidewalk to the front door, or weatherproofing and insulating the residence.

Accessibility. The residence must accommodate the child's disability. This includes the delivery of equipment, mobility, and transportation.

Space Requirements. Any area of the house can be used as the child's room. The most important consideration is that the child not be isolated

Exhibit 1-4 Criteria for DME Vendor Selection

1. Ability to supply all DME equipment and disposable supplies
2. Availability of reliable services 24 hours a day, including preventive maintenance
3. Fair and reasonable charges and billing practices
4. Provider status with appropriate state or federal agencies or third-party payers
5. Experience in providing care to pediatric patients
6. Provision of written instructions for operation and maintenance of equipment*
7. Provision of "loaner" or replacement equipment if equipment malfunctions*
8. Ability to train home care personnel
9. Timely responses to telephone calls regarding problems*

Source: "Selecting Equipment Vendors for Children on Home Care" by M.B. Hartsell and J.H. Ward, *American Journal of Maternal Child Nursing,* Vol. 10, pp. 26–28, American Journal of Nursing Company, © January/February 1985.

from the family. Storage space must be able to accommodate hourly, daily, and monthly supplies. A nightstand can be used to store equipment and supplies that are required within an 8-hour period. A large closet can be used to store equipment and supplies that are required during a 24-hour period (e.g., diapers, scale, water bottles, suction catheters). Items requiring bulk storage can be placed in the basement or garage. There should be enough room to store up to 1 month's worth of supplies and equipment. Storage areas should be free of dampness, have moderate temperatures, and not contain toxic chemicals.

Electrical Requirements. An electrician may be required to evaluate the structure for accommodation of electrical needs. This is especially important if the child is ventilator dependent. There must be adequate power to maintain the equipment and the household appliances. Spare fuses should always be available.

Special Equipment. The house should be equipped with a telephone and a smoke alarm. A battery-powered floodlight and power failure alarm system should also be considered if the child is dependent on a ventilator.

Preparation of Written Care Plan

A detailed care plan should be written prior to discharge. It should include a brief medical history, medical discharge plan, and nursing care plan. The nursing care plan should include a step-by-step instructional guide for procedures. The following elements should also be included: arrangements for rehospitalization; medications, including dose, routes, and frequency indicated; type of diet with special equipment and assistance needs; activity level, noting limitations, disabilities, and assistance required; sleeping pattern and duration, noting problems and concerns; elimination needs; special problems; equipment; personal care needs, including bathing, grooming, dressing, communication; sensory problems, listing disabilities and aids; special needs, including emotional, behavioral, developmental, and educational; financial assistance; potential emergency care needs; and signs and symptoms to alert the family that major changes have occurred in the child's health that make it important for medical care to be sought. Telephone numbers for the hospital emergency department, medical equipment supplier, ambulance service, and home care agency should also be provided. A daily routine should be developed with input from the child, family, and health care team. This schedule should reflect the child's needs and be adaptable to the family's life style. A sample schedule is listed in Exhibit 1-5.

Communication with Community Agencies

Community agencies include all resources and agencies that provide support to the family and ensure the child's adjustment within the family (Bilotti 1984). Community services must be available if care in the home is to be cost effective and of high quality, if the child is to access education and recreation services, if the care is to be safe, and if the parents can be expected to assume long-term responsibility for home care (Nelson et al. 1987). Long-term home care should not be attempted if community services are not available to the child and family. These services would include public service agencies, home health care agencies (or available health care providers), respite care providers, and educational services.

Public Service Agencies. Public service agencies play a vital role in assuring safe care for the pediatric patient in the home. If the child is dependent on life support equipment or has special needs that are affected by the use of public

Exhibit 1-5 Daily Routine

7:00 – 9:00	Awake, morning care, breakfast
9:00 – 10:00	Physical therapy
10:00 – 12:00	School
12:00 – 1:00	Lunch
1:00 – 3:00	Rest period/free time
3:00 – 4:00	Speech therapy
4:00 – 5:00	Watch TV
5:00 – 6:00	Dinner
6:00 – 9:00	Family time
9:00 – 10:00	Bedtime, evening care, physical therapy

Source: Reprinted from ''Tucson's First Homebound Ventilator Child: Kim Nichols'' by P.A. McCoy and W.L. Votroubek, *Caring*, with permission of National Association for Home Care, © December 1986.

services, the following agencies should be notified prior to discharge: gas and electric company, fire department, telephone company, ambulance service, snow removal, and public works. Written communication should state politely and clearly the request for service before an emergency occurs (Bilotti 1984). It should include a description of the child's diagnosis, age, medications, and hospital identified for emergency transport. Notifying these agencies of the child's needs will facilitate a quick response in emergencies. Exhibit 1-6 is a sample letter that can be used as a guide for communicating with community agencies.

Nursing Care. Nursing care is the foundation of home care programs. It is neither fair nor realistic to expect parents to care for their child indefinitely 24 hours per day, 7 days per week (Shannon 1983). Therefore, the family must have assistance in the home. The amount of assistance required is contingent on the dependency requirements of the child. Prior to discharge, the family and health care team should discuss the need for nursing care in the home. If nursing care is required, the family must select a method of providing that care. The family can choose between independently hiring nursing staff or selecting a home care agency (funding sources may place restrictions on the type of nursing service provided).

Independent contracting occurs when the family and individual nurses, without the use of a home care agency or other intermediary, enter

Exhibit 1-6 Sample Letter to a Community Agency

November 15, 1989

Tucson Electric Company
200 Park Street
Tucson, AZ 85730

Dear Sir or Madam:

My daughter is coming home at the end of November following hospitalization at University Medical Center. The purpose of this letter is to inform you that she requires electrically powered life support equipment. The social worker at the hospital suggested that I write to you and inform you of our acute need for electrical power. She indicated that you could expedite power lines and equipment repairs in my area if you were aware of such a medical need. We will have a temporary backup power source but will feel much more comfortable knowing that your company is aware of the need for continual electricity. Please feel free to call me or, if necessary, I can stop by your office and discuss the situation in greater detail. Our physician is John Smith; his phone number is (602) 555-9237. He is willing to discuss our daughter's care in more detail if you feel it is required.

Thank you for your consideration of this matter, which is very important to my family.

Sincerely,

Mrs. Jackie Nichols

Source: Adapted from "Tucson's First Homebound Ventilator Child: Kim Nichols" by P.A. McCoy and W.L. Votroubek, *Caring,* with permission of National Association for Home Care, © December 1986.

into an agreement for home care services (Kaufman and Lichtenstein 1985). Independent contracting for nurses may reduce costs and result in use of insurance resources at a slower pace. However, the parents must perform all employment functions.

The agency recruits and selects nurses to work in the home. The agency may also identify a primary nurse for the child. This individual assumes the coordination of care for the child in the home and may also help order and inventory supplies, communicate changes in the care plan to other staff, and participate in training new staff in the home. The advantages and disadvantages of each method are listed in Table 1-1.

Parents often have many concerns and questions about selecting a home care agency. They lack the necessary information required to determine if an agency is suitable for providing the care their child requires. A thorough examination of the agency should be completed prior to authorizing the agency for the provision of service. Considerations that parents should discuss with any prospective health care agency are identified in Exhibit 1-7.

Parents also voice concerns regarding the competency of the agency's nursing staff. This often results when parents are not consulted about the personnel. Parental rights of approval and disapproval of personnel will help alleviate these concerns. In addition, parents should be permitted to review the agency's application process and skills list if so desired. Open communication between the agency and the parents will help ensure a successful home care experience.

Educational Services. Educational provisions for the child requiring home care should not be neglected. Children requiring long-term specialized home care will vary in their need for educational services. Infants and small children may benefit from home-based intervention programs. Older children will need school experiences or special education services. The case coordinator or the discharge planner should be in constant contact with the school district personnel to inform them of the child's need for educational services and to plan strategies to accomplish the child's education. Further discussion on educational services is found in Chapter 17.

Respite Care. Families will occasionally require temporary relief from caregiving responsibilities. Respite care services to provide that relief should be identified prior to discharge. This will help ensure that the child remains in the community.

Table 1-1 Nursing Care in the Home: Independent Contracting versus Agency

	Advantages	Disadvantages
Agency	Provides personnel Responsible for scheduling personnel Submits reimbursement forms to insurance company Assumes educational responsibility Can assume case manager role Responsible for sick time and holiday coverage Costs include malpractice and liability coverage, Social Security, workers' compensation, bonding Supervision provided on cases	Expensive Family has less control over personnel
Independent Contracting	Less expensive Family decides on personnel	Family must advertise for nurses Family must interview and hire nurses Family is responsible for education after child is discharged Family must accommodate sick calls Family assumes employer responsibility, including providing Social Security and billing

Discharge Teaching

Thorough teaching is essential. All caregivers, including home care nurses, should be instructed in every aspect of routine and emergency care. The teaching method should incorporate adult learning principles and should be geared toward the learning needs of the family and caregivers. Teaching methods should include discussion, instructional materials, and demonstration by a nurse or therapist with a return-demonstration by the caregivers (McCarthy 1985). Caregivers should be required to demonstrate all aspects of care prior to discharge. The nurse should also observe for appropriate levels of confidence and competence required for routine performance (McCarthy 1985).

Teaching home care skills can be complex and demanding. The teaching process is best accomplished by allowing plenty of time for learning, individualizing the learning process for different learners, and developing a complete and thorough discharge plan (Chadderdon and Johnson 1986). The goal of discharge teaching is to validate mastery of tasks and ensure that parents and caregivers are able to function competently.

Nursing Care Plan. The written care plan serves as the basis for education of home care nurses and the family. Education should begin early in the discharge planning process. Orientation to care should begin by teaching simple tasks, then progressing to more complex tasks. Mastery of tasks should be documented on separate teaching forms for each person who will provide care. This form includes a checklist of procedures that is marked by a team member (with date and initials) on four occasions: (1) at the time that the procedure is discussed and demonstrated, (2) when the caregiver being trained performs a return-demonstration, (3) when the caregiver being trained performs the procedure with assistance, and (4) when the caregiver performs the procedure independently. Procedures and skills can be practiced in a learning situation away from the child so that the caregiver can gain confidence in the use of equipment and supplies. All procedures need to be performed with the child prior to discharge.

Documentation of discharge teaching is extremely valuable. It provides a mechanism for hospital staff and home care agency review of caregiver competencies and identifies additional training needs. It is also important to note the degree of understanding and skill that can be verbalized and demonstrated by the caregivers. Teaching checklists facilitate both the measurement and documentation of the skills and knowl-

Exhibit 1-7 Considerations in Choosing an Agency

---

1. What type of experience does the agency have in caring for children with special needs?
2. How does the agency recruit qualified nurses?
3. Will the agency sign a contract/written agreement for care provision?*
4. Will the agency accept the insurance plan and do the paperwork required?*
5. What is the agency's policy for covering sick calls, vacations, and holidays?
6. Is the agency willing to send nurses to the hospital for training prior to discharge? (This service should be free of charge.)*
7. Does the agency have written standards of care for the pediatric population?
8. Is there a nursing supervisor available?
9. Will the nursing supervisor visit nurses in the home on a regular basis?*
10. Is the nursing supervisor available to assist with problems that might arise?*
11. Who is responsible for providing updated training needs for the nurses?
12. Does the agency provide other services?
13. What are the costs involved?*
14. Is someone available at the agency 24 hours a day?*
15. What if I (parent) don't like a nurse?
16. Am I (parent) allowed to interview a nurse?
17. What about lunch breaks? Do I (parent) provide coverage?
18. Do I (parent) stay at home while the nurse is there?

Source: "The Family as Care Manager: Home Care Coordination for Medically Fragile Children" by J. Kaufman and K. Lichtenstein. Prepared by Georgetown University Child Development Center, p. 12. 1985.

---

edge acquired by the caregivers (McCarthy 1985). Exhibit 1-8 is an example of a teaching documentation form.

Discharge Teaching for Parents. Early positive reinforcement of parental participation in care will help build skill and confidence (Levine and Rice 1984). Training and education in providing care is multifaceted. Parents and caregivers must develop technical skills as well as judgment.

The family and caregivers must be carefully trained in all aspects of the child's care. Parents should be given progressive responsibility prior to their child's discharge. During this time, staff should offer assistance, advice, and support. Some programs strongly recommend contract-ing with parents and caregivers for a series of specific teaching sessions in order to accomplish discharge teaching. Parents must demonstrate competence in operating equipment, performing procedures, and administering medicine. They must also learn to cope with emergencies. Educational efforts should include classroom exercises, hands-on training in the hospital, and postdischarge instruction.

Written discharge instructions should be developed and given to the parents and caregivers prior to discharge. These instructions should include a summary of all aspects of the child's care, including steps of procedures, medication guidelines (dose, route, side effects), and equipment checklists. Information should be easy to read and understand. It is helpful if all necessary information is placed in a looseleaf notebook so that the information stays together and is easily accessible. A family member or caregiver should be designated to maintain and update the manual for future teaching needs.

Home Care Nurses. The home care agency must be completely familiar with the teaching instructions that occur in the hospital so that consistency can be maintained in the home environment. This can be accomplished by including the home care nurses in the discharge teaching sessions. This supervision will also help the parents relax with the staff providing care to their child.

Development of Discharge Plan

Caregiver readiness for discharge is an important component of the discharge plan. A rooming-in period provides an excellent method for assessing readiness. Prior to discharge, the parents or significant caregiver spends 24 to 72 hours in the hospital assuming full care for the child. This allows the parents or caregivers to assume control of their child's care using the skills learned in discharge teaching, with assistance from professional staff if required. Observation of the parents' skills during this time period can help identify any additional preparation needs. The nurse can also offer the family support and positive recognition for providing care.

The social worker or discharge planner should arrange for discharge transportation during this time. Arrangements should also be made for professional staff, if required, to accompany the

Exhibit 1-8 Sample Discharge Teaching Documentation Form

Patient's Name: _____

Name of Caregiver: _____

Instructions: Instructor should place date and initials into box under each column when completed by caregiver.

Skills and Procedures	Discussion about Procedure by Instructor	Demonstration by Instructor	Return-demonstration by Caregiver	Review of Procedure Principles by Caregiver	Performed with Assistance	Performed Independently
Handwashing						
Suctioning						
Equipment Cleaning						
Medication Administration						
Chest Physical Therapy						
Tracheostomy Care						

Instructor: _____ Date Completed: _____

Name of Caregiver: _____ Date Completed: _____

child on the transport home. The DME vendor should be present on the day of discharge to assist with equipment assembly once the child has arrived home.

It is helpful for the child to be discharged during the early part of the week. This allows for availability of the discharge team to solve minor problems that will arise during the first few days at home (Giovannoni 1985).

Program Evaluation

Evaluation of the discharge planning process is essential if home care is to be a safe and successful alternative for children and families (McCarthy 1985). Discharge planners, health care professionals, and parents are responsible for evaluating all aspects of the discharge planning process. One effective method for program evaluation is to enclose a follow-up evaluation form in initial correspondence to the parents. This form can be mailed back to the hospital, and information can be shared with the staff. In addition, telephone calls during the first few weeks can serve as an important method for gathering information in the evaluation process.

Program evaluation must be an ongoing process, with continuous evaluation of the home care program. A routine for coordinated review of the child's needs, how the family is managing, and other available findings can be useful in future endeavors of discharge planning.

REFERENCES

American Academy of Chest Physicians. *Discharge Planning: Resources and Equipment for Home Care of Ventilator-assisted Individuals*. Chicago: American Academy of Chest Physicians, 1986.

American Academy of Pediatrics. "Ad Hoc Task Force on the Home Care of Chronically Ill Infants and Children: Guidelines for Home Care of Infants, Children, and Adolescents with Chronic Disease." *Pediatrics* 74(1984):434–436.

American Hospital Association. *Guidelines for Discharge Planning*. Chicago: American Hospital Association, 1984.

American Nurses' Association. *Code NP-49, 3000-3*. Chicago: American Nurses' Association, 1975.

Bilotti, Gene. *Getting Children Home: Hospital to Community,* prepared by Georgetown University Child Development Center for the Division of Maternal and Child Health, May 1984.

Brook Lodge Invitational Symposium on the Ventilator-Dependent Child, sponsored by American Academy of Pediatrics, Children's Home Health Network of Illinois, La Rabida Children's Hospital and Research Center, and Upjohn Healthcare Services, October 16–18, 1983.

Burr, B.H.; Guyer, B.; Todress, I.D.; Abrahams, B.; and Chiodo, T. "Home Care for Children on Respirators." *New England Journal of Medicine* 309(1983): 1319–1323.

Cabin, B. "Cost Effectiveness of Pediatric Home Care." *Caring* 4(1985):48–51.

Chadderdon, Carolyn, and Johnson, Dawn L. "Teaching the Patient and Family about Home Care." In *Ventilator-assisted Patient Care: Planning for Hospital Discharge and Home Care,* edited by D.L. Johnson, R.M. Giovannoni, and S.A. Driscoll. Rockville, Md.: Aspen Publishers, Inc., 1986.

Childress, Josephine; Diamond, Linda; Knapper, Joni; McCarthy, Michael; McLaughlin, Mary; Ridley, Mary Ann; Shanahan, Elaine; Simmons, Laura; and Tuths, Carmel. "Discharge Planning to Home Care for the Ventilator-dependent Patient." *Baton,* Upjohn Healthcare Services, 1, no. 3 (1984):11.

Giovannoni, Rita. "Chronic Ventilator Care: From Hospital to Home." *RX Home Care.* January 1985:51–55.

Gittler, Josephine, and Colton, Milo. *Community-based Case Management Programs for Children with Special Health Care Needs.* U.S. Department of Health and Human Services Public Health Service, 1986.

Kaufman, Joanne, and Lichtenstein, Karen-Ann. *The Family as Care Manager: Home Care Coordination for Medically Fragile Children,* prepared by Georgetown University Child Development Center for the Division of Maternal and Child Health, 1985.

Kirkhart, Kathryn, facilitator. "Encouraging Early Family Involvement." In *Home Care for Children with Serious Handicapping Conditions.* A report on the conference sponsored by the Association for the Care of Children's Health and the Division of Maternal and Child Health, Public Health Service, U.S. Department of Health and Human Services, Houston, Texas, May 27, 1984.

Levine, Sunni, and Rice, Nancy, facilitators. "Facilitating Transition from Hospital to Home." In *Home Care for Children with Serious Handicapping Conditions.* A report on the conference sponsored by the Association for the Care of Children's Health and the Division of Maternal and Child Health, Public Health Service, U.S. Department of Health and Human Services, Houston, Texas, May 27, 1984.

McCarthy, Maureen F. "A Home Discharge Program for Ventilator-assisted Children." *Pediatric Nursing* 12 (1986):331–335.

McCarthy, Sally. "Discharge Planning for the High Risk Infant." In *Home Care for the High Risk Infant,* edited by Elizabeth Ahmann. Rockville, Md.: Aspen Publishers, Inc., 1985.

Nelson, Richard P.; Moore, Brenda Rae; Bowers, Kathy; Beckett, Julianne; and Hulme, Thomas S. *Iowa's Home Care Monitoring Program.* Conducted by the Iowa Mobile and Regional Health Specialty Clinics, a division of the Department of Pediatrics, University of Iowa Hospitals and Clinics, The University of Iowa, Iowa City, Iowa, March 1986, revised April 1987.

Omnibus Budget Reconciliation Act of 1986, P.L. 99-509, S 9441(c)(2)(D) October 21, 1986.

Shannon, Karen. "Sick Kids Need Involved People." In *Brook Lodge Invitational Symposium on the Ventilator-Dependent Child,* sponsored by American Academy of Pediatrics, Children's Home Health Network of Illinois, La Rabida Children's Hospital and Research Center, and Upjohn Healthcare Services, October 16–18, 1983.

Stein, Ruth E.K. "Home Care: A Challenging Opportunity." In *Home Care for Children with Serious Handicapping Conditions.* A report on the conference sponsored by the Association for the Care of Children's Health and Division of Maternal and Child Health, Public Health Service, U.S. Department of Health and Human Services, Houston, Texas, May 27, 1984.

Chapter 2

Health History, Interviewing, Nursing Process, Care Plan, and Documentation

Patricia A. McCoy

Nurses involved in home care programs enter the home for two reasons: (1) initial assessment and (2) health maintenance and illness prevention. The functions of the home care nurse in relation to these two areas are reviewed in Exhibit 2-1.

Responsibility of the home care nurse has increased because care is provided outside the support structure of the inpatient setting. Coordination of care and assurance of timely communication between all health care professionals working with the child and family are important elements of this responsibility. In this chapter several topics that help in the coordination of care and processing of information are addressed, including the principles of health history interviewing, the use of the nursing process, and guidelines for documentation and care plan development so that pertinent information is communicated to necessary personnel.

HEALTH HISTORY

Obtaining the health history is often the first interaction that the home care nurse has with the child and family. It is the first step in establishing and promoting a relationship that helps promote partnership with the parent and significant caregivers in the care of the child. To accomplish this, the professional must establish and promote a therapeutic relationship with the child and the family during this initial visit. The interview should be a two-way process in which the nurse gains information from as well as gives information to the child and family. During this visit the goals for the home care program and the expectations of the parents and child should be discussed. Boundaries of interaction regarding discipline, normal patterns of behaviors, and any other significant concerns should be addressed.

Time management for the initial home visit can be a challenge given the amount of information that must be gathered. The initial interview will be more successful if it is scheduled in advance. Advance notice allows parents to plan and set aside time in their busy schedule. The initial visit should be limited to 1½ to 2 hours. Longer periods of time may impinge on the family's routine and result in fatigue and frustration for the child and family.

The initial visit to the home may require any or all of the following: in-depth interview; assessment of the child, special care requirements, and parent–child interactions; evaluation of the safety of the home environment; equipment checks for proper functioning; assurance of adequate supplies; review of care plans and interventions; review and perhaps demonstration of emergency procedures; and answering the family's and child's questions. The home care nurse is often not given adequate time to meet with the child and the family prior to the child's discharge. In these cases, it is essential that the professional takes time during the first visit to complete the health history and physical assessment to obtain baseline information. If the child has been seen

Exhibit 2-1 Functions of the Nurse in the Home

Initial Assessment
1. Obtain a history.
2. Perform physical examinations.
3. Delineate a care plan with specific short- and long-term goals (assess how family members perceive their roles and clarify roles and responsibilities).
4. Identify and develop a system for ordering, delivering, and storing of supplies or review devised system for accuracy and completeness.
5. Establish or review emergency protocols specifying roles and functions of each family member in terms of priorities.
6. Identify strength and availability of internal and external resources, including professional referrals.

Health Maintenance and Illness Prevention
1. Consult periodically with physician regarding ongoing physical examination findings.
2. Provide physical nursing care for the child.
3. Assess and assist in managing deteriorating physical/mental status and consult with appropriate health care professionals for further evaluation.
4. Assess and initiate emergency care if necessary and assist in the coordination of care during transports.
5. Evaluate nursing and medical aspects of the care plan and revise as necessary.
6. Counsel, advise, and teach patient and family members regarding health maintenance and illness prevention.
7. Collaborate with family, school, church, and community in administering plan of care.
8. Encourage the mobilization of internal family resources in the delivery of care.
9. Maintain ongoing clinical records.
10. Keep current on latest research findings, which will assist in the delivery of high-quality care.
11. Develop educational programs and inservice education for care providers and family.

Source: Fran Farrell, R.N., M.S.W. Used with permission.

Exhibit 2-2 Elements of a Pediatric Health History*

- Home and family data
- Family health history
- Past health history—prenatal, birth, newborn, allergies, accidents, illnesses, previous hospitalizations
- Health maintenance—immunizations, screening procedures, dental care
- Developmental history
- Personal history—friends, activities, hobbies, parent–child interactions
- School history—present and past schooling, grade, and performance
- Daily patterns—feeding, sleep, elimination habits, special needs for activities of daily living
- Special care needs—equipment, treatments, diet, medications
- Review of body system[†]

*See Appendix 2-A.
[†]See Appendix 2-B.

information is necessary for continual monitoring and evaluation of the child's changing status. The elements of a pediatric health history are listed in Exhibit 2-2.

PRINCIPLES OF INTERVIEWING

Interviewing the child and family is a complex process that requires skill in communication and interpersonal relationships. An attentive, nonjudgmental approach is essential for fostering an environment that allows the family to discuss concerns and problems openly. A common ground must be established to help the family relax during the interview. An assessment of the family's knowledge and understanding of the child's diagnosis, including an understanding of medical terminology, is helpful in establishing this common ground. The family may not understand all the medical terminology, especially if the child's problem has been recently diagnosed, and may not be able to provide accurate information. The home care nurse should clarify terminology and provide information to help the family gain understanding about the child's illness. In addition, some questions that seem important to the home care nurse may seem unnecessarily prying to the parents, who then become reluctant to reply (Ahmann 1986). This

by the home care nurse prior to discharge, most of the initial information will have been gathered and only baseline data of the child's status in the home will need to be obtained.

The health history (see Appendixes 2-A and 2-B), in conjunction with the physical assessment, observations of parent–child interactions, and growth and development assessment form the basis for identification of nursing diagnosis and development of the initial plan of care. This problem can be avoided by explaining the reasons for the question prior to asking it.

Successful interviewing requires a combination of strategies to elicit pertinent information. Open-ended questions provide one effective approach. Questions such as "Can you tell me about your child's illness?" or "Can you describe your child's daily routine?" may help provide better information than objective questions. Methods of helping and guiding—facilitation, clarification, empathic responses, and interpretation—may encourage the family and child to respond with more detail. Occasionally, the need for specific details to complete the health history will require direct questioning. Bernstein and colleagues (1974) have outlined the most appropriate way to use direct questioning: (1) questions should progress from the general to the specific; (2) questions should progress from the less personal to the more personal; (3) questions should be worded to elicit answers of at least a sentence, avoiding the "yes" and "no" response; and (4) questions should be worded to avoid bias.

Parents are often the primary source of information, especially for the young child. As the child grows older, he or she will be able to add significantly to the health history and more accurately describe the severity of the symptoms and his or her level of concern about them (Bates 1979). Information accuracy may be improved by interviewing the adolescent without the parents being present. Whenever possible, the wishes of the adolescent should be respected. If confidential information must be shared with the parents, the adolescent should be informed of this need prior to discussion of it with the parents.

Knowledge is the home care professional's most powerful tool. Careful and meticulous data collection when combined with a sound knowledge base in normal growth and development (see Chapters 13 and 14) and family dynamics and family systems (see Chapter 19) will adequately prepare the nurse to plan the care for the child and the family.

THE NURSING PROCESS

The nurse must analyze and synthesize the information that has been collected in order to identify the nursing diagnosis and develop inter-

ventions. The nursing process helps accomplish this through a systematic approach to analysis of the patient's health problems and allows development of a comprehensive treatment plan. The nursing process consists of six orderly and disciplined steps that allow for change as warranted by the child's changing condition.

1. *Assessment.* Nursing care must be based on adequate information and analysis of that information. The interviewing and observation process gathers information that helps the nurse identify the nursing diagnosis.
2. *Nursing diagnosis.* Nursing diagnosis is a method of identifying a problem based on data analysis. It places judgment on the assessment data.
3. *Goal setting.* Goal setting establishes a broad statement of direction to resolve the situation identified by the nursing diagnosis. Short- and long-term goals should be identified. This helps demonstrate actual progress to the child and family.
4. *Plan.* Alternative solutions must be considered so the best choice can be made for the child and family. This phase involves the development of a careful "blueprint" for carrying out the goals determined in step 3. The nurse uses the collective knowledge of all health care professionals involved in the child's care to develop the plan.
5. *Implement.* The nurse will implement strategies designed to facilitate the execution of stated goals.
6. *Evaluate.* Evaluation is a continuous process. Major factors to be considered are how the nurse's actions brought about changes in the child's condition and whether identified goals were fulfilled.

CARE PLAN

Detailed plans outlining specific interventions are essential in establishing continuity for the many providers that come into contact with the patient and family. A detailed care plan also assists in allaying feelings of anxiety, insecurity, inadequacy, and apprehension in the caregiver who feels less than prepared to care for the child. Care plans should be formulated by using the nursing process. Areas for assessment, nursing diagnosis, goal setting, planning, and evaluation should be included on the care plan document. The care plan should be well documented and easily understood, with a copy available to the family in the home (Ahmann 1986) and should be updated and changed to provide current information about treatment modalities.

Teaching is an important aspect of the home care nurse's role. The goal is to develop the parent's and caregiver's ability to care for the child. The care plan should include detailed teaching objectives and strategies wherever necessary. The demonstration–return-demonstration method is a helpful tool for instruction, and it can easily be incorporated into the nursing care plan. As caregivers become proficient in an area, notation should be recorded on the nursing care plan so that subsequent health care providers will be aware of the caregiver's abilities. This teaching interaction between the home care nurse and parents or significant caregivers can help them overcome insecurities or feelings of inadequacy.

DOCUMENTATION

Documentation of care delivered in the home has taken on greater significance owing to the increased potential for litigation, the increasing number of professionals in the home, and the increased sophistication of technology in the home. Documentation is also a critical factor for home care agencies meeting state licensure and certification requirements and is the basis for Medicare and third-party reimbursements (Con-

naway 1985). The clinical record serves a variety of purposes in the home care agency. These include billing for services rendered, maintaining continuity of care by providing a tool to communicate care to other professionals involved with the patient, and providing the basis for research, audits, and statistical information. Most importantly, the clinical chart serves as a legal document that provides a mechanism for ensuring that the nurse has met professional standards of practice when delivering patient care (Connaway 1985).

Increasingly, providing pediatric home care requires home care professionals to deal with a variety of technology. It is the home care nurse's responsibility to document meticulously the maintenance of this equipment to ensure the child's safety. Flow sheets and graphics have been developed that can be used when hourly notation of equipment settings or maintenance checks are required. The medical team or the home care agency should define the parameters for documentation of high-tech equipment.

REFERENCES

Ahmann, Elizabeth. *Home Care for the High Risk Infant*. Rockville, Md.: Aspen Publishers, Inc., 1986.

Bates, Barbara. *A Guide to Physical Examination*. 2d ed. Philadelphia: J.B. Lippincott Co., 1979.

Bernstein, L.; Bernstein, R.S.; and Dana, R.H. *Interviewing: A Guide for Health Professionals*. 2d ed. New York: Appleton-Century-Crofts, 1974.

Connaway, Nancy. "Documenting Patient Care in the Home: Legal Issues for Home Health Nurses." *Home Healthcare Nurse* 3, no. 5 (1985):6–8.

Pediatric Health History

Name: _____   Nickname: _____
Age: _____ Sex: _____   Date of Birth: _____
Address: _____   Phone: _____
_____
Mother's Name: _____   Work Phone: _____
Father's Name: _____   Work Phone: _____
Parents living together: _____

PHYSICIANS

Doctor: _____   Phone: _____
_____   Phone: _____
_____   Phone: _____
_____   Phone: _____
_____   Phone: _____
Diagnosis: _____
_____
_____
_____

FAMILY AND HOME DATA

Family Members (list names and ages)
Mother _____   Age _____
Father _____   Age _____
Sibling _____   Age _____
Sibling _____   Age _____
Sibling _____   Age _____
Sibling _____   Age _____
Description of home and community (observation for safety, location of equipment, availability of telephone, transportation) _____
_____
_____
_____
_____

Caregiver Skills and Family Adjustment

Growing confidence and competence _____

Generally comfortable in caregiver role, relaxed, seems confident _____

_____

Seems overwhelmed _____   Many questions _____

Lack of interest _____   Anxious _____

Parents' participation as Caregivers:

Mother _____   Father _____

Siblings: Adjusting Well _____Not Adjusting _____

Support systems (involvement with agencies) _____

Comments: _____

_____

Family Health History

Source of Information _____

Note the occurrence within the family of any of the following conditions: asthma/allergies, diabetes, heart disease, hypertension, renal disease, stroke, cancer, alcoholism, drug abuse, hearing/vision loss, mental illness, mental retardation, deaths, headaches, anemia

Mother _____

_____

_____

Father _____

_____

Siblings _____

_____

Maternal grandmother _____

_____

Maternal grandfather _____

_____

Paternal grandmother _____

_____

Paternal grandfather _____

_____

PAST HEALTH HISTORY

Prenatal History

Age of mother _____ Gr _____ Para _____ AB _____

Prenatal care (frequency, source) _____

_____

Complications of pregnancy (infections, bleeding, etc.) _____

_____

Alcohol (frequency, amount) _____Smoking (packs/day) _____

_____ Injury _____Weight gain _____

Caffeine _____ X-rays _____

Medications _____

Birth History

Hospital _____Address _____

Gestational age _____ Type of delivery _____ Length of labor _____
Labor: _____ Spontaneous _____ Induced _____
Presentation: Vaginal _____ Breech _____ Vertex _____
Medications used _____
Apgars ___/___ Birth weight _____ Length _____ Head circumference _____
Comments: _____
_____
_____
_____

Newborn History
(Place a check mark near applicable items and explain in comment section.)
Respiratory difficulties _____ Infections _____ Surgical procedures _____ Jaundice _____
Seizures _____ Anemia _____ Physical abnormalities _____ Feeding problems _____
Temperature instability _____
Length of hospitalization: Newborn nursery _____
Intermediate nursing _____ ICU _____
Comments: _____
_____

Allergies
Foods _____
Medications _____
Other _____

Accidents

_____
_____
_____
_____

Illnesses

Measles _____	Rubella _____
Chickenpox _____	Mumps _____
Scarlet fever _____	Strep throat _____
Meningitis _____	Hepatitis _____
Pneumonia _____	Otitis _____
Tuberculosis _____	Abscesses _____
Febrile convulsions _____	Pertussis _____

Other _____
_____
_____

Previous Hospitalizations

_____
_____
_____
_____

Brief history of the most recent hospitalization _____
_____

HEALTH MAINTENANCE

Immunizations
DT or DPT (circle)   1   2   3   Booster   1   2
TOPV   1   2   3   Booster   1   2
MMR _____
Tetanus _____Booster _____
Tine test _____
Other _____
Reactions _____

Screening Procedures
Hct. _____ Hbg. _____ T.B. _____Eye exam _____
Hearing exam _____ Dental exam (source and frequency) _____

DEVELOPMENTAL HISTORY

Reflexes (indicate presence with a check mark.)
Moro _____ Stepping _____ Rooting _____ Sucking _____ Tonic Neck _____
Grasp _____ Blinking _____
Development milestones: (list age acquired)
Hold up head _____   Responds to name _____
Smiles responsively _____   Cruise _____
Roll prone to supine _____   Walk _____
Roll supine to prone _____   Babble _____
Voluntary grasp–release   First word _____
    of toys _____   Finger feed _____
Sit alone _____   Cup drink _____
Four-point crawl _____   Spoon feed _____
Pull to stand _____

PERSONAL HISTORY

Activities/hobbies/play/toys (note special security toy) _____
_____
_____

Caregiver's description of the child's usual personality (include how child usually expresses emotion)
_____
_____

Parent–child interactions _____
_____

Special fears/concerns of child _____
_____
_____

Peer relationships _____
_____
_____

Idiosyncratic behaviors or habits (e.g., thumb sucking, nail biting, temper tantrums, head banging)
_____
_____

SCHOOL HISTORY

Does child attend school? _____ Name of school _____
Current grade _____ Address _____
Favorite subjects _____
_____

Least favorite subjects _____

History of past performance _____

General attitudes about school/career plans _____

DAILY PATTERNS

Feeding Patterns
Bottle _____ Special nipple _____ Breast fed _____ Cup _____ Nasogastric tube _____
Gastrostomy _____
Appetite _____ Schedule _____
Type of formula (amount, frequency) _____
Juices (amount, frequency) _____
Concerns/problems _____
_____
_____
_____

Sleep Patterns
Sleep schedule (include naps) _____
Crib _____ Bed _____ Bedwetter _____ Climber _____ Pacifier _____
Bedtime routine and/or sleeping positions _____
_____
Problems/concerns _____
_____

Elimination Patterns
Toilet trained: Urine _____ Bowel _____ Cloth diapers _____ Disposable diapers _____
Training pants _____ Potty chair _____ Other _____
Urinary habits (frequency, amount, color, odor) _____
Bowel habits (frequency, type, color) _____
Word(s) for bowel movements _____ Urination _____
Problems/concerns _____
_____
_____

Special Needs for Activities of Daily Living
Crutches _____ Wheelchair _____ Braces _____
Other _____
Braces for teeth or other oral appliances _____
_____
Glasses _____ Contacts _____ Hearing aid _____ Wig _____
Bathing (frequency, method) _____
Discipline _____
_____
Self-care: Feeding _____ Bathing _____
        Dressing _____ Toileting _____
Do you have any problems/concerns with managing your child in the home? _____
_____
_____
_____
_____

SPECIAL CARE NEEDS

Source of information _____

Parental description of child's medical problems _____

_____

_____

_____

_____

Equipment (type, location, arrangement, and prescribed settings) _____

_____

_____

_____

_____

_____

Suppliers

Name _____   Phone _____

Name _____   Phone _____

Name _____   Phone _____

Name _____   Phone _____

Treatments

Name _____   Frequency _____   Schedule _____

Name _____   Frequency _____   Schedule _____

Name _____   Frequency _____   Schedule _____

Name _____   Frequency _____   Schedule _____

Name _____   Frequency _____   Schedule _____

Medications

Name _____   Frequency _____   Schedule _____

Name _____   Frequency _____   Schedule _____

Name _____   Frequency _____   Schedule _____

Name _____   Frequency _____   Schedule _____

Name _____   Frequency _____   Schedule _____

R.N. Signature _____Date Completed _____

Note: Modified with permission from "Nursing Intake History" (Ahmann, Peck, and Lierman), Children's Hospital National Medical Center Home Care Program, as printed in *Home Care for the High Risk Infant: A Holistic Guide to Using Technology* by Elizabeth Ahmann, Aspen Publishers, Inc., © 1987.

Appendix 2-B

Review of Systems

List Areas of Concern or Areas within Normal Limits

Review of Systems (Circle if Present)

1. **SKIN:** Itching, dryness, rashes, acne, bruises easily, hypersensitivity to tactile input, hyperpigmented spots, nodules

2. **EYES:** Glasses _____ Last eye exam
   _____

   Itch, water, tire easily, redness, stands close to TV, clumsy, sensitive to light, cross, rubs eyes, squints, slanted downward, slanted upward, epicanthal folds, wide spacing. Other _____
   _____

   Risk factors from history:
   _____
   _____

3. **EARS:** Earaches, hearing loss, infections, sensitive to noise, drainage, ringing, fears strangers, wakens from sleep when called, low-set, malformed. Other _____
   Risk factors from history:
   _____
   _____

4. **NOSE:** Frequent colds, itching, discharge, infections, paroxysmal sneezing, nosebleeds, broad flat bridge. Other _____
   _____

5. **MOUTH–THROAT:** Dental cavities, toothache, bleeding gums, sore throat, strep, hoarseness, swollen glands, loss of color of teeth, pitted teeth, thin upper lip. Other _____
   _____

6. **CARDIORESPIRATORY:** Coughing, wheezing, shortness of breath, cyanosis, tires easily with running, hyperventilates. Other _____

_____

7. **GASTROINTESTINAL:** Diarrhea, constipation, bleeding, abdominal pain, vomiting. Other _____

8. **GENITOURINARY:** Strong stream, dribbling, dysuria, burning, frequency, odor, color, undescended testes. Other _____

_____

9. **MUSCULOSKELETAL:** Pain, swelling, leg pains, redness in joints, limited range of motion in joints, back pains, fractures easily or multifractures, lax joints, nails malformed, webbing of digits, hypermuscle or hypomuscle tone.

10. **NEUROLOGICAL:** Headaches, dizziness, twitches, blackout spells, tremors, fainting spells, reflexes appropriate for age.

11. **ENDOCRINE:** Deviation in growth pattern, hyperactivity or hypoactivity, excessive thirst, frequent voiding, coarse hair texture, hair pattern whorls, excessive body/facial hair.

12. **GENETIC:** Family history of delays, seizures, mental retardation, stillbirths, diagnosed genetic or congenital defect, failure to thrive. Other _____

_____

Note: Reprinted from *FAT: The Family Assessment Tool for School Nurses and Other Professionals* by Sandra Holt and Thelma Robinson, revision authors, Thelma Robinson (school-aged) and Melissa Van Wey (infant/preschool) with permission of Family Assessment Tools, ©1979, 1985.

Chapter 3

Financing Pediatric Home Care

Wendy L. Votroubek

Financing of pediatric home care can be considered a problem that results from success (Gibbons 1987). The success is the technological and medical science advancements that have dramatically increased survival rates for children who would not have survived even 20 years ago. The problem is that many of these children are dependent on technology, and funds available to finance their long-term care are limited. Payment sources have not kept pace with the needs of these children, whose families face total health care costs significantly higher than what many individuals will pay in a lifetime.

Issues discussed in this chapter include costs of home care, methods of financing, and funding considerations or strategies before the initiation of home care and during the provision of home care. Sample cost-comparisons and cost analysis are also included.

COSTS OF HOME CARE

Home care costs can be divided into two categories. Start-up costs, the first category, are one-time costs incurred before or at the time of discharge. They include the costs of home improvements, supplies and equipment, and caregiver training. The second category, on-going costs, includes items such as supplies and services needed for the duration of home care. Some of the items included in this category are nurses, therapists, and disposable equipment.

Start-up Costs

A common start-up cost is financing of home improvements or modifications required to accommodate special equipment and/or nursing staff. These modifications may include widened doorways and ramps, room additions or remodeling, wiring and other electrical work, and special needs such as generators. Occasionally home modifications are not sufficient and the family may need to move to a home that is more sanitary or closer to a medical facility.

Frequently, supplies and equipment are the largest component of the start-up costs. Equipment will either be rented or purchased, depending on the length of its use and/or insurance benefits.

The last component of start-up costs is family and caregiver training. The family must be trained to perform all aspects of the child's care even when professional home care is not deemed necessary. The amount of training depends on the diagnosis, the child's condition, and the family's ability to understand the components of the care. The family of a ventilator-dependent child, for example, will normally require at least 2 to 3 weeks of training by nursing and therapy staff and a rooming-in period (see Chapter 1).

Ongoing Costs

Ongoing supplies and services are the items the family purchases on a continuing basis to provide care for the child at home. These may include oxygen, ventilator tubings, suction catheters, formulas and feeding bags, dressings and diapers. The most costly ongoing supplies are probably incurred by children requiring total parenteral nutrition (TPN). This is because the nutrient formulas are individualized, require special handling and storage, and have expensive components such as predigested fats, carbohydrates, protein solutions, vitamins, and minerals (U.S. Congress 1987).

Certain funding sources will pay for the ongoing medical supplies as long as they are necessary. Other sources will pay for them as long as there is professional nursing care in the home. Families should review their insurance policies to determine the durable medical equipment and supplies coverage. If there is a choice of vendors, families should compare costs to obtain the best combination of price and service. Occasionally, diagnostic specific organizations (e.g., the Muscular Dystrophy Association) or community agencies will assist with the purchase of various medical supplies.

Nursing is the most expensive component of ongoing home care costs. Nursing care assistance is directly related to the amount of care the family is willing and able to provide and the funding source benefits. Nursing care for the technology-dependent child depends on three factors: (1) the complexity of the care required (ventilator-dependent child), (2) the amount of paid nursing care required (8 hours per day as compared with 24 hours per day), and (3) the registration level of nurse in the home (RN or LPN) (U.S. Congress 1987). For example, home care for a ventilator-dependent child requiring nursing care 16 to 24 hours per day will cost more than a child receiving intravenous antibiotic therapy requiring visits by a registered nurse every 6 hours.

Treatments performed by occupational, physical, or speech therapists form another major expense. Many funding sources will pay for these therapists if they are prescribed by a physician and there is an observable patient gain. If the funding sources will not pay for these therapists, state or local agencies or schools may provide care (see Chapter 17). Therapies performed by a respiratory therapist usually are not covered by third-party payers; thus, the family

and/or home care nurses must perform required respiratory treatments.

Outpatient costs, including physician and laboratory services, are also incurred on an ongoing basis. Outpatient care may include well child follow-up, such as immunizations; management of the disease process, including specialty care; and laboratory tests, especially for children on TPN or chemotherapy. Follow-up care may also include a dietitian for the child with nutritional needs.

The costs of recurrent hospitalization must also be included in ongoing expenses. Although home care nursing is usually in lieu of hospitalization, a child may require brief periods of hospitalization for treatment of new problems, evaluation and assessments, or respite. These hospitalizations are often not included when comparing costs of home care and institutionalization.

Case management is extremely beneficial to the home care process, but often an optional ongoing cost because funding may not cover this aspect. It includes organizing, appropriating, and coordinating services received and equipment used. Another major element is to monitor patient progress continuously so necessary changes to the treatment program can be initiated. Case management also includes organizing and using available community resources. This type of management is appropriate for chronically ill and medically needy children and their families. Further information on case management is available in Chapter 2 and Appendix A.

The final ongoing cost that should be considered is respite care. Respite care will increase the total costs of home care, but it gives the family relief from ongoing nursing care and may allow them to care for their child at home for a longer period of time. Respite care can be paid for by third-party payers or, in some cases, by state or county funds. Often though, funding is not available and the child is hospitalized, put in temporary foster care, or cared for by relatives.

Cost Analysis/Cost Comparison

Most payers will require a cost analysis/cost comparison that outlines the components and costs of the home care program. This analysis provides the funding source with a breakdown of the services to be delivered and their costs. Funding sources may solicit cost analyses from more than one agency to determine which agency will provide the most effective cost-saving strategy. Cost analysis includes both start-up and ongoing costs. It is not necessary to include the costs of outpatient visits and rehospitalization because these are not provided by the home care agency (Exhibit 3-1).

Cost comparisons examine the relative costs of hospitalization and equivalent care provided at home. Most cost comparisons are not true comparisons of equivalent costs because normally only reimbursable costs are included. Indirect costs to the family such as room and board, increased utility costs, time off from work for which parents are not paid, and other costs of caregivers are not included. True hospital costs may not be reflected if quoted hospital rates do not reflect discounts negotiated by third-party payers. A typical cost comparison is shown in Exhibit 3-2.

METHODS OF FINANCING

The population of technology-dependent and medically needy children is relatively small but uses a large percentage of health care resources. One source states that children with disabilities incur medical costs between 3 and 38 times greater than children without disabilities (Fox 1984). The costs are incurred by both third-party payers and families.

The extent to which health care, including home care, is available for medically needy and technology-dependent children depends largely on the availability of financing. This availability can be broken down into three factors: (1) the degree to which this population is covered by private insurance or public health care programs, (2) whether the funding source covers home care for the population (for the technology-dependent child it is ideal to have long-term coverage), and (3) whether the home care benefits are sufficient to finance most of the medical needs of the child (U.S. Congress 1987).

The various sources of financing for home care are private insurance, health maintenance organizations, Medicaid, individual and community-based waivers, Department of Defense—CHAMPUS, and other programs and services. In addition to describing what each program typically pays for, the potential problems specific to each source of payment are discussed.

Private Insurance

Private insurance is the main source of health care coverage for children with serious illnesses (Fox 1986a). The purpose of private insurance is not to provide comprehensive health care; it is pooled protection against the risk of unexpected medical and financial demands (Weeks 1985).

This type of insurance coverage varies with the benefits and coverages written into the policy. Some states mandate certain benefits such as coverage for a newborn child or handicapped child over the age of 18; however, most coverage is dependent on the individual or group policy. The most extensive insurance benefit packages are provided through group policies (Fox 1986a). Data from the Department of Health and Human Services has shown that a large percentage of privately insured chronically ill or disabled children have group policy coverage. The remaining percentage that has individual insurance policies is likely to have substandard coverage. The individual insurance for these children might include insurance with riders that exclude coverage for treatment of the child's specific preexisting condition and any isolated problems. The riders may be temporary or lifetime, depending on the severity and type of diagnosis (Fox 1986a). The terms commonly used with private insurance that outline insurance benefits and limitations are defined in Exhibit 3-3.

The main features of insurance coverage that can affect long-term home care are lifetime maximums, stop-loss provisions, and covered or limited services. Insurance companies have expanded home coverage benefits within the past 5 years to include higher maximum lifetime benefits and annual catastrophic stop-loss provisions. On the other hand, a large number of medium-sized and large business firms have no provisions for home health care benefits and most home care coverage is not sufficient to meet the needs of a child requiring ongoing nursing care (U.S. Congress 1987). In addition, some employers have increased cost sharing requirements, with resultant higher employee copay-

Exhibit 3-1 Cost Analysis for Care of a Ventilator-Dependent Child

Ms. Zee Apple
Department of Utilization Review
ABC Health Plan
Tucson, AZ 85701

Re: Joshua Wita

Dear Zee,

Enclosed is PDQ Home Care's cost estimate of home care services for Joshua Wita. We made the following assumptions in preparing our estimate:

1. Services require 30 days per month.
2. R.N. services are quoted based on two 12-hour shifts, 7 AM–7 PM and 7 PM–7 AM, using Monday through Friday bill rate. The prices reflect case management and all necessary taxes and insurances.
3. In the interest of cost reduction, we explored the benefits of purchase, rather than rental, of the enteral pump. PDQ Home Care does not inventory our respiratory and enteral supplies. We obtained our pricing for these items from Zodiac Medical Supply.

Please let us know if you need any additional information.

Sincerely,

Nancy Matler, MS, RN
Pediatric Manager

Enclosures
cc: Lori Gainer, MD—University Hospital
    Pamela Wilson, MSW—University Hospital

PDQ HOME CARE

Joshua Wita Home Care
COST ANALYSIS
April 2, 1988

Home Nursing Care

	7 AM–7 PM	7 PM–7 AM	Monthly
Registered Nurse	$400	$450	$25,500
Licensed Practical Nurse	$250	$270	$15,600

Equipment Purchase

Ventilator	$8,995
External battery and cable	$ 300
Ambu Bag	$ 358
Medimist	$ 263
Total equipment purchase price:	$9,916

Enteral Feeding

Cost: $42/day; $1,260/month
Includes enteral pump, IV pole, feeding bags with tubing (quantity 31), formula (Isomil 24 cal. w/iron), clamps, catheter plugs, and three-way connector.
Alternate Cost: $28.60/day; $858/month
This reduced cost can be achieved by purchasing the enteral pump and IV pole for a one-time charge of $480.

Monthly DME Rental

Suction machine	$120
Liquid oxygen system	$372
(includes contents)	
Infant monitor with intercom	$355
Total monthly rental	$847

Exhibit 3-1 continued

Monthly Disposable Supplies

Cost: $826.50/month
　Includes 3 feet of ventilator tubing, 6 to 7 inches of flex tubing, swivel tracheostomy adapter, tracheostomy tube, IPPB circuit, pall filter, proximal T adapter, air intake filter, 100-ft. roll of corrugated flex tubing, De-Lee suction catheters, disinfectant, 3-mL sterile saline vials, and infant monitor supplies.

Total Supply and Equipment Cost

Monthly ongoing cost	$ 2,531
Purchase cost	$10,396 (includes enteral pump)
Total cost	$12,927

Total Start-up Cost Including Personnel

Registered nurses	$25,000
Licensed practical nurses	$15,600
Total Start-Up Cost with Registered Nurse	$37,927
Total Start-up Cost with Licensed Practical Nurse	$28,527

Exhibit 3-2 Cost Comparison for Care of Patient with Cystic Fibrosis at Home

Patient: Aaron Wilson
Date:　4/88

Procedure	*University Hospital*	*Home Care*
Room charge	$550	High-tech nurse, $344/day Visits, $86/day; 　four visits daily
Respirator treatment		
Percussion and postural drainage	$176/day ($44 each, 4 × day)	No additional charge
Aerosol treatment nebulizers	$12 each	$4 each (do not need new 　one daily)
Bronchodilator	$3.50/day	$1.50/day
Disinfectant	N/A	$10
Oxygen	$100	$15
IV antibiotic therapy		
IV solution	$33/day	$20/day
IV administration set	$33/day	$14/day
IV pump rental	$38/day	not necessary
IV cassette rental	$30/day	not necessary
IV antibiotic	$240/day	$240/day
Total	$1,215.50/day	$648.50/day

ments and deductibles. Greater cost-sharing requirements undoubtedly place a financial hardship on many families with chronically ill or handicapped children (Fox 1986a).

State regulations have assisted insurers requesting home care benefits. Some states have laws requiring health insurance plans to include home care coverage (American Medical Association 1986). The laws, however, do not apply to employers who self-insure; only those policies written by health insurance companies are affected.

Individual benefits management is a program offered by many insurers that recognizes the potential savings of home care. This program allows for reimbursement of a wide range of home and community-based services, provided that their total cost is less than hospitalization (Fox 1986a). Almost all large carriers offer this kind of benefit. It may be found under titles such

Exhibit 3-3 Terms Commonly Used with Private Insurance

- *catastrophic stop loss*—upper limits on client's out-of-pocket payment for services received

- *copayment or coinsurance date*—percent of the total cost of services received that insured is responsible for; an example is 20 percent of the first $5,000.

- *first dollar deductible*—the amount the insured must pay each year before insurance coverage begins; depending on the insurance carrier there will be either a single or a family deductible.

- *lifetime maximum*—maximum amount of dollars for all medical care per insured, may be per diagnosis; common lifetime maximums are $50,000–$2 million.

- *limitations to services*—usually this is in regard to equipment, therapies, and home nursing care; for example, the limitation would be 2 hours of nursing care per day by a registered nurse.

- *preexisting conditions*—any condition that insured has been diagnosed and received treatment for at the time of application of insurance policy; length of treatment exclusion of the preexisting condition varies per insurance company.

- *premium*—stated annual cost of insurance policy; payments may be per month or quarterly.

- *probationary limitations*—period of delay for insurance to receive benefits after joining new policy; for example, 30 to 60 days.

- *riders*—statement of insurance coverage that specifically states what is excluded or limited, usually in relation to preexisting condition.

- *stop loss*—insured annual upper limit on out-of-pocket expenditures.

as individual case management, large claims management, or medical care management (Fox 1986a). The case manager, in many instances, is a registered nurse who assists the family and home care agency in providing effective services.

Reimbursement Strategies

Home health agencies must follow certain guidelines during home care initiation to ensure payment is received for care provided. When the referral is made, the home care agency obtains the name of the insurance company, its telephone number, and applicable policy and group numbers. The insurance company is then called to verify home care benefits, including coverage of services, deductible, stop-loss amount, and lifetime maximum. If the insurance company

has a case management person, required care and expected costs should be discussed at this time.

Home care agencies must also determine which of the following are required for billings: assignment of benefits, insurance claim, and/or nurse's notes. Many insurance companies also require physician's orders and a letter of medical necessity (Exhibit 3-4). Insurance companies will not normally guarantee payment over the telephone. Continuing communication with the insurance company is necessary to avoid problems in procuring payment.

Health Maintenance Organizations

Health maintenance organizations (HMOs) are another source of home care financing. HMOs provide comprehensive health care for members and their families for a fixed prepaid premium (Leonard 1986). HMOs function as both provider of care as well as insurer. Salaried staff members or independent physician associations (IPAs) under contract provide care.

HMOs outline the specific care that is available for subscribers. Inpatient care is provided through hospitals that have a contract with the HMO; outpatient care is available through contracted physicians and therapists. Home care is normally available through contracted home care agencies with varying limitations on amount and type of nursing care provided. Occasionally HMO benefits are not appropriate to care for the medically needy or technology-dependent child at home.

The primary advantages of coverage through an HMO are lower or predictable costs and assured access to care. The family's indirect costs are lower than with traditional insurance. Ongoing care decisions can be made on an individual basis by local coordinators and discharge planners. The disadvantages are the limitations imposed by contractual providers and services. Occasionally the mandated home care providers do not have the experience or expertise required to provide care for medically fragile children. In addition, home care may be a more costly alternative to hospitalization because of the discount contractual arrangements between the local hospital and HMO.

Exhibit 3-4 Sample Letter of Medical Necessity

Star Insurance Company
609 Brodie Drive
Tucson, AZ 85700

Attn: Medical Case Management   Re: Jason Miner
                                                                Number 023507 D

To whom it may concern,

　　Jason Miner has been my patient since his birth at University Hospital. I anticipate discharging him to home care within the next 10 to 14 days if proper arrangements can be made.

　　Jason's medical problems are bronchopulmonary dysplasia, tracheal stenosis, and failure to thrive. Currently he has a tracheostomy and requires supplemental oxygen, frequent tracheal suctioning, and respiratory therapy. In addition, he has a gastrostomy tube and receives frequent tube feedings.

　　Jason will need nursing care for at least 8 hours a day for the first month. As Jason continues to improve and his parents get accustomed to the extensive home care procedures, we anticipate less home care will be needed.

　　Please let me know if additional information is needed.

Sincerely,

Frederick Burton, MD
Pediatric Pulmonologist
University Hospital

Reimbursement Strategies

HMOs usually provide discharge coordinators at a local level, thus streamlining the process of providing payment for home care services. The case coordinator is in contact with the patient and family and performs cost analysis of services to be provided by the contractual home care agency and durable medical equipment company (Briggs and Cummings 1986). Authorization for services occurs at the time of referral with issuance of an authorization number for the expected duration of treatment. Ongoing care is authorized at regular scheduled intervals.

Medicaid

Medicaid is the largest public sector financing program that involves children. Medicaid provides health insurance to financially disadvantaged persons through state-administered programs that are funded with a mix of state and federal monies. As a condition of federal funding, the federal government mandates that the states designate eligible populations for specific programs and limit federal support of services. States, however, are able to tailor programs on a local level to fit their needs (U.S. Congress 1987). Arizona is the only state that does not have a formal Medicaid program. It has a demonstration project, Arizona Health Care Cost Containment System (AHCCCS), that does not contain all the services mandated by the federal government.

Medicaid eligibility requirements vary from state to state. The eligibility is "piggybacked" to various welfare statutes, Aid to Families with Dependent Children (AFDC), and Supplemental Security Income (SSI). Eligibility is also dependent on severe financial and categorical eligibility standards (Rosenbaum 1986).* The linkage of Medicaid eligibility to SSI and of SSI to institutionalization allowed a child with long-term disability and inadequate private insurance to receive hospital services under Medicaid regardless of the family's income and assets. The eligibility criteria established a system by which a technology-dependent child could receive hospital care, covered under Medicaid, without impoverishing the family. Medicaid had an incentive for hospital care instead of home

---

*SSI eligibility standards include a patient with a disability that is expected to last _____ (or until death) and with an income or assets below a certain limit. Income and resources are not considered though if the individual has been institutionalized for _____.

care because once home, the family's resources would be deemed available to Medicaid.

The situation changed in 1981 after a family appealed to the president and Congress for home coverage for their medically needy daughter. The federal government now permits states to waive certain eligibility criteria and provide home care outside their regular Medicaid program.

Some states do provide pediatric home care as a part of the Medicaid program. The services include home nursing visits, medical equipment, and supplies. Home nursing services may be intermittent or part-time home care, with a limitation of 50 visits per year (U.S. Department of Health and Human Services 1984). Seldom are the services adequate to provide home care for a technology-dependent child.

Medicaid Options

Four options exist under the Medicaid program to provide home care for the technology-dependent/medically needy child. Three options require that states obtain a federally approved waiver of Medicaid rules to provide additional services. The fourth does not require a waiver approval; it allows changes in the eligibility rules (Fox 1986b).

1. The individual "Katie Beckett" waiver (no longer used)
2. The regular 2176 home- and community-based waiver
3. The model 2176 home- and community-based waiver
4. The state plan amendment

Eligibility requirements for each waiver vary, including categorical and income requirements. In the following section the Medicaid waivers and their advantages and disadvantages are discussed. A summary of each option and the criteria specific for that plan are provided in Table 3-1.

Individual Waiver. The individual waiver program and the "Katie Beckett" waiver were created in 1982* by the secretary of the Department of Health and Human Services in response to the need for home care for a technology-dependent child. The waiver was the first Medicaid plan to address the problems of loss of Medicaid and SSI eligibility for patients who could be discharged to the home to receive less costly care. The waiver was intended as a temporary strategy to permit specific persons to retain Medicaid coverage for home care. It was a stopgap measure implemented while states pursued other long-range options, including state amendments or 2176 waivers (Fox 1986b).

"Katie Beckett" waiver requests were accepted between June 1982 and December 1984 from state Medicaid agencies. A board determined whether the SSI deeming rules should apply in each case. These rules consider family income and resources to assess eligibility for SSI payments and Medicaid. Waiver of the deeming requirements was based on two factors: (1) home-based care would result in reduced Medicaid expenditures and (2) quality of the care would be as good or better than that provided in an institution (U.S. Congress 1987).

Medicaid eligibility at home continued until the waiver was no longer appropriate. It included all services that were part of the state's routine Medicaid plan. States were not able to expand Medicaid programs that may be needed for the technology-dependent child.

The waiver had many attractions and one drawback. The benefits included cost savings of home care versus hospitalization, the opportunity for disabled children to receive care at home, the use of Medicaid benefits as an insurance backup, and the opportunity for the medically needy child to earn higher income. The major drawback was that many states did not provide Medicaid home care benefits. Unless other financing sources were available to pay for private duty nursing care, the waiver did not provide adequate care for the medically needy child.

Regular 2176 Waivers. The home- and community-based waivers enable states to finance noninstitutional services for Medicaid recipients in lieu of hospitalization. The waiver program was enacted in 1981 as part of the Omnibus Budget Reconciliation Act in response to states' demands for flexibility in dealing with decreased federal funds (Rosenbaum 1986). The waivers designate specific target populations, broaden the usual income eligibility process, and expand the range of home- and community-based services available under the state's Medicaid plan.

---

*As part of the Tax Equity and Fiscal Responsibility Act of 1982 (TEFRA) Amendment.

Table 3-1 Comparison of State Medicaid Options for Extended Home- and Community-Based Care

Option	Categorical Eligibility	Income Eligibility	Number of Persons Able to Participate	Geographical Areas	Allowable Services	Time Period
Individual waivers (no longer newly awarded)	Disabled persons who, because of relatives' income, would otherwise be eligible for Medicaid only if institutionalized	Deeming rules are waived	One person per waiver	Not applicable	Regular state Medicaid services only	Persons eligible until waiver no longer needed
Regular 2176 waiver	State may target to aged or disabled, mentally retarded or developmentally disabled, or mentally ill. Persons must require level of care provided in Intermediate Care Facility (IFC), Intermediate Care Facility for the Mentally Retarded (ICF/MR), Skilled Nursing Facility (SNF), or hospital	States may waive deeming rules; may increase income eligibility to 300% of SSI standard	All persons meeting eligibility criteria	May be less than statewide	Can offer certain services otherwise not authorized under Medicaid law; can provide more extensive coverage of regular services	3-year waiver; 5-year renewal
Model 2176 waivers	States can define specific categories of disabled persons. Patients must require level of care provided in ICF, ICF/MR, SNF, or hospital	States must waive deeming rules.	50 or fewer slots per waiver program	May be less than statewide	Similar to regular 2176 waivers; must offer at least one service in addition to those provided by regular Medicaid	3-year waiver; 5-year renewal
State plan amendment	Disabled persons younger than age 19 who, because of relatives' income, would otherwise be eligible for Medicaid only if institutionalized; patient must require level of care provided in a hospital, ICF, ICF/MR, or SNF	Deeming rules are waived	All persons meeting eligibility criteria	Statewide	Regular state Medicaid services only	State option

Source: Technology-Dependent Children's Access to Medicaid Home Care Financing by H.B. Fox and R. Yoshpe, Office of Technology Assessment, U.S. Congress, August 1986.

The population eligible for the regular 2176 waiver comprises those likely to require long-term care in a skilled nursing facility, intermediate care facility, or hospital (Rosenbaum 1986). The individuals served under the waiver program must be from one of the following Medicaid target groups: aged, disabled, or both; mentally retarded, developmentally disabled, or both; or mentally ill. States can serve more than one group by having more than one waiver. Three additional restrictions to eligibility are applied. First, persons must reside within certain geographical areas of the state. Second, patients must be discharged from a long-term care institution. Finally, eligibility is restricted to persons for whom the Medicaid cost of providing home- and community-based services is less than the cost of institutional care (Fox 1986b; U.S. Congress 1987).

Income eligibility for the waiver population can be amended beyond the regular Medicaid program. The first method increases the income eligibility limits to three times the maximum Social Security payments. Persons would be obligated under the income criteria to contribute to the cost of the care. The other option is to consider a portion of the parents' or spouses' income unavailable to the child or adult receiving home care services. Once the eligibility criteria are established, all those who apply for the waiver are accepted until the project limit is reached.

Services provided under the regular 2176 waiver include those not allowed by Medicaid or that are to some degree not covered and include nursing, medical supplies and equipment, therapies, homemaker/home health aide personal care services, adult day care, habitation, case management, respite services, and minor home modifications and utility expenses.

Technology-dependent and medically needy children may receive services as a result of the waiver following a cost comparison. This comparison must use a special cost-effectiveness formula developed for the waiver. The reason is twofold: (1) the waiver system increases the number of Medicaid recipients receiving long-term care and (2) for a state to receive waiver approval, it must show its proposed program is no more costly to Medicaid than institutional care.

The regular 2176 waiver has many advantages. One is the flexibility of target groups. Small, selective populations can be served across state or regional areas. The waiver can potentially serve a small group of disabled children who would otherwise be institutionalized. A disadvantage is that the SSI deeming rules provide waiver eligibility for a specific number of technology-dependent patients who have high care costs. States fear that surpassing original cost estimates will lead to denial of waiver renewal requests.

Model 2176 Waivers. The model 2176 waiver program was developed in December 1982 by the Health Care Financing Administration. It was designed to encourage states to provide home- and community-based services for disabled persons who would lose Medicaid eligibility with noninstitutional care (Fox 1986b). The model waiver is more restrictive than the regular waiver in that the state may apply it to no more than 50 children or adults at one time. The model waiver also must waive SSI income deeming rules to permit Medicaid eligibility for noninstitutional services. Eligibility is based not on the parents' income but on the child's income (Galten 1986).

States applying for the model waiver must meet the same requirements as with the regular 2176 waiver with one exception. They need offer only one home- or community-based waivered service. Population subgroups such as ventilator-dependent persons may be targeted under model waivers as they are under regular home- or community-based waivers.

Eligibility for the model waiver is limited to cases where the cost of home care is equal to or less than institutional care. Covered services may include respite care, skilled nursing care, case management, private duty skilled nursing care, home modifications, personal care, and homemaker/home health aide care (Galten 1986).

The model waiver offers the state several advantages over the regular waiver. It provides a cap on home care services and is usually approved by the Health Care Financing Administration more often than the regular waiver. If the model waiver is targeted to the medically needy/technology-dependent child exclusively, the requirement to document nursing home resident reduction can be avoided. The major draw-back is that the 50-person limitation may require the state to apply for more than one waiver to adequately serve the home care population.

State Plan Amendment. The state plan amendment provides an additional source of home care for children younger than the age of 19. This amendment provides home care through Medicaid for disabled children who would be eligible for Medicaid if they were institutionalized. It allows Medicaid home care benefits for children who require the level of care provided by a hospital, skilled nursing facility, or intermediate care facility and whose needs can be met at lower cost through home care. Services include only regularly covered Medicaid benefits; special services cannot be added. All children who meet the eligibility criteria are accepted, although the state can discontinue coverage at any time.

The state plan offers options for children who might not otherwise be able to live at home, but states agree there are disadvantages. The state plan is too broad and may offer home care to an overly large population. Parents and providers, on the other hand, feel the plan is not extensive enough and does not adequately care for a technology-dependent or medically needy child at home.

Medicaid Waiver Limitations

There are problems associated with each of the four Medicaid options discussed previously that limit the availability of home care services for technology-dependent or medically needy children. However, even with insufficient information available to providers and planners, restricted state monies, and restrictive federal regulations, the waivers do provide alternative settings of care for children who would otherwise receive care in institutions.

The problems associated with the waivers range from the basic design restricting needy services to limited public awareness for persons who refer children to the waiver system. The problems include state reluctance to apply the waivers because of the time-consuming and confusing federal application process; state-imposed limitations due to inadequate numbers of case managers and/or home care agencies; and the hospital discharge planners, health care pro-

Exhibit 3-5 State Regulations that Hinder or Limit Access of Medical Services

- Not waiving SSI deeming rules (possible only under the regular 2176 waivers, since these rules must be waived under the model waiver)
- Restricting eligibility for a waiver only to certain disease categories (possible only under model waiver)
- Allowing waivered services only to a person actually discharged from an institution
- Not allowing home care costs to be compared against the costs of hospitalization (as opposed to skilled nursing facilities or intermediate care facilities)
- Limiting reimbursable hospital days (which make it difficult to show program cost savings from home care to Medicaid)
- Not covering skilled shift nursing (i.e., private duty nursing) as a regular or a waivered service
- Not expanding in other ways the range of regular Medicaid home services available when relying on an individual waiver or state plan amendment to serve the needs of the technology-dependent population

Source: Technology-Dependent Children: Hospital vs. Home Care—A Technical Memorandum, Office of Technology Assessment, U.S. Congress, May 1987.

viders, and families who remain unaware of the possibilities raised by the local waiver program. Specific state regulations that tend to limit or hinder access of medical services to technology-dependent children are listed in Exhibit 3-5.

Children who require ventilator or nutritional support comprise 60 percent of the children served under the three waiver programs (state plan amendment information not available). Twenty-five percent have central nervous system disorders, including cerebral palsy, multiple sclerosis, quadriplegia, and spina bifida. Ten to 15 percent are children with accidental injuries, congenital diseases, or metabolic and immune disorders, such as cystic fibrosis, congenital heart disease, and multiple congenital anomalies (Fox 1986b).

Early Periodic Screening and Diagnosis and Treatment Programs

The waiver system is not the only route to home care services through Medicaid. A few states use early periodic screening and diagnosis and treatment programs (EPSDT) to provide services to children who fall under the basic Medicaid program. Federal Medicaid law makes EPSDT available to all categorically needy beneficiaries younger than the age of 21 (Rosenbaum 1986). Program services include comprehensive health assessments; immunizations; vision, dental, and hearing care; and treatment for any conditions discovered by the assessment. Additional services include administrative services, including outreach and case management, transportation, scheduling, and referrals for uncovered services (Rosenbaum 1986).

States also have the option to provide the services necessary for comprehensive home care for children under EPSDT even though those services are not available to adults. These additional services include private duty nursing care, medical equipment and supplies, and therapies.

EPSDT offers advantages to states while potentially providing full medical and remedial services for children. States can "waive" comparability for disabled children without providing Medicaid services to recipients of all ages. States can also shift cost from state appropriations to federally matched Medicaid funds.

Children with Special Health Care Needs

Children with Special Health Care Needs (CSHCN), formally Crippled Children's Services, is the nation's oldest, most direct, and sustained effort for support of children with chronic health problems (Hobbs et al. 1985). Started in 1935, it was the only major public source of support (state and federal mix) until Medicaid and other programs were started in the 1960s. Maternal and child health block grants in 1981 (under the Omnibus Budget Reconciliation Act) removed federal requirements for state services with resultant individual state appropriations and control—a state match of four federal dollars with three state dollars.

The range of conditions covered by the state program includes orthopedic problems, conditions requiring surgical procedures, leukemia, asthma, diabetes, renal and cardiac disorders, and, most recently, ventilator-dependent children. Services range from basic hospitalization and surgical care to supported clinics and special health teams that address the wide range of medi-

cal, emotional, and social needs of enrolled children (Hobbs et al. 1985). Conditions and services covered vary from state to state.

CSHCN provides care primarily through specialty clinics, as opposed to the Medicaid method of reimbursing for services provided. Medicaid will often pay for the services provided to eligible recipients in the specialty clinics. CSHCN eligibility policies parallel those of the Medicaid program almost exactly; the program will reimburse only for services after the spend down requirement is met and the child is receiving Medicaid services (Fox 1986b). Fees charged are based on the family's size, income, and resources, with low-income women and children receiving services free of charge.

The major focus of CSHCN services is clinic based, but some home care services are available. Services include skilled nursing care, extended home care services, outpatient visits, medications, supplies, and equipment. Some states provide certain services to fill gaps not covered by Medicaid, such as case management, other purchased equipment, special formulas, medications, and 1 month of skilled nursing care (Fox 1986b). The wide discretion available in implementation of state-covered CSHCN services can dramatically impact the availability of home care options.

The CSHCN programs in three states have served as an important source of financing care for ventilator-dependent children. Illinois, Louisiana, and Maryland were recipients of maternal and child health demonstration project funds— Special Project of Regional and National Significance (SPRANS)—between 1983 and 1986. The program objectives were to develop a regionalized system of care for technology-dependent children and to develop a comprehensive, coordinated model of care (U.S. Congress 1987). The programs, aimed at long-term care, included case management, coordination of care, and caregiver training.

The SPRANS grant programs have made CSHCN more aware of the need for case coordination for medically fragile children. The care of chronically ill children, and more importantly, technology-dependent children, is both fragmented and disease specific, and CSHCN programs need to become more involved in the coordination of care. As a result, CSHCN's programs in a few states are willing to take on the responsibility of expanding services.

Department of Defense Methods of Financing

The Department of Defense (DOD) directly provides or pays for medical care for active-duty and retired military personnel and their dependents (U.S. Congress 1987). Care is provided through DOD hospitals and the Civilian Health and Medical Program of the Uniformed Services (CHAMPUS), which pays for care that is not available at the military hospitals.

The DOD pays for long-term care through the regular home health benefits available through CHAMPUS, the Program for the Handicapped (PFTH), and the Home Health Care (HHC) Demonstration Project. The benefits of the regular home health care program include durable medical equipment, including ventilators; oxygen; parenteral and enteral nutrition therapies; physical therapy; skilled nursing care; and medications, medical supplies, and physician visits. Custodial care, however, is not paid or provided. Custodial care is care for a patient who (1) has a mental or physical disability that is expected to be prolonged; (2) requires a protected, monitored, or controlled environment, whether in an institution or in the home; (3) requires assistance to support the essentials of daily living; or (4) is not under active treatment that will reduce the disability to the extent necessary to enable the patient to function outside the protected environment (U.S. Department of Defense 1986). If a child is considered to be receiving custodial care he or she is eligible for only a small part of the usual home benefits. The benefits available in this case include medications, medical supplies, and up to 1 hour of nursing care per day.

The PFTH is a CHAMPUS program for handicapped dependents of military personnel. Persons, to be eligible, must demonstrate that services from public programs or institutions are not available. This program requires prior approval for coverage of all supplies and services. The services covered include institutional, outpatient, and home care and physical, occupational, and speech therapy. The ceiling for benefits is $1,000 per month (U.S. Congress 1987).

Skilled nursing care, homemaker care, and custodial care are not covered.

CHAMPUS' third program for providing home care is the HHC Demonstration Project. This program provides comprehensive home care services for technology-dependent children in lieu of hospitalization. Services include medical and skilled nursing care, home health aides, medications, durable medical equipment and supplies, therapies, and related services (Potter 1987).

The majority of persons who have received care through the HHC Demonstration Project are technology-dependent, supported by ventilators, oxygen therapy, TPN and/or intravenous antibiotic therapy. Initial reports show an initial cost savings of 25 to 45 percent; ongoing care costs savings were 55 to 59 percent (Potter 1987).

The original HHC Demonstration Project provided care from July 1986 to July 1988. CHAMPUS extended the program in 1988 to continue to provide home care benefits for at least another 1 to 2 years. In addition, CHAMPUS initiated Project CARE (Coordinate Appropriate Resources Effectively) to provide home care case management. This program allows a full range of benefits using the case management approach. Project CARE has a catastrophic cap of expenditures: $1,000 for active-duty military personnel and $10,000 for retired military personnel (Potter 1988). Additional information on the Demonstration Project and Project Care can be obtained from the CHAMPUS office in Aurora, Colorado (see Appendix A).

Reimbursement Strategies

The HHC Demonstration Project makes home care services available after a determination that home care (including all medically necessary services, supplies, and equipment) is less expensive than hospitalization. All costs except the cost-share (under $10 per day) is paid by CHAMPUS. Unless a preauthorization is made, the service request is denied. Items that must be included in requests for home care are listed in Exhibit 3-6.

Reports must be submitted to CHAMPUS every 30 days. These ongoing reports must have a current physician progress report, which includes justification for home care, current

Exhibit 3-6 Items for Requests for Home Care

- A medical statement signed by a physician
- Itemized cost of inpatient care per day versus itemized cost of home care per day (all drug therapies, supplies, equipment needs, professional services, and institutional charges must be included)
- Complete name and address of any insurance company
- An explanation as to the percentage of hospital bill covered by other insurance and the amount the other insurance pays toward home care
- Signed copy of the most current claim form including itemized statement of charges
- Detailed proposed plan of management for home care
- Make and model number of equipment and accessories to be purchased
- Name and address of supplier(s)
- Itemized cost of equipment and accessories to be purchased/rented
- Names and addresses of all providers of care and alternatives

Source: Guidelines Regarding the Information To Be Submitted for Home Health Care Benefits under the CHAMPUS Home Health Care Demonstration, Office of Civilian Health and Medical Program of the Uniformed Services, U.S. Department of Defense, September 1986.

response to treatment, changes in condition, cost, treatment plan, and estimated length of service. Daily nursing notes, therapy progress notes, and treatment plan must also be included.

Disease-Oriented Voluntary Agencies

Disease-oriented voluntary agencies are a source of support for chronically ill children. Assistance with hands-on home care service is usually not available, but some important services are available, including limited medical services, therapies, special equipment, transportation, community services, family education and support, political lobbying, and research. Agencies often focus on one disease or a group of associated diseases, such as muscular dystrophy, spina bifida, or cystic fibrosis.

The disease-oriented organizations occasionally may be a source of payment of last resort. Even then, the services provided would be family education and support. Many of these organizations have very small budgets and have been faced with a decrease in amount of available monies in the past few years.

Grass Roots Funding

Grass roots fund raising has been used by some families to help pay for the cost of home care. Local fund raising may be successful for a specific piece of equipment; however, it is difficult to raise the funds necessary for ongoing nursing care. The methods include bake sales, raffles, media coverage, and specialty projects for ventilator-dependent children. Local groups will occasionally assist by donating time instead of money.

FINANCIAL CONSIDERATIONS

Financing must constantly be considered during provision of home care. A financial assessment is a major requisite for home care. This assessment should ensure the adequacy of funding and outline the family's financial responsibility. Assessments are then performed at regular intervals to monitor payment of services, evaluate the family's ability to pay out-of-pocket expenses, and determine if the funding source can continue payment.

In this section information is provided to help the family find funding necessary for care. Much of this information has been presented throughout this chapter, but the important points are summarized to provide a more concise reference to the financing pitfalls associated with home care.

- *Anticipate home care needs at the time of hospital admission.* Home care must now be considered as an option for technology-dependent children and children with acute or chronic health care problems who have traditionally been cared for in hospitals. Examples include the newly diagnosed diabetic, the child with cystic fibrosis, and an infant with hyperbilirubinemia. Physicians, discharge planners, and primary nurses should anticipate and plan home care for many children who are admitted to the pediatric unit.
- *Determine home care benefits early in the child's hospitalization.* Will Medicaid, the insurance company, or an HMO pay for

home care? What level of skill is required and/or provided? Does the state have a waiver program? If so, what are its limitations? Does the physician need to intervene with the funding source and outline home care needs? These questions must be addressed early in the child's hospitalization.

• *Choose an appropriate home care agency.* Does the funding source have a preferred home care agency? Does the home care agency have experience with providing care to pediatric patients? Does the agency have qualified caregivers on call 24 hours a day? A cost analysis from one or more agencies may be required by the funding source and should be done early in the discharge planning process. If an agency has a proven track record with technology-dependent children, the discharge planner should advocate accordingly.

• *Take advantage of the various funding programs available to help finance home care.* Insurance companies may have case managers to help provide home care for certain medically needy children. The discharge planner and/or home care agency should query the funding sources to determine the availability of this service. Discharge planners and families also need to be aware of an additional program that may help finance care: the Federal Consolidated Omnibus Reconciliation Act (COBRA). This allows persons to continue insurance coverage either through group membership or individual policy conversions at a reasonable premium. This is especially important for families in which one or both parents have changed jobs and/or insurance carriers.

• *Check benefits thoroughly when negotiating a new insurance policy.* The insurance benefits should be reviewed thoroughly, especially if a person has the option of choosing from more than one policy. The areas of consideration are immediate coverage at time of birth, duration of coverage after birth, conditions of policy renewal and cancellation, and total benefits. An insurance agent or financial planner should be able to assist in the translation of various insurance policies.

• *Be cost conscious, especially with suppliers and equipment.* Equipment may be leased or purchased based on the child's prognosis and estimated length of equipment use. The funding source, durable medical equipment company, and family should negotiate rental or purchase prices. Supplies may often be reused, saving the family and funding source money. Feeding pump bags and tubing, urinary catheters, and even insulin syringes can be reused. A durable medical equipment company or home care agency can instruct the family regarding the cleaning and storage of the various reusable supplies.

• *Documentation is essential in payment of home care services.* Some funding sources will not pay for "instruction" or "teaching" of certain elements of care. Home care agencies need to communicate with funding sources to determine what services may be billed. In addition, many funding sources require a copy of the nurses' notes with each bill. Home care nurses must include all care provided for protection of liability as well as for reimbursement.

Families, discharge planners, and home care agencies should maintain frequent communication with the payment sources before and during the initiation of home care. Funding for home care will continue to be an issue in the future. Almost all children who use private insurance for long-term care will reach the lifetime maximum of their benefit coverage. Medicaid is not available in all states. CHAMPUS will not pay for custodial care. Some HMOs will not pay for long-term home care. Problems and hurdles still abound, but the information presented here will help in planning for financing home care and will minimize the problems that have risen out of success (Gibbons 1987).

REFERENCES

American Medical Association. Department of State Legislation, Public Affairs Group. *State Health Legislation Report*. Vol. 14, no. 1. Chicago: American Medical Association, 1986.

Briggs, N., and Cummings B. "Insurance Reimbursement of Pediatric Home Care." *Pediatric Nursing* 12(1986):449, 457.

Fox, H. *A Preliminary Analysis of Options to Improve Health Insurance Coverage for Chronically Ill and Disabled Children*. Washington, D.C.: Fox Health Policy Consultants, 1984.

Fox, H. *Private Health Insurance Coverage of Chronically Ill Children*. Washington, D.C.: Fox Health Policy Consultants, 1986a.

Fox, H. *Technology-dependent Children's Access to Medicaid Home Care Financing*. Washington, D.C.: Fox Health Policy Consultants, 1986b.

Galten, R. "Funding Pediatric Home Care." *Caring* V, no. 12 (1986):43–45, 51.

Gibbons, J. "Foreword." In U.S. Congress Office of Technology Assessment. *Technology-dependent Children: Hospital vs. Homecare—A Technical Memorandum*. Washington, D.C.: U.S. Government Printing Office, May 1987.

Hobbs, N.; Perrin, J.; and Ireys, H. "Patterns of Paying for Care." In *Chronically Ill Children and Their Families*, edited by N. Hobbs, J. Perrin, and H. Ireys. San Francisco: Jossey-Bass Publishers, 1985.

Leonard, A. *A Guide to Health Care Coverage for the Child with a Chronic Illness or Disability*. Madison, Wis.: Center for Public Representation, July 1986.

Potter, M.C. *A Report on the Department of Defense Office of Civilian Health and Medical Program of the Uniformed Services Home Health Care Demonstration Project*. Aurora, Colo.: Department of Defense, 1987.

Potter, M.C. Department of Defense, Office of Civilian Health and Medical Program of the Uniformed Services, Aurora, Colorado. Personal communication, February 1988.

Rosenbaum, B. *Medicaid as a Source of Health Care Financing for Children with Technological Needs*. Washington, D.C.: Children's Defense Fund, 1986.

U.S. Congress, Office of Technology Assessment. *Technology-dependent Children: Hospital vs. Home Care—A Technical Memorandum*. Washington, D.C.: U.S. Government Printing Office, 1987.

U.S. Department of Defense, Office of Civilian Health and Medical Program of the Uniformed Services. *Guidelines Regarding the Information to be Submitted for Home Health Care Benefits under the CHAMPUS Home Health Care Demonstration*. Washington, D.C.: U.S. Government Printing Office, 1986.

U.S. Department of Health and Human Services, Health Care Financing Administration. *Health Care Financing Program Statistics: Analysis of State Medicaid Program Characteristics 1984*. Baltimore, Md.: Department of Health and Human Services, 1984.

Weeks, K.H. "Private Health Insurance and Chronically Ill Children." In *Issues in the Care of Children with Chronic Illness*, edited by N. Hobbs and J. Perrin. San Francisco: Jossey-Bass Publishers, 1985.

Part II

A Systems Approach to Home Care

Chapter 4

Alterations in Neurological Function

Adele Lee Entz

The most common type of neurological concerns in children include head injuries, hypoxic injuries, spinal cord injuries, and seizures. Any injury is a crisis to the child, family, and staff caring for the child. Following initial care and stabilization, extensive planning is necessary in preparation for discharge. The clinical assessment of the child and family is crucial to establish an effective care plan. Second, a basic understanding of the physiology and pathophysiology of the problem is necessary. Third, the nursing care with applicable nursing diagnoses needs to be identified to assist nurses and other health care personnel in guiding care. Finally, the pharmacology and "mechanics" involved in caring for these children must be incorporated into the care plan.

The most common neurological disorders that occur in the pediatric population are discussed in this chapter. Topics include head injury and hypoxic injury, spinal cord injury, and seizures.

HEAD INJURY

Head injury is one of the most prevalent and complex neurological injuries occurring in children. Falls are the major cause of injury in young children while vehicular accidents are most likely the cause of injury in older children (Deutsch and Sawyer 1985). Hypoxic injuries, such as near-drowning and aborted sudden infant death syndrome are other causes of brain injury.

Pathology

Head injuries are classified as open or closed. Open injury refers to a fracture of the skull and confines the level of damage of the brain to the specified site of injury. Closed injury may be identified from a mild concussion, in which the brain is slightly bruised with little or no loss of consciousness, to a severe closed-head injury, which is usually accompanied by extensive loss of consciousness, relative to the degree of trauma. The patient suffering a greater degree of "contrecoup" or bouncing of the brain within the skull, resulting in multiple bruising and injury, will have greater long-term deficits.

When considering the child with a severe head injury and loss of consciousness, the main initial concerns are centered around saving the child's life and preventing any secondary problems and complications that may occur related to multiple trauma that coincides with the head injury. Within this initial period the main medical and nursing concerns revolve around the respiratory status, level of consciousness, increased cerebral edema, musculoskeletal functioning, and family crisis. Concerns regarding skin integrity, bowel and bladder elimination, nutrition, and infection are also included within the care plan. Many of these same concerns will be included in the care plan for the child on discharge.

The Glasgow Coma Scale (Exhibit 4-1) is used in acute care settings to assist health care professionals to identify the child's level of con-

Exhibit 4-1 Glasgow Coma Scale

Eyes Open
  4 = Spontaneously
  3 = To speech
  2 = To pain
  1 = None

Best Verbal Response
  5 = Oriented
  4 = Confused
  3 = Inappropriate words
  2 = Incomprehensible sounds
  1 = None

Best Motor Response
  6 = Obeys commands
  5 = Localize pain
  4 = Flexion to pain—withdrawal
  3 = Flexion to pain—abnormal
  2 = Extension to pain
  1 = None

Source: Reprinted with permission from *Lancet*, Vol. 2, p. 81, © 1974.

sciousness. If the child is discharged in a non-alert state, this scale will be useful in evaluating any changes the child experiences.

In addition to level of consciousness, it is important to identify what part(s) of the brain suffered greatest injury. Specific tests used to determine the extent of damage include computed tomography, magnetic resonance imaging, arteriography, and electroencephalography.

Symptomatology

Common symptoms displayed by children with head injury include loss of speech, hemiparesis, spasticity of muscles with subsequent posturing and potential contractures, and difficulty with chewing and swallowing. A short attention span may also be noted. Seizures may be present, depending on the injury.

These children should be involved in a rehabilitation program as soon as they are released from an intensive care situation. The scope of rehabilitation is discussed later in this chapter.

SEIZURE DISORDERS

Seizure disorders represent an array of symptoms from absence to twitching to total tonic-clonic movements. They may result in unconsciousness or impaired consciousness. Recurring seizures are frequently referred to as epilepsy.

A description of seizures and symptoms can be found in Table 4-1.

Pathology

Seizures arise from an abnormal or excessive neuronal discharge in the brain. In infancy the cause of seizures may be related to cerebral trauma (e.g., anoxia), cerebral abnormality, or malformation. Brain tumors, head injury, degeneration of brain tissue, and infections such as meningitis or encephalitis preclude seizures in children.

Seizures caused by either trauma or infections may be delayed in appearance by as much as 24 months after the insult (Livingston 1974). The degree of functional area involvement may be determined by an electroencephalogram. This test is also helpful in determining the child's progress and response to medication.

Symptomatology

The clinical features of seizures vary. Some of the typical features found with specific types of seizures are listed in Table 4-1. These manifestations can be grouped into two main categories: (1) presence of anoxia evidenced by cyanosis and (2) the degree of muscle involvement. Anoxia is a major concern, since it can lead to additional tissue damage within the brain. Cyanosis is the main symptom of hypoxia and is noted mainly around the eyes (periorbital) and the mouth (circumoral). Muscle involvement varies from staring episodes to loss of tone to strong jerking muscle contractions with loss of consciousness. It is important that the child's caregiver keep a record of seizures because of the different possible manifestations.

Two important components involved in caring for the child with seizures are administering the appropriate treatment (both medications and diet) and keeping a precise record of seizures for the physician and other health care professionals to assist in monitoring the effects of the therapy. Exhibit 4-2 is a sample chart that may assist the parents and caregivers in recording this information.

Table 4-1 Seizures

Type	Old Terms	Description
Partial		
Simple		Motor, sensory, or autonomic; the child is aware, can talk, and remembers all parts of the seizure
Complex	Psychomotor, limbic, temporal lobe seizure	Motor, sensory, somatosensory autonomic, and psychic (hearing voices, etc.), a combination-type seizure
Partial	Jacksonian	Begins in one part of the body as a localized jerking but may spread to the entire body and become generalized
Generalized		
Absences	Petit mal	Brief absences or staring spells, usually without falling
Myoclonic jerks	Infantile seizures	Sudden quick jerks or muscle spasms
Atonic	Akinetic, drop seizures	Complete and sudden loss of postural tone
Tonic	Tonic	Stiffening of muscles; child normally falls
Clonic	Clonic	Repetitive muscle jerking
Tonic-clonic	Grand mal	Stiffening phase followed by muscle jerking; aura precedes (sensation—visual or auditory) and sleep follows (postictal stage)

SPINAL CORD INJURY

A spinal cord injury (SCI) with major neurological involvement is an uncommon cause of physical handicap in children. However, there are an increasing number of children with SCIs admitted to medical centers. There are no studies that have been conducted nor are there statistics that can assist the nurse in providing hope or support for full recovery with children experiencing an SCI. The greatest concern with these children, who are usually teenagers, is emotional and psychological support, while providing for their physical needs.

Pathology

Fracture of the vertebrae with subsequent severing or compression of the spinal cord is the most common reason for an SCI. This may be the result of a vehicular accident, a diving injury, or possibly a gunshot wound. More rarely, a spinal cord tumor may lead to an SCI as a result of surgical treatment.

When an SCI has occurred, the extent of injury needs to be determined based on the location of the injury on the spinal column. A high cord injury, one involving the cervical and upper thoracic nerves, will create a greater deficit of function. Persons injured at the C-2 level will more than likely be dependent on a ventilator. In addition, these children will have mobility and elimination deficits. Children injured in the thoracic range may regain some use of their arms/shoulders, depending on the exact level of the injury. Children injured in the lower thoracic and lumbar region will experience deficits with mobility and elimination but will have use of their upper torso. Concerns regarding sexuality are very great with all levels of injury and must be considered no matter how young the person is at the time of injury. These fears become an overwhelming concern during adolescence and as one becomes older.

Exhibit 4-2 Sample Chart for Recording Medications and Seizures

Medication Administered	Time of Onset	Seizures		Cyanotic?	Need O$_2$
		Duration	Symptoms		

Symptomatology

Movement is of great concern in assessing the level of injury and abilities of function. Voluntary movements require an intact spinal cord to transfer the messages to the brain and back to the sensorimotor source. Reflexive movements occur from the point of sensation, through the spinal cord, and then back to the point of sensation. Therefore, those movements that occur distal to the injury on the spinal column are considered to be reflexive rather than voluntary. When patients return home, this difference will need to be assessed throughout their recovery period.

Sensation is a concern with children with SCI because it may relate to possible injury. Prevention of hot water scalds, cuts, or injury to the lower extremities must be taught to the child and parents.

Muscle spasticity is a third symptom and a concern related to aberrant nerve-to-muscle impulses. These impulses may cause flaccid muscles as well as spastic muscles, both of which have potential concerns for caregivers.

A complete musculoskeletal assessment every 1 to 2 months is essential. Once a thorough assessment has been made and the level of involvement determined, progress may be possible with an aggressive rehabilitation program. This program will assist the child and family in dealing with the activities of daily living in as normal a way as possible.

Care for these children is physical and psychological. Physically, they will work to become mobile again. This frequently requires the use of a wheelchair, which creates many hurdles and barriers that need to be confronted and overcome. Psychologically, the child needs support to grow and mature in a positive and realistic manner. Depression regarding the lack of independence is the most common psychological concern experienced. Specific concerns are discussed in the rehabilitation and nursing care sections.

REHABILITATION

Rehabilitation refers to "the restoration to a disabled individual of maximum independence commensurate with his limitations by developing his residual capabilities" (Osol 1973).

Rehabilitation is a multiphasic process that includes identifying many levels of functioning to delineate the appropriate type of program for the child. Each process is very specific to the child's disability.

Disability is frequently designated as severe, moderate, or minimal when the recovery is good. Severe disability refers to children who are dependent on 24-hour care. These children may have spastic paralysis, dysarthria, and dysphasia. Children with moderate disability are considered independent but still disabled. They are able to meet their own activities of daily living, use public transportation, and may be able to participate in the labor force, although this may be in a sheltered form. The level of employment is relative to the extent of their cognitive impairment. Minimal disability refers to children who have restoration of all normal function, even though there may be some existing sequelae that continue (Deutsch and Sawyer 1985).

Once the extent of disability has been defined, the sequelae that are experienced from the neurological impairment should be assessed (Exhibit 4-3). The following is a brief description of some of the sequelae encountered when dealing with a neurologically impaired child. The identification of these problems will assist in planning for the child's rehabilitation care within the home.

Comprehensive and well-organized care is the key to an optimal recovery. Since injuries vary to such a degree, the rehabilitation program for each child will be varied. Choosing appropriate services is a major concern for both the family and the health care professionals. Many factors need to be addressed regarding (1) the presence of a program in the local community, (2) its adequacy to provide services to the child, (3) the willingness of this program to address the complete scope of needs for the neurologically injured child and not just the physical needs, and (4) the parents' desires and abilities to have the child remain in the community or to transfer elsewhere. If there is no rehabilitation program or support personnel in the area where the child lives, the family must consider taking the child to a facility that will meet the specific rehabilitation and developmental needs or else devise their own program in the home. The nurse is an excellent coordinator for these types of programs.

Exhibit 4-3 Possible Sequelae for the Neurologically Impaired Child

Physical:

- Confinement to a wheelchair
- Other motor deficits, such as hemiplegia, wide-based gait, or poor balance
- Sensory integration impairment—impaired perception of temperature, changes in tactile sensation, or problems with visuomotor integration
- Visual deficits leading to muscle imbalance and neurological damage causing severe visual field impairment
- Motor speech disorders (e.g., dysarthria, oral apraxia)

Cognitive:

- Reduced attention and concentration
- A variety of types of memory impairment
- Difficulty in problem solving and decision making
- Reduced processing speed
- Impaired organization and planning
- Difficulty with concept formation
- Rigidity of response (e.g., alternative solutions are not sought)
- Impaired auditory and/or visual processing abilities
- Difficulty in making appropriate judgments on major life decisions

Behavioral:

- Inability to engage in purposeful activity
- Disinhibition
- Inability to respond appropriately to environmental cues
- Socially inappropriate behavior
- Impulsivity
- Poor initiation

Emotional:

- Personality regression
- Denial, i.e., inability to recognize deficits that are present or perceive their impact on their family (older children and adolescents, young adults)
- Reduced self-esteem
- Depression

Source: Copyright © 1985 by Matthew Bender & Company, Inc., and adapted with permission from *A Guide to Rehabilitation.*

Each discipline can be contacted and then together the team members can develop an appropriate program for the child. Team members important within the rehabilitation of a neurologically injured child include the physician, primary nurse, occupational therapist, physical therapist, speech–language pathologist, teacher, recreational therapist, and the family. Specific medical and related professionals who become involved with these children include pediatricians, orthopedic surgeons, ophthalmologists, podiatrists, social workers, psychologists, psychiatrists, nurses, child life specialists (play therapists), neurologists, neurosurgeons, orthotists, and many others.

The organization of all disciplines intervening to care for the child is a complex process. The nurse can assist the parents to create a notebook detailing those involved with their child's care as well as identifying goals and progress made toward those goals. Evaluations should occur periodically to assess (1) neurological status, (2) levels of function, (3) special nursing and medical needs, (4) strengths and weaknesses in motor function, (5) speech and intellectual development, and (6) equipment and treatment needs. New goals and objectives are identified as progress is made. A primary care physician in association with a primary care nurse who is aware of the needs of the family and the child is invaluable in developing a cohesive system.

Children with SCI require special equipment to facilitate activities of daily living. Support equipment required to care for children with moderate to severe disabilities is discussed in Chapter 16.

Various medications are used to control seizures and muscle tone and to facilitate respiratory status. Some of the most common medications are listed in Table 4-2. A description of the action, dosages, and common side effects is included.

Nutrition is another concern and treatment modality. Some children will eat "normal" foods, while others will have food pureed to varying consistencies, and still others will be fed by either a gastrostomy tube or a jejunostomy tube. An in-depth description of diet therapy can be found in Chapter 7.

Rehabilitation is very comprehensive and involves not only extensive planning but also intensive nursing care. In the next section the

Table 4-2 Medications

Category/Drug (Trade/Generic)	Action/Uses	Dosages	Side Effects
Skeletal Muscle Relaxants			
Hydroxyzine hydrochloride (Atarax)	Depresses the central nervous system at the limbic and the subcortical levels of the brain	50–100 mg po daily in divided doses	Drowsiness, dry mouth, decreased alertness
Diazepam (Valium)	Depresses the central nervous system at the limbic and subcortical levels of the brain	Children > 6 mo: 1–2.5 mg po, tid or qid Adult: 2–10 mg po tid or qid	Drowsiness, lethargy, hangover, ataxia, nausea, vomiting, rash, cardiovascular collapse
Dantrolene sodium (Dantrium)	Acts directly on skeletal muscle to interfere with intracellular calcium movement	1 mg/kg/day po bid–qid Adult: 25 mg po daily to 100 mg bid–qid	Muscle weakness, drowsiness, severe diarrhea, hepatitis, sweating, fever; give with meals; possible photosensitivity
Methocarbamol (Robaxin)	Reduces transmission of impulses from spinal cord to skeletal muscle	1 g po tid	Nausea, anorexia, gastrointestinal upset, some drowsiness, anaphylactic reaction
Clorazepate dipotassium (Tranxene)	Depresses the central nervous system at the limbic and subcortical levels of the brain	Child 9–12 yr: max 7.5 mg po bid Child > 12 yr: begin 7.5 mg po tid to max 90 mg daily	Drowsiness, lethargy, hangover, dry mouth
Baclofen (Lioresal)	Reduces transmission of impulses from the spinal cord to skeletal muscle	5 mg tid up to 80 mg daily	Drowsiness, dizziness, weakness, nausea, urinary frequency
Anticonvulsants			
Diazepam (Valium)	See above		
Chlorazepate dipotassium (Tranxene)	See above		
Primidone (Mysoline)	Unknown, but some activity may be due to phenobarbital, which is an active metabolite For grand mal seizures, complex-partial (psychomotor) seizures	Child <8 yr: 125 mg po daily up to 1 g daily qid Adult/child >8 yr: 250 mg po daily qid	Drowsiness, ataxia, diplopia, nausea, vomiting, edema
Phenytoin sodium (Dilantin)	Stabilizes neuronal membranes and limits seizure activity by either increasing efflux or decreasing influx of sodium ions across cell membranes in the motor cortex during generation of nerve impulses For generalized tonic-clonic (grand mal) status epilepticus, nonepileptic seizures (posthead trauma, Reye's syndrome)	Child: 15 mg/kg IV in q8–12h intervals (loading) Maintenance: 5–7 mg/kg po or IV q12h	Agranulocytosis, ataxia, slurred speech, confusion, ventricular fibrillation, nystagmus, nausea, diplopia, vomiting, gingival hyperplasia, exfoliative dermatitis, hirsutism; urine may turn pink or brown

Table 4-2 continued

Category/Drug (Trade/Generic)	Action/Uses	Dosages	Side Effects
Mephenytoin (Mesantoin)	Stabilizes neuronal membranes and limits seizure activity by either increasing efflux or decreasing influx of sodium ions across cell membranes in the motor cortex during generation of nerve impulses Hydantoin derivative For generalized tonic-clonic (grand mal) seizures, complex-partial (psychomotor) seizures	Child: 50–100 mg po daily up to 200 mg po q8h	Leukopenia, drowsiness, fatigue, agranulocytosis, rashes, gingival hyperplasia, nausea, vomiting
Clonazepam (Clonopin)	Appears to act on the limbic system, thalamus, and hypothalamus to produce anticonvulsant effects For absence (petit mal) and atypical absence seizures, akinetic and myoclonic seizures	Child up to 10 yr: 0.01–0.03 mg/kg po daily in three divided doses; max = 0.1–0.2 mg/kg daily	Drowsiness, ataxia, behavioral disturbances, increased salivation, nystagmus, constipation, urinary retention; use contraindicated in patient with hepatic disease
Phenobarbital (Luminal)	Depresses monosynaptic and polysynaptic transmission in the central nervous system and increases the threshold for seizure activity in the motor cortex For all forms of epilepsy, febrile seizures in infancy	Child: 4–6 mg/kg po daily, divided q12h Adults: 100–200 mg daily or divided tid	Drowsiness, lethargy, hangover, rash; may interfere with liver metabolism
Ethosuximide (Zarontin)	Increases seizure threshold; reduces the paroxysmal spike-and-wave pattern of absence seizures by depressing nerve transmission in the motor cortex For absence (petit mal) seizures	Child 3–6 yr: 250 mg po daily or 125 mg po bid, up to 1.5 g daily Adult/child > 6 yr: 250 mg po bid to 1.5 g daily	Agranulocytosis, aplastic anemia, drowsiness, fatigue, dizziness, euphoria, lethargy, nausea, vomiting, anorexia, epigastric and abdominal pain, hirsutism, rashes; use with caution
Carbamazepine (Tegretol)	Stabilizes neuronal membranes and limits seizure activity by either increasing efflux or decreasing influx of sodium ions across cell membranes in the motor cortex during generation of nerve impulses For generalized (tonic-clonic) seizures, complex-partial (psychomotor) seizures, mixed seizure patterns	Child < 12 yr: 10–20 mg/kg daily in two to four divided doses Adult and child > 12 yr: 200 mg po in 6 to 8 hr intervals	Aplastic anemia, agranulocytosis, thrombocytopenia, vertigo, ataxia, drowsiness, nausea, stomatitis, dry mouth, rash, Stevens-Johnson syndrome, abnormal liver function

nursing care that is involved with neurologically impaired children as applied to nursing diagnosis is described. Comprehensive care plans, established by a nurse, should exist for all patients on discharge from the hospital. These plans will assist both home care nurses and the family to care for the child.

NURSING CARE

In caring for the child with an alteration in neurological function due to head injury, seizures, or SCI the goals are to (1) return the child to an optimal state of neurological functioning; (2) prevent/identify potential complications; (3) promote adequate nutritional intake and optimal growth; (4) promote adequate patterns of elimination; (5) provide optimal mobility; (6) support the family/child's positive self-esteem and coping related to altered neurological functioning; and (7) promote optimal sexual functioning in the patient with an SCI.

Nursing Care to Return the Child to an Optimal State of Neurological Functioning

Goal: Assess Neurological Status

Assessment of the neurological function of a child with a head injury is multifaceted. Assessing the cranial nerves will be possible to the extent of the child's level of consciousness. Frequently the child will experience hemiparesis in which the one side of the body will be void of voluntary movement and the opposite side of the face will have decreased sensation and movement. The side of the face that is affected indicates the side of the brain that has suffered greater damage.

Assessment of the child's perception of sensation and movement in all extremities is important to perform on a regular basis. Over time, varying degrees of function will return and must be monitored and recorded. Children with SCI may regain some sensation depending on the type and level of cord injury. Cranial nerve assessment in a patient with an SCI will be of interest in the determination of upper cord injuries and may assist health care professionals to determine the degree of deficit.

Intracranial pressure will also need to be assessed. Injured brain cells that have died shrink and slough into the system. During the recovery period, fluid accumulates to adjust for the spaces within the skull owing to the process of the brain shrinking. If this fluid is produced too rapidly and is not absorbed as it would be under normal circumstances, then increased intracranial pressure results. The pressure may continue and result in double vision, headaches, vomiting, and lethargy. Medical attention should be sought immediately if any combination of these symptoms is identified. Treatment for increased intracranial pressure is the reduction of the fluid. If the fluid accumulation is chronic, a shunt may be surgically placed to take the fluid from the ventricle of the brain to the abdomen.

Goal: Provide Appropriate Cognitive Training

It is not uncommon for children with head injuries and seizures to need to relearn cognitive skills. This can be accomplished through the public school system in many states. Federal law mandates that all children must receive an education to their optimum level of ability through 18 years of age. This can be either in the classroom or in the home.

Computers can assist all neurologically injured children as an alternate means of communication and a learning tool. Some children can be helped to improve their attention span and visual fields through the use of computers. Other uses for computers with neurologically injured children are being developed.

Nursing Care to Prevent/Identify Potential Complications

Goals: Assess for Respiratory Complications

Children who are neurologically impaired may need assistance in maintaining adequate oxygen needs. They may not be mobile enough to prevent pulmonary stasis or to clear their own airway. Therefore, professionals may need to assist families with helping the child maintain adequate oxygenation. This process may include postural drainage and clapping, suctioning, oxygen administration, oral bronchodilators, and aerosol bronchodilators (small-volume nebulizers). Some patients have a tracheostomy and may also require a ventilator. Nurses should evaluate the appropriate functioning and the cleaning of the apparatus. In providing tracheostomy care, the caregiver should clean the inner cannula and the site around the outer cannula and provide new tracheostomy ties at least twice a day. This procedure is recommended to be done under sterile conditions although some physicians do not believe that anything more than "clean" is needed (see Chapter 5).

To prevent complications of the respiratory tract, upper respiratory tract infection, or pneumonia, the prescribed respiratory therapy should be performed and an adequate amount of fluids should be administered. The fluids assist the lungs in liquefying respiratory secretions and aid in their expectoration.

Goal: Assess for Alterations in Cardiac Function

Cardiovascular complications that may occur include orthostatic hypotension and generalized poor circulation. These problems are secondary to the lack of mobility present in many of these children. Assessment of blood pressure when lying down, sitting, standing, and walking can determine how the child is able to compensate for levels of immobility. If a significant drop in blood pressure occurs, as during standing, the child's legs should be moved in a pumping fashion to facilitate blood return. Assessing pedal pulses as well as capillary refill in nail beds of the hands and feet is always valuable.

Nursing Care to Promote Adequate Nutrition and Optimal Growth

Goal: Assess Nutritional and Fluid Intake

Nutritional and fluid intake is extremely important to monitor and assess in all children. The caregiver must be aware of the child's ability to obtain and swallow fluids and to monitor this intake. If the intake is inadequate and the child's swallowing is intact, offering the child an 8-ounce glass of water every 2 hours will be of value. When the child has an altered route of feeding, smaller amounts of fluids offered more frequently may need to be administered. The average amount of fluids needed can be calculated using the following formula: 125 mL/kg/day. As the child becomes an adolescent fluid needs decrease to 80 to 90 mL/kg/day. It is

Exhibit 4-4 Routes and Types of Foods Appropriate per Route

- Oral—table food, pureed food
- Gastrostomy—pureed food, formulas, nutritional supplements
- Nasogastric—pureed food, formulas, nutritional supplements
- Jejunostomy—nutritional supplements

---

important that these needs are monitored and adjusted as the child grows or is losing water, which occurs with high environmental temperatures, fever, upper respiratory tract infections, vomiting, and diarrhea.

Goal: Monitor Altered Routes of Feeding

Feeding methods are varied for altered routes. *Bolus* feeding consists of feedings of 240 mL or 8 ounces over 20 minutes three to six times a day administered by gravity or syringe.

The second method is termed *intermittent* feeding and may be regulated by a feeding pump for 6 to 10 hours a day, usually while sleeping.

The third method is defined as *continuous* feeding. A feeding pump is used, and the child receives feedings at a rate of 50 to 100 mL/hr. The types of food and usual routes are listed in Exhibit 4-4. Further information is available in Chapter 7.

Goal: Assess Growth Patterns

Growth patterns of all children should be monitored using the following indicators:

- Height and weight charts (updated monthly)
- Skin fold fat and protein analysis (when growth percentile is low)
- Caloric analysis as appropriate for age and stage of growth

A dietitian can perform these assessments.

Goal: Monitor Administration of Special Diets

Special diets are an important consideration in working with neurologically impaired children. Children with specific types of seizures, myoclonic or akinetic, may benefit from the use of a ketogenic or medium-chain triglyceride diet. The ketogenic diet is composed of a high ratio of fat to protein and carbohydrate, normally a 4:1

ratio. The patient undergoes a starvation period usually lasting from 3 to 6 days until there is a 10 percent body weight loss, 4+ acetone and diacetic acid in the urine, and carbon dioxide values between 10 and 12. This means that there are four times greater amounts of fats in the diet than the carbohydrates and proteins combined (*Manual of Applied Nutrition* 1981). Medium-chain triglycerides have a high caloric value, are easily absorbed from the gastrointestinal tract, are water miscible, and are tasteless (Huttenlocher et al. 1971). Frequently, dietitians have incorporated the use of medium-chain triglyceride oil in milk to provide an increased source of these fats in the diet (Anderson et al. 1985).

Nursing Care to Promote Adequate Patterns of Elimination

Goal: Promote Adequate Bowel Elimination and Prevent Constipation and Incontinence

Bowel patterns need to be monitored since constipation is common. A bowel training program may be established when there is lack of control of the bowels. These programs can range from specific nutrients (bran) or juices (prune) that promote adequate bowel movements. If these measures are not successful, alternatives such as cathartics and laxatives may be used. The use of glycerine suppositories for the timing and stimulation of bowel movements is a widely used practice. Sufficient fluid intake is also important in preventing constipation.

If the child experiences diarrhea, a physician should be consulted to determine the cause and treatment regimen.

Goal: Prevent Urinary Tract Infections and Promote Normal Patterns of Urinary Elimination

Incontinence is a major concern in many children with neurological impairment. Diapers are the most common method of dealing with incontinence. Bladder training programs may be instituted when children become aware of the results of voiding in a toilet or commode.

Children with SCI and their parents or caregivers may be taught to perform intermittent catheterization every 4 to 6 hours. Sterile or clean technique may be used during catheterization. Catheters that are reused must be cleaned in an antiseptic solution, rinsed, and then stored in a clean/sterile container. Many catheters are used once and discarded. Some children have indwelling Foley catheters, while older males may use an external catheter that affixes to the outer skin of the penis.

It is important to assess frequency, volume, and clarity of the urine since an increase in frequency, a decrease in volume, and a decrease in clarity may represent a urinary tract infection. Fluid intake is the most important treatment and often may prevent urinary tract infection.

Nursing Care to Provide for Adequate Mobility

Goal: Protect From Injury

Safety is essential when a child has difficulty with ambulation, balance, and motor control. Children with seizures are at high risk for injury when there is a loss of postural tone. Children with frequent seizures need to wear a helmet to protect themselves from possible head injury. Their beds should have padded side rails, and their main play areas should be free of sharp objects. These children should be observed at all times.

Goal: Promote Optimal Mobility

Providing for mobility will depend on the child's level of injury. Movement is important for respiratory and cardiovascular status. Standing is important for weight bearing on the long bones to decrease the degree of demineralization. Children who do not have motor control in their lower extremities should use a standing frame approximately twice a day for 30 to 60 minutes. These frames may be made or purchased.

If the child is not mobile, a wheelchair is necessary to allow the child to get from one place to another. Transfers with good body mechanics are taught to the caregivers and to the children to assist the caregivers. Posture chairs are of value for those children with more severe involvement. These are custom-made wheelchairs that attempt to keep the child in alignment (see Chapter 16).

Hemiparesis with increased tone or spasticity will lead to scoliosis, which must be monitored and treated if the degree of curvature exceeds the normal range since lung capacity may become compromised.

Goal: Assess Range of Motion

Maintaining range of motion in all joints will decrease the level of contractures as well as promote development of independence with activities of daily living. When contractures occur due to disuse and increased tone and spasticity, casts may be applied. Following this procedure, splints are made by occupational therapists (hands) and physical therapists (feet, legs, and trunk) to maintain neutral positioning. If the child's muscle tone is excessive, breakdown of the skin may occur if muscles work against the splint. These areas will need to be assessed at least twice daily. Splints on the feet are a plastic/metal combination that may have a joint at the ankle if the child walks. These splints provide support and keep the foot in a neutral position.

Goal: Prevent Alteration in Skin Integrity

When working with an immobile child, skin integrity must be monitored and assessed at least twice a day. The child's weight must be shifted at least once an hour for 5 to 10 minutes while in the wheelchair to prevent skin breakdown from occurring. The bedridden child can be moved from side to side and back to front every 2 hours as tolerated. A change of scenery as well as the relief of pressure over bony prominences is also beneficial.

Many therapists will be involved in the care of these children. Physical therapists help to facilitate sitting, transfers, standing, and walking. Their main focus includes the trunk and legs. Occupational therapists deal with fine motor skills and the arms and neck. Their area of focus involves the activities of daily living: feeding, dressing, bathing, toileting, and communicating (see Chapter 16).

Nursing Care to Support the Family/Child in Positive Family Processes, Parenting, and Self-esteem

Goal: Prevent Social Isolation

Social isolation is common in families with children experiencing neurological problems. Children with head injury and spinal cord injury are usually confined to a wheelchair which must be accommodated during any travel. Children with frequent or uncontrolled seizures may remain at home because of fear of a seizure occurring in public. Support groups and other families with children with seizures may be of assistance in providing ideas on safe ways to "venture out."

Goal: Promote Positive Self-Concept

A child's self concept may be altered when he or she remains aware of his or her condition related to previous abilities. It is important to encourage appropriate goals to regain previously held skills. Supporting the child as a "good child" will help to promote a positive self-concept.

Goal: Promote Level of Control and Parenting

Another nursing concern is alteration in parenting. Parents may not be able to interact with their child as in the past. Therefore, altered patterns of interaction and parenting need to be established. Transfer of care from hospital to parents is another challenging step to home care for the neurologically injured child. Parents need to be assessed for overprotection, rejection, abuse, and depression. Counseling and support groups assist the parents in coping with the variety of challenges they must face. In many areas of the country, state-supported agencies provide respite care for the child to allow the parents time off.

Family processes may be altered as well. Decision making within the family changes when money is needed for the injured child's care. Time and energy is spent in different ways to support the child. Siblings need to be included and supported. Family therapy may be valuable to reestablish family cohesiveness and functioning (see Chapter 19).

Many families and children experience powerlessness related to their inability to control symptoms and predict the outcome of the condition of their child. Allowing the family and child to participate in care and make decisions will greatly enhance their perception of power.

Nursing Care of Sexual Dysfunction in Spinal Cord Injury

Goal: Promote Satisfactory and Positive Identity with Sexual Function

A special problem for children and adolescents with SCI is the sexual dysfunction experienced related to the neurosensory deficits. Although the child may not perceive his or her loss when young, this perception will change as adolescence is reached. Those injured as teenagers may feel this loss immediately. Some specific problems that occur in females include loss of libido, fatigue, and decreased perineal sensation. They have not lost their ability to have children strictly related to the SCI. Males, however, have extensive repercussions from the SCI since they are unable to achieve or sustain an erection for intercourse. Secondary problems relating to these concerns include limitations on sexual performance, value conflicts regarding sexual expression, decreased libido, altered self-concept, depression/anxiety, and often an unwilling or uninformed partner.

As the patient with SCI grows and matures there is a variety of information available from the National Spinal Cord Injury Foundation.

Additional resources for SCI patients can be found in Appendix A.

REFERENCES

Anderson, L.; Dibble M.; Turkki, P.; Mitchell, H.L.; and Rynbergen, H. *Nutrition in Health and Disease*. 17th ed. Philadelphia: J.B. Lippincott Co., 1985.

Deutsch, P., and Sawyer, H. *Guide to Rehabilitation*. New York: Matthew Bender, 1985.

Huttenlocher, P.; Wilbourn, A.; and Signore, J. "Medium-chain Triglycerides as Therapy for Intractable Childhood Epilepsy." *Neurology* 21(1971):1097–1103.

Livingston, S. "Diagnosis and Treatment of Childhood Myoclonic Seizures." *Pediatrics* 53(1974):542–548.

Manual of Applied Nutrition. 6th ed. Baltimore: Johns Hopkins University Press, 1981.

Osol, Arthur (ed.). *Blakiston Medical Dictionary*. New York: McGraw-Hill Book Company, 1973.

Chapter 5

Alterations in Respiratory Function

Patricia A. McCoy
Lynn M. Feenan

The number of children with chronic respiratory conditions being cared for in the home is increasing rapidly. Treatment modalities for these children include pulmonary physiotherapy, intravenous antibiotics, and high-tech ventilator support. The home care nurse must be familiar with the respiratory disease seen in home care and must also have a thorough knowledge of treatment methods to maintain a safe therapeutic environment for these children.

Information is provided in this chapter on the most common respiratory diseases in children that can be managed in the home: asthma, bronchopulmonary dysplasia (BPD), cystic fibrosis, and apnea. In addition, home care guidelines for management of the ventilator-dependent child are outlined. Finally, nursing care plans for the home care of the children are presented.

DISEASE PROCESSES

Asthma

Asthma is probably the most common cause of recurrent respiratory symptoms in children. It is estimated that of the 15 million asthmatics, 2 to 5 million are children (Evans et al. 1987).* The incidence of childhood asthma is highest during the first few years of life. During adolescence there are few new cases of asthma diagnosed and most cases of childhood asthma improve. However, by late adolescence, only 20 percent of childhood asthmatics are asymptomatic (Martin et al. 1980). The remainder continue to have some respiratory complaints.

The definition of asthma is still controversial. Definitions range from describing clinical symptoms to cellular mechanisms. The American College of Chest Physicians and the American Thoracic Society (1975) define asthma as "a disease characterized by an increased responsiveness of the airways to various stimuli and manifested by slowing of forced expiration which changes in severity either spontaneously or as a result of therapy." Researchers examining asthma have helped health care providers understand the mechanisms and pathophysiology of asthma. It is now recognized that, irrespective of etiological factors and clinical classifications, the airways of almost all children with asthma are hyperreactive to both specific and nonspecific stimuli (Boushey et al. 1980; Platts-Mills et al. 1985).

There are two categories of bronchial asthma: instrinsic and extrinsic. Extrinsic asthma usually begins in childhood. It occurs in persons who have allergies and is precipitated by an antibody–antigen reaction. The reaction releases chemical mediators, which causes bronchoconstriction, bronchospasm, and increased capillary permeability, leading to mucosal edema and the hypersecretion of mucus into the airway (Luck-

---

*The wide range in the prevalence of asthma is due to the variations in definitions used to describe the disease.

mann and Sorensen 1987). Nonallergic asthma (intrinsic) is most often found in adults and follows recurrent respiratory tract infections.

Many factors can precipitate an intrinsic or extrinsic asthma attack. These include infection, ill health, stress, fatigue, emotional distress, physical exercise, exhaustion, allergens, irritants, and climate. The control of asthma depends on recognizing the factors that cause the condition and minimizing contact with them.

The main symptom of asthma is respiratory distress. During an asthma attack, airways constrict and the mucous membranes swell and secrete increased amounts of mucus. The narrow airways become filled with mucus and become partially or completely blocked. Breathing requires great effort. Symptoms vary with the severity of the attack and include chest tightness, dry cough, wheeze, and dyspnea. Cyanosis may occur in severe cases.

The length of an asthma attack can vary. Most asthma attacks can be treated at home. Some attacks, however, will not respond to the usual medications and therapy. This situation is termed *status asthmaticus* and normally requires hospitalization.

Medications

The main group of drugs used in the treatment of asthma are bronchodilators. These medications reverse the constriction of the bronchioles. Medications can be given intravenously, orally, or by inhalation therapy. The child requiring intravenous medications is often placed in the hospital for observation.

The inhaled route is the primary choice because it provides a lower dosage of therapy, has direct action on the lungs, and gives rise to fewer side effects. The inhaler is convenient, and the child will gain full benefit provided he or she can coordinate inspiration with triggering the inhaler. The procedure for using an inhaler is outlined in Exhibit 5-1. It should be noted that this procedure is a guideline for inhaler therapy and the patient should follow the manufacturer's instructions or those of the nurse or physician.

Inhalers are often difficult for children to use because of the precise coordination between the release of medication and inspiration. Holding chambers are available for use with inhalers and have assisted many children with the use of metered-dose inhalers. Holding chambers catch

Exhibit 5-1 How to Use an Inhaler

Administering Medication

1. Shake inhaler.
2. Breathe out slowly, a little more than normal. Do not force all the air out of lungs.
3. Tip head back slightly.
4. Place mouthpiece of inhaler in mouth. Be sure inhaler is upright and that tongue and teeth do not block the mouthpiece.
5. Close lips around mouthpiece.
6. Inhale slowly while simultaneously squeezing the inhaler once.
7. After inhalation is completed, hold breath for 5 to 10 seconds.
8. Remove inhaler from mouth and exhale.
9. Wait 5 minutes before administering second inhalation. Always use the total number of inhalations prescribed.

General Care of Inhaler

1. Wash plastic mouthpiece daily.
2. Check opening of mouthpiece to ensure patency.
3. If obstructed, opening can be cleared with a needle or pin.

the medication released from the inhaler and hold it until the child starts to breathe in. The child can then breathe the medication in at a slower rate, eliminating the need for a coordinated inspiratory effort.

Nebulized preparations are available for patients who are too young to use any other device. Nebulizers are designed to deposit airborne droplets of water and a specific bronchodilating agent, decongestant, or mucolytic agent into the airways. The exact amount of medication is added to a measured amount of saline in the nebulizer cup. The air flow through the mixture in the cup produces the mist. This treatment is usually timed to take place before chest physiotherapy. The procedure for nebulizer therapy is outlined in Exhibit 5-2.

Corticosteroids can also be used in the treatment of asthma. Their principal action is to decrease bronchiolar inflammation.

The goal of drug therapy is to obtain and maintain therapeutic blood levels. Therapeutic blood levels take time to reach and, once established, can be maintained by taking medications on a regular basis. Medications should be taken on time and in the dose prescribed. Doses should not be ''made up'' if one is skipped. In addition

Exhibit 5-2 How to Use a Nebulizer

1. Position child in a comfortable position.
2. Place prescribed dose of medication into nebulizer cup. Measure carefully. A syringe can be helpful.
3. Place prescribed amount of saline into nebulizer cup.
4. Place nebulizer cap on cup.
5. Turn on the compressor or other source of power.
6. Place mist mask over tracheostomy tube opening or place mouthpiece into child's mouth. Mouthpiece should be placed between child's teeth.
7. If mist mask is used, medication will be inhaled as child breathes. If mouthpiece is used, have child breathe in slowly, pause momentarily, and exhale slowly while the medication is being administered.
8. For mouthpiece administration, this procedure should be repeated until all the medication is used.
9. Periodically tap the nebulizer cup so that medication accumulating on the side of the nebulizer cup falls to the bottom of the nebulizer to be nebulized.

to medication, children should be reminded to drink plenty of fluids. This helps keep mucus in the bronchioles from becoming thick and sticky and thus more difficult to expectorate.

The main objective of therapy is to allow the asthmatic to lead as normal a life as possible. The treatment approach should be appropriate to the child and his or her condition. This includes both the type of drugs prescribed and routes of administration. There are a wide range of drugs available to treat asthma. Information on the most common medications is summarized in Table 5-1.

Bronchopulmonary Dysplasia

Bronchopulmonary dysplasia (BPD) is a chronic respiratory disease of infants. The disorder commonly follows the treatment of respiratory distress syndrome with mechanical ventilation but may also occasionally occur following pneumonia, meconium aspiration syndrome, tracheoesophageal fistula, and congenital heart disease (Farrell and Palta 1986). The incidence of BPD is uncertain because the published data are variable. The average incidence is approximately 20 percent but rates as

high as 68 percent have been noted (Harrod et al. 1974). Differences in the incidence of BPD between hospitals and controversies over the relative importance of risk factors are partially attributable to the lack of precise universally accepted diagnostic criteria for BPD. Symptoms include tachypnea, dyspnea, hypoxemia, and hypercapnia.

The duration of mechanical ventilation and the degree of prematurity appear to be important factors in the etiology of BPD. Changes in lung function include decrease in lung compliance, an increase in pulmonary resistance, and variable degrees of hypoxemia and hypercapnia (Bancalari and Gerhardt 1986).

The goal of therapy is to assist lung growth. Treatment for these infants includes optimizing nutrition, restricting fluids, and maintaining oxygen therapy at 50 to 55 mm Hg. Bronchodilators, such as theophylline and metaproterenol, and diuretics, including furosemide, chlorothiazide, and spironolactone are used. Higher caloric requirements have been documented in children with BPD, making nutritional management crucial. These children may have a gastrostomy tube placed if there is frequent occurrence of emesis or demonstration of gastric reflux or rumination, since aspiration may contribute to the continued need for oxygen or ventilatory support.

Oxygen-dependent infants with BPD can be cared for at home. Intensive home care requires meticulous attention to nutrition; chest physiotherapy; occupational, physical, and speech therapy; appropriate immunizations; and medications.

Oxygen

Oxygen therapy is essential to decrease the work of breathing, maximize nutrition, and prevent pulmonary hypertension or hasten its resolution (Taussig 1986). Meeting oxygen requirements and decreasing the work of breathing reduces caloric demands and facilitates weight gain in the infant with BPD. Compressed, liquid, or oxygen concentrators are available for home use.

Nasal cannulas are frequently used for oxygen therapy. Cannulas are used to deliver oxygen under 40 percent. Humidification is required for chronic use of oxygen in the home. Nasal prongs can be shaped to fit the facial contour, and equipment must be tested on the infant/child prior to

Table 5-1 Common Medications

Common Name	Administered Form	Indications
Bronchodilators (Sympathomimetics)		
Epinephrine	Subcutaneous injection	To relieve acute symptoms of
Isoproterenol (Isuprel)	Aerosol	bronchospasm and on a regular basis
Isoetharine (Bronkosol)	Aerosol	to prevent bronchospasm. Inhalers
Metaproterenol (Alupent)	Inhaler, pill, liquid, aerosol	work in minutes. Pills and liquids take
Terbutaline (Brethine, Bricanyl)	Aerosol, pill	30 to 45 minutes. Duration of action
Albuterol (Ventolin, Proventil)	Aerosol, pill	varies.
		Potential complications: palpitations, heart pounding, flushing of face, shakiness, nausea
Bronchodilators (Theophylline drugs)		
Aminophylline	Intravenous injection, pill, liquid	To relax smooth muscle in the walls of
Oxtriphylline (Choledyl SA)	Pill, capsule, liquid	the airways and relieve spasms; used
Theophylline Aerolate, Constant-T Respbid	Pill, capsule, liquid	on a regular basis to prevent bronchospasm; must be taken
Slo-Bid, Slo-phyllin, Somophyllin	Pill, capsule, liquid	regularly to be effective.
Theobid, Theo-Dur, Theolair	Pill, capsule, liquid	*Potential complications:* nausea, vomiting, headache, insomnia, diarrhea, restlessness, and irritability
Cromolyn sodium (Intal, Aarane)	Capsule: to be placed in spin-inhaler Liquid for nebulizer	To prevent bronchospasm; does not stop the bronchospasm once it has occurred; most helpful for those who have relatively symptom-free periods between attacks. *Potential complications:* cough, irritation, wheezing, nasal congestion
Corticosteroids		
Cortisone, Methylprednisolone (Medrol), prednisone	Pill	Used when bronchodilators do not provide adequate relief. These do not
Dexamethasone (Decadron)	Pill	give immediate relief of symptoms.
Beclomethasone (Vanceril, Beclovent)	Inhaler	*Potential complications:* vary with dose: appetite stimulation; weight gain; full, round face; increased sense of well-being; sleep difficulty; fluid retention; acne; increased bruising
Atropine sulfate	Liquid for aerosol Pill; dissolve for aerosol	Used as a bronchodilator for acute relief; occasionally used on a chronic basis. *Potential complications:* Dry mouth, tachycardia

Source: Adapted from Pediatric Pulmonary Section, Arizona Health Sciences Center, Tucson, Arizona.

discharge. The cannula should be removed at least once every 8 hours and cleaned with a moist cloth. Skin care should also be done at this time.

Certain situations may cause an increase in oxygen requirements. These include persistent cyanosis, crying spells or tantrums, labored breathing, chest physiotherapy, or feedings. Parents should be instructed in the proper use of oxygen equipment and parameters for increasing oxygen based on the assessment of the child. Oxygen should be decreased as soon as possible after the child's assessment returns to baseline.

If oxygen cannot be decreased to the original level, the physician should be called.

Parents need to be instructed in safety issues for home administration of oxygen prior to discharge. The home care nurse should assess the home environment for compliance with safety guidelines.

Medications

There are several medications used in the treatment and management of BPD. These include bronchodilators, diuretics, electrolytes, digitalis, and vitamins. Parents should be instructed in the dosage and administration of these medications. The home care nurse should review the purpose, dosage, and administration methods for each medication with the parents or significant caregiver. Side effects and safety issues regarding proper storage of medications should also be discussed, and side effects of medication treatment should be brought to the attention of the physician immediately.

Water retention is an important symptom for a child with BPD. The basis for diuretic therapy for this problem is the observation of dilated lymph vessels and interstitial pulmonary edema. Infants with severe obstructive lung disease may have increased venous return and pulmonary artery pressure that may result in pulmonary edema. Parents should be taught to observe for signs of water retention and report these findings to the home care nurse. These signs include irritability, poor feeding, increased work of breathing, color changes, and edema.

Some infants with BPD may be treated with corticosteroids. The use of these drugs is limited to infants who are not dependent on a ventilator for respiration. The numerous potential benefits that have been noted must be balanced against the numerous side effects of long-term therapy.

Postural Drainage and Chest Percussion

Postural drainage and chest percussion involve positioning the child to use gravity to loosen and drain excess mucus from specific sections of the lung. The aim of therapy is to reduce airway obstruction and improve gas exchange. The positions used for chest percussion will differ from child to child based on which area of the lung requires draining. Each postural drainage position requires a specific area on the chest to be percussed. Percussion is done by placing a cupped hand or a percussion cap against the child's chest (Westphal-Larter et al. 1977). The vibration caused by this movement loosens the mucus from the walls of the airways.

Parents or caregivers should be taught the specific positions of chest physiotherapy required for their child prior to the child's discharge. Several important points to remember when performing chest physiotherapy are listed in Exhibit 5-3. Postural drainage positions and the areas of the lung that should be percussed for each position are shown in Figure 5-1.

Exhibit 5-3 Guidelines for Chest Physiotherapy

1. Always do postural drainage and chest percussion before meals or 2 hours after meals to reduce the risk of vomiting. The best times are usually in the early morning and 1 hour before bedtime.
2. Chest physiotherapy can be started in any position. Following a set routine will encourage that all positions are treated.
3. Avoid doing percussion on bare skin. Protect the skin with one layer of soft clothing or blanket.
4. Do percussion over the ribs only. Percussion should be avoided over the sternum, vertebrae, kidneys, and abdominal organs.
5. Percuss for at least 1 minute over the specific area on the chest for each position.
6. Entire treatment should take 30 minutes.
7. Percuss anterior, posterior, and lateral chest.
8. Small children usually swallow mucus, which may cause vomiting. Children can be taught to spit out mucus when they reach age 3 to 4.
9. Young children may fall asleep during chest physiotherapy. It is important to complete the procedure.
10. Coughing several hours after chest physiotherapy is not uncommon. It can occasionally take several hours to have mucus loosen from smaller airways and move into larger airways where it can be coughed out.
11. Tissues should be handy for the older child to spit mucus into or to wipe the mouth of the younger child.

Source: Adapted from *Postural Drainage and Percussion for Infants and Small Children* by N. Westphal, K. Lefevre, and J. Barry, Pediatric Pulmonary Section, Department of Pediatrics, Arizona Health Sciences Center, Tucson, Arizona, 1977.

Conditions of the Newborn—Apnea

Home care for children who require monitoring for apnea is increasing. Reasons for monitoring include documented apnea, respiratory obstruction, neuromuscular disorders, tracheostomy, ventilator dependency, and family history of sudden infant death. Ball (1984) describes apnea as the cessation of respiration for more than 15 seconds or the time without respiration after which functional changes are noted, such as cyanosis, hypotonia, or metabolic acidosis. This must be differentiated from periodic breathing, which is a frequent and normal finding in infants. Periodic breathing is characterized by sporadic episodes in which respirations cease for up to 10 seconds and is not

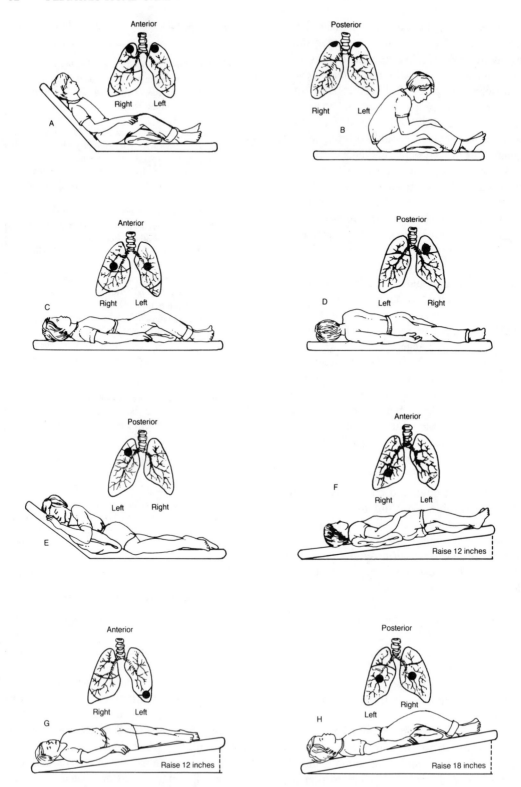

Figure 5-1 Positions for postural drainage. A. Anterior apical segment; sitting. B. Posterior apical segment; sitting. C. Anterior segment; lying flat on back. D. Right posterior segment; lying on left side. E. Left posterior segment; lying on right side. F. Right middle lobe; lying on left side. G. Left lingula; lying on right side. H. Anterior segments; lying on back.

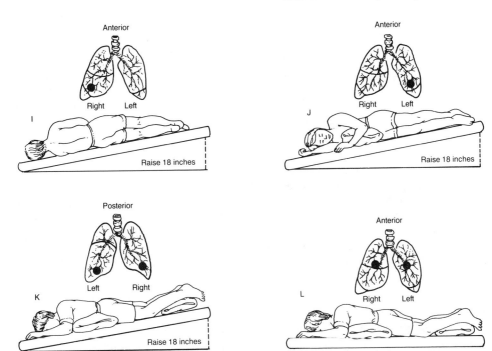

Figure 5-1 continued I. Right lateral segment; lying on left side. J. Left lateral segment; lying on right side. K. Posterior segments; lying on stomach. L. Superior segments; lying on stomach. *Source:* Reproduced by permission from *Mosby's Manual of Clinical Nursing Procedures* by J. Hirsch and L. Hannock, St. Louis, 1981, The C.V. Mosby Company.

associated with cyanosis or bradycardia (Korones 1981).

The three main forms of apnea are central, obstructive, and mixed. In central apnea there is no movement of the abdominal or thoracic muscles. Air flow is absent. In obstructive apnea, there is movement of the respiratory muscles but no air exchange. Mixed apnea is a combination of central apnea followed by obstructive apnea (Ahmann 1986). All three types of apnea can occur in premature and term infants. Factors precipitating apnea can include central nervous system disorders, metabolic alterations disturbing central nervous system metabolism, extreme immaturity, infections and fevers, vasovagal stimulation, and Valsalva maneuvers. Apneic episodes may be accompanied by bradycardia, changes in blood pressure, decreased peripheral blood flow, hypoxemia, and hypotonia (Ahmann 1986). Prolonged apnea without intervention can lead to respiratory arrest, brain damage, and death (Ahmann 1986).

There are three main elements in apnea management. The first is to prevent gastroesophageal reflux and accommodate any anatomical abnormalities. This is achieved through proper positioning of the infant. Second, cardiorespiratory monitoring assists in alerting caregivers to apneic episodes. The third element is intervention appropriate to the apneic episode. This can range from tactile stimulation for mild apneic episodes to vigorous resuscitation for severe episodes lasting 30 seconds or longer.

Home Care Routines

Parents should be instructed in the use of the monitor, trouble-shooting procedures, and emergency procedures, including cardiopulmonary resuscitation, prior to discharge. They should also be taught to observe the pattern of the apnea episodes and to count pulse and respiration. Instruction should emphasize the importance of observing frequency, duration, and symptoms associated with the episode. Caregivers must be aware of the level of intervention required for specific types of episodes, including the need for resuscitation, and must be aware of any possible precipitating factors.

Record keeping should be demonstrated and performed. A sample document is displayed in Exhibit 5-4.

The home care nurse should complete a thorough assessment of the infant with each visit. Pulse and respiration rates should be obtained and documented. Monitor accuracy should be checked. The nurse should review the apnea flow record to ascertain patterns or areas of concern. The number, type, and duration of alarms and associated symptoms should be noted on each visit. The infant's color and respiratory patterns should be observed and noted. Normal color changes related to sleep, feeding, room air temperature changes, and stooling should be discussed with parents. Safety precautions (such as no baths with the monitor in place) should be reviewed.

The home care nurse should assess the area of electrode placement for skin breakdown. Skin care should be discussed. Caregivers should be instructed not to use oils or lotions over areas where electrodes will be placed since this decreases electrode adhesiveness. Electrodes should be repositioned every 3 days or when they become loose.

The nurse should observe the parents obtain an apical pulse and respiratory rate. Caregivers should be assessed for proper placement of electrodes and safe use of the monitor, including discussion of monitor use during all sleep periods and whenever the infant is out of sight. Additionally, the nurse should assess the caregiver's response to each type of monitor alarm and encourage the family to keep a careful record (see Exhibit 5-4). The possible causes of alarms and situations when intervention is necessary should be discussed and documented. A review of the types of interventions required in particular situations may be appropriate. Caregivers may need periodic refreshers regarding emergency plans.

The home care nurse should take extra time to discuss any concerns the parents may have about the monitor. Use of this equipment usually precipitates anxiety for parents and positive reinforcement is often required. A thorough assessment of the caregiver's knowledge and confidence in the management of equipment and assessment techniques is essential. Review of alarms, electrode placement, and troubleshooting equipment should be performed and documented. Additionally, an assessment of the effect of home monitoring on caregiver's daily schedules is often helpful. The home care nurse can teach and review procedures as necessary and may be able to help the family develop new patterns of family member responsibility based on the assessment. Emergency telephone numbers placed near the infant's bedside and home telephone often add to parental security.

Home Monitoring

Impedence monitoring is most commonly used in the home. This type of monitor will not sound an alarm during periods of obstructive apnea, in which the chest wall still moves and deadspace air flow occurs in the upper respiratory tract. The alarm sounds only when central apnea occurs. To compensate, most apnea monitors are designed to monitor heart rate in addition to respiratory rate. The monitor must be chosen carefully to ensure that it will meet the needs of the child. It should be in use for 3 to 4 days prior to discharge, and instruction should include the manufacturer's troubleshooting and basic maintenance guide. A good monitor is easy to operate, accurate, and portable. Minimum controls will make user errors less frequent. Many companies now make monitors that are sensitive to the chest movements of the pediatric patient.

Electrode placement is important for proper monitor performance. The electrodes must make contact with the sides of the chest wall in order to sense the movement of breathing and should be placed symmetrically. Electrodes should be replaced as their attachment becomes less secure and should be repositioned at least every 2 to 3 days to prevent skin breakdown.

Loose lead alarms must be distinguished from apnea alarms. Most home monitors have some method of indicating that an alarm is due to a loose lead. Factors that can contribute to loose lead alarms include a loose electrode patch, a dirty electrode, oil on the infant's skin, a loose belt, detachment of electrode wires from the cable, malfunctioning wires, a defective cable, or a monitor malfunction. A systematic approach to checking for loose leads should be followed: start at the infant and check the electrodes and then check all connections in the line between the child and the monitor. Many manufacturers have instruments that can help parents

Exhibit 5-4 Apnea and Bradycardia Event Sheet

Date/Time	Episode				Color				Stimulation				Activity				Breathing				Position				Choking	Additional Comments
	Apnea (Breathing)	Bradycardia (Heart Rate)	Apnea Duration (Seconds)	Bradycardia Duration (Seconds)	Normal	Pale (White)	Dusky	Blue	Self	Gentle	Vigorous	Vigorous/ CPR	Sleeping	Feeding	Awake/Resting	Not Sure	Normal	Shallow	None/Difficult	Couldn't Tell	Stomach	Back	Infant Seat	Other	Yes or No

Source: Pediatric Apnea Center, University of Arizona Health Sciences Center, Tucson, Arizona.

Exhibit 5-5 Response to Apnea Alarms

1. Observe for respiratory movement.
2. If no respiratory movement is noted or infant/child appears lethargic, attempt to stimulate breathing by calling loudly to and then touching the infant/child. Start with a gentle touch and proceed to a vigorous touch if necessary.
3. If there is no response, proceed with mouth-to-mouth resuscitation and cardiopulmonary resuscitation if necessary. The response for a bradycardia alarm is similar, but stimulation of the infant/child is sufficient in most cases.

Source: Home Care for the High Risk Infant: A Holistic Guide to Using Technology by E. Ahmann, pp. 137–138, Aspen Publishers, Inc., © 1986.

check to make sure that the wires are not faulty. These look like pen flashlights and test the entire circuit to the lead. The presence of a specific light indicates a properly functioning circuit. Appropriate responses to an apnea alarm are discussed in Exhibit 5-5. Potential monitor problems and recommended actions are outlined in Table 5-2.

Discontinuing the Monitor

Approximately 90 percent of infants cared for in major referral centers have concluded monitoring by the time they reach 1 year of age. Ariagno (1984) has described five general criteria for discontinuation of a monitor for a child with documented apnea:

1. The infant has been free of events requiring prolonged, vigorous stimulation or resuscitation for at least 3 months, or at least 2 months if there have been no critical problems since the presenting episode.
2. The infant has not experienced a real monitor alarm for at least 2 months. This should be based on an apnea setting for 20 seconds and a heart rate of 60 beats per minute.
3. During the asymptomatic period, the infant must have experienced the stress of nasopharyngitis and/or diphtheria-pertussis-tetanus immunization without a recurrence of symptoms.
4. A clinical evaluation (neurological, developmental, and physical examination) shows that the problem or the initial reasons behind the decision to use a monitor on the child have been resolved.
5. The infant has shown no abnormalities on cardiopulmonary recordings, if these were present at the time of the child's initial evaluation. In addition, two normal sleep tests spaced at 2- to 3-month intervals are often recommended.

Discontinuing the monitor may often be stressful for parents. Despite the initial anxiety, most parents come to rely on the monitor as a source of security and safety. A weaning program allowing time to relinquish the monitor may be necessary. Caregivers should also be

Table 5-2 Apnea Monitor Troubleshooting Guide

Problem	Possible Cause	Action
1. False apnea alarms	• Loose belt • Infant may be shallow breather	• Tighten belt. • Check electrode placement. Placement should be between nipple and armpit.
2. Lead alarm—indicates that lead is disconnected or that a piece of equipment is broken	• Loose belt • Disconnected lead wires • Disconnected cable • Broken lead wires • Dead electrodes • Dirty cable and/or jack	• Tighten belt. • Check that lead wires are attached to monitor and to electrode. • Check that cable is securely inserted into back of monitor. • Replace wires. • Replace electrodes. • Clean with cotton swab and alcohol.
3. Battery alarm	• Battery needs recharging	• Plug battery charger into monitor and wall plug. • Always charge monitor when not in use.

helped to recognize the infant's stable condition and to view the infant as no longer at risk.

Medications

Theophylline is often administered to infants with apnea. It is a central nervous system stimulant that increases the respiratory drive. It is important to administer this medication regularly. It can be given with meals. Dosage is usually 2 mg/kg every 8 hours (Thach 1985). A tuberculine (TB) syringe should be used to measure dosage. The infant should receive monthly follow up for evaluation of theophylline levels. Adverse reactions can include gastrointestinal problems, central nervous system effects, and cardiac effects and should be reported to the physician immediately.

Cystic Fibrosis

Cystic fibrosis is a congenital disease characterized by multiple exocrine gland dysfunction involving the lungs and pancreas. Specifically, the sweat glands are unable to conserve salt; the pancreas is unable to produce enzymes for fat digestion, with subsequent steatorrhea and malnutrition; and the pulmonary disorder interferes with normal ciliary action, plugs airways, and creates a medium for bacterial growth and infection. Pancreatic changes are due to obstruction of the acini and ducts. Obstruction leads to atrophy, which is replaced by connective tissue, resulting in fibrosis of the gland. Insulin production usually remains unaffected. Recent advancements in the treatment of children with cystic fibrosis have resulted in increased life expectancy.

Clinical Manifestations

Cystic fibrosis is usually diagnosed prior to 6 months of age. The infant may present with a failure to gain weight. Stool characteristics may be the first indication of this pathology. They are usually described as loose but not fatty or frequent; foul-smelling; frothy; and light in color. However, it is the formation of thick mucus that is the major concern with this disease. Viscous intestinal mucus may cause a thick mass within the bowel that can precipitate an ileus, intussusception, fecal impaction, and/or rectal prolapse (Luckmann and Sorensen 1987). Pancreatic

involvement includes replacement of acinar cells by cysts, fibrotic tissues, thick mucus, and fat. The lack of pancreatic enzymes causes steatorrhea. Obstruction of biliary ducts from the mucus may cause cirrhosis or portal hypertension. Pulmonary complications such as bronchopneumonia and chronic bronchitis are common. The sweat of patients with cystic fibrosis contains a large amount of sodium, and salt depletion can occur during periods of warm weather (Luckmann and Sorensen 1987).

Treatments

Intervention for patients with cystic fibrosis includes (1) prophylactic pulmonary support, including bronchodilators, expectorants, and postural drainage; (2) administration of pancreatic enzymes; and (3) nutritional management (Luckmann and Sorensen 1987).

Prevention of pulmonary infection is of the utmost importance. Interventions aimed at removal of thick secretions should be administered prophylactically. This includes chest percussion and vibration. Aerosol treatments can also be used to enhance secretion removal. When the child requires antibiotic therapy for treatment of pulmonary infections, home care is an alternative to hospitalization after initial stabilization.

Pancreatic supplements are the foundation for nutritional management. These supplements provide digestive enzymes that the patient with cystic fibrosis cannot produce in sufficient amounts. Pancreatic enzymes should be administered with each meal. The small child or infant may take medications easier if they are mixed with a small portion of food. Enzymes should never, however, be mixed with formula. Older children may be able to tolerate capsules or tablets.

Good nutrition is essential for children with cystic fibrosis, and the home care nurse should reinforce teaching started with the parents while the child was hospitalized. Nutritional management includes a diet that is high in proteins, calories, and salt. There is some difference of opinion as to whether calories should be increased through the use of fats. Many major medical centers are now prescribing diets unlimited in fat. Replacement of fat-soluble vitamins is essential because absorption is decreased. Salt intake will need to be increased during periods of warm weather or of excessive exercise when sweating is increased to prevent salt depletion, heat prostration, and cardiovascular collapse (Luckmann and Sorensen 1987).

Feeding the small child afflicted with cystic fibrosis may require special attention. These children may be irritable and fussy with feedings. Breathing may be difficult, and coughing and vomiting may be common. The home care nurse should assess the parent–child interaction during feeding time. Careful assessment may lead to identification of interventions that can ease the potential feeding dilemmas.

Intravenous Therapy in the Home

The management of cystic fibrosis has progressed dramatically. Use of pancreatic enzymes and vitamins has provided effective management of gastrointestinal manifestations of the disease. Pulmonary infection and its sequelae remain the primary concern. Complications include atelectasis, bronchiectasis, abscess formation, cor pulmonale, and respiratory failure (Rucker and Harrison 1974). Many of the pulmonary infections require intravenous administration of antibiotics in conjunction with intensive chest physiotherapy for successful treatment.

To prevent long hospital stays solely for antibiotic administration, health care providers have been using home care programs. Studies document the cost effectiveness and favorable response on home intravenous antibiotic therapy for patients with cystic fibrosis, osteomyelitis, and endocarditis (Jeejeebhoy et al. 1976; Ingram et al. 1979; Antoniskis et al. 1978; Striver et al. 1982; Rucker and Harrison 1974). In addition, compliance, infection rates, therapeutic efficacy, and safety were documented as "remarkably good" (Striver et al. 1982). Home care programs are initiated only after the child has been admitted to the hospital to establish therapeutic levels of antibiotic therapy. Monitoring intravenous therapy is conducted by the home care nurse, in conjunction with the child and/or family.

Venous Access Sites. A critical element for an effective antibiotic home care program is maintenance of trouble-free venous access. The selection and placement of either a peripheral or central venous catheter prior to discharge is required. The most common type of indwelling central venous catheters are Broviac or Hickman catheters (see Chapter 11). These lines are most convenient for long-term intravenous therapy. Heparin locks are the most frequent type of peripheral catheter used and are ideal for short-term intravenous therapy. However, the use of peripheral veins is limited by many factors, including repeated venipuncture, frequent changes of the intravenous site (every 2 to 3 days), and frequent clotting and infiltration. The type of catheter placed should be based on patient needs, nursing convenience, and duration of therapy (Kasmer et al. 1984).

Drug Delivery Systems. There are three main types of delivery systems that can be used in the home. The selection of a delivery system must be based on the caregiver's abilities, drug therapy, and the need for nursing care.

The first type of system is gravity infusion. This is the simplest, least expensive system to use. Proper flow rate is ensured by regulating the required drops per minutes through manual adjustment of the roller clamp. This type of system has several limitations. First, it must be watched closely for accuracy of the flow rate. There are no safety devices for informing caregivers if the infusion is proceeding too fast or slow. Second, since there is no method of automatically stopping the infusion once it has been completed, it must be closely monitored so that air does not infuse into the vein. Third, the infusion is affected by the position of the catheter in relation to the height of the bag of fluid. The lower the catheter site is from the infusion bag, the faster the infusion rate. The higher the position of the catheter site in relation to the bag, the slower the infusion rate.

The second type of delivery system is an infusion pump. This type of system is necessary in situations that require a sustained, slow flow rate over a long period of time. There are several brands on the market. An IVAC pump is an example of an infusion controller. Its mechanism is propelled by gravity, and the infusion flow rate is constantly monitored by a photoelectric eye. The flow rate is adjusted by a valve that mechanically pinches the intravenous tubing to increase or decrease the lumen size (Kasmer et al. 1984).

True infusion pumps (IMEDs) administer the prescribed volume through mechanical piston action that forces fluid through the intravenous tubing at a constant rate. These type of pumps are used to deliver fluids at a high flow rate (100 to 300 mL). Both types of pumps have safety features that sound an alarm when it detects air in the line, occlusions, and completion of infusion. Infusions will automatically stop whenever the alarm sounds.

The third type of delivery system is an ambulatory infusion device. This system is advantageous because patients can be fully ambulatory during therapy. The equipment is small and light and can be attached to a belt or carried in a shoulder holster. Examples of this type of system include syringe pumps, Cormeds, and Pancreatec. Syringe pumps work on the principle of the pump depressing the plunger of an antibiotic-filled syringe at a fixed rate. Major drawbacks with this system include limited volume infusions (most syringes are 20 to 50 mL) and lack of an adequate alarm system to indicate problems other than complete infusion and occlusion. Peristaltic type pumps (Cormeds, Pancreatec) must be used only with central venous lines because of the pressure created by the pump. The pumps operate by having the antibiotic bag attached to intravenous tubing and threaded through the pump. Infusion can be continuous or intermittent depending on the type of pump. The use and maintenance of any equipment for intravenous therapy should be taught to the parents and caregivers prior to the child's discharge.

The following are guidelines for antibiotic therapy in the home:

1. Intravenous sites should be rotated every 48 to 72 hours or when evidence of inflammation or infiltration is present.
2. Intravenous antibiotic tubing should be changed every 24 hours. All supplies and equipment should be evaluated during each home visit and reordered as necessary.
3. Intravenous site should be assessed each visit or at each administration of drug, whichever is more frequent, for the following: redness or streaking of the vessel, swelling, tenderness, drainage, slow drip when fluid is allowed to infiltrate by gravity, and evidence of blood return when bag is lowered below the intravenous site.
4. All information should be documented according to agency guidelines.

Antibiotic Administration. Initial training in antibiotic therapy in the home is the responsibility of the discharging hospital. However, the home care nurse is responsible for ensuring that the parents are sufficiently trained in the administration of intravenous therapy on days when the home care nurse is not present. Review and reinforcement of critical elements of the teaching plan should include handwashing, aseptic technique, intravenous site care, infusion pump operation, storage of antibiotics, signs and symptoms of adverse reactions, administration of medications including preparation of the drug and flushing of the heparin lock, disposal of needles and syringes, and record keeping. The home care nurse should refer to agency guidelines or instructions provided to parents at the time of discharge from the hospital.

The home care nurse should monitor vital signs, laboratory tests, equipment operations, supplies, adverse drug effects, and complications. Maintenance of a clinical record and documentation of pertinent information should be completed on each visit. Routine discussion with the physician of the child's progress is essential to ensure quality patient care in the home.

CARE OF THE CHILD REQUIRING MECHANICAL VENTILATION

Increasingly, children requiring mechanical ventilation are being cared for in the home. To provide a successful experience, an organized approach to patient care management must be used. The purpose of this portion of the chapter is to cover routine home care procedures necessary for safe management of the child requiring ventilation. Goals of therapy should be maintenance of a patent airway, protection from infection, integrity of skin, speech development, and feeding. Determining ventilator requirements, selection of a ventilator, and education on the types of ventilators available is beyond the scope of this book.

Tracheostomy Care

Children requiring long-term ventilation are discharged home with a tracheostomy tube in place. Prior to discharge parents should be instructed in proper management of the tube and ventilator. The home care nurse should be familiar with the child's equipment prior to working with the child in the home setting. Ideally, the home care nurse should participate in discharge teaching at the same time the parents are learning. This provides for continuity of care and similar knowledge base in procedures and clinical management. A nursing care plan should be developed while the child is still hospitalized. It should clearly outline the care required and steps for procedures.

Tracheostomy changes are often ordered by physician preference. Time frames vary from weekly to monthly. Changing the tracheostomy tube can be an anxiety-provoking experience for parents. The home care nurse should be supportive to the parents during this procedure; however, parents should be encouraged to change the tube with the home care nurse assisting as necessary. This allows the parents to remain skilled in this procedure and offers confidence in any emergency situations. Many physicians order the child to receive 10 to 15 percent higher oxygen prior to tracheostomy tube changes. In addition, the child should receive extra breaths from the ventilator or manually prior to changing the tracheostomy tube. Several helpful guidelines in the management of tracheostomy tube changes are listed in Exhibit 5-6. The procedure for changing a tracheostomy tube is detailed in Exhibit 5-7.

The most common tracheostomy tubes used in home care are either plastic or metal. Metal tracheostomy tubes (Figure 5-2) have three parts: (1) the outer cannula, (2) the inner cannula, and (3) the obturator. The outer cannula is placed into the child's tracheostomy stoma to keep it open. The outer cannula has a neck plate that fits flush with the neck and has holes on each side to attach tracheostomy ties that will hold the outer cannula in place. The inner cannula fits inside the outer cannula. It is designed so that it can be removed and cleaned as needed. Care of the inner cannula is outlined in Exhibit 5-8.

The obturator fits into the outer tube before insertion. Its rounded tip smooths the end of the cannula and facilitates nontraumatic insertion of the tube into the stoma. The obturator is immediately removed after insertion to open the tube for air passage. Once the obturator is removed, the inner cannula fits into the outer cannula. It must be locked into place to prevent accidental removal. The inner cannula maintains airway

Exhibit 5-6 Helpful Hints for Tracheostomy Tube Changes

1. A small infant or child can be wrapped securely in a blanket (mummy wrap) to help prevent wiggling.
2. Never change a tracheostomy tube alone. A second person should assist in steadying the child.
3. A small towel should be rolled and placed under the shoulders of the child to facilitate exposure of the tracheostomy stoma.
4. After cutting the tracheostomy ties, place thumb and index finger on wings of tracheostomy tube to steady.
5. The child should be given three to five breaths with the Ambu bag (if dependent on ventilator) prior to removing the tube. Oxygen should be used if ordered.
6. The end of the tube should be lubricated with a water-soluble agent prior to insertion.
7. Tracheostomy ties should be placed on the tube before insertion.

patency. The obturator should be placed in a plastic bag at the head of the bed so that it can be used in case of extubation.

Plastic one-piece tracheostomy tubes are also available and frequently used in home care. These may be used once and then discarded. The most common brand name is Shiley. This tube is more convenient because it is one piece; however, airway patency may be more difficult since there is no inner cannula. Tube changes must be more frequent to maintain airway patency.

Tracheostomy tubes can be cuffed or uncuffed. Inflated cuffs permit mechanical ventilation and protect the lower airway by creating a seal between the upper and lower airways (Figure 5-3). Cuffed tubes seal the area between the outer cannula and the tracheal wall. The use of cuffed tubes carries risks. Excessive cuff pressures can cause tracheal mucosal damage. The nurse must be familiar with managing cuffed tracheostomy tubes to help avoid this type of problem.

To inflate a cuff, the caregiver will inject a prescribed amount of air into the cuff line. Once the syringe is removed, the one-way valve in the line ensures that the air will not escape. A balloon indicates the presence or absence of air in the cuff. However, it cannot be considered an absolute indicator of cuff inflation. Most children at home will not have cuffed tracheostomy

Exhibit 5-7 Changing the Tracheostomy Tube

Supplies

Tracheostomy tube
Twill tape
Scissors
Clean tracheostomy tube dressing
Suction equipment
Sterile water or distilled water
Sterile basin or paper cup
Hydrogen peroxide
Cotton-tipped swabs for cleaning stoma

Procedure

1. Wash hands.
2. Assemble equipment.
3. Open new tracheostomy tube package, but do not remove tube from the package. (Remember that the tube is sterile.) Insert and secure twill tape through one flange (wing) while tube is still in package.
4. Suction before changing tube. Child should be given three to five breaths (with oxygen, if ordered) and allowed to "recover" from suctioning before proceeding.
5. Hold tracheostomy tube in place and cut tape with scissors.
6. Remove tube with smooth motion.
7. Stoma area can be cleaned at this time or after new tube is placed depending on age of child, medical stability, and airway stability.
8. Touching only the flanges (wings) of the new tube, remove tube from package and lubricate with water-soluble agent. Put obturator in place. Hold exterior portion of obturator in place with thumb.
9. Gently insert tube into stoma following the contour of the trachea, first upward, then in a downward, curved motion.
10. Remove obturator.
11. Fasten tracheostomy ties. This should be done loosely at first to accommodate placement of new dressing. Then, ties should be pulled snug; little finger should fit between the tie and the patient's neck.
12. Insert inner cannula, if used.
13. If tracheostomy tube is to be reused, be sure to clean just the inner cannula immediately with hydrogen peroxide and water. After the tube has dried, store it in a clean, sealed plastic package. One-piece disposable tubes can be discarded.

Source: Adapted with permission from *Taking Care of Your Trach at Home* by Gayle A. Traver from the Division of Respiratory Therapy and the Otorhinolaryngology Section of the University of Arizona College of Medicine, Arizona Health Sciences Center, Tucson, Arizona, 1977.

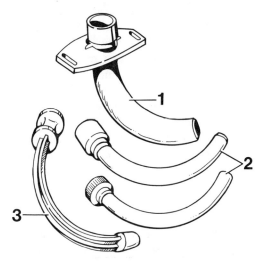

Figure 5-2 Metal tracheostomy tube showing the outer cannula (1), inner cannula (2), and obturator (3). *Source:* Reprinted with permission from *Taking Care of Your Trach at Home* by Gayle A. Traver from the Division of Respiratory Therapy and the Otorhinolaryngology Section of the University of Arizona College of Medicine, Arizona Health Sciences Center, Tucson, Arizona, 1977.

Exhibit 5-8 Care of Inner Cannula of Tracheostomy Tube

Supplies

Clean bowl or paper cup
Hydrogen peroxide
Distilled water
Brush or pipe cleaner

Procedure

1. Wash hands.
2. Prepare equipment: pour about ¼ cup hydrogen peroxide into a basin and dilute with ¼ cup distilled water.
3. Remove inner cannula: hold neck plate in place with one hand and use the other to unlock inner cannula. Tilt patient's head slightly backward and pull inner cannula out in a smooth downward motion.
4. Clean inner cannula: place inner cannula in cup with hydrogen peroxide and water. Gently scrub the inside and outside of the cannula with a brush or pipe cleaner.
5. Rinse thoroughly under running tap water. Make sure all hydrogen peroxide is removed since it is irritating to lungs.
6. Inspect cannula to make sure it is clean.
7. Shake off excess water.
8. Reinsert cannula, being sure to lock it in place.

Source: Adapted with permission from *Taking Care of Your Trach at Home* by Gayle A. Traver from the Division of Respiratory Therapy and the Otorhinolaryngology Section of the University of Arizona College of Medicine, Arizona Health Sciences Center, Tucson, Arizona, 1977.

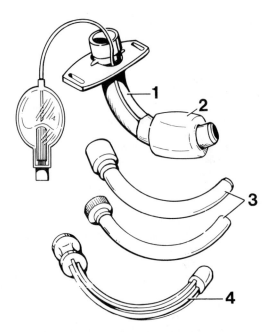

Figure 5-3 Cuffer tracheostomy tube showing outer cannula (1), cuff (2), inner cannula (3), and obturator (4). *Source:* Reprinted with permission from *Taking Care of Your Trach at Home* by Gayle A. Traver from the Division of Respiratory Therapy and the Otorhinolaryngology Section of the University of Arizona College of Medicine, Arizona Health Sciences Center, Tucson, Arizona, 1977.

tubes in place; however, the occasional cuffed tube may be required. It is important to alternate periods of inflation and deflation to decrease trauma to the tracheal wall from pressure exerted by the cuff. The use of minimal leak technique and minimal occluding volume can help decrease tracheal wall pressure. In minimal leak technique, the cuff pressure is adjusted to allow for minimal air leak around the cuff at the end of inspiration. Minimal occluding volume represents the smallest amount of air used to inflate the cuff that will allow no air leak around the cuff (Becker and Shea 1986).

Fenestrated tracheostomy tubes allow the child to communicate. This is managed by an opening between the flange and the distal tip of the tube. Air flow passes through the opening during exhalation, allowing air to pass over the vocal cords for speech. In order to use this type of tube, the child must be able to breathe spontaneously or with minimal assistance. If a child

is off the ventilator for any period of time, the cuff (if present) should be deflated and the tube plugged.

Stoma Skin Care

The stoma site must be kept clean to prevent infections. Moisture and secretions can cause irritation and may lead to skin breakdown. Stoma care should be done at least twice a day to remove secretions from around the tube and to examine the appearance of the stoma. Cleaning should be done more frequently if an odor is present. The dressings, if used, should be changed at least twice daily and when they become soiled or dampened. Precut gauze dressings are available and convenient to use (Figure 5-4). Gauze sponges should never be used for tracheostomy dressings because filaments can easily be inhaled into the trachea. The procedure for daily stoma care is outlined in Exhibit 5-9.

All tracheostomy tubes must be secured to prevent accidental extubation, excessive movement, or misalignment. Changing tracheostomy

Figure 5-4 Precut gauze dressing. *Source:* Reprinted with permission from *Taking Care of Your Trach at Home* by Gayle A. Traver from the Division of Respiratory Therapy and the Otorhinolaryngology Section of the University of Arizona College of Medicine, Arizona Health Sciences Center, Tucson, Arizona, 1977.

Exhibit 5-9 Stoma Care

Supplies

Cotton-tipped swabs
Hydrogen peroxide
Distilled water
Clean bowl or paper cup
Tracheostomy dressing
Ointment (if prescribed)
For tubes with inner cannula: a tracheostomy kit containing a sterile two-part basin, brush, pipe cleaner, cotton-tipped swabs, gloves, gauze sponges, and sterile drape (Exhibit 5-8)
For cuffed tubes: one sterile 10- to 20-mL syringe for inflating cuff
Sterile forceps (for emergencies—either to remove foreign objects or to keep stoma open)

Procedure

1. Wash hands.
2. Assemble equipment.
3. Pour hydrogen peroxide into bowl and moisten the cotton-tipped swabs in it. (Some physicians order ½ strength hydrogen peroxide to be used.) Mix ½ ounce hydrogen peroxide with ½ ounce distilled water.
4. Remove old dressing and examine stoma for redness, bleeding, or drainage. If dressing is stuck to skin, moisten it with distilled water for easier removal.
5. Use swab to clean around the stoma site. Clean from stoma area outward using circular motion.
6. Allow skin to dry.
7. Apply ointment if ordered.
8. Apply new precut gauze dressing. Do not use a regular gauze sponge and cut a slit in it since the frayed edges can be inhaled through the tracheostomy opening. The use of a dressing is optional.

Source: Adapted with permission from *Taking Care of Your Trach at Home* by Gayle A. Traver from the Division of Respiratory Therapy and the Otorhinolaryngology Section of the University of Arizona College of Medicine, Arizona Health Sciences Center, Tucson, Arizona, 1977.

ties should be a part of the routine care (Exhibit 5-10). The knot used to secure a tracheostomy tube is shown in Figure 5-5. There should always be a complete tracheostomy tube set at the patient's bedside for emergency replacement.

Suctioning

The purpose of suctioning is to remove secretions that accumulate in the lungs and large airways that cannot be coughed out. Suctioning of the tracheostomy tube should be done only when it is necessary to avoid damage to the lining of the trachea. This is usually done in the early morning, before meals, and before going to bed. Clinical indications for suctioning include moist, noisy breathing; increased stridor and/or respiratory rate not caused by activity; frequent coughing; nasal flaring; restlessness, irritability, or crying; and color changes. Too frequent suctioning causes increased secretion production. The procedure and equipment for suctioning is outlined in Exhibit 5-11, and the procedure for cleaning suction equipment is outlined in Exhibit 5-12.

A bulb syringe can be used for suctioning the nose and mouth and also the tip of the tracheostomy tube when secretions are coughed up but cannot be cleared from the tube. Bulb syringes must be cleaned thoroughly every 24 hours. This can be done by filling the bulb with warm soapy water, letting it sit momentarily, and squeezing the water out of the bulb. This procedure should be repeated several times until the water returns clear.

There continues to be controversy regarding the use of a clean versus a sterile suctioning technique. Clean suction technique (Exhibit 5-13) requires the reuse of disposable suction catheters. The recommendation for clean versus sterile technique must be decided by the medical provider. Nationwide standards differ and range from clean technique to duplication of hospital procedures. Theoretically, bacterial contamination would be a concern since the lumen of the suction catheters are too small to clean adequately. The probability of adhesion of mucus to the wall of the lumen causes great concern for risk of infection. The technique to

Exhibit 5-10 Changing Tracheostomy Ties

Supplies

Twill tape

Scissors

Procedure

1. Wash hands.
2. Clear secretions from airway and lungs by coughing or suctioning. This will decrease the possibility of coughing while the tube is untied.
3. Cut one length of twill tape long enough to go slightly more than twice around the neck.
4. Holding the tube in place with one hand, cut the old tape with scissors and remove old tape.
5. Thread tape through hole in side of neck plate.
6. Pull through a little more than half of the tape and bring this end around neck.
7. Thread bottom tape through opposite neck plate hole.
8. Take the other end of tape and bring it around back of head to opposite shoulder.
9. Tie ends of tape in a square knot at the side of the neck, snug enough so that only one finger can fit between tapes and neck.

Source: Adapted with permission from *Taking Care of Your Trach at Home* by Gayle A. Traver from the Division of Respiratory Therapy and the Otorhinolaryngology Section of the University of Arizona College of Medicine, Arizona Health Sciences Center, Tucson, Arizona, 1977.

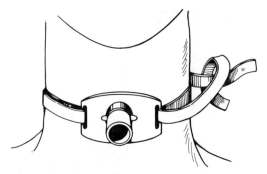

Figure 5-5 Knot used to tie tracheostomy tube. *Source:* Reprinted with permission from *Taking Care of Your Trach at Home* by Gayle A. Traver from the Division of Respiratory Therapy and Otorhinolaryngology Section of the University of Arizona College of Medicine, Arizona Health Sciences Center, Tucson, Arizona, 1977.

clean suction catheters at home for reuse is outlined in Exhibit 5-14.

Secretions should be observed for color, consistency, and odor. Blood-tinged mucus could indicate that suctioning is being done too often. Infection will cause odor or color changes to the mucus. If this persists for more than 24 hours, the physician should be notified.

Ventilator Maintenance

The type of ventilator to be used in the home will be decided while the child is still hospitalized. Parents and caregivers should be trained in ventilator maintenance, troubleshooting, and emergency care prior to discharge. The ventilator selected for use in the home is dependent on the child's diagnosis, required oxygen concentration, daily requirements for mechanical ventilation, availability of equipment, and repair service. The ideal home ventilator is inexpensive, portable, small, and lightweight. The pur-

pose of this section is to give the reader insight into routine home procedures for managing the ventilator. An example of a weekly schedule for care of the ventilator-dependent child is shown in Table 5-3.

Troubleshooting Equipment

Regular and systematic monitoring of ventilator equipment is essential for the safe delivery of care.* Regular and frequent ventilator checks are mandatory, allowing for close follow-up of the child's respiratory status, as well as detection of mechanical flaws (Parrell and O'Connor 1986). Daily routines for equipment maintenance include ventilator checks, cleaning and changing the ventilator circuits, and cleaning the suction machine and resuscitation bag. Established routines for ventilator checks are facilitated by the use of a ventilator check flowsheet (Exhibit 5-15). As well as hospital instructions, most manufacturers provide detailed troubleshooting guidelines. These guidelines list problems, possible causes, and corrective actions.

The most common nonmedical problems encountered with ventilator equipment include humidifier malfunction, electrical power failure, suction machine malfunction, frozen oxygen gauge, and holes in ventilator tubing. Consistent problems with the ventilator require the home

---

*Ventilator equipment refers to all pieces of equipment used with a ventilator: oxygen analyzers, oxygen storage containers, and suction equipment.

Exhibit 5-11 Suctioning the Tracheostomy Tube (Sterile Technique)

Supplies

Suction machine with connecting tubing
Suction catheter kit (clean or sterile may be ordered)
Paper cup or sterile cup
Sterile saline or distilled water for cup
Sterile saline for insertion into tracheostomy tube
Resuscitation bag
Oxygen

Procedure

1. Assemble equipment.
2. Wash hands.
3. Open sterile suction kit.
4. Pour sterile saline into sterile cup.
5. Turn suction machine on. Suction pressure should not exceed 120 mm Hg and should be checked before suctioning.
6. Put on glove.
7. Attach suction catheter to suction tubing making sure not to handle sterile end of catheter.
8. Suction a small amount of water from the cup. This ensures that suction is working and lubricates the catheter.
9. Place prescribed amount of sterile saline into tracheostomy tube. This will help loosen secretions.
10. If ordered, administer five to ten breaths with resuscitation bag at the prescribed oxygen concentration.
11. Insert catheter gently into the trachea until child coughs or resistance is felt. *Do not* apply thumb to suction at this time.
12. Remove suction catheter about ½ inch once resistance is felt.
13. Put thumb over suction port to apply suction.
14. Withdraw suction catheter slowly. Suction should not last for more than 5 seconds.
15. Administer five to ten breaths with resuscitation bag, if required.
16. Clear secretions from catheter by suctioning a small amount of sterile saline from the sterile cup.
17. Listen to child's breathing; observe child's color; observe secretions in tubing. Repeat suctioning as needed.
18. When finished suctioning, clear suction tubing by suctioning the rest of the water from the sterile cup.
19. Discard catheter, glove, and sterile water.
20. Document per agency policy.

Exhibit 5-12 Cleaning Suction Machine

Clean jar daily.

1. Empty jar. Contents may be flushed in toilet.
2. Clean jar and connecting tubing with warm soapy water and rinse.
3. Reassemble.

Disinfect once a week.

1. After cleaning, soak jar and tubing in Control-III (mixed according to instructions on label) for 10 to 15 minutes.
2. Empty Control-III and air dry parts.
3. Reassemble.

Source: Adapted with permission from *Taking Care of Your Trach at Home* by Gayle A. Traver from the Division of Respiratory Therapy and the Otorhinolaryngology Section of the University of Arizona College of Medicine, Arizona Health Sciences Center, Tucson, Arizona, 1977.

care nurse to observe how the equipment is used, cleaning practices, and daily maintenance. This may help identify interventions to decrease problem areas.

Oxygen Delivery Systems

Some ventilator-assisted children require supplemental oxygen. The oxygen system chosen for use in the home is based on the pressure input requirements of the ventilator, required flow rates, portability of oxygen system, and availability of supplier. The three most frequent types of oxygen delivery systems are discussed.

Oxygen Cylinders

Oxygen cylinders are made from aluminum or steel and are available in various sizes. These are high-pressure tanks that must be secured either

Exhibit 5-13 Suctioning the Tracheostomy Tube (Clean Technique)

Supplies

Suction machine with connecting tubing
Suction catheter
Paper or plastic cup with distilled water
Resuscitation bag
Oxygen
Box of clean gloves
Sterile saline for insertion into tracheostomy tube

Procedure

1. Assemble equipment.
2. Wash hands for at least 30 seconds with soap and warm water. Dry hands with a clean towel or paper toweling. Place glove on suctioning hand (optional).
3. Turn suction machine on. Suction pressure should not exceed 120 mm Hg and should be checked before suctioning.
4. Attach suction catheter to suction tubing making sure not to handle sterile end of catheter. 'If the catheter has been used previously, suction water from the cup before suctioning the tracheostomy tube.
5. If needed, use shallow suction on the tracheostomy adaptor only. Suction secretions visible in the tracheostomy and do not leave in airway for more than 5 seconds. Rinse catheter with water.
6. If secretions are thick, place prescribed amount of sterile saline into tracheostomy tube. This will help loosen secretions.
7. If ordered, administer five to ten breaths with resuscitation bag at the prescribed oxygen concentration.
8. Insert catheter gently into the trachea until child coughs or resistance is felt. *Do not* apply thumb to suction at this time.
9. Remove suction catheter about ½ inch once resistance is felt.
10. Put thumb over suction port to apply suction.
11. Withdraw suction catheter slowly. Suction should not last for more than 5 seconds.
12. Administer five to ten breaths with resuscitation bag, if required.
13. Suction enough water from the paper cup to clear the secretions from the catheter.
14. Listen to child's breathing; observe child's color; observe secretions in tubing. Repeat suctioning as needed.
15. When finished suctioning, clear suction tubing by suctioning the rest of the water from the sterile cup.
16. Turn off suction machine. Turn off oxygen if used. Wash hands.
17. One suction catheter may be used for 1 to 2 hours, or up to 24 hours. Some suggest that the suction catheter be discarded after each use. Use the recommendation from your local children's hospital.
18. After you are finished suctioning, rinse the catheter with distilled water, shake off excess water, and store catheter wrapped in clean paper towel. Remember to discard suction catheter after the agreed length of usage.
19. Document per agency policy.

in stands or with chains to minimize the danger of a "torpedo" effect if the tank is tipped over and the yoke is broken. This system is most cost effective when the child requires small amounts of oxygen for less than 15 hours per day (Becker and Shea 1986). A single cylinder can be supported in a stand and transported easily. Multiple cylinders can be manifolded together to form a bank of oxygen, which can be kept in a storage room or garage. A bank of oxygen cylinders can power a positive-pressure ventilator with a high gas requirement for a stationary child (Becker and Shea 1986).

Liquid Oxygen

Liquid oxygen can be used with a low-flow oxygen delivery system. This system is safer than the cylinder method because it is a low pressure system. It may be more cost effective for low to moderate continuous-flow use, and bulk liquid systems are available if a large amount of oxygen will be used. Liquid oxygen is stored in large metal cannisters and smaller portable units can be filled from it. Spillage often occurs each time the portable unit is filled, and evaporation may occur when the unit is not in use.

Oxygen Concentrators

An oxygen concentrator separates oxygen from room air. This system is most cost effective when the child requires low flow oxygen over more than 15 hours per day (Becker and Shea 1986). Concentrators are powered by 115 volts

Exhibit 5-14 Cleaning Suction Catheters for Reuse

1. Suction enough water through the catheter to clear it of mucus.
2. Wipe off the outside of the catheter.
3. Wash in warm soapy water and rinse.
4. Soak in prescribed cleansing solution for 10 minutes. (Make sure to follow manufacturer's instruction for mixing of this solution.)
5. Remove from cleansing solution, shake off excess fluid, and air dry.
6. Put in sealed plastic bag for storage.

Discard catheters if:

1. Mucus cannot be cleared from catheter.
2. There are signs and symptoms of a chest infection.

Source: Adapted with permission from *Taking Care of Your Trach at Home* by Gayle A. Traver from the Division of Respiratory Therapy and the Otorhinolaryngology Section of the University of Arizona College of Medicine, Arizona Health Sciences Center, Tucson, Arizona, 1977.

of alternating current at a frequency of 60 Hz, draw from 2.5 to 15 amperes, and will increase the electric bill accordingly (Becker and Shea 1986). A cylinder or liquid oxygen system must be available for back up in case of power failure.

Humidification

All children receiving home mechanical ventilation via tracheostomy require a means for warming and humidifying inspired air to prevent drying and inspissation of tracheobronchial secretions, insensible water loss, and loss of body heat (American College of Chest Physicians 1975). Humidification can be provided by jet nebulizer, cascade, or regenerative humidifier. The type of humidifier should be selected and tested prior to the child's discharge.

Monitors/Alarms

Some ventilators do not come equipped with the necessary monitors to ensure the child's safety. Additional monitoring equipment may be necessary. Minimally, the ventilator alarms should include apnea monitors, high and low pressure alarms, CO_2 alarms, oxygen analyzer/monitor, and spirometers.

Supplies

Equipment for the ventilator will need to be ordered periodically. The home care nurse can assist the parents with this function. Supplies required for home ventilation are listed in Exhibit 5-16.

Travel

Many children requiring mechanical ventilation are able to attend school, go to movies, and spend time outside. This is because ventilators are becoming more portable and mechanically operated wheelchairs with space available for mounting a battery-powered ventilator are allowing children more flexibility. Trips away from home need to be carefully planned. Equipment needed for travel is similar to equipment needed at home. The home care nurse should plan for emergencies during travel and prepare equipment accordingly.

Table 5-3 Weekly Schedule for Care of Ventilator-Dependent Child

Tasks	Sun	Mon	Tues	Wed	Thurs	Fri	Sat
Clean suction machine	X	X	X	X	X	X	X
Tracheostomy change		X					
Stoma care	X	X	X	X	X	X	X
Change tracheostomy ties	X	X	X	X	X	X	X
Check ventilator settings	X	X	X	X	X	X	X
Chest physiotherapy	X	X	X	X	X	X	X
Clean suction jar	X	X	X	X	X	X	X
Soak suction equipment		X					
Clean Ambu bag and valve	X	X	X	X	X	X	X
Check oxygen level in tanks			X		X		
Inventory supplies		X					
Order supplies			X				
Rinse cascade on ventilator and refill	X		X		X		X

Exhibit 5-15 Ventilator Check Flowsheet

Things to Check	Date/Times							
Ventilator:								
Mode								
Volume								
Low alarm								
High alarm								
Respiratory rate								
Inspiratory time								
PEEP								
Tidal volume								
FIO_2								
Inline temperature								
Water level								
Circuits:								
Circuit change								
Circuit cleaning								
Equipment Cleaning:								
Suction machine								
Resuscitation bag								
Other:								
Suctioning								
Aerosols								

NURSING CARE PLANS IN THE HOME

This section provides some general guidelines for nursing care of children with cystic fibrosis, BPD, asthma, tracheostomies, and ventilator dependency. It is important to remember that the needs of the child and family will vary greatly from case to case. Information from the facility referring the child is vital in constructing specific, individual care plans. It is likely that parents have been instructed to some extent on providing medical and nursing care for their child. They, along with the primary and/or specialty care providers should be used as resources. This will ensure and maintain consistent, safe, effective, and individualized care.

A broad range of skills are required to care for children with alterations in respiratory function. In addition to clinical skills, the home care nurse must be able to assess family coping ability, parental stress, self-esteem (child and parents), need for privacy and control, general health maintenance, and enmeshment of child, family, community, and primary, secondary, and tertiary health care providers. Effective intervention is based on a sound understanding of these concepts. These areas are addressed in this section. General nursing diagnosis and patient outcomes that apply to all five previously mentioned disease states are outlined. The care plans in Appendixes 5-A through 5-E address specific problems of each disease entity (Carpentio 1983; Nelson and Beckel 1987).

Alterations in Respiratory Function

This broad category includes impaired gas exchange, ineffective airway clearance, and/or

Exhibit 5-16 Supplies for Ventilation in the Home

Suction machine
Precut gauze dressings
Cotton-tipped swabs
Hydrogen peroxide
Suction catheters
Clean or sterile gloves
Paper cups or suction kits
Twill tape
Scissors
Tracheostomy tubes
Distilled water or sterile saline
Pipe cleaners or brush (for inner cannula)
Sterile saline for irrigation
Oxygen
Ventilator circuits
Resuscitation bag

ineffective breathing patterns. The goal of care is to maintain optimal respiratory function with proper gas exchange, effective respiratory patterns, and adequate airway clearance. Assessment of the child's respiratory status must be continuous owing to the dynamic state of these diseases. This begins by establishing the child's baseline. For example, it is often common for children with cystic fibrosis to have a cough or for infants with BPD to have a slightly elevated respiratory rate. Breathing patterns may solely be the result of the cycle of the mechanical ventilator and may therefore appear to be different from "normal" respiratory excursions. This baseline should allow the home care nurse to make a thorough respiratory assessment of the child within the first few minutes of the visit. This should include inspection for signs of respiratory distress: a tense, drawn, or worried facial expression; nasal flaring; chest retractions; altered rate or depth of respirations; change in skin color (noting duration, degree, and location); or altered chest movement (Kendig and Chernick 1983). The child's cough and secretions should also be evaluated.

Notation of sputum color, consistency, odor, and amount can be of great importance in detecting a potential infection. A change in the child's cough should also be noted during the assessment. A recent history from either the previous shift's nurse, the parent, or the child will be necessary to determine the significance of any changes that may be noted on the examination.

Auscultation is another important part of the initial respiratory assessment. The presence of any adventitious sounds is significant in the final evaluation of the child's respiratory status. Complete thoracic auscultation with a reliable stethoscope is often the best way to identify potential alterations in gas exchange or airway clearance. There continues to be debate in the medical arena in defining specific sounds heard through the stethoscope, such as rales, crackles, rhonchi, wheezes, or squeaks (Fox 1978). Precise terminology is less important than recognition of an abnormal sound that is not a part of the child's baseline assessment. The location of the sound and the point at which it occurs in the respiratory cycle are both important. For example, a "crackle" noted in the right upper lobe during both inspiration and expiration or "wheezes" found bilaterally on expiration are important data that can help determine the action required in a given situation.

The initial respiratory assessment is the basis for determining the care plan for the day. If there is no alteration from the child's previous condition, then the nurse can proceed with specific daily treatments and interventions as outlined in the general nursing care plan. If an alteration in any respiratory parameter is noted, it may mandate changes to the care plan for that day. For example, if the child with a tracheostomy or with cystic fibrosis has an increased cough or has lungs that sound congested, he or she may benefit from extra chest physiotherapy, extra suctioning, and perhaps a consultation with the physician regarding a potential infection. If the asthmatic child is noted to be more dyspneic or wheezy, he or she may require an additional dose from a metered-dose inhaler. If the child with BPD has been found to have rales, he or she may benefit from extra chest physiotherapy or an extra dose of diuretic (an action requiring a physician's order and using further data, such as the child's weight and most recent intake and output).

The initial respiratory assessment of the infant/child with a pulmonary disorder is the standard used to identify complications or improvements in the child's status. This information allows caregivers to detect, respond to, and prevent progression of complications and to note positive response to therapy leading toward an improvement in the child's status.

Alterations in Nutrition: Less Than Body Requirements

Nutritional deficits can be observed in varying degrees in children with alterations in respiratory status. The desired patient outcome is adequate nutritional intake that supports proper growth and development. In some instances this is crucial to the ultimate resolution of the pulmonary ailment. The child with BPD must grow in order to generate new alveoli and lung tissue to eventually "grow out" of the disease (Fox 1978). The child with cystic fibrosis must maintain adequate nutrition to ward off impending pulmonary infections; yet at the same time the pulmonary disease increases the difficulty of maintaining adequate caloric intake for growth and healing. Compounding the problem, particularly for the infant with BPD, is the need for increased calories. These infants have increased caloric expenditure because of their lung disease and may also need to maintain fluid restriction. For this reason, 24 or 28 calorie formulas are often prescribed. Another means of providing more calories without added volume is by adding nutritional supplements such as medum-chain triglyceride oil or high-glucose polymers. The home care nurse should know how to mix the formulas correctly and should monitor the family's preparation of formula because this is often an aspect of care where errors are made. Directions for mixing formula should be written in the child's discharge orders. If they are not, the physician or nutritionist should be contacted for such instructions.

Infants who have had recurrent oral intubations, oral or nasopharyngeal suctioning, or sucking deprivation secondary to their critical illness as a neonate may have developed a feeding aversion (Palmer et al. 1975). Such children may require feeding from a nonoral route. These sites include gastrostomy, jejunostomy, or nasogastric tube. The home care nurse must be knowledgeable in the care of such tubes (see Chapter 7). Tubes should be patent at all times. This can be achieved by administering a small (10–30 mL) water flush after each feeding or medication. Some tubes require routine changes to maintain patency and to avoid deterioration. Parents should be observed and/or aided during the process of changing the feeding tube, checking for placement and patency, and daily use. A child with a nasogastric tube will need more frequent tube changes (i.e., every 2 to 3 days) than a child with a gastrostomy tube (i.e., every 4 to 8 weeks). A tube replacement schedule should be recommended by the discharging health care team.

A speech therapy consultation should be recommended for an infant or child with a feeding difficulty, particularly if it is found to be behavioral (Lierman et al. 1987). Parental education regarding oral stimulation and the slow introduction of pacifiers, nipples, and food is a crucial element of care for the child with a feeding aversion. Some tertiary care centers may have a "feeding team" or program specifically designed to care for infants and children who will not eat. Speech therapy can normally be conducted in the home. Identified interventions should be integrated into the daily care plan.

Providing adequate nutritional intake for the infant/child with a chronic pulmonary disorder can often be a challenging task. Parents need encouragement and positive feedback. Consultations with appropriate health care professionals, including counselors and/or social workers, may help those families frustrated by what is often perceived as the most difficult aspect of care.

Skin Integrity and the Potential for Impairment

There are several factors involved that can help lead to skin difficulties. The first is the child's chronic condition, often complicated by an impaired nutritional state. Second, the child may require additional apparatus that impairs skin integrity. Oxygen nasal cannulas, tracheostomy tubes and ties, gastrostomy tubes, and/or monitor leads are all potential harbingers to skin irritation or breakdown. In addition, the underlying disease state may cause skin problems. For example, the asthmatic child may also present with atopic dermatitis or the infant with cystic fibrosis may have perineal breakdown from frequent, malabsorbed stools. Finally, various treatments such as antibiotics or mist to a tracheostomy may cause skin irritation, rashes, or breakdown. A thorough examination of the skin must be done on a routine basis to ensure the child has intact skin free of breakdown or areas of infection. Stomas should be clean without erythema, edema, or drainage. Various equipment (nasal cannulas, ventilator tubings, monitor leads, gastrostomy tubes) should be secured so that there is minimal traction or torque that can cause undue pressure on the skin. Tubes that need to be taped in place should, whenever possible, be taped onto something other than the skin itself (e.g., a small piece of gauze, another piece of tape). This minimizes the number of times tape is put on and pulled off the skin itself. For example, placing two thin strips of adhesive tape on the cheeks of a child requiring oxygen via nasal cannulas allows the oxygen tubing to be taped onto the tape, which can stay in place for days. Rotation of tape, monitor leads, and tracheostomy tie knots will also decrease irritation. Thorough cleansing and drying of areas of potential skin breakdown is also crucial. A hair dryer set on low/cool can help dry areas of skin that are difficult to reach (e.g., the back of an infant's neck) without causing abrasion from rubbing with a towel. Finally, when an area of skin breakdown is noted, the physician should be notified. Antibiotic creams and ointments or hydrocortisone cream might be very useful treatment but should not be used without a physician or nurse specialist's recommendation.

Impaired Growth and Development

Impaired growth and development can include both physical and psychosocial aspects. The desired patient outcome is normal growth and development. Inadequate nutritional intake is the precipitant of impaired physical growth and development. Children with cystic fibrosis are often thinner and smaller than their peers (Nussbaum and Galant 1984). Adolescents with cystic fibrosis also tend to enter puberty later, delaying the onset of secondary sexual characteristics (Nussbaum and Galant 1984). Severe asthmatics may be smaller in stature if they have required long-term corticosteroid therapy. The etiology of the impaired physical growth must be identified and efforts made to correct it whenever possible. For example, if the problem is inadequate caloric intake, then a nutritional plan to increase calories is appropriate. If the child with

cystic fibrosis has significant malabsorption, then measures should be taken to correct it. Accurate records should be kept at specific intervals to plot the child's true physical growth. These data will help physicians and nutritionists plan future interventions.

Delayed psychosocial growth and development can result from isolation if the child has had long or frequent hospitalizations, immobility, repeated painful stimuli from required medical/nursing interventions, and dissociation from peers and family (McCollum 1975). Infants with BDP are often found to be developmentally delayed, particularly in the area of gross motor development (Koops et al. 1984). Children on ventilators or with tracheostomies are often less mobile than their peers, decreasing their opportunities to play, explore, and interact appropriately for their age group. The signs and symptoms of delay can be obvious or may be manifested in more covert ways. Awareness for signs of chronic anxiety, irritability, and depression can be manifestations of the frustrations that often accompany isolation (Aradine 1980). Symptoms can also be exhibited by family members.

Identification of developmental delays requires formulation of a plan of care. A written care plan should be completed prior to discharge so that family, home care nurses, school personnel, and home care physical and occupational therapists can partake in a program appropriate for that child's developmental stimulation. If developmental delays are detected during home care, the care plan should be developed in conjunction with the referring medical center. A physical or occupational therapy consultation will help quantify and qualify the delay. Interventions should then be identified. Interventions should incorporate family participation in delivery of care (Koops et al. 1984). Involving the family augments therapy for both the child and family by allowing them time together.

It is important for the home care nurse to be able to perform a developmental assessment in order to identify a developmental delay. This need not be a formal test (i.e., performing a standard developmental test) but should be part of the initial nursing evaluation. Based on knowledge of normal growth and development (see Chapter 13), and given the boundaries of the child's physical limitations and medical history, the home care nurse may recognize delays that could be treated. A referral should be made through the local physician or pulmonary specialist in order to verify the suspicions of developmental delay and plan care accordingly.

Knowledge Deficit

Knowledge deficit related to the disease process and necessary treatment regimens is a common problem recognized by home care nurses. It is hoped that parents and child have been educated prior to the patient's discharge. However, it must be recognized that hospitalization is a stressful period and a certain disruption. Inability for the child or family to incorporate all necessary information during that time is not unusual (Redman 1976). It is crucial to assess a family's level of knowledge regarding the disease and treatment interventions. This is especially true since families and patients are often expected to be independent in carrying out the entire treatment regimen at some point. Accurate assessment must be based on education done prior to discharge. Communication with the primary nurse or physicians will provide information to use as a basis for assessment of the patient and family's level of knowledge. For example, one cannot assume that parents did not incorporate information on how to position a child for chest physiotherapy if in fact they were never taught. Home care nurses have the unique opportunity of relatively frequent exposure to patient and family. Reinforcement of education and an ongoing assessment of the patient and family's knowledge base will serve as a basis for quick identification of knowledge deficits so that they can be corrected.

Once an accurate assessment has been made, the obvious intervention is to educate the family or patient in any deficient areas. Communication with the discharging facility will ensure that consistent teaching is being conducted. Consistency in teaching will help assimilate information as well as decrease confusion and frustration.

Parents or patients should be encouraged to ask questions and to write down questions for later discussion. Many families and patients find the use of a journal invaluable for keeping track of day-to-day changes, assessments, occurrences, and questions. Some tertiary care settings provide families with records to facilitate follow-up visits and future hospitalizations.

Ineffective Coping

Ineffective coping can be manifested by recognition and verbalization of the inability to cope, role confusion, inability to make decisions or ask for help, and inappropriate use of defense mechanisms. Ineffective coping will affect the patient and family's ability to comply with any part of the home care plans and therapeutic regimens. Contributing factors can be pathophysiological, situational, and maturational. The home care nurse must be aware of the signs of ineffective coping and must use assessment skills to ascertain the degree of impact on the family's ability to care for the child. Patient outcomes include recognition of ineffective coping strategies, facilitation for support and guidance in stressful situations, and patient/family use of appropriate, effective coping strategies.

Many authors have examined the effect of chronic illness on the child and family (Green and Solnit 1964; McCollum 1975). Theories may vary in specifics, but it is generally accepted that the chronic illness of a child is a lifelong source of stress, anxiety, fear, and guilt. Families and children have been able to master effective coping strategies if provided with proper training and skills. The home care nurse may be the pivotal point for recognition and facilitation of effective coping.

Home care is more cost effective than hospital care, and the impact of chronic hospitalization and separation is often devastating to both the child and family. We cannot, however, assume that sending the child home will solve all problems (Solnit and Stark 1961; Lancaster 1981; Donn 1982; Burr et al. 1983). It may precipitate new stressors and hardships for the family to cope with. Once home, the multiple sources of support in the hospital are no longer available and the family is left with the overwhelming responsibility of caring for their child day to day, month to month, year to year.

Nursing care in the home is a mechanism that promotes effective coping. It prevents parent "burnout" from shouldering the burden of 24-hour nursing care. It allows the parent time to truly "parent" rather than consistently tend to medical, technical, or nursing needs of the child.

Home nursing should also allow the parents time away from the child to spend as a couple or to spend with other children. Siblings must be recognized for their importance as members of the family (McCollum 1975). Nurses in the home can also affect family coping strategies by being an educational resource. Often families experience stress because they feel unknowledgeable regarding aspects of their child's care. The home care nurse can reinforce education and promote self-assurance for parents.

Home nursing care is often a great relief for families, but it can also be a source of stress. Suddenly, families have strangers in the home. Issues of privacy, independence, and role confusion surface. Parents often feel awkward disagreeing in front of the nurse. They may avoid disciplining their children for fear of being seen or heard and judged incorrectly. They may not trust the nurses. They may resent such an intrusion, although it is obviously necessary and helpful to them. Home care nurses must be aware and sensitive to these issues. Frequent care meetings can help keep communication lines open and lead to strategies for coping with the presence of nurses in the home.

Ineffective coping can be an ongoing, fluctuating problem for children and families impacted by chronic illness. Recognition and assessment of the problem and contributing factors is the first step toward resolution. Providing support, facilitating communication, and encouraging appropriate coping strategies will serve to maintain effective stress management and coping abilities for these children and families facing countless, yet surmountable odds.

REFERENCES

Ahmann, Elizabeth, *Home Care for the High Risk Infant.* Rockville, Md.: Aspen Publishers, Inc., 1986.

American College of Chest Physicians. "American Thoracic Society Pulmonary Terms and Symbols." *Chest* 67(1975):583–593.

Antoniskis, A.; Anderson, B.C.; Van Volkinberg, E.J.; Jackson, J.M.; and Gilbert, D.N. "Feasibility of Outpatient Self-administration of Parenteral Antibiotics." *Western Journal of Medicine* 128(1978):690–693.

Aradine, C.E. "Home Care for Young Children with Long Term Tracheostomies." *American Journal of Maternal-Child Nursing* 5(1980):121–125.

Ariagno, R.L. "Evaluation and Management of Infantile Apnea." *Pediatric Annals* 13(1984):210–217.

Ball, Barbara A. "Apnea/Bradycardia Flow Sheets in a Neonatal Setting." *Focus on Critical Care* 11, no. 4(1984):13.

Bancalari, E., and Gerhardt, T. "Functional Alterations in the Acute Phase of Bronchopulmonary Dysplasia." In *Bronchopulmonary Dysplasia and Related Chronic Respiratory Disorders: A Report to the Nineteenth Ross Conference on Pediatric Research.* Ross Laboratories, 1986.

Becker, E.A., and Shea, T.A. "Airway and Ventilation Accessories." In *Ventilator-assisted Patient Care: Planning for Hospital Discharge and Home Care,* edited by D.L. Johnson, R.M. Giovannoni, and S.A. Driscoll. Rockville, Md.: Aspen Publishers, Inc., 1986.

Boushey, H.A.; Holtzman, M.J.; Sheller, J.R.; and Nadel, J.A. "Bronchial Hypersensitivity." *American Review of Respiratory Disease* 121(1980):389–413.

Burr, B.H.; Guyer, B.; Todress, I.D.; Abrahams, B.; and Chiado, T. "Home Care for Children on Respirators." *New England Journal of Medicine* 309(1983):1319–1323.

Carpentio, L.J. *Nursing Diagnosis: Application to Clinical Practice.* Philadelphia, J.B. Lippincott Co., 1983.

Donn, S. "Cost Effectiveness of Home Management of Bronchopulmonary Dysplasia." *Pediatrics* 70(1982):330–331.

Evans, R.; Mullally, D.I.; Wilson, R.W.; Gergin, P.T.; Rosenberg, H.M.; Gtauman, J.S.; Chevailey, F.M.; and Feinleib, M. "National Trends in the Morbidity and Mortality of Asthma in the U.S." *Chest* 91(1987):655–745.

Farrell, P.M., and Palta, M. "Bronchopulmonary Dysplasia." In *Bronchopulmonary Dysplasia and Related Chronic Respiratory Disorders: A Report to the Nineteenth Ross Conference on Pediatric Research.* Ross Laboratories, 1986.

Fox, W.W. "Bronchopulmonary Dysplasia (Respirator Lung Syndrome): Clinical Course and Outpatient Therapy." *Pediatric Annals* 1(1978):40–45.

Green, M., and Solnit, A.J. "Reactions to the Threatened Loss of a Child: A Vulnerable Child Syndrome." *Pediatrics* 34(1964):58–66.

Harrod, J.R.; L'Heureux, P.; Wagensteen, O.D.; and Hunt, C.E. "Long Term Follow-up of Severe Respiratory Distress Syndrome Treated with IPPB." *Journal of Pediatrics* 84(1974):277.

Ingram, G.I.C.; Dykes, S.R.; Creese, A.L.; Mellor, P.; Swan, A.V.; Kaufert, J.K.: Rizza, C.R.; Spooner, R.J.D.; and Biggs, R. "Home Treatment in Haemophilia: Clinical, Social, and Economic Advantages." *Clinical and Laboratory Haematology* 1(1979):13–27.

Jeejeebhoy, K.N.; Langer, B.; Tsallas, G.; Chu, R.C.; Kuksis, A.; and Anderson, G.H. "Total Parenteral Nutrition at Home: Studies of Patients Surviving 4 Months to 5 years." *Gastroenterology* 71(1976):943–953.

Kasmer, Richard J.; Hoisington, Lisa M.; and Yukniewicz, Steve. "Home Parenteral Antibiotic Therapy: II. Drug Preparation and Administration Considerations." *Home Healthcare Nurse* 5(1984):19–29.

Kendig, E.L., and Chernick, V. *Disorders of the Respiratory Tract in Children* Philadelphia: W.B. Saunders, 1983.

Koops, B.L.; Abman, S.H.; and Accurso, F.J. "Outpatient Management and Follow-up of Bronchopulmonary Dysplasia." *Clinics in Perinatology* 11(1984):101–122.

Korones, S.B. *High Risk Newborn Infants: The Basis for Intensive Nursing Care*. 3d ed. St. Louis: C.V. Mosby Co, 1981.

Lancaster, J. "Impact of Intensive Care on the Parent–Infant Relationship." In *High Risk Newborn Infants: The Basis for Intensive Nursing Care*, edited by S. Kornes. Toronto: C.V. Mosby Co., 1981.

Lierman, C.; Wolff, R.; Hazelton, J.; Pesquera, K.; and Wilson, E. "Multidisciplinary Treatment of Feeding Disorders in the Home." *Pediatric Nursing* 13(1987): 266–270.

Luckmann, Joan, and Sorensen, Karen. *Medical-Surgical Nursing: A Psychophysiologic Approach*. Philadelphia: W.B. Saunders Co., 1987.

Martin, A.J.; McLennan, L.A.; Landau, L.I.; and Philan, P.D. "The National History of Childhood Asthma to Adult Life." *British Medical Journal* 280(1980): 1397–1400.

McCollum, A.T. *The Chronically Ill Child: A Guide for Parents and Professionals*. New Haven, Ct.: Yale University Press, 1975.

Nelson, N.P., and Beckel, J. *Nursing Care Plans for the Pediatric Patient*. Philadelphia: C.V. Mosby Co., 1987.

Nussbaum, E., and Galant, S.P., eds. *Pediatric Respiratory Disorders: Clinical Approaches*. Orlando, Fla.: Grune & Stratton, 1984.

Palmer, S.; Thomson, R.J.; and Linschied, T.R. "Applied Behavior Analysis in the Treatment of Childhood Feeding Problems." *Developmental Medicine in Children's Neurology* 17(1985):333–339.

Parrell, S.J., and O'Connor, M.H. "Managing Equipment and Supply Needs in the Home." In *Ventilator-assisted Patient Care: Planning for Hospital Discharge and Home Care*, edited by D.L. Johnson, R.M. Giovannoni, and S.A. Driscoll. Rockville, Md.: Aspen Publishers, Inc., 1986.

Platts-Mills, T.A.; Heymann, P.W.; Chapman, M.D.; and Mitchell, E.B. *Progressive Respiratory Research*. (1985) 276–284.

Redman, B.K. *The Process of Patient Teaching in Nursing*. St. Louis: C.V. Mosby Co., 1976.

Rucker, R.W., and Harrison, G.M. "Outpatient Intravenous Medication in the Management of Cystic Fibrosis." *Pediatrics* 54(1974):358–360.

Solnit, A.J., and Stark, M.H. "Mourning and the Birth of a Defective Child." *Psychoanalytic Study of the Child* 16(1961):521–535.

Striver, H.G.; Trosky, S.K.; Cote, D.D.; and Oruck, J.L. "Self-administration of Intravenous Antibiotics: An Efficient, Cost-effective Home Care Program." *Canadian Medical Association Journal* 127(1982):207–211.

Taussig, L.M. "Long-term Management and Pulmonary Prognosis in Bronchopulmonary Dysplasia. In *Bronchopulmonary Dysplasia and Related Chronic Respiratory Disorders: A Report to the Ninetieth Ross Conference on Pediatric Research*. Ross Laboratories, 1986.

Thach, B. "Sleep Apnea in Infancy and Children." *Medical Clinics of North America* 69(1985):1294.

Westphal-Larter, Nanci; Lefevre, Karen; and Barry, John. *Postural Drainage and Percussion for Infants and Small Children*. Respiratory Therapy, Department of Respiratory Services, Pediatric Pulmonary Section, Department of Pediatrics, Arizona Health Sciences Center, Tucson, Arizona, 1977.

Appendix 5-A

Nursing Care Plan for a Child with Asthma

Nursing Diagnosis/ Patient Problem	Defining Characteristics	Nursing Interventions	Expected Outcomes
1. Alteration in respiratory status: ineffective airway clearance and gas exchange *Etiology:* • bronchoconstriction or spasm • Increased mucus production • Airway inflammation • Environmental "triggers" or allergens	Signs of respiratory distress: • Abnormal breath sounds (wheezes, crackles) • Cough • Tachypnea • Dyspnea • Anxiety • Irritability • Cyanosis	Assess respiratory status frequently during respiratory distress (every 15 minutes). *Administer medications as prescribed: daily bronchodilators, prn metered-dose inhalers (MDI), corticosteroids. *Administer oxygen as ordered and indicated. Remove or avoid environmental allergens or "triggers" when possible. Assess for side effects of bronchodilators, beta agonists, corticosteroids, etc. Perform chest physiotherapy as tolerated for mobilization of mucus. Remain calm and be supportive and reassuring during crisis.	Patient is free from respiratory distress. Patient is free from side effects of asthma medications.
2. Anxiety related to ineffective gas exchange *Etiology:* • Actual or perceived threat to biological integrity • Acute change in health status	Restlessness Irritability Tension Fear Nervousness Increased respiratory distress	Stay with child during acute asthma attack. Maintain calm, quiet environment when possible. Allow patient to assume comfortable position. Reassure patient and family. Encourage use of relaxation techniques if familiar to child.	Patient and family demonstrate decreased anxiety during acute onset of symptoms.

*Denotes nursing intervention requiring a physician's order.

Nursing Diagnosis/ Patient Problem	Defining Characteristics	Nursing Interventions	Expected Outcomes
3. Knowledge deficit related to • Pathophysiology of disease • Treatment regimen • Proper use of metered-dose inhalers (MDIs) and medications • Environmental "triggers" and allergens	Verbalization of questions, concerns, fears, misconceptions related to asthma and prescribed treatment Inability to verbalize rationale for medications Inability to demonstrate proper use of MDIs, nebulizers, and/or oxygen if needed Noncompliance with treatment regimen Environmental "triggers" and allergens still present in home	Reinforce proper use of equipment and medications. MDIs: • Exhale. • Tilt neck to straighten airway. • Inhale puff. • Hold breath 10 seconds. • Exhale. • Wait 5–10 minutes and repeat second puff. • Use holding chambers as appropriate for ease of administration. Assist family in finding ways to avoid or control environmental "triggers" or allergens. Reinforce signs and symptoms of respiratory distress and medication toxicity/side effects. Encourage follow-up for further education and reinforcement of teaching.	Patient and family are knowledgeable about disease process, treatment regimen, and environmental triggers to avoid. Patient and family can verbalize appropriate treatment regimen and demonstrate proper use of MDI, nebulizer, and/ or oxygen.
4. Coping: ineffective— patient and family *Etiology:* • Chronicity of illness • Ever-present possibility of acute onset of symptoms	Use BPD care plan.	Use BPD care plan.	Patient and family use appropriate coping mechanisms. Patient and family form trusting relationship with health care providers. Patient and family use support resources as appropriate.

*Denotes nursing intervention requiring a physician's order.

Nursing Care Plan for a Child with Bronchopulmonary Dysplasia

Nursing Diagnosis/ Patient Problem	Defining Characteristics	Nursing Interventions	Expected Outcomes
1. Alteration in respiratory status related to impaired gas exchange	Signs of respiratory distress: • Tachypnea • Tachycardia • Paleness/cyanosis • Adventitious breath sounds • Diaphoresis • Irritability • Retractions • Nasal flaring • Hypoxia • Hypercapnia	Assess respiratory status every 8 hours. *Administer oxygen via nasal cannula or tent as ordered. *Perform chest percussion and postural drainage as needed. *Administer respiratory medications (bronchodilators, corticosteroids) as ordered. Notify physician of any change from baseline respiratory status.	Patient is adequately oxygenated.
2. Alteration in nutritional status: less than body requirements *Etiology:* child has increased caloric needs and is unable to meet these secondary to: • Compromised respiratory status • Feeding aversions • Fluid restrictions • Gastroesophageal reflux	Inadequate weight gain for age (corrected for prematurity) Inability to take nourishment by mouth Slowed alveolar regeneration secondary to nutritional status If feeding aversions are questioned, consult feeding team, if available, or nutritionist.	*Nutritional consultation should be provided by referring facility. *Weigh frequently, as ordered by physician. Monitor accurate intake and output. Maintain dietary record complete with symptoms of aversions or reflux and report to physician. *Establish hyperosmolar calorie-dense feedings (maintaining fluid restriction as needed). Report compromised respiration status during feedings.	Patient has gradual, appropriate growth, concomitant with improved respiratory status. Patient is free from oral feeding aversions. Mealtime is positive experience for child and family.

*Denotes nursing intervention requiring a physician's order.

Nursing Diagnosis/ Patient Problem	Defining Characteristics	Nursing Interventions	Expected Outcomes
		*Increase oxygen during feedings. If patient is unable to tolerate oral feedings, maintain feedings via gastrostomy, jejunostomy, or nasogastric tube. Maintain reflux precautions after feedings.	
3. Fluid volume excess	Respiratory distress: • Labored respirations • Cyanosis • Retractions • Decreased breath sounds • Rales • Tachypnea • Cough • Decreased urine output • Edema	Monitor intake and output every 4–8 hours. Daily weights (or more frequent if ordered) *Maintain fluid restriction. Assess for signs of respiratory distress due to fluid overload: • Monitor vital signs including blood pressure. • Auscultate breath sounds. • Note signs of respiratory distress. • Note edema. • Note increased oxygen requirement. *Administer diuretics. *Administer potassium supplement. Assess for side effects of diuretics as needed.	Patient has appropriate ratio of fluid intake and urine output. Patient is without signs of respiratory distress. Patient has no untoward side effects from diuretics or electrolyte supplements.
4. Skin integrity: potential for impairment	Skin irritation from tape needed to secure tubes or leads: • Redness • Edema • Rash • Abrasions • Actual breakdown	Minimize amount of tape on skin. Minimize tension of tubes or lines. Rotate monitor lead or tape sites. When possible, tape onto something other than skin (e.g., another piece of tape, small gauze pad). Maintain clean, dry skin around tube sites. Maintain adequate nutritional state. *Treat rashes or breakdown with antibiotic ointments or corticosteroid creams as ordered and appropriate.	Patient has clear skin with no rashes, breakdown, or infection.
5. Impaired growth and development: physical and psychosocial	Inability to maintain steady growth curve Inability to reach appropriate developmental milestones	Encourage parents to maintain active involvement in playful, stimulating activities. Maintain consistent caregivers.	Patient maintains steady, appropriate growth. Patient progresses through developmental milestones at appropriate pace (as outlined by

*Denotes nursing intervention requiring a physician's order.

Nursing Diagnosis/ Patient Problem	Defining Characteristics	Nursing Interventions	Expected Outcomes
Etiology: • Isolation due to long-term and/or repeated hospitalizations • Immobility • Sensory deprivation and/or overload • Altered nutritional status • Decreased energy level from increased work of breathing • Repeated painful stimuli • Separation from parents • Inconsistent caregivers	Inappropriate muscle tone—may be increased or decreased Irritability Chronic anxiety or depression	Maintain consistent daily schedule. *Provide organized program of audiovisual tactile stimulation via occupational or physical therapy. Maintain record of developmental milestones.	developmental specialists).
6. Knowledge deficit related to • Pathophysiology of BPD • Treatment regimen • Signs and symptoms of infecton, respiratory distress, fluid overload *Etiology:* • Inaccurate information given to family • No explanations given for rationale of treatments • Family unable to absorb all information at once	Inaccurate compliance to specified treatment regimen Verbalization of questions or problems regarding aspects of BPD and required interventions Inability to articulate rationale for treatment Inappropriate expectations of recovery from disease state Inability to independently care for child	Assess reasons for inaccurate compliance or noncompliance. Provide accurate information to parents at rate that is appropriate to promote learning. Reinforce all teaching frequently. Assess return-demonstrations for accuracy. Encourage follow-up with pulmonary center or physician knowledgeable in care of BPD. Encourage parents to keep journal of questions or concerns. Continually assess for further knowledge deficit.	Family verbalizes and demonstrates understanding of disease process and treatment regimen. Family forms trusting relationship with care providers and feels comfortable asking questions in future.
7. Coping: ineffective—family *Etiology:* • Chronicity of illness and very slow improvement of health status • Frequent hospitalizations	Verbalization of inability to cope Infrequent visiting when child is hospitalized Role confusion Inability to meet basic care needs of child Inability to make decisions Chronic sadness, depression Anger	Determine etiology of ineffective coping and/or noncompliance. Assess coping mechanisms and encourage use of appropriate mechanisms. Determine alternate strategies for ineffective coping mechanisms. Encourage involvement with support groups or other	Family: • Demonstrates decreased anxiety and stress. • Demonstrates increased ability to care for child. • Develops trusting relationship with care providers.

*Denotes nursing intervention requiring a physician's order.

Nursing Diagnosis/ Patient Problem	Defining Characteristics	Nursing Interventions	Expected Outcomes
• High care demands of patient • Isolation • Inability to appropriately bond with infant in neonatal period	Noncompliance with medical regimens	families in similar situations whenever possible. Use resources such as social workers, family counselors, community aides, hospice, respite care, etc. as available and appropriate. Allow family opportunity to verbalize stress, frustration, fatigue, and anxiety.	• Uses healthy, appropriate coping mechanisms.

Nursing Care Plan for a Child with Cystic Fibrosis

Nursing Diagnosis/ Patient Problem	Defining Characteristics	Nursing Interventions	Expected Outcomes
1. Alteration in coping related to chronic illness (patient and family) *Etiology:* • Recurrent, frequent pulmonary exacerbations and/ or hospitalizations • Significant change in life style with progressiveness of disease and time-consuming treatment regimens • Shortened life span related to prognosis	Demonstration of feelings of anxiety, fear, sadness, depression Inappropriate coping mechanisms Noncompliance to treatments	Encourage verbalization of feelings. Assess coping mechanisms and encourage use of appropriate mechanisms. Assess reasons for noncompliance. Encourage involvement with support groups if available. Use resources such as social workers, counseling, community aide, hospice, etc., as appropriate. Check with CF Center or CF Foundation re further suggestions of sources of support. Provide information re more aesthetically pleasing devices (e.g., internal venous access device vs. Hickman gastrostomy button vs. tube) to maintain positive body image. Encourage verbalization of feelings of sexuality, body image, peer relationships. Encourage independence with treatments.	Patient and family: • Demonstrate decreased anxiety, fear, and/or sadness. • Develop trusting relationship with caregivers. • Use healthy, appropriate coping behaviors.
2. Knowledge deficit related to • Pathophysiology of CF	Inaccurate compliance to treatment regimen Inability to articulate rationale for treatments	Assess reasons for inaccurate or noncompliance. If knowledge deficit, then provide information to patient and family.	Patient and family demonstrate and verbalize understanding of the disease process and treatment regimen.

Nursing Diagnosis/ Patient Problem	Defining Characteristics	Nursing Interventions	Expected Outcomes
• Treatment regimen • Signs and symptoms of infections	Verbalization of problems or questions regarding CF and/or treatment interventions	Contact CF Center or CF Foundation for more in-depth information. Arrange and/or encourage follow-up care with CF Center. Encourage parents and patient to write down further questions. Reinforce all education prn. Assess on continual basis for further knowledge deficit.	Patient and family feel comfortable asking questions and will admit knowledge deficit in future.
3. Alteration in skin integrity Etiology: • Frequent malabsorbed stooling in infants • Rectal prolapse (from malabsorption and frequent stooling) • Stoma sites of various catheters: Hickman, gastrostomy tubes, jejunostomy tubes	Excoriation in perineal area of infant Prolapse of rectal mucosa through anus Signs of infection or irritation at catheter insertion site (edema erythema, drainage, tenderness	*Administer pancreatic enzymes as ordered. Change soiled diapers frequently. Apply protective layer of ointment (Desitin, Vaseline, etc.) to buttocks. Notify physician of rectal prolapse. Frequently assess catheter insertion sites for signs of infection. *Provide catheter site care as outlined by physician.	Patient has decreased stooling with minimal skin irritation and no rectal prolapse. Catheter insertion site is clean with no signs of infection.
4. Self-concept: disturbance in role performance, body image, and self-esteem Etiology: • Physical changes from cystic fibrosis: clubbing, cachexia, cyanosis, barrel chest • Activity intolerance	Change in social involvement—resistance to interact with peers Verbalization of • Negative body image • Fear of rejection • Feelings of helplessness, hopelessness, sadness, depression Noncompliance or uninvolvement with treatment regimen.	Educate parents and preadolescents for likelihood of delayed maturation and physical changes accompanying CF. Relay sense of acceptance for the patient, despite physical appearance. Encourage interaction with other CF patients as source of support. Encourage interaction with peers. Provide privacy whenever possible for chest physiotherapy, coughing and expectoration, and elimination.	Patient has positive feelings of self and body demonstrated by independence, motivation, participation in care, and verbalization of self-acceptance.
5. Alteration in respiratory status related to ineffective airway clearance and impaired gas exchange Etiology: • Unusually thick, tenacious	Increased cough from baseline Increased production of mucus Change in thickness or color of respiratory secretions Dyspnea Tachypnea	Encourage and/or perform chest physiotherapy before meals and at bedtime (2–4 times) *Administer medications as ordered (antibiotics [IV or po] aerosolized medications, bronchodilators, corticosteroids.)	Patient has decreased cough and sputum production, no fever, and no hemoptysis, tachypnea, chest pain, nor adventitious breath sounds.

*Denotes nursing intervention requiring a physician's order.

Nursing Diagnosis/ Patient Problem	Defining Characteristics	Nursing Interventions	Expected Outcomes
respiratory secretions • Frequent respiratory infections • Eventual lung scarring and fibrosis	Hemoptysis Chest pain	Encourage hydration to decrease viscosity of secretions. *Administer oxygen as ordered and needed. Assess for further deterioration of respiratory status and notify physician of significant changes. If hemoptysis, estimate volume; notify physician; transport to emergency department or physician's office if greater than 2 tablespoons.	
6. Alteration in nutrition: less than body requirements *Etiology:* • Malabsorption of nutrients fats/ proteins/fat-soluble vitamins • Decreased appetite secondary to infection • Emesis secondary to coughing	Frequent loose, foul-smelling, bulky stools Inconsistent or inadequate weight gain Weight loss Abdominal pain and cramping Emesis after cough Increased signs of respiratory tract infections	*Administer supplemental pancreatic enzymes before or scattered throughout meals and snacks. *Administer supplemental vitamins (multivitamin, water-soluble vitamin E, vitamin K) Monitor stooling pattern. *1. If there is increased stooling, enzymes may need to be increased. *2. If there is decreased stooling or constipation, enzymes may need to be decreased. Encourage diet high in proteins and calories. Monitor weight gain or loss pattern. *Treat symptoms of respiratory tract infection if present. Administer chest physiotherapy *before* meals. Encourage smaller, more frequent feedings if emesis with cough. *Administer supplemental nutrition as ordered.	Patient maintains or gains weight as outlined by physician. Enzyme supplementation is adequate to control malabsorption. Patient is in well-nourished state.

*Denotes nursing intervention requiring a physician's order.

Appendix 5-D

Nursing Care Plan for a Child with a Tracheostomy

Nursing Diagnosis/ Patient Problem	Defining Characteristics	Nursing Interventions	Expected Outcomes
1. Alteration in respiratory status: ineffective airway clearance *Etiology:* • Potential for airway obstruction due to ineffective cough, thick secretions, or mucus plugging	Signs of respiratory distress: • Adventitious breath sounds • Change in secretions: Amount Thickness Color change • Increased cough • Tachypnea • Cyanosis • Retractions • Nasal flaring • Dyspnea	Encourage coughing to clear airway. Suction tracheostomy tube *when needed* (avoid excess suctioning). Suction length of tracheostomy tube *only*: if unable to clear airway, *then* deep suction beyond end of tube. *Provide continuous humidified air or oxygen to tracheostomy tube via air compressor or heat/moisture exchanges ("artificial noses") Instill drops of sterile normal saline as needed, to loosen secretions.	Patient has a clear airway. Patient and family are able to recognize signs of potential airway obstruction and to provide necessary intervention.
2. Impaired skin integrity: *Etiology:* • Tracheostomy stoma, tracheostomy ties, secretions, humidity	Moisture from secretions and humidity Mechanical irritation from pressure of tracheostomy ties, humidity mask, and/or tubing Presence of excoriation, rash, pressure sites	Assess every 8 hours for areas of pressure or skin breakdown. Change tracheostomy ties and pad at least once a day and prn for moistness or looseness. *Clean stoma with half-strength hydrogen peroxide and rinse with water at least twice a day and prn. Dry stoma area and area under ties *thoroughly*. (Hair dryer on cool setting can be helpful to dry hard-to-reach areas on side or back of neck.)	Patient has intact skin without breakdown or signs of infections.

*Denotes nursing intervention requiring a physician's order.

Nursing Diagnosis/ Patient Problem	Defining Characteristics	Nursing Interventions	Expected Outcomes
		Rotate knot of tracheostomy ties to avoid consistent area of pressure. Pad area of humidity mask if resting against chin. *Humidity setting should be 30–40 mm H_2O (to avoid excess moisture to skin). If rash is present, call physician for advice.	
3. Injury: potential for • Hypo-oxygenation • Tracheal mucosa irritation, tracheal stenosis, tracheitis • Decannulation *Etiology:* • Excessive or deep suctioning • Insecure tracheostomy ties • Mechanical irritation from movement of tube	Cyanosis: • Intolerance of suctioning procedure • Microatelectasis	*Hand ventilate with oxygen or room air before and after suctioning (*required* for mechanically ventilated patient). Apply suction on withdrawal of catheter only. Limit suctioning to 5–10 seconds. Use proper-sized suction catheter. Check breath sounds before and after suctioning.	Patient is without injury secondary to tracheostomy: • No respiratory distress • No tracheal irritation • Secure tracheostomy tube
	Bleeding during or after suctioning • Presence of granulation tissue (internally viewed only via bronchoscopy) • Difficulty replacing tracheostomy tube during routine change • Excessive secretions (secondary to excessive suctioning)	Suction only when child cannot clear secretions independently. Suction only length of tracheostomy tube (if unable to clear airway, *then* deep suction). Report bleeding or difficulty changing tube to physician. Report presence of external granulation.	
	Displaced tracheostomy tube • Loosened ties • Signs of respiratory distress	Assess adequate gas exchange through tracheostomy tube at least every 8 hours. Change tracheostomy ties at least once a day and more often if wet, loose, soiled. Ties should be one fingerbreadth loose. Tie changing procedure should be performed by two persons unless emergency. Emergency kit (extra tube, ties, scissors, suction catheter, saline) should *always* be within reach in case of obstruction or decannulation.	

*Denotes nursing intervention requiring a physician's order.

Nursing Diagnosis/ Patient Problem	Defining Characteristics	Nursing Interventions	Expected Outcomes
4. Ineffective communication related to tracheostomy *Etiology:* • Patient is unable to effectively verbally communicate to caregivers, family, and peers because tracheostomy bypasses vocal cord vibration necessary for speech.	Ineffective attempts at communication Unwillingness to use alternate modes of communicaton other than vocal speech Family or patient: • Frustration • Anger • Sadness • Depression	*Speech therapy consultation should be made for inpatient and outpatient therapy (infancy to adolescence). *Tracheostomy tube can be "downsized" to allow for air movement around tube and vocalization. *Encourage use of alternative modes of communication (sign language, communication board, mouthed speech, computer/robotic speech). Assess patient's and family's adaptation to method of communication. Assess coping skills related to communication. Reinforce recommendations from speech therapist.	Patient is able to effectively communicate with family, peers, and caregivers. Patient and family are satisfied with mode of communication.
5. Knowledge deficit related to tracheostomy care *Etiology:* • Family, patient, or designated caregiver is unable to safely, independently care for child based on knowledge deficit.	Questions regarding tracheostomy care/ procedures Verbalization of problems, fears, misconceptions, and hesitation to care for child with tracheostomy Noncompliance with care regimen Inability to independently care for child Inaccurate return-demonstrations of cares	Thorough discharge teaching should be carried out by referring facility before discharge. Reinforcement of teaching to be done by home nurses (consistent with teaching done by referring facility). Ensure that *anyone* responsible for child's care is *thoroughly* educated (e.g., babysitters, other family members, school personnel) regarding tracheostomy care. Community agencies, emergency personnel, electricity and phone company, and local hospital emergency department personnel are notified of presence of tracheostomized child in community. Encourage follow-up with pulmonary center/referral facility. Contact facility with any questions/concerns.	Patient is safely cared for at all times by knowledgeable caregiver. Caregivers demonstrate ability to properly carry out care regimen. Patient and family feel comfortable asking questions and will admit knowledge deficit in future.
6. Coping: ineffective—patient and family *Etiology:* • Changes in body integrity	Verbalization of inability to cope Role confusion Inability to meet basic care needs Inability to make decisions	Determine etiology of ineffective coping and noncompliance. Assess coping mechanisms and encourage use of appropriate mechanisms.	Patient and family: • Demonstrate decreased anxiety, fear, and stress. • Develop trusting relationship with caregivers.

*Denotes nursing intervention requiring a physician's order.

Nursing Diagnosis/ Patient Problem	Defining Characteristics	Nursing Interventions	Expected Outcomes
• High care needs of patient • Frequent hospitalizations • Inability to vocalize • Isolation	Noncompliance with medical regimens	Determine alternate strategies for ineffective coping mechanisms. Encourage involvement with support groups if available. Use resources such as social workers, counselors, community aides, hospice, respite care as available and appropriate. Allow patient and family opportunity to verbalize stress, frustration, fatigue, and anxiety.	• Use healthy, appropriate coping behaviors.

Nursing Care Plan for a Child with Ventilator Dependency

Nursing Diagnosis/ Patient Problem	Defining Characteristics	Nursing Interventions (see also Appendix 5-D)	Expected Outcomes
1. Alteration in respiratory status: ineffective breathing patterns *Etiology:* • Neuromuscular impairment • Loss of functional lung tissue • Fatigue, anxiety • Central nervous system impairment	Signs of respiratory distress: • Shortness of breath • Dyssynchrony with ventilator • Use of accessory muscles • Retractions • Nasal flaring	Check all ventilator settings connections. Correct any problems. Monitor effects of any ventilator setting changes. Provide emotional support during periods of anxiety. Teach relaxation techniques used at times of anxiety. Show patient how to become synchronous with ventilator. Optimize patients' position to facilitate use of diaphragm and to maintain open airway.	Patient has no signs of respiratory distress. Patient is able to initiate relaxation techniques to decrease anxiety. Patient can describe optimal position of effective breathing.
2. Alteration in respiratory status: ineffective airway clearance *Etiology:* • Excessive, thick secretions • Ineffective cough due to weakness/ fatigue • Bronchoconstriction • Infection • Immobility	Change in secretions: • Color • Amount • Consistency • Odor Signs of respiratory distress: • Cyanosis • Tachypnea • Dyspnea • Retractions or flaring • Diaphoresis • Tachycardia Temperature elevation Difficulty suctioning secretions Intermittent elevated peak inspiratory pressures or "high pressure" alarms on ventilator Restlessness, anxiety	Monitor for signs of ineffective airway. Encourage coughing when possible. Suction tracheostomy tube as needed. Notify physician of signs of infection. *Administer antibiotics or bronchodilators as ordered. Provide adequate humidification to airway. Provide adequate hydration. Initiate chest physiotherapy to aid airway clearance.	Patient has open airway and can clear secretions either by cough or by suctioning. Patient has no signs of respiratory distress. Patient has no signs of infection. Patient is adquately hydrated and humidified to keep secretions loose and manageable.

*Denotes nursing intervention requiring a physician's order.

Nursing Diagnosis/ Patient Problem	Defining Characteristics	Nursing Interventions	Expected Outcomes
3. Altered respiratory status: impaired gas exchange *Etiology:* • Loss of functional lung tissue • Neuromuscular impairment • Central nervous system impairment • Increased secretions • Anxiety or fear • Fatigue	Signs of respiratory distress: • Tachypnea • Dyspnea • Cyanosis • Tachycardia Change in mental status Somnolence Headaches Night sweats Disorientation in morning Diaphoresis	Monitor for signs of respiratory distress. Monitor ventilator settings and functions. Check for disorientation or change in mental status after naps or in morning. Maintain clear airway. Observe for change in sleep patterns due to CO_2 retention.	Patient is without respiratory distress. Patient shows no signs of hypoxia or hypercarbia. Patient maintains adequate gas exchange with properly functioning ventilator.
4. Immobility: impaired *Etiology:* • Physical limitations due to attachment of ventilator • Neuromuscular impairment	Muscle atrophy or decreased muscle tone Limited range of motion Dyspnea or fatigue with exertion Anxiety Anger Depression	Ensure use of portable mechanical ventilator whenever possible. Ensure use of wheelchair with mount for ventilator to increase mobility. Encourage use of adaptive devices to operate wheelchair (e.g., P-switch, ''sip and puff'' device). Maintain daily range of motion exercises. Follow physical therapy recommendations for mobility exercises. *Initiate physical therapy referral if needed. Observe for signs of respiratory distress with exertion/exercise. Position and reposition patient frequently for optimal use of extremities.	Patient is as independently mobile as possible. Patient is able to maintain optimal position or can direct others to do so. Patient maintains baseline range of motion whenever possible.
5. Impaired verbal communication *Etiology:* • Tracheostomy tube • Mechanical ventilator	Impaired ability to phonate: • Anger • Depression • Anxiety • Frustration	*Provide periods of phonation via cuff deflation and increased volumes whenever possible and if tolerated. Provide alternate methods of communication (e.g., paper and pencil, letter board, picture board, computer, sign language). *Consult with speech therapist regarding use of adaptive communication devices.	Patient is able to adequately communicate using most appropriate method for him or her. Patient demonstrates decreased frustration when communicating.
6. Coping: ineffective— patient and family	Verbalization of inability to cope Role confusion Inability to meet needs of patient, family, or self	Assess causative or contributing factors for ineffective coping. Assess use of coping mechanisms: encourage	Patient and family: • Demonstrate and use appropriate coping mechanisms.

*Denotes nursing intervention requiring a physician's order.

Nursing Diagnosis/ Patient Problem	Defining Characteristics	Nursing Interventions	Expected Outcomes
Etiology: • Changes in body integrity • Changes in life style • 24-hour care/ supervision of patient demands • Social isolation • Loss of independence • Loss of privacy • Prolonged hospitalization • Unsatisfactory support systems • Exhaustion	Inability to follow suggested treatment regimen Inability to make decisions Chronic sadness or depression Anger Hopelessness/helplessness expressed by patient or family Fatigue or exhaustion	those that are appropriate and discourage those that are inappropriate. Offer anticipatory guidance and problem-solving techniques. Encourage use of relaxation techniques or stress-reducing activities. Allow as much independence and privacy as possible. Maintain consultation with social worker or counselor on ongoing basis. Encourage *all* family members (including siblings and involved extended family members) to seek support that they feel is appropriate and comfortable for them. Allow patient and family time to verbalize concerns, sorrows, feelings, and issues.	• Demonstrate ability to care for patient and self. • Develop trusting relationship with professional (nurse, social worker, counselor, teacher). • Verbalize anxieties and fears. • Problem solve situations that are anxiety producing. • Have as much independence and privacy as is possible and safe.
7. Knowledge deficit related to • Care of tracheostomy • Care of ventilator • Medications • Treatment schedule • Equipment care and cleaning • Signs of respiratory distress *Etiology:* • Inaccurate information given to family • Patient and family unable to absorb all information required due to volume of information, shock, and inability to cope • Ineffective or incomplete education	Verbalization of questions or deficiency in knowledge of skills Inability for correct return-demonstration of skills Inaccurate compliance with specified treatment Inability to articulate rationale for treatment	Provide individualized teaching plan to patient and family. Provide accurate information at rate appropriate to promote learning. Reinforce all teaching on regular basis. Encourage practice of all skills, particularly those needed in an emergency situation. Assess return-demonstrations for accuracy of skills. Consult tertiary care center or discharging facility for questions regarding routines of care and specifics of what family was taught. Provide inservice education to home nursing staff on regular basis regarding care of tracheostomy, ventilator and emergency procedures (use tertiary care center prn). Ensure that *all* care providers are educated in *all* aspects of care before independently caring for child.	Patient and family are able to participate accurately and independently in all dimensions of care. Care providers can describe and demonstrate accurate skills required for care. Patient is, *at all times*, with knowledgeable care provider trained in all aspects of care. Family feels comfortable asking questions about care. Family trusts all care providers.

Chapter 6

Alterations in Cardiac Function

Karen C. Uzark

Each year approximately 30,000 children enter the health care system in this country with a structural abnormality of the heart (Roland 1979). Nearly one third of all infants with congenital heart defects (2.6 per 1,000 live births) are born with a critical cardiac anomaly leading to cardiac catheterization, cardiac surgery, or death within the first year of life. During the past 3 decades, the prognosis for the majority of these infants has improved dramatically. Referral from the pediatric cardiac center for home care services is often indicated to promote optimal health and functioning of the children now surviving with congenital heart disease.

DISCHARGE PLANNING ISSUES

The diagnosis of significant congenital heart disease is often made soon after birth. The physiological and psychological impact of the infant's heart defect has important implications for discharge planning. Clearly the individual infant's needs following discharge will be related to the physiological consequences or clinical features of the specific cardiac defect and will be influenced by the parents' response to the cardiac diagnosis.

Impact of the Cardiac Diagnosis

The two cardinal signs of serious congenital heart disease are cyanosis and congestive heart failure.

Cyanotic Heart Disease

Cyanotic defects usually produce symptoms at birth or within the first months of life. Cyanosis is found in patients with cardiac lesions associated with significant obstruction to pulmonary blood flow or with mixing of the systemic and pulmonary blood through a right-to-left cardiac shunt. Heart defects resulting in cyanosis (Table 6-1) include tetralogy of Fallot, transposition of the great arteries, tricuspid atresia, total anomalous pulmonary venous connection, pulmonary atresia with intact ventricular septum, truncus arteriosus, and Ebstein's anomaly of the tricuspid valve. Tetralogy of Fallot and transposition of the great arteries are the most prevalent cyanotic defects, each responsible for about 10 percent of all cases of congenital heart disease, and will be discussed in greater detail (Adams and Emmanouilides 1983).

In tetralogy of Fallot the site of obstruction to pulmonary flow may involve the infundibulum of the right ventricle, the pulmonic valve, the annulus of the pulmonic valve, or the branches of the pulmonary artery. The degree of obstruction also varies, ranging from mild, allowing net left-to-right shunting through a large ventricular septal defect (pink tetralogy), to severe, as in pulmonary atresia. The age at onset of the dominant symptom of cyanosis varies according to the degree of obstruction to pulmonary flow. A life-threatening symptom in children with tetralogy of Fallot is paroxysmal hyperpnea or hypoxic spells. A "spell" usually consists of an initial period of irritability or inconsolable crying, followed by paroxysms of hyperpnea, deep cyanosis, and decreased level of consciousness or sometimes convulsions. Hypoxic or anoxic spells frequently occur early in the morning after a good night's sleep. It has been suggested that the spell occurs when a sudden spasm of the right ventricular outflow tract causes a rapid decrease in pulmonary blood flow (Gunterroth et al. 1983). If a child has a history of "spells," surgical palliation or correction is required on an *urgent* basis. The Blalock-Taussig shunt, a subclavian artery to pulmonary artery anastomosis, seems to be the preferred procedure for palliation in infants with tetralogy of Fallot and tricuspid atresia. Complete repair of tetralogy of Fallot is usually accomplished before the child enters school.

In transposition of the great arteries, the systemic and pulmonary circulations function in parallel; hence, the greatest portion of the output of each ventricle is recirculated to that ventricle. Prominent cyanosis is usually evident soon after birth since systemic arterial oxygen saturation is dependent on the relatively small amount of blood that is exchanged between the two circulations through a patent foramen ovale, an atrial septal defect, a ventricular septal defect, or a patent ductus arteriosus. While the systemic arterial oxygen saturation is generally improved by balloon atrial (Rashkind) septostomy during cardiac catheterization, the infant usually remains very cyanotic until surgical correction is accomplished within the first year of life. This cyanosis increases with crying, bathing, cold temperatures, and exercise. Parents are often very anxious about their infant's cyanosis and may be afraid to let the infant cry. An increase in cyanosis unrelated to activity, however, may be insidious and thus difficult for parents to notice. Recently, surgeons have been able to relocate the great vessels to their appropriate ventricles (Jatene operation) during the first days or weeks of life. While the great vessels can be moved, the coronary arteries are more difficult to reimplant into the new aorta in small neonates. Many cardiovascular surgeons therefore prefer to perform the Senning or the Mustard procedure when the infant is 6 to 12 months of age. These procedures provide redirection of systemic and pulmonary venous return using an intra-atrial baffle

created from atrial septum (Senning) or pericardium (Mustard). Following these surgical interventions children are generally asymptomatic and appear healthy. Some patients may develop atrial arrhythmias following placement of intra-atrial baffles.

The surgical management of the other cyanotic heart defects previously mentioned is summarized in Table 6-1. With hypoxia prior to surgical correction of cyanotic heart defects, the requirement for increased oxygen-carrying capacity requires increased iron for hemoglobin. In general, the hemoglobin level in a moderately cyanotic patient should be above 15 to 16 g/dL and a normal hemoglobin level indicates a "relative" anemia. In cyanotic children, anemia may cause increased dyspnea with decreased exercise tolerance, as well as increasing the frequency of hypoxic spells and the risk of cerebrovascular accident. With chronic arterial desaturation, however, red blood cell formation is stimulated and polycythemia results. As the central hematocrit reaches 65 to 70 percent (or hemoglobin near 20 g/dL), a marked increase in blood viscosity elevates peripheral vascular resistance and decreases oxygen delivery to the tissues. Children may complain of headaches, chest pain, fatigue, and muscle cramps and are also at increased risk of cerebrovascular accident. If the child with cyanotic heart disease and polycythemia becomes dehydrated, the hematocrit may rise sharply, increasing the risk of spontaneous cerebrovascular accident. Dental caries and periodontal disease are also more common in children with cyanotic heart disease, and there is increased risk of developing infective endocarditis, even following surgical repair.

Congestive Heart Failure

Acyanotic defects that cause congestive heart failure include those causing large left-to-right shunts and those causing severe obstruction of the left side of the heart or of the aorta. Heart defects that commonly result in congestive heart failure (Table 6-2) include ventricular septal defect, patent ductus arteriosus (especially in premature infants), complete atrioventricular septal defect (endocardial cushion defect), severe coarctation of the aorta, and hypoplastic left heart syndrome. Critical aortic stenosis in the neonate and total anomalous pulmonary venous connection without obstruction also cause

Table 6-1 Cyanotic Heart Defects

Defect	Anatomy	Surgical Management
Transposition of the great arteries	The aorta arises from the right ventricle and the pulmonary artery from the left ventricle.	Arterial switch (Jatene) operation in neonatal period or intra-atrial baffle (Mustard or Senning procedure) later in infancy
Tetralogy of Fallot	Combination of four defects: (1) pulmonary stenosis, (2) ventricular septal defect, (3) overriding aorta, and (4) right ventricular hypertrophy	*Palliative:* Blalock-Taussig or other aortopulmonary shunts in infancy *Repair:* patch closure of VSD and resection of infundibular pulmonary stenosis ± pulmonary valvulotomy if necessary
Tricuspid atresia	Complete agenesis of the tricuspid valve with no direct communication between the right atrium and a hypoplastic right ventricle	*Palliative:* shunt (or pulmonary artery banding if increased pulmonary blood flow via a ventricular septal defect) *Repair:* pulmonary artery connected to right atrium (Fontan procedure), usually around school age
Total anomalous pulmonary venous connection	Pulmonary veins do not enter the left atrium but are connected either directly or indirectly to the right atrium	*Repair:* pulmonary venous trunk connected to left atrium in infancy
Truncus arteriosus	Single arterial trunk forms the aorta and pulmonary artery, overriding the ventricles and receiving blood from them through a ventricular septal defect	*Repair:* Closure of ventricular septal defect, removing the origin of the pulmonary arteries from the trunk, and connecting the pulmonary arteries to the right ventricle with a conduit in infancy
Pulmonary atresia with intact ventricular septum	Complete atresia of the pulmonary valve and varying degrees of hypoplasia of the right ventricle	*Palliative:* Blalock-Taussig shunt ± pulmonary valvulotomy *Repair:* Right ventricular outflow tract reconstruction or Fontan procedure
Ebstein's anomaly of the tricuspid valve	Redundant tricuspid valve tissue with the septal and posterior leaflets displaced downward into the right ventricle for a variable distance	*Repair:* Tricuspid valve replacement or modified tricuspid annuloplasty (Patients with less severe forms do not require surgery.)

Table 6-2 Acyanotic Heart Defects Commonly Causing Congestive Heart Failure in Infancy

Defect	Description
Hypoplastic left heart syndrome	Aortic atresia and underdevelopment of the left ventricle, mitral valve, hypoplastic aortic arch, and/or coarctation
Coarctation of the aorta	Constriction of the aorta usually located slightly distal to the origin of the left subclavian artery
Ventricular septal defect	An abnormal opening between the right and left ventricle that may result in congestive heart failure if the left-to-right shunt is large
Atrioventricular septal defect (endocardial cushion defect)	A defect in the lower part of the atrial septum (ostium primum) and the membranous ventricular septum and a single common atrioventricular valve
Patent ductus arteriosus	A connection between the pulmonary artery and the aorta that fails to close after birth, allowing increased blood flow to the lungs

congestive heart failure. In children with these congenital heart defects, heart failure is most likely to develop within the first weeks or months of life, about 90 percent within the first year of life. With the exception of hypoplastic left heart syndrome, surgical repair in the first year of life generally relieves congestive heart failure symptoms. Children without structural heart defects may also present with congestive heart failure due to cardiomyopathy.

Congestive heart failure is the failure of the cardiac output, because of the inadequacy of myocardial performance, to meet all the metabolic demands of the body. This state arises as a consequence of the excessive work load imposed on cardiac muscle by the structural defects. The principal manifestations of congestive heart failure are tachycardia, tachypnea, and dyspnea. The striking feature of congestive heart failure in the infant is a respiratory rate over 60 per minute and often as high as 100 to 120 per minute, sometimes associated with nasal flaring, retractions, and even wheezing. Expiratory grunting may be noted in some infants. A chronic "hacking" cough may be present in children secondary to congestion of bronchial mucosa, as well as an increased frequency of respiratory infection. Increased sweating has been noted in infants with cardiac failure, probably reflecting increased activity of the autonomic nervous system in the presence of impaired myocardial performance. The sweating is usually found on the face, neck, and head and is not related to the environment. Pallor or even cyanosis may also be present, even if the heart defect is not associated with intracardiac right-to-left shunting, and the infant in failure may appear grayish or more

mottled, especially with crying or feeding. The infant may have trouble sucking, swallowing, and breathing simultaneously, needing to rest frequently during a feeding, and thus the feeding takes longer. Sometimes the infant falls asleep exhausted before the intake is adequate, and, in older infants, poor weight gain may be the most prominent and, for the parents, the most worrisome feature of heart failure. Facial edema is more common in infants and children than peripheral edema, while ascites and generalized anasarca are rare.

Psychosocial Responses

The diagnosis of significant congenital heart disease, often made soon after birth, is a traumatic emotional experience for parents. The initial reactions of the family to the child's defect have been described as acute fear and anxiety, immediate shock followed by mourning the loss of a healthy child, anger or resentfulness, and guilt over causing the child's heart defect. Because the exact cause of the child's defect is usually not known, parents tend to fantasize about the etiology. The initial diagnosis often represents a family crisis, and health care professionals play a key role in supporting parents during their emotional ordeal of accepting a child with congenital heart disease. Parents often do not appreciate the differences between congenital and acquired heart disease. Bergman and Stamm (1967) found that two thirds of the parents interviewed believed the child had the same type of heart disease encountered in adults. Related to this misconception, parents fear the child's sudden death from a "heart attack."

Parental reactions to the diagnosis may also interfere with their ability to cooperate with the therapeutic regimen and even threaten their ability to provide optimal care for their child (Rozansky and Linde 1971). The loss of self-esteem that may accompany having produced an infant with a cardiac defect hinders the attainment of the parenting role. Development of the parental role is influenced by characteristics of the infant such as physical appearance and behavior. The infant with heart disease may be cyanotic, small for gestational age, tire easily, or feed poorly. The infant's expected weight gain or motor development may not be achieved at a level sufficient to promote parental self-esteem. Also, when the child differs so greatly from expectations, parents may miscalculate the child's needs. One study confirmed that parents have negative feelings about their infant with congenital heart disease as well as various misconceptions, especially with regard to cyanosis, sudden death, and vulnerability to infection, that may hinder optimal parenting behaviors (Uzark et al. 1985). As the child grows, these emotional reactions often further interfere with the parent's ability to set limits for acceptable behavior and administer disciplinary measures that are necessary parental functions, whether or not the child has heart disease.

The impact of a child with a congenital heart defect is not limited to parents as individuals but also affects marital ties, sibling relationships, and the entire family as a unit. Prior to discharge following diagnosis of heart disease it is essential to assess the family's stress level and coping strategies, their abilities or strengths, and their resources. Lewandowski (1980) has suggested some parameters for assessing possible coping strategies of parents of children with congenital heart defects requiring surgery. These include the following:

- Parent's perception of the situation (realistic or distorted)
- Available situational supports, such as parents' relationships with each other, other family members and friends, hospital staff, and other possible support systems
- Family's interaction with each other
- Ways parent has coped with stress in the past

- Decision-making abilities
- Parent's interaction with others
- Parent's interaction with child
- Types of questions and repetition of questions
- Types of concerns voiced or voicing no concerns
- Verbalizations about own anxiety level, coping strategies
- Brief attention span or inability to focus on any one thing
- Amount of involvement in child's care that parent desires or accepts
- Parent's outward physical appearance
- Nonverbal behaviors (restlessness, rocking, tightly clasped hands, rigid posture, wringing of hands, shaking, crying)
- Somatic signs and symptoms (headache, gastrointestinal upset, frequent urination, backache)

Besides personal coping resources, it is also important to assess the family's social support network and potential financial needs. Parents need support from extended family members or mature friends who express not only emotional concern but also willingness to provide periodic assistance with child care. Community resources, including the local heart association, state crippled children's services, parent support groups, school systems, and other agencies may offer valuable services to families of children with heart disease. Primary physicians and nurses play a critical role in offering meaningful support to parents and promoting comprehensive health care for these children. Unfortunately, the actual cardiac pathology may assume such overwhelming importance for health care professionals that anticipatory guidance regarding ''normal'' child behavior and needs is omitted and even the administration of immunizations and adequate dental care have been found to be neglected (Uzark et al. 1983).

The responses of significant others to the diagnosis of heart disease can have lasting, deleterious effects on the child's psychosocial well-being. Studies have suggested that behavioral disorders and poor adjustment of the child are more highly related to maternal attitudes (anxiety, protectiveness, and overindulgence) than to the severity of the heart disease. In a study of young adults who had been asymptomatic for almost 7 years from congenital heart disease, Garson and associates (1974) found that psychopathology derives not so much from the direct effects of the disease or the severity of the physical symptomatology as from life experiences associated with the diagnostic label of congenital heart disease. Degree of psychopathology appeared to be related to the disparity between how the child perceives his or her illness and how others view the child's disease. In discharge planning, accurate information regarding the child's physical and emotional needs will facilitate the home care nurse's ability to promote the child's physical health and help prevent or reduce untoward psychosocial consequences of the cardiac diagnosis. To ensure optimal planning and care, all referrals to the nursing agency from the pediatric cardiac center should include (1) discharge data regarding the child's pulse, respiratory rate, color, and weight; (2) assessment of the family's responses to the child's diagnosis and care and their existing resources; and (3) information regarding the patient's medications, diet, activity, any special treatments, and plans for medical follow-up.

TEACHING ISSUES PRIOR TO DISCHARGE

Since the child with congenital heart disease frequently does not have the defect surgically corrected at the time of diagnosis, parents require essential guidance and direction to provide optimal care for their child. Discharge preparation should generally include information regarding symptoms of cardiac distress, medications, diet/feeding, activity, and health maintenance needs. The family also needs support and encouragement to recognize and meet their own psychosocial needs.

Cardiac Distress

Parents should be taught symptoms of increasing cardiac distress so that these can be promptly reported and treated. Since a paroxysmal hyperpneic attack or hypoxic spell can result in death of the infant with cyanotic heart disease, a spell or suspicion of spells should be reported to the cardiologist immediately. When the parent observes a hypoxic spell, as previously described, the child should be placed in the knee–chest position to attempt to alleviate the attack. A severe spell, however, may only be relieved by administration of oxygen and morphine or may even require surgical therapy.

Parents should also be aware of other signs of increasing cardiac distress that require less urgent therapy. While increased cyanosis associated with crying, activity, and cold temperature is expected in infants with cyanotic heart defects, parents can observe over time increased cyanosis of lips or nailbeds at rest. Increasing symptoms of congestive heart failure may also occur over several days, not suddenly as parents sometimes anticipate. Parents should note increased perspiration unrelated to the environment, slower feeding or decreased oral intake, cough, edema, and decreased urinary output. The symptoms should be reported to the cardiologist or primary care physician, who may increase the child's medications. Positioning the child at a 45° angle can help alleviate the respiratory distress associated with congestive heart failure by decreasing the pressure of the viscera on the diaphragm. This can be accomplished by placing the child in an infant seat or by elevating the head of the mattress. Older children may be more comfortable using several pillows. It is very rarely necessary to keep oxygen in the home.

Medications

Cyanotic infants or children are often discharged on no medications. An iron preparation may be prescribed in the treatment of anemia, which frequently occurs in 4- to 24-month-old infants. (Besides the increased risks to the cyanotic child associated with anemia, anemia also increases the work of the heart and may aggravate congestive heart failure.) Treatment for anemia is usually an oral form of ferrous sulfate: Fer-in-sol drops (25 mg Fe/mL), Feosol elixir (8 mg Fe/mL), or tablets. The dose is carefully based on weight and should only be given for a prescribed length of time with periodic checking of hemoglobin or hematocrit levels. Administration between meals or with a vitamin C–fortified juice helps increase iron absorption. Parents should be aware of possible side effects of iron therapy, including temporary staining of the teeth, darker stool, and occasional constipation.

Digoxin is the most frequently used cardiac medication for the treatment of congestive heart failure. The primary action of digitalis is to improve the force of ventricular contractility. Digitalization is usually done in the hospital and children are sent home on maintenance doses. In children under 10 years of age, the daily maintenance dose is generally 0.01 to 0.015 mg/kg but is also individualized based on the patient's needs and serum digoxin levels. Premature infants and patients with impaired renal function should receive lower doses. Digoxin elixir contains 0.05 mg/mL and is usually administered every 12 hours. Digitalis toxicity does not occur very often, especially since appropriate maintenance doses are generally established and monitored with serum digoxin levels. Toxicity should be considered however when observing decreased appetite, nausea, vomiting, bradycardia, and other arrhythmias. Hypokalemia may augment toxicity. Besides knowledge of the drug's dose, administration, and potential adverse effects, parents need information about what actions to take if the child vomits the medication, if the parent forgets to give a medication dose as scheduled, if a child accidentally receives too much medication, and if there are questions or concerns. A form with these instructions for parents regarding digoxin is presented in Exhibit 6-1. Written medication instructions are most helpful and should be reviewed with parents.

Diuretics are frequently also employed to facilitate the removal of accumulated fluid and sodium when there is considerable pulmonary or systemic edema associated with congestive heart failure. Commonly prescribed diuretics are furosemide (Lasix), chlorothiazide (Diuril), and

---

Exhibit 6-1 Information on Digoxin for Parents

Digoxin is a medicine frequently given to infants and children with heart disease when they have congestive heart failure or a very rapid heart rate. This heart failure developed because of a heart defect and does not mean that the heart will stop beating; it means that the heart muscle is weak and cannot pump as forcefully as it should. The action of digoxin is to slow and strengthen the pumping of the heart muscle.

Some guidelines for parents giving digoxin are presented below:

1. *How to give digoxin at home:* Digoxin should be given twice a day, morning and evening, at times you can easily remember. Draw up the digoxin liquid in the syringe or dropper provided. Check amount carefully. With infants it is easiest to then place the dropper in the child's mouth so that it rests halfway back on the tongue or the side. Then give the medication slowly, allowing the child time to swallow.
2. *If your child vomits the digoxin*, do *not* repeat that dose of medicine unless the child vomited immediately (within 5 minutes) after the digoxin was given *and* you are sure all the medicine has come up. If it has been more than 5 minutes, just give the normal dose of digoxin at the next *regular* time. Digoxin starts to be absorbed shortly after being given.
3. *If you forget to give the digoxin dose*, you may give it up to 2 hours later. If it is more than 2 hours late, just give the next dose at the regular time. It is important for your child to receive the digoxin every day.
4. *If your child becomes ill with severe loss of appetite or frequent vomiting or diarrhea for longer than 24 to 48 hours*, encourage ingestion of fluids, especially fruit juices, and contact the child's physician. Digoxin's effect on the heart can be changed by loss of body fluids and salt, especially potassium.
5. *If your child is absorbing too much digoxin (digoxin toxicity)*, you may notice that the child's appetite is much less than normal, vomiting is frequent, or the heart rate is slower than usual or irregular. Call the child's physician or the Pediatric Cardiology Department (see below).
6. *If the child accidentally swallows too much digoxin*, call the physician or take the child to the nearest emergency department *immediately*. Digoxin should *always* be kept in a safe place, if possible in a locked cabinet, out of any child's reach.
7. The dosage of digoxin is increased as a child grows. Your child's present dose is _____ mL per day.

Should you have any questions or concerns, please feel free to call _____ and ask for a pediatric cardiology nurse, clinician, or any member of the cardiology staff. At night or on weekends, call the paging operator and ask for the pediatric cardiology fellow on call.

Source: Reprinted with permission from C.S. Mott Children's Hospital, University of Michigan, Ann Arbor, Michigan.

Table 6-3 Usual Pediatric Doses of Diuretics

Drug	Dose
Furosemide (Lasix)	1–2 mg/kg/dose
Chlorothiazide (Diuril)	20–30 mg/kg/day
Spironolactone (Aldactone)	2–3 mg/kg/day
Aldactazide (Chlorothiazide + Spironolactone)	2–3 mg/kg/day
Triamterene (Dyrenium)	3 mg/kg/day

spironolactone (Aldactone). Usual doses are presented in Table 6-3. Diuretics can produce electrolyte imbalance, the most serious being potassium depletion. In many instances children who receive a potassium-wasting diuretic will also take a potassium-sparing diuretic, such as spironolactone, to offset excessive potassium loss. Excessive fluid loss and potassium depletion can occur when the child becomes ill with prolonged vomiting, diarrhea, poor fluid intake, and fever. Parents of children receiving diuretics should notify the physician if these symptoms appear and observe for signs of dehydration of electrolyte imbalance (dry lips, decreased urination, weakness, lethargy).

More recently, systemic *vasodilator drugs* that serve to alter ventricular preload and/or afterload have been employed in infants and children who have not shown a satisfactory response to treatment with digitalis and diuretics. These vasodilator drugs, which include hydralazine (Apresoline), Captopril (Capoten), and prazosin (Minipress), decrease the work of the heart by lowering the resistance to flow in the blood vessels of the body. Hydralazine, at present, is probably the most commonly prescribed arteriolar vasodilator (dose = 0.5 mg/kg/day orally every 6 to 8 hours). Possible side effects include headache and dizziness.

Antibiotics should be prescribed for prophylaxis against bacterial endocarditis prior to any bacteremia-producing orodental, genitourinary, or gastrointestinal procedures or surgery. The American Heart Association has published recommendations for prophylaxis in the form of a card to be carried by parents or patients (Exhibit 6-2). Virtually all congenital heart disease requires prophylaxis, with the exception of atrial septal defect secundum, partial anomalous pulmonary venous return, and trivial pulmonary stenosis.

Diet/Feeding

Nutritional management of infants or children with uncorrected congenital heart disease can present a difficult challenge for parents and health care providers. Poor weight gain is especially common in infants with congestive heart failure, when fatigue and tachypnea interfere with adequate food intake. These infants should be fed more frequently, in early infancy perhaps as often as every 2 hours during the day and every 4 hours at night. Prolonging the duration of each feeding beyond 30 minutes frustrates both parents and infants. Swallowing and breathing will be easier if the infant is held in a semi-upright position for feeding, and frequent burping is helpful. When the infant is bottle fed, energy expenditure can also be reduced by using a soft nipple designed for premature infants or one that has a hole large enough to allow easy flow of the formula.

When the bottle-fed infant cannot take an adequate volume of formula, the health care professional may recommend increasing the caloric concentration. This may be accomplished by adding less water to formula concentrate (13 ounces of formula concentrate + 9 ounces of water = 24 calories/ounce) or adding caloric supplements such as Polycose, MCT oil, or corn oil to the formulas or breast milk. Attention must be paid to water balance in high-density formulas, and infants may develop diarrhea or vomiting when the high calorie formula is not tolerated. Low sodium formulas are commercially available and may occasionally be used, but some are not palatable, provide too little sodium to satisfy growth requirements, or may be associated with electrolyte disturbances. In pediatric cardiology it is now common practice to promote caloric and protein intake *without* strict sodium and fluid restrictions, even if this means more rigorous diuretic therapy.

When the breast-fed infant does not grow well or tires quickly at the breast, the mother can pump her breasts and offer breast milk (with a calorie supplement) in a bottle for one or more feedings each day or after nursing. Breast milk is naturally lower in sodium than many commercial formulas and is easily digested. Many mothers who prefer breast feeding become anxious about their inability to monitor/measure the infant's intake of breast milk. It is usually possi-

Exhibit 6-2 Recommendations for Prophylaxis for Bacterial Endocarditis

Name: _____

needs protection from
BACTERIAL ENDOCARDITIS
because of an existing
HEART CONDITION

Diagnosis: _____
Prescribed by: _____
Date: _____

For Dental Procedures and Surgery of the Upper Respiratory Tract

1. For most patients: Oral Penicillin	**Adults:** 2.0 g of penicillin V one hour prior to procedure and then 1.0 g six hours after initial dose. **Children less than 60 pounds:** 1.0 g of penicillin V one hour prior to procedure and then 500 mg six hours after initial dose.
2. For those allergic to penicillin (may also be selected for those receiving oral penicillin as continuous rheumatic fever prophylaxis): **Erythromycin**	**Adults:** 1.0 g orally one hour prior to procedure and then 500 mg six hours after initial dose. **Children:** 20 mg/kg orally one hour prior to procedure and then 10 mg/kg six hours after initial dose.
3. For those patients at higher risk of infective endocarditis (especially those with prosthetic heart valves) who are not allergic to penicillin: **Ampicillin** plus **Gentamicin**	**Adults:** Ampicillin 1.0-2.0 g plus gentamicin 1.5 mg/kg IM or IV, both given 30 minutes before procedure, then penicillin V 1.0 g (500 mg for children under 60 lb) orally six hours after initial dose. **Children:** Timing of doses is same as for adults. Dosages are ampicillin 50 mg/kg and gentamicin 2.0 mg/kg.
4. For higher risk patients (especially those with prosthetic heart valves) who are allergic to penicillin: **Vancomycin**	**Adults:** Vancomycin 1 g IV over 60 minutes, begun 60 minutes before procedure; no repeat dose is necessary. **Children:** Vancomycin 20 mg/kg IV over 60 minutes, begun 60 minutes before procedure; no repeat dose is necessary.

For Gastrointestinal and Genitourinary Tract Surgery and Instrumentation

1. For most patients: **Ampicillin** plus **Gentamicin**	**Adults:** 2.0 g ampicillin IM or IV plus gentamicin 1.5 mg/kg IM or IV given 30 minutes before procedure. May repeat once eight hours later. **Children:** Same timing of medications as adult schedule. Dosages are ampicillin 50 mg/kg and gentamicin 2.0 mg/kg.
2. For patients allergic to penicillin: **Vancomycin** plus **Gentamicin**	**Adults:** 1.0 g vancomycin IV given over 60 minutes plus 1.5 mg/kg gentamicin IM or IV, each given 60 minutes before procedure. Doses may be repeated once 8-12 hours later. **Children:** Timing as above. Doses are vancomycin 20 mg/kg and gentamicin 2.0 mg/kg.
3. Oral regimen for minor or repetitive procedures in low-risk patients: **Amoxicillin**	**Adults:** 3.0 g amoxicillin one hour before procedure and 1.5 g six hours after initial dose. **Children:** Same timing of doses: 50 mg/kg initial dose and 25 mg/kg follow-up dose.

Note: In patients with compromised renal function, it may be necessary to modify or omit the second dose of antibiotics. Intramuscular injections may be contraindicated in patients receiving anticoagulants. Children's doses should not exceed adult doses.

Please refer to these Joint American Heart Association–American Dental Association recommendations for more complete information as to which patients and which procedures require prophylaxis.

Source: Adapted from "A Statement for Health Professionals" by the Committee on Rheumatic Fever and Infective Endocarditis: Prevention of Bacterial Endocarditis, *Circulation*, Vol. 70, pp. 1123A–1127A, by permission of the American Heart Association, Inc., © 1985.

ble to work out an effective schedule that combines breast and bottle feeding, and mothers need to be supported in their decision regarding feeding their infant. When faster respiratory rates interfere with the infant's ability to suck from the bottle or breast, it may be easier for the infant to take cereal/food from a spoon. In this case, early introduction of solid foods may be suggested when the infant appears ready. Even if the infant or child seems to have an adequate caloric intake, children with heart defects may still have delayed growth during infancy and childhood for reasons not yet fully understood. Heart surgery can result in catch-up growth, but again this is unpredictable. Parents need support for their persistent efforts to meet their child's nutritional needs.

As previously mentioned in the section on medications, children with congenital heart disease may also experience iron deficiency or potassium depletion. Infants can be fed iron-fortified formulas and cereals. Parents of children eating table foods should include foods high in iron- and potassium-rich foods, such as bananas and orange juice, in the daily diet of these children. Parents must be encouraged to prepare well-balanced meals to ensure adequate nutritional intake and discouraged from constantly urging foods with little nutritional value in their desire to achieve weight gain in their child with heart disease.

Activity

Children with most heart defects may lead normal, active lives. An infant should be allowed to cry, crawl, and walk. It is unnecessary to restrict the young child's activity in any way, as long as he or she is allowed to rest as desired. No matter how active these children may appear, they will rest or seek less active play if needed. Parents and professionals need to promote realistic developmental behaviors among young children with heart disease.

School-age children will have often already had successful surgical repair at an early age and should be permitted to participate in physical education classes and all recreational activities to their level of tolerance. Activities will be restricted for 6 to 8 weeks following surgery.

Some children are advised, based on cardiac status and diagnosis, to avoid participation in strenuous sports and highly competitive games since their pride may force them to continue beyond their physical capabilities. Older children with pulmonary artery hypertension and pulmonary vascular obstructive disease should avoid strenuous physical activity and competitive sports since such activity increases the pulmonary artery pressure and may accelerate the development of pulmonary vascular obstructive disease. Isometric activities (weight lifting, gymnastics) are contraindicated in children with marked left-sided obstructive disease (aortic stenosis, coarctation) or cardiomyopathy because such work tends to disproportionately increase systemic blood pressure relative to myocardial oxygen uptake. When the cardiac lesion tends to be progressive with age, as in aortic stenosis, aortic regurgitation, and mitral regurgitation, children should be encouraged to develop skill in activities and sports that will be able to be continued in adulthood. Acceptable activities may include swimming, golf, cycling, bowling, horseback riding, archery, and fishing. These children may often participate in less strenuous team games such as baseball, badminton, or volleyball. The American Heart Association (1986) has published recreational and occupational recommendations for young patients with heart disease, classified by diagnosis and severity. Unnecessary restrictions should not be imposed by parents, schools, community organizations, or health care professionals. A written recommendation from the pediatric cardiac center is helpful to the patient and community agencies.

Provision of written discharge instructions is always helpful and prevents confusion. The parents should also have a written schedule of follow-up appointments and a phone number available to notify the physician of problems or questions.

NURSING CARE PLANS IN THE HOME

In caring for the child with an alteration in cardiac function due to a congenital heart defect, the goals are to (1) maintain optimal cardiac output and alleviate cardiac distress, (2) prevent/identify potential complications, (3) promote adequate nutritional intake and optimal growth, (4) support the family/child's effective coping with stress associated with the cardiac diagnosis and hospitalization experiences, and (5) foster primary health care and the psychosocial development of the child with heart disease. Since corrective surgery is increasingly being performed at an earlier age, especially in symptomatic children, the nursing interventions to follow are primarily directed toward the infant or very young child who requires home care before definitive repair. Pertinent nursing implications for each goal are presented.

Nursing Considerations to Maintain Optimal Cardiac Output and Alleviate Cardiac Distress

Assessment of the child's cardiovascular status is a vital component of the home care nurse's role. The assessment process not only provides ongoing evaluation of the efficacy of the therapeutic regimen following discharge to allow early identification of problems or increased needs but also provides tremendous reassurance to parents regarding their child's health status. A careful history should include assessment of the child's respiratory status, feeding behavior, activity level, and color. Suggested questions to be addressed at each visit are presented as Exhibit 6-3. Key elements of the physical assessment include heart rate, respiratory rate, color of lips and mucous membranes and extremities, and weight changes. A persistent respiratory rate of more than 60 per minute and a heart rate greater than 160 beats per minute in a *quiet* infant suggest cardiac distress and should be reported to the physician. The nurse who has not observed the child daily may also be able to detect any subtle changes in color. The nurse should note increased cyanosis of lips and mucous membranes or a generalized gray color in a child with congestive heart failure. Such findings may not be appreciated by parents and should be shared with the cardiologist. A weight gain in infants of 50 g or more per day may suggest fluid accumulation.

It is important to assess the parent's accuracy and confidence in administering medications. The amount and method of administration of

Exhibit 6-3 Questions for Parents of Infants with Symptomatic Cardiac Disease

- Does the infant consistently breathe rapidly even while at rest?
- Does the infant have retractions or nasal flaring with breathing?
- Does the infant appear to be working harder just to breathe?
- Does the infant tire easily with feedings?
- Does the infant have to rest frequently while feeding?
- How many ounces does the infant take each feeding? Over what length of time?
- Does the infant vomit frequently?
- Does the infant always seem to have a cold?
- Does the infant's color become increasingly blue, gray, or mottled with feeding, crying, or other forms of exertion?
- Is the infant unduly lethargic or unusually irritable?
- Does the infant respond appropriately, according to age, to stimuli in the environment?
- What new behaviors (milestones) has the infant accomplished?

every medication should be reviewed. An understanding of the medication's purpose may help facilitate compliance, and barriers to compliance should be identified. Barriers may be related to difficulty in administration (measurement, taste), medication cost, scheduling problems, or anxiety regarding side effects. Recently, more cardiologists believe that asking parents to count the heart rate prior to giving the digoxin causes unnecessary anxiety. This practice has been abandoned by many cardiac centers, since serum levels are monitored and infants are likely to outgrow the dosage. The nurse, however, should report any arrhythmia or a significant decrease in heart rate and should be more suspicious of digitalis toxicity if there is a history suggesting possible potassium depletion.

Measures to reduce energy requirements or expenditure include maintaining a comfortable environmental temperature, positioning, and planning daily care to ensure adequate periods of rest. As previously mentioned, children with congestive heart failure are more comfortable in a semi-Fowler's position, elevated 45° to 60°. Hypoxic infants may sleep best in the prone position and may breathe more comfortably in the knee–chest position. Smaller, more frequent feedings and other feeding practices discussed earlier in this chapter can reduce energy expenditure with feeding.

Nursing Considerations to Prevent or Identify Potential Complications of Heart Disease

For all children with hemodynamically significant congenital heart disease, anemia can result in increased symptoms. If the cyanotic child becomes anemic, the risk of cerebrovascular accident increases. Whole cow's milk and infant formulas not supplemented with iron cannot generally meet the increased iron needs of cyanotic infants. The total amount of iron available in breast milk, although efficiently absorbed, may also be insufficient. The nurse should be aware of the child's most recent hematocrit or hemoglobin level and periodically evaluate dietary intake. The nurse can provide parents with information concerning good food sources of iron. When an iron supplement is prescribed the nurse should review with parents the dose and method of administration and can recommend measures to help increase iron absorption.

When the cyanotic child becomes dehydrated, the hematocrit or viscosity of the blood can rise sharply, potentially leading to thrombus formation and cerebrovascular accident. In patients receiving digoxin or diuretics, fluid and electrolyte imbalances associated with gastroenteritis could also be catastrophic. The nurse should emphasize the importance of adequate fluid intake to avoid these complications. In children with diarrhea or vomiting who cannot tolerate clear liquids or oral electrolyte solutions, intravenous fluids may be necessary to maintain hydration. Parents should be instructed to seek prompt medical attention for illnesses causing any degree of dehydration from fever, lack of intake, or increased fluid losses.

Respiratory infections are common in infants with large intracardiac left-to-right shunts and congestive failure. Exposure to persons with infections should be minimized, and parents should avoid taking young infants to crowded places where they are more likely to acquire contagious illnesses. Good handwashing is important by family members who are ill. The nurse should be sure a thermometer is available in the home and that the parents can take the child's temperature properly. Fevers should be reported to the primary care physician, and infections should be treated with the appropriate antibiotic when an organism is isolated or strongly suspected. Antibiotics are not needed when the infection is viral, and when patients are maintained on chronic antibiotic therapy or receive frequent courses of broad-spectrum antibiotics they may be at increased risk for infections from resistant organisms or fungi. (Some patients with congenital heart disease however have associated immunodeficiency syndromes such as asplenia or DiGeorge's syndrome and require daily antibiotic prophylaxis.)

Infective endocarditis (subacute bacterial endocarditis) is an infection of the valves or inner lining of the heart and is a potential sequela of bacteremia in the child with a cardiac defect. Instruction in the use of prophylactic antibiotic therapy is essential and should be periodically reviewed. Penicillin should be administered 30 minutes to 1 hour before dental work or any surgical procedure, including tonsillectomy or any manipulation of the urinary or intestinal tracts. A second dose is given 6 hours later. Good oral hygiene is also important for these children since dental caries may be an added source of bacteria. Symptoms and signs of endocarditis are somewhat nonspecific, and the onset is usually insidious. There is usually unexplained fever (may be low grade), and malaise and anorexia are commonly noted in children. Other signs may be petechiae, Janeway's spots (painless hemorrhagic areas on the palms and soles), or splinter hemorrhages (thin black lines) under the nails. Some children develop headaches or other neurologic symptoms. Blood cultures should be obtained from any child with unexplained fever.

Nursing Considerations to Promote Adequate Nutritional Intake and Optimal Growth

Adequate nutritional management requires careful assessment of the child's dietary intake and parental feeding practice at each home visit. If the infant is bottle fed, 24-hour formula intake and formula preparation methods should be reviewed. Infants with heart disease may require as much as 70 calories per pound (or 150 calories per kilogram) of body weight daily for growth. A desirable weight gain for young infants is 0.5 to 1 ounce per day. Weighing the child daily is not necessary and should be discouraged, since fluctuations are common and influenced by nondietary factors. Periodic, perhaps weekly, weight checks by the home care nurse, however, can be helpful to assess growth (or identify excessive fluid accumulation).

Observation of infant feeding practices is especially important to identify potential measures to facilitate caloric intake or reduce energy expenditure. As previously discussed, the nurse may recommend holding the infant in a more upright position for feeding, more frequent burping, or a softer nipple. Changes in the caloric concentration of formulas should only be instituted at the direction of the physician. A guide for parents in feeding infants with congenital heart disease is available from the American Heart Association (1984) and most cardiac centers.

The nurse can assist the parents of older infants and children by analyzing a 3-day dietary record to be certain that nutritional requirements are being met. The parents can be provided with appropriate information regarding foods high in sodium, potassium, or iron, as indicated by the specific child's needs. Parents should be encouraged to prepare well-balanced meals to ensure adequate nutritional intake.

Nutritional management of infants with uncorrected significant heart defects can present a tremendous challenge for parents and health care providers. It can be frustrating and disheartening for parents when their child fails to gain weight despite their persistent efforts. Parents can be reminded that some children with heart defects have slow weight gain, regardless of the feeding method or caloric intake. Feeding by nasogastric tube will be instituted if the infant is unable to consume enough food to meet nutritional requirements. In these instances, it is important for the nurse to review tube feeding procedures and to encourage parents to continue to provide their infants with satisfaction derived from sucking and caressing. The nurse can offer invaluable support to these parents who are diligently working to meet their child's nutritional needs.

Nursing Considerations to Support the Family and Child's Effective Coping with Stress Associated with the Cardiac Diagnosis and Hospitalization Experiences

The diagnosis of congenital heart disease has a significant emotional impact on the child and family. The nurse can support the parents during the initial period of grief or mourning and recognize the parents' limited ability to understand information regarding the cardiac diagnosis during this process. The nurse's sensitivity and warmth may enable the parents to express their reactions and emerge with a sense of reassurance or acceptance of their feelings of loss, denial, anger or resentfulness, and guilt. Furthermore, parents are able to assimilate only the information about their child for which they are emotionally prepared and they are often apt to exaggerate and misinterpret the physician's explanations. Parents seem to be primarily interested in two kinds of medical information: prognosis and surgery. It is important therefore to assess the family and child's level of understanding and to explore the meaning of the child's diagnosis to them. Parents appreciate receiving written information and may have questions at home related to information received at the cardiac center. They should be encouraged to contact the pediatric cardiology service with urgent questions and write down questions to be answered at their child's next clinic visit. Parents often cannot anticipate the meaning or implications of their infant's heart defect prior to the child's discharge from the hospital. In an effort to increase knowledge and promote a more positive, less anxious attitude among parents of newborns with serious congenital heart disease, a videotape entitled "Your Baby with a Congenital Heart Defect" was developed at the University of Michigan and is used at some cardiac centers (Uzark and White 1981). In this videotape, three families relate common feelings, problems, and infant care experiences from their home settings. It is suggested that the videotape transmits information about infant behavior that may not be included in the usual course of discussion with hospital personnel. Parents need affirmation of their child's normal attributes and behaviors, and routine child care issues should be discussed, including bathing, feeding, elimination, sleep habits, and comfort measures in response to crying. The parents should be encouraged to treat the child in as normal a manner as possible. Parents also often need permission and considerable encouragement to meet their own needs for rest and recreation and should recognize the special needs and concerns of the child's siblings.

The cardiac diagnosis, heart surgery, poor prognosis, or perceived extraordinary home care requirements may create significant stress in the family. This anxiety or stress can create a barrier that not only prevents parents from comprehending explanations but may even interfere with their ability to provide optimal care to the child. The home care nurse is in a unique position to assess concurrent stresses in the family outside the hospital environment. Some parameters for assessing parental coping behaviors have been outlined earlier in this chapter. Recognizing the emotional stress involved in caring for a child with a heart defect and helping parents to express their feelings and manage their stress may enable parents to then direct their energies toward caring optimally and realistically for their child. The nurse can explore the personal and social supports the parents have, including the presence of other family members and friends, recreation and activities for stress management, finances, ability to find babysitters, and access to other support services. The nurse can observe and assess the supportiveness of interactions among family members and the use of the identified resources. Stress and perceived social isolation can sometimes be alleviated through parent groups, which have developed in many areas of the country. When such groups are not available or approachable, meeting another parent of a child with a similar problem in the community can often provide unequaled support to the new parent, and such empathetic information sharing seems to be readily received and valued. The home care nurse is often in a position to introduce parents directly or identify an appropriate parent through the cardiac center. Referral to the local heart association, state crippled children's services, and other community agencies may also provide helpful resources.

Parents may experience loss of self-esteem and perceive helplessness in response to the birth of their infant with a heart defect. Clear affirmation of positive parenting behaviors and effective coping strategies not only reinforces these behaviors but can promote feelings of greater control and confidence. Most families are capable and resilient in handling even complex problems related to the child's cardiac diagnosis.

It is also essential to provide psychological support and information to the child and family to help them cope with the increased stress of hospitalization. While surgical repair of serious heart defects is often now accomplished during infancy, some children will require later hospitalization for heart surgery or heart catheterization. Preexisting conditions that influence the child's response to hospitalization include the parent's attitude toward the child's condition, the child's age or stage of development, and the child's unique past experiences with any aspect of health care. Based on the assessment of these and other factors, such as the child's knowledge and identified fears, an individualized teaching plan can be developed. Important nursing considerations include the following:

- Involving the parents in assessment and preparation
- Adapting information to the child's cognitive level and level of psychosocial development
- Responding to the child's fears and past experiences
- Providing the parents and child with role information
- Describing sensations at appropriate times
- Answering questions simply and honestly

The communication of accurate information about the events of hospitalization can reduce stress. Several methods of preparation, including tours, books, or videotapes, may be necessary to effectively communicate information to children. Videotapes and films seem to be powerful and acceptable media for communicating supportive information to children. These educational aids are available through many cardiac centers or bookstores in the community.

Nursing Considerations to Foster Primary Health Care and the Psychosocial Development of the Child with Heart Disease

While the provision of comprehensive health care is the goal for every child, the added burden of cardiac disease reinforces our concern for the primary and preventive health care needs of these children. The child's cardiac diagnosis however may interfere with the delivery of primary health care services related to lack of involvement by primary physicians, uncertainty regarding responsibility for certain aspects of care, or parental and provider anxiety or misconceptions. The presence of congenital heart disease is not a contraindication to administration of immunizations. The home care nurse should inquire about the child's immunization status and can facilitate communication between health care providers regarding the child's primary care needs. Parents should be assured that the chances of side effects in their child will not be increased and the immunizations should be encouraged to minimize the incidence of very devastating preventable diseases. Parents may need encouragement to consult the local physician for matters not related to the cardiac problem and may be apt to attribute any symptom to the child's cardiac condition. Parents may also not recognize their child's need for dental health services, in spite of the child's increased susceptibility to infective endocarditis when dental or periodontal disease is not controlled. Visits to the dentist should start by 3 years of age or sooner if dental caries are apparent. If a particular dentist is reluctant to treat the child with heart disease, referral should be made to another dentist or the cardiac center. The nurse should also educate or reinforce information regarding scrupulous dental hygiene, including frequent teeth brushings, reduction of cariogenic sugars in the diet, and use of appropriate fluoride supplements.

The cognitive development of children with congenital heart disease is usually within normal limits. Delayed development, particularly in gross motor milestones, has been attributed to congestive heart failure, decreased arterial oxygen saturation, and/or psychological and social factors (Alsenberg et al. 1982). Symptomatic infants may have limited energy for accomplishing gross motor tasks, but parents often tend to anticipate the infant's every need and to inhibit the child's developmental striving. Parents should be informed about expected developmental milestones so that they can recognize strengths and progress. The importance of a stimulating environment and of avoiding an overly protective or restrictive parental attitude at home should be emphasized. Professionals and parents need to promote realistic developmental behaviors among these children. The nurse can assist the parents in fostering optimal development by encouraging parents to stimulate the infant toward feasible goals through specific age-appropriate activities such as placing the infant in a prone position to encourage motor development or allowing older infants to explore in a safe environment to encourage mobility instead of being held. Referral to a developmental stimulation or early intervention program may be appropriate in some instances.

Parents of children with congenital heart disease may also tend to be overly permissive in the home, avoiding conflict and failing to establish consistent rules or limits for the child's behavior. When different expectations for behavior are expected for well siblings who also may receive less attention, sibling jealousy and resentment can create additional stress in the family. Siblings often can understand and accept some special needs if explanations are given. Anticipatory guidance regarding these known problem areas should be given to prevent potential behavior problems and to foster independence and feelings of self-confidence in the child with heart disease.

Surgical repair is now likely to be accomplished before school age, so that treatment does not interfere with school attendance and performance. Teachers and parents should not be overprotective and lower expectations but provide realistic optimal educational opportunities. Legislation exists (P.L. 92-112) to guarantee the availability of special education programming when it is needed, and early referral is important. Some children may need homebound teaching for a period of time because of illness or recovery from surgery. Education is extremely important to children with heart disease especially when future occupational decisions may be affected by decreased physical endurance. Although the majority of patients with congenital heart disease are functionally quite normal, early vocational guidance is important to prevent occupational choices that are unreasonable in relation to the person's potential work capacity.

REFERENCES

Adams, Forrest H., and Emmanouilides, George C. (eds.). *Heart Disease in Infants, Children, and Adolescents*. Baltimore, Md.: Williams & Wilkins, 1983.

Aisenberg, Ruth B.; Rosenthal, Amnon; Nadas, Alexander S.; and Wolff, Peter H. "Developmental Delay in Infants with Congenital Heart Disease." *Pediatric Cardiology* 3 (1982):133.

American Heart Association. *Feeding Infants with Congenital Heart Disease*. Dallas, Tex.: American Heart Association, 1984.

American Heart Association. "Recreational and Occupational Recommendations for Young Patients with Heart Disease." *Circulation* 74 (1986):1195A.

Bergman, A.B., and Stamm, S.J. "The Morbidity of Cardiac Nondisease in School Children." *New England Journal of Medicine* 276 (1967):1008.

Garson, Arthur; Williams, Redford B.; and Reckless, John. "Long-term Follow-up Patients with Tetralogy of Fallot." *Journal of Pediatrics* 85 (1974):429.

Gunterroth, Warren G.; Kawabori, Isamu; and Boum, David. "Tetralogy of Fallot." In *Heart Disease in Infants, Children, and Adolescents*, edited by Forrest H. Adams and George C. Emmanouilides. Baltimore, Md.: Williams & Wilkins, 1983.

Lewandowski, Linda A. "Stress Coping Styles of Parents of Children Undergoing Open-heart Surgery." *Critical Care Quarterly*, Vol. 3. 1980:78–81.

Roland, Thomas W. "The Pediatrician and Congenital Heart Disease." *Pediatrics* 64, no. 2 (1979):180.

Rozansky, Gerald I., and Linde, Leonard H. "Psychiatric Study of Parents of Children with Cyanotic Congenital Heart Disease." *Pediatrics* 48 (1971):450.

Uzark, Karen; Collins, James; Meisenhelder, Kimberly; Macdonald, Dick; and Rosenthal, Amnon. "Primary Preventive Health Care in Children with Heart Disease." *Pediatric Cardiology* 4 (1983):259.

Uzark, Karen; Rosenthal, Amnon; Behrendt, Douglas; and Becker, Marshall. "Use of Videotapes to Promote Parenting of Infants with Serious Congenital Heart Defects." *Pediatric Cardiology* 7 (1985):111.

Uzark, Karen, and White, Stewart. *"Your Baby with a Congenital Heart Defect."* Ann Arbor, Mich.: Biomedical Media Productions, 1981.

Chapter 7

Alterations in Metabolic Functions

Loretta Forlaw
Marilee Thompson Tollefson

Children with gastrointestinal disease often suffer from metabolic and nutritional alterations that affect normal growth and development, body image, and life style. Home care can help provide a normalization of the child's feeding patterns, peer socialization, and family involvement. The chronicity of these diseases and the need for frequent hospitalization require ongoing cooperation and communication between hospital staff and home care providers.

In this chapter an overview of the gastrointestinal diseases that the home care nurse is likely to encounter is presented. Broad guidelines for care are provided because specific treatment and techniques are determined on a case-by-case basis. The home care nurse provides reinforcement, evaluation, and suggestions for improving care in the home setting. The guidelines in this chapter will help the home care nurse ensure that appropriate nursing issues have been addressed and that parent teaching is reinforced after the child is discharged from the hospital.

GASTROINTESTINAL DISORDERS

Inflammatory Bowel Disease

Inflammatory bowel disease is the term used to designate ulcerative colitis and Crohn's dis-

ease (regional enteritis). The cause of inflammatory bowel disease is unknown. Current theory postulates that it results from a genetic susceptibility to one or more environmental factors. Psychological factors may influence symptoms and the severity of the attack (Silverman and Roy 1983).

Ulcerative colitis affects the mucosa and submucosa of the colon and rectum. Approximately 15 percent of all cases occur in children younger than 16 years old. The mean age in this group is 11 years. It occurs in both sexes. Signs and symptoms to be monitored in the home setting include cramping, abdominal pain, and distention followed by bloody diarrhea (20 – 30 stools per day); fever; anorexia; nausea and vomiting; apthous stomatitis; joint pain; and conjunctivitis (Silverman and Roy 1983; Whaley and Wong 1987).

Crohn's disease may affect any part of the gastrointestinal tract but usually affects the terminal ileum. It is most common in the adolescent and young adult. Signs and symptoms to be monitored in the home setting include fever, nonbloody diarrhea, constant abdominal pain frequently localized in the right lower quadrant, anorexia, nausea and vomiting, apthous stomatitis, joint pain, conjunctivitis, and uveitis.

Medical Interventions

Medical management of inflammatory bowel disease focuses on promoting optimal nutritional status and reducing bowel inflammation.

The opinions or assertions contained herein are the private views of the author and are not to be construed as official or as reflecting the view of the Department of the Army or the Department of Defense.

Nutritional therapy is directed toward providing a diet that meets the patient's increased caloric, protein, vitamin, and mineral requirements. Patients may require avoidance of lactose-containing foods during exacerbations. Parenteral nutrition and/or tube feedings may be required when the patient is malnourished and/or during any prolonged period of inadequate oral intake.

The drug of choice is sulfasalazine, which is postulated to inhibit both the synthesis and degradation of prostaglandins (Silverman and Roy 1983; Whaley and Wong 1987). Sulfasalazine contains 5-aminosalicylic acid (5-ASA), which acts locally on the mucosa to reduce inflammation. Colonic bacteria must be present to split the molecule for release of 5-ASA; therefore, oral antibiotics are contraindicated. The major side effects (anorexia, nausea and vomiting, abdominal distention, fever, and bloody diarrhea) are similar to the symptoms that occur during exacerbations. If the child develops any of these symptoms, it must be determined if they are due to exacerbation of the disease or if the sulfasalazine dosage needs to be reduced or stopped. Corticosteroid therapy dramatically reduces the symptoms. The child must be observed closely for recurrence of symptoms during tapering of corticosteroid therapy. Careful consideration must be given to the benefits of corticosteroids versus their negative impact on growth.

Surgical procedures, including total colectomy and ileostomy, may benefit patients with ulcerative colitis. The continent (Koch) ileostomy and continent colectomy are options in some cases. Crohn's disease responds poorly to surgical intervention, with recurrence of disease within 2 to 4 years.

Psychological support is often critical. Many patients will benefit from individual or group interactions with their peers. Patients and families should be made aware of the services of the National Foundation for Ileitis and Colitis, Inc., and the United Ostomy Association. Further information is located in Appendix A.

Short Gut Syndrome

Short gut syndrome occurs after extensive resection of the small bowel. Motility, absorp-

tion, and digestive functions are altered. The degree of resection is critical in determining the child's ability to adapt to an oral diet or tube feeding. Presence of the ileocecal valve and of greater than 40 cm of the small bowel contributes significantly to survival and later compensatory adaptation by the remaining small bowel (Silverman and Roy 1983).

Long-term outcomes for children with massive bowel resections resulting in short bowel syndrome are difficult to predict because of the previously small number of survivors. This uncertainty creates stress in children and families whose futures are unknown. Frequent rehospitalizations may be an anticipated pattern due to need for manipulation of medications, feedings, and management of infection. Developmental considerations are critical in preparing patients for readmissions. Continuity of care is essential, requiring ongoing communication between home care and hospital team members.

Hirschsprung's Disease

Hirschsprung's disease is a congenital anomaly characterized by the absence of ganglion cells in an intestinal segment. Lack of peristalsis and failure of the internal sphincter to relax leads to mechanical obstruction.

Medical Interventions

Surgical intervention is the most effective therapy. A three-stage approach is used. The first stage includes removal of the aganglionic segment and a temporary colostomy. The colostomy allows the bowel to rest and resume its normal caliber and tone. Reanastomosis, which "pulls" the end of the intact bowel down to a point near the rectum (pull-through procedure) is the next stage. This is performed when the child is 8 to 12 months of age or weighs approximately 20 pounds. The third stage, closure of the colostomy, is usually performed within a few months of the reanastomosis procedure. About 90 percent of patients are free of symptoms after completion of surgical intervention (Silverman and Roy 1983; Whaley and Wong 1987).

Home care issues focus on the child's nutritional status and ostomy care. After colostomy, closure attention is directed to promotion of a normal diet for age and of bowel control.

Biliary Atresia

Biliary atresia is the congenital absence of a portion of the bile ducts. The most common abnormality is complete atresia of the extra-hepatic structures. Evidence suggests it may be caused by a viral infection shortly before or after birth (Silverman and Roy 1983). Irreversible obliteration of the bile ducts usually leads to death within 18 months unless early surgical intervention is successful.

Medical Interventions

Infants with extrahepatic atresia may benefit from the Kasai procedure, which involves form-ing a substitute duct from a segment of jejunum. The infant has a postoperative double stoma. Once bile drainage is greater than 50 mL/day, the bile is re-fed through the distal stoma to aid fat metabolism.

Medical management for infants with intra-hepatic lesions is similar to postoperative fol-low-up after the Kasai procedure. Formulas containing medium-chain triglycerides (Por-tagen, Pregestimil) are usually well tolerated. Water-miscible forms of vitamins A, D, and E are required. If there is decreased bone density, 1,24-dihydroxy vitamin D is given. Cho-lestyramine may decrease the pruritic symptoms by binding bile acids and preventing their reab-sorption. It may also interfere with absorption of other medications, particularly fat-soluble vitamins. Phenobarbital may decrease irri-tability. Antibiotics are used prophylactically during the first year in an attempt to decrease the number of episodes of cholangitis. Diuretics are necessary once ascites occurs. Spironolactone (Aldactone) and furosemide (Lasix) are usually effective (Silverman and Roy 1983).

Home care issues include aggressive efforts to maintain nutritional status, frequent physical therapy to prevent motor development delays, ostomy care, early recognition of the signs of cholangitis and ascites, skin care measures to relieve pruritis, and psychological support.

Liver transplantation is the definitive treat-ment for biliary atresia. Constant attention to all details that optimize these childrens' health and continued growth increases their chance of sur-viving long enough to become candidates for a liver transplant.

TEACHING ISSUES PRIOR TO DISCHARGE

The wide age range of pediatric patients with gastrointestinal alterations requires that the home care provider be knowledgeable about growth and development to meet age-related needs. The infant may have prolonged periods of hospitalizations with limited or no opportunities for oral feeding. These circumstances can lead to interrupted maternal bonding and may affect the trust relationship. The adolescent whose body image is essential to his or her sense of well-being is on the other end of the spectrum. The presence of a stoma or the need for total parenter-al nutrition can be emotionally devastating.

The home care nurse must know the common critical principles and techniques for ostomy care, parenteral and enteral nutrition, and medi-cation administration. Guidelines are broad and are provided to ensure the child and caregiver have been taught, understand, and can perform all critical measures for safe care in the home. The proliferation of formulas and equipment requires caregivers to consult the information provided by manufacturers for specific details. A vendor, for example, may deliver parenteral nutrition, but the family must still check the label and store the solution appropriately. The family or the home care nurse must be able to contact a resource person if there are any questions or problems.

NURSING CARE PLANS IN THE HOME

The goals in caring for the child with altera-tions in metabolic function are to (1) identify and promote developmental issues, (2) maintain optimal nutritional status, and (3) identify/pre-vent potential complications. The following dis-cussion provides information to help develop nursing care plans (Table 7-1).

Nursing Considerations to Promote Understanding of Developmental Issues

The infant with a congenital anomaly or dis-ability is at high risk for developmental delay

Table 7-1 Nursing Care Plan for the Child with Alteration in Metabolic Function

Patient Problem/Need (Nursing Diagnosis)	Outcome Criteria	Nursing Intervention(s)
Alteration in nutrition, secondary to weight loss, related to poor oral intake, diarrhea	Patient demonstrates no weight loss or appropriate weight gain for age or consumes appropriate calories.	Obtain daily weights same time every day, same scale, before meals, recorded on permanent record. Record specific quantity of intake every feeding and record on permanent record.
Alteration in elimination secondary to diarrhea	Patient demonstrates regularity in bowel pattern	Document volume, type, frequency, color, and odor for each stool and record. Report bowel pattern changes to physician.
Alteration in coping, secondary to disabling medical condition	Patient and family verbalize knowledge of community resources and demonstrate use of support system.	Use home care agency social worker if deficits noted. Initiate social work referral, social history, and determination of risk factors. Ensure introduction to support groups, financial assistance.
Knowledge deficit, secondary to newly diagnosed condition	Patient and family verbalize understanding of disease and treatment.	Assess patient and family's readiness for learning. Use age-appropriate educational aids. Ensure access to commercially printed literature: inflammatory bowel disease, etc. Use medication instruction sheets, individualized to patient's needs. Use teaching checklists: total parenteral nutrition, Broviac catheter care, nasogastric feedings, stoma care. Developmental level used in teaching: infant and toddler ages need total parental involvement with emphasis on establishing trust relationship between care taken and infant, encouraging autonomy in toddler; school-aged and adolescent ages use emphasis on body image and independence; school-age and preschool-age children often fear body mutilation; adolescents can learn to perform care independently and are best motivated with a positive self-image.
Alteration in skin integrity, secondary to presence of stoma, diarrhea	Patient demonstrates no erythema, edema, or tenderness at stoma or perianal area.	Document skin condition daily; record and report erythema, edema, and tenderness. Expose erythematous area to air four times a day.

continues

Table 7-1 continued

Patient Problem/Need (Nursing Diagnosis)	Outcome Criteria	Nursing Intervention(s)
Knowledge deficit relative to need for total parenteral nutrition	Patient demonstrates no signs of infection, dislodged catheter, or air embolus and gains weight at prescribed rate.	Do not use TPN line for medications. Use aseptic technique for catheter care. Assess for hyper/hypoglycemia: ensure constant infusion rate; assess blood and urine glucose checks. Assess for hydration: record and report decrease in urine/stool volume, decreased skin turgor, eyes sunken, increased urine specific gravity, weight loss or excessive weight gain. Assess for signs of mineral/electrolyte deficiency: monitor laboratory values. Assess for catheter rupture/breakage or occlusion. Ensure presence of padded hemostat to clamp central line during a change. Check pump for function and correct flow rate at least every 4 to 6 hours. Record and report fever, lethargy, irritability, vomiting, erythema or edema at insertion site, loose suture, fluid leaking. Ensure cardiopulmonary resuscitation certification for caretakers. Obtain Medic Alert warning tags. Assess electrical safety in home. Write emergency notification letter to power company.

due to prolonged hospitalization and limited sensory stimulation. When the infant is ready for home care an assessment of the infant's developmental level and of maternal bonding is required to determine if intervention is needed. The infant with gastrointestinal alterations can represent the less than ideal infant that causes parental grief and mourning. This must be recognized and handled through therapeutic intervention to reduce the risk of neglect and abuse. The presence of a stoma, Broviac catheter, or feeding tube can be highly traumatic for parents and can interfere with normal developmental experiences. Failure to adjust or cope with these issues in the home requires a nursing care plan with multidisciplinary psychosocial dimensions, including occupational therapy.

Pediatric nurses are especially sensitive to the preschool-aged and school-aged child whose developmental milestones incorporate acquired skills of initiative and industry. Their increased reasoning ability and verbal expertise make teaching and planning for home care both challenging and rewarding. This age group is characterized by egocentricity. They often feel responsible for their illness or hospitalization, so an accurate assessment of their understanding of their illness is critical. The child and family can be taught, using audiovisual aids, to explain the altered anatomy, special diet requirements, and the technology required for care. Maximizing learning in children in this age group requires frequent reinforcement that they are not responsible for the situation. Their fear of body mutilation makes it essential that every invasive procedure should be carefully explained. Home care for this age group should include close coordination with preschool or school administrators. This coordination should include preparation of the peer group and any special arrangements required for administration of medications, stoma care, feeding, or emergency care. Mealtimes at home or school require special attention for children receiving tube feedings or parenteral nutrition.

Adolescents with alterations in gastrointestinal function demand continuity for a successful hospital plan to be incorporated into home care. Most individuals in this age group will have demonstrated their degree of acceptance and understanding of their illness before discharge. Psychological or social work needs should be identified prior to the discharge planning process. Many hospitals have established support groups that adolescents can join prior to discharge. The hallmark of the adolescent developmental level is independence, so all teaching should be done directly with the child whenever possible. Adolescents should participate in decision making about their home care, such as scheduling tube feeding or delivery of total parenteral nutrition, and diet modifications. Sexuality is an issue that must be assessed and addressed on an individual basis. The adolescent's primary concerns with any treatment method will be its effect on body image and peer relationships.

Nursing Considerations to Promote Optimal Nutritional Status

Assessment of Nutritional Status

A dietitian should provide the child's estimated nutritional requirements prior to discharge. The home care nurse should know what the child should consume daily to promote weight gain. Specific volumes of formulas should be provided for the infant and child

requiring tube feedings. Sample menus with specific guidance related to the child's needs (especially for supplements) and preferences should be provided for the older infant and child. Growth curves should be initiated on discharge and continued throughout home care. Measurement differences can be controlled by using the same scale, obtaining nude weights (especially in infants), and always weighing before feeding and at the same time of day. Stoma bags should be empty before weighing. A dietitian should be consulted if weight gain is not appropriate or if the parent is having difficulty with food choices. Dietary requirements may occasionally decrease from those estimated at the time of discharge (resolution of infection, decreased corticosteroid dosage) and the diet, tube feeding, or delivery of total parenteral nutrition will need to be modified to prevent excessive weight gain.

Children with gastrointestinal disease should be assessed for the physical signs and symptoms associated with nutrient deficiency. These children are prone to developing electrolyte, vitamin, and mineral deficiencies from inadequate intake, malabsorption, or excessive losses. The signs and symptoms listed in Table 7-2 are not usually apparent until there is significant nutrient deficiency. They should be brought to the attention of the physician as soon as they are identified.

Oral Alimentation

Oral alimentation is the preferred method of providing nutrition. Children with biliary atresia and Hirschsprung's disease can usually meet their growth requirements with proper attention on adequate oral nutrition. Children with biliary atresia experience fat malabsorption and require a formula high in medium-chain triglycerides (MCT). Children or adolescents with inflammatory bowel disease may require low-residue, lactose-free diets during mild exacerbations of their disease. Corticosteroid therapy, particularly during exacerbation, may make it difficult for them to eat enough to meet their nutritional needs. Children with colostomies or ileostomies require attention to the mineral and electrolyte content of their fomulas and/or oral diet to prevent sodium, zinc, or potassium deficiencies. Cold liquids that increase peristalsis and gas producing foods should be avoided. Tube feeding and/or total parenteral nutrition are essential

Table 7-2 Signs and Symptoms Suggestive of Nutritional Deficiencies

Type of Deficiency	Sign/Symptom	Deficient Nutrient
Protein–calorie malnutrition		
Hair	Dullness	
	Easy pluckability	
	Sparse	
Lips	Cheilosis	
Tongue	Edema	
Glands	Parotid enlargement	
Muscles, extremities	Interosseous muscle wasting	
	Temporal muscle wasting	
	Intercostal muscle wasting	
	Calf muscle wasting	
	Edema	
Water- and Fat-Soluble Vitamin Deficiencies		
Skin	Follicular hyperkeratosis	Vitamin A
	Petechiae	Vitamin C
	Purpura	Vitamins C and K
	Pellagrous dermatitis	Niacin
Face	Nasolabial seborrhea	Riboflavin
Eyes	Xerosis of conjunctivae	Vitamin A
	Keratomalacia	Vitamin A
	Corneal vascularization	Riboflavin
	Blepharitis	Vitamin B complex, biotin
	Bitot's spots	Vitamin A
	"Spectacle eye"	Biotin
Lips	Cheilosis	Vitamin B_6, niacin
	Angular stomatitis	Riboflavin, iron
Tongue	Bald	Niacin, vitamin B_{12}, iron, riboflavin, vitamin B_6, folic acid
	Magenta tongue	Riboflavin
Muscles, extremities	Painful calves, weak thighs	Thiamine
	Edema	Thiamine
Neurological	Absent vibratory sense in the feet	Vitamin B_{12}
	Hyporeflexia	Thiamine
	Decreased position sense	Vitamin B_{12}
	Confabulation, disorientation	Vitamin B_{12}
	Weakness, paresthesias	Thiamine, pyridoxine, pantothenic acid, vitamin B_{12}
Essential Fatty Acid Deficiency		
Hair	Alopecia	
Extremities	Scaly dermatitis located primarily over the legs and feet	
Electrolyte/Mineral Deficiency		
Face	Seborrheic dermatitis	Zinc
Hair	Alopecia	Zinc
Neurological	Weakness	Potassium, magnesium
	Lethargy	Potassium, calcium, iron
	Confusion	Magnesium, phosphorus
	Flaccid paralysis	Potassium
	Irritability	Potassium, calcium, magnesium
	Convulsions	Calcium

Source: Adapted from *Modern Nutrition in Health and Disease*, 6th ed., by R.S. Goodhart and M.E. Shils (Eds.) with permission of Lea & Febiger, © 1980.

when nutritional requirements cannot be met orally. Either of these modalities can be delivered at night to avoid interference with normal activities.

Meeting nutritional requirements of children with gastrointestinal disease may require the use of both parenteral and enteral nutrition during exacerbation of their disease or when oral intake is inadequate. Delivery of parenteral or enteral nutrition requires that the parents and/or child perform all associated care in a meticulous and safe manner.

Enteral/Tube Feeding Formulas

Factors to be considered in the selection of the correct formula include the current manifestation of the disease, feeding tube diameter, placement, and cost. Enteral formulas are presented in Table 7-3. A variety of formulas are available owing to the variation in formula requirements in different gastrointestinal disease processes, other medical conditions, and the child's individual requirements. Children with short gut syndrome may be on a defined formula such as Progestimil and then progress to a complete formula such as Osmolite. Children with biliary atresia require Portagen for its high percentage

of MCT oil. Supplements such as Polycose and/or MCT oil may be used to increase the caloric density of these formulas. Commercial formulas are recommended, especially for infants, because they provide a fixed nutrient profile and their low viscosity allows delivery through small bore tubes. Noncommercial blenderized formulas can only be delivered via large-bore tubes, and the optimal nutrient profile may be difficult to obtain. Inappropriate osmolarity will also cause problems in children requiring tube feedings. Gastrointestinal complications associated with enteral feedings are listed in Exhibit 7-1.

Cost is often a problem due to the requirement for expensive formulas and supplements. If the formulas are not covered by insurance or Medicaid, the child may become eligible for Women/Infant/Children (WIC). The parents may be able to decrease cost by arranging bulk purchase. Local organizations such as the Lions Club may provide funds to purchase a given amount of the formula and/or the enteral pump and supplies.

Tube Feeding Types and Routes

Nasogastric tubes are passed through the nose, down the esophagus, and into the stomach. The most common tubes are made of polyvinyl

Table 7-3 Enteral/Tube Feeding Formulas

Trade Name	kcal/oz	Special Features/Comments
Infant Formulas		
Mature human milk	21.5	Lactose source of CHO*
Whole cow's milk	19.5	Lactose source of CHO; butterfat source of fat
2% lowfat milk	15.5	Butterfat source of fat
Skim milk	10.5	Butterfat source of fat
Enfamil 20/Enfamil w/Iron 20	20	Contains lactose for CHO; nonfat milk source of protein; coconut and soy oils source of fat
Enfamil w/Iron 24	24	Contains lactose for CHO; nonfat milk source of protein; coconut and soy oils source of fat; also for premature infants
Isomil	20	For cow's milk protein and/or lactose intolerance; CHO source is corn syrup and 40% sucrose.
Isomil sf	20	For cow's milk protein, lactose, and/or sucrose intolerance; CHO source is glucose polymers.
Nursoy	20	For cow's milk protein and/or lactose intolerance
Prosobee	20	Soy protein and soy oils; use for lactose and cow's milk protein intolerance, sucrose intolerance, galactosemia.

*CHO = carbohydrate

Table 7-3 continued

Trade Name	kcal/oz	Special Features/Comments
Similac 20/Similac w/Iron 20	20	Nonfat cow's milk source of protein; coconut and soy oils source of fat
Similac 24	24	For premature infants with fluid intolerance†
SMA	20	Nonfat cow's milk and whey source of protein; coconut, safflower, and soybean oils source of fat
Specialized Infant Formulas		
Nutramigen	20	Source of CHO is corn syrup, cornstarch; source of protein is casein hydrolystate; hypoallergenic formula, nutritionally complete; use for infants and children intolerant to food proteins and/or lactose intolerance.
Portagen	20	Source of fat is MCT oil 87% and corn oil 12%; nutritionally complete; for impaired fat absorption secondary to pancreatic insufficiency, bile acid deficiency, intestinal resection, lymphatic anomalies (liver disease).
Pregestimil	20	CHO source is cornsyrup and tapioca; fat content is MCT oil and corn oil; nutritionally complete; easily digestible protein, CHO, and fat; used for malabsorption syndromes.
RCF (Ross Carbo-hydrate Free)	20	Use for infants with CHO intolerance; CHOs are added according to amount infant will tolerate.
Vital	30	Decreased amount of fat (9.4%) and increased amount of CHO (74%); nutritionally complete hydrolyzed diet, used for impaired digestion or absorption
Nutritional Supplements and Complete Diets		
Alimentum	20	Source of CHO is glucose polymers; lactose free; protein source is polymers casein hydrolysate; 50% of fat from MCT oil; comes in ready-to-feed can.
Enrich	30	High dietary fiber, lactose free; source of CHO is sucrose and cornstarch.
Ensure	30	Lactose free; use for supplemental feedings; requires digestion.
Ensure Plus	45	Increased kcal density, otherwise same as Ensure
Jevity	31	High fiber, isotonic solution; fat content is 50% MCT oil.
Isocal	30	Requires digestion; fat content has MCT oil; source of CHO is maltodextrine.
Osmolite	30	Source of protein is soy isolate and casein; fat source has medium-chain triglycerides, corn, and soy oils; isotonic accessible.
Pediasure	30	RDAs for ages 1–6 years in approximately 1,100 mL lactose free; MCT oil is 20% of fat source.
Polycose	23 cal/tbs	CHO supplement; add to liquids for calories.
Pulmocare	45	Decreased CHO, increased fat; decreases metabolic CO_2 production
Promod	4.2 kcal/g 28 kcal/ scoop	Protein supplement, use in milk to increase caloric and protein intake.
Vivonex	30	Elemental formula, decreased fat and increased CHO

†If a formula is labeled as a premature formula, the source of fat is medium-chain triglycerides, which allows for easier fat absorption.

Exhibit 7-1 Gastrointestinal Complications Associated with Enteral Nutrition/Tube Feeding

I. Nausea and Vomiting

   A. Potential causes
      1. Offensive smell
      2. High osmolality—gastric retention
      3. Rapid rate of infusion
      4. Lactose intolerance
      5. Excessive fat in formula
   B. Prevention/therapy
      1. Add flavorings to formula if osmolality is not critical
      2. Elevate head of bed to at least 45°
      3. Use isotonic formula
      4. Begin at slow rate; increase rate in slow increments
      5. Use low or no lactose formula
      6. Maintain fat at 30 to 40 percent of total calories

II. Diarrhea

   A. Potential causes
      1. Hyperosmolar solution or medications
      2. Lactose deficiency
      3. Fat malabsorption
      4. Cold feedings
      5. Protein malnutrition
      6. Other: primary malabsorption; antibiotics
   B. Prevention/therapy
      1. Use isotonic formula
      2. Use slow rate initially
      3. Increase rate in 24- to 48-hour increments
      4. Decrease to rate at which patient was not having diarrhea and advance slowly
      5. Use low or lactose-free formula
      6. Use low-fat products in patient with primary cause for malabsorption
      7. Stop formula for 12 to 24 hours if above measures unsuccessful
      8. Antidiarrheal agents may be necessary
      9. Albumin or supplemental parenteral nutrition may be required in patient with serum albumin level less than 2.5 mg/dL
     10. Dilute hypertonic medications

III. Constipation

   A. Potential causes
      1. Dehydration
      2. Impaction
      3. Obstruction
      4. Fiber-free formulas
   B. Prevention/therapy
      1. Strict monitoring of intake and output
      2. Additional free water by enteral formula or intravenously to maintain output greater than input by 500 to 1,000 mL
      3. Digital removal
      4. Decompression/surgery for obstruction
      5. Addition of fiber to diet

Source: Adapted from *Support Nursing—Core Curriculum* by C. Kennedy-Caldwell and P. Guenter (Eds.) with permission of the American Society for Parenteral and Enteral Nutrition, © 1988.

chloride, polyurethane, and Silastic. Silastic or polyurethane tubes are preferable when removal of the tube is not desirable.

Nasoduodenal tubes are passed through the nose, down the esophagus, and into the duodenum. They are appropriate if the child cannot tolerate intermittent gastric feedings, has difficulty with regurgitation, or is at high risk for aspiration of formula. Polyurethane or Silastic tubes are preferred for this route since they remain soft for long periods and are not likely to cause intestinal perforation.

Gastrostomy tubes are surgically placed through a small opening in the skin and abdominal muscles directly into the stomach. This tube is used in children who require tube feeding for an extended period.

A gastrostomy button is now available for children who require long-term tube feeding. It replaces the Malecot tube or Foley catheter once the gastrostomy site is established. The shorter length of this tube decreases the risk of obstruction associated with other gastrostomy tubes. The button has an antireflux valve that decreases the possibility of gastric contents irritating the skin. A safety plug remains in place between feedings and eliminates the need for a clamp. The button is usually placed while the child is in the clinic setting. The site should be observed closely for any evidence of pressure necrosis. This can occur if the button is too small. General guidelines for site care, button care, and management of complications are presented in Exhibit 7-2.

Delivery Methods

The most common methods of delivering enteral formulas are the continuous or intermittent (bolus) methods. We prefer the term *intermittent feeding* rather than *bolus feeding* because it more effectively indicates that all noncontinuous feedings should be given slowly. Continuous delivery is required when enteral formula is delivered into the jejunum or duodenum.

An enteral pump is usually required when continuous feedings are necessary. Slow, constant delivery of formula into the jejunum or duodenum is necessary to prevent "dumping syndrome" symptoms (dizziness, tachycardia, diarrhea, and nausea). These symptoms result from the rapid movement of extracellular fluids into the bowel to dilute the hypertonic formula to an isotonic mixture. Circulating blood volume is decreased by this rapid fluid shift. Portable backpack pumps are available that allow continuous enteral pump feeding without limiting the child's activities. (See Exhibit 7-3 for home delivery techniques.)

Total Parenteral Nutrition

Total parenteral nutrition (TPN) formulas are designed to meet individual requirements for calories, protein, vitamins, and minerals. Fat requirements are met through the use of lipid (fat) emulsions. Parenteral nutrition is usually provided in a cyclic fashion in the home setting. The child will receive the TPN and fat emulsion over a 12- to 18-hour period, usually during the evening. This child will normally be adapted to the optimal time and fluid delivery rate while in the hospital. Daily discontinuation of the TPN includes a 2-hour weaning period to prevent hypoglycemia. Adolescents and/or children receiving corticosteroids may require a 3-hour weaning period. If a child required 1,150 mL of TPN and 250 mL of lipid emulsion per day over a 12-day period, the following schedule would be typical:

1. Begin TPN and fat emulsion at 8 PM.
   TPN rate: 107 mL/hr from 8 PM to 6 AM
   Lipids rate: 20.8 mL/hr from 8 PM to 8 AM
2. Decrease TPN rate to 54 mL/hr from 6 AM to 7 AM.
3. Decrease TPN rate to 26 mL/hr from 7 AM to 8 AM.
4. Discontinue TPN and lipids at 8 AM.

Suggested procedures for starting and discontinuing the TPN and lipids are outined in Exhibits 7-4 and 7-5.

These solutions are usually delivered to the home on a weekly or monthly basis depending on the child's metabolic stability. Vitamin preparations have limited stability and must be added to the TPN daily. The TPN should be removed from the refrigerator approximately 30 minutes before infusion, the vitamins should be added using strict aseptic technique, and the TPN should then be gently mixed. The bottle or bag should be spiked and should be allowed to hang

Exhibit 7-2 Gastrostomy Feeding Button Care

Site Care

1. No dressing required.
2. Site can be cleansed with a mild soap and water. Turn the button in a full circle while cleansing site.
3. Allow the site to dry thoroughly before covering with clothing.

Button Care

1. Flush with 5 to 10 mL of water after feeding or medication administration.
2. Clean the inside tube with a cotton-tipped applicator and flush with water.

Complications

1. Nonfunctional antireflux valve
   a. Lubricate the obturator with water-soluble lubricant.
   b. Insert the obturator into the shaft of the button until the valve makes a popping sound indicating the closed position. Leakage of gastric content should cease.
   c. If unsuccessful, tape the safety valve and notify physician.
2. Occlusion
   a. Attempt to flush gently with 2 to 3 mL of water.
   b. Gently insert an 8 or 10 F suction catheter into shaft of button.
3. Dislodgement
   a. Lubricate obturator with water-soluble lubricant.
   b. Insert obturator and distend button several times to ensure patency of antireflux valve.
   c. Lubricate the stoma and the button dome with water-soluble lubricant.
   d. Insert the button through the gastrostomy into the stomach.
   e. Remove the obturator. (If antireflux sticks to the obturator, rotate the obturator slowly during removal. If this is unsuccessful, gently push the obturator back into the button until the valve is closed.)
   f. Check visually for closure of antireflux valve.
   g. Insert the flip-top safety plug.

Exhibit 7-3 Tube Feeding: Home Delivery Techniques

Formula and Delivery System

Commercial powder formula

1. Labeling
   a. Check for match with your prescription. The same brand of formula may be available in different concentrations and with different additives.
   b. Check expiration date on container.

2. Preparation and storage for formula requiring mixing
   a. Wash hands.
   b. Clean area and utensils and blender for mixing.
   c. Wipe top of container before opening.
   d. Measure exact amount of formula, liquid, and other additives. Mix well.
   e. Cover and refrigerate any used formula. Use within 24 hours. If medications are added to 24-hour volume, label formula prior to refrigeration. If unsure whether medication was added, start with fresh formula. Most manufacturers recommend discarding any formula remaining at room temperature for 8 to 12 hours.
   f. Keep unmixed formula powder covered and in an air-tight container.

Exhibit 7-3 continued

3. Preparation of ready-mixed formula
   a. Wash hands.
   b. Rinse and wipe the top of the container.
   c. Shake formula container before opening.
   d. Cover and refrigerate any unused formula.
   e. If medications are added to 240-mL volume, label formula prior to refrigeration. If unsure whether medication was added, start with fresh formula.

4. Formula delivery
   a. Equipment
      1) Toomey syringe
      2) Container for water
      3) Feeding bag and tubing
      4) Pump

5. Delivery technique
   a. Wash hands.
   b. Check for placement of tube:
      1) Balloon pulled up against skin
         a) Mark tube with pen or tape to indicate where tube is even with skin.
         b) Attach through a nipple to keep against skin and prevent movement into jejunum or duodenum.
         c) Return gastric contents that are aspirated into the stomach.
      2) Nasoenteric
         Attempt to aspirate gastric contents; this may not always be successful with small-bore tubing.
   c. Check residual volumes for intermittent feeding
      1) Residual volume _____ mL or less—refeed
      2) Residual volume _____ mL or greater
         May hold feeding. Refeed aspirate (if large amount curdled formula or oral secretions, discard). Wait 30 minutes.
   d. Delivery of formula
      Attach syringe without plunger or feeding bag with filled tubing (to prevent excessive air into stomach) to clamped gastrotomy or nasoenteric tube.
   e. Flushing feeding tube
      Flush tubing with at least 5 mL of water and clamp while injecting last 0.5 mL. Remove syringe or feeding bag. Close tubing. Gastrostomy tube and syringe without plunger may be elevated and left to air dry.

6. General measures
   a. Oral hygiene
      1) No lemon-glycerine swabs
      2) Lip lubrication
      3) Teeth
         Notify dentist if child has intravenous device (Broviac/Hickman catheter or intravenous ports). May require prophylactic antibiotic before routine care or delay in care. *Gentle* brushing or use of rinses only.
   b. Periodic reassessment of growth parameters and immunizations
   c. Reevaluation of nutritional requirements
      1) with each gain or loss of 1 to 2 kg body weight
      2) with intercurrent illnesses
      3) every 3 months
      4) with change in medications
      5) after institution of formula changes
   d. Safe storage of all medications
      1) Do not put in bathroom medicine cabinets because of exposure to humidity.
      2) Childproof caps.
      3) Tape bottles to be discarded securely or discard via sink.
   e. Safe destruction of all needles and syringes.

Source: Wendy Votroubek.

Exhibit 7-4 Procedure for Starting TPN and Fat Emulsion Solution

Supplies

Alcohol swabs (70% isopropyl)
———— mL of fat emulsion
———— mL of TPN solution and fat emulsion
Intravenous tubing and/or cassette for TPN
Extension tubing without stopcock
Tape
Occluding or rubber-shod clamp
Povidone-iodine or chlorhexidine cleanser

Procedure

1. Wash hands.
2. Organize supplies.
3. Remove cap from TPN bottle.
4. Wipe top of TPN bottle with 70% isopropyl alcohol swab.
5. Add vitamins to TPN bottle.
6. Insert intravenous tubing (cassette) into TPN bottle and fat emulsion and connect intravenous tubing (cassette) to intravenous pumps.
7. Connect TPN and fat emulsion tubing to y-connector; hang TPN bottle and fat emulsion bottle on intravenous pole.
8. Connect extension tubing to y-connector.
9. Set pump at 000 and purge until all tubing is filled. Be sure to fill y-site closest to bottle of TPN and bottle of fat emulsion.
10. Place cap on extension tubing.
11. Check to see that all tubing is filled and *no air is present*.
12. Set rate and volume to be infused on intravenous pump.
13. Clamp catheter with occluding clamp.
14. Remove intermittent infusion plug.
15. Wipe hub with alcohol swab.
16. Plug extension tubing into catheter.
17. Release clamp.
18. Turn pump on and push start button.
19. Be sure red light is flashing.
20. Tape connections.
21. Initial rate of infusion: *Rate volume to be infused*
       9 PM – 7 AM   ————————
       7 AM – 8 AM   ————————
       8 AM – 9 AM   ————————

for at least 10 minutes. Three-in-one delivery systems that combine the TPN and lipid in one bag have become available for home use. Parents and/or the child will continue to add the vitamin preparation shortly before infusion of the solution. Formula changes are usually only required to meet growth requirements or correct metabolic alterations.

Frequency of metabolic monitoring (weekly or monthly) is determined by the child's physiological stability. Parents should be aware of the signs and symptoms of common metabolic alterations that indicate the need for more frequent monitoring (Forlaw 1980) (Exhibit 7-6).

Home TPN is usually delivered via a Broviac/ Hickman catheter. Strict aseptic technique is required to prevent catheter-related infection. Handwashing is critical prior to any care associated with a catheter. The full dressing procedure is usually performed until the catheter exit site is fully healed. The full procedure is also recommended for children who have an ostomy in addition to their central line. The modified dressing procedure can be used once the catheter exit site is healed. Frequency of the dressing change varies from daily to three times per week. We prefer daily to every-other-day dressing changes since this maintains a lower bacterial count. The dressing should always be changed immediately if it becomes wet or soiled and after bathing or swimming. See Exhibits 7-7 and 7-8 for suggested dressing procedures.

Exhibit 7-5 Daily Discontinuation of TPN and Fat Emulsion Solution Procedure

Supplies

Heparin solution _____ units/mL
3 mL sterile syringe
22-gauge sterile needle
Rubber-shod or occluding clamp
70% isopropyl alcohol swab
Sterile catheter cap
Small bottle povidone-iodine scrub or chlorhexidine skin cleanser

Procedure

CATHETER MUST ALWAYS BE CLAMPED WHEN OPEN TO AIR.

1. Wash hands thoroughly with povidone-iodine or chlorhexidine skin cleanser or use soap in dispenser.
2. Wipe top of heparin solution vial with alcohol swab.
3. Check label on heparin solution vial; it should read heparin _____ units/mL.
4. Withdraw _____ mL of heparin solution into syringe. Use a new sterile syringe and needle. Remove air from syringe.
5. Recheck heparin solution label.
6. Clamp catheter.
7. Clamp filter (if used).
8. Turn off intravenous pump.
9. Remove extension tubing from catheter.
10. Wipe catheter hub with alcohol swab.
11. Remove needle from syringe.
12. Insert syringe into hub of catheter.
13. Check for tight fit of syringe into catheter.
14. Release clamp but hold in place.
15. Inject _____ mL of heparin solution.
16. Clamp catheter while pushing in last _____ mL of heparin. This step is *very important!* You must always be *pushing* in the heparin solution as you clamp the catheter.
17. Remove syringe; leave clamp on catheter.
18. Connect sterile catheter cap or intermittent infusion plug filled with sterile saline.
19. Remove clamp.
20. Tape catheter in comfortable position.

The central line catheter must be heparinized when not in use for continuous infusions. Correct heparinization of the catheter is critical to prevent occlusion. The catheter is Silastic, and the softness of this material allows blood to be aspirated into the lumen if it is clamped without continuing a gentle forward injection of the heparin solution (Exhibit 7-9).

It is important to see that the young child or infant does not have direct access to the catheter. A 4 × 4-inch gauze pad placed over the looped and secured catheter is helpful. The child or infant should always wear clothing that minimizes access to the catheter. We frequently fashion an undershirt from tubular Spandex to hold a 4 × 4-inch gauze pad in place and thus decrease the child's access to the catheter. All connections should be securely taped during infusions even when Luer-lok tubing is used. A clamp should either be attached to the catheter or worn by the child at all times. It is important to stress to the child and parents that if a problem develops the catheter can easily be occluded by bending it rather then searching for a missing clamp.

Nursing Considerations for Identifying/Preventing Complications

Complications Associated with Enteral/ Tube Feeding and TPN—Mechanical Complications

Enteral Nutrition. Mechanical complications associated with enteral nutrition are influenced by the size and position of the feeding tube. The mechanical complications described in Exhibit 7-10 are usually preventable. Adolescents are more likely to use the nasoenteric tube than younger children.

Exhibit 7-6 Metabolic Complications Associated with Parenteral/Enteral Nutrition/Tube Feeding

---

I.   Hypoglycemia

    A. Causes
       Sudden cessation of feeding, most common in patients on medications for hyperglycemia.
    B. Signs and symptoms
        1. Weakness
        2. Diaphoresis
        3. Hunger
        4. Nervousness
        5. Irritability
        6. Palpitations
        7. Tremors
        8. Headache
        9. Blurring or double vision
      10. Numbness of lips/tongue
    C. Prevention and therapy
        1. Monitor blood glucose level during initiation of therapy.
        2. Provide glucose if feeding is abruptly interrupted.

II.   Hyperglycemia

    A. Causes
        1. Excessive carbohydrate administration
        2. Glucocorticoids
        3. Insulin lack
        4. Chromium deficiency
    B. Signs and symptoms
        1. Fatigue
        2. Thirst
        3. Polyuria
        4. Dry, hot, flushed skin
    C. Prevention and therapy
        1. Use of formulas with higher fat content
        2. Insulin or oral hypoglycemia agents

III. Hyperosmolar Nonketotic Dehydration

    A. Causes
        1. Untreated hyperglycemia resulting in increasing urine output with dehydration
        2. Each molecule of glucose carrying two molecules of water
    B. Signs and symptoms
        1. Dry skin
        2. Dry mucous membranes
        3. Fever
        4. Polydipsia
        5. Osmotic diuresis
        6. Hypovolemia
        7. Somnolence
        8. Seizures
        9. Coma
    C. Prevention and therapy
        1. Daily monitoring of blood glucose level during initiation of feeding, at least twice daily in patient with diabetes or other reason for insulin lack.
        2. Discontinue feeding until blood glucose level is controlled.

IV.   Prerenal Azotemia

    A. Causes
        1. Dehydration
        2. Calorie/nitrogen imbalance

Exhibit 7-6 continued

      B. Signs and symptoms
          1. Poor skin turgor
          2. Dry mucous membranes
          3. Decreased urine output
          4. Increased specific gravity
          5. Weight loss
      C. Prevention and therapy
          1. Adequate hydration
          2. Correct calorie–nitrogen ratio

V.   Essential Fatty Acid Deficiency

      A. Causes
          1. Inadequate intake of linoleic acid
      B. Signs and symptoms
          1. Scaly dermatitis
          2. Poor wound healing
          3. Alopecia
      C. Prevention and therapy
          1. Provide 4% calories as linoleic acid.
          2. Safflower oil most common source.

VI.   Hypovolemia

      A. Causes
          1. Inadequate fluid replacement
          2. Hyperglycemia
          3. Excessive gastrointestinal losses
          4. Systemic infection
          5. Renal disease
          6. Intestinal obstruction
          7. Blood loss
          8. Burns
          9. Diuretics
      B. Signs and symptoms
          1. Poor skin turgor
          2. Dry mucous membranes
          3. Decreased urine output
          4. Increased specific gravity
          5. Weight loss
          6. Increased pulse
          7. Lethargy—coma
          8. Convulsions
          9. Hypotension
        10. Tachycardia
        11. Abdominal distention
        12. Decreased or increased temperature
        13. Feeble to absent peripheral pulses
      C. Prevention and therapy
          1. Close monitoring of intake and output, weight
          2. Adequate fluid replacement
          3. Treatment of underlying cause
          4. Daily biochemical monitoring during initiation of feeding

VII.   Hypervolemia

      A. Causes
          1. Excessive fluid replacement
          2. Postoperative antidiuretic hormone effect of renal disease
          3. Corticosteroid therapy
          4. Excessive sodium
          5. Excessive sodium bicarbonate

continues

Exhibit 7-6 continued

   B. Signs and symptoms
      1. Rales
      2. Headache
      3. Muscle weakness
      4. Fatigue
      5. Apathy
      6. Postural hypotension
      7. Nausea, vomiting
      8. Abdominal cramps
   C. Prevention and therapy
      1. Check electrolytes daily as feeding is initiated, at least once weekly.
      2. Strict intake and output
      3. Weight
      4. Urine specific gravity
      5. Fluid restriction (free water)

VIII.   Hyponatremia

   A. Causes
      1. Dilutional
      2. Excessive urinary or gastrointestinal losses
      3. Inadequate replacement in formulas
   B. Signs and symptoms
      1. Headache
      2. Muscle weakness
      3. Fatigue
      4. Apathy
      5. Nausea, vomiting
      6. Abdominal cramps
      7. Seizures
   C. Prevention and therapy
      1. Careful monitoring of intake and output—include urine, nasogastric, ostomy electrolytes in patients who may have excessive losses.
      2. Fluid restriction
      3. Sodium replacement if true deficit

IX.   Hypernatremia

   A. Causes
      1. Dehydration
      2. Excessive infusion of sodium ion
      3. High protein feeding
      4. Diabetes insipidus
      5. Inability to perceive thirst
   B. Signs and symptoms
      1. Dry skin
      2. Dry mucous membranes
      3. Thirst
      4. Decreased urine output
      5. "Rubbery" tissue turgor
      6. Tachycardia
      7. Excitement
      8. Weight loss
   C. Prevention and therapy
      1. Strict intake and output
      2. Daily electrolytes with initiation of feeding and then at least weekly
      3. Adequate hydration

Exhibit 7-6 continued

X.   Hypokalemia

    A. Causes
        1. Anabolism
        2. Deficit of potassium in solution
        3. Excessive urinary or gastrointestinal losses
        4. Metabolic alkalosis
        5. Diuretics
    B. Signs and symptoms
        1. Anorexia
        2. Nausea, vomiting
        3. Abdominal distention
        4. Paralytic ileus
        5. Muscle weakness
        6. Cardiac arrhythmias
    C. Prevention and therapy
        1. Check electrolytes daily while initiating feeding, then at least weekly.
        2. Provide adequate potassium supplementation.

XI.   Hyperkalemia

    A. Causes
        1. Excessive replacement of potassium
        2. Metabolic acidosis
        3. Renal failure
        4. Crushing injury
        5. Acute digitalis poisoning
        6. Mineralocorticoid deficiency
    B. Signs and symptoms
        1. Nausea and vomiting
        2. Diarrhea
        3. Muscle weakness
        4. Muscle irritability
        5. Oliguria, anuria
        6. Numbness, tingling
        7. Cardiac arrhythmia
    C. Prevention and therapy
        1. Monitoring of potassium delivery
        2. Monitoring of potassium losses (urine, nasogastric, ostomy)

XII.   Hypophosphatemia

    A. Causes
        1. Anabolism
        2. Inadequate formula
        3. Insulin administration
        4. Alcoholism
        5. Chronic use of phosphate binding antacids
    B. Signs and symptoms
        1. Paresthesias
        2. Hyperventilation
        3. Lethargy
        4. Coma
    C. Prevention and therapy
        1. Check serum levels daily during initiation of feeding, then at least weekly.
        2. Phosphate supplementation

continues

Exhibit 7-6 continued

XIII. Hyperphosphatemia

    A. Causes
        1. Excessive delivery of phosphate
        2. Renal insufficiency
    B. Prevention and therapy
        1. Check serum level daily during initiation of feeding, then at least weekly.
        2. Use enteral formula with low or no phosphate content.

XIV. Hypocalcemia

    A. Causes
        1. Insufficient calcium in formula
        2. Rapid correction or hypophosphatemia
        3. Vitamin D deficiency
        4. Increased urinary excretion
        5. Decreased parathyroid hormone
        6. Respiratory acidosis
        7. Acute pancreatitis
        8. Large amounts of citrated blood
    B. Signs and symptoms
        1. Numbness and tingling of nose, ears, fingertips, or toes
        2. Carpopedal spasm
        3. Muscle twitching
        4. Convulsions
        5. Tetany
        6. Positive Trousseau's sign
        7. Positive Chvostek's sign
        8. Nausea, vomiting
        9. Diarrhea
      10. Cardiac arrhythmias
    C. Prevention and therapy
        1. Adequate provision of calcium
        2. Adequate provision of vitamin D
        3. Slow correction of hypophosphatemia

XV. Hypomagnesemia

    A. Causes
        1. Insufficient magnesium in formula
        2. Excessive urinary and gastrointestinal losses
        3. Hypercalcemia
        4. Elevated aldosterone levels
        5. Chronic alcoholism
        6. Impaired gastrointestinal absorption
    B. Signs and symptoms
        1. Agitation
        2. Depression
        3. Confusion
        4. Convulsions
        5. Paresthesias
        6. Tremor
        7. Ataxia
        8. Muscle cramps
        9. Tetany
      10. Tachycardia
      11. Hypotension
      12. Positive Chvostek's sign
    C. Prevention and therapy
        1. Check serum levels initially; repeat as necessary, especially in patient with diarrhea.
        2. Provide adequate delivery of formula.

Exhibit 7-6 continued

XVI. Hypermagnesemia

A. Causes
1. Excessive amount in formula
2. Renal failure
3. Severe dehydration
B. Signs and symptoms
1. Lethargy—coma
2. Hypotension
3. Loss of deep tendon reflexes
4. Respiratory depression
5. Cardiac arrhythmia
6. Tachycardia—bradycardia
C. Prevention and therapy
1. Monitor serum levels during initiation of therapy.
2. Use formula with decreased or no magnesium in patient with hypermagnesemia.

XVII. Hypozincemia

A. Causes
1. Inadequate amount in formula
2. Impaired absorption—short bowel syndrome, Crohn's disease
3. Increased losses (diarrhea, ostomy output)
4. Increased uptake by reticuloendothelial system
B. Signs and symptoms
1. Anorexia
2. Impaired sense of taste
3. Erythematous rash—perinasal area, genitalia
4. Poor growth
5. Hypogonadism
6. Impaired wound healing
7. Diarrhea
C. Prevention and therapy
1. Provide adequate amounts of zinc.

XVIII. Hyperzincemia

A. Causes
1. Excessive amounts in formula
B. Signs and symptoms
1. Pallor
2. Fatigue
3. Scurvy-like bone lesions
4. Pathologic fractures
C. Prevention and therapy
1. Decrease zinc provision with decreased stool output, ostomy losses, or postinfectious states.

Source: Adapted from *Support Nursing—Core Curriculum* by C. Kennedy-Caldwell and P. Guenter (Eds.) with permission of The American Society for Parenteral and Enteral Nutrition, © 1988.

TPN. The most common mechanical complications that occur during TPN are related to the central line. Occlusion and/or rupture of the central line can be prevented with careful attention to correct flushing procedures. Should the central line catheter become obstructed, the family or caregiver should know how to attempt to aspirate the clot. If this is not successful, the physician or appropriate nursing personnel should be called immediately. The child should be taken to the hospital to have urokinase placed into the catheter to dissolve the obstructing clot or fibrin sheath. The effectiveness of the urokinase is diminished by the length of time the catheter remains obstructed.

Rupture or tearing of the central line catheter requires immediate clamping to prevent blood loss or air embolism. The catheter can be

Exhibit 7-7 Broviac Dressing Care—Full Procedure

This procedure should be done for the first 7 days after Broviac/Hickman insertion or until the site is healed.

Supplies

Povidone-iodine scrub/chlorhexidine
Mask

Tray containing:

    Sterile drape
    Sterile gloves (2) pair
    10% Acetone/70% isopropyl alcohol swabsticks (3)
    Povidone-iodine scrub swabstick (3)
    Povidone-iodine ointment
    2 × 2-inch gauze pads (4)
    Sterile scissors
    Tincture of benzoin swabstick
    Elastoplast
    Dressing label

Tape (not in tray)

Procedure

1. Explain procedure to patient. If this is first dressing change, check for povidone-iodine allergy.
2. Organize supplies at bedside.
3. Put on mask.
4. Wash hands for 1 minute with povidone-iodine scrub or chlorhexidine. Turn off faucet with paper towel.
5. Remove old dressing carefully and place in bag.
6. Inspect catheter site and surrounding skin for signs of irritation, leakage, edema, erythema, or altered position of catheter. Notify appropriate contact person if any of above are present.
7. Secure catheter to chest wall forming a loop so that swabs can easily be used under the catheter.
8. Don sterile gloves.
9. Cleanse the area with acetone/alcohol swabsticks. Always work from the exit site toward the periphery in a circular motion cleansing a 2- to 3-inch diameter. Repeat three times. NEVER GO BACK OVER THE SITE WITH THE SAME SWAB. BE SURE TO CLEAN UNDER THE CATHETER ALSO.
10. Cleanse skin with each sterile povidone-iodine scrub swabstick. Again, cleanse with friction using a circular motion from center to periphery. Repeat three times.
11. Remove povidone-iodine scrub with sterile alcohol swabstick. Allow skin to dry.
12. Paint area from center to periphery with povidone-iodine *solution* swabstick. Blot any pooled solution, especially from under catheter. Allow to dry.
13. Apply povidone-iodine ointment to exit site. Apply ointment from first 3 days only.
14. Apply sterile 2 × 2-inch gauze pad "cut" to fit around catheter at insertion site.
15. Cover 2 × 2-inch gauze pad and catheter near exit site with two 2 × 2-inch gauze pads.
16. Paint skin at periphery of pad with tincture of benzoin. Allow to dry.
17. Cut Elastoplast to approximately 3 × 3-inch size. Round edges of Elastoplast.
18. Apply Elastoplast to cover 2 × 2-inch dressing site. Tape edges of Elastoplast in a window fashion and anchor remaining catheter to dressing. Apply tape in a chevron fashion at catheter–Elastoplast interface.
19. Ensure that the catheter is looped and attached to the skin or dressing. Tape may be used to do this, or the clamp may be used to attach it to the dressing, or the patient may wear a chain around the neck with the clamp on the catheter and the chain. Any of these methods may be used provided that the catheter is secured so that if it is accidentally pulled on the catheter will not be pulled.
20. Label dressing. Include date of change and initials of person performing dressing change.
21. Remove supplies and clean work area.

Exhibit 7-8 Exit Site Care—Modified

This procedure should be done after the exit site is healed. It is done every other day and after showering. The patient may shower after the stitches have been removed if the exit site is healed. Immediately after the shower, clean and dress the exit site following this procedure.

Supplies

Povidone-iodine scrub/chlorhexidine
10% acetone/70% isopropyl alcohol swabsticks (2)
Povidone-iodine swabstick (3)
2 × 2-inch gauze pads (4)
Tape

Procedure

1. Wash hands. Turn off faucet with paper towel.
2. Remove old dressing. Deposit in trash basket.
3. Inspect catheter site and surrounding skin for signs of irritation, leakage, edema, erythema or altered position of catheter. Notify physician if any of the above are present.
4. Secure catheter to chest wall forming a loop so that swabs can easily be used under the catheter.
5. Cleanse the area with acetone/alcohol swabsticks. Always work from the exit site toward the periphery in a circular motion, cleansing a 2- to 3-inch area. Repeat twice using a sterile acetone/alcohol swabstick.
6. Paint the area with a povidone-iodine swabstick, starting at the exit site and working outward in a circular motion until the skin is cleaned 2 to 3 inches around the exit site. Repeat once using a sterile povidone-iodine swabstick. Allow the povidone-iodine to dry or blot area dry. Check under catheter.
7. Using the third sterile povidone-iodine swabstick, clean the catheter in a circular motion starting from the exit site and cleansing 2 to 3 inches of the catheter. *Blot* dry.
8. Fold a 2 × 2-inch gauze pad in half, taking care not to touch the portion that will touch the exit site. Place the folded pad on the skin under the catheter at the exit site.
9. Take a second 2 × 2-inch pad and cover the folded pad and the entire exit site.
10. Tape the gauze pads in place.
11. Ensure that the catheter is also looped and attached to the skin or dressing. Tape may be used to do this, or the clamp may be used to attach it to the dressing, or the patient may wear a chain around the neck with the clamp on the catheter and the chain. Any of these methods may be used provided that the catheter is secured so that if it is accidently pulled on it will not be pulled out.
12. Label dressing. Include date of change and initials of person performing dressing change.
13. Remove supplies and clean working area.
14. Chart dressing change, appearance of catheter site, and any problems encountered.

occluded by bending it if a clamp is not available. The family can do a temporary repair in the home and return to the hospital immediately for a temporary or permanent repair. The temporary repair in the home may decrease the risk of infection and clotting of the catheter (Exhibit 7-11).

Metabolic Complications

Metabolic complications often reported in children with gastrointestinal disease were presented in Exhibit 7-6. These metabolic complications may occur with either parenteral or enteral nutrition. The possibility of occurrence increases with the addition or deletion of drugs or if the child has changes in fluid losses or gains without strict attention to replacement. This is a particular concern if the child is only on tube feeding or TPN. For example, attention must be paid not only to increased ostomy losses but also to increased fluid and electrolyte requirements due to losses from summer activities or variances in temperatures in the home.

Infectious Complications

Enteral Nutrition. Contaminated formulas and aspiration pneumonia are the infectious complications most often associated with enteral nutrition. The complications are usually avoidable with good assessment of the family's ability to administer the feedings. The child's potential risk factors for aspiration should be identified (e.g., tracheostomy, chronic reflux) and addressed in the nursing care plan. The family

Exhibit 7-9 Heparinization of Broviac/Hickman Catheter

Flushing Requirements

1. If the child is receiving continuous infusions into the catheter, no flushing is required.
2. If the child is receiving intermittent infusions (12-hour TPN, antibiotics) the catheter should be flushed with 5 mL of normal saline, then 3 mL 10 units/mL heparinized saline after each use. No additional flushing with heparinized saline is required.
3. If the child is not receiving any infusions through the catheter, the catheter must be flushed with heparinized saline twice daily according to this procedure. It is not necessary to use normal saline for routine flushes.

Supplies

Heparinized saline (10 units/mL)
3 mL syringe
22-gauge, 1-inch needle
Sterile 70% isopropyl alcohol pad

Procedure

1. Wash hands thoroughly. Turn off faucet with paper towel.
2. Draw up 3 mL of heparinized saline (10 units/mL) using sterile technique.
3. Clamp the catheter.
4. Clean the top of the intermittent injection port with a 70% isopropyl alcohol wipe. Allow to dry.
5. Insert needle of syringe containing heparinized saline through the intermittent injection port.
6. Release the occluding clamp.
7. Flush the catheter with 3 mL heparinized saline (10 units/mL).
8. Clamp the catheter with the occluding clamp while instilling the last 0.5 mL of heparinized saline. This creates positive pressure, which will prevent the backflow of blood into the tip of the catheter.
9. Remove the needle and syringe and discard appropriately.
10. Check that the connections are securely taped.

should be aware that the child may require readmission to the hospital if aspiration occurs.

The home care nurse is in the best position to evaluate the family's ability to maintain the clean environment, techniques, and equipment necessary to prevent formula contamination.

Local infection may occur at the gastrostomy tube site if it is not kept clean and dry or if there is continuous drainage. Daily cleansing of the site and changing the gastrostomy tube when needed will prevent these complications. Irritation of the skin at the gastrostomy exit site may require the use of stoma wafer or zinc oxide.

TPN. Infectious complications associated with TPN are related to the delivery system or the central line catheter. Proper handwashing technique is critical when dealing with solutions, tubing, catheter, and skin care.

Medications

Medications used most commonly in children with gastrointestinal disease have been discussed under the appropriate disease heading. A discussion of specific medications to include functions, side effects, and drug–nutrient interactions is in Table 7-4. It is important to pay attention to whether the medication must be given on an empty stomach, especially in the child who is receiving continuous feedings. With continuous feedings, higher doses of certain drugs (e.g., phenytoin) may be necessary since some of the drug may be bound to the protein in the enteral formula. Certain drugs (e.g., cholestyramine) may decrease absorption of other drugs. Medications with high osmolality, such as potassium chloride or sodium chloride, require dilution before administration via nasoenteric tube or gastrostomy tube to avoid diarrhea. It is essential that the child remain well hydrated with medications such as cholestyramine or antibiotics that may affect renal function.

Ostomy Care

The home care nurse should be familiar with and follow the ostomy care procedures taught to the parents and/or child during hospitalizations. The enterostomal therapist should be consulted

Exhibit 7-10 Mechanical Complications Associated with Enteral Nutrition/Tube Feeding

I.　Nasopharyngeal Discomfort

　A. Causes
　　1. Absence of chewing, which is the normal stimulus to salivary secretions
　　2. Mouth breathing as a result of the tube being in place
　B. Signs and symptoms
　　1. Sore throat
　　2. Difficulty with swallowing
　　3. Hoarseness
　　4. Dry mucous membranes
　C. Prevention
　　1. Use of soft, small-bore tubes
　　2. Use of therapeutic nursing measures
　D. Therapy
　　1. Lubrication of lips
　　2. Chewing sugarless gum
　　3. Gargling with warm water and a mouthwash solution
　　4. Physiologic saliva or analgesic and/or anesthetic lozenges for severe discomfort (anesthetic lozenges may decrease swallowing or gag reflexes)

II.　Nasal Erosions and Necrosis

　A. Cause:
　　1. Pressure on nasal ala from tube
　B. Sign:
　　1. Erosions of nasal ala
　C. Prevention
　　1. Use of soft, small-bore tube
　　2. Proper taping of tube
　D. Therapy
　　1. Tape tube so that no pressure is exerted against nasal ala.
　　2. Apply tincture of benzoin to area where tape will be applied.

III.　Abscess—Nasal Septum

　A. Causes
　　1. Pressure against the nasal cartilage, especially in the malnourished.
　　2. Dehydrated patient with subsequent sloughing of nasal cartilage and dropping of the dorsum of the nose.
　　3. If bacterial organisms are present, an abscess may develop.
　B. Signs and symptoms
　　1. Complaints of continual pain and pressure from the tube.
　　2. Fever, chills
　C. Prevention
　　1. Soft, small-bore tubing
　　2. Proper taping of small- or large-bore tube
　　3. Evaluation of patient's nose size in relation to tube size

IV.　Acute Sinusitis

　A. Cause:
　　1. Sinus tract occluded by the nasoenteric tube
　B. Signs and symptoms
　　1. Pain
　　2. Nasal congestion with or without purulent drainage
　　3. Malodrous breath
　　4. Mild fever
　C. Prevention
　　1. Soft, small-bore tubing
　　2. Evaluation of patient's nose size in relation to tube size
　D. Therapy
　　1. Removal of nasoenteric tube
　　2. Bed rest

continues

Exhibit 7-10 continued

    3. Analgesics
    4. Hot compresses to face
    5. Nonsurgical drainage

V.   Acute Otitis Media

    A. Cause: pressure at the Eustachian tube opening from the nasoenteric tube, with entry of pathogenic bacteria into the middle ear
    B. Signs and symptoms
        1. Severe, dull throbbing ear pain
        2. Fever, chills
        3. Slight dizziness
        4. Nausea and vomiting
        5. Child may pull on affected ear
    C. Prevention: use of soft, small-bore tubing
    D. Therapy
        1. Nasoenteric tube changed to other nostril
        2. Antibiotic therapy if appropriate
        3. Myringotomy if severe

VI. Hoarseness

    A. Cause: irritation of mucous membranes of the larynx from presence of nasoenteric tube
    B. Sign: hoarseness
    C. Prevention
        1. Use of soft, small-bore tube
        2. Adequate hydration
        3. Mouth care
    D. Therapy
        1. Soft, small-bore tube
        2. Steam or aerosol therapy
        3. Warm gargle
        4. Anesthetic lozenges

VII. Excessive Gagging

    A. Cause: anxious patient or hypersensitive gag reflex
    B. Signs and symptoms: excessive gagging; anxiety
    C. Prevention: careful explanation prior to placement of tube
    D. Therapy: reassurance

VIII. Esophagitis

    A. Causes: predisposing factors: intestinal obstruction, persistent vomiting, poor nutritional status, supine position with an increase in acid reflux into the distal esophagus, large-bore tube obstructing the esophageal lumen
    B. Signs and symptoms
        1. Heartburn
        2. Sour stomach
        3. Substernal and epigastric burning sensations with pain referred to the head, neck, and arms
    C. Prevention
        1. Use of soft, small-bore tubing
        2. Elevation of the head of the bed
        3. Early recognition of patients at risk and those with symptoms of developing esophageal irritation
    D. Therapy
        1. Removal of tube
        2. Esophagoscopy and dilation.

Source: Adapted from *Support Nursing—Core Curriculum* by C. Kennedy-Caldwell and P. Guenter (Eds.) with permission of The American Society for Parenteral and Enteral Nutrition, © 1988.

Exhibit 7-11 Temporary Repair—Pediatric

The immediate response if the Broviac/Hickman catheter should become cut or punctured is to clamp the catheter between the cut or puncture and the chest wall. This procedure should then be performed as soon as possible. A temporary repair kit containing the following supplies should be available in the home and taken on trips.

Supplies

Masks
Blunt needle adaptor: 23-gauge blunt needle, 20-gauge blunt needle
Sterile scissors   Small padded tongue blade
70% isopropyl alcohol pads   3-0 silk suture
Povidone-iodine swabsticks   Tape
Vial of normal saline   Sterile intermittent injection plug
Heparinized saline 10 units/mL   Sterile gloves
3-mL sterile syringes (2)   Sterile barrier
22-gauge sterile needles (3)   Masks

Procedure

1. Check that the catheter is clamped.
2. If intravenous fluid tubing is attached to Broviac/Hickman catheter, turn off pump or flow control device.
3. Wash hands. Turn off faucet with paper towel.
4. Explain procedure to child as you prepare to repair catheter.
5. Obtain and set up equipment.
6. Put on mask. Have child put on mask.
7. Set up sterile field. Fill 3-mL sterile syringe with normal saline.
8. Place the sterile drape on the patient's chest.
9. Prep the catheter area of the cut or puncture with 70% isopropyl alcohol pad. Allow alcohol to dry.
10. Prepare the catheter area of the cut or puncture with povidone-iodine solution. Blot dry.
11. Using sterile scissors, cut portion of the catheter with cut or puncture. Clamp should remain in place proximal to tear or fracture.
12. Place the catheter on the sterile barrier.
13. Put on sterile gloves.
14. Attach syringe normal saline to blunt needle. Fill blunt needle with normal saline. Insert blunt needle into the Broviac/Hickman catheter.
15. Remove the clamp and pull back on the plunger on the syringe until blood is obtained. This will ensure that there is no air in the catheter.
16. Flush the catheter with the syringe filled with 3 mL of normal saline.
17. Replace the clamp.
18. Remove the syringe.
19. Flush the catheter with 3 mL of 10 units/mL heparin solution.
20. With clamp in place, remove syringe and attach sterile intermittent infusion port or reconnect *sterile* filled intravenous tubing.
21. Clamp catheter.
22. Release clamp.
23. If intravenous tubing is reattached, ensure correct infusion delivery.
24. Tie the blunt needle adaptor to catheter using 3-0 silk suture; then tape the blunt needle to the catheter.
25. Place padded tongue blade under area of Broviac/Hickman catheter with blunt needle adaptor. This will ensure that the catheter cannot bend and be punctured by blunt needle. Tape to the padded tongue blade in a fashion that allows changing sterile intermittent infusing port or intravenous tubing.
26. Tape sterile intermittent infusion port.
27. If intravenous fluid is not infusing, flush catheter with 3 mL of 10 units/mL heparinized saline.
28. If intravenous tubing has been connected to the Broviac/Hickman catheter, it should be taped in a joint-to-joint fashion. Be sure intravenous fluid is infusing at appropriate rate and that intravenous infusion pump is functioning properly if in use.
29. The appropriate resource person should be notified as soon as possible to arrange for permanent repair.

Table 7-4 Medications Commonly Used for Alterations in Metabolic Functions

Drug	Purpose	Precautions	Drug–Nutrient Interaction	Side Effects
Sulfasalazine (Asulfadine)	Bowel disease (inflammatory) suppressant	Patients hypersensitive to one sulfonamide may be hypersensitive to others. Patients hypersensitive to furosemide, sulfones, thiazide diuretics, sulfonylureas, carbonic anhydrase inhibitors, or salicylates may react to this medication. Use is not recommended for children under 2 years of age. Excreted in breast milk; may cause hemolytic anemia in glucose-6-phosphate dehydrogenase–deficient neonates. Caution needed when general anesthesia is required. Take with meals; maintain adequate fluid intake.	Anticoagulants Anticonvulsants Antidiabetic agents Methotrexate Digitalis Folic acid Hemolytics Methenamine Oxyphenbutazone	Diarrhea, dizziness, loss of appetite, nausea or vomiting, headache, increased sensitivity to light or sunlight, itching or rash, aching of joints or muscles, difficulty in swallowing, fever, sore throat, unusual bleeding or bruising, jaundice, blood in urine, lower back pain, discolored urine (no medical significance)
Chole-styramine (Questran)	Binds with bile acids in the intestine preventing their reabsorption Antipruritic Antidiarrheal	Children are more likely to develop metabolic acidosis. *Cautions with use:* Renal function impairment Constipation Complete atresia or biliary obstruction Peptic ulcer Patient may absorb more of other medications when cholestyramine is stopped.	Anticoagulants Chenodiol Digitalis Thiazide diuretics Penicillin G (oral) Tetracycline (oral) Vancomycin (oral) Thyroid hormones Fat-soluble vitamins Potential decreased absorption of any other medication	Constipation, nausea or vomiting, weight loss, belching, bloating, diarrhea
Vitamin D	Promotes intestinal calcium and phosphate absorption; mediates the mobilization of calcium from bone	Infants may be sensitive to small doses.	Cholestyramine Glucocorticoids Phenobarbital Phenytoin	Vitamin D toxicity associated with hypercalcemia; arrested growth in children; constipation common in children and adolescents; diarrhea,

Vitamin	Uses/Dietary sources		Drug interactions	Signs/symptoms of toxicity

Vitamin A

Dietary sources: fish liver oils, egg yolks, butter, fortified milk products

To prevent and treat vitamin A deficiency, evidenced by follicular hyperkeratosis, xerosis of conjunctiva, keratomalacia, and Bitot's spots

Best dietary sources: liver, fish liver oils, egg yolks, yellow-orange fruits and vegetables, dark green, leafy vegetables, whole milk, Vitamin A–fortified skim milk, butter, margarine

Pregnancy
Breast feeding
Evaluate:
Doses delivered by diet
Parenteral nutrition
Enteral nutrition

Mineral oil
Barbiturates
Digitalis

Antacids
Anticoagulants
Cholestyramine
Mineral oil
Neomycin
Sucralfate
Oral contraceptives
Isotretinoin
Vitamin E

headache, loss of appetite, metallic taste, nausea or vomiting common in children; unusual increase in thirst; unusually dry mouth; unusual tiredness or weakness; bone pain, hypertension, mood changes

Acute overdose
In children, hydrocephalus and increased intracranial pressure

General
Bleeding from gums or sore mouth, diarrhea, dizziness or drowsiness, double vision, headache, irritability, seizures, peeling of skin, vomiting

Chronic overdose—children
Premature closure of epiphysis; bone or joint pain; drying or cracking of skin or lips; fever; general feeling of body discomfort or weakness; headache; increased sensitivity of skin to sunlight; irritability; loss of appetite; loss of hair; stomach pain; tiredness; unusual increase in frequency of urination (especially at night) or in amount of urine; vomiting; yellow-orange patches on soles of feet, palms of hands, or skin around nose and lips; hepatomegaly

if there is difficulty with appliance fit, maintenance, or skin care.

Care of the colostomy and ileostomy sites is similar, with protection of the skin and prevention of dehydration being the primary requirements for nursing interventions. The infant or small child with a stoma may not require an appliance; a small 2 × 2-inch gauze pad kept in place by a diaper may be sufficient. Gauze pads saturated with petroleum jelly are used if the stoma is friable and bleeds easily. The gauze is changed after each stool; the skin is cleansed well and dried; and a protective barrier (zinc oxide, karaya products) is applied. The parent should know to wet the gauze with a small amount of water if there is any resistance to removal. In the older child an appliance is used and should remain in place for at least 24 hours to decrease or prevent skin irritation. An infant urine collecting bag can be used in the infant with a large volume of output. The skin is cleansed well and dried, and tincture of benzoin or a skin preparation is applied. A karaya product and/ or stomadhesive is then applied to prevent skin breakdown and promote adherence of the appliance. The correct size appliance is then applied.

REFERENCES

Forlaw, L. "Parenteral Nutrition in the Critically Ill Patient." *Critical Care Quarterly* 3–4 (1980).

Goodhart, R.S. and Shils, M.E. (eds). *Modern Nutrition in Health and Disease*. Philadelphia: Lea & Febiger, 1980.

Silverman, A., and Roy C.C. *Pediatric Clinical Gastroenterology*. St. Louis: C.V. Mosby, 1983.

Whaley, L.F., and Wong, D.L. *Nursing Care of Infants and Children*. St. Louis: C.V. Mosby, 1987.

Chapter 8

Alterations in Endocrine Function

Janice A. Greer

The endocrine system includes eight glands that produce hormones that exert influence on specific tissues or target organs. Hormones carried throughout the body by the circulatory system control and regulate growth and sexual development, metabolism, and physiological stress response (Anthony and Thibodeau 1983).

Endocrine dysfunctions in children can affect not only the child's general health and well-being but also the family and community. Treatment is life long and requires long-term follow-up. It often requires changes in life style. The goals of the treatment plan are correction of the hormonal imbalance, maintenance of normal growth and development, prevention of short- and long-term complications, and the adjustment of the child and family to the disease process and treatment regimen.

Home nursing care is directed toward achieving treatment plan goals through education, use of community resources, identification of problems, and development of strategies to cope with these problems. In this chapter the more common endocrine dysfunctions seen in children are addressed along with the role of the home care nurse in caring for the child and the family.

ALTERATION IN GROWTH: GROWTH HORMONE DEFICIENCY

Growth is an important indicator of a child's mental and physical health as well as the quality of the environment. A chronic problem in any of these areas may affect the growth rate.

Factors that influence the child's growth are genetic, prenatal, endocrine, nutritional, and psychological and the presence of systemic chronic illness. The endocrine system influences growth through the activity of growth hormone and of other hormones, such as thyroxine, glucocorticoids, estrogen, and testosterone.

The general pattern of growth in children is relatively consistent. By 2 or 3 years of age, children have established their own growth pattern based on their genetic potential. Standardized growth charts have been developed for plotting the child's growth against established norms.

Accurate measurement of height is essential in the assessment of growth. Supine length is the preferred position for measuring children younger than 2 years of age. The child is placed on an unyielding horizontal surface with the soles of the feet in a plane perpendicular to the body axis. The head is placed in the Frankfurt position, a line drawn from the outer canthus of the eye to the external auditory meatus is placed perpendicular to the body axis. Children older than age 2 years should be measured while standing against a wall with feet bare, medial malleoli touching, and the heels, buttocks, and shoulders in contact with the wall. With the head held in the Frankfurt position a rigid, right-angled device is rested on the child's crown.

The height attained is plotted on the appropriate standardized growth chart for age and sex. A deviation in the established percentile channel or a decrease in growth rate or velocity signals the need for referral. The expected growth rates or growth velocity per year of the child's age are shown in Table 8-1. The referral is made to the child's primary health care provider or an endocrinologist.

Children with documented growth hormone deficiency are currently being treated with synthetic growth hormone. This medication is given subcutaneously or intramuscularly three times a week or daily. The dose is individualized to achieve maximum growth. To achieve this maximum growth, the growth hormone preparation is administered until growth is complete.

Nursing Care Plans in the Home

Potential for Knowledge Deficit Related to Administration of the Growth Hormone Preparation

Education may include initial instruction on the administration of growth hormone or assessment of the child's or family's technique and their re-education. Home care nurses are beginning to provide the initial instruction.

Growth hormone preparations are packaged as a powder and must be diluted with the accompanying diluent. The medications are obtained through the child's hospital or home care agencies designated by the manufacturers.

The manufacturers have patient education materials that can be helpful in the education process. The behavioral objectives for administration of the growth hormone are listed in Exhibit 8-1. The child's participation in the injections should be appropriate for develop-

Exhibit 8-1 Behavioral Objectives for Administration of Growth Hormone

1. State the rationale for receiving the growth hormone medication.
2. List equipment and materials needed.
3. Describe the care and storage of the needles, syringe, and growth hormone preparation.
4. State the schedule of administration.
5. Demonstrate understanding of the concept of sterility.
6. Demonstrate ability to correctly mix and draw up amount of growth hormone preparation.
7. Demonstrate ability to correctly inject the growth hormone preparation.
8. Identify sites for growth hormone injection.
9. Describe rationale for site rotation.
10. Demonstrate ability to record injection given and site used in log book.
11. State resources to contact when questions or problems arise.
12. Identify follow-up plans.

mental age. Adolescents wishing to take on more responsibility may give their own injections. Educating the adolescent is indicated particularly for patients whose parents have had primary responsibility for the injections. Preschool- and school-aged children's participation in the injections is limited to sitting still for the procedure. Play therapy and a positive reinforcement system should be used to help the nurse and parents promote sitting still behavior. It is important to address parental anxiety about giving their child injections and causing pain. This can be accomplished by having the parent give another adult a subcutaneous injection of normal saline and receiving an injection of normal saline prior to giving an injection to the child.

The average annual cost of growth hormone therapy is $15,000. The cost may place financial burden on the family. Some states offer financial assistance through Children with Special Health Care Needs. The manufacturers also offer a program for financial assistance.

Potential for Disturbance in Self-Concept Related to Short Stature

School-aged children and adolescents struggle to achieve a sense of identity and of belonging with a peer group. Children with growth delays are at risk for the development of disturbances in self-image. Compounding the

Table 8-1 Growth Rates per Year of Age

Age	Growth Rate
0–6 months	16–17 cm
7–12 months	8 cm
13–24 months	10 cm
25–36 months	>8 cm
37–48 months	7 cm
4 years to puberty	5–6 cm

Source: Reprinted from *Clinical Pediatric and Adolescent Endocrinology* by S.A. Kaplan (Ed.), p. 3, with permission of W.B. Saunders Company, © 1982.

problem is the accompanying delay in the development of secondary sexual characteristics. It is important to assess the child and family's feelings about the growth delay and the child's self-image, relationships with peers, and performance in school.

Children with growth delays are frequently treated as if they are younger. The family, teachers, and peers may need assistance in developing expectations and interactions appropriate for the child's age not stature. The child may need assistance in developing realistic expectations of himself or herself, particularly in relationship to physical activities and athletics. Activities in which size is not of consideration should be encouraged.

The child and family must be realistic in their expectations of the probable response to the treatment. If unrealistic expectations fail to materialize, the child and family may experience frustrations that interfere with their psychological well-being.

ALTERATION IN WATER BALANCE: DIABETES INSIPIDUS

Diabetes insipidus is a disorder of water balance, an inability to concentrate urine that results from a lack of antidiuretic hormone (ADH). ADH is synthesized by the hypothalamus and stored and released by the posterior pituitary. It increases permeability of the collecting tubules of water, promoting reabsorption of water.

The characteristic signs and symptoms of diabetes insipidus are polydipsia, polyuria, nocturia, enuresis in a child who is toilet trained, and preference for iced water. The constant thirst and frequent urination interfere with play, school, sleep, and the intake of appropriate nutrients. When fluid is withheld, the child with diabetes insipidus becomes irritable and may seek out other sources of fluid, such as drinking out of the toilet bowl.

The clinical manifestations include increased 24-hour urine output, specific gravity below 1.005, serum osmolarity above 290 mOsm/kg, and mild hypernatremia above 145 mEq/L.

There are three classifications of diabetes insipidus: central, nephrogenic, and psychogenic. Central diabetes insipidus is caused by a deficiency in ADH. The major causes are

trauma, tumors, infection, or surgical procedure or it may be idiopathic. In fact, diabetes insipidus may be the presenting complaint of a child with an intracranial lesion. Nephrogenic diabetes insipidus results from renal insensitivity to ADH. This disorder can result from a variety of forms of chronic renal disease, from various drugs and toxins, and, in rare instances, from an X-linked inheritance pattern. Psychogenic diabetes insipidus, compulsive water drinking, is rare in children and is associated with a number of psychological disturbances.

Water deprivation tests and challenge with ADH are used to confirm the diagnosis. Dietary sodium and protein restrictions and the use of chlorothiazide are helpful in reducing the polyuria associated with nephrogenic diabetes insipidus. Desmopressin acetate (DDAVP) administered intranasally using a soft, calibrated plastic catheter is the drug of choice for the treatment of central diabetes insipidus. The usual dosage is 0.05 to 0.20 mL every 12 to 24 hours and is adjusted according to the child's pattern of response. In those children receiving a single dose, the hormone is usually administered in the evening so that the polyuria and polydipsia do not interfere with sleep and school.

Short periods of polyuria, polydipsia, and decreased urinary specific gravity (breakthrough) should occur 30 minutes to 1 hour prior to the administration of the next dose of DDAVP to prevent fluid intoxication. Older children usually can identify when breakthrough occurs. In infants and children who cannot make that determination, the assessment of specific gravity is essential.

Nursing Care Plans in the Home

*Potential for Fluid Volume Deficit
   Related to Polyuria Secondary to
   Diabetes Insipidus*

Assessment of the child's level of hydration provides important information on the efficacy of the treatment plan as well as the early identification of problems. The history should include the intake, the output, specific gravity readings if ordered, and dose and timing of the DDAVP administered, and the timing of the breakthrough. Changes in the child's behavior and school performance should also be noted. Increased irritability and decreased attention span are frequently evident in children with poorly controlled diabetes insipidus. The physical assessment should include weight (particularly changes in weight over time); the integrity of the mucous membranes, skin, and extremities; and specific gravity. Rapid weight gain or loss, signs of dehydration, and breakthrough occurring more than 1 to 2 hours prior to the next dose should be communicated to the health care provider.

Assessment of the method of administration of DDAVP is important since incorrectly administered DDAVP will cause increased polyuria and polydipsia. It must be administered with the child in a sitting position with the head hyperextended so the nasal bridge is flattened. The catheter is inserted filled with the medication halfway up the nares. The other end is placed in the mouth, and with a quick puff the medication is blown into the nares. Blowing too hard will blow the medication into the nasopharynx, and the DDAVP will be deactivated by the gastric juices. A bad taste in the mouth after administration indicates that the medication has entered the nasopharynx. The child must not sniff or blow the nose immediately after administration of the drug.

Potential for Knowledge Deficit Related to Disease, Administration of Medication, Signs and Symptoms of Dehydration or of Fluid Overload, and Prevention of Dehydration

It is important that the nurse assess the family's understanding of diabetes insipidus, ability to administer the DDAVP, and knowledge of the signs and symptoms of dehydration and fluid overload. The family's ability to measure specific gravity and to maintain the equipment must also be observed. When the refractometer is used to measure specific gravity, quality control testing with distilled water is essential to ensure that the readings are accurate.

The family must understand the potential for dehydration during illness. The absorption of DDAVP may be impaired when the mucous membranes become engorged owing to a cold or allergic rhinitis. Vomiting and decreased fluid intake also place the child at risk. Dehydration generally will not occur as long as the child drinks sufficient amounts of fluid. Infants and children who do not have ready access to fluids

are at greater risk. Parents should be instructed to contact the health care provider whenever persistent vomiting and decreased fluid intake occur. Hospitalization for intravenous administration of fluids may be necessary to ensure adequate hydration.

Alteration in Patterns of Urinary Elimination Related to Polyuria Secondary to Diabetes Insipidus

Polyuria frequently interferes with the child's play, sleep, and school performance. Bedwetting can be particularly distressing for the child and can be reduced or eliminated with proper administration of DDAVP, timing of administration, and dosage. An increase in bedwetting should be communicated to the health care provider.

For the school-age child, frequent trips to the rest room can lead to admonishment from the teacher and teasing from the other children. Assisting school personnel and other students in understanding diabetes insipidus and the need for frequent trips to the rest room can make the school experience less stressful.

ALTERATION IN ADRENAL FUNCTION: ADRENAL INSUFFICIENCY

Deficient adrenal glucocorticoid and mineralocorticoid production results from dysfunction of the adrenal cortex, deficiency in production of adrenocorticotropic hormone (ACTH), or suppression of endogenous adrenal function due to exogenous glucocorticoid therapy.

Congenital adrenal hyperplasia is an autosomal recessive genetic disorder in the biosynthesis of cortisol due to a specific enzymatic defect. The most common form of this disorder is caused by hyperproduction of ACTH, leading to hyperplasia of the adrenal gland and excessive adrenal androgen secretion. This leads to prenatal virilization of the female (enlargement of the clitoris and fusing of the labia) and postnatal virilization of both female and male (enlargement of the clitoris or penis, development of pubic hair and acne, and acceleration of growth). Aldosterone deficiency may also be present, leading to low serum sodium levels, high serum potassium levels, and vascular collapse (New et al. 1985). Affected females are usually recognized at birth owing to their ambiguous genitalia. Affected males, who generally appear normal at birth, present at 7 to 14 days of age in adrenal crisis.

Adrenal insufficiency due to ACTH deficiency is generally caused by tumors, infections, cranial irradiation, or surgical procedures in the hypothalamus or pituitary region. Aldosterone secretion is normal.

The administration of glucocorticoids suppresses ACTH secretion and produces atrophy of the adrenal cortex. Glucocorticoids taken for more than 2 weeks at or above physiological levels will suppress cortisol production. It may take 1 to 18 months for the function of the pituitary-adrenal axis to return to normal (Migeon and Lanes 1985).

Hydrocortisone is the drug of choice for chronic glucocorticoid replacement therapy. The dosage is normally 12 to 25 mg/m² in divided doses given two to three times daily (Migeon and Lanes 1985) and should be individualized. The treatment for mineralocorticoid deficiency is replacement therapy with oral fludrocortisone (Florinef), 0.10 to 0.15 mg/day as a single dose (Migeon and Lane 1985). In infants receiving formula only, carefully regulated amounts of salt will be added to the formula.

Nursing Care Plans in the Home

Potential for Knowledge Deficit Related to Disease, Administration of Medication, Signs and Symptoms of Complications, and Prevention of Adrenal Crisis

The family, and when appropriate the child, must be educated about the disease process, administration of the replacement medication, and adjustment of the hydrocortisone dose during times of physiological stress. They also must be able to recognize the signs and symptoms of adrenal insufficiency (undertreatment), hypercortisolism (overtreatment), and adrenal crisis.

The hydrocortisone preparation comes in a liquid form as Cortef and in pill form as Florinef. If Cortef is used, the parents must be instructed to shake the bottle vigorously before use to ensure that the preparation is thoroughly mixed. To ensure correct dosage, Cortef should be

Table 8-2 Signs and Symptoms Associated with Adrenal Dysfunction

Hypercortisolism	Adrenal Insufficiency	Adrenal Crisis
Moon facies	Lethargy	Nausea
Increased body fat	Anorexia	Vomiting
Retarded growth	Weakness	Dehydration
Muscle weakness	Occasional vomiting	Lethargy
Hypertension	Weight loss	Hypotension
	Hyperpigmentation	Shock
	Virilization (in children with congenital adrenal hyperplasia)	

administered using a syringe. Florinef can be crushed and dissolved in a small amount of formula or food. In children with congenital adrenal hyperplasia, the hydrocortisone is given three times daily, preferably every 8 hours. The mid-afternoon dose is the dose most frequently forgotten. The school nurse's assistance can be enlisted in giving this dose.

Adrenal crisis occurs when the adrenal cortex cannot produce the additional levels of cortisol needed to prevent widespread vasodilation, shock, and death during times of physiological stress. Physiological stress includes trauma, surgery, and illness, especially when associated with high fever. The signs and symptoms of adrenal crisis are vomiting, dehydration, lethargy, hypotension, and shock. Signs and symptoms associated with adrenal dysfunction are listed in Table 8-2.

The parents must be instructed to double or triple the dose of hydrocortisone for several days during times of illness, especially when associated with high fever. Parents should be instructed to contact the health care provider immediately when the signs and symptoms of adrenal crisis are present. Injectable hydrocortisone is available that can be used under the direction of the health care provider during significant illnesses, especially persistent vomiting. Children should wear Medic-Alert identification tags stating they have adrenal insufficiency.

Potential for Disturbance in Self-Concept Related to Appearance Changes Secondary to Early Onset of Pubic Hair, Enlargement of Clitoris or Penis, and Increased Height for Age

Children with precocious virilization are at risk of developing disturbances in self-concept. Precocious virilization can occur in poorly controlled 21-hydroxylase deficiency, the most common form of congenital adrenal hyperplasia. In the school-age years, children begin to struggle with peer identity and the need for peer acceptance. Precocious development of pubic hair and enlargement of the penis or clitoris can make the child feel different and can interfere with developing peer relationships and development of a healthy self-concept.

The child's feelings and understanding about the disease must be assessed. Explanations must be directed toward the child's developmental level. Play therapy can help the child explore and express feelings. The home care nurse can work with school personnel in developing programs to help students understand and accept differences among them.

Acceleration in growth may cause adults to have unrealistic expectations of the child. Parents and teachers may need assistance in developing appropriate expectations for the child based on age and not stature.

*Potential for Alterations in Family
Processes Related to Having a Child
with Congenital Adrenal Hyperplasia
or 21-Hydroxylase Deficiency*

The diagnosis of congenital adrenal hyperplasia has an emotional impact on the family. It can be particularly stressful when the child has ambiguous genitalia or when the sex assigned to the child at birth is incorrect. The nurse can support the family through the grieving process in which the parents grieve for the loss of the perfect child.

It is important to assess the family's level of understanding, coping mechanisms, feelings about the child's diagnosis, and support systems. The parents are particularly interested in information concerning corrective surgery for the ambiguous genitalia. Surgery, depending on the defect, occurs anywhere from 3 months to 3 years of age. The parents need reassurance that the child will look normal after surgery, and they may need assistance in explaining the disease to other family members.

ALTERATION IN THYROID FUNCTION: HYPOTHYROIDISM

Hypothyroidism results from the inability of thyroid hormone production to meet the patient's need. Hypothyroidism may be congenital, resulting from a defect in or absence of the thyroid gland or deficiency in thyroid stimulating hormone or thyroid releasing hormone. The incidence of congenital hypothyroidism is 1 in 4,000 live births (La Franchi 1982). Neonatal screening for hypothyroidism is part of the newborn screening tests in most states. Early identification and initiation of therapy has reduced the significant developmental delays previously associated with congenital hypothyroidism. The signs and symptoms of congenital hypothyroidism are listed in Table 8-3.

Hypothyroidism acquired in childhood and adolescence is caused most often by an autoimmune process known as Hashimoto's thyroiditis. Hypothalamic or pituitary disease may result in deficiencies of thyroid releasing hormone or thyroid stimulating hormone with subsequent development of hypothyroidism. The signs and symptoms of acquired hypothyroidism are listed in Table 8-4.

The treatment for hypothyroidism is replacement therapy with L-thyroxine. The dose is 100 $\mu g/m^2$/day but must be individualized (La Franchi 1982). The dose of L-thyroxine is adjusted for growth throughout childhood and adolescence.

Nursing Care Plans in the Home

*Potential for Knowledge Deficit Related
to Disease, Administration of
Medication, and Complications*

Home care nursing of a child with hypothyroidism requires educating the family about the disease including the importance of giving the medication daily and the signs and symptoms of both hypothyroidism and hyperthyroidism (overtreatment).

For infants the pill is crushed in a small amount of formula or strained food and administered by a spoon. The medication should not be placed in a bottle of formula since the infant may not drink all the formula and not receive the full dose of L-thyroxine. For older children and adolescents, the nurse may need to assist the family in identifying methods of remembering the medication, such as a calendar or a weekly reminder pill box.

Behavioral changes may occur in children with acquired hypothyroidism after replacement

Table 8-3 Symptoms and Signs of Congenital Hypothyroidism

Symptoms	Signs
Prolonged jaundice	Skin mottling
Lethargy	Umbilical hernia
Constipation	Jaundice
Feeding problems	Macroglossia
Cold to touch	Large fontanelles, wide sutures
	Distended abdomen
	Hoarse cry
	Hypotonia
	Dry skin
	Slow reflexes
	Goiter

Source: Reprinted from *Pediatric Clinics of North America,* Vol. 26, p. 46, with permission of W.B. Saunders Company, © 1979.

Table 8-4 Symptoms and Signs of Acquired Hypothyroidism

Symptoms	Signs
Slow growth	Decreased growth velocity
Puffiness	Increased upper to lower segment ratio
Decreased appetite	Delayed dentition
Constipation	Myxedema, mildly overweight
Swollen thyroid gland	Goiter
Lethargy	Delayed reflex return
Drop in school performance	Dull, placid expression
Cold intolerance	Pale, thick, carotonemia or cool skin
Galactorrhea	Muscle pseudohypertrophy
Menometrorrhagia	Delayed puberty
	Precocious puberty

Source: Reprinted from *Clinical Pediatric and Adolescent Endocrinology* by S.A. Kaplan (Ed.), p. 92, with permission of W.B. Saunders Company, © 1982.

therapy begins. The child may become hyperactive in comparison with previous behavior as well as experiencing sleep disturbances and emotional lability. Parents and teachers need to be aware of anticipated behavioral changes. These symptoms of hyperthyroidism may be present for several weeks until the child's system adjusts to a normal thyroid state.

Potential for Self-Care Deficit Related to Developmental Delays Secondary to Low Thyroid Levels during First 2 to 3 Years of Life

Because of the increased incidence of developmental delays associated with congenital hypothyroidism, periodic assessment of the child's development is important. Some experts recommend that children with congenital hypothyroidism have serial developmental testing until the child reaches school age (La Franchi 1982).

The Denver Development Screen Test (DDST), a standardized tool used to assess development in children from infancy through the preschool years, is one screening tool that can be used. Children with suspected delays should be referred to the primary health care provider or a developmental center for further evaluation. The home care nurse should assist the family in using developmentally appropriate play activities with the child.

ALTERATION IN CARBOHYDRATE METABOLISM: DIABETES MELLITUS

Diabetes mellitus is a syndrome of altered carbohydrate metabolism that results from an absolute or functional deficiency of insulin. The incidence of diabetes in childhood is 1:500, making it the most common childhood endocrine disorder (Sperling 1982).

There are two major classifications of diabetes mellitus: insulin-dependent diabetes mellitus (IDDM), or type I, and non–insulin-dependent diabetes mellitus (NIDDM), or type II. The type of IDDM most common in children, adolescents, and young adults results from an absolute deficiency of insulin due to destruction of the beta cells. An exogenous source of insulin is necessary for life. NIDDM occurs more frequently in obese adults over 40 years of age and results from insulin resistance or decreased tissue sensitivity to insulin. Treatment of NIDDM may or may not include insulin. Meal plans directed toward weight loss and oral hypoglycemic agents may also be used.

The classic symptomatology of diabetes in childhood is polydipsia, polyphagia, nocturia, and bedwetting in children who are toilet trained. Weight loss, lethargy, and candidal vaginitis may also be present. The plasma glucose concentration is elevated above 200 mg/dL (Drash 1986).

Insulin acts on target cells in tissues by binding to receptor sites located on the cell membrane, facilitating glucose uptake by the tissues.

Tissues that do not require insulin for glucose uptake are the brain, kidney tubules, red blood cells, and intestinal mucosa.

Deficiency of insulin leads to hyperglycemia with resultant glucosuria. Glucosuria occurs when the renal threshold of approximately 160 mg/dL is exceeded. Polyuria and an osmotic diuresis result in losses of sodium and potassium and in dehydration. Polydipsia occurs secondary to the dehydration and a hyperosmolar state. Intracellular glucose deficiency causes appetite increases. Weight loss occurs despite a normal or increased appetite.

Protein and fat stores are broken down to maintain energy supplies. Gluconeogenesis (glucose formed from protein) occurs, adding to the hyperglycemia, osmotic diuresis, and dehydration. Fat catabolism accelerates, with increased formation of ketone bodies. Accumulation of ketoacids leads to metabolic acidosis and compensatory rapid, deep (Kussmaul) breathing to "blow off" excess carbon dioxide. The characteristic fruity odor is due to these ketone bodies. Progressive dehydration, hyperosmolarity, and acidosis impair the level of consciousness and result in coma. The effect of insulin deficiency is shown in Figure 8-1.

Diabetic ketoacidosis (DKA) is defined as hyperglycemia (usually with a plasma glucose concentration above 200 mg/dL), glucosuria, ketonemia, ketonuria, and acidosis (pH below 7.30 and bicarbonate less than 15 mg/L) (Sperling 1982). Precipitating factors include emotional stress, trauma, and infections. Treatment is correction of the fluid and electrolyte imbalance, the acidosis, and hyperglycemia. One of the best treatments of diabetic ketoacidosis is

prevention through education of the child and family.

The diagnosis of IDDM is based on an elevated plasma glucose concentration, glucosuria, ketonuria, and history of polyuria and polydipsia. Oral glucose tolerance tests are rarely used in children. Because of increased public awareness, the diagnosis in children and adolescents occurs in many cases before the development of DKA.

The goal of the treatment plan for children is to achieve normoglycemia while avoiding severe hypoglycemia, maintenance of normal growth and development, and maintenance of the emotional well-being of the child and the family. The goals for each child and family are individualized. For example, the primary goal for a child with recurrent episodes of DKA may be to keep the child out of the hospital.

Preliminary evidence indicates that good metabolic control may prevent the development of complications and may reverse their early stages (Leslie and Sperling 1986). The complications associated with diabetes include retinopathy, cataracts, nephropathy, peripheral neuropathy, autonomic neuropathy, coronary artery disease, and peripheral vascular disease. Growth failure has also been documented in children with poorly controlled diabetes (Chase 1985). The complications usually appear following 10 to 15 years of established diabetes (Leslie and Sperling 1986).

Insulin Therapy

Multiple daily injections are usually required to achieve normoglycemia in children and ado-

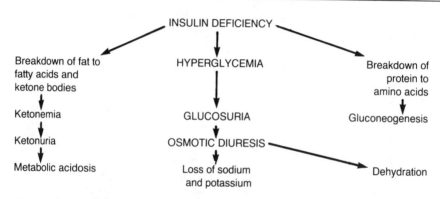

Figure 8-1 Effects of Insulin Deficiency

lescents. A common therapy regimen includes a combination of short- and intermediate-acting insulin given before breakfast and the evening meal. Regular and NPH insulin are commonly used. The commercially available types of insulin are listed in Table 8-5.

Insulin is identified not only by its action but also by its degree of purity. Purity refers to the parts per million of animal proinsulin (another pancreatic hormone). Human insulin is the purest, with pork insulin a close second. Beef/pork and beef mixtures are the least pure. Human insulin is recommended for children and adolescents because it decreases local skin reactions, the development of antibodies against insulin, and lipoatrophy.

Insulin is given subcutaneously using sites on the upper arms, thighs, buttocks, and abdomen. Insulin infusion pumps are available to provide a continuous basal infusion of regular insulin with bolus infusion before meals and snacks. A small needle is placed subcutaneously and is replaced every 48 hours. Infusion pumps have not been widely used in children because of increased risk of hypoglycemia, the need for frequent monitoring of blood glucose levels, and the need for frequent adjustment of the meal plan and insulin dosage. Devices are available for jet injection of insulin, in which insulin is forced through a fine nozzle at high pressure. These devices cost $650 to $1,000, which may be covered by insurance plans.

Nutrition Therapy

Nutrition is an important component of the treatment regimen. The goals of nutrition therapy are appropriate blood glucose and blood fat levels, reasonable weight, and good nutrition (American Diabetes Association 1987). These goals are achieved through eating well-balanced meals with foods from all the food groups; eliminating foods high in simple sugars, salt, and fat; maintaining consistency in the timing of the meals and snacks; and maintaining consistency in the amount of food eaten at each meal and snack. The current recommendations from the American Diabetes Association (1987) are as follows:

1. *Calories*: Calories should be prescribed to achieve a desirable body weight.

2. *Carbohydrates*: The amount of carbohydrates should ideally be 55 to 60 percent of the total calories. The use of complex carbohydrates and foods high in fiber is recommended.

3. *Protein*: The recommended dietary allowance for protein is 0.08 gm/kg of body weight.

4. *Total fat and cholesterol intake*: The total fat and cholesterol intake should be restricted, with the total fat intake less than 30 percent of the total calories and cholesterol intake less than 300 mg/day. Saturated fats should be replaced with unsaturated fats.

5. *Alternative sweeteners*: The use of sweeteners is acceptable.

6. *Salt intake*: The recommended sodium intake is 1,000 mg/100 kcal, not to exceed 3,000 mg/day.

The goals of nutrition therapy are achieved through the use of a meal plan individualized for the child and family. The meal plan provides a guide for food choices at meals and snacks. The types of meal planning used include the exchange meal plan, high carbohydrate–high fiber–low fat meal plan, constant carbohydrate meal plan, and the glycemic index meal plan. It is important that the family have in-depth understanding of the meal plan. The child and/or adolescent with diabetes should see a dietitian every 3 to 6 months so the meal plan can be evaluated and adjusted as the child grows (American Diabetes Association 1987).

In order to maintain appropriate blood glucose levels and prevent hyperglycemia, a pattern of three meals and three snacks is recommended. The timing of the snacks takes into account the peak action of the insulins and the periods of exercise. Insulin injections are given 30 minutes before the meal to prevent a postprandial rise in the blood glucose level.

Exercise

Exercise is another important component of diabetes management. Exercise not only affects blood glucose levels but also increases circulation, body stamina, and cardiac and pulmonary output and promotes a sense of well-being. Current data suggest that vigorous exercise should

Table 8-5 Commercially Available Insulin

Product	Manufacturer	Onset (Hours)	Peak (Hours)	Duration (Hours)	Strength	Form
Rapid Acting						
Humulin Regular	Lilly	½–1	2–4	5–7	U-100	Human
Novolin Regular	Squibb/Nova	½–1	2–4	5–7	U-100	Human
Velosulin Regular	Nordisk-USA	½–1	2–4	5–7	U-100	Human
Iletin II Regular	Lilly	½–1	2–4	6–8	U-100 U-500	Pork
Iletin II Regular	Lilly	½–1	2–4	6–8	U-100	Beef
Purified Pork R	Squibb/Novo	½–1	2–4	6–8	U-100	Pork
Velosulin Regular	Nordisk-USA	½–1	2–4	6–8	U-100	Pork
Iletin I Regular	Lilly	½–1	2–4	5–7	U-40 U-100	Beef/pork
Regular	Squibb/Novo	½–1	2–4	5–7	U-40 U-100	Pork
Purified Pork S (Semilente)	Squibb/Novo	1–2	2–4	12–16	U-100	Pork
Iletin Semilente	Lilly	1–2	4–6	12–16	U-40 U-100	Beef/pork
Semilente	Squibb/Novo	1–2	4–6	12–16	U-100	Beef
Intermediate Acting						
Humulin N (NPH)	Lilly	1–3	6–12	12–16	U-100	Human
Novolin N (NPH)	Squibb/Novo	1–3	6–12	12–16	U-100	Human
Insulatard	Nordisk-USA	1–3	6–12	12–16	U-100	Human
Iletin II NPH	Lilly	1–3	6–12	18–24	U-100	Beef/pork
Insulatard (NPH)	Nordisk-USA	1–3	6–12	18–24	U-100	Pork
Purified Pork (NPH)	Squibb/Novo	1–3	6–12	18–24	U-100	Pork
Iletin I (NPH)	Lilly	1–3	6–12	18–24	U-100	Beef
NPH	Squibb/Novo	1–3	6–12	18–24	U-40 U-100	Beef/pork
Humulin L (Lente)	Lilly	1–3	6–12	12–28	U-100	Human
Novolin L (Lente)	Squibb/Novo	1–3	6–12	12–28	U-100	Human
Iletin II (Lente)	Lilly	1–3	6–12	12–28	U-100	Pork/pork
Purified Pork Lente	Squibb/Novo	1–3	6–12	12–28	U-100	Pork
Iletin I Lente	Lilly	1–3	6–12	12–28	U-40 U-100	Beef/pork
Long Acting						
Iletin II PZI (Protamine Zinc and Iletin II)	Lilly	4–6	14–24	36	U-100	Pork/beef
Iletin I PZI	Lilly	4–6	14–24	36	U-40 U-100	Beef/pork
Purified Beef U (Ultralente)	Squibb/Novo	4–6	14–24	36	U-100	Beef
Iletin I (Ultralente)	Lilly	4–6	14–24	36	U-40 U-100	Beef/pork
Ultralente	Squibb/Novo	4–6	14–24	36	U-100	Beef
Humulin U (Ultralente)	Lilly	4–6	14–24	36	U-100	Human
Mixtures						
Mixtard (30% regular, 70% NPH)	Nordisk-USA	½–1		24	U-100	Pork
Novolin 70/30	Squibb/Novo	½–1		24	U-100	Human

be undertaken only when the blood glucose level is in the range of 100 to 200 mg/dL and no urinary ketones are present (American Diabetes Association 1987). If the pre-exercise blood glucose level is elevated, exercise may cause an increased blood glucose level and ketosis.

The major complication of exercise is hypoglycemia. One contributing factor to the hypoglycemia is the increased rate of absorption of insulin from the exercising limb. Injection of the pre-exercise insulin dose in a nonexercising area is recommended. Adjustment of insulin dose and the use of supplemental carbohydrate-containing snacks may also prevent exercise-induced hypoglycemia. Frequent monitoring of blood glucose levels should occur before, during, and after the exercise period to prevent hypoglycemia and to determine the efficiency of the insulin dose and the meal plan.

Monitoring

Self-monitoring of blood glucose has become a major adjunct to diabetes care in the past decade. In 1986, the Consensus Development Conference on Self-Monitoring of Blood Glucose ("Consensus Statement" 1987) recommended that blood glucose monitoring be used by all persons treated with insulin. The goal of normoglycemia cannot be achieved safely without self-monitoring. In children it is also necessary for the recognition and prevention of severe hypoglycemia and for decisions related to adjustment of the various components of the treatment plan.

Blood glucose monitoring is performed with a chemically impregnated strip that changes color when in contact with glucose. These reagent strips can be compared visually with a graded color chart or can be read by a meter. Blood glucose meters are recommended for those persons who are color blind or have difficulty with visual interpretation. The meters do provide a more objective method and cost approximately $150, which may be at least partially covered by most insurance plans. Devices that operate by a spring-loaded release of a lancet are available to obtain the blood sample. These devices reduce the pain and discomfort associated with the use of the traditional metal lancet. The blood testing products available are listed in Table 8-6.

Table 8-6 Blood Testing Products

Name (Distributor)	Test Strip Used
Blood Glucose Meters	
Accuchek I (Boehringer Mannheim)	Chemstrip bG
Accuchek II (Boehringer Mannheim)	Chemstrip bG II
Beta Scan B (Orange)	Trend Strips
Diascan (Home Diagnostics)	Diascan
Exac Tech (Baxter)	ExacTech Test Strips
Glucochek SC (Larkin)	Chemstrip bG
Glucometer I (AMES)	Dextrosticks
Glucometer II or Glucometer M (AMES)	Glucostix
Glucoscan 2000 or 3000 (Lifescan)	Glucoscan Test Strips
One Touch (Lifescan)	One Touch Test Strips
Tracer (Boehringer Mannheim)	Tracer Strips
Trends Meter (Orange)	Trend Strips
Test Strips for Visual Reading	
Chemstrip bG (Boehringer Mannheim)	
Dextrosticks (AMES)	
Glucostix (AMES)	
Trend Strips (Orange)	
Visidex II (AMES)	
Spring-Loaded Devices	
Autoclix (Boehringer Mannheim)	
Autolance (Becton Dickinson)	
Auto-lancet (Palco)	
Autolet (AMES or Ulster Scientific)	
Glucolet (AMES)	
Monojector (Sherwood Monoject)	
Penlet (Lifescan)	

Blood glucose monitoring usually occurs two to four times daily: before breakfast, lunch, evening meals, and/or bedtime snack. It is important that results are obtained at all four times during a week's time in order to determine if adjustment in insulin dose is warranted. Monitoring may also be performed at 2 to 3 AM to detect nighttime drops in blood glucose levels (Somogyi effect) or rises in blood glucose levels (dawn phenomenon).

Urine glucose testing, the traditional method of monitoring, does not accurately reflect the blood glucose level. Factors that influence the results include overall kidney function, volume of urine excreted, and medications such as ascorbic acid, penicillin, salicylates, cephalosporins, and chloralhydrate (Rotblatt and Koda-Kimble 1987). Hypoglycemia is difficult to detect when urine glucose testing is used.

Urine ketone testing is an essential part of monitoring to detect ketosis and prevent diabetic ketoacidosis. Ketone testing should be done when blood glucose levels are above 240 to 300 mg/dL and when the child is ill.

Nursing Care Plans in the Home

Potential for Knowledge Deficit Related to Initial Phase and In-depth Continuing Phase of Education

Knowledge assessment and education of the child and family are important components in caring for the diabetic child. The initial phase provides the child and family basic education and skills needed for coping and participating with diabetes management. The behavioral objectives for the initial stage developed by the American Diabetes Association are listed in Exhibit 8-2 (Franz et al. 1986). The continuing education phase provides the family with skills and knowledge needed to master self-sufficiency in daily management.

The goal is to assist the child and family with flexibility, insight, motivation, and skills needed to make life-style changes. This phase continues throughout the life of the person with diabetes (Exhibit 8-3). The child's participation in the education phases is essential. The education must be appropriate for the child's development level.

Assessment of the child and family's knowledge and beliefs about diabetes, social situation, life style, health beliefs, and readiness to learn must be completed before an educational plan can be developed. Individualization of the teaching plan based on the assessment is crucial for the success of diabetes education.

Initial Stage

Because children are diagnosed in the early stages of the disease, the setting for the initial phase can be the hospital, the outpatient area, or the home. The effectiveness of the education process may be diminished if sufficient time is not allowed for the child and family to work through the grief and turmoil experienced at diagnosis.

Play therapy using needle play is often helpful in assisting the child in adjusting to the treatment regimen. Children love to "poke" the fingers of others, especially the health care provider's. A reinforcement system using stickers and praise helps the child develop good "sitting still" behavior. For the older child the stickers may be cashed in for special treats or special time with family members. The key is to reinforce appropriate sitting still behavior while ignoring other behaviors. This system can also be used to encourage use of alternate injection sites.

Good technique is required to achieve accurate results in blood glucose monitoring. Directions for specific reagent strips and meters must be followed closely to ensure accurate results. Problems frequently arise in covering the reagent pad completely with blood. Too little blood leads to false low results. Washing the hands with warm soapy water, milking the finger, and poking the outer aspect of the finger are techniques that result in increased blood flow. Adequate handwashing cleanses the finger of substances such as fruit juices that may lead to false high results.

The risk of hypoglycemia increases when near normoglycemia is achieved. Severe hypoglycemia resulting in seizure or loss of consciousness must be avoided at all costs. The early recognition and prompt treatment of hypoglycemia is important. Older children and adolescents usually recognize the symptoms and take appropriate action. The typical symptoms include shakiness, dizziness, hunger, drowsiness, headache, sweating, and blurred vision. These symptoms are not expressed in young children. Symptoms in these children are paleness and sudden changes in behavior, such as irritability and lethargy.

If equipment is available, checking the blood glucose is important to confirm hypoglycemia prior to initiation of treatment. If equipment is unavailable, treatment should be initiated immediately to prevent development of severe hypoglycemia.

The treatment includes the use of a simple carbohydrate to cause a rapid rise in blood sugar and a protein snack to prevent recurrent hypoglycemia. The goal is to raise the blood glucose

Exhibit 8-2 Behavioral Objectives: Initial Education for Children with Type I Diabetes Mellitus and Their Families

Definition

- Define diabetes.
- Identify components of the treatment plan (meal plan, insulin therapy, and exercise).
- Explain the effect that a lack of insulin has on the body.
- Explain the difference between type I and type II diabetes.

Meal Plan

- Explain interrelationship between food, insulin, and exercise.
- State importance of good nutrition.
- Explain importance of meal plan in relationship to diabetes control.
- Identify types and amounts of food to be included in the meal plan.
- Explain modification of meal plan during sick days, party, travel, and eating out (especially dining in fast food restaurants).

Exercise

- Explain benefit of exercise.
- Explain the influence of exercise on blood glucose levels.
- Explain when exercise is not recommended.
- Describe need to test blood glucose before, during, and after changes in exercise.
- Explain foods (amount and type) to be used to prevent hypoglycemia associated with exercise.
- Explain need to inform appropriate person concerning the possibility of hypoglycemia with exercise along with its recognition and treatment.

Insulin Therapy

- Explain effect insulin has on blood glucose level.
- Explain type, species, concentration, and amount of insulin to be taken.
- Demonstrate ability to draw up amount of insulin using proper technique, including two types of insulin.
- Demonstrate ability to inject insulin using proper technique.
- Explain importance of rotating insulin injection sites and use of rotation schedule.
- Explain daily administration of insulin and times of injection.
- Explain schedule for giving insulin.
- Explain peak action, onset, and duration of insulin used.
- Inform patient and family where to purchase insulin and syringes.

Monitoring

- Explain benefit of self-monitoring of blood glucose.
- Demonstrate ability to perform self-monitoring of blood glucose.
- Demonstrate ability to document results of self-monitoring of blood glucose in record book.
- State schedule for self-monitoring of blood glucose.
- Explain when to contact health care provider: blood glucose levels consistently above and below guidelines.
- Explain honeymoon period and its effect on blood glucose and insulin dosages.
- Explain rationale for monitoring urine ketone levels.
- Demonstrate ability to perform urine ketone testing.
- Demonstrate ability to record results of urine ketone testing.
- Explain when to perform urine ketone testing.
- Explain when to contact health care provider: test is positive for ketones.
- Explain optimal blood glucose and urine ketone results in relationship to time of day and various situations.
- Explain rationale for urine glucose testing (if this method is used).
- Demonstrate ability to perform urine glucose testing (if this method is used).

continues

Exhibit 8-2 continued

- Demonstrate ability to record results of urine glucose testing (if this method is used).
- Explain when to contact health care provider: persistent glucosuria.

Acute Complications

- State possible symptoms of hypoglycemia and its treatment.
- Explain possible causes of hypoglycemia.
- Explain ways to prevent hypoglycemia.
- Explain how and when to use glucagon.
- Demonstrate ability to administer glucagon.
- Explain need to carry a form of simple sugar at all times.
- Describe possible symptoms of hyperglycemia.
- Explain causes of hyperglycemia and methods of prevention.
- Explain sick day rules and the need to continue insulin administration during illness.
- State when and how to contact health care provider in case of hypoglycemia, hyperglycemia, illness.
- Explain ketoacidosis, its causes and treatment.

Psychosocial Adjustment

- Parents verbalize that child has diabetes.
- Patient verbalizes that he or she has diabetes when developmentally appropriate.
- Patient verbalizes feelings about having diabetes and/or parents verbalize feelings about having a child with diabetes.
- Patient and family state that daily injections, meal planning, and exercise are the necessary treatment of diabetes.

Activities of Daily Living

- Explain how to fit routine into school setting and work.
- Explain importance of Medic Alert tag for a form of diabetic identification.

Health Habits

- Explain need for good personal hygiene, daily foot care, and daily dental care.

Community Resources

- List resources in community for diabetes support and education.

Use of Health Care System

- Describe when and how to obtain emergency care.
- State follow-up plans.

Source: Goals for Diabetes Education by M. Franz et al., pp. 7–9, American Diabetes Association, Inc., © 1986; ''Instruction Plan, Day 1—Day 7,'' Diabetic Home Care Program, Medical Personnel Pool, Inc., 1987.

level into the normal range without rebound hyperglycemia. The current recommendation for treatment in adults is the use of 20 g of carbohydrate (Brodows et al. 1984). Twenty grams of carbohydrate is equivalent to 13.3 fluid ounces of cola, 12 ounces of juice, or 4 glucose tablets. Ten to 15 g of carbohydrate generally is sufficient to treat hypoglycemia in children and young adolescents. A treatment plan of hypo-glycemia in children is presented in Table 8-7. The symptoms of hypoglycemia generally subside in 10 to 15 minutes after treatment has been initiated. The use of candy to treat hypoglycemia is not recommended in children because some children may be tempted to report false episodes in order to obtain candy.

As the blood glucose level drops to very low levels, the child may become combative and/or

Exhibit 8-3 Behavioral Objectives: In-Depth Continuing Education and Counseling for Children with Type I Diabetes Mellitus and Their Families

Definitions

- Explain the cause of type I diabetes mellitus.
- Explain the symptoms of poorly controlled diabetes.
- Explain how diabetes is diagnosed.
- Explain what is good diabetes control.
- Explain the benefit of good diabetes control.
- State behaviors necessary to achieve good diabetes control.
- Explain the effects of insulin deficiency.
- Explain the dawn phenomenon.
- Describe treatment of the dawn phenomenon.
- Explain the Somogyi effect.
- Describe how to prevent the Somogyi effect.
- Explain the effect of the counterregulatory hormones on blood glucose.
- Explain the honeymoon period and its effect on blood glucose.

Nutrition

- Plan appropriate meals from meal plan.
- Describe benefit of food in controlling blood glucose and lipids.
- Explain importance in maintaining consistency in caloric intake.
- State caloric level in percentage of fat, protein, and carbohydrates in meal plan.
- List nutrients in foods (carbohydrate [simple, complex, refined, fiber], fat, protein, vitamins, minerals, and water).
- Explain the function of these nutrients.
- Explain effects of these nutrients on blood glucose and lipid levels.
- List sources of fiber in meal plan.
- Explain differences between saturated and unsaturated fats.
- Explain benefit of reducing total fat, saturated fat, and cholesterol in meal plan.
- Explain benefit of reducing salt in meal plan.
- Explain how to modify meal plan in relation to changes in activity.
- Plan appropriate meals based on meal plan when eating out (especially with dining in fast food restaurants).
- Explain how to incorporate ''special treats'' in the meal plan.
- Demonstrate ability to evaluate food products from information on food labels.
- Identify those dietetic and low calorie foods that may be incorporated into meal plan.
- Explain how to incorporate dietetic and low calorie foods in meal plan.
- Explain how to incorporate sweetening agents in meal plan.
- Describe effect that alcohol has on blood glucose.
- Explain how to modify meal plan during illness.
- Explain when to adjust (increase/decrease) caloric intake.

Exercise

- State benefits of exercise.
- Explain benefits of exercise on blood glucose and lipid levels.
- Identify types of exercise that could be incorporated into diabetes treatment plan.
- Explain the relationship between exercise, injection sites used, and blood glucose level.
- Explain the effect that timing of exercise has on blood glucose level.
- Explain the relationship between exercise, timing of meals, and blood glucose level.
- Explain how to choose injection sites to prevent hypoglycemia during and after periods of exercise.
- Explain effect that exercise has when hyperglycemia and/or ketosis are present.

continues

Exhibit 8-3 continued

- Explain how to adjust meal plan to prevent hypoglycemia during and after exercise.
- Explain benefit of monitoring blood glucose level before, during, and after exercise.
- Explain benefit of carrying concentrated carbohydrate source during periods of exercise.
- State that strenuous exercise can affect blood glucose levels for up to 12 to 24 hours.
- Explain the benefit of exercising with a companion and wearing appropriate identification outlining emergency care.

Medication

- Describe sources of insulin (beef/pork, pork, human).
- Identify the different types of insulin.
- State the time of onset, peak, and duration of insulins used.
- Explain benefit of site rotation.
- Explain plan for site rotation.
- Define lipohypertrophy.
- Define lipoatrophy.
- Explain how to prevent lipohypertrophy and lipoatrophy.
- Explain when insulin dose should be adjusted.
- Explain how to adjust insulin dosage based on guidelines.
- Explain effect other medications have on blood glucose levels.
- Explain care and storage of insulin during travel.
- Explain when insulin dosage should not be adjusted.
- Explain the proper way to reuse insulin syringes as well as the benefits and risks.

Monitoring

- Explain how to adjust treatment plan (exercise, meal plan, insulin dose) based on results of blood glucose monitoring to achieve desired blood glucose levels.
- Identify factors that cause fluctuations in blood glucose levels.
- Explain benefit of glycosylated hemoglobin in maintaining diabetes control.
- Explain how to relate results of glycosylated hemoglobin to treatment plan.
- State when to notify health care provider.

Acute Complications

- State causes of hypoglycemia.
- Explain how to prevent hypoglycemia.
- Explain mechanism of ketone production.
- Explain causes of ketosis.
- Explain treatment of ketosis.
- Define diabetic ketoacidosis.
- Explain how to prevent diabetic ketoacidosis.
- Explain signs and symptoms of diabetic ketoacidosis.
- Explain effect stress (emotional and physical) has on diabetes control.
- State sick day roles: adjustment in meal plan, monitoring, and insulin dose.
- State need to take insulin during illness.
- State when to notify health care provider.

Psychosocial Adjustment

- Patient states concerns about having diabetes.
- Parents state concerns about having child with diabetes.
- Patient explains the effect that diabetes has had on life style.
- Patient and family state situations that cause stress.
- Patient and family state methods used to manage stress.

Exhibit 8-3 continued

Health Habits

- Explain proper care of skin.
- Explain proper care of feet and nails.
- Explain proper dental care.
- Explain when to communicate with health care provider.
- Explain deleterious effect of smoking.
- Explain deleterious effect of drug abuse (alcohol and illicit drugs).

Long-Term Complications

- Explain benefit of good diabetes control.
- Explain complications that can be associated with diabetes.
- State need for annual ophthalmological examination.
- State need for regular blood pressure monitoring.
- State when to notify health care provider.

Community Resources

- List community resources available to assist with special needs and concerns.
- Encourage visit to local American Diabetes Association chapter.

Use of the Health Care System

- State need for routine follow-up to health care provider.
- State need for periodic nutritional assessments.
- State need for continuous diabetic education.

Source: Goals for Diabetes Education by M. Franz et al., pp. 15–20, American Diabetes Association, Inc., © 1986.

semiconscious. Glucose paste or gel can be squeezed into the pouches of the cheek and rubbed into the gums to speed absorption into the mucous membranes. Glucagon is available to treat persons who have severe reactions. Glucagon is a hormone that when injected causes a rise in blood glucose by releasing glucose from glycogen stores in the liver. The usual dose is 0.5 to 1.0 mg subcutaneously or intramuscularly (Sperling 1982). Nausea and vomiting may occur after administration of glucagon owing to the rapid rise in the blood glucose level. All parents must be instructed in the use of glucagon.

Prevention is the best treatment for hypoglycemia. A program of prevention includes eating meals and snacks on time, following the meal plan, and eating an extra snack when extra exercise occurs. The rapid onset of hypoglycemia requires that parents, older children, and adolescents carry a readily available source of rapid-acting carbohydrate. Glucose tablets, gels,

and sugar packets are convenient items. The wearing of a Medic Alert tag is also essential.

It is important to elicit the support and cooperation of school personnel. The school nurse and teacher need information about the meal plan, the timing for the meals and snacks, the appropriate handling of special treats, the treatment of hypoglycemia, and the monitoring of blood glucose and urine ketone levels. The goal is to incorporate the diabetes treatment regimen into the school schedule so the child can participate in all activities. Attempts should be made to incorporate special treats into the child's regularly scheduled snacks. Some parents send a special treat such as diet soda or special cookies with the child on those days. Others allow the child to eat a small portion of the treat. If cake or cupcakes are the treat, the icing should be removed because it is very high in simple sugars.

The chronicity of diabetes and the ongoing nature of the education process make follow-up essential. Adjustments in the treatment regimen

Table 8-7 Signs and Symptoms and Appropriate Treatment of Hypoglycemia

Signs and Symptoms	Treatment
Mild:	
Hunger	4–6 ounces fruit juice
Dizziness	or
Shakiness	2–3 glucose tablets
Blurred vision	or
Drowsiness	½ can regular soda
Sweating	or
Headache	2 teaspoons sugar
Paleness	or
Irritability	2 teaspoons honey
	Followed with a protein snack
Moderate:	
Behavioral changes such as lethargy, irritability, and refusal to take juice, glucose tablets, or soda	½ tube Instaglucose
	or
	⅓ bottle Glucose
	or
	1 small tube cake icing
	Rub into gums and follow with a protein snack
Severe:	
Seizure	0.5–1.0 mg glucagon intramuscularly or subcutaneously
Loss of consciousness	
	Followed with a protein snack when child regains gag reflex

may be necessary as the child resumes a regular schedule of activities. Follow-up plans should include return visits to the physician, dietitian, and nurse.

Continuing Education Phase

Site rotation is an important component of insulin injection therapy. Injecting into the same area causes a build-up of fat that interferes with the absorption of the insulin. Sites used should be examined for signs of lipohypertrophy (lumps or thickening of the skin) and lipoatrophy (concave areas associated with the breakdown of fat). Repeated use of one area also decreases sensation in the area, unfortunately encouraging the overuse of an area because it "hurts less." A plan for site rotation must be incorporated in the schedule. The current recommendations are that all sites in one area be used before changing to another (Thatcher 1987). This pattern may improve consistency in insulin absorption. It has been found that insulin is absorbed at different rates from different regions: fastest from the abdomen, intermediate from the arm, and slowest from the thigh (Koivosto and Felig 1980).

Figure 8-2 is a guide for site rotation. Sites most frequently used by children are the arms, thighs, and buttocks. Buttocks are often the easiest sites to use in young children. Many children resist using the abdomen out of fear.

Periodic reassessment of monitoring technique is important. Problem areas frequently encountered include failure to obtain sufficient blood to cover reagent pad, inaccurate timing of the test, errors in removing the blood from the strip, and poor maintenance and care of the meter. Another problem frequently encountered is the fabrication of results. One study showed that 40 percent of the children listed fabricated results and 18 percent failed to record some test results (Wilson and Endres 1986). It may be that the children's desire to please the parents and health care providers contribute to this problem. Results in the desired range frequently elicit praise while results in the hyperglycemia range far too often elicit accusations of "cheating" on the meal plan.

Self-monitoring of blood glucose levels in and of itself will not affect diabetes control. The family and child must have knowledge of and guidelines for adjusting the treatment plan based on the results obtained. The guidelines for adjustment are individualized to reflect the insulin regimen used, the specific meal plan used, and the desired range of blood sugars to be achieved.

The development of diabetic ketoacidosis in children with IDDM is a continual concern. Proper education and medical supervision can help avoid this complication. The following general sick day rules must be followed to prevent the development of diabetic ketoacidosis:

1. Never omit insulin. The dosage may need to be adjusted depending on the blood glucose level, the presence of ketones, and the ability to follow the meal plan.
2. Monitor the blood glucose and urine ketone levels every 2 to 4 hours.
3. Follow the meal plan. If the child is vomiting or will not eat, provide foods high in carbohydrate, such as regular soda, Gatorade, regular Jello, and Popsicle.
4. Notify the physician when vomiting or ketones persist or early signs of diabetic ketoacidosis are present (abdominal pain, nausea, vomiting, Kussmaul breathing, change in level of consciousness).

Potential for Nonadherence as Related to Complexity of Treatment Plan

Ensuring that patient and families adhere to a specific treatment plan is a frequent problem for the health care provider. The following factors have been associated with a lower adherence rate: a behavioral restriction or life-style change, a lengthy duration of treatment, no immediate consequence from the nonadherence, and treatment behaviors required several times a day (Rapoff and Christophersen 1982). The demanding and complex diabetes treatment plan places the child and family at risk for adherence problems. One of the primary goals of home care is to promote adherence to the treatment plan.

The first step is to determine how fully the child and family are adhering to the treatment plan. Assessment tools include a self-report, observation of the child's and parent's behaviors as related to the treatment plan, and physical examination. To promote honesty in the self-report, health care providers should take a non-judgmental approach. Interviewing the child and

parent separately may also yield more accurate information since children may be more reluctant to share information in front of their parents. During the home visit, the nurse has an opportunity to observe the child and parents' technique in injections and monitoring. Education can occur on the elements of the procedure omitted or performed incorrectly. Review of the child's record book can give information on the frequency of monitoring and the handling of problems. Results written in the same ink and handwriting should make the nurse suspicious of falsified results. Lastly, examination of the injection sites can provide useful information on site rotation.

Several strategies can be used to promote adherence. One of the major causes of nonadherence is lack of understanding. Education should be selective, brief, and written. The child and parent should be involved in developing the treatment plan, and it should be tailored to the child and family's characteristics. This includes developing a schedule for injections and meals, creating a meal plan around the family's food preferences, and choosing an exercise program that the child enjoys. Strategies for behavioral change should be based on goals that are specific and easily attainable. For example, if the child is not monitoring the blood glucose level, one should lower the expectations and require the child to check the blood glucose level five times per week. Meaningful rewards can be given after each improvement. The reward must be individually tailored and may include praise, material objects, money, or special time with a family member. It is important to reward the testing and not the blood glucose results. A behavioral contract is another technique that can be used. Contracting is a written agreement between the child and family and another person that clearly and specifically states the behavior to be changed and the reward to be provided for the specifically desired behavior. For example, Susan will check her blood glucose level before breakfast each day, and in return her mother will pay her $5.00 at the end of each week.

For those children and families with complex emotional or behavioral problems, the health care provider should be notified. A referral should be made to a psychologist or therapist experienced in dealing with medical and behavioral problems.

Injection Log

This BODY MAP is designed to help you record your insulin injections. Write down the date that you start an area. Place an X in the space on the map to show which site you used. One suggested pattern for using the map is to rotate your injections in one area for one week or until you have used each site in the area once. This system will help you rotate insulin injection sites over the 12 body areas and avoid using any one area or site too often.

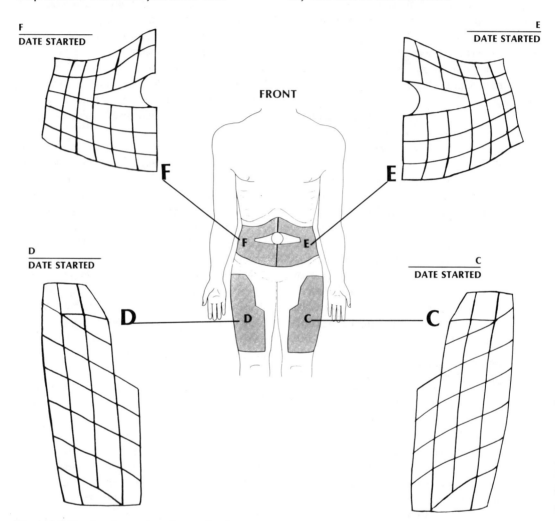

Figure 8-2 Plan for site rotation. *Source:* Reprinted from the GETTING STARTED "Site Selection" brochure with permission of Becton Dickinson Consumer Products, Becton Dickinson and Company, Franklin Lakes, New Jersey, © 1985.

Potential for Disturbances in Self-concept Related to Chronic Illness and Feeling Different from Peers

The young child is most concerned with the daily routine of injections and finger pokes. The child's cognitive development may result in the perception that the painful procedures are a result of his or her wrongdoing. The parent and nurse need to provide play activities to assist the child in working through these feelings and must also provide careful explanation directed toward the child's developmental level. Older children might have difficulty accepting why they must behave differently than their peers. They are constantly reminded of their chronic illness by the need to interrupt play for a snack, a premeal blood test, or an injection and by their require-

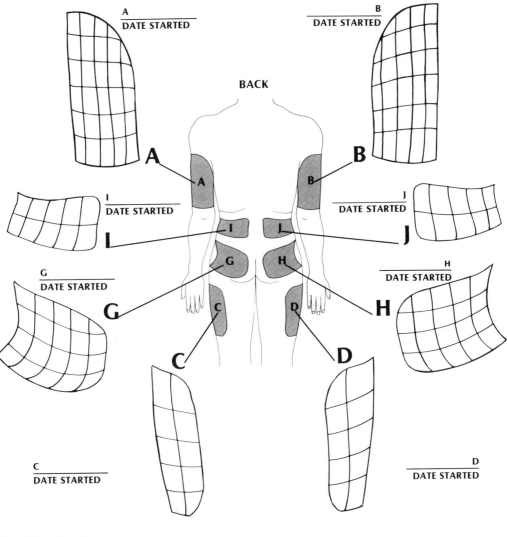

BACK

A
DATE STARTED

B
DATE STARTED

I
DATE STARTED

J
DATE STARTED

G
DATE STARTED

H
DATE STARTED

C
DATE STARTED

D
DATE STARTED

Figure 8-2 continued

ment to follow a schedule for meals and the need to eliminate high sugar foods (especially at parties). As the children become more independent, parents fear the child will inadvertently do something that will compromise the diabetes control. The adolescent is far more concerned about being different from peers. He or she is also trying to accomplish the developmental task of separating from the parents in the face of a potentially life-threatening disease. The diabetes treatment may be resisted by the adolescent as he or she searches for independence. Parents may have a difficult time encouraging independence especially when the teenager is not following the treatment plan.

In young and school-aged children, positive reinforcement for small goals accomplished will promote cooperation and interest in the treatment plan. The children's activities should not be restricted but should be encouraged. Expectations regarding their participation in the diabetes treatment plan must be realistic. School-aged children cannot be expected to assume complete control of their diabetes regimen. It is a shared responsibility with the parents. They need supervision and guidance. Since the treatment plan becomes tedious over time, children should be allowed ''vacations'' in which the parents resume some aspects of the care. Guidelines for self-care management are outlined in Table 8-8.

Table 8-8 Guidelines for Self-care Management of Diabetes

Age (Years)	Diet	Insulin	Testing
4–5	Helps pick foods based on likes and dislikes	Helps pick injection sites; pinches up skin; wipes skin	Collects blood or urine; watches parent do testing; colors test results on records
6–7	Can tell if food has no sugar, some sugar, or lots of sugar	Pushes plunger in after parent gives shot	Performs blood or urine test; records results; may need reminding; will need supervision
8–9	Selects foods based on exchanges	Gives own shot (at least one/day)	Does own blood test
10–13	Knows meal plan	Rotates sites; measures insulin	Looks for patterns in test results
14 +	Plans meals and snacks	Mixes two insulins in one syringe (if needed)	Suggests insulin changes based on test patterns

Source: Reprinted from GETTING STARTED "My Child Has Diabetes: A Book of Questions and Feelings for Parents" brochure with permission of Becton Dickinson Consumer Products, Becton Dickinson and Company, Franklin Lakes, New Jersey, © 1985.

One of the common causes of poorly controlled diabetes in adolescents is the adolescent's inability to assume full responsibility for all aspects of the treatment plan. Parents must be available to assist with problem solving and decision making. Education must accompany the gradual transfer of responsibility.

Recurrent episodes of diabetic ketoacidosis are life threatening. Most cases are associated with poor psychosocial adjustments and emotional stress (White et al. 1984). In some children, ketoacidosis may result from missed injections. Parents and health care providers should be alert to this possibility if the child is giving injections behind a locked door and statements are made indicating that the child hates the injections. In some of these cases, having the parent give or supervise the injections has reduced the ketoacidosis episodes. Children experiencing recurrent episodes of ketoacidosis may benefit from psychosocial intervention.

Support groups can be important resources for the child, the siblings, and the parents. It is an opportunity to share fears and concerns as well as to identify possible solutions. The local offices of the American Diabetes Association or Juvenile Diabetes Foundation may have a listing of support groups. Diabetes camps are another excellent source of support for children. In camp, new skills are attempted and learned in an atmosphere of support and acceptance. Physical activity, fun, and peer support are encouraged. Many camps are sponsored by the American Diabetes Association.

REFERENCES

American Diabetes Association. "Nutritional Recommendations and Principles for Individuals with Diabetes Mellitus." *Diabetes Care* 10 (1987):126–132.

Anthony, C.P., and Thibodeau, G.A. *Textbook of Anatomy and Physiology.* 11th ed. St. Louis: C.V. Mosby Co., 1983.

Brodows, R.G.; Williams, C.; Amatreeda, J.M. "Treatment of Insulin Reactions in Diabetics." *Journal of the American Medical Association* 252 (1984):3378–3381.

Chase, H.P. "Avoiding the Short- and Long-Term Complications of Juvenile Diabetes." *Pediatrics in Review* 2 (1985):140–149.

"Consensus Statement on Self-Monitoring of Blood Glucose." *Diabetes Care* 10 (1987):95–99.

Drash, A.L. "Diabetic Mellitus in the Child and Adolescent: I." *Current Problems in Pediatrics* 16 (1986):413–466.

Franz, M.; Krosnick, A.; Maschak-Carey, B.J.; Parker, T.; and Wheeler F. *Goals for Diabetes Education.* New York: American Diabetes Association, 1986.

Koivosto, V.A., and Felig, P. "Alterations in Insulin Absorption and in Blood Glucose Control Associated with Varying Insulin Injection Sites in Diabetic Patients." *Annuals of Internal Medicine* 92 (1980):59–61.

La Franchi, S. "Hypothyroidism: Congenital and Acquired." In *Clinical Pediatric and Adolescent Endocrinology,* edited by S.A. Kaplan. Philadelphia: W.B. Saunders Co., 1982.

Leslie, N.D., and Sperling, M.A. "Relation of Metabolic Control to Complications in Diabetes Mellitus." *Journal of Pediatrics* 108 (1986):491–497.

Migeon, C.I., and Lanes, R. "Adrenal Cortex: Hypo- and Hyper-function." In *Pediatric Endocrinology,* edited by P. Lifshitz. New York: Marcel Dekker, Inc., 1985.

New, Mi; Pang, S.; and Levine, L.S. An Update of Congenital Adrenal Hyperplasia." In *Pediatric Endo-*

crinology, edited by P. Lifshitz. New York: Marcel Dekker, Inc., 1985.

Rapoff, M.A., and Christophersen, E.R. "Compliance of Pediatric Patients with Medical Regimens. In *Adherence, Compliance and Generalization in Behavioral Medicine*, edited by R.B. Stuart. New York: Brunner/Mazel, Inc., 1982.

Rotblatt, M.D., and Koda-Kimble, M.A. "Review of Drug Interference with Urine Glucose." *Diabetes Care* 10 (1987):103–110.

Sperling, M.A. "Diabetes Mellitus." In *Clinical Pediatric and Adolescent Endocrinology*, edited by S.A. Kaplan. Philadelphia: W.B. Saunders Co., 1982.

Thatcher, C. "An Update on Insulin Site Rotation." *Diabetes Self-Management*, 1987, pp. 26–27.

White, K.; Kolman, M.D.; Wexler. P.; Polin, G.; and Winter, R.J. "Unstable Diabetes and Unstable Families: A Psychosocial Evaluation of Diabetic Children with Recurrent Ketoacidosis." *Pediatrics* 731 (1984): 749–750.

Wilson, D.P., and Endres, R.K. "Compliance with Blood Glucose Monitoring in Children with Type I Diabetes Mellitus." *Journal of Pediatrics* 108 (1986):1022–1024.

Chapter 9

Alterations in Renal Function

Lynn R. Anderson

Renal failure can be acute or chronic and affects all age groups. Acute renal failure is a sudden and severe impairment of kidney function over a short period of time (Brundage 1980). Chronic renal failure is a slow, degenerative disease that affects the kidneys over a much longer period of time. The life expectancy for children with these diseases has greatly improved over the past 2 decades owing to medications, diet, and dialysis. Therefore, referral for home care services is often indicated to enhance the health and functioning of these children. In this chapter the features of chronic and acute renal failure are discussed, a home dialysis program is presented as an alternative to hospital care, and nursing concerns in the home are identified.

ACUTE RENAL FAILURE

Acute renal failure can often be reversed through medical or surgical treatment. It is caused by impairment of renal perfusion (prerenal), diseases of the renal parenchyma (renal), and/or obstruction to urine outflow (postrenal). Prerenal causes can be circulatory collapse, as in hemorrhaging or anaphylactic shock, or from prolonged vomiting or diarrhea. Renal causes include acute infections such as acute glomerulonephritis, vascular disorders, and nephrotoxicity. Postrenal problems are related to blood clots, an enlarged prostate, or tumors.

Diagnosis of acute renal failure is relatively certain due to well-defined symptoms. The kidneys abruptly cease to function, as opposed to chronic renal failure in which kidney function slowly degrades. The body cannot adapt to the abrupt onset. This causes the patient to present with acute manifestations of renal failure in a short period of time. Uremic symptoms can occur within 72 hours. The symptoms the child presents with can affect every system of the body and include acidosis, pulmonary edema, hypertension, decreased urinary output, anorexia and vomiting, mental aberration, rashes and itchiness, anemia, elevated white blood cell count and elevated potassium, urea, and creatinine levels (Brundage 1980).

The prognosis of acute renal failure varies with the cause and severity of the disease. Adequate and prompt treatment greatly improves the survival rate. The outcome, however, for reversible acute renal failure is unpredictable. Most children with acute renal failure remain in the hospital until proper kidney function returns.

CHRONIC RENAL FAILURE

Chronic renal failure is often characterized by progressive irreversible damage to both of the kidneys over an extended period, and it becomes apparent when kidney function can no longer meet the demands of the body (Brundage 1980). Blood urea nitrogen (BUN) accumulates in the bloodstream, hypertension develops, red blood cell production decreases, electrolyte values are elevated, and urinary output begins to diminish. Symptoms often will not appear until kidney function is reduced to 10 percent of normal.

Many diseases or anomalies can result in chronic renal failure. Renal disease can develop from idiopathic nephrotic syndrome, diabetic nephropathy, polycystic kidney disease, medullary cystic disease, glomerulonephritis, and drug-induced disorders. The clinical picture and treatment of these diseases are often similar.

There are a few classic symptoms of chronic renal failure. Renal failure often presents as polyuria and an inability to concentrate the urine. Eventually oliguria and anuria develop and the kidneys may become enlarged, contracted, or irregularly shaped. The major symptoms are hypertension due to fluid overload and renin production. BUN and creatinine levels increase because the kidneys can no longer effectively filter waste products. Serum potassium levels may increase because of oliguria. Anemia may develop due to decreased renal production of erythropoietin.

Treatment of Chronic Renal Failure

Nutrition and Medication

Controlled diet and good nutrition are extremely important in treating children with chronic renal failure. A proper diet is based on basic nutrition. Proteins, carbohydrates, fats, vitamins, and minerals are important in developing and maintaining a healthy body. Using these building blocks is highly important in controlling end-stage renal disease.

Medications are required to enhance the functions of the failing kidneys. Vitamins, calcium supplements, antacids, iron, and antihypertensive medications are important in controlling the major kidney functions. The common medications used to treat children with chronic renal failure and the purpose for each medication are listed in Table 9-1.

Continuous Ambulatory Peritoneal Dialysis

When medications and diet can no longer control the severity of chronic renal failure, the disease is often treated with continuous ambulatory dialysis (CAPD). This relatively safe procedure alters abnormalities of blood composition resulting from renal failure (Brundage 1980). CAPD enables the exchange of waste products almost as effectively as hemodialysis by controlling the levels of creatinine and urea in the blood. It also corrects fluid and electrolyte imbalance.

CAPD is an acceptable form of treatment for both acute and chronic renal failure. It is generally used in cases of chronic renal failure to allow the child to return home and undergo dialysis away from the hospital environment.

The advantages of peritoneal dialysis over hemodialysis are that it is safer, easier to assemble, less likely to cause fluid and electrolyte imbalance, and less confining to the child and requires no heparinization (Brundage 1980). The major disadvantages are higher protein losses and peritonitis.

CAPD exchanges fresh dialysate fluid through a small tube (Tenckoff catheter) that is surgically inserted into the peritoneal cavity. Normally four exchanges are performed each day. Dialysate fluid is drained from the peritoneal cavity and replaced with fresh dialysate fluid every 4 hours during the day. The fourth exchange is left in the peritoneal cavity overnight.

Dialysate is administered in either 0.5-L or 1-L bags. The bags are connected under sterile conditions to tubing connected to the Tenckoff catheter. The dialysate is then drained into the child's abdomen and left for the next 4 hours. The empty bag connected to the tubing is rolled up and hidden under the child's clothing. At the completion of the four hour dwell, the bag is unrolled and placed on the floor so the dialysate can drain into the bag. When the dialysate bag is full, the bag is disconnected and discarded. A fresh dialysate bag is then attached. This procedure generally takes 20 to 30 minutes.

The tubing connected to the Tenckoff catheter is generally changed every 6 weeks. The catheter can remain in the peritoneal cavity for 2 to 3 years if no complications occur. Instructions on performing CAPD are given in Exhibit 9-1.

Peritoneal dialysis is based on diffusion, osmosis, and filtration. The solution used to dialyze is a glucose concentration called dialysate. The peritoneal cavity is used as a type of semipermeable membrane. Metabolic waste

Table 9-1 Medications used in Treatment of Chronic Renal Failure

Drug or Nutritional Supplement	Function
Vitamin D (Rocaltrol), 0.25–0.5 µg/day	Permits calcium absorption from the intestine.
Multivitamin supplement	Dialysis removes all the water-soluble vitamins including vitamin C and the entire B complex group. Vitamin C promotes the health of mucous membranes that provide protection against infection. Vitamin C assists in tissue repair. Vitamin B maintains optimum cellular metabolism.
Calcium carbonate	Required when calcium intake is less than recommended. Primarily used as a phosphate binder; at the same time provides supplemental calcium.
Iron	Sometimes needed due to anemia.
Antacids	Help maintain a proper level of phosphorus. Antacids containing magnesium (e.g., Maalox®, Mylanta®) should not be used routinely. Bind phosphorus in the intestine, which is then excreted in the stool. If the phosphorus level is too high, calcium will not be absorbed.
Laxatives and stool softeners	Patients with renal disease taking antacids often have constipation. However, many laxatives contain magnesium, which does not dialyze out. Follow a physician's recommendations.
Androgens	Help treat anemia associated with dialysis by stimulating the production of erythropoietin, which stimulates the production of red blood cells.
Antihypertensive agents	Decrease blood pressure and will need periodic readjustment according to dietary intake and dialysis.

Source: Reprinted with permission from the *Home Care Training Manual* by the University of Virginia Medical Center Pediatric Renal Department.

---

products are exchanged intravascularly into the peritoneal cavity and drained out of the body in the dialysate solution (Brundage 1980).

Three types of dialysate solution are available for peritoneal dialysis. There are 1.5, 2.5, and 4.25 percent dialysate solutions. The higher the percentage of dialysate, the greater the oncotic force. Higher percentages increase the amount of fluids and waste products that leave the intravascular area and pass into the peritoneal cavity. Therefore, monitoring the child's weight is very important in determining the type of dialysate to be used. Each child should be given a target weight. Maintaining target weight is important in controlling the child's blood pressure and fluid and electrolyte balance. Dialysate containing 1.5 percent solution should be used when the child is at or below the target weight. Dialysate containing 2.5 percent solution should be used with slight weight increases of 2 to 3 pounds. Children with significant weight gains should use 4.25 percent solution. Parameters should be

given to the child and parents on discharge from the hospital.

Tenckoff catheter care is important for children on CAPD. The Tenckoff catheter is the tube that is sutured into the child's abdomen and used to administer dialysis. Most institutions require a sterile dressing over the insertion site. This helps to prevent contamination of the site. This dressing should be changed every day and/or if it becomes dirty or wet. It is a protective device against infection, and keeping the area clean is critical. Instructions on catheter dressing change are presented in Exhibit 9-2.

The major complications of CAPD are peritonitis, leakage of fluid from the Tenckoff catheter site, hypervolemia, hypovolemia, atelectasis, and pneumonia (Brundage 1980). The general signs and symptoms of peritonitis are cloudy dialysate, fever, and abdominal discomfort. This is generally associated with poor sterile technique. Children are generally expected to have peritonitis one to two times per

Exhibit 9-1 CAPD Bag Exchange

Purpose: To remove waste products and correct fluid and electrolyte balance through peritoneal dialysis on a continual basis.

Supplies:

IV pole
CAPD Prep Model 7
Dialysate bag (heated to body temperature only with a heating pad)
Outlet port clamps
Additional masks
Blue pad (absorbant pad with a plastic lining)
Alcohol
Medication supplies as required

Special Instructions: The area used for a bag exchange needs to be protected from any contaminates or drafts of air. Anyone within 10 feet of the exchange should wear a mask.

Steps:

1. Clean off tabletop with alcohol.
2. Gather supplies.
3. Put on mask.
4. Wash hands well.
5. Remove bag and tubing from clothing and place bag on blue pad on floor or on IV pole drainage rack; open roller clamp to begin drain.
6. Prepare new bag during the draining phase:
   a. Remove bag from overwrap and dry off excess moisture.
   b. Check the following five items:
      1) Concentration
      2) Size
      3) Expiration date
      4) Leaks (discard bag if present)
      5) Secure covering over medication and outlet ports (discard bag if not secure)
   c. Add medications if required (see procedure for adding medications).
   d. Position outlet port clamp at the "step" of the administration port. Close clamp.
7. Once drainage has stopped, close roller clamp. Place drainage bag on table to the left of the new bag (reverse position if left handed).
8. Position outlet port clamp on drainage bag at the step of the administration port.
9. Open new povidone-iodine connection shield package.
10. Remove connection shield from drainage bag. Be careful not to touch and contaminate the bag/spike connection.
11. Remove covering from the administration port of new bag.
12. Slowly and carefully remove spike from drainage bag and insert into new bag.*
13. Place new connection shield on bag/spike connection.
14. Hang bag in infusion position. Tap bag so that air will rise to top.
15. Open roller clamp to initiate infusion. Adjust flow to comfort.
16. Close roller clamp when infusion is complete. Leave a few milliliters of liquid in the bag to facilitate folding.
17. Fold bag so that the spike and bag connection is on the inside. Secure the bag in a manner that provides support and prevents catheter movement.
18. Documentation: chart vital signs, weight (as filled weight), drainage appearance and solutions instilled on CAPD flow sheet.
19. To discard drainage: hold bag up and remove clamp and allow fluid to drain into toilet (cutting the administration port off speeds up the process).

*If during the insertion of the spike to the bag for connection the spike touches anything except the inside of the bag opening, it is to be considered contaminated.

You must do the following:

a. Make sure the roller clamp is closed *completely*.
b. Clamp with a Kelly (rubber shod) clamp or tie two knots in the tubing if a Kelly clamp is not available.
c. Call renal unit or person on call to come in for tubing change.

Warm new bag in heating pad in preparation for next exchange.

Source: Reprinted with permission from the University of Virginia Medical Center Pediatric Renal Department.

Exhibit 9-2 Tenckoff Catheter Dressing Change and Exit Site Care

Purpose: To clean the catheter and examine the exit site to make sure the skin is not infected.

Supplies:

Alcohol
Hydrogen peroxide
Four sterile 4 × 4-inch gauze sponges
Cotton-tipped swabs
Povidone-iodine swabsticks
Paper tape (1-inch width)
Two sterile 2 × 2-inch gauze sponges
Air strip

Steps:

1. Clean work area with alcohol.
2. Gather supplies.
3. Wash hands.
4. Open all sterile packages. Pour hydrogen peroxide solution over one opened package of sterile 4 × 4-inch gauze sponges.
5. Remove old catheter dressing, being careful not to pull on catheter.
6. Check exit site around catheter for signs of infection, such as redness, tenderness, or drainage.
7. Saturate cotton-tipped swabs with hydrogen peroxide and clean around catheter exit site, moving in a circular motion; if crust is present, gently clean area, being careful not to force crust off, which may cause bleeding.
8. Rinse area around catheter exit site with hydrogen peroxide–soaked gauze sponge. Hold gauze sponge only by its four corners. Clean an area 3 inches from the exit site. Always clean from catheter out, and never return to cleaned area with the same gauze sponge.
9. Repeat step No. 8 with second hydrogen peroxide–soaked gauze sponge.
10. Dry entire exit site area completely with second opened package of 4 × 4-inch gauze sponges, using the four-corner technique.
11. Clean area around the catheter exit site with a povidone-iodine swabstick. Work in a circular motion, from exit site outward.
12. Repeat step No. 11 two more times.
13. Let povidone-iodine dry on area around catheter exit site.
14. Make a loop with the catheter and tape it with 1-inch paper tape, bridging tape for safety. Place a 2 × 2-inch gauze sponge under the titanium adaptor to protect the skin.
15. Apply air strip (similar to a large Band-Aid) over the exit site.
16. If not using the air strip, be sure dressing is covered with a sterile 4 × 4-inch gauze pad and taped securely. However, leave some gauze exposed to allow the skin to breathe.

This procedure should be done daily or every other day.

Source: Reprinted with permission from the University of Virginia Medical Center Pediatric Renal Department.

year owing to the high number of tube disconnects and reconnections. However, peritonitis is not life threatening if it is caught at an early stage. Awareness of the signs and symptoms of peritonitis and maintaining accurate records of vital signs aid early detection. Fever, abdominal pain, redness around the Tenckoff catheter site, and cloudy dialysate are the classic signs of infection.

The treatment for peritonitis is antibiotics and heparin, which are usually administered with dialysate. The medications generally are in vials and are inserted into the dialysate bag under sterile conditions with a needle. The procedure for adding medications to the dialysate bag is outlined in Exhibit 9-3. The antibiotic chosen will depend on the infection.

The child usually remains on antibiotic therapy for 10 to 14 days. It is important to continue to record vital signs and the color of the dialysate (Exhibit 9-4). In addition to monitoring the dialysate color, it is important to examine the dialysate for small fibrin clots, which may clot off the tubing and are a sign of possible infection. These clots are pieces of irritated tissue that have broken down from the infection. Elimination of fibrin clots is easily accomplished by adding heparin to the fresh dialysate before each

Exhibit 9-3 Addition of Medication to CAPD Bags

Supplies:

Mask
Medication vial
Povidone-iodine swabs
Povidone-iodine
2×2-inch gauze pad
Syringe with needle
Extra 23-gauge $\times$ 1-inch needle

Steps:

1. Put on mask.
2. Wash hands.
3. Read medication vial carefully to check if medication is correct, if medication has not expired, and if reconstitution is suggested on the vial.
4. Prepare medication vial and medication port of bag as follows:
   a. Scrub vial and bag's medication port for 1 minute with povidone-iodine swabs.
   b. Drop a drop of povidone-iodine solution on vial and medication port and allow it to stay there for 5 minutes.
   c. At the end of 5 minutes blot off excess povidone-iodine with a sterile gauze pad.
   d. Draw up medication from vial.
   e. Insert medication carefully into the medication port of bag.
   f. Mix solution.

Source: Reprinted with permission from the University of Virginia Medical Center Pediatric Renal Department.

Exhibit 9-4 Record Sheet for Home Dialysis

Date/ Time	Vital signs twice a day	Weight	Dialysate IN OUT	% Used	Color

Source: Adapted from the Record Sheet for Home Dialysis with permission from the University of Virginia Medical Center Pediatric Renal Department.

pass. Each liter of dialysate usually has 250 units of heparin added.

Continuous Cyclic Peritoneal Dialysis

Continuous cyclic peritoneal dialysis (CCPD) is a form of peritoneal dialysis that uses a cycler machine for dialyzing. The machine is small enough to be used in the home and can be used for dialysis of the child while he or she sleeps. The child's tubing is connected to the dialysate bags on the machine. The machine switches the bags to allow the child's peritoneal cavity to drain and infuse dialysate without waking during the night. Five to six cycles are performed during the night, and in the morning the child is disconnected from the machine and is free from dialysis until the following evening. The child must undergo dialysis for at least 10 hours for the dialysis to be effective. The final exchange is left in the abdomen for a prolonged dwell during the day. Opening and closing the catheter twice in 24 hours reduces the potential for peritonitis and reduces the involvement of the child and family with the dialysis (Brem and Toscano 1984).

Families have found the cycler to be an ideal solution for a number of reasons. It is less complicated, set up is easy and efficient, the machine is small and easy to handle, and the instillation of fluid is by gravity while the child sleeps (Fieldon and Johnson 1981). The cost of the cycler has in the past deterred patients from use of the machine but is now comparable to CAPD.

The decision to use CCPD or CAPD is generally left to the child and family. Some families prefer to use CCPD to allow the child to live "normally" during the day. Others have found CCPD confining and would rather continue with CAPD. Each family and each situation is different. However, there do not seem to be any major medical differences between the two methods (Fine et al. 1985).

Both CAPD and CCPD provide adequate treatment for children unable to undergo transplantation and as a method of maintenance until transplantation is performed. Both types of dialysis are more acceptable than hemodialysis. They can easily be interchanged and adapted into the child and family's life style. Many families prefer CCPD when staying at home and CAPD for vacations, when transporting the machine could become burdensome. Fluid and dietary restrictions are minimized when using CAPD or CCPD, and both methods free the child from the hemodialysis machine (Wilson et al. 1983).

Hemodialysis

Hemodialysis is another method of treatment for pediatric renal patients. It requires certified trained professionals. Few children undergo hemodialysis in the home because of this requirement for expertise. Therefore, the major focus of this section is concentrated on the basic mechanisms of hemodialysis and on fistula care.

Hemodialysis uses a machine that has a blood compartment and a dialysate compartment that are separated by semipermeable membrane. This membrane allows water and solutes to move to and from the blood. The blood first enters the system from an arteriovenous fistula or cannula. It then moves through a compartment walled by a semipermeable membrane. Dialyzed fluid surrounds this compartment, permitting water, electrolytes and nitrogenous wastes to pass freely across the membrane by diffusion, osmosis, and ultrafiltration.

The patient's blood enters the hemodialysis machine through an internal or external cannula or fistula. Cannulas are surgically inserted under local or regional block anesthesia. They are usually placed in the inner surface of the forearm 1 to 2 inches above the wrist. The surgeon avoids joints and uses more distal arteries to prevent interference with circulation (Gutch and Stoner 1983). Most patients have internal cannulas, because they are more aesthetically pleasing and decrease the risk of infection.

The major problems with external shunts are the risk of infection and the risk of tubing separation causing bleeding from the artery. Shunts also cause erosion on the skin and infection at the site (Gutch and Stoner 1983). Therefore, it is important to assess them appropriately throughout the day. Assessment for adequate blood flow is accomplished by auscultating over the blood vessel near the venous cannula tip for a buzzing sensation. This technique for ensuring proper cannula function should be taught to the patient prior to discharge.

The internal cannula has largely replaced the external cannula. Its location under the skin reduces complications resulting from infection and clotting. Cannula access is accomplished by inserting a needle through the skin for each dialysis procedure. The skin gradually becomes less sensitive with each dialysis. Pressure must be applied to the site for 20 to 30 minutes after the needle is removed.

The most important areas to stress for the pediatric patient requiring hemodialysis are diet, medication administration, and cannula care. Hemodialysis is only performed three times per week. Therefore, it is particularly important to limit the child's intake of protein, sodium, fluids, phosphorous, and potassium. Excessive accumulation of any one of these substances can be fatal. Medications are just as important as they are for children on peritoneal dialysis and should be monitored appropriately.

Renal Transplantation

Renal transplantation has become an accepted therapeutic procedure for patients with chronic renal failure. Children faced with death are able to regain a healthy, active life style after receiving a kidney from a cadaver or a living relative. Kidney transplantation frees the child from dialysis and enables him or her to live a "normal" life.

After the kidney has been surgically implanted, the recovery period begins. The child may require dialysis for a short period of time until the kidney is functioning properly. Some children remain in the hospital for weeks or months. The length of stay depends on reaction to medications, stability of blood pressure, signs of rejection, and reliability of the family in caring for the child.

The child who receives a kidney may face significant problems following the transplant. Teaching, both before and after discharge, will help solve those problems. Instruction on diet, medications, signs and symptoms of infection and rejection, health habits, and continuing medical supervision are all extremely important (Brundage 1980). Some of the important signs of infection are fever, flank pain, and fatigue. Signs of rejection are hypertension, decreased urinary output, lethargy, and fluid retention.

Prior to discharge, the child should be instructed on maintaining good hygiene and skin care to decrease bacterial growth. Routine eye, dental, and physical examinations are also highly stressed. The eyes should be closely monitored because they are affected by hypertension, uremia, and calcium in the bloodstream. The teeth are affected by the lack of calcium absorp-tion in the body. This causes dental problems in children with renal disease.

Children with kidney transplants must monitor their physicial activity level. Some physicians prefer the child to avoid contact sports for the first year in order to avoid any trauma to the kidney. However, protective supports are now available for children who want to participate in contact sports.

The child discharged with a functional kidney must be closely monitored for transplant rejection and for compliance with diet, medications, weight, vital signs, and activity level. These children are required to take azathioprine, prednisone, or cyclosporine to help the body accept the kidney. These drugs control the body's immune system. It is important, therefore, that these children avoid communicable diseases if possible.

The major fear after transplantation is rejection, which can occur weeks, months, or years after the procedure. The emotions associated with receiving a new kidney can be overwhelming for the child and family. They often forget the child's health is tenuous and must be monitored closely. The home care nurse must stress the importance of the child's medications, weight control, vital signs, and signs and symptoms of hypertension. Hypertension, decreased urinary output, nausea, and lethargy are indicators of kidney failure. Monitoring these signs closely can save a kidney from being rejected.

DISCHARGE PLANNING

The diagnosis of specific renal disorders can occur at any time and will usually indicate major physiological and psychological problems for the child and require some adjustment by each family member. Effective discharge planning should be based primarily on the child's prognosis and the treatment. The plan can be tailored to meet specific family needs.

The discharge training process will vary from hospital to hospital. The child's length of stay in the hospital, the number of days needed for training, and the teaching tools used for instructing the families will all affect the process. Most institutions, however, will use the same basic structure and will normally teach both CAPD and CCPD to provide families with a choice.

Teaching begins with basic instructions on handwashing, infection control, renal anatomy and physiology, and the general principles of peritoneal dialysis (Fieldon and Johnson 1981). Vital signs, diet, medications, catheter care, and weight assessment are all taught before beginning hands-on teaching (Fieldon and Johnson 1981).

Parents are generally taught how to perform dialysis in the clinic or hospital, and children learn as they gain greater knowledge at home. The child should be at least 10 years old to assume self-care. Children younger than age 10 need assistance in sterile technique, and some children older than age 10 may need supervision. The earlier the child can assume his or her own care, the easier it is for the family. The home care nurse should participate in teaching the child self-care.

The teaching program in the hospital normally requires about 2 weeks to teach both CAPD and CCPD. The child undergoes dialysis Monday through Friday with four to six exchanges per day, giving the parents ample opportunity to assimilate necessary information.

The first week is spent learning CAPD. The parents practice dressing changes, monitor vital signs and weights, add medications to the dialysate, and perform CAPD. They are also taught to monitor for kinks in the line, increased weight gain, poor drainage, and signs and symptoms of peritonitis. By the end of the first week, the entire dialysis is performed by the parents. This includes the catheter care, set up, hook up, and disconnect (Fieldon and Johnson 1981).

Proficiency in the use of the cycler normally requires an additional week of teaching. Each machine has a handbook that explains the mechanics of the machine, trouble-shooting solutions, and the alarm system. From day 2 of the second week of training, the parents are required to set up the machine, decide on the dialysate to be used, monitor vital signs, monitor weight changes, and keep records. Prior to the child's discharge the parents take a short written quiz and solve situational problems. They are encouraged to ask questions and are reminded that a renal nurse or home care nurse will be available if problems arise.

The renal nurse should arrange for all needed equipment to be sent to the family's home during the in-house training period. The hospital will select a durable medical equipment vendor to supply the machine and supplies. Arrangements for insurance coverage will be made before the materials are sent to the home. The home care nurse should be responsible for ensuring all necessary items are received.

FAMILY CONCERNS

Chronic renal failure and the resultant constant stress of dialysis, medications, and diet often strain the coping abilities of both the family and child. They grow tired of the daily schedules of dialysis and their altered life style. The home care nurse must be able to recognize the signs of this stress. Symptoms include late clinic appointments, shifting the responsibility of dialysis to the child when the child is too young for this responsibility, failure to take medications or perform exchanges, being consistently unavailable by telephone, being unable to make decisions, and frequent episodes of infection (see Chapter 19).

Children or adolescents on hemodialysis or peritoneal dialysis are often segregated from their peers because of fatigue, dialysis schedule, and alteration in self-image. Parents often have an underlying guilt about the disease that results in overprotective behavior. This can prevent the child from developing a sense of independence. The parents feel responsible for their child's handicap and believe they must keep the child comfortable at all costs.

The home care nurse must encourage parents to help their child learn self-care by offering the child the responsibility for changing dressings, learning dialysis, and taking medications. The home care nurse can guide children and adolescents in self-care techniques. Patients should be encouraged to verbalize their feelings, hopes, dreams, and anxieties. Isolation from school and peers (especially for children on hemodialysis) often leaves the child with no one to turn to for guidance, reassurance, and friendship. The parents and home care nurse are often the persons with whom the child can most easily relate. They are the consistent caregivers and are able to recognize academic successes, social skills, and talents and provide avenues of pride and accomplishment (Williams 1978). These children require a tremendous amount of acceptance and support in their attempts to gain independence and a sense of self-worth.

Support groups can help families deal with stress (see Chapter 19). Talking with someone in a similar situation can help in times of anxiety and fear. The home care nurse managing these families should help seek out appropriate support groups. The National Kidney Foundation is an excellent support group that offers information and support to persons of all ages in all areas of the country.

Summer camps are also helpful by offering an opportunity for the child and parent to live apart for a few weeks. These camps allow children on peritoneal dialysis and/or hemodialysis to spend a few weeks with counselors, medical staff, and children their own age in a different environment. The camps offer activities such as swimming, horseback riding, and arts and crafts. The medical staff and counselors are trained to take care of children's physical and emotional needs. This is an excellent opportunity for the children to become more independent and for parents to get a break from the daily routines of dialysis.

NURSING CARE PLANS IN THE HOME

The goals in caring for the child with impaired renal function are to (1) maintain optimal kidney function, (2) prevent potential complications, (3) promote adequate nutritional intake and optimal growth, (4) support the family/child's coping mechanism, (5) encourage self-care, and (6) support the child's psychological development.

Nursing Considerations to Maintain Optimal Renal Function

Assessment of the child's renal function is a vital role for the home care nurse. The assessment process provides ongoing, accurate information to help the family and physician recognize problems or needs of both the child and family. Assessment of the child's vital signs, weight, growth pattern, skin, and eyes are all highly important. An increase in temperature is an early sign of infection. Weight gain may indicate a problem with the dialysis solution. An increase in blood pressure may indicate additional problems. The skin and eyes often indicate the effectiveness of dialysis or kidney function. Such findings should be shared with the child's nephrologist.

It is important to assess the child's ability to administer medications accurately and confidently. Amounts and types of medication should be reviewed before discharge. Explaining the importance of these medications may facilitate cooperation by families and children in meeting medication schedules. Hypertensive medications, calcium supplements, and phosphate binding medications are extremely important in helping the child maintain optimal health.

The child with renal failure is required to monitor his or her diet to some degree. The extent of monitoring will depend on the type of dialysis the child has chosen and the severity of the renal failure. Monitoring weight gain is also important in assessing renal function and the efficiency of the dialysis.

Nursing Considerations to Prevent/ Identify Potential Complications of Renal Disease

The major complication of dialysis is infection. Peritoneal dialysis requires insertion of a Tenckoff catheter into the peritoneal cavity. Hemodialysis requires that a cannula be inserted into the radial artery and vein. Both areas offer sites for infection. It is, therefore, important to monitor the child's temperature, level of activity, and cannula insertion site. Color changes in the discarded dialysate fluid can indicate infection. Redness or irritation around the Tenckoff catheter or cannula sites may also indicate infection. Close attention to these areas is critical.

Monitoring the child's intake of phosphorus and calcium is highly important in preventing growth retardation. Elevated phosphorus levels decrease calcium levels. Therefore it is important to keep these electrolytes balanced. Calcium is critical in bone growth and development. When calcium levels are below normal, the bones become weak and brittle. Phosphorus can be controlled with phosphorus binding medications such as aluminum hydroxide (Amphojel) and by decreasing the child's intake of cheese, which is high in phosphorus.

Children with renal failure often experience weight gain and should be closely monitored. Weight should be measured once a day and recorded on the flow record. An increase in weight may cause an increase in blood pressure and may also indicate that the dialysate concentration prescribed is no longer effective and should be changed.

Hypovolemia is a complication often associated with hemodialysis. The renal staff should closely monitor for hypovolemia during dialysis, particularly during the summer. When the weather is warmer the child's activity is generally increased, which can result in increased fluid loss and potential dehydration.

Promote Adequate Nutritional Intake and Optimal Growth

Adequate nutritional intake should be carefully monitored by the home care nurse. Children on peritoneal dialysis generally have fewer problems with nutrition. They should be encouraged to monitor their weight and their intake of salty foods. Intake of foods high in calcium and phosphorus should also be monitored to maintain a balance between the two to promote optimal skeletal development.

Children on hemodialysis should monitor the intake of proteins, salts, fluids, phosphorus, and potassium. Dialysis three times per week allows more time for toxins to accumulate in the bloodstream. When these toxins reach high levels, the child can become very sick and should undergo dialysis immediately.

Support the Family and Child's Coping Mechanism

Families of children diagnosed with renal disease are often anxious and frightened. The nurse is able to offer support and understanding as the family begins to ask questions and understand the problems that they will encounter. It is important to assess the family's level of understanding of the disease and of the consequences of renal failure. Families often hear selectively and require time and support until they begin to grasp the total reality of their child's disease (see Chapter 19).

Families often appreciate reading materials regarding their child's illness. Support groups are also helpful for families wishing to express their feelings. The library may have videotapes that help explain the pathophysiology of the kidneys and the complications of renal failure.

Parents need reinforcement in treating the child normally and continuing basic family routines. The dialysis schedule should be incorporated into the family and child's life to permit the child to attend school and extracurricular activities. CAPD can be done in the school bathroom or the nurse's office during a break.

Parents need to be encouraged to attend to their own needs, taking time away from the child. Rest and relaxation are important in keeping the stress level at a minimum. Parents should be encouraged not to feel guilty if they express a need to get away. This is a normal and healthy feeling.

Encourage Self-Care and Support the Child's Psychological Development

Most children enjoy caring for themselves and being responsible for their own lives. The home care nurse can enhance this by working with the child in the home and teaching dietary, hygiene, and medication needs. Younger children may want to change their own Tenckoff catheter dressing or set up for a dialysis exchange. It is important to assess their cognitive development and motivational level and then use their skills.

The school system should be interested in helping the child adapt to the academic environment. The school nurse can help the child with dialysis exchanges. She can also act as a support person when the child is overwhelmed with the responsibilities of dialysis. Tutors are available for children who are unable to attend school for long periods of time.

It is important to know how the child is physically adapting to changes brought about by renal disease. The renal clinic keeps accurate records of the child's blood and urine tests. They are also aware of the child's physical condition and the psychological problems the child may be facing. In addition, the child will often act differently at home than in the clinic. It is important, therefore, that the home care nurse communicate with the renal health care team. This enables both teams to promote better quality care. When both teams are able to understand the child they will be able to offer the child and family the support they need.

REFERENCES

Brem, Andrew S., and Toscano, Alice M. "Continuous Cycling Peritoneal Dialysis for Children: An Alternative to Hemodialysis Treatment." *Pediatrics* 74(1984): 254–257.

Brundage, Dorothy J. *Nursing Management of Renal Problems*. St. Louis: C.V. Mosby Co., 1980.

Fieldon, A., and Johnson, Susan. "Home Training Peritoneal Dialysis in Pediatric Patients." *Journal of the American Association of Nephrology Nurses and Technicians* (1981):41–43.

Fine, R.N.; Scharer, K.; and Mehls, O. *CAPD in Children*. Berlin: Springer-Verlag, 1985.

Gutch, C.F., and Stoner, M.H. *Review of Hemodialysis for Nurses and Dialysis Personnel*. St. Louis: C.V. Mosby Co., 1983.

Williams, J. "Loss of Autonomy for the Late Adolescent with End-stage Renal Disease." *Journal of the American Association of Nephrology Nurses and Technicians* 5(1978): 145–149.

Wilson, Danna; Conley, Susan; and Brewer, Eileen. "Adaptation to Home Dialysis: The Use of CAPD and CCPD in Infants and Small Children." *Journal of the American Association of Nephrology Nurses and Technicians* 10(1983):49–50.

Chapter 10

Impairment of the Musculoskeletal System

Patricia A. Edwards
Cheree Matta Posch

The most frequently encountered musculoskeletal problems requiring complex long-term home care are cerebral palsy and muscular dystrophy. The estimated incidence of cerebral palsy varies from one and one-half to five cases per 1,000 live births. The muscular dystrophies are the largest group of muscle diseases that occur during childhood. Duchenne's dystrophy, the most common and most extensively studied type, occurs in approximately 0.14 per 1,000 children. In this chapter, following a review of cerebral palsy and muscular dystrophy, the care of children with these disorders in the home is described with a discussion of specific interventions based on nursing diagnoses.

CEREBRAL PALSY

Cerebral palsy refers to a collection of neuromotor disorders of central origin (motor cortex, basal ganglia, or cerebellum), with the essential clinical finding being neuromotor impairment. Prenatal, perinatal, and postnatal factors that contribute to the development of cerebral palsy include asphyxia and infection. Studies indicate, however, that a large proportion of the cases of cerebral palsy remain unexplained (Nelson and Ellenberg 1986). This fact may be especially disconcerting to the parents, who ask "Why was my child affected?" Despite earlier optimism that cerebral palsy was likely to disappear with improvements in obstetric and neonatal care, there has reportedly been no consistent decrease in its frequency in the past 2 decades and cerebral palsy continues to be the most frequent childhood disability (Molnar 1985).

During the neonatal period an infant who has sustained a severe insult to the brain may display a weak suck and uncoordinated swallow. Parents may describe a "floppy" or hypotonic infant. There are often abnormalities of the grasp, Moro, and stepping reflexes. Abnormal posturing and muscle tone may be present. Seizures occur in about one half of the children but less frequently in children with diplegia and dyskinetic cerebral palsy (Molnar 1985).

Cerebral control of movement develops as the infant matures. Failure to attain motor milestones and a change in muscle tone from hypotonic to hypertonic may become evident. Evaluation of delayed or abnormal motor development must take into account the wide range in variability and quality of performance in achievement of milestones (Taft and Barabas 1982). Thus establishing an early definitive diagnosis of cerebral palsy is difficult in some children since specific manifestations indicating neuromotor impairment may not be present.

Variations of clinical manifestations in the continuum of this disorder are a result of differing degrees of involvement. Children with spastic hemiplegia (one side of body) or spastic quadriplegia (all four extremities) make up the largest group. Clinical manifestations include increased muscle tone, increased stretch reflexes, and muscle weakness. Contractures of the affected joints occur due to spasticity, which may be mild to severe. In hemiparetic cerebral palsy, which is the most frequent clinical type, fine motor function of the hand is the most severe impairment. Sensory deficits, cortical neglect, and unawareness of the paretic side may also be present. Despite the limited function of the hemiparetic hand, these children are expected to become independent in daily activities unless perceptual or cognitive deficits interfere with self-care skills (Molnar 1985). Greater involvement of the lower extremities is more common in the child with quadriparetic cerebral palsy. A "scissoring" gait results as bilateral contractures rotate the hips inward. The usual motor pattern also includes plantarflexion of the feet, poor trunk control, and flexion contractures of the wrist and fingers. Oromotor involvement, manifested by tongue protrusion, impaired swallowing, and dysarthric speech may be present to varying degrees.

Spastic diplegia is the common term applied to a variation of spastic quadriparesis in which the upper extremities are only mildly affected.

Athetoid cerebral palsy, the second most common type of neuromotor dysfunction, manifests as writhing, uncontrolled muscular activity that appears when the child is 18 months of age or older. These abnormal involuntary movements include facial grimacing, tongue and mouth dystonic movements, and rotary or twisting movements of the hands and feet. Muscle tone fluctuates, and abnormal movements may disappear during sleep. If the child is anxious or physically stimulated, the abnormality of the movements may intensify. A mixed pattern of cerebral motor deficit may occur with elements of spasticity and athetosis.

Cerebellar impairment of balance and coordination characterizes ataxic cerebral palsy, which is the least frequent clinical type. Clinical manifestations include a wide-based, unsteady gait and uncoordinated upper extremity function. "Overshooting" when reaching for a toy is characteristic. Speech may be monotonous and drawling.

Management of spasticity includes specialized treatment techniques aimed at inhibition of the patterns of abnormal reflex activity and facilitation of normal motor patterns. Orthopedic management includes the use of positioning devices (braces, splints) and, in selected cases, surgery (heel cord lengthening, hamstring release, obturator neurectomy, and adductor myotomy).

Injection of phenol or alcohol solution into the peripheral nerve or motor points of a spastic muscle results in a decrease in tone due to chemical neurolysis. Although the effects are transient, good results and no significant side effects have been reported (Molnar 1985). Occasionally children undergoing tibial nerve block will experience painful paresthesias, which may last from 3 to 4 weeks and can almost always be managed with mild analgesics. Hydrotherapy can have a soothing effect. The relative benefits and goals of each treatment regimen must be communicated effectively to the family to avoid unrealistic expectations since the underlying motor dysfunction is not corrected.

Use of medications for the control of spasticity requires careful monitoring for adverse side effects. Adjunctive medication may be required for control of seizures and other associated conditions.

Auditory and visual deficits are reportedly more common in the child with cerebral palsy as compared with nonhandicapped children. Early recognition and correction of these deficits will minimize interference with the child's functioning to the extent possible. One should remember, however, that the child with cerebral palsy may have normal intellect capabilities.

A comprehensive care plan and follow-up must be developed for infants identified as "high risk" in addition to those infants with a known neurological dysfunction. Infant research studies support the concept of early intervention during infancy and the first 3 years of life (Cruikshank 1976). An infant's responsiveness to a wide variety of stimuli and enjoyment of social contacts has also been found to correlate highly with the capacity to cope with frustrations and challenges presented by the environment (Murphy 1986). Notable achievements in this area include the use of specially adapted electromechanical toys. As a result more severely multihandicapped children (developmental level, 6 months to 8 years) can experience increased opportunities for interaction and exploration, enhancing their motor and perceptual development. Through the use of specially designed switches the child can control, often for the first time, some part of the environment. In addition, the concept of cause and effect, a foundation for future learning, is within their realm of experience. Similarly designed switches can eventually be used to drive an electric wheelchair or operate an environmental control device. The toys also serve as an introduction to the use of augmentative communication devices.

In summary, goals for children with cerebral palsy and their families include the following:

- Maximize the child's potential for achieving independence in movement and mobility, communication, and self-care.
- Minimize the deleterious effects of associated conditions (e.g., seizures, auditory and visual deficits, cognitive impairments).

- Assist the family to deal with the special demands in caring for their child through education, emotional support, and communication/coordination of the necessary resources.

Treatment includes adaptive devices to facilitate movement and self-care abilities, augmentative communication devices, therapeutic handling and positioning, and modification of spasticity with medications, such as dantrolene (Dantrium), diazepam (Valium), baclofen (Lioresal), benztropine (Cogentin), and clonazepam (Clonopin), peripheral nerve blocks, and orthopedic surgery.

Additional nursing goals are included in Exhibits 10-1 through 10-11.

MUSCULAR DYSTROPHY

Progressive muscle weakness and increasing disability characterize the four types of muscular dystrophy. All four have a genetic origin; how-

---

Exhibit 10-1 Impaired Physical Mobility

Goals:

- Maintain independent movement within the environment to the fullest extent possible.
- Recognize complications of immobility and prevent or treat.
- Participate in activities within limitations.
- Minimize potential for injury.

Interventions:

- Assess the degree of neuromuscular impairment and assess functional abilities, including activity tolerance, coordination, strength, endurance, level of discomfort/pain, joint range of motion. Document using scale indicating independent, independent with equipment, assistance from another person, assistance from another person and equipment, dependent.
- Assess the effects of perceptual and cognitive impairment.
- Discuss purposes of mobility, prevention of disuse phenomena, stimulation and motivation, and ability to complete activities of daily living.
- Meet child's safety needs and minimize potential for injury by supervised ambulation, helmets, seat belts, correct-fitting wheelchairs with appropriate safety features, and restrainers to assist with positioning. Assess for presence of risk factors for injury.
- Use assistive devices (orthotics, splints, braces) to facilitate protection and stimulation of weak muscles, relaxation of tight muscles, joint support, functional positioning, prevention of contractures, and delay in progression of abnormal postures.
- Establish home recreation/exercise program.
- Teach proper positioning to prevent complications and encourage compliance with treatment program to delay or prevent complications.
- Assess for complications of immobility and note effects in the following areas: integumentary (skin breakdown), respiratory (infection, decreased vital capacity), neuromuscular (circulation, weakness, contractures), gastrointestinal (appetite, digestion, elimination), genitourinary (infection, continence), and psychosocial (attitude, self-concept, socialization). Discuss, teach, and reinforce with caregivers.

Exhibit 10-2 Potential Impairment of Skin Integrity

Goals:

- Minimize risk for skin breakdown.
- Prevent, recognize and treat complications.

Interventions:

- Plan with the family and patient an effective skin care regimen to prevent breakdown and to recognize and treat problems. Some children may be able to use/position a mirror to inspect less accessible parts of their body.
- Discuss use of methods to increase circulation and alter or eliminate pressure: exercise including active and passive range of motion, position change, positioning devices, lotions or ointments, skin barriers, alternate pressure mattresses or waterbeds, and flotation pads or gel cushions for wheelchairs.
- Observe pressure areas, institute effective care, and begin treatment when problems arise.

Exhibit 10-3 Ineffective Airway Clearance/Breathing Pattern

Goals:

- Minimize risk for occluded airway or respiratory distress.
- Prevent or recognize and treat complications.
- Effectively clear secretions within level of ability.

Interventions:

- Assess for signs and symptoms of increased respiratory effort and respiratory distress, including secretions audible/visible in airway that cannot be independently cleared, change in breath sounds, retractions, use of accessory muscles, asymmetrical chest wall movement, tachypnea, tachycardia, diaphoresis, pallor, and cyanosis.
- Discuss/review with caregivers the indications for calling the physician and/or rescue squad. Assess plans for emergency intervention and assist in their development.
- Use adaptive seating and positioning to improve pulmonary function.
- Use aggressive pulmonary toilet, assisted coughing and postural drainage when required.
- Instruct in use and side effects of prescribed antibiotics.

---

ever, the most common form, Duchenne's, is found only in males and is transferred as a recessive, sex-linked trait. Elevated enzyme levels in this type have led to speculation that a biochemical deficit in the muscle tissue may be a causative factor. Additionally, early recognition of this exceptionally high enzyme activity level will facilitate genetic counseling.

Onset of symptoms in Duchenne's dystrophy start during the preschool phase when weakness in the legs, stumbling, and flat feet are noted. For other types the onset of symptoms may not occur until late childhood, adolescence, or early adult life. Wasting of the muscles occurs, but the muscles actually seem to grow larger, especially in the calves, because of increased fat and fibrous tissue. The weakness progresses to the pelvic area, leading to a waddling gait, difficulty in getting up from the floor (Gower's sign), toe walking, and difficulty in climbing stairs. Lordosis and scoliosis develop. As more areas become involved, ambulation becomes difficult and confinement to a wheelchair is necessary. The disease continues on a steady, downhill course until almost all voluntary muscles are affected and the child is bedridden. Most children do not survive past age 21, with death resulting from respiratory or cardiac complications. Goals in nursing care of these children include the following:

- Maintain safe ambulation.
- Maintain function and independence through range of motion, surgery to release contracture deformities, bracing, and performance of activities of daily living.

Exhibit 10-4 Alteration in Nutrition

Goals:

- Maintain body weight in relation to metabolic need while maintaining optimal health.
- Attain desirable body weight with optimal health.

Interventions:

- Assess for consumption of adequate fluids and calories, including the use of assistive devices. Encourage self-feeding using long-handled utensils, drinking tubes, and other devices as recommended.
- Assess effectiveness of swallowing facilitation techniques, including use of verbal cueing, modification of food type/consistency, positioning.
- Observe caregivers' ability to tube feed, including preparation of equipment, placement of tube, position check, safety, and administration of feeding. Assess knowledge of common tube feeding problems such as constipation, diarrhea, abdominal cramping, vomiting, plugged tube, and aspiration.
- Note behavior, response, and tolerance of dietary regimen. Provide adequate diet teaching emphasizing the need for food with high fiber content to facilitate normal elimination.
- Assess hydration status by reviewing pattern of weight gain, intake versus output, skin turgor, and condition of mucous membranes.
- Note condition of teeth, compliance/ability to provide effective oral hygiene program to include flossing and brushing, as well as avoidance of cariogenic foods.

Exhibit 10-5 Alteration in Bowel Elimination

Goals:

- Establish regular pattern in bowel functioning.
- Resume elective bowel function pattern.

Interventions:

- Assess usual/current pattern of bowel function.
- Evaluate dietary intake.
- Determine use of medications, enemas, or natural laxatives.
- Promote normalization of bowel function with use of bowel program including diet high in fiber and bulk, adequate amount/type of fluid intake (using some type of incentive/reward program here may be helpful for some children), activity exercise as tolerated, stool softeners/laxatives as prescribed, privacy and scheduled times for defecation, and normal and comfortable position.

Exhibit 10-6 Self-care Deficit: Feeding, Bathing, Hygiene, Dressing, Grooming, Toileting

Goals:

- Achieve self-care to the fullest possible extent.
- Achieve activities of daily living within limits of situation.

Interventions:

- Continually assess and evaluate potential for self-care capabilities and activities.
- Change daily routines as indicated.
- Identify barriers and assist in the provision of necessary adaptations and assistive devices to facilitate self-care activities. Help with the selection and modification of clothing.
- Review/reinforce instructions from the interdisciplinary team; continually evaluate care plan with patient/family to identify progress and needed modifications.
- Assess patient/family response to level of and/or changes in functioning. Provide support/referral to appropriate resources as needed.

Exhibit 10-7 Anticipatory Grieving

Goals:

- Feelings are appropriately expressed.
- Difficulties in the process of grieving are identified and resolved.

Interventions:

- Assess current needs and behaviors involving patient and family. Note family interaction patterns and alterations imposed by disease.
- Provide assistance to patient in expressing feelings and dealing with changes in familiar patterns. Incorporate family and significant others in support structure.
- Give information, identify strengths, and refer to other resources as appropriate (counseling, support groups, spiritual resources).

Exhibit 10-8 Sensory-Perceptual Alteration (Visual, Auditory)

Goals:

- Improve ability to interact with the environment and respond to it adaptively.

Interventions:

- Assess level of functioning through periodic ophthalmological and auditory screening.
- Provide opportunities for self-initiated activities such as specially adapted toys. General concepts for provision of stimuli: individually tailored for infant or child; variable over time and in intensity; must capture the child's attention to elicit a response. Placement of such stimuli should present a challenge, however, within the scope of the child's ability.
- Review environmental safety aspects and use of assistive devices, including hearing aids, communication devices to promote acquisition of language skills, and/or effective communication patterns.

Exhibit 10-9 Diversional Activity Deficit/Powerlessness

Goals:

- Engage in meaningful activities appropriate for tolerance and abilities.
- Initiate coping actions appropriate for identified problems.
- Maintain appropriate level of social interaction.

Interventions:

- Determine ability to participate, mobility requirements, and interest in leisure activities that are available.
- Identify patient's locus of control.
- Motivate/stimulate patient's involvement in needs identification and activity planning; acknowledge reality of situation and patient's perceptions/concerns and provide for physical and mental activities.
- Explore options for activities given patient's strengths and abilities.
- Show respect and concern for the child and family and assist in dealing with feelings of hopelessness and anger.
- Continue school as long as possible and encourage socialization and diversional activities.

Reduce preventable complications by early recognition and intervention.

- Help child and family understand and cope with the nature of the condition and to deal with the restrictions imposed on their lives.

Treatment includes supportive measures, supervision, special braces, aids, and equipment. A lightweight body brace, individually constructed, may help to delay deterioration and abnormality. Physical therapy and orthopedic

Exhibit 10-10 Impaired Home Maintenance Management

Goals:

- Is able to function in home environment with use of available resources and appropriate modification.
- Has environment that is clean and safe and facilitates optimal growth and development.

Interventions:

- Assess level of physical functioning as well as cognitive and emotional functioning.
- Reduce architectural barriers in as many areas as possible.
- Identify learning needs, available support systems, and financial resources.
- Support patient and family in their ability to maintain a safe environment that promotes and encourages independence. This includes establishment of a realistic home care plan, identification and acquisition of necessary equipment, structural modifications to facilitate care, as well as discussion and planning with family opportunities to have respite from care of patient. Modify plans as disease state changes or progresses.

Exhibit 10-11 Disturbance in Body Image/Self-Concept

Goals:

- Verbalize understanding of body differences and acceptance of self.
- Recognize and incorporate changes into self-concept in an accurate manner with preservation of self-esteem.

Interventions:

- Assess level of knowledge about present condition/diagnosis and patient/family responses to changes in function.
- Assess adaptation to grief response related to changes in function and/or prognosis; modify as disease progresses.
- Acknowledge and accept adaptation/grief response while setting limits on maladaptive behavior.
- Provide information, reinforce explanations, and refer to support groups/counseling as appropriate.
- Encourage positive attitudes and effective communication patterns.

procedures can minimize deformities. Exercise, rest, and diet needs are normal. Assistance in activities of daily living is required, along with reduction of architectural barriers and modification of clothing. Relationships with staff should be supportive, with assistance provided in decision making as care needs increase. Long-term support is necessary in dealing with fears of death and grieving. The parents should be given genetic counseling.

The therapy program should be tailored to the child's needs and abilities. Active participation of the family in a home program of activities and exercises and school, social, and recreational activities is encouraged. The patient should be helped to develop and enhance self-help skills for maximum independence. The home care nurse can provide supportive interactions for the family and child.

The child with muscular dystrophy and cerebral palsy requires the combined services and involvement of an interdisciplinary health care team. The home care nurse can assist the family to clarify roles and responsibilities and to coordinate various services. The use of nursing diagnoses provides a focus for discharge and home care planning. It facilitates communication with nurses in community agencies and other resources for continuing care (Gordon 1987). Goals and interventions to be included in the care plan are presented in Exhibits 10-1 through 10-11 and should be viewed in relation to the specifics of the disease condition and the assessed needs and problems of the child and family (Doenges and Moorhouse 1985).

REFERENCES

Cruikshank, W. *Cerebral Palsy: A Developmental Disability*. 3d ed. Syracuse, N.Y.: Syracuse University Press, 1976.

Doenges, M., and Moorhouse, M.F. *Nurse's Pocket Guide: Nursing Diagnoses with Interventions*. Philadelphia: F.A. Davis Co., 1985.

Gordon, M. *Nursing Diagnosis Process and Application*. 2d ed. New York: McGraw-Hill Book Co., 1987.

Molnar, G.E. "Cerebral Palsy." In *Pediatric Rehabilitation*, edited by G.E. Molnar. Baltimore: Williams & Wilkins, 1985.

Murphy, L.B.; Helder, G.M.; and Small, C.T. "Individual Differences in Infants, Zero to Three." *Bulletin of the National Center for Clinical Infant Programs* December (1986):6.

Nelson, K.B., and Ellenberg, J.H. "Antecedents of Cerebral Palsy: Multivariate Analysis of Risk." *New England Journal of Medicine* 315 (1986):86.

Taft, L.T., and Barabas. G. "Infants with Delayed Motor Performance." *Pediatric Clinics of North America* 29, no. 1 (1982):148.

Chapter 11

Impairment of the Hematopoietic System

Sharon A. Frierdich

Hematologic disorders manifested in children and adolescents encompass a wide spectrum of clinical pathologies. Causation of the illnesses are related to functional abnormalities, production failure, or depletion of specific cellular components of the blood. The symptoms, course of the illness, and management strategies will vary with each clinical problem. Subsequently, the home care needs of children with these disorders require an individualized approach.

In developing a care plan for a child with a hematologic disorder, the nurse should have knowledge of the normal variances in cellular production throughout childhood. An understanding of the pathophysiology and treatment of the specific diseases is also required. Finally, it is important to assess the impact of illness on the child and the family.

CHILDHOOD HEMATOPOIETIC DISORDERS

Hyperbilirubinemia

Hyperbilirubinemia is an elevated bilirubin level that produces jaundice. Clinical jaundice is visible at serum bilirubin levels of 5 to 7 mg/dL. Approximately 50 percent of all newborns, and a higher percentage of premature infants, develop physiologic jaundice (Buchanan 1978).

There are several factors that contribute to a physiologic increase in bilirubin levels. First, in extrauterine life, there is an increase in red blood cell breakdown due to decreased oxygen requirements in the extrauterine environment. Second, there is an impaired ability in the first few days of life to excrete bilirubin. The increased breakdown load cannot be handled by the liver owing to an intermittent deficiency of glucuronyl transferase. Last, intestinal bacteria, which breaks down indirect bilirubin, is not present at birth, so it remains in the conjugated form (Goodman 1987). Physiologic jaundice usually does not exceed safe bilirubin levels greater than 12 mg/dL and is corrected after 4 days.

Breast-fed infants can also develop increased bilirubin levels. Substances in breast milk (i.e., pregnandiol and free fatty acid) inhibits glucuronyl transferase in the liver (Kivlahan et al. 1984). Discontinuation of breast feeding usually reduces the bilirubin level to normal, although mothers can continue to breast feed their infants if bilirubin remains at safe levels.

Phototherapy is used to treat physiologic jaundice and some cases of pathologic jaundice. Phototherapy is the use of intense fluorescent light on the infant's exposed skin. A blue range light source is known to decompose bilirubin by the process of photo-oxidation. This light source changes unconjugated bilirubin to water-soluble bilirubin that is excreted in bile (Whaley and Wong 1987).

Home care agencies are presently making phototherapy a viable treatment option in the home. Infants who have uncomplicated, non-progressive hyperbilirubinemia are eligible for this alternative rather than remaining hospitalized.

Discharge Teaching Issues

The appearance of jaundice in the newborn may be anxiety producing to parents, especially if this is their first born. Parents of children with physiologic jaundice need information concerning cause and potential treatment. They need assurance regarding the benign nature of the condition and that the golden yellow color will eventually disappear. Mothers who are breast feeding need to know that jaundice may last longer in their infants than in bottle-fed infants. Infants with pathologic jaundice may require longer hospitalizations than the mother for treatment. Parents should be encouraged to visit frequently to promote parent–infant bonding and allow the mother to continue to breast feed.

Home phototherapy is an option for children who have nonprogressive hyperbilirubinemia and require only a few days of treatment. The nurse needs to assess the ability as well as the desire of the parents to perform this treatment in the home. The benefit of home phototherapy is that it allows the child to be discharged with the mother, which fosters parent–infant bonding. In addition, it allows the mother to continue breast feeding and there are less interruptions in the family unit.

Parents will require instruction on equipment use, schedule of treatments, and special care of infants. A nursing care plan for home phototherapy is found in Appendix 11-A.

All infants who develop jaundice should be followed frequently with an initial visit 1 week after discharge. They should be checked for signs of anemia. If kernicterus occurred, the child will require periodic evaluations for observation of developmental delays and auditory and neuromuscular abnormalities. If problems exist, parents will require rehabilitative counseling to maximize the abilities of their child.

Anemias in Childhood

Anemias are the most common hematologic disorders seen in infancy and early childhood. Anemia is defined as a reduction in the number of red blood cells or blood hemoglobin concentration. This results in a decrease in the oxygen-carrying capacity of the blood; therefore, the signs and symptoms are reflective of decreased oxygenation to the tissues.

Signs and symptoms are also dependent on the rapidity in the development of the anemia. Most chronic disorders have an insidious onset and therefore the body is allowed time to compensate for the decrease in the number of red blood cells.

The most prevalent signs and symptoms noted with all anemias include pallor of skin and mucous membranes and an increased cardiac output and heart rate to meet the demand for oxygen. When anemia progresses, the child may show signs of weakness, shortness of breath, anorexia, irritability, dizziness, headaches, and fatigability with exertion. In severe anemia, signs of cardiac failure, dyspnea, edema, increasing weakness, and weight gain may occur.

Diagnosis of the specific cause of the anemia is assisted by the history of occurrence of symptoms and laboratory data. A complete blood cell count is usually the first test to be performed. Evaluation of these results can determine the extent of the anemia, decrease of other cellular components, and morphology of erythrocytes (size, shape, and amount of hemoglobin). Other tests that may be essential in determination of the cause of anemia include bone marrow aspiration, hemoglobin electrophoresis, reticulocyte count, bilirubin, and iron values.

Iron-Deficiency Anemia

Iron-deficiency remains the most common cause of anemia in childhood. It is most frequently reported between 6 months and 3 years of age and again in adolescence. The factors that most often lead to iron deficiency in children are rapid growth, insufficient absorption, and blood loss (Dallman 1987).

The normal newborn usually has sufficient iron derived from breakdown of maternal red blood cells for up to 3 to 4 months. After this time, because of the rapid growth of the infant, the iron stores need to be replenished. Therefore, iron-deficiency anemias are most frequently seen in premature infants and infants who, after 4 months of age, consume a diet of non-iron-containing cow's milk with little solid food. Adolescents, especially females, experiencing rapid growth with the onset of puberty are also at risk for development of iron-deficiency anemia.

Iron deficiency can occur as a result of loss of blood through the intestines due to intolerance or hypersensitivity to milk. Ingestion of drugs that cause gastrointestinal bleeding, such as salicylates, and parasitic infections can also lead to intestinal blood loss.

Malabsorption syndrome or prolonged diarrhea can prevent absorption of iron even with sufficient intake.

Children with iron-deficiency anemia usually present with symptoms of anemia and may also have dark tarry stools in the case of gastrointestinal blood loss. A history of dietary and elimination patterns is essential in making a diagnosis. The complete blood cell count will show hypochromic (pale) and smaller (low mean corpuscular hemoglobin [MCH]) erythrocytes with a decreased hemoglobin value. Ferritin levels are usually low: the total iron binding capacity may be elevated with low serum iron levels.

The goals of treatment of iron-deficiency anemia are to replace the tissue iron deficits and correct the underlying cause of the anemia (Robinson et al. 1978). The treatment of choice is oral supplementation of iron for 5 to 6 weeks. Instructions should be provided to correct practices that contributed to the development of the anemia (e.g., inadequate fortified diet, use of salicylates and other drugs that cause gastrointestinal bleeding). Malabsorption syndromes and milk hypersensitivity often require discontinuation of milk products or a trial with a non-milk formula.

Sickle Cell Anemia

Sickle cell anemia is the most common hemolytic disease in the United States, affecting predominately the black population and those of Mediterranean ancestry. Sickle cell trait is present in 8 percent of the population, and the disease is present in 1 percent (Whaley and Wong 1987). Children with sickle cell traits are usually asymptomatic except at times of prolonged hypoxic episodes, whereas sickle cell disease is associated with multiple acute and chronic problems.

Sickle cell anemia is an autosomal-recessive disorder in which adult hemoglobin (HbA) is partly or completely replaced by sickle hemoglobin (HbS). The gene is partially expressed in the heterozygous state, or sickle cell trait, as part normal hemoglobin and part sickle hemoglobin (HbSA). Sickle cell anemia is the complete expression of sickle hemoglobin (HbSS), variant combinations with sickle cell–hemoglobin C disease (HbSC), or sickle cell–thalassemia B disease.

The abnormality results from the replacement of an amino acid on the hemoglobin chain from glutamine in hemoglobin A to valine in sickle hemoglobins. This abnormal amino acid will affect the shape (crescent or sickle shape) and solubility of the hemoglobin molecule, especially under conditions of low oxygen and pH. The transformation of red blood cells to a rigid, crescent shape causes them to become lodged in blood vessels of decreased blood flow, resulting in vessel infarction, thrombosis formation, and ischemia to surrounding tissues. This is known as sickle cell crisis. A crisis may be brought on by infection, fever, cold exposure, hypoxia, strenuous physical activity, and extreme fatigue. During periods of adequate oxygenation and hydration, the red blood cells retain their normal shape.

There are several types of episodic sickle cell crises. Vaso-occlusive crisis is the most common crisis experienced, resulting in veno-occlussion and ischemia. The symptoms manifested are fever, extremity and abdominal pain, and swelling of the extremities, usually without anemia. Splenic sequestration crisis results in pooling of blood in the spleen, causing a drop in blood volume. This can lead to cardiovascular collapse. Viruses or other infectious agents can depress red blood cell production, which, superimposed on red blood cell destruction, can lead to an aplastic crisis.

Short- and long-term complications occur in the organs as a result of multiple episodes or crises. The spleen initially becomes enlarged due to congestion and sequestration of sickle cells. Over time, the splenic sinuses will become compressed and fibrinotic until they become a shrunken fibrotic mass. Consequently, the spleen is unable to filter bacteria and children become more susceptible to infection.

Cirrhosis of the liver can be the sequelae of impaired hepatic blood flow and capillary obstruction. The liver becomes enlarged and tender. Gallstones occur as frequently as one in four patients by age 25 due to accretion of calcium bilirubinate in the gallbladder. Surgical removal of the gallbladder may be indicated.

The glomerular capillaries of the kidney may become congested with sickle cells, leading to fibrosis and eventually to nephrotic syndrome. The initial symptoms of ischemia are hematuria, enuresis, dysuria, and inability to concentrate urine.

Orthopedic complications, which occur due to hyperplasia of the bone marrow and hypoxia, include osteoporosis, osteomyelitis, and aseptic necrosis of the femoral epiphysis. Hand–foot syndrome, characterized by pain and swelling over hands and feet, is common. Children with sickle cell anemia may be shorter in stature than normal children.

Thrombosis and ischemic episodes of the central nervous system can lead to headaches, convulsion, aphasia, and, most serious, cerebrovascular accident. Retinopathy and retinal detachment may occur owing to ischemia to the vessels in the eye.

Cardiopulmonary problems result from the increased demand on these organs from chronic anemia and vessel infarction. Congestive heart failure, myocardial infarction, and pulmonary infections and fibrosis may occur.

Sickled cells are rapidly destroyed, causing hemolysis. Increased erythropoiesis to compensate for anemia results in production in extramedullary sites. Prominence of the face and skull are due to this fact. Increased hemolysis results in jaundice and hemosiderosis, which is the storage of iron by the liver, spleen, and bone marrow. Often, children with sickle cell anemia will also have deficits in folic acid and vitamin B_{12}. Evaluation of these deficiencies is essential to avoid progressive anemia.

The diagnosis of sickle cell disease is determined by evidence of normocytic, normochromic anemia and sickle cells on the complete blood cell count. Elevations in the reticulocyte count and the bilirubin level are also noted. Hemoglobin electrophoresis can make a definitive diagnosis by detection of hemoglobin abnormality, thus differentiating sickle cell trait versus the disease.

The aim of treatment is supportive since there is no cure for the disease. Treatment includes prevention of sickling episodes through adequate oxygenation and hemodilution. Crisis interventions usually require hospitalization for pain control, hemodilution with intravenous hydration, electrolyte replacement, blood transfusion, and antibiotics for an infectious source. Oxygen therapy may be helpful, especially when the child is in cardiac failure.

Aplastic Anemia

Aplastic anemia is a serious disorder caused by a production failure of red blood cells, white blood cell, and platelets. Aplastic anemia may be an acquired or congenital defect.

Fanconi's anemia is the most common congenital aplastic anemia. This condition is genetically transmitted. In addition to pancytopenia, symptoms include microcephaly, defects in the radii and thumb, cardiac and renal abnormalities, deafness, dwarfism, and hyperpigmented rash (James and Hinoki 1987).

Acquired aplastic anemia can occur as a result of exposure to benzene and hydrocarbons often found in glue, paints, and petroleum solvents. In addition, bone marrow depression can be related to certain drugs (e.g., chemotherapy, certain antibiotics) or large doses of radiation. In some cases, aplastic anemia can be the sequelae of contracting viral infections, such as hepatitis and measles. Idiopathic aplastic anemia is the term designated when no etiology is identified.

The complete blood cell count will show a decrease in circulating erythrocytes, white blood cells, and platelets. Confirmation of aplastic anemia is made by a hypocellular bone marrow. The exhibiting signs and symptoms are related to the degree of severity of anemia, thrombocytopenia, and leukopenia.

The treatment of choice for moderate to severe anemia in children with an Histocompatibility Locus Antigen (HLA)-matched sibling is a bone marrow transplant. This option has a 60 percent cure rate. The odds are increased to 80 percent when the child has not received prior transfusions that would have caused sensitization to histocompatible antigens (Fitchen 1983).

Patients who have minor symptomatology or who do not have a compatible donor may have stimulation of cellular production by various therapies. Antithymic globulin (ATG) is a sera produced by immunization of horses or rabbits with human peripheral blood and is a cytotoxic reagent with activity against marrow cells (Alter 1987). ATG has been shown to induce a remission in 50 percent of patients. It is usually administered intravenously on ten consecutive days. Due to the potential for adverse reactions (allergic reactions, serum sickness), children are hospitalized for this therapy.

There are several other controversial therapies including oral use of androgens, steroids, and cyclosporin A. A trial of several months may be initiated, but with failure should be discontinued due to adverse side effects. Table 11-1 outlines the medication used in hematopoietic disorders, dosages, and side effects.

Children with aplastic anemia require supportive therapy of red blood cells and platelet transfusions. Unfortunately, many patients develop antiplatelet antibodies and become refractory to platelet transfusions. More conservative limits are set as criteria for transfusions. Aminocaproic acid (Amicar®) is usually prescribed to decrease use of platelet transfusions and prevent bleeding. Chelation therapy may be necessary for iron overload due to multiple red blood cell transfusions. Blood products should be irradiated to deactivate lymphocytes that may cause graft-versus-host disease after repeated transfusions.

Infections are a major problem in this population. These children are usually placed on prophylactic trimethoprim sulfamethoxazole to prevent pneumocystis infections and oral antifungal therapy. Intravenous administration of broad spectrum antibiotics is required for febrile episodes. Granulocyte transfusions are indicated for life threatening infections not responsive to antibiotics.

Children who have severe anemia, thrombocytopenia, and neutropenia and are not

Table 11-1 Hematopoietic Medications Used in Disorders

Medication	Purpose	Dosage	Side Effects
Aminocaproic acid (Amicar®)	Stabilize a clot and prevent lysis	100 mg/kg every 6 hours to maximum dose of 6 gm	nausea, cramps, skin rash, diarrhea, hypotension, dizziness, tinnitus, malaise, headache, nasal stuffiness, conjunctival suffusion, renal toxicity
Amphotericin B	Antifungal	0.5–1.0 mg/kg/day IV diluted in 500 ml of D5W	fever, chills, hypotension, dyspnea, renal toxicity, flushing, anaphylaxis, generalized pain
AZT	Reverse transcriptase inhibitor	100–200 mg everyday 4° po (dose not determined for under 12 years of age)	fevers, chills, myalgias, fatigue, neutropenia, anemia, headaches, abdominal discomfort, tremors, confusion
Clotrimazole	Antifungal	10 mg lozenge 4–5 × daily (suck until it disappears)	abnormal liver function, nausea/vomiting (5%)
Corticosteroids	Stimulation of bone marrow production	Dosage is dependent on specific disorder	mood swings, shortened stature, masks signs of infection, hypertension, water retention, "moon face," trunkal obesity, acne, decreased glucose tolerance

Cryoprecipitate

$$\text{Expected Factor VIII increase (in \% of normal)} = \frac{\text{Units administered}}{\text{Body weight (in kg)}} \times 2$$

$$\text{Units required} = \text{body weight (in kg)} \times 0.5 \times \text{desired Factor VIII increase (in \% of normal)}$$

Replacement of factor VIII, and factor IX concentrate

$$\text{Expected Factor IX increase (in \% of normal)} = \frac{\text{Units administered}}{\text{Body weight (in kg)}} \times 1 \text{ to } 1.3$$

$$\text{Units required} = \text{body weight (in kg)} \times 0.8 \text{ to } 2 \times \text{desired Factor IX increase (in \% of normal)}$$

Table 11-1 continued

Medication	Purpose	Dosage	Side Effects
Cyclosporine	Stimulation of marrow production	5–10 mg/kg/day	hirsutism, seizures, renal toxicity, hypertension, gum hyperplasia
Desferoxamine	Chelation of excess iron	20–40 mg/kg/day (over 8–24 hours) slow intravenous or subcutaneous infusion over 8–10 hrs daily	allergy, tinnitus, tubular neuropathy, hypotension with rapid infusion, dysesthesia, cataracts, optic neuritis, visual disturbances
Desmopressin	Promote release of Factor VIII and von Willebrand from vessel wall	0.03 μg/kg/dose IV slowly	headaches, nausea, nasal congestion, flushing, abdominal cramping
Ferrous sulfate Fer-in Sol Syrup Ferosol Elixer Fer-in-Sol Drops	Increase serum iron	Therapeutic replacement: 5–6 mg/kg/day Maintenance: 1.0 mg/kg/day to maximum 15 mg (age: 4 mo–3 yrs) 2.0 mg/kg/day (age-low birth weight infants starting at 2 months) 10 mg/day (age 4–10) 18 mg/day (puberty)	nausea, vomiting, diarrhea (5% cases), constipation (10% cases), dental stains, false positive stool guiac, dark stools
Folic acid	Replacement of folic acid	1–5 mg daily for 7 days Maintenance: 0.1 mg infants -0.3 children less than 4	allergic sensitization
Gammaglobulin	ITP and aplastic anemia Provide pooled donor plasma stores of immunoglobulin	100 mg/kg per month (0.6 mL/kg) IV or IM	nausea, vomiting, flushing, chills, facial swelling, abdominal pain, loss of consciousness, anaphylactic reaction
Ketoconazole	Antifungal	200–400 mg/day	nausea/vomiting, headaches, epigastric pain, anorexia, rash, hepatotoxicity
Nystatin	Antifungal	400,000–600,000 U swish and swallow 3 × day	diarrhea, GI distress, nausea/vomiting
Oxymethalone	Androgen stimulation of bone marrow production	1–5 mg/kg/day	hepatotoxicity, virilizing effects, hepatocellular cancer, CNS excitation, insomnia, premature closure of epiphysis in children, edema, retention of electrolytes, decrease of glucose tolerance
Penicillin	Antibiotic prophylactic post splenectomy	125 mg bid po (<5 yr) 250 mg bid po (>5-<12 yr)	Abdominal discomfort, rash, allergic reaction, anaphylaxis
Trimethoprim Sulfamethoxazole	Prophylaxis against *Pneumocystis carinii* pneumonia	6 mg/kg trimethoprim and 30 mg/kg of sulfamethoxazole per day × 3 days per week	pancytopenia, allergic reactions, hepatitis, neurologic changes, renal failure, arthralgia, weakness, insomnia
Vitamin B_{12}	Replacement of vitamin B_{12}	Initial: 100 mcg IM 1–2 wks Maintenance: 30–50 mcg IM monthly	pulmonary edema, congestive heart failure, anaphylactic reaction, transient diarrhea, itching, exanthema, pain after injection

responsive to therapy have an extremely poor prognosis. Life expectancy is from several months to five years.

Discharge Teaching Issues

Anemias caused by nutritional deficiencies have a short course if the proper nutrients are replaced. Sickle cell disease and aplastic anemia are chronic disorders and require life time management. The major issues for discharge teaching for a family of a child with anemia include (1) disease and treatment plan; (2) nutritional counseling; (3) conservation of physical energy; (4) avoidance of infection; (5) pain relief and comfort measures; (6) genetic counseling, if applicable to disease transmission; and (7) coping with the impact of disease on child and family.

Disease and Treatment. Since there are specific variables related to the source of anemia, family members require an explanation of the disease, causative factors, prognosis, and potential complications. They also need instruction on interpretation of laboratory values and frequency of medical follow-up visits. The specific treatment plan should be outlined, and the route of administration and dosage of medications should be explained. Expected side effects of therapy should be reviewed as well.

Written information on the disease and treatment should be provided. Many of the support organizations have prepared instructional material useful in the teaching process.

Parents should receive information on contacting health care personnel who will assist in the management of their child's care.

Nutritional Counseling. Nutritional counseling should focus on the dietary sources to replenish nutrients causing the anemia, such as iron, vitamin B_{12}, and folic acid. All children with anemia benefit from suggestions to increase nutrients, especially foods high in vitamin B_{12} and folic acid required for regeneration of red blood cells. The nurse should assist the parents in assessing sources of dietary insufficiencies. Parents should receive assistance in planning meals based on the developmental needs of the child and on cultural and food preferences. Resources should be provided to assist families with budget restraints impacting on proper nutrition. Methods to increase dietary intake, such as small frequent meals, should be offered when the child has chronic fatigue.

Conservation of Physical Energy. Methods to conserve the child's energy and promote adequate tissue oxygenation are a primary instructional need. Young children, when allowed, will self-regulate their activities and not overextend their tolerance capacity. Older children may become exhausted when trying to maintain the same level of activity as their peers. Parents and children require information to maximize the child's energetic periods in order to meet the child's developmental needs. Most children with chronically low hemoglobin levels are able to adapt to lower than normal oxygen concentrations. The effects are most noted during periods of strenuous exercise or periods of stress. Therefore, children should participate in activities that are interesting and challenging yet require minimal energy expenditure.

The adolescent requires additional information on methods to conserve energy with sexual intercourse. Pregnancy may place additional demands on the female; therefore, specialized counseling is required during the prenatal period.

Additional oxygenation may be efficacious in certain situations. If home oxygen is to be used, parents require instruction on proper use and safety measures.

Red blood cell transfusions infused in the home setting are a growing practice for patients requiring frequent transfusion therapy. The nurse must receive specific physician orders on the type and amount of blood product to be infused. The product should be checked for correct typing and other significant data (e.g., irradiation and expiration time) prior to initiation of transfusion. The child should be closely monitored for potential complications associated with red blood cell transfusions. Any symptoms indicative of a transfusion reaction should prompt the nurse to discontinue the transfusion and report the incident immediately to the physician. Protocols for administration of emergency medications should be developed to expedite interventions when transfusion reactions do occur.

Parents should be instructed to report symptoms of advancing anemia, especially severe fatigue, headaches, weight gain and edema, and shortness of breath. These manifestations may indicate congestive heart failure.

Avoidance of Infection. Avoidance of infection should be stressed owing to the increases in oxygen demand during infectious periods. These precautions are especially important for children with sickle cell disease to prevent initiation of crisis and for children with aplastic anemia who are immunosuppressed.

Maintenance of good health practices, such as good hygiene, regular dental care, and updating immunizations, should be encouraged. Children with aplastic anemia require special instruction when neutropenic.

Children with sickle cell disease are prone to the development of skin ulcerations due to tissue ischemia. This problem is most often seen in the lower extremities. Skin breakdown should be reported immediately, and proper care of the area should be taught.

The importance of pneumococcal prophylaxis should be stressed when the child has a nonfunctioning spleen or a splenectomy. Compliance to daily antibiotic therapy should be assessed.

Parents should be alerted to report signs and symptoms of infection immediately, especially when their child becomes febrile.

Pain Relief and Comfort Measures. Pain is a symptom primarily related to children with sickle cell disease noted during hand–foot syndromes and crisis episodes. Other children with anemia may experience headaches and also abdominal pain due to enlargement of the liver and spleen. The prevention of vasoconstriction through limited exertion, good hydration, and avoidance of cigarette smoking and alcohol use is the primary intervention to reduce painful episodes.

All pain should be carefully assessed. Medication schedule and dosage should be explained. Around-the-clock scheduling of analgesics is advocated for chronic pain. Narcotic use may be necessary for moderate to severe discomfort. Parents need reassurance that their child will not become addicted to narcotic use if medications are taken for pain alone. Children with concurrent platelet disorders should not receive aspirin products.

Comfort measures, especially during sickle cell crisis, should be employed. Keeping the child warm and providing rest and support to areas of discomfort are helpful. Warm packs should only be used when advocated by the physician. Parents should check for proper temperature before applying warm packs on the child. Cold applications should not be used because of the resulting vasoconstriction.

Genetic Counseling. When a child is diagnosed with a genetic anemia, all family members should also be tested. The results of the testing should be provided in a clear, honest manner while being sensitive to the impact this may have on the parents. Parents and older children should be encouraged to express their concerns and feelings regarding the transmission of the disease to offspring. If family planning options are requested, information should be provided.

Coping with the Impact of Anemia. Children with chronic anemia have to cope with the physical restraints on their activity, body alterations, decreased growth, sexual immaturity, and decreased life expectancy. These impairments and stressors will present different issues as the child grows. They need the opportunity to express their concerns, feelings, and attitudes. They require an evolving explanation of the disease, tests, and purpose of treatment. Due to frequent hospitalizations, outpatient checkups, or home illnesses, school personnel need to be alerted to the special needs of the student. Anemia may also result in a decreased level of attention or learning deficits. Tutorial programs should be implemented when necessary to sustain academic performance.

The family must learn to adjust when a child has a chronic and life-threatening disorder. Parents may feel guilt over the transmission of the disease that may create additional coping burdens. Parents may also be expected to perform technically advanced procedures such as daily deferoxamine infusions or monthly vitamin B_{12} injections in the home. The nurse can assist the family in maintaining a sense of normalcy, set realistic expectations for the child, and encourage expression of all the individual members' concerns. Support organizations and resources to assist with financial concerns should be offered. Since the life expectancy may vary with the chronic anemia, the family needs to be kept abreast of new therapies and recommendations. Family members should be aware that anticipatory grief is a normal emotion, and open honest communication should be fostered especially in dealing with such topics as death.

Home care plans for children with anemia are presented in Appendixes 11-B through 11-D.

COAGULATION DISORDERS IN CHILDHOOD

Bleeding disorders in children can be caused by abnormal structure or function of blood vessels; decreased production, destruction, or sequestration of platelets or abnormal platelet function; and congenital or acquired coagulation deficiencies (Lusher 1987). A complete history, a physical examination, and a laboratory evaluation are essential in the diagnosis of the specific cause of the disorder.

The signs and symptoms of increased bleeding tendency include local to generalized bleeding. The skin and mucous membranes are frequent sites of bleeding. Bruising and petechiae (flat, non-tender, red spots) may be evident on the skin, especially on dependent areas, bony prominences, and areas of trauma. Prolonged epitaxis and gum bleeding are also common symptoms. Patients with more severe disorders may show signs of conjunctival or retinal hemorrhage, melena, hematuria, gastrointestinal bleeding, and menorrhagia. Intracranial hemorrhage, a life-threatening consequence, may occur spontaneously.

Idiopathic Thrombocytopenic Purpura

Thrombocytopenia, a decrease in circulating platelets, may result from known etiology such as platelet loss, hemolysis, infection, and specific autoimmune disorders. Certain drugs such as aspirin, indomethacin, sulfonamide derivatives, and chemotherapeutic agents depress platelet production. The origin of idiopathic thrombocytopenic purpura (ITP) is related to the development of IgG antibody directed against platelets, although the source of immune alteration is unknown (Rosove 1983).

There are two forms of ITP: acute and chronic. Most cases of ITP are of the acute form, with duration lasting for only a few weeks or months (Rosove 1983). Approximately one half of these cases are preceded by viral infections a few weeks before onset (Ablin and Wong 1976). ITP lasting longer than 6 months usually results in a chronic, long-term course.

Presenting symptoms of ITP are dependent on the degree of thrombocytopenia. The complete blood cell count reveals a reduced number of platelets, although the bone marrow examination reveals normal to slight increase in megakaryocytes. Results of coagulation studies are also normal.

Treatment of the acute form involves supportive measures to prevent bleeding (e.g., avoidance of aspirin, intramuscular injections, and traumatic activities).

Usually, acute ITP does not require medications due to spontaneous remission. Corticosteroid therapy is started in severe cases and tapered slowly following response. Chronic ITP may require chronic use of corticosteroids. Recently, intravenous γ-globulin has been shown to be beneficial in 50 percent of patients refractory to other therapies. Splenectomy is reserved for patients not responding to corticosteroids. Platelets are transfused only for active bleeding. Many patients with chronic ITP are advised to take aminocaproic acid (Amicar®) to stabilize clot formation.

Hemophilia

Hemophilia A (factor VIII deficiency) and hemophilia B (factor IX deficiency) are genetically transmitted disorders inherited as X-linked recessive traits. Therefore, only males are affected, but females may be carriers. Hemophilia has similiar frequency in all racial and socioeconomic populations.

Hemophilia A is the most common form of hemophilia occurring in 1 in 10,000 males in the United States. It is characterized by the congenital absence of antihemophilia factor, which is required in the formation of thromboplastin. The severity of the disorder is dependent on the plasma level of factor VIII.

Hemophilia B is also known as Christmas disease. The incidence of hemophilia B is 0.25 in 10,000 in males (Ashenhurst et al. 1979). The defect results from deficiency of factor IX coagulant activity.

When factor levels are 1 percent or less of normal the bleeding tendency can be noted in infancy (e.g., cephalhematoma at birth or excessive bleeding during circumcision). Bleeding episodes are most commonly initiated during the toddler years when the child begins to walk and has frequent bumps and falls. Oral lacerations are often seen at this time and present difficulty in bleeding control.

As children grow older, they frequently have bleeding into joints, known as hemarthrosis. This condition produces a swollen, hot, painful joint with restricted mobility. Repeated incidences of hemarthrosis causes degeneration of the synovial membrane with ankylosis, contracture, and atrophy of joint.

Other frequent sites of bleeding are into the muscles of the extremities, retroperitoneal area, and right iliopsoas region, which may manifest as symptoms of appendicitis. Central nervous system hemorrhage may occur from trauma and accounts for the major cause of death in children with hemophilia.

Children who have mild hemophilia (between 5 and 25 percent plasma level deficiency) may not show symptoms until they have a severe injury, surgery, or tooth extraction.

In most children with hemophilia, small cuts and abrasions will stop in a few minutes with application of firm pressure. Treatment for deeper lacerations, trauma, and joint bleeding requires replacement of the deficit plasma factors to control bleeding. Two forms of plasma extracts are being used: (1) concentrated factor VIII and factor IX and (2) cryoprecipitate. These products must be infused intravenously.

Glycine-precipitated concentrates are freeze dried from frozen plasma. They can be stored 2 years if refrigerated. Since multiple donors are used in the production of these concentrates, infections such as hepatitis and acquired immunodeficiency syndrome (AIDS) have been transmitted through frequent use of this product. Better screening of donors and heat-treated or monoclonal derivatives of concentrate are methods for reducing the risk of infections.

Cryoprecipitate, a precipitant formed when fresh frozen plasma is frozen and slowly thawed, is also frequently used. This product needs to be stored in a freezer. Cryoprecipitate requires fewer donors and usually contains 100 units of factor VIII per bag.

The half-life of factor VIII is 8 to 12 hours and that of factor IX is 24 hours; therefore, prolonged or subsequent bleeding episodes require repeated infusions (Aledort 1986). Calculation of the amount of product to be infused is dependent on the degree of bleeding. Life-threatening situations require 100 percent replacement, while other bleeding episodes only require 20 to 50 percent replacement (Lusher 1987). Evaluation of the success in replacement therapy should be monitored by appropriate laboratory tests.

Desmopressin acetate (DDAVP) is receiving increased use for mild to moderate hemophilia A when the child has minor bleeding episodes, minor surgical procedures, and tooth extraction. An intranasal form is being used in Europe but presently is not concentrated enough for use in the United States.

Approximately 10 percent of patients with severe hemophilia will develop inhibitors to factor VIII or factor IX that destroy the factor replacement when infused. When the child does not respond after replacement therapy, inhibitor levels should be tested. In addition, these levels should be checked prior to surgical procedures. Although therapy becomes more difficult, alternative products may be successful (Aledort 1986).

As children grow they often require orthopedic surgery for (1) simple joint or bruise aspiration, (2) debridement and/or synovectomy, (3) osteotomy, (4) arthrodesis or joint fusion, and (5) arthroplasty or joint replacement. Such procedures should be discussed in detail prior to surgery. A physical therapist should be consulted to provide rehabilitation after surgery (Cotta et al. 1987).

Discharge Teaching Issues

The child and family require instruction on the source of the bleeding tendency. Genetic counseling should be provided for family members when the disorder is inherited.

The major goals of discharge planning of a child with a defect in hemostasis are instruction on (1) prevention of bleeding, (2) treatment and care with bleeding episodes, (3) rehabilitation after bleeding occurs, and (4) the impact of the disease on child and family.

Prevention of Bleeding

Parents need to learn to maintain a balance for their child by providing a safe environment while at the same time fostering normal development and a sense of independence. They usually benefit from specific suggestions on the types of activities to promote at various stages of their child's growth.

Young children are most vulnerable to bleeding when they begin to stand and walk. Extra padding should be applied to the elbow and knee areas. Gates should be placed to prevent access to stairs. Carpeting of floors and pads on the side of cribs and playpens will cushion falls. Throw rugs are often a hazard and should not be used. A helmet should be worn by the child when play may result in a head injury. Toys should be selected that are soft, especially those that may be chewed. "Big Wheels" are preferable to tricycles since they are less likely to tip over.

Older children should be involved in making wise choices in participation sports, hobbies, and careers that will not increase their risk of bleeding. Regular physical activity is encouraged to build strong musculature and normal weight, which will ultimately decrease bleeding in muscles and joints. Involvement in specific sports activities should be discussed with the physician. School personnel should be informed of the child's limitations in physical activities.

Oral care should be performed with a soft toothbrush, and flossing is discouraged when bleeding results. Rectal temperatures, enemas, and suppositories should be avoided. Tight, constricting clothing should not be worn. Older children should be taught to handle sharp objects with caution.

Adolescents should be instructed to shave with an electric shaver. Adolescent females should refrain from tampon use and should report increased or prolonged menstrual flow.

Parents should receive instruction to not administer aspirin products to their child. Nonsteroidal analgesics should be used only with the consent of a physician. A Medic Alert emblem should be worn by the child to alert others to the child's risk of bleeding, especially in emergency situations.

Parents should consult their physician prior to a child's dental work or surgery. Special precautions may be necessary at these times even if the child has had no prior major hemorrhage.

Treatment and Care during Bleeding Episodes

Action should be initiated immediately when bleeding occurs. Superficial cuts and abrasions usually respond to firm pressure applied for 10 to 15 minutes. When epitaxis occurs, the child should lean forward and apply pressure to the bridge of the nose. Hemarthrosis requires immobilization of the area with elevation above the heart and application of cold packs to the area to promote vasoconstriction. "Ready-to-apply" cold packs are recommended and should be kept easily accessible.

Symptoms that indicate a potential intracranial hemorrhage, such as headaches, loss of consciousness, slurred speech, and loss of sensation or movement, should be *immediately* reported to the physician. Black tarry stools, hematemesis, and hematuria should also be reported, as should hip pain, throat or neck swelling, chest injury or pain, abdominal pain, and eye injury.

Children who have chronic thrombocytopenia will require platelet transfusion when signs and symptoms of bleeding are evident. Platelet transfusions are usually administered in a medical setting.

Parents of children who require factor replacement can be taught to manage minor hemorrhages through administration of the appropriate factor product. Home management requires specialized instruction. Parents need to demonstrate the correct procedure in mixing, dose calculation, venipuncture technique, and administration. A proper storage facility (refrigerator for concentrate and a non-frost-free freezer for cryoprecipitate) is necessary to maintain efficacy of the product.

Usually, the first few bleeding episodes are traumatic for the family. Parents should receive anticipatory guidance to remain calm and supportive to decrease anxiety in their child. Telephone numbers of contact personnel should be kept near the telephone. Other caregivers should receive instruction on actions if bleeding occurs. Parents will feel more comfortable in taking respite leaves when they know their child will be supervised and appropriately cared for.

Rehabilitation after Bleeding Occurs

Children with chronic coagulation disorders benefit from a comprehensive interdisciplinary team approach. An essential component of the program is incorporation of physical therapy. Such a program should be initiated at diagnosis, and the child should have intervention throughout childhood into adult life.

Joints are a common site of bleeding. Repeated bleeding in joint spaces can result in chronic synovitis and cartilage destruction. Osteoporosis, subchondral bone cysts, malalignment of bones, and limb asymmetry are often late sequelae. Repeated muscle hemorrhage may cause fibrotic tissue and shortened muscles, leading to joint contractures. After bleeding in the joints and muscles, a physical therapist should be consulted to suggest appropriate splinting and a progressive exercise and strengthening program. Pain relief measures should be initiated after bleeding since pain will often interfere with increasing mobility and participation in exercise programs.

Children who survive an intracranial hemorrhage may have multiple temporary or permanent physical and/or sensory defects. They require a complete assessment to determine their specialized needs by speech, occupational, and physical therapists.

The Impact of the Disease on Child and Family

Growing up with a disorder that places significant restriction on participation in activities can be stressful for the child. In addition, children with thrombocytopenia may be on therapy that alters their appearance. Children should receive counseling to develop strategies for interacting with peers and the development of positive self-esteem.

Parents require guidance in setting limits with their child and providing appropriate discipline. They also need to avoid overprotecting their child. Parents often express concerns over being suspected of child abuse, when their child has multiple bruises, by persons who are not aware of the child's disorder. They also state they feel guilt when the child's disorder is genetically transmitted. Fathers often express coping difficulties when a son with bleeding tendencies cannot engage in male stereotypical activities. Anticipatory counseling regarding these concerns should be addressed at diagnosis.

Unfortunately, a current concern by family members is the threat of contracting the acquired immunodeficiency syndrome (AIDS) from the use of blood products and blood factor replacement. The child or adolescent should receive instruction on the risk and benefits of testing for the virus, and follow-up counseling is essential if the test is positive.

Parents should receive information on resource organizations and support services. Many medical centers and organizations sponsor summer camps for children with coagulation disorders and support groups for family members.

Home care plans for children with coagulation disorders are presented in Appendixes 11-E and 11-F.

IMMUNODEFICIENCY IN CHILDREN

Altered immune function in children is the result of absence or deficiencies of components required for cellular immunity, humoral immunity, or both.

Combined Immunodeficiency

Several syndromes have combined deficiencies in cellular and humoral immunity.

Several combined immunodeficiency syndrome (SCIDS) is a congenital disorder that occurs as an X-linked recessive or autosomal recessive disorder. The disease may be related to abnormal DNA metabolism with deficiencies in adenosine deaminase or purine nucleoside phosphorylase.

Children with SCIDS usually manifest the disease in the first few months of life with multiple episodes of bacterial, fungal, and viral infections. Failure to thrive, dermatitis, and diarrhea are common. Bone marrow transplantation from a histocompatible sibling donor is the most promising treatment of this otherwise fatal disease. Fetal liver and thymus transplants as well as parental haploidentical bone marrow transplantation are being investigated (Rosen et al. 1984).

Ataxia-telangiectasia is an autosomal recessive disorder. Cerebellar ataxia is usually noted when the child begins to walk. Telangiectases occur around age 5 and are evident on exposed areas of the skin. The immunologic findings are usually low levels of IgG, IgE, and IgA. There is also a dysfunction in T-helper cells. This disorder is uniformly fatal (Rosen et al, 1984).

Wiskott-Aldrich syndrome is an X-linked disorder characterized by (1) thrombocytopenia,

(2) eczema, (3) recurrent infections, (4) IgM deficiency, and (5) progressive dysfunction of the thymus gland (Whaley and Wong, 1987). Children with this disorder have episodes of bleeding and infection and are prone to the development of lymphoreticular malignancies. Some success has occurred in treatment of this syndrome with bone marrow transplantation. Splenectomy may improve the platelet count and decrease the bleeding tendency (Lum et al. 1980).

Children with immunodeficiencies are often placed on prophylactic antifungal and sulfisoxazole oral medications as well as monthly doses of γ-globulin.

A home care plan for the immunosuppressed child is presented in Appendix 11-G.

Acquired Immunodeficiency Syndrome

Acquired immunodeficiency syndrome (AIDS) is a fatal disease that is transmitted by contact with a retrovirus called human immunodeficiency virus (HIV). This retrovirus, an RNA virus, enters the host cell of the T-helper lymphocyte. HIV carries an enzyme, reverse transcriptase, that converts viral RNA into the DNA genetic material of the cell. These viral genes are duplicated, and a new generation of defective T-helper lymphocytes is produced that contain the viral gene (Boland and Klug, 1986). The retrovirus can inhabit the cell for years. The incubation period in children is relatively shorter than in adults, ranging from 1 month to 2 years (Rodgers 1985).

The HIV virus is transmitted by contamination from blood, semen, urine, or vaginal secretions of the infected person. The infectious agent has also been noted in bone marrow, lymph nodes, spleen, cerebrospinal fluid, brain, and neural tissues. Although HIV has been isolated in tears and saliva, these secretions are not believed to be significant in the transmission of AIDS (Selwyn 1986).

Several laboratory tests can assist in the diagnosis of AIDS. The enzyme-linked immunosorbent assay (ELISA) can detect antibodies to HIV. A second test, the Western blot, employs electrophoretically banded proteins to differentiate antibodies according to molecular size (Blattner et al. 1985). This test is used to rule out false-negative results of the ELISA test. Labora-

tory values indicate abnormalities in cellular immunity, including lymphopenia, which is a decrease in the number of T-helper lymphocytes relative to T-suppressor lymphocytes. In addition, there is a decrease in the number of natural killer lymphocytes. B-cell lymphocyte production is normal or accelerated (Robinson 1984).

The Centers for Disease Control defines pediatric AIDS as a "child who has had a reliably diagnosed disease at least moderately indicative of underlying cellular immunodeficiency and no known cause of underlying immunodeficiency of any reduced resistance reported to be associated with that disease." Primary and secondary immunodeficiency diseases must be ruled out prior to the diagnosis of AIDS.

In 1986, 0.125 percent of all reported cases of AIDS in the United States were in youths younger than 19 years of age (Selwyn 1986). Seventy-eight percent of these pediatric cases occur in infants whose mothers have AIDS. These women have a history of intravenous drug use or have had sexual contact with an infected partner. Fifteen percent of the cases affect children who receive contaminated blood tranfusions. Four percent occur in children with hemophilia who received coagulation replacement therapy. Six percent of children have an unknown source in which risk factors are incomplete (Boland & Klug 1986).

Mortality in children with AIDS is primarily due to infection or malignancy. Children with AIDS are vulnerable to multiple opportunistic infections such as *Pneumocystis carinii* pneumonia, *Candida*, herpesviruses, and cytomegaloviruses. Kaposi's sarcoma and B-cell lymphomas are potential malignancies.

Abnormal cranial and facial characteristics have been observed in children infected with HIV in utero. These features include increased distance between the medial aspect of the eyes, increased distance between the outer aspects of eyes (canthal distances), prominent triangular philtrum (fold between lip and nose), and patulous lips. These features should alert health care professionals to potential HIV infection.

Often patients experience a period of time prior to the acute clinical course known as the prodrome period. In infants, this period is characterized by failure to thrive, persistent episodes of thrush, diarrhea, and hepatosplenomegaly. Older patients may experience fever, malaise, night sweats, diarrhea, lymphadenopathy, arthralgia, and oral candidiasis (Rodgers 1985).

At present, there is no cure. Research has investigated several approaches without complete success. Antiviral agents that prevent replication of the virus through inhibition of reverse transcriptase are encouraging. One such agent is Zidovudine (3'-azido-3'deoxy-thymidine [AZT]). Other treatments with immune modulators (interferon, interleukin-2, and thymic and bone marrow transplants) have limited applicability and success (Selwyn 1986).

The major focus of therapy is supportive. Prophylactic antibiotics, antifungal agents, and γ-globulin infusions can retard development of septic episodes. Nutritional supplementation is often required owing to increased caloric requirements. Good pulmonary hygiene such as daily postural drainage is recommended.

The major emphasis in care of children with AIDS is to prevent transmission of the virus. Since the virus cannot be transmitted by casual contact, the child is encouraged to maintain normal activities.

A home care plan for the child with AIDS is presented in Appendix 11-H.

Discharge Teaching Issues

Family members of a child with a defect in cellular or humoral immunity will benefit from an understanding of the normal function of the immune system and the implications the specific defect will have on the health of their child. The primary discharge teaching goals are to (1) prevent (or minimize the incidence) of infections, (2) promote early reporting of signs and symptoms of infection and initiation of therapy, (3) avoid disease transmission, and (4) foster healthy adaptation of the family members during the chronic and life-threatening phases of the disease.

Prevent or Minimize Infections

Total prevention of infection may not be a practical expectation since the majority of infections are opportunistic or have an endogenous source. Therefore, most health care centers do not recommend social isolation of the child and encourage as normal life style as possible.

The home environment should be evaluated for proper appliances (e.g., refrigerator, stove),

heat, and electricity. In addition, proper disposal of garbage, cleanliness, and toileting facilities should be evaluated. Pets in the home should have had their "shots," and the child should not come in contact with the pet's excreta. Vaporizers or home humidifiers should be cleaned frequently to prevent dispersion of fungus.

Good physical hygiene of the child is recommended. Handwashing after play, contact with animals, and toileting should be taught. Routine oral care after meals and at bedtime is necessary. The oral cavity should be assessed frequently for evidence of oral candidiasis, ulcerations, or dental caries. Nystatin suspension or clotrimazole troches are usually prescribed prophylactically to prevent oral yeast infections. Dental care is important, and often antibiotic coverage is indicated for the period dental work is to be performed.

Parents should be instructed that their child must not receive live viral vaccines, which include measles, mumps, rubella, and Sabin oral polio. The Salk polio, which is a killed virus, may be administered. Siblings should also receive the Salk polio vaccine since the live virus, which inhabits the gastrointestinal tract of the recipient for approximately 3 weeks, may be passively transmitted to the immunosuppressed child.

Precautions against contracting chickenpox should be discussed. Parents need to immediately report exposure of their child to persons who have chickenpox lesions or who break out with lesions 48 hours after contact. These precautions also apply to persons with active shingles. Varicella zoster immunoglobulin (VZIG) is an intramuscular injection that, when administered within 72 hours after exposure, will prevent or attenuate the course of chickenpox. School personnel should be informed to contact parents if there is an outbreak of chickenpox in the classroom. Parents should receive information to report any rash on their child. If the child develops chickenpox, the child usually requires approximately 10 days of intravenous acyclovir therapy in the hospital.

Children exposed to measles may receive pooled serum immune globulin within 48 hours after exposure.

Children with immunoglobulin deficiency are usually administered γ-globulin. Indwelling central line catheters now allow the child to receive larger doses of intravenous immunoglobulin, which may be given weekly. Parents who will administer γ-globulin in the home require teaching on dilution and administration of the product as well as instruction on potential side effects.

Children with immunodeficiency diseases often have recurrent pulmonary infections, which can lead to bronchiectasis. Parents should be taught pulmonary percussion and drainage therapy to assist in secretion removal during infections. Percussion is not advised when the child has thrombocytopenia. Prophylactic use of trimethoprim sulfamethoxazole is usually prescribed to prevent *Pneumocystis carinii* pneumonia. Pulmonary function tests are performed annually to evaluate the lung capacity of the child.

Children with immunodeficiency diseases often present with failure to thrive and have an increased caloric demand. In addition, children with oral lesions or chronic diarrhea will require special attention to maintain proper nutrition and fluid and electrolyte balance. A nutrition consultation is warranted for these children. Parents should be instructed to report weight loss in their child. Supplemental nutrition via nasogastric or hyperalimentation routes is often required, and parents will need to learn the administration for the method selected.

Information regarding food preparation is important. All fresh fruits and vegetables should be cleaned or avoided depending on physician preference. All meats should be well cooked. Foods that can easily spoil should be kept refrigerated.

Fatigue and stress has been shown to adversely affect the immune system; therefore, the child should have adequate rest and situations of stress should be avoided.

Promote Early Reporting and Treatment

Children who are immunosuppressed may be unable to elicit the usual symptoms of infection, or initiation of symptoms may indicate the infection is already progressive. It is therefore essential that infectious episodes are identified early and treatment initiated immediately.

Parents should be instructed to report any sign or symptom of infection. Since a fever may be the initial sign, parents should be taught to use and read a thermometer. A glass thermometer is the most dependable method to measure fever. Children running low-grade fevers should not receive antipyretics, since these drugs will mask an elevation for several hours.

The specific symptoms to report are discussed in the care plan located in Appendix 11-G. The child should be immediately evaluated by a physician and appropriate cultures and tests performed to establish the source of infection. Usually children are hospitalized initially to begin therapy and be observed for response. Home administration of intravenous antibiotics or antifungal medications can then be used once an organism has been identified and the child is noted to be responsive. Parents will require specialized instruction or administration guidelines. They also need to report breakthrough fevers since infections not responsive to therapy may occur while on treatment.

Avoidance of Disease Transmission

Parents of children with primary immunodeficiency disease require genetic counseling when the disease is inherited. Family planning conferences should be provided if requested.

Family members of children with AIDS need special information to eliminate contamination of the infectious source to themselves or others. They need to understand that transmission only occurs when there is close, intimate contact with mucosal surfaces or body fluids, such as blood, semen, or saliva. The special home care precautions are reviewed in Appendix 11-H. These precautions include methods to prevent infection through avoidance of contact with the child's blood and body secretions directly or from contaminated materials. Other caretakers and school personnel should also receive information on these precautions.

Once the child is diagnosed with AIDS it is important to identify the source of transmission of HIV to the child. All family members should be tested. When AIDS is transmitted to an infant in utero, it is not unusual for the mother to be unaware that she carries the disease. If the parent has poor health or when transmission of HIV to the child was caused by unhealthy practices (intravenous drug use), the parents need to be evaluated as to their ability to care for the special needs of their child. Often, the child may need to be cared for by relatives or placed in foster care in these situations.

Foster Healthy Adaptation of Child and Family

There is a tendency for parents of a child who is immunosuppressed to isolate their child from "normal" social interactions. Parents require guidance to promote independence and provide a life style as normal as possible for the child. These children can attend school and participate in most activities when precautions are relayed to the appropriate persons supervising the child.

Parents and children benefit from meeting other families in similar situations. Parents should also receive information on agencies and organizations that can provide information, resources, and support.

Families of children with AIDS often require additional support. They may be ostracized by their community because of the mistaken fear that transmission can occur by casual contact. Parents may require advocacy and education by health personnel and knowledge of their legal rights.

Parents should be informed of experimental treatments and the risks and benefits to their child. Treatments, such as bone marrow transplantation, may require that members of family be treated far away from home. This may cause temporary disruption in the home. Counseling should be provided to decrease emotional and financial stress on the family.

Since most of these disorders are fatal, the family should be encouraged to express their feelings and concerns. Guilt is a common emotion expressed by parents who transmitted the disease genetically or through the acquired route. Anticipatory grief, especially when the child has a serious infection, is often expressed. The family members should be enouraged to express their feelings regarding the death of their child. A hospice care referral may be helpful if the terminally ill child is cared for in the home.

THE CHILD WITH CANCER

Approximately 6,600 children are diagnosed with cancer each year in the United States (American Cancer Society 1988). Although cancer remains the leading cause of death due to disease in children aged 3 to 14, it is important to emphasize that the long-term survival rate exceeds 50 percent (American Cancer Society 1988). Therefore, the goal to successful man-

agement of the child with cancer and the family is to develop a support network between the medical center, home, and community in order to promote individual growth and development.

The epidemiology of the majority of childhood cancers remains unknown and most often is the "end result of numerous influences at the cellular level" (Higgins and Muir 1979). Unlike adult cancers, the importance of routine screening for early detection has minimal significance in children owing to the rarity of the cancer types and the often rapid onset of the cancer. Many presenting symptoms mimic common childhood maladies, which are ruled out prior to the diagnosis of cancer. These factors are important to stress to parents who may be feeling the burden of guilt on causing the cancer or not seeking early medical care.

Childhood cancer encompasses a variety of diseases (Figure 11-1), each unique in treatment approach and overall prognosis.

Discharge Planning Issues

The agenda for discharge teaching is established by the specific cancer type, prognosis, forms of therapy, and the short- and long-term effects of the disease and treatment. The psychosocial and financial impact of the diagnosis of a child with cancer on the child and family necessitates anticipatory counseling and referral to support services.

Childhood Cancers

Acute Leukemia

Acute leukemia is the most frequently occurring cancer in children, accounting for approximately 40 percent of all the cancer types. The two major types of leukemia are acute lymphoid leukemia (ALL) and acute nonlymphoid leukemia (ANLL).

Leukemia involves a malignant transformation of a blood cell with duplication in the bone marrow and infiltration through the peripheral blood system. Initial symptoms are due to this process and include bone marrow failure (bleeding and easy bruising, fatigue and pallor, and infections); involvement of the liver, spleen, and lymph nodes; increasing organ size; and arthralgia related to leukemia infiltration in bones and joint spaces. Neurological symptoms may be

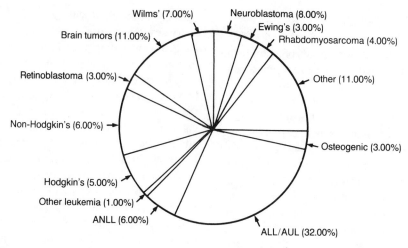

Figure 11-1 Approximate percent distribution of common pediatric cancers from Children's Cancer Study Group data. *Source:* Data taken from *Cancer in the Young* by A.S. Levine (Ed.), p. 4, Masson Publishing, © 1982.

present in patients with central nervous system leukemia. The absolute diagnosis is made by microscopic evaluation of the bone marrow contents.

The average age at onset of ALL in children is 3 to 5 years (Miller 1980). The disease-free survival rate is now 70 to 80 percent at 5 years (Niemeyer et al, 1985). Classification of ALL, according to immunological and cytogenic tests as well as prognostic factors (e.g., initial white blood cell count, age, presence of central nervous system disease) have assisted in tailoring treatment regimens for selected groups. Children with poor prognostic features require more aggressive therapy, while children with good features will require less therapy, thus minimizing their risk for secondary late effects.

The phases of treatment usually include a 1-month induction of chemotherapy to obtain a remission of the leukemia. Remission is obtained in approximately 95 percent of all children, but it is not a cure. The following month is the consolidation phase, and the treatment includes weekly intrathecal chemotherapy. Some children may require cranial irradiation. The focus of this phase of therapy is on the leukemia in the central nervous system. Maintenance therapy will usually last for a period of 2 to 3 years and consists of low-toxicity drugs, requiring fewer visits to the medical center. Investigations are supporting more aggressive maintenance regimens with patients at higher risk.

Patients who have a relapse of ALL while on chemotherapy, or within 6 months after discontinuation of therapy, have a poor long-term survival. However, more aggressive treatment regimens or a matched allogeneic bone marrow transplant has improved outlook to 30 to 50 percent disease-free survival (Johnson et al. 1981).

Acute nonlymphoid leukemia can occur at any age of childhood. Treatment results are not as optimistic as with ALL, with the 5-year disease-free survival rates being 40 to 56 percent in children younger than 18 years of age (Weinstein et al. 1980). Chemotherapy is very aggressive. It requires support for long periods of severe marrow suppression. The course of therapy usually lasts 9 to 12 months. Children in remission who have an allogeneic bone marrow transplant from a matched sibling have a 60 percent long-term survival (Thomas et al. 1979).

Lymphomas

Cancer of the lymphoid system include Hodgkin's disease and non-Hodgkin's lymphoma. Hodgkin's disease is primarily a disease of adolescents, while non-Hodgkin's lymphoma commonly occurs between the ages of 5 and 15 (Gardner and Graham-Pole 1983).

Hodgkin's disease usually presents as painless lymphadenopathy. Systemic symptoms such as malaise, anorexia, fever, night sweats, and pruritus occur in advanced disease. It is important to know the full extent of the disease and histological type to determine staging, prognosis, and the treatment plan. Radiography, nodal biopsy, lymphangiography, and, in most cases, an exploratory laparotomy with splenectomy are performed to determine tumor involvement. Children who have a splenectomy will require daily penicillin prophylaxis as well as immunization with pneumococcal vaccine to prevent susceptibility to bacterial infections.

Children with Hodgkin's disease are treated with radiation therapy. Advanced cases require a combination of radiation therapy and chemotherapy. Long-term survival for stage I and II disease is 90 percent, and for stage III and IV it is 80 percent (Sullivan et al, 1984).

Non-Hodgkin's lymphoma is differentiated from ALL by a percentage of lymphoblasts in the bone marrow being less than 25 percent. There are three major forms of pediatric lymphoma: lymphoblastic, undifferentiated (Burkitt's and non-Burkitt's), and large cell lymphoma. Non-Hodgkin's lymphoma has a rapid onset with disseminated lymph node involvement at diagnosis. Symptoms are dependent on pressure to tissues caused by the space-occupying tumor. Emergency radiation therapy may be required if the tumor is pressing on vital organs (i.e., trachea). Chemotherapy with intrathecal therapy is the main method of treatment and has increased the 5-year disease-free survival to 80 percent (Weinstein et al, 1979).

Brain Tumors

Brain tumors are the most common form of solid tumor in children, predominately occurring between 5 and 10 years of age (Van Eys 1984). Infratentorial brain tumors are the most frequent tumors occurring in pediatric population. These tumors include cerebral astrocytomas, medulloblastomas, brain stem gliomas, and ependymomas. Less common supratentorial tumors include craniopharyngiomas, optic nerve gliomas, and pineal tumors (Ertel 1983).

Signs and symptoms of a brain tumor are influenced by tumor size, rate of growth, and location. Disruption in cerebrospinal fluid (CSF) flow will lead to signs of increased intracranial pressure. Neurological examination and imaging studies (computed tomography and magnetic resonance imaging) are usually the most effective methods of diagnosis.

Surgery is usually indicated to biopsy, debulk, or remove the tumor if possible. Surgery is also required for placement of ventricular shunts or reservoirs when CSF flow is obstructed. Radiation therapy and, more recently, chemotherapy offer increasing hope for cure. The 5-year survival rate is presently only 20 percent (Ertel 1983). Unfortunately, many children with brain tumors suffer some degree of physical and/or learning disability.

Wilms' Tumor

Most children diagnosed with Wilms' tumor, or nephroblastoma, are younger than 7 years of age (Belasco et al. 1984). This tumor is frequently reported with rare congenital anomalies such as aniridia, hemihypertrophy, cryptorchidism, and hypospadias (Pendergrass 1976). Usually one kidney is involved, although there are rare bilateral presentations. Most children are noted to have a large abdominal mass. Other symptoms include abdominal pain, malaise, anorexia, fever, anemia, hematuria, and hypertension (Belasco et al. 1984).

Surgical removal of the tumor with nephrectomy of the involved kidney is the major method of diagnosis and treatment. The extent of tumor involvement and histological type will determine adjuvant treatment. Chemotherapy is required in all cases for 10 weeks to 15 months (D'Angio et al. 1983). Radiation therapy and more aggressive chemotherapy are necessary when there is evidence of metastatic spread.

The prognosis for children with Wilms' tumor is approximately 90 percent, with the best outcome in those who present with local involvement and favorable histology (D'Angio et al. 1983). Follow-up management includes evaluation of the function of the remaining kidney.

Neuroblastoma

Neuroblastomas are tumors that most often arise from the neural crest cells of the adrenal gland and the sympathetic nervous system (Altman and Swartz 1983). This tumor is most often seen in children younger than 5 years of age. Signs and symptoms are dependent on the size of the tumor and its location. A large abdominal mass is the most frequent initial sign, although 70 percent of patients have widespread metastatic disease at diagnosis (Hayes and Green 1983). Head and neck tumors are other common sites.

Radiological studies and evaluations of urinary catecholamine levels are diagnostic of the tumor extent and provide information for clinical staging and treatment. Surgical removal of the tumor followed by radiation therapy to residual disease is the primary method of treatment. Chemotherapy is used when the disease is more advanced (Voute 1984). Since most children present with progressive disease, the 2-year survival rate is less than 10 percent. Spontaneous regression of the tumor has been reported in young infants with localized disease (Seegar et al. 1982).

Rhabdomyosarcoma

Rhabdomyosarcoma is a tumor that arises from striated muscle tissue. This tumor can occur anywhere there is striated muscle and presents as a soft tissue mass. The peak ages of occurrence are from early childhood to adolescence (Pizzo 1982).

Signs and symptoms are dependent on the size of the tumor and location. The most common sites are the head and neck, genitourinary tract, limbs, trunk, and retroperitoneum (Maurer et al. 1977).

Diagnostic evaluation to determine the extent of disease and clinical staging includes radiographical studies and histological findings of biopsy and bone marrow biopsy. Cerebrospinal fluid examination is usually required for tumors located in the head and neck region.

Complete surgical removal of the tumor is always attempted when possible. Radiation therapy to primary and metastatic sites and aggressive chemotherapy regimens are also used. Patients with central nervous system involvement receive intrathecal chemotherapy (Heyn et al. 1974). Today, children with localized disease have a 70 to 80 percent long-term survival, while children with widespread disease have a 20 percent chance for cure (Altman and Swartz 1983).

Bone Tumors

The two most common bone tumors are osteogenic sarcoma and Ewing's sarcoma. Bone tumors are most often seen during adolescence.

Osteogenic sarcoma is a cancer arising from the bone-producing mesenchymal cells most often occurring in the shafts of large bones such as the distal femur, proximal tibia, and proximal humerus (Ettinger 1983). Patients usually complain of a painful mass and diagnosis is made by biopsy of the tumor. Metastatic workup includes bone scan and computed tomography of the chest.

Surgical removal of the tumor usually involves amputation of the involved limb, although advances in limb salvage procedures have made this an option for selected patients who have nearly completed bone growth, have tumors that are easily resected, and have no evidence of metastatic disease (Ettinger 1983). Surgical removal of metastatic lung disease is also indicated to maximize cure.

Preoperative chemotherapy is a new approach to evaluate tumor response and is used to select the appropriate postoperative chemotherapy (Rosen 1976). The survival rate for osteogenic sarcoma is approximately 50 percent (Ettinger 1983).

Ewing's sarcoma is a small cell malignancy of the bone. It most commonly involves the femur or pelvis but can occur in any bone. The initial symptoms are similar to osteogenic sarcoma, and the diagnosis involves tumor biopsy and radiographic tests for metastatic workup. Complete surgical excision of the tumor is attempted.

Unlike osteogenic sarcoma, Ewing's sarcoma is responsive to high-dose radiation delivered to residual disease. Adjuvant chemotherapy is also effective (Swartz and Levine 1983).

Approximately 60 percent of patients with nonmetastatic disease have 3-year disease-free survival (Ettinger 1983). Unfortunately, patients with metastatic disease at diagnosis have an extremely poor prognosis.

Retinoblastoma

Retinoblastoma is an embryonic tumor of the retina. Most children are diagnosed prior to 5 years of age. Retinoblastoma may be bilateral in 20 percent of cases (Dyment and Jaffe 1983). The unique significance of this tumor is its genetic transmission in some cases and the potential susceptibility of children to secondary malignancies regardless of treatment (Foley 1982).

Retinoblastoma can extend beyond the retina into the vitreous fluid, choroid, optic nerve, and subarachnoid space. Metastases can occur to the central nervous system, bone marrow, lymph nodes, and liver (Tapley et al. 1984).

Leukocoria (''cat's eye reflex'') and strabismus are common signs of retinoblastoma. Other signs and symptoms include a red, inflamed eye and visual impairment. Ophthalmological examination can diagnose the location of the tumor. Radiography and bone marrow aspiration can determine the extent of the metastatic disease.

The goal of therapy is to try to maintain the child's vision while eradicating the tumor. Radiation therapy, cobalt plaques, phototherapy, photocoagulation and cryotherapy are attempted for localized disease. Enucleation of the eye is required in advanced cases (Tapley et al. 1984). Chemotherapy is used for metastatic spread.

The survival rate for children with retinoblastoma averages 85 to 90 percent, with the majority of children maintaining useful vision in the treated eye (Foley 1982). Unfortunately, metastatic disease is usually fatal.

Cancer Treatment and Associated Side Effects

The use of a combination of treatment modalities has played a major role in increasing the survival in children with cancer. Specific treatment is based on the disease, stage of disease, age of child, and prognosis.

Surgery

The role of surgery may be diagnostic, curative, or palliative. Most often surgery is performed to biopsy the tumor for diagnosis and clinical staging. When appropriate, partial and complete removal of solid tumors is important to facilitate the action of radiation therapy and chemotherapy against a smaller tumor mass. Surgery has a role in palliative care to reduce patient discomfort (e.g., tumor removal or nerve blocks).

Surgical procedures are often indicated to diagnose infectious complications or to insert therapeutic devices (central line catheters, ventricular reservoirs, and shunts). The goals of postoperative care are to prevent complications, such as infection and hemorrhage, and to provide pain relief. Most surgical procedures require short-term physical restraints, while other surgeries (enucleation, amputation, colostomy) have a permanent impact on the physical and psychological adjustment of the child.

Radiation Therapy

Selection of radiation therapy as a primary treatment modality is dependent on the radiosensitivity of the tumor and the age of the child. The potential gains of radiation therapy must be weighed against the late effects on the child and availability of alternative therapy.

The type of radiation used, the field to be irradiated, the maximal dose, and the fractionation of total dose need to be determined to maximize effectiveness while limiting complications. Young children will often require sedation and molds to decrease movement and exposure outside the field to be irradiated. Parents should be instructed on the importance of maintaining skin markings.

Side effects of radiation therapy are dependent on the site irradiated and the dose of radiation. Cranial irradiation may result in partial or complete alopecia. The hair loss could be permanent in that area if high doses are used. Learning disabilities may be a late sequelae of cranial irradiation, especially in the young child (McCalla, 1985).

Irradiation to the head and neck region may result in irritation and dryness of the eyes, dryness and stomatitis of oral mucosa, and esophagitis. Abdominal irradiation can cause nausea, vomiting, and diarrhea. Skin irritation may become intensified in patients receiving anthracycline chemotherapy (doxorubicin, daunomycin, or dactinomycin) or through prolonged sun exposure (Fachtman et al. 1982). Immunosuppression can occur if large areas of marrow are included in the field.

Other late effects of radiation may include skeletal defects, decrease in muscle mass, endocrine abnormalities, sterility, and secondary cancer (McCalla 1985). Awareness of these potential long-term effects have guided the design of therapy.

Chemotherapy

Chemotherapy has a primary role in the treatment of most childhood cancers. Treatment protocols often use repeated doses of a combination of antineoplastic agents to produce a greater antitumor effect, prevent development of tumor resistance, and minimize toxic effects on normal tissues.

The choice of antineoplastic drugs, dose, route of administration, and schedule are dependent on the specific disease protocol. Each drug will have unique side effects, which are summarized in Table 11-2.

Table 11-2 Chemotherapy Used in Pediatric Cancer Treatment

Drug	Route	Side Effects
Asparaginase (Elspar)	IM	Organ involvement: hepatotoxicity, pancreatitis Other: allergic reactions, fever, chills, urticaria, anaphylaxis, malaise, coagulation abnormalities, hypoalbuminemia
5-Azacytidine	IV	Skin: pruritus, rash Gastrointestinal: nausea, vomiting, diarrhea Bone marrow depression Organ involvement: hepatotoxicity Other: hypotension with rapid infusion, fever, hypophosphatemia
Bleomycin	IV, IM, SC	Skin: alopecia, erythema, hyperpigmentation Gastrointestinal: nausea, vomiting, anorexia, stomatitis Organ involvement: pulmonary fibrosis Other: fever, chills, allergic and hypotensive reactions, pain at injection site
Busulfan (Myleran)	PO	Skin: hyperpigmentation Gastrointestinal: nausea, vomiting, diarrhea Bone marrow depression Organ involvement: pulmonary fibrosis, adrenal insufficiency, gynecomastia, amenorrhea, impotence, sterility
Cisplatin (CDDP, Platinol)	IV	Gastrointestinal: nausea, vomiting, anorexia Neurological: peripheral neuropathy, seizures Bone marrow depression Organ involvement: ototoxicity, renal tubular damage Other: allergic reactions, magnesium wasting
Cyclophosphamide (Cytoxan, Endoxan)	IV, IM, PO	Skin: alopecia, dermatitis Gastrointestinal: nausea, vomiting, anorexia, stomatitis Bone marrow depression Organ involvement: hepatotoxicity, hemorrhagic cystitis, cardiomyopathy, pulmonary fibrosis, azoospermia, amenorrhea Other: inappropriate antidiuretic hormone secretion, sinus congestion
Cytarabine (ARA-C, arabinosylcytosine, cytosine arabinoside)	IV, IM, SC, IT	Skin: alopecia, rash, flushing, sensitivity to sunlight Gastrointestinal: nausea, vomiting, diarrhea, anorexia, stomatitis Neurological: neuritis, headaches Organ involvement: hepatotoxicity Other: fever, arthralgia, dizziness, pain at injection site
Dacarbazine (DTIC)	IV	Skin: facial flushing, rash, alopecia Gastrointestinal: nausea, vomiting, anorexia Bone marrow depression Neurological: facial paresthesia, headache Organ involvement: hepatotoxicity, renal toxicity Other: fever, chills, malaise, myalgia, edema, electrolyte abnormalities, pain during infusion
Dactinomycin (actinomycin D, Cosmegan)	IV	Skin: alopecia, acne, hyperpigmentation, radiation recall reaction, tissue vesicant Gastrointestinal: nausea, vomiting, anorexia, diarrhea, stomatitis Bone marrow depression Other: fever, malaise, mental depression, abdominal pain
Daunomycin hydrochloride IV (daunorubicin, DNR, cerubidine)	IV	Skin: alopecia, rash, tissue vesicant Gastrointestinal: nausea, vomiting, anorexia, stomatitis Bone marrow depression Organ involvement: cardiotoxicity Other: red-colored urine, fever, abdominal pain
Doxorubicin hydrochloride (Adriamycin)	IV	Skin: alopecia, facial flushing, urticaria, hyperpigmentation of nails and dermal creases, tissue vesicant, radiation recall reactions Gastrointestinal: nausea, vomiting, anorexia, stomatitis, diarrhea

Table 11-2 continued

Drug	Route	Side Effects
		Bone marrow depression Organ involvement: cardiotoxicity Other: red/orange-colored urine, fever, chills
Etoposide (VP-16-213)	IV	Skin: alopecia, tissue vesicant Gastrointestinal: nausea, vomiting, diarrhea Bone marrow depression Neurological: headaches, hypotension, peripheral neuropathy Other: allergic reaction
5-Fluorouracil (Efudex, 5-FU)	IV, PO	Skin: alopecia, rash, hyperpigmentation Gastrointestinal: nausea, vomiting, anorexia, diarrhea, stomatitis Bone marrow depression Other: conjunctival irritation, visual disturbances
Hydroxyurea	PO, IV	Skin: rash Gastrointestinal: nausea, vomiting, stomatitis, diarrhea Bone marrow depression Neurological: neurological disturbances Organ involvement: renal toxicity
Lomustine (CCNU CeeNu)	PO	Skin: alopecia Gastrointestinal: nausea, vomiting, anorexia, diarrhea, stomatitis Bone marrow depression Organ involvement: hepatotoxicity, renal toxicity, pulmonary toxicity
Mechlorethamine (nitrogen mustard, Mustargen)	IV	Skin: alopecia, tissue vesicant Gastrointestinal: nausea, vomiting, anorexia, diarrhea Bone marrow depression Organ involvement: hepatotoxicity Other: vertigo, tinnitus, amenorrhea, decreased spermatogenesis
6-Mercaptopurine (6-MP, Purinethol)	PO	Gastrointestinal: nausea, vomiting, stomatitis, anorexia, diarrhea Bone marrow depression Organ involvement: hepatotoxicity, renal toxicity Other: fever
Methotrexate (MTX, Amethopterin)	PO, IV, IM, IT	Skin: alopecia, acne, telangiectasia, furunculosis, rash, depigmentation, sensitivity to sunlight Gastrointestinal: nausea, vomiting, stomatitis, anorexia, diarrhea Bone marrow depression Neurological: arachnoiditis intrathecal use, headache Organ involvement: pulmonary toxicity, renal toxicity, hepatotoxicity Other: fever, chills, amenorrhea, impaired spermatogenesis, osteoporosis
Prednisone	PO	Skin: acne, striae, facial flushing Gastrointestinal: increased appetite, gastric ulcers Neurological: personality changes, headaches, vertigo Organ involvement: pancreatitis Other: moonface, trunk obesity, osteoporosis, muscle weakness, hypertension, hyperadrenocorticism, fluid and electrolyte disturbances, immunosuppression, growth suppression
Procarbazine	PO	Skin: rash, hyperpigmentation Gastrointestinal: nausea, vomiting, anorexia, stomatitis, diarrhea Bone marrow suppression Neurological: hyperirritability, euphoria, headache, dizziness, insominia, nightmares, hallucinations, peripheral neuropathy, tumors, coma, seizures Organ involvement: renal toxicity, pulmonary fibrosis Other: chills, fever, angioedema

continues

Table 11-2 continued

Drug	Route	Side Effects
Teniposide (VM-26, thenylidene)	IV	Skin: alopecia, tissue vesicant Gastrointestinal: nausea, vomiting, stomatitis, diarrhea Bone marrow suppression Other: allergic reaction, hypotension
6-Thioguanine	PO	Skin: rash Gastrointestinal: nausea, vomiting, anorexia, stomatitis, diarrhea Bone marrow depression Organ involvement: hepatotoxicity
Vinblastine sulfate (VLB, Velban)	IV	Skin: alopecia (rare), tissue vesicant Gastrointestinal: nausea, vomiting, anorexia, constipation, stomatitis Bone marrow depression Neurological: paresthesia, ataxia, peripheral neuropathy, ileus, mental depression, seizures Organ involvement: hepatotoxicity Other: aspermia
Vincristine sulfate (VCR, Oncovin)	IV	Skin: alopecia, tissue vesicant Gastrointestinal: nausea, vomiting, abdominal pain, constipation Bone marrow depression (mild) Neurological: paresthesia, peripheral neuropathy, ileus, areflexia, ptosis, diplopia, seizures, headache, ataxia, depression Organ involvement: hepatotoxicity Other: inappropirate antidiuretic hormone secretion

Source: Handbook of Oncology Nursing by B. Johnson and J. Gross (Eds.), pp. 38-59, John Wiley and Sons, Inc., © 1985.

Biological Therapies

Biological therapies are receiving recognition for their potential role in cancer treatment. The premise for using these agents is that the human immune system can recognize and destroy malignant cells. Therefore, stimulation of the natural immune system or infusion of immune components may assist the body's natural defense mechanism and make it work more effectively.

Active immunotherapy involves injection of tumor cells from the patient or cells from another patient who has the same tumor type. This inoculation will stimulate one or more components of the immune system to make antibodies against the tumor.

Active nonspecific immunotherapy involves injection of a noncancerous antigen that will stimulate the immune system against the malignant cells. Several substances are being studied for effectiveness in potentiating the immune system. Among these substances are interferon inducers and transfer factors. Transfer factors are natural products of the immune system that, in higher concentrations, can stimulate a more impressive immune response.

The side effects that can occur with injection of these substances include localized pain, edema, and necrosis. Systemic effects include generalized malaise, chills, and fever. Anaphylaxis can occur. Gastrointestinal and cardiopulmonary complications have also been identified.

Although immunotherapy is not a new method of treatment, researchers are identifying potentially more active agents that can be used as an adjuvant treatment option with conventional therapy.

Bone Marrow Transplantation

Bone marrow transplantation is a treatment option offered when conventional therapy has been unsuccessful in eradication of a malignancy, especially in ALL and selected solid tumors. Bone marrow transplantation may be the primary treatment modality for children in remission of ANLL and chronic myelogenous leukemia.

The process of bone marrow transplantation involves the patient receiving aggressive ablative therapy (chemotherapy and/or total body irradiation) to destroy the cancer. This therapy also destroys normal bone marrow cells. The patient will then need to receive hematopoietic "rescue" through an infusion of bone marrow harvested from his or her own body at an earlier time (autologous) or from a compatible donor (allogeneic).

Autologous donation is performed if the patient's bone marrow is free of malignancy or the cancer cells can be destroyed prior to infusion back into the body. Allogeneic donation is usually from a sibling who is histocompatibly matched by testing human leukocyte antigen and mixed leukocyte culture. Each biological sibling has a 25 percent chance of matching the patient.

The donation of bone marrow is usually performed under general anesthesia. The donor undergoes multiple bone marrow aspirations from the anterior and posterior iliac crests. The major risks to the donor are anesthesia, pain at the aspiration site, infection, and blood loss. Most donors have stored several units of their blood prior to surgery for postoperative transfusions and are able to be discharged within 1 to 2 days after donation.

The aspirated bone marrow is filtered and bagged, ensuring sterility, and delivered to the patient similar to a blood transfusion. It remains a mystery how the infused bone marrow cells migrate and engraft in the recipient's bone marrow.

Aggressive supportive care is essential during the bone marrow transplantation. Engraftment of the bone marrow may not occur for 1 to 4 weeks. During this aplastic period the patient requires red blood cells and platelet transfusion, an infection controlled environment, medication prophylaxis, and prompt initiation of antibiotics or antifungal drugs if fever occurs. Other toxicities associated with the ablative therapy, such as nausea, vomiting, skin irritation, diarrhea, mucositis, and alopecia need appropriate care. Most children receive total parenteral nutrition due to poor oral intake.

Graft-versus-host reaction can occur after engraftment. This reaction is the recognition of the donor's lymphoid cells to the recipient's body as foreign, resulting in tissue destruction. It is graded on the severity of skin involvement, liver dysfunction, and gastrointestinal symp-

toms. Approximately 60 percent of all patients receiving allogeneic bone marrow will demonstrate some degree of graft-versus-host reaction (Glucksberg et al. 1974).

The child remains susceptible to infections due to prolonged immunosuppression. Pneumonia caused by cytomegalovirus or *Pneumocystis* can occur. The child is very susceptible to acquiring herpes simplex, herpes zoster, or varicella zoster. Other late effects from the ablative chemotherapy can result in hemorrhagic cystitis or cardiac toxicity. Total body irradiation can result in cataracts, postirradiation pneumonitis, endocrine problems, and second malignancies. Adverse effects related to the numerous antibiotics, antifungal agents, and drugs used to control graft-versus-host reaction can often result in renal or neurological impairments.

Chronic graft-versus-host reaction may develop after 100 days after the procedure. Symptoms of this condition include skin dryness and thickening, sicca syndrome causing dryness of eyes and oral mucosa, and intestinal and liver abnormalities.

When the bone marrow has successfully engrafted and the child demonstrates adequate oral intake, resolution of infection, and other problems, discharge planning can be initiated. Relapse of the disease remains the major concern after bone marrow transplantation.

Psychosocial and Financial Impact on Family

The diagnosis of cancer in a child will impact every member of the family. Often, cancer is initially perceived as ending in a fatal course. Parents are overwhelmed with grief and associated feelings of guilt, anger, shock, denial, and depression. Treatment usually needs to be initiated immediately. Information regarding the disease, treatment options, and potential side effects of therapy is relayed to obtain "informed consent" for treatment. The retention of information is likely to be limited.

Differences in coping patterns between parents, communication styles, or separation of the mother and father during their child's hospitalizations may increase marital stress. There may be role changes in the family that require adjustment. Relatives and friends may be supportive or add additional stress by offering unsolicited advice or undermining the parents' coping (Hall et al. 1982). The reader is referred to Chapter 19 for further discussion on stress tolerance.

These children are placed in an environment in which they have little control and are subjected to multiple intrusive and painful procedures. They may perceive the distraught reactions of their parents as frightening. Depending on their developmental age, they can fantasize about the seriousness of their illness and eventual outcome. Regression and depression are common reactions. Older children may seek control through noncompliance to the therapeutic regimen. Many children fear school reentry and peer contact owing to changes in appearance or level of physical ability.

Siblings are also affected by the diagnosis of cancer in their brother or sister. They may feel they may have caused the disease, or that they can contract it. They may be angry and jealous over the parental attention and gifts the sick child is receiving. They may be embarrassed by the child's change in appearance. Often siblings are affected by the change in family routine and their usual participation in activities. They may perceive the child with cancer as not having the same expectations or receiving discipline for wrongdoings. Siblings often are burdened with providing progress reports on the sick child's condition to friends and relatives, instead of engaging in conversations focused on them (Sourkes 1980).

Most children with cancer are often diagnosed and treated at distant medical centers. Frequent hospitalizations and clinic visits add financial burdens due to travel costs, food, lodging, and extraneous expenses. Job-related stressors include increased absences and retention of insurance coverage. The insurance may or may not provide full coverage for inpatient or outpatient costs or will have a "pay later" policy. There may be restrictions on coverage of prosthetics devices or supportive resources.

Teaching Issues Prior to Discharge

Discharge teaching should incorporate content specific to the disease, treatment, anticipated short- and long-term effects, related home care, and precautions. In addition, counseling is directed toward decreasing family stress, maintenance of as normal a life style as possible, and access to support and financial resources.

A family conference is usually planned once the diagnosis of cancer is made. This conference is to provide initial information and address concerns and questions. Significant others, such as grandparents, are encouraged to attend.

After the family conference, several teaching sessions are required. Adolescents and parents can be instructed together. Younger children will need a modified teaching approach geared to their developmental age. Parents are encouraged to audiotape the sessions for future reinforcement. Written instructions should be provided for reference.

Disease and Prognosis

Parents are provided information regarding the etiology of cancer, concept of metastasis, and prognosis. The treatment modalities and side effects are explained. A treatment schedule or time table should be provided. If the child is eligible for a research study, parents require protocol information and explanation regarding the benefits and risks in participating. They should also receive the schedule of planned tests and procedures.

Side Effects of Therapy

Teaching issues related to the side effects of therapy should emphasize preventive measures when applicable and care of the child when symptoms occur. Parents should receive information on "when" and "who" to contact when problems arise in the home.

Hair Loss. Alopecia, or hair loss, may involve not only scalp hair but also eyelashes, eyebrows, and axillary and pubic hair. Instructions should include the anticipated degree, duration, and time hair loss will begin. Hair regrowth may occur in some cases while on therapy. The child and family need to know that the color and texture may vary from that prior to treatment. Parents and child should be encouraged to express their fears and concerns regarding this change in appearance. Suggestions for protective and cosmetic coverings, such as wigs, scarves, or hats, should be provided.

Skin Changes. Care for potential skin problems, such as rashes, acne, irritated skin, hyperpigmentation, and photosensitivity should be discussed. Rashes and skin erythema are usually transient but should be reported. The causative agent may or may not be the cancer therapy. Other sources, such as tape sensitivity, other drugs, or infection should be investigated.

Acne is usually the result of corticosteroid therapy or a side effect of dactinomycin. The skin should be kept clean. The use of benzoin peroxide topical cream is usually advised. Oral or topical antibiotics are prescribed when there is widespread folliculitis.

Hyperpigmentation is the result of increased levels of melanin-stimulating hormone. The areas most often affected are nail beds, teeth, gingiva, and along veins used for chemotherapy. Skin may also be hyperpigmented in areas of irradiation. This discoloration may take several months to fade after discontinuation of therapy. Photosensitivity is increased along with sensitivity of skin to ultraviolet rays. Even short exposure in direct sunlight can lead to severe sunburn. Parents are instructed to apply a No. 15 to 25 hypoallergenic, waterproof sunscreen to their child's exposed skin surface when the child is out in sunlight longer than 30 minutes. Protective clothing and hats are also recommended.

Dry, irritated skin may be a result of certain drugs and radiation. Frequent applications of nonalcohol base moisturizing cream such as Eucerin may be helpful. No harsh soaps, creams, powder, or cosmetics should be used on an irritated area. Avoiding direct contact with heat and cold is essential. Tight-fitting clothes and harsh fabrics can exacerbate the condition. Antipyretic medications may be necessary if the child scratches the area. A moisturizing lip balm should be applied frequently to prevent dryness of lips. Children often prefer flavored lip balms.

Gastrointestinal Effects. Gastrointestinal side effects most commonly reported are stomatitis, anorexia, nausea and vomiting, diarrhea, and constipation. These symptoms are usually temporary but can be the source of discomfort for children undergoing cancer therapy.

Routine oral care is encouraged. The recommended procedure is brushing teeth after meals with a soft toothbrush and fluoride toothpaste. Flossing is discouraged when the platelet count is below 2,000/cu mm and the absolute neutrophil count is below 500/cu mm. The oral cavity is rinsed after brushing with a baking soda

mouthwash (1 tsp/1 qt of H_2O). Parents and older children should inspect the mouth for signs of yeast infection or ulcerations. If the child has oral candidiasis (thrush), nystatin suspension is swished and swallowed or a clotrimazole troche is sucked for 20 minutes. These medications should be taken after routine mouth care.

Chewing sugarless gum can assist in stimulating saliva production, a natural infection control measure. Artificial saliva is available for use when production is diminished due to therapy. Dental care is also emphasized, although children usually require prophylactic antibiotics during dental work to prevent opportunistic infections.

Stomatitis is the result of damage to the epithelial cells of the mucosa by therapy and results in painful ulcerations, hemorrhage, and often secondary infections. This condition may interfere with adequate oral intake. With minor ulcerations, parents are instructed to apply a topical anesthetic (benzocaine [Ora-Jel, Anbesol] viscous lidocaine, dyclonine [Dyclone]) to the area, especially prior to eating. A mixture of dyclonine, Maalox, and diphenhydramine (Benadryl) is effective. Children should be encouraged to eat cool, bland foods during this time and avoid spicy, acidic, or irritating foods and liquids. Medications may be needed for pain control. If the child is unable to eat or drink sufficient amounts or is experiencing severe pain, hospitalization may be indicated for parenteral pain control and temporary total parenteral nutrition.

Esophagitis, or ulceration of the esophagus, is less easily managed than stomatitis. Swallowing topical anesthetics is not recommended in children due to potential for aspiration from loss of gag reflex. The recommendations for oral care, nutrition, and pain control are the same as for stomatitis.

Nausea and vomiting are symptoms frequently seen as a consequence of chemotherapy and abdominal irradiation. Antiemetic medications are used cautiously with younger children because of their extrapyramidal reactions. Chlorpromazine (Thorazine), diphenhydramine, hydroxyzine (Vistaril), and promethazine (Phenergan) have been noted to be efficacious in young children. Older children and adolescents often receive a combination of drugs, including diphenhydramine, haloperidol (Haldol), metoclopramide (Reglan), prochlorperazine (Compazine), and dexamethasone (Decadron).

Chemotherapy-related nausea usually will last approximately 24 hours after administration of the causative agent. Good antiemetic control around the clock is advised, especially with older children and adolescents who may develop anticipatory nausea and vomiting. Parents need to be instructed on interventions if an extra-pyramidal reaction (stiffness of jaw, tremors) occurs. Prophylactic diphenhydramine is usually prescribed for use 24 to 48 hours after the last antiemetic drug was given to prevent this reaction.

Children should not be forced to eat or drink when nausea or vomiting is expected to be of short duration (24 to 48 hours). Small frequent feedings or a clear liquid diet are better tolerated. Minimizing sights, sounds, and adverse smells, while providing enjoyable, relaxing distractions are recommended. Young children should be positioned in a semi-upright position or in a face-down position to prevent aspiration if vomiting occurs.

Anorexia can occur for multiple reasons. These include taste alterations, nausea and vomiting, stomatitis and esophagitis, oral infections, dryness of oral mucosa, or as a direct effect of cancer.

Alterations in taste are not uncommon, and children often request different foods than prior to treatment. They may experience a decrease in the acuity of their taste sensations. Common taste changes are aversions for bitter foods, such as beef, pork, and chocolate. Poultry and fish are often preferred as are salty foods and fewer sweets. Parents should experiment with various food types and elicit suggestions on what foods the child likes to eat. Taking older children grocery shopping allows them choices in food selection. Mealtime should be a pleasant experience for the child.

Children on high-dose corticosteroid therapy will have an increase in appetite and sodium retention. The parents and child should be prepared to expect weight gain, especially facial and truncal obesity. They should receive nutritional guidance on limiting their child's intake of salty foods.

The weight and growth of the child should be monitored closely. A nutritional consultation may be necessary if the child is consistently losing weight. Suggestions for nutritional supplements are usually not tolerated well in younger children. Many children on aggressive therapy may suffer from anorexia and weight loss and will require total parenteral nutrition at home. This usually requires hospitalization for a few days to educate caregivers in the technique. Nasogastric feedings are also used, although the passage of the tube is often perceived as traumatic by many children.

Diarrhea may occur as a side effect of therapy and can be a sign of a gastrointestinal infection or a malabsorption syndrome. Parents are instructed to report persistent diarrhea in their child. Suggestions should be provided for a low residue diet and avoidance of high-bulk foods, caffeine beverages, and milk or milk products. The child should be encouraged to drink plenty of liquids, such as Pedialyte or Gatorade to replace lost electrolytes. Severe diarrhea may require more aggressive monitoring and interventions.

During periods of diarrhea, the rectal area should be kept clean and dry. Skin irritation should be treated with a topical cream such as Desitin or Vaseline Constant Care. Antidiarrheal medications such as Kaopectate may be needed but should be prescribed by the oncologist.

Constipation may result from *Vinca* alkaloid chemotherapy (vincristine, vinblastine) but may also be related to decreased activity, stress, narcotic use, or decreased roughage in the diet. Parents are encouraged to provide more bulk in their child's diet and increase the child's intake of liquids. Encouraging mobility and exercise is also recommended. Stool softeners such as Colace, Pericolace, or Naturcil are often prescribed for routine use when constipation is an expected symptom to prevent impaction. Parents are advised to avoid laxatives, enemas, and suppositories unless specifically prescribed by the oncologist. Parents should receive suggestions on tailoring the child's meals and activities to correspond with times of most energy. If the child's best time is in the morning, he or she may wish to attend school at that time and come home and rest in the afternoon.

Hematologic Changes. Bone marrow suppression may result from tumor invasion of bone marrow, irradiation to bone marrow sites, and chemotherapy. The result is a decrease in the number of circulating blood cells. Parents should be instructed in the interpretation of a complete blood cell count, platelet count, and differential of the percentage of white blood cells and in the resulting care based on the values. A decrease in red blood cell production, bleeding, or hemolysis can cause symptoms of anemia. Hemoglobin or hematocrit levels are indicative of the degree of anemia. Parents are instructed to report symptoms such as paleness, fatigue, poor appetite, irritability, headaches, dizziness, and shortness of breath, which may be symptoms of anemia in their child. Most children will receive a packed red blood cell transfusion when the hemoglobin value is less than 8 g/dL.

A decrease in the number of platelets can predispose the child to bleeding. Platelet counts lower than 5,000 to 20,000/cu mm usually indicate the potential for bleeding and the need for platelet transfusion. Parents are instructed to report any signs of spontaneous bleeding: epitaxis, bleeding gums, blood in urine or stool, bleeding around central line exit sites, or prolonged menstrual periods. Multiple bruises or petechiae are usually symptoms of thrombocytopenia and should be reported.

Preventive measures against bleeding should be advised. Children should avoid rough contact sports, wear loose fitting clothes, and avoid flossing teeth during periods of low platelet counts. Adolescents are encouraged to avoid shaving with straight razors and use electric shavers. Children should not receive aspirin products, which may alter platelet function. During bleeding episodes, firm pressure should be applied for 5 minutes. If bleeding persists longer than 10 minutes, the parents should notify the physician. If the child suffers a head injury, parents should notify the physician immediately owing to the potential for a central nervous system hemorrhage.

Infectious Complications. Infection is a frequent complication in children with cancer and is one of the major causes of morbidity and mortality in this population. Children are predisposed to infections due to immunosuppression caused by the disease and its treatment. Bone marrow suppression by chemotherapy results in neutropenia, with the nadir occurring at approximately 1 week after therapy and lasting for 4 to 10 days or longer.

Parents are initially very fearful of exposing their child to potential sources of infection (school, shopping malls, church). They need to be reassured that most infections children contract are from within their own bodies (endogenous infections). Therefore, placing them in a protective bubble would not prevent the occurrence of infection.

Parents are instructed on the importance of the absolute neutrophil (granulocyte) count. This count is calculated by multiplying the percentage of neutrophils (segs, bands) times the total white blood cell count. When the result is less than 500/cu mm, the child is at increased risk for infection. Parents are also informed that the child may not demonstrate the usual signs and symptoms of infection in a neutropenic state. Parents should have a thermometer in the home and be instructed in reading the thermometer correctly. They should immediately notify the physician if child develops a temperature greater than 101°F (38.3°C) . In addition, they should report frequent cough or shortness of breath. Any sign of skin breakdown, pain, rash, erythema, or drainage on any area of the body should be reported. The physician should be notified when oral stomatitis, esophagitis, and oral candidiasis are present. Pain on defecation or rectal area skin breakdown may indicate a rectal abscess that requires immediate attention.

Good handwashing is the best preventive measure against infection. Children should be taught to wash hands after using the toilet, after playing outside or with pets, and prior to eating. Other members of the family should take the same precautions.

Children should not be responsible for cleaning up pet's excreta, such as in cages, fish bowls, or litter boxes. Household humidifiers and vaporizers should be cleaned daily with a chlorine-based solution or Lysol.

Fresh fruits and vegetables should be washed well. Some institutions recommend cooking all unpared fruit and raw vegetables. Raw meats should be cooked well. Children are instructed to avoid drinking unpasteurized milk or milk products.

Children should not receive live vaccinations (measles, mumps, rubella, and oral polio) because of the risk of contracting the illness in immunocompromised patients. It is often recommended that siblings not receive the oral live polio (Sabin vaccine) but instead receive the inactivated polio vaccine (Salk vaccine) since the live virus is excreted in the stool. Diptheria-pertussis-tetanus (DPT) and influenza vaccines may be given to the child, but these vaccines may produce an ineffective therapeutic defense response. Catch up on immunizations is advocated 6 months to 1 year after completion of all therapy.

Children exposed to measles who have not received prior immunization may receive pooled serum immune globulin within 48 hours after exposure.

Varicella (chickenpox) and herpes zoster (shingles) may be a serious disease in children receiving cancer therapy. Parents are instructed to immediately report their child's exposure to these viral infections. An exposure is defined as 1 hour in direct contact with a person who has chickenpox lesions or develops chickenpox within 2 days after contact. An exposure also includes contact with a person who has shingles. Varicella zoster immunoglobulin (VZIG) can be administered within 72 hours after exposure to eliminate the risk of developing chickenpox or to attenuate the course of the disease. The half-life of VZIG is short, and the immunoglobulin must be readministered if the child is subsequently exposed after 3 weeks.

Children on aggressive therapy are often instructed to receive trimethoprim-sulfamethoxazole daily or 3 times a week to prevent the development of *Pneumocystis carinii* pneumonia, a common infection acquired by immunosuppressed patients.

Neurological Effects. Neurological changes, such as peripheral neuropathy, are common in children receiving *Vinca* alkaloids. Early signs of this side effect include jaw pain, tingling of fingers and toes, decreased reflexes, tremors, and weakness of extremities. Parents are encouraged to report problems with coordination such as stumbling or toe-walking. Modifications in therapy and physical therapy exercises may be initiated if the symptoms become severe.

Cardiac Effects. Cardiopulmonary complications may occur as a consequence of cancer, infection, or direct toxicity of therapy. Parents are instructed to report symptoms in their child, such as shortness of breath, frequent cough, and fatigue, which may indicate a problem. Periodic evaluation of cardiac function, with an ejection fraction or echocardiographic scan, should be performed when the child is receiving drugs that have been known to cause cardiotoxicity. Pulmonary function tests are recommended to evaluate lung function prior to drugs that may cause fibrosis.

Renal Effects. Renal effects by tumor involvement, cancer therapy, other drugs, or infection may adversely affect the child's excretory function. Parents are instructed to promptly report oliguria, dysuria, or blood in the urine.

Some chemotherapy agents will temporarily discolor the urine to a reddish hue. Parents should be informed of this fact prior to administration of the drug. Kidney function determined by urinalysis (creatinine clearance) or serum analysis (blood urea nitrogen, creatinine) are measured prior to initiation of therapy known to be nephrotoxic. Irritation of the bladder wall due to by-products of cyclophosphamide chemotherapy may result in bleeding or hemorrhagic cystitis. Children should be encouraged to drink plenty of fluids and void frequently while receiving this drug. Most children are hospitalized during administration of cyclophosphamide to receive adequate intravenous hydration after administration. Cisplatin therapy may cause magnesium wasting from the renal tubules. Therefore, many children receiving this drug require nutrition counseling on intake of foods with high magnesium content or instructions on supplemental oral intake of magnesium.

Hepatic Effects. Many of the drugs are associated with hepatotoxicity. Children are monitored for this effect by checking for elevations in liver function tests. Parents should be instructed to report jaundice.

Endocrine Effects. Endocrine abnormalities may occur with certain drugs. Abnormality in pancreatic function may result in usually transient diabetes especially with high doses of corticosteroids or use of asparaginase, which may require insulin therapy.

Reproductive Effects. Adolescents should receive counseling around sexuality issues. It is important to assess the sexual knowledge and behavior of the adolescent. All adolescents who are sexually active should be informed of birth control measures while receiving therapy. It should be remembered that certain antibiotics may impede the efficacy of birth control pills.

Postpubescent females should be prepared for potential amenorrhea while on therapy and that this condition does not ensure they will not conceive during this period. Vaginal candidal infections are not uncommon; therefore, vaginal discharge should be reported.

Males should be informed of potential transient impotence with the use of certain drugs, such as the *Vinca* alkaloids. Both males and females should be instructed to avoid sex practices that may potentially cause infections, specifically anal sex.

Safety Issues

Family members should also receive information on safe handling of chemotherapeutic drugs in the home to decrease their exposure to these potentially harmful agents (Exhibit 11-1).

Late Effects of Disease and Therapy

In recent years there has been increasing awareness of the need for long-term follow-up of survivors of childhood cancer. Late complications have developed as a consequence of the disease, specific therapies, or complications of therapy. Screening for potential problems and early management may prevent or minimize the impact on the physical functioning of the child. The psychological sequelae to the child and family should also be assessed.

Alterations in growth, musculoskeletal abnormalities, and hormone deficiencies have been seen as a result of specific therapies. Organ damage (i.e., liver, heart, lung) from therapy may become more evident later in life when these organs are stressed (e.g., pregnancy). Central nervous system effects should be considered especially in children with a history of tumor, infection, or hemorrhage in the brain or who have received cranial irradiation or intrathecal medication. Periodical neurophysiological testing is recommended to evaluate central nervous system impairments in these children.

Gonadal function and sexual ability may be impaired. Genetic predisposition to cancer has been seen in rare cases, specifically with retinoblastoma. When appropriate, genetic and fertility counseling should be provided to the parents and adolescents.

It has been documented that persons who have been treated for childhood malignancies have an increased risk for the development of a second neoplasm (Meadows et al. 1980). This has been seen most often when the child received high doses of radiation or alkylating chemotherapy agents.

The psychological impact on the patient and family members also needs to be assessed, even after the "cure." Parents and siblings may have suffered adverse psychological effects due to the experience of cancer in the family. As children grow into adulthood, they may have evolving concerns related to their cancer experience. Adolescents have reported difficulty in obtaining jobs and health insurance. They may require guidance regarding social discrimination and their legal rights.

As children who have cancer enter adolescence they should receive information of the potential late consequences of cancer and the treatment. They should be encouraged to continue to seek routine health care and receive a summary of their disease and treatment history, especially if they move to another area. Anticipatory counseling, periodic physical examinations, and testing are ideally directed by a multidisciplinary health care team familiar with the late effects of childhood cancer.

Psychosocial and Financial Issues

The diagnosis of cancer in a child, regardless of prognosis, represents an extremely stressful experience for each member of the family. Although childhood cancer is now termed a chronic illness due to the high survival rates, the course is intermined with often numerous acute episodes. Coping styles, additional stressors, areas of strengths, and the quantity and quality of the family's support network will vary. If the parents are divorced or separated, the impact of the illness may affect two family units.

The coping tasks that parents confront have been identified by Hoffman and Futterman (1971):

- Anticipatory mourning for the loss of the "well" child

- Maintaining a sense of mastery over their grief to be able to continue to respond to day-to-day responsibilities

- Helping their child cope and adapt to the illness, while encouraging normal development

- Maintaining the integrity of the family and responding to each of the needs of the individuals

Exhibit 11-1 Safe Handling of Chemotherapy in the Home

Several studies have documented that antineoplastic agents are potentially mutagenic, carcinogenic, and teratogenic to health care personnel who handle these agents. Therefore, in 1986, the U.S. Occupational Safety and Health Administration (OSHA) issued protective guidelines for mixing and administration of antineoplastic agents and proper disposal of contaminated equipment. Although little is known about the potential hazards to family members of children being treated with chemotherapy, it is advised to be cautious and limit exposure to contamination. *Note:* Most chemotherapy is excreted in the body secretions (urine, vomit, stool) while receiving chemotherapy and for 48 hours after the last dose of therapy.

Hygiene

1. Wash hands with soap and water after going to the bathroom.
2. Close toilet lid and flush after use.
3. Wash hands with soap and water after handling urine, vomit, and stool.

Oral Chemotherapy

1. Wash hands well with soap and water.
2. Remove plastic cover from medication containers.
3. Pour out the prescribed number of pills into cover. You can also use a ''medication cup'' or other small container. Use the cup only for medication.
4. If crushing pills, crush the pills in a plastic wrap.
5. Wash hands well with soap and water after administration.
6. Return extra medicine to your hospital pharmacy.

Intravenous Chemotherapy

1. Ideally, all intravenous chemotherapeutic agents should be mixed and properly labeled by the pharmacist using safety precautions.
2. If mixing chemotherapeutic drugs in the home, receive dilution and dosage instructions from health care providers.
3. Select a room that is well ventilated and has a good light source.
4. Select a flat, uncluttered, clean surface.
5. Only the person mixing or drawing up the drugs should be in the room.
6. No eating, drinking, smoking, or gum chewing should be done while mixing. Do not mix drugs in an area where there are uncovered foods or cosmetics.
7. Latex gloves and reading or safety glasses should be worn.
8. All mixing of drugs should be performed over a plastic absorbent disposable covering.
9. When drawing a chemotherapeutic agent from a vial, wrap a sterile gauze around the junction of the needle and top of the vial.
10. Before removing needle from the vial, raise needle above liquid and allow excess air to escape into syringe. This will prevent spraying of the drug from the vial when the needle is removed.
11. Put gloves, plastic covering, alcohol pads, etc., into a plastic bag and secure tightly. Discard in home trash.
12. Place vials of drugs, infusion bag, tubing, needles, and syringes used in mixing the drugs in a leakproof, shatterproof, and puncture-proof container (e.g., coffee can). Seal container and return to hospital pharmacy for proper disposal.

Cleaning up Urine, Vomit, or Stool

1. Use latex gloves and paper towels to clean up vomit, urine, or stool. Wash area with paper towel, soap, and water, and then rinse area with another paper towel.
2. Place latex gloves and paper towels in a plastic bag. Seal tightly. Throw out in home trash.
3. Wash hands well with soap and water after removing gloves.
4. If assistive devices (bedpans, urinals, commodes, or emesis basins) are used, use latex gloves to rinse item thoroughly. Avoid spilling or splashing on skin.

Diapers

1. Wear latex gloves when changing diapers.
2. For cloth diapers: wash separately from other laundry.
3. For disposable diapers: place in plastic bag, secure tightly, and dispose of as usual.

Clothing and Linens

1. Wear latex gloves while handling clothing or linen soiled with urine, vomit, or stool. Avoid having soiled articles come in contact with your clothing.
2. Wash soiled linens and clothing separately.

Exhibit 11-1 continued

Medication Spills on Floor or Furniture

1. Wear latex gloves and use paper towel to pick up or wipe up spilled medication.
2. Clean area with another paper towel and soap and water and rinse area with another paper towel.

Medication Spills on Skin or in Eyes

1. Wash skin with soap and water immediately after contact.
2. Immediately rinse out eye(s) with fast running water for 15 minutes. Keep affected eye(s) open while rinsing it out.
3. Contact health care provider for follow-up care.

Johnson and colleagues (1979) state, "The keys to easing the initial stress are gentle, honest communication, patience, empathy, and education." Helping parents to problem solve and make their perceived mountains into mole hills (e.g., who will babysit the other children when we go to clinic?) will restore their need to feel in control.

Parents often require guidance in dealing with their children about the disease and treatment. Role modeling communication techniques and providing informational materials is helpful. They often require information in responding to the reactions and comments of well-meaning friends and relatives. Other family members and friends may be pessimistic in their outlook of the child's health or offer suggestions that may weaken the parents' ability to cope with the reality of the situation. Other persons, unable to cope themselves, may withdraw from relationships with the family. Parents should be informed of these potential reactions. Methods to redirect these reactions into constructive assistance by providing information and suggestions of support are helpful.

Parents should also receive anticipatory counseling on common issues that result in additional marital stress. Continued open communication between couples is essential. There is no room for blaming the partner for the illness in the child or for the additional burdens as a result of illness. Respect for the roles that the father and mother assume in maintaining the income and needs of the family should be addressed. Parents should try to find private time to share their feelings and strengthen their union. Often, parents find association with other parents of children with cancer beneficial for recognition of the normalcy of their feelings and responses, as well as for additional support and information. Self-help parent groups such as the Candlelighters should be

identified as a potential aid to parents. It is not uncommon for the family to have additional financial concerns related to cancer in a child. Financial counselors should be consulted initially to assist the family. Agencies that can provide financial support should be identified. Some parents may hesitate to receive assistance due to pride; therefore, tact is required in offering support while maintaining their feeling of self-esteem.

Parents should also receive counseling in fostering the normal development in their child with cancer and the impact the illness may have on their other children. The nurse should stress that the child with cancer should not be treated as "special," since this may influence the expectations of the child later in adult life. Parents should continue to provide consistent limits and appropriate discipline. They should foster the child's independence rather than promote overprotectiveness.

Children who receive information about disease and treatment at an age-appropriate level are able to respond amazingly well. Their questions should be answered as honestly and calmly as possible. They should be encouraged to express their fears and concerns. Whenever possible, they should be allowed choices to assist them in maintaining control.

The major issue in coping for young children is fear of separation from parents. Parents should be allowed to accompany their child during treatment visits or to provide a close surrogate, such as a grandparent. Parents should be aware that often young children may perceive the intrusive procedures performed on them as a result of their bad deeds. They need reassurance that these events are not a consequence of wrongdoings.

School-age children and adolescents often fear the reactions of their peers to their change in appearance, predominately hair loss. Most pediatric oncology centers have developed school reentry programs to communicate with school personnel. School reentry programs should share information regarding the following:

- Disease, treatment, and expected absences
- The child's physical and learning limitations
- Psychological adaptation of the child and family members
- Importance of notification of parents of chickenpox or measles exposure of the child and avoidance of live virus immunization
- Designing a tutorial program when necessary
- Preparation of classmates for the child's return to school
- Continued communication with parents and health care providers to assess the child's changing needs

The teacher, school nurse, home care nurse, or a member of the pediatric oncology team should share information with the classmates prior to the child's return to the school. These visits are beneficial in reducing the fears the friends and fellow students may express about the cancer, such as ''cancer is contagious'' or ''that everyone who gets cancer dies.'' With simplistic explanations, students can understand cancer, its treatment, and reasons for side effects of therapy. Students are encouraged to be empathetic (e.g., ''How would you want to be treated if you had to get medicine that made you lose your hair?''). Preparation of the classmates helps reduce the embarrassment and social isolation often felt by the child with cancer that may lead to school phobia.

Older children and adolescents often benefit from participation in support groups, camps, and other activities designed to acquaint them with other children sharing the cancer experience. Camps for children with cancer are designed to encourage independence and stress normalcy, rather than the sick role.

As previously cited, the siblings of children with cancer are often emotional victims of the disease. Parents require counseling on supporting their children who are not sick. The siblings may have fantasies about the disease, its cause,

and side effects of treatment. They require age-appropriate information and the assurance that nothing they did or did not do caused the cancer. They should receive special time to reaffirm they are also loved and receive attention and praise for their accomplishments. Parents should encourage the children to express their feelings in acceptable ways. Changes in the siblings' roles and responsibilities should be minimized, and maintenance of their usual routine and activities is encouraged. Parents should receive information on special programs for assisting siblings to cope with a brother or sister with cancer.

Nursing Care Plan in the Home

Discharge from the security of the hospital after the diagnosis of cancer is often perceived by most families as stressful. Parents are frequently unsure of their capability to meet the demands that cancer in the family entails. Often, children have additional care needs, such as central line catheters. In addition, due to insurance policies, administration of supportive therapies, such as antibiotics and total parenteral nutrition, is increasingly being performed in the home. The home care nurse can assist families in the psychological transition to the home, as well as offer support in providing care to the child with cancer.

A method of communication should be established between the pediatric oncology nurse and home care nurse. The initial referral should relate information on the cancer, treatment plan, discharge teaching, and home care needs. Periodic updates should follow, especially after acute episodes or change in treatment plan.

The primary goals in caring for a child with cancer in the home are (1) reinforcement of discharge teaching; (2) prevention and early identification of complications; (3) rehabilitation to optimal physical ability; (4) access to community resources; and (5) promotion of family cohesion, communication, and positive adaptation of each individual to the chronic illness.

Reinforcement of Discharge Teaching

Family members may have retained little information after diagnosis due to the stress. The home care nurse needs to assess the knowledge of the family and identify areas for reinforcement of teaching. Specific areas of reinforcement include the following:

- Information regarding cancer type
- Various therapies and schedule
- Purpose and schedule for medications in the home
- Expected side effects of current therapy
- Home care of and precautions related to side effects of therapy
- Frequency of tests (e.g., blood sampling)
- Additional care needs of child (e.g., central line care, home total parenteral nutrition or antibiotics, postoperative care)

Often, parents need assistance in differentiating between normal deviations in health, side effects of therapy, and recurrence of cancer. For example, the parents of a 2-year-old girl were concerned by her irritability, low-grade fever, and diarrhea. They thought her symptoms were due to her therapy or relapse of the leukemia, but careful examination revealed the child was breaking in her molars and "teething," and this was her usual response to this normal physical milestone.

It cannot be assumed that parents and children will be compliant in taking chemotherapy and other prescribed medications. Parents should be encouraged to watch their young children take their medication, because they may throw the medication away or "feed it to the cat." Adolescents may become so involved in their daily activities or seek to gain control over the cancer and therefore purposefully forget to take their medications. This high-risk group requires special attention in determining their compliance without inferring guilt.

Prevention and Early Identification of Complications

Minor problems may quickly become oncologic emergencies in a child receiving therapy for cancer. Any concerns about the child's health status should be immediately reported to the pediatric oncologist or nurse.

Infection continues to be the leading cause of death in children with cancer. Since most children are receiving immunosuppressive therapy it is unlikely they will complete their treatment course without an infectious episode. It should be stressed to patients and parents that any fever or signs of potential infection (pain, redness or drainage of skin, cough or shortness of breath) be immediately reported. The neutropenic patient may not be able to elicit an inflammatory response; therefore, subtle signs should not be ignored.

The nurse can assist in identification of risk factors in the child's environment that could increase the potential for infection. Reinforcement of teaching regarding personal hygiene, chickenpox exposure, and avoidance of live immunizations should be stressed.

Dry skin and rashes may be avenues for development of infection. The nurse can assist in assessment of the cause. Irritation due to tape or dry skin due to weather exposure are examples in which the nurse can suggest interventions. Rashes should always be reported to the physician.

Children with central line catheters may receive home antibiotic therapy after initial stabilization of infection in the hospital. The home care nurse should review the infusion procedure with parents or may be responsible for the administration of the medication.

Signs and symptoms of thrombocytopenia and anemia should be reported immediately. The home care nurse can provide suggestions for safe play and energy conservation measures to reduce fatigue. Activities such as school can be planned during periods of most tolerance. Other reasons for fatigue should be explored, including pain, sleep disturbances, or anxiety, and appropriate interventions initiated to reduce these problems.

Weight loss and anorexia should be monitored closely. Small amounts of weight loss in a young child should be considered significant. The nurse should assess the cause of decreased intake and provide nutritional counseling. Children who are unable to take an adequate caloric intake may require supplementation through nasogastric feedings or total parenteral nutrition. Parents will require follow-up observation if these interventions are performed in the home.

The home care nurse can provide nutritional guidance for diarrhea, constipation, and nausea and vomiting. Medications may provide relief when there is prolongation of symptoms, which should be reported to the physician.

Any change in neurological functioning of the child should be reported immediately. There may be numerous causative factors, most requiring prompt medical interventions.

Children who are experiencing pain require careful assessment of the location, intensity, and possible cause. All painful episodes should be reported. The home care nurse should collaborate with the health care team to assist in the management toward pain relief.

Rehabilitation to Optimal Physical Ability

Cancer may result in temporary or permanent physical disabilities in some children. Children may have impairment due to amputation or neurological sequelae. There may be loss of sensory function due to blindness or decreased hearing. Each child will require assessment of his or her special needs. Additional home care or school services may be required, such as occupational, physical, and speech therapy. Special supplies and appliances may be necessary to provide care in the home. The home care nurse is in a position to assist the family in providing for these special care needs.

Provision of Access to Community Resources

The home care nurse may be more aware of local resources and agencies that may benefit the families of children with cancer. In addition, the nurse can act as patient advocate in the community to assist in acquisition of the required resources.

The nurse may be aware of parent support groups, such as the Candlelighters. Other organizations in the geographical area may be identified that provide educational materials, as well as psychological support.

The nurse or local social worker may be familiar with local agencies or organizations that provide financial support, assistance with transportation, respite care, or babysitting services. The nurse can also assist parents with completion of numerous and often complicated agency forms.

Promotion of Family Cohesion, Communication, and Positive Adaptation to the Chronic Illness

The home care nurse is in a unique position to evaluate potential problems in the adjustment of family members. A visit planned immediately after diagnosis can establish a relationship with the family and address their initial questions, concerns, and feelings related to the cancer.

The ongoing role of the nurse is to foster a sense of control and independence and encourage the family members to take it "one day at a time." If adjustment problems are identified the nurse can provide counseling or make referrals for psychological support.

Unfortunately, not all children will remain in remission of their disease or respond favorably to treatment. Recurrences of the disease add additional stress on the family system with the threat of the death of the child. At this time, many parents may seek unproven methods of cancer treatment (Johnson et al. 1979) and health care professionals need to share realistic optimism on treatment options and assist family members in making decisions.

When all therapy options are exhausted and the child's condition is terminal the parents may require assistance in discussing this fact with their children. They require guidance in making choices surrounding their preference in care of their child who is dying. If they want their child to die in the home, the home care nurse and/or hospice nurse will have a pivotal role in providing comfort measures for the child and emotional support for the family, relatives, and friends. Discussion on the care of the terminally ill child is located in Chapter 12.

HOME CARE OF CENTRAL LINE CATHETERS

Central line catheters have become increasingly popular for use in children with hematologic and malignant disorders and other chronic health problems. The catheters facilitate ease in treatment administration as well as enhance the quality of life for the patients. The catheters are designed for long-term use (months to years) with proper maintenance.

Children who benefit from placement of a central line catheter include those who require intensive chemotherapy, consecutive days of therapy, or frequent administration of vesicant drugs. Other considerations for the insertion of a central line catheter are for children requiring long-term therapy of blood products, antibiotics, or total parenteral nutrition. Children who have traumatic reactions to venipuncture and have difficult access should also be considered as candidates for placement of central line catheters. The catheters have the additional advantage of being used for blood sampling.

The two major types of central line catheters are the external right arterial catheter (external catheter) and the implanted infusion port catheter (implanted port). Both catheters are made of flexible Silastic rubber and are surgically inserted into a large vein, usually a cephalic or external jugular vein, with the end of the catheter resting in the right atrium of the heart. For intensive combination therapy, double-and triple-lumen catheters are available.

The external catheter allows easy accessibility since several inches of the tube extend outside the chest wall. This catheter is tunneled through the subcutaneous tissue from the anterior chest (exit site). A Dacron cuff wrapped around the tunneled portion of catheter allows growth of tissue to the cuff anchoring the catheter securely in the chest. This process takes approximately 2 weeks. Another purpose of the cuff is to impede infection up the tunnel. The catheter is then inserted into the vein (entrance site) (Figure 11-2).

There are several advantages for the selection of the external catheter. This type provides convenience in accessing the device for frequent use

and access is not traumatic. It is usually easily repaired and does not require surgical removal. The disadvantages include minor restrictions in activities (swimming in natural bodies of water) and necessitate securing the catheter to the chest to prevent pulling or accidental removal of the catheter. This catheter also requires more maintenance and therefore more supplies.

The implanted port catheter comprises a self-sealing silicone port encased in a plastic or steel chamber. This chamber is attached to the catheter. The chamber is usually placed in the tissue near the anterior wall of chest and sutured in place. The catheter is tunneled through the subcutaneous tissue and introduced into the vein. The skin above the port is sutured closed (Figure 11-3).

Implanted ports have several advantages. They may be more cosmetically appealing for older children. They do not limit activity and require less maintenance. The major disadvantages of this catheter type include less convenience for frequent port access and requirement of a special Huber-point needle for port entry. This catheter requires port access be accom-

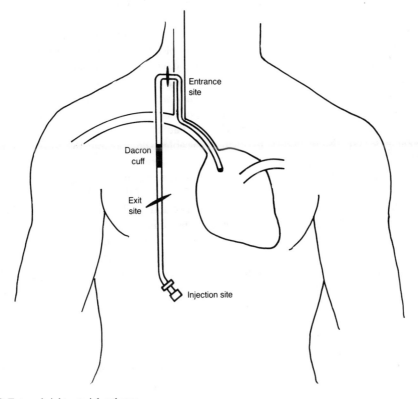

Figure 11-2 External right arterial catheter.

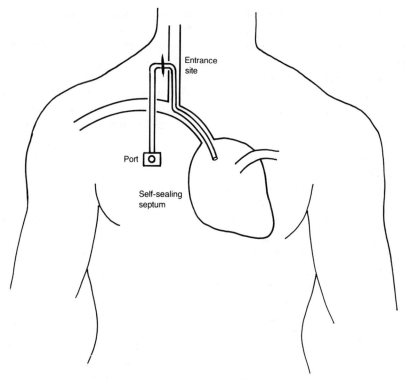

Figure 11-3 Implanted infusion port catheter.

plished by passage of the needle through the skin, and this may be perceived as painful or traumatic for younger children. The needle has the potential for dislodging from the port during long infusions especially with active, young children. In addition, the catheter requires surgical removal. Parents and older children should be involved in the selection of the type of catheter to be inserted. They should be informed of the advantages and disadvantages of each catheter. They often benefit in talking with other children who have had catheters and their parents. Preoperative therapeutic play with a doll that has a catheter can reduce the fear young children may experience with placement of the device.

Central line catheters are surgically placed under general or local anesthesia. A postoperative chest film should confirm proper placement of the catheter. Patients should be initially observed for bleeding, signs of infection at the incision sites, pneumothorax, hemothorax, or arterial puncture. They may have slight discomfort, especially at the entrance site, for approximately 2 days.

Discharge Planning Issues

A major role of nursing is to instruct parents and older children in the proper maintenance of the device. The catheter care involved, in order to maintain patency and prevent infection, will vary with the type of catheter and institutional policies.

Parents and other primary caretakers should be able to demonstrate the correct method of care and maintenance prior to discharge. Written instructions on care should be provided for home reference. If the child attends school, the school nurse and teacher should receive information on the catheter and emergency care if problems should occur (Exhibit 11-2).

Supplies required for maintenance should be provided. Instructions on storage and disposal of supplies should emphasize the need to maintain sterility prior to use and in keeping sharp objects out of the reach of children. Used needles and syringes should be placed in a leakproof, puncture-proof, and/or shatter-resistent container. Most institutions encourage the return of used needles and syringes for proper disposal.

Exhibit 11-2 Important Information on Central Line Catheters for School Personnel

Your student, _____, has a central line catheter inserted into a large vein and tunneled under the skin exiting at the chest. There are several types of catheters (Broviac, Hickman, or Raaf). The purposes for the catheter are as follows:

1. Administration of drugs, blood products, and/or intravenous nutrition
2. Drawing blood samples for testing

Many teachers are concerned about the catheter and are interested in information and precautions they should take. The child's parents have been instructed in the care of the catheter and can be an excellent resource for your questions and concerns. The central line catheter is secured under the skin by a special cuff and is difficult to pull out. The catheter should be securely taped down for activities such as gym or recess. The following actions should be taken *if the catheter is pulled out:*

1. Apply pressure to the exit and entrance sites of the catheter for 20 minutes and keep the child in a sitting position.
2. Contact the parents or call the number below.

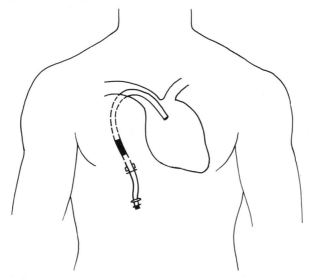

Small children should have the catheter covered when using scissors. The following actions should be taken *if the catheter is cut:*

1. Place a clamp above the site of the cut.
2. Wrap the cut area in sterile gauze.
3. Contact the parents or call the number below.

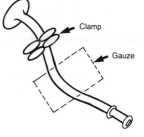

Students who swim in school have been instructed to apply a special plastic wrap over their catheter prior to swimming.

The following supplies should be kept in the classroom to use if problems arise:

1. A clamp
2. A catheter cap
3. Tape
4. Sterile gauze

Contact person for questions, concerns, or problems:

_____ Telephone No.

Exhibit 11-3 Removal of Central Line Catheter

The central line catheter is removed when it is no longer needed or when the central line or tunnel has become infected. This handout will explain how the catheter is removed and care instructions to follow at home. If you have any questions, please ask your nurse or physician.

What Will Happen

1. Your child will change into a hospital gown. The dressing over the catheter will be removed.
2. Your child may be given medication to make him or her sleepy.
3. The exit site will be cleansed. Your child will receive an injection to numb the exit site area.
4. The skin that has grown around the catheter and cuff will be loosened. This will make it easier to remove the catheter.
5. The catheter is pulled out. Your child may feel some discomfort as this happens.

After Removal

1. Right after the catheter is removed, your child will be placed in an upright sitting position.
2. Pressure will be applied to the entrance site for 20 minutes. (This is important in order to collapse the vein in which the catheter was placed.)
3. Pressure will also be applied to the exit site until bleeding has stopped.
4. The exit site will then be cleansed and bandaged.
5. If your child received sedation, you will need to wait to leave the clinic until your child can at least be aroused from sedation.

Initiation of a home care nurse referral should occur when there is question of care compliance by the caregiver. Home care nurses should receive a copy of the care instructions to guide their observations and teaching in the home.

Nursing Care Plans in the Home

Meticulous care of the catheter is essential to prevent complications and maintain proper utilization. There are significant variations in the procedures for home care of central line catheters from one institution to another. Good handwashing should always precede caring for the catheter. Sterile gloves should always be worn with the entry into an implanted port, but few institutions recommend sterile gloves in handling external catheters. Procedures for care of the central line can be found in Chapter 7.

Blood Drawing from Catheter

Often family members are instructed on obtaining blood specimens from the catheter. The procedure is easily taught and has the advantage of decreasing the number of visits to the medical center. The procedure for drawing blood from the external catheter involves cleaning the juncture of the injection cap and catheter with an alcohol swab. The cap is removed and a sterile syringe is connected to the catheter. The clamp is released and 5 mL of fluid is aspirated

back. Since this fluid is a mixture of blood and heparinized solution it is discarded after reclamping the catheter. A second syringe is attached and the amount of blood needed for the test is aspirated. The catheter is clamped, the syringe removed, and a sterile injection cap is applied. The catheter is then flushed with heparinized solution. The blood sample is put in the appropriate tube.

To draw blood from the implanted port, the sterile supplies are prepared and sterile gloves are applied. The area above the port is prepped with a povidone-iodine swab. As with the flushing technique, one hand is the sterile hand and opposite is the clean hand. The Huber needle is inserted and held by sterile hand. A 5 cc syringe is attached to the Huber needle and 3 to 5cc of solution is aspirated and syringe removed. Another sterile syringe is connected to the needle and the blood sample is obtained. The syringe is removed and the catheter is flushed with 5 cc of saline followed by 1 mL of 1000 U Heparin. The Huber needle is removed and pressure is applied over site with sterile gauze. The syringe containing the blood specimen is emptied into the appropriate tube.

Venous Thrombosis

A child who has a central line catheter and develops edema of the neck and face, predominately on the side of the catheter, should be

Exhibit 11-4 Home Care After Removal of Central Line Catheter

---

Observation of Entrance Site

1. Your child should remain in a semi-upright position for 6 hours after the catheter is removed.
2. Check the entrance site every hour for 6 hours. Check for swelling and/or bruising under the skin.
3. If swelling occurs, apply firm pressure to the entrance site for 20 minutes. Then call the phone number provided below.

Care of the Exit Site

1. Clean the exit site daily for 3 days. Wash hands first. Then clean site with soap and water. Apply triple antibiotic ointment to the site and cover with a bandage.
2. After 3 days the exit site can be left open to the air.
3. Your child can bathe and shower the day after the catheter is removed.
4. Call your physician if you see these signs of infection at the exit site: redness or drainage.

General Notes

1. Was your child's cuff removed (   ) Yes   (   ) No
   Sometimes the cuff will stay under the skin when the catheter is removed. Usually this will not cause any problems. In rare cases, though, the cuff may become infected and need to be removed. (Redness and swelling in the cuff area may be signs of infection.) Children should be told when they are older if they have the cuff under the skin in case any problems arise.
2. Your child may want to keep the catheter. If so, it should be soaked overnight in bleach or Hibaclens.

If you have any questions or concerns, please call _____.

---

suspected of venous thrombosis. This problem occurs due to thrombus formation around the catheter obstructing venous circulation to the upper neck and head regions. This results in venous occlusion and edema.

Urokinase infusion and systemic heparin therapy is necessary for lysis of the clot. The catheter may require removal after the urokinase therapy if there is only partial lysis of the clot.

Removal of the Central Line Catheter

The central line catheter is removed when it is no longer needed or complications develop that necessitate removal. External catheters are usually pulled forcefully while the child is sedated. Lidocaine is injected around the exit site, and the skin is loosened from the exit site. Occasionally, especially when there is a tunnel infection, the tissue adhering to the cuff is loosened to ensure cuff removal when pulling the catheter. As the catheter is pulled back, pressure is applied to the entrance site for 20 minutes to collapse the vein in which the catheter was placed. Pressure is also applied to the exit site with a sterile gauze until bleeding has stopped. Catheter removal information and home care after removal of the exter-

nal catheter are outlined in Exhibits 11-3 and 11-4.

The implanted port catheter is removed through a surgical procedure. An incision is made over the area of the port, and the sutures around the port are released. The port and catheter are removed. Pressure is applied immediately to the entrance site, and the incision area is sutured closed. Parents are instructed on cleaning of the incision site. Sutures are removed in 1 week.

REFERENCES

Ablin, A, and Wong, W. "The Blood and its Disorders." In *Nursing Care of Children*, edited by E. Waechter, F. Blake, and J. Lipp. Philadelphia: J.B. Lippincott Co., 1976.

Aledort, L. *Current Management in the Treatment of Hemophilia: A Physician's Manual*. National Hemophilia Foundation, 1986.

Alter, B. "The Bone Marrow Failure Syndromes." In *Hematology of Infancy and Childhood*, edited by D. Nathan and F. Oski. Philadelphia: W. B. Saunders Co., 1987.

Altman, A., and Swartz, A.D., "The Soft Tissue Sarcomas." In *Malignant Diseases in Infancy, Childhood and Adolescence*. Philadelphia: W.B. Saunders Co., 1983.

American Cancer Society. *Cancer Facts and Figures—1988*. New York: American Cancer Society, 1988.

Ashenhurst, J.; Green, D.; Hruby, M.; Langenhenning, P.; Sapko, M.; Seeler, R.; and Telfer, M. *Understanding Hemophilia: A Guide for Parents*. Hemophilia Foundation of Illinois, 1979.

Belasco, J.; Chatten, J.; and D'Angio, G. "Wilms' Tumor." In *Clinical Pediatric Oncology*. 3d ed., edited by W.W. Sutow, D.J. Fernbach, and T.J. Viette. St. Louis: C.V. Mosby Co., 1984.

Blattner, W.; Biggar, R.; Weiss, S.; Melby, M.; and Goedert, J. "Epidemiology of Human T-lymphotropic Virus Type III and the Risk of Acquired Immunodeficiency Syndrome." *Annals of Internal Medicine* 103 (1985):665–670.

Boland, M., and Klug, R. "AIDS: The Implications for Home Care." *MCN: American Journal of Maternal Child Nursing* 11(1986):404–411.

Buchanan, G.R. "Neonatal Coagulation: Normal Physiology and Pathophysiology." *Clinical Haematology* 7(1978):85.

Cotta, S.; Jutras, M.; and McQuarrie, A. *Physical Therapy in Hemophilia*. New York: National Hemophilia Foundation, 1987.

D'Angio, G. "The Treatment of Wilms' Tumor: Results of 2nd National Wilms' Tumor Study." *Cancer* 47(1983): 2302.

Dallman, P. "Iron Deficiency and Related Nutritional Anemias." In *Hematology of Infancy and Childhood*, edited by D. Nathan and F. Oski. Philadelphia: W.B. Saunders Co., 1987.

Dyment, P.G., and Jaffe, N. "Retinoblastoma." In *Pediatric Oncology: A Treatise for Clinicians*, edited by P. Lanzkowsky. New York: McGraw-Hill Book Co., 1983.

Ertel, L.J. "Malignant Bone Tumors: Ewing's Sarcoma." In *Cancer Therapy in Children*, edited by C. Pochedly. Thorofare, N.J.: Charles B. Slack, Inc., 1983.

Ettinger, L.J. "Osteosarcoma." *Pediatric Annals* 12(1983): 374–382.

Fachtman, D.; Fergusson, J.; Ford, N.; and Pryor, A. "The Treatment of Children with Cancer." In *Nursing Care of the Child with Cancer*, edited by D. Fochtman and G. Foley. Boston: Little, Brown & Co., 1982.

Fitchen, J. "Pancytopenia and Bone Marrow Failure." In *Practical Hematology*, edited by W.G. Hocking. New York: John Wiley & Sons, 1983.

Foley, G. "Retinoblastoma." In *Nursing Care of the Child with Cancer*, edited by D. Fochtman and G. Foley. Boston: Little, Brown & Co., 1982.

Gardner, R.V., and Graham-Pole, J. "Non-Hodgkin's Lymphoma." *Pediatric Annals* 12(1983):322–335.

Glucksberg, H.; Storb, R.; Fefer, A.; et al. "Clinical Manifestations of Graft-versus-Host Disease in Human Recipients of Marrow from HLA-matched Sibling Donors." *Transplantation* 18(1974):295–304.

Goodman, J. Nursing Care of the High Risk Infant. In *Child and Family: Concepts of Nursing Practice*, edited by M. Smith, J. Goodman, and N. Ramsey. New York: McGraw-Hill Book Co., 1987.

Hall, M.; Hardin, K.; and Conatser, C. "The Challenges of Psychological Care." In *Nursing Care of the Child with Cancer*, edited by D. Fochtman and G. Foley. Boston: Little, Brown & Co., 1982.

Hayes, F.A., and Green A.A. "Neuroblastoma." *Pediatric Annals* 12(1983): 366–373.

Heyn, R.; Holland, R.; Newton, W.A.; Tesst, M.; Bresslow, N.; and Hartment, J.R. "The Role of Combined Chemotherapy in Treatment of Rhabdomyosarcoma in Children." *Cancer* 34(1974):2128.

Higgins, J., and Muir, C. "Environment Carcinogenesis: Misconceptions and Limitations to Cancer Control." *Journal of the National Cancer Institute* 63(1979): 1290.

Hoffman, E., and Futterman, E.M. "Coping with Waiting: Psychiatric Intervention and Study in the Waiting Room of a Pediatric Oncology Clinic. *Comprehensive Psychiatry* 12(1971):67–80.

James, J., and Hinoki, K. "Hematologic Function." In *Child and Family: Concepts of Nursing Practice*, edited by M. Smith, J. Goodman, and N. Ramsey. New York: McGraw-Hill Book Co., 1987.

Johnson, F.L.; Thomas, E.D.; Clark, B.S.; Chard, R.L.; Hartman, J.R.; and Storb, R. "A Comparison of Marrow Transplantation with Chemotherapy for Children with Acute Lymphoblastic Leukemia in Second or Subsequent Remission." *New England Journal of Medicine* 305(1981):846–851.

Johnson, L.; Rudolph, L.; and Hartman, J. "Helping the Family Cope with Childhood Cancer." *Psychosomatics* 4(1979):241–251.

Kivlahan, C., and James, E.J. "The Natural History of Neonatal Jaundice." *Pediatrics* 74, no. 3(1984): 364-370

Lum, L.G.; Tubergen, D.G.; Corash, L.; and Blaese, R.M.. "Splenectomy in the Management of Thrombocytopenia of the Wiskott-Aldrich Syndrome." *New England Journal of Medicine* 302(1980):892–896.

Lusher, J. "Diseases of Coagulation: The Fluid Phase." In *Hematology of Infancy and Childhood*, edited by D. Nathan and F. Oski. Philadelphia: W.B. Saunders Co., 1987.

Maurer, A.; Moon, T.; Donaldson, M.; Fernandez, C.; Gehan, E.; Hammond, D.; Hays, D.; Lawrence, W.; Newton, W.; Ragab, A.; Reney, B.; Soule, E.H.; Sutow, W.; and Tesst, M. "The Intergroup Rhabdomyosarcoma Study: A Preliminary Report." *Cancer* 40(1977):2015.

McCalla, J. "A Multidisciplinary Approach to Identification and Remedial Intervention for Adverse Late Effects of Cancer Therapy." *Nursing Clinics of North America* 20(1985):117–130.

Meadows, A.; Krejmas, N.L.; and Belasco, J.B. "The Medical Cost of Cure: Sequelae in Survivors of Childhood Cancer." In *Status of the Curability of Childhood Cancers*, edited by J. Van Eys and M.P. Sullivan. New York: Raven Press, 1980.

Miller, D. "Acute Lymphoblastic Leukemia." *Pediatric Clinics of North America* 27(1980):1980.

Niemeyer, C.M.; Hitchcock-Bryan, S.; and Sallan, S.E. "Comparative Analysis of Treatment Programs for Childhood Acute Lymphoblastic Leukemia." *Seminars in Oncology* 12(1985):122–130.

Pendergrass, T. "Congenital Anomalies in Children with Wilms' Tumor." *Cancer* 37(1976):403.

Pizzo, P.A. "Rhabdomyosarcoma and the Soft Tissue Sarcomas." *Cancer in the Young*, edited by A.S. Levin. New York: Masson, 1982.

Robinson, L. "Acquired Immunodeficiency Syndrome (AIDS)—An Update." *Critical Care Nursing* 4(1984):75–83.

Robinson, L.; Brown, A.; and Underwood, T. "Iron Therapy: Helps and Hazards." *Pediatric Nursing* 4(1978): 9–13.

Rodgers, M. "AIDS in Children: A Review of the Clinical, Epidemiologic, and Public Health Aspects." *Pediatric Infectious Disease* 4(1985):230–236.

Rosen, F., Cooper, M., and Wedgwood, R. "The Primary Immunodeficiencies: I and II. *New England Journal of Medicine* 311(1984): 240, 303.

Rosen, G. "Management of Malignant Bone Tumors in Children and Adolescents." *Pediatric Clinics of North America.* 23(1976):183–213.

Rosove, M. "Bleeding Disorders." In *Practical Hematology*, edited by W.G. Hocking. New York: John Wiley & Sons, 1983.

Seegar, R.C.; Siegel, S.E.; and Sidell, N. "Neuroblastoma: Clinical Perspectives, Monoclonal Antibodies, and Retinoic Acid." *Annals of Internal Medicine* 97(1982):873–884.

Selwyn, P. "AIDS: What is not Known About a History and Immunovirology." *Hospital Practice* 21(1986):69.

Sourkes, B. "Siblings of the Pediatric Patient." In *Psychological Aspects of Childhood Cancer*, edited by J. Kellerman. Springfield, Ill.: Charles C Thomas, 1980.

Sullivan, M.P.; Fuller, L.M.; and Butler, J.J. "Hodgkin's Disease." In *Clinical Pediatric Oncology.* 3d ed., edited by W.W. Sutow, D.J. Fernbach, and T.J. Viette. St. Louis: C.V. Mosby Co., 1984.

Swartz, A., and Levine, A. "Primary Bone Cancer." In *Malignant Diseases of Infancy, Childhood, and Adolescence.* 2d ed., edited by A. Altman and A. Swartz. Philadelphia: W.B. Saunders Co., 1983.

Tapley N.V.; Strong, L.C.; and Sutow, W.W. "Retinoblastoma." In *Clinical Pediatric Oncology.* 3d ed., edited by W.W. Sutow, D.J. Fernbach, and T.J. Viette. St. Louis: C.V. Mosby Co., 1984.

Thomas, E.D.; Buckner, C.D.; Clift, R.; Fefer, A.; Johnson, F.L.; Neiman, P.; Sale, G.; Sanders, J.; Singer, J.; Shulman, H.; Storb, R.; and Weiden, P. "Marrow Transplantation for Acute Non-lymphocytic Leukemia in First Remission." *New England Journal of Medicine* 301(1979):597–599.

Van Eys, J. "Malignant Tumors of the Central Nervous System." In *Clinical Pediatric Oncology.* 3d ed., edited by W.W. Sutow, D.J. Fernback, and T.J. Viette. St. Louis: C.V. Mosby Co., 1984.

Voute, P. "Neuroblastoma." In *Clinical Pediatric Oncology.* 3d ed., edited by W.W. Sutow, D.J. Fernbach, and T.J. Viette. St. Louis: C.V. Mosby Co., 1984.

Weinstein, H.J.; Mayer, R.J.; and Rosenthal, D.S. "Treatment of Acute Myelogenous Leukemia in Children and Adults." *New England Journal of Medicine* 303(1980): 473.

Weinstein, H., and Link, M.P. "Non-Hodgkin's Lymphoma in Childhood." *Clinical Haematology* 8(1979):699–717.

Whaley, L., and Wong, D. "The Child with Hematologic Dysfunction." In *Nursing Care of Infants and Children*, edited by L. Whaley and D. Wong. St. Louis: C.V. Mosby Co., 1987.

The Child with Hyperbilirubinemia Receiving Phototherapy

Nursing Diagnosis	Expected Outcomes	Nursing Interventions
1. Knowledge deficit related to hyperbilirubinemia and purpose and procedure of phototherapy	Parents verbalize knowledge of disease and purpose and procedure of phototherapy Parents communicate their concerns and feelings about home phototherapy Parents demonstrate ability to assemble and use phototherapy unit Child does not develop any harmful effects due to phototherapy Bilirubin level returns to normal	Assess prior knowledge, ability and desire to learn. Assess support in home for respite (someone will need to be with child at all times). Assess instructional needs of other significant caregivers. Instruct parents in • Cause of hyperbilirubinemia • Normal breakdown mechanism of hemoglobin and excretion (urobilinogen in urine—dark urine; stercobilinogen in stool—brown stool) • Purpose of phototherapy Instruct parents in documentation in log every 2 hours during phototherapy • Child's temperature • Hours of treatment • Oral intake • Output • Specific gravity • Position change • Eye patches Instruct on use of phototherapy unit • Assembly and use of unit • Reading temperature probe • Light source remains 30 inches from bed • Reading of fluorometer • Plexiglass shield intact over light source to prevent ultraviolet rays and protection of child from bulb breakage

Nursing Diagnosis	Expected Outcomes	Nursing Interventions
		• Unit placement should be away from drafts, heat vents, and heavy traffic areas
		• Caretaker should avoid prolonged exposure under light and wear sunglasses near light source
		Instruct in preparation of child
		• Application of eye patches over closed eyes of child, then secured with mask and checked hourly
		• Mouth and nose are not obstructed
		• Methylcellulose eye drops application (if prescribed)
		• Report eye drainage to physician
		• Turn every 2 hours to maximize skin exposure
		• Child is placed on abdomen and sides, propped with blankets to prevent aspiration
		• Child is without clothes placed on disposable diaper
		• Child is never fed in unit
		• Paper mask covers gonads (optional)
		RN to draw daily bilirubin levels by heel stick as prescribed by physician.
		Laboratory to call physician with results.
		Home care nurse to communicate with physician for further orders.
2. Potential for impairment of skin integrity related to phototherapy	Child has normal skin reactions as a reaction of phototherapy	Instruct parents about
		• Avoidance of skin lotion
		• Appearance of maculopapular rash is common and disappears spontaneously
		• A severe gray-brown discoloration (bronze baby syndrome) occurs and clears 3 weeks after therapy is discontinued
		• Report extreme skin erythema, dryness, or blistering to physician
3. Potential for altered body temperature related to hypothermia or hyperthermia	Child does not develop hypothermia or hyperthermia	Instruct parents to
		• Maintain temperature in room at 72°F
		• Check child's temperature every hour (physician to specify expected temperature) If too warm, reduce temperature in room If too cold, wrap child in three blankets and increase room temperature
		• Recheck temperature in 30 minutes: if normal return to unit; if still abnormal, call physician

Nursing Diagnosis	Expected Outcomes	Nursing Interventions
4. Potential for fluid volume deficit related to insensible loss due to heat and frequent loose stools	Child does not become dehydrated	Instruct parents to • Offer frequent feeding • Child should take 4 or more extra ounces of formula or water • If breast feeding, encourage at least 8 feedings plus additional water • Record number and color of stools • Weigh infant every 4–8 hours • Call physician if decreased intake of fluids or urine output or projectile vomiting
5. Potential for alteration in parental role related to phototherapy and fatigue of caregiver	There is a period of infant bonding. The child is not affected by sensory deprivation	Child is removed from unit every 2 hours, and eye patches are removed for feedings and interaction with parents Parents are provided with suggestions for stimulation of infant when eye patches are applied (music, voice, and touch) and when out of unit (visual stimulation)

Appendix 11-B

Anemias in Childhood (General)

Nursing Diagnosis	Expected Outcomes	Nursing Interventions
1. Health maintenance: risk factors for anemia	Appropriate referrals are made with suspected anemia in children.	Assess for sign and symptoms of anemia • Pallor • Irritability • Poor feeding and weight loss • Decreased attentiveness • Weakness • Fatigability with exertion Assess for inadequate diet Assess for other contributing causes such as chronic diarrhea or intestinal blood loss Assess decreased financial resources or cultural preferences that may influence proper nutrition
2. Knowledge deficit related to cause and treatment plan for anemia	The parents verbalize knowledge as to cause of anemia and home therapy. Child takes medications.	Instruct in cause of anemia. Instruct in expected signs and symptoms Instruct in meaning of laboratory results and frequency of tests Instruct in treatment plan Instruct in importance of follow-up medical checkups
3. Potential for infection related to increased risk due to tissue hypoxia	Child exhibits no sign of infection or skin breakdown.	Instruct in good hygiene measures Report elevated temperature and other signs of infection to physician
4. Alteration in tissue perfusion related to anemia	Child remains active and alert appropriate for age and capability Parents demonstrate safe and proper use of oxygen in home environment (if required)	Assess level of child's activity tolerance Counsel parents concerning maximizing child's energy

Nursing Diagnosis	Expected Outcomes	Nursing Interventions
	Administer transfusions in the home safely (if required)	• Assist child with activities of daily living • Support activities during peak energy time that stimulate development and independence • Provide sedentary projects when child is most exhausted but prevent boredom and withdrawal • Alert significant others (babysitter, teacher, tutor) to child's physical tolerance • Plan rest periods between activities Report progressive signs of anemia, especially cardiac failure • Shortness of breath • Extreme weakness and fatigue • Edema and weight gain Provide oxygen for use if ordered by physician • Instruct on proper oxygen setting determined by need and physician's order • Stabilize oxygen equipment against falling or puncture • Check contents of container and refill before empty • Do not smoke in area of oxygen use • Apply oxygen tubing correctly to maximize benefits; may need to secure with tape to prevent dislodgement • Provide humidification if nasal/oral mucosa becomes dry and irritated; lubricate nasal mucosa with water-soluble lubricant Obtain order for blood product administration from physician Obtain order for premedications and emergency care from physician Check compatibility of blood product with ABO and Rh factor of patient Check if product was irradiated if ordered Check expiration date and time Infuse product as ordered by physician Check vital signs according to protocol Document according to protocol Notify physician of any adverse reaction
5. Alterations in nutrition related to fatigue and anorexia	Child maintains or gains weight as appropriate Child consumes foods required to correct anemia	Instruct parents to provide frequent small meals to conserve child's energy Counsel parents on deficiency in child's diet

Nursing Diagnosis	Expected Outcomes	Nursing Interventions
		Counsel parents on importance of mealtime as a pleasant experience Check child's weight periodically
6. Potential for ineffective child coping related to decreased physical ability and multiple intrusive procedures	Child is less anxious and adjusts to altered abilities Child demonstrates less fear with procedures	Counsel child, at age-appropriate level in • Cause of symptoms • Purpose of tests and procedures • Importance of medication • Reasons for certain home precautions Observe parent's ability to meet the needs of the child Encourage child to assist in planning activities appropriate to capability
7. Potential for ineffective family coping related to additional stressors to family members	Family members communicate their fears and concerns	Encourage expression of feelings and concerns of parents, siblings, and significant others Discuss feelings of parental guilt for potentially causing anemia in the child Inform family members of signs of progress Anticipate stressful periods and need for respite care for child Counsel parents regarding the special needs of other children for attention and maintenance of as normal routine as possible Assist in providing resources for family

The Child with Sickle Cell Anemia

Nursing Diagnosis	Expected Outcomes	Nursing Interventions
1. Potential for alteration in tissue perfusion related to sickle cell crisis	Child participates in life style that avoids physical and emotional stress. Child drinks adequate amounts of fluid. Child remains free of infection. Child has adequate rest Parents report symptoms of crisis immediately to physician	Instruct on avoidance of factors that promote crisis: • Strenuous physical activity • Infection • Low oxygen environment • Prolonged exposure to heat or cold • Emotional stress Calculate daily recommended intake for age of child. Instruct in minimal daily intake. Instruct that child should drink frequently, every 30–60 minutes Provide suggestions to encourage child to drink • Make drinking enjoyable (e.g., games, pictures on bottom of paper cups, sticker after drinking) • Allow child to select fluid preference • Promote understanding that drinking will make child feel better. Restrict cola and tea (increases diuresis) and cranberry juice (promotes acidosis). Increase fluid intake during warm weather and with increased exercise. Keep temperature in home comfortable. Instruct in signs and symptoms of dehydration • Irritability • Dark, concentrated urine • Poor skin turgor • Dry oral mucosa

Nursing Diagnosis	Expected Outcomes	Nursing Interventions
		Report problems to physician that can lead to dehydration (e.g., vomiting and diarrhea)
		Instruct on early signs and symptoms of infection
		Stress all febrile episodes should be reported to physician.
		Provide health maintenance
		• Periodic pneumococcal vaccine after age 2
		• Updated immunizations
		• Routine dental care
		Stress importance of avoiding known source of infection
		Instruct in importance of rest periods and minimizing activities of overendurance
		Instruct parents in signs and symptoms of crisis episodes
		• Severe pain (abdominal and extremity)
		• Persistent fevers
		• Extreme fatigue
		Instruct parents to report crisis to physician.
2. Potential for alterations in nutrition related to megaloblastic disorders	Child eats well-balanced meals	Instruct on importance of meals
		Provide nutritional counseling on foods high in folic acid and vitamin B_{12} (if deficient)
3. Altered comfort related to sickle cell crisis	Child is free of pain	Administer analgesics for pain as advised by physician
		Use warm compresses to extremities for arthralgia (do not use cold, which produces sickling)
4. Health maintenance	Child does not experience complications related to sickle cell anemia	Encourage routine eye examination
		Encourage follow-up visits in a comprehensive sickle cell clinic for routine evaluation of all systems
	Family members and older children verbalize understanding of genetic transmission	Provide genetic counseling to family and growing child
		Encourage testing of other family members

Appendix 11-D

The Child with Aplastic Anemia

Nursing Diagnosis	Expected Outcomes	Nursing Interventions
1. Knowledge deficit related to medications, schedule, and side effects	Parents verbalize knowledge of medication, schedule, and side effects	Instruct in medications, schedule, and side effects. Provide suggestions for decreasing water retention and increased weight gain on corticosteroid therapy • Low sodium diet • Limit high caloric snacks • Promote nutritious meals
2. Disturbance in self-concept related to masculinization (androgen therapy), weight gain, acne (corticosteroid therapy) hirsutism (cyclosporin A)	Child discusses feelngs and concerns and participates in activities with peers	Provide opportunities for child to discuss feelings about disease, treatment, and impact on self and social interactions. Encourage parents to promote independence and participation in activities that child is successful
3. Potential for ineffective family coping related to feelings of guilt and potential fatal course of disease	Family members communicate feelings and concerns	Introduce family to another family with a child with aplastic anemia. If child is to have a bone marrow transplant, introduce to a family whose child has had a bone marrow transplant. Encourage expression of feelings regarding disease, transmission (Fanconi's anemia), potential causes, and anticipatory grieving. Provide genetic counseling in case of Fanconi's anemia

Appendix 11-E

The Child with Thrombocytopenia

Nursing Diagnosis	Expected Outcomes	Nursing Interventions
1. Potential for bleeding related to thrombocytopenia	The nurse assesses the status of child The nurse performs interventions while minimizing risk of bleeding Parents (older children) verbalize knowledge of disease, treatment, and side effects of therapy Child shows no signs or symptoms of bleedings Parents (older children) initiate protective measures to prevent bleeding	Assess for signs and symptoms of bleeding Avoid use of tourniquet or pad tourniquet and apply loosely If an injection is necessary, use the smallest needle possible and apply pressure for 5 minutes after needle removal Avoid pumping up blood pressure cuff above usual systolic range Instruct parents in cause of disorder and treatment measures Review schedule of home medication and side effects Instruct parents (if applicable) on corticosteroid therapy • Avoid high sodium diet • Limit snacking; provide low calorie snacks • Anticipate mood swings • Taper medication slowly after prolonged use • Take corticosteroids with meals to prevent gastrointestinal ulceration Review common signs and symptoms of bleeding to report to physician • Bruising and petechiae • Bleeding from nose or gums • Hematemesis, coffeeground emesis • Hematuria • Gross blood or tarry stools • Significant increase in menstruating blood flow

Nursing Diagnosis	Expected Outcomes	Nursing Interventions
		• Change in level of consciousness, headaches, or blurred vision
		Instruct parents in protective measures to minimize bleeding
		• Use soft toothbrush; rinse toothbrush under hot water before brushing to soften fibers
		• Measures to keep stools soft (e.g., high bulk diet, use of stool softener)
		• Avoid rectal temperatures, suppositories, and enemas
		• Avoid vaginal douching
		• Avoid tight, constricting clothing
		• Use electric razor, not blades for shaving
		• Avoid use of aspirin, or nonsteroidal analgesics
		• Menstruating females should consult with physician about use of birth control pill or progestational agents to prevent bleeding
		Assist parents in acquisition of Medic Alert tag for child
2. Potential for injury related to thrombocytopenia	The child participates in activities that minimize trauma Parents demonstrate correct procedure when bleeding occurs	Instruct parents to pad side rails of infant's bed Assist parents in structuring activities that avoid trauma, especially falls and contact with hard objects Assist in acquiring a helmet for use by active young children Assist parents in teaching child to wipe nose rather than blowing Instruct school personnel in precautions, especially in relation to degree of physical activity (gym, recess) Instruct parents in steps to take if bleeding occurs • Apply pressure to site (bridge of nose for epitaxis) for 10 minutes; if bleeding continues, call physician and continue to apply pressure
3. Potential for infection (if applicable) related to splenectomy	Parents help child to take prophylactic antibiotic daily	Instruct parents in the importance of compliance in taking antibiotic (penicillin) daily to avoid sepsis
4. Disturbance in self-concept of child related to restricted activities, evidence of bruises, weight gain or corticosteroid therapy	Child verbalizes feelings and concerns about disease, treatment, and restrictions in activities	Assess child's social interaction with peers Encourage the child to verbalize feelings and concerns Instruct parents to provide activities that promote independence and challenges while not initiating trauma Discuss with teacher, coach, or gym teacher methods to encourage participation in activities with peers

Nursing Diagnosis	Expected Outcomes	Nursing Interventions
		(e.g., make junior coach, official score keeper) Offer suggestions on discipline, such as limit setting and "time out"
5. Potential for ineffective family coping related to fears of spontaneous bleeding, hemorrhagic signs on child, restrictions on siblings to avoid rough contact with brother or sister	Family members verbalize their fears and concerns	Encourage expression of feeling and concerns by family members Provide suggestions to parents on coping with episodes of staring of strangers at child with bruises since they may think parents are abusive to child Assist parents in instructing respite, babysitter, or other relatives in care of child so they feel comfortable leaving child in care of others Assist parents in instructing siblings on types of behavior (no hitting) and activities with ill child. *Note:* They should report to parents if ill child is taking advantage of disorder (e.g., "I can hit you but you can't hit me back.")

Appendix 11-F

The Child with Hemophilia

Nursing Diagnosis	Expected Outcomes	Nursing Interventions
1. Potential for injury related to deficiency of clotting factors	Child has few bleeding episodes. Parents recognize early signs of bleeding. Parents initiate appropriate treatment at signs of bleeding. Parents recognize and report early signs of bleeding. Parents initiate appropriate treatment at signs of bleeding.	Make the child's environment as safe as possible: • Pad infant's crib. • Supervise activities of toddlers and young children. • Set appropriate limits. • Choose safe toys • Pad elbow and knee area of clothing of young children. • Assist older children in choice of activities that limit risk of trauma. • Consult with school personnel on participation in activities • Obtain Medic-Alert tag for child to wear. • Use soft toothbrush for oral hygiene. • Use electric shaver rather than straight blade. • Wear loose clothing. • Avoid use of aspirin products. • Keep stools soft with high-bulk diet or stool softener. • Notify physician prior to surgery or dental visits. • Participate in physical therapy program to maintain strong musculature. • Eat well-balanced diet to prevent weight gain and stress on joints. Instruct parents and older children on recognition of bleeding episodes: • Stiffness, tenderness, heat and swelling in joints and muscles

Nursing Diagnosis	Expected Outcomes	Nursing Interventions
		• Pain in groin, flexion of thigh, and resistance to extend extremity
		• Change in level of consciousness, headaches
		• Nasal or oral mucosa bleeding
		• Hematuria
		Discuss methods to assist parents to remain calm and of support to child during bleeding.
		Instruct parents to report all bleeding episodes to physician, especially those involving throat, neck, or central nervous system *immediately*.
		Instruct parents on initial interventions with bleeding:
		• Skin abrasions—apply pressure for 5 to 10 minutes with clean gauze.
		• Nose bleed—apply firm pressure for 5–10 minutes to bridge of nose; keep child in sitting position with head tilted slightly forward.
		• Muscle and joint bleeding—apply ice to affected area; apply padded splint to posterior area (maintain a functional comfortable position); elevate and rest extremity (may need to use crutches for lower extremity hemorrhage).
		• Hematuria—drink 6–8 mL of fluid every 2–3 hours.
		Instruct parents in home administration of concentrate or cryoprecipitate:
		• Assess parents' ability and readiness to learn procedure.
		• Provide access to frost-free freezer (cryoprecipitate) and refrigerator (concentrate) to store product.
		• Observe ability to draw up correct dosage of factor replacement.
		• Observe ability to do venipuncture with aseptic technique.
		• Observe ability to correctly prepare factor replacement product.
		• Observe administration of slow infusion.
		• Apply pressure to site for 5–10 minutes after needle removal.
		Instruct parents to keep a log documenting bleeding episodes:
		• Time of onset
		• Mechanism of injury
		• Treatment
		• Infusion dose
		• Results of treatment
		• Nature of pain

Nursing Diagnosis	Expected Outcomes	Nursing Interventions
2. Alteration in comfort related to painful effusions, arthropathy	Child is free of pain.	Instruct parents to administer analgesics according to physician's orders. Maintain splinting and rest until bleeding stops. Initiate physical therapy program after acute phase and surgery.
3. Disturbance in self-concept related to disruption in normal activities, joint deformities, current threat of AIDS	Child expresses feelings and concerns. Child participates in appropriate activities. Child develops social relationships with peers.	Provide age-appropriate information about hemophilia, treatment, and complications. Encourage expression of disease and restrictions on activities. Instruct parents to encourage independence and include in decisions concerning activities. Encourage competition in sports with peers (supported by physician). Encourage parents to provide stimulating sedentary activities during periods of immobilization. Encourage parents to allow child to participate in care and treatment. Assist older children in decisions regarding jobs and career.
4. Potential for ineffective family coping related to guilt of transmission, fear of hemorrhage in child, financial burden, and other stressors	Family members discuss their feelings and concerns.	Provide instruction to all family members on genetic transmission, special needs of treatment, and complications. Members of the family should be referred for testing and genetic counseling. Parents should be encouraged to express feelings regarding guilt, having a son who cannot participate in male stereotypical sports, the stress on family routine, etc. Provide access to resource and support organizations.

Appendix 11-G

The Immunosuppressed Child

Nursing Diagnosis	Expected Outcomes	Nursing Interventions
1. Potential for infection: related to immunosuppressive disorders	Nurse identifies potential sources of infection Parents and other caregivers verbalize knowledge of disease and treatment Parents verbalize signs and symptoms of child to report to physician Parents verbalize precautions to reduce infection Parents provide a safe environment for child Parents perform central line catheter care Parents demonstrate postural drainage technique	Assess child's medical history, past infections, especially contagious diseases (e.g., chickenpox, mumps, measles), allergies, immunization status Obtain information about home environment: telephone, electricity, home hygiene system, kitchen/bathroom facilities, sleeping arrangements, pets, etc. Assess pattern of daily living of home occupants Obtain information on child's diet, pattern of daily living, school, hobbies Obtain history on siblings: immunization status, exposure to contagious diseases, pattern of daily living Assess knowledge of disease, prognosis, and treatment Review purpose and schedule of prophylactic medications. Review laboratory tests and meaning of values Assess instructional needs of significant caregivers: relatives, home care aides, sitters, and school personnel Instruct on the following • Method and times to obtain child's temperature • Symptoms to report to physician: Temperature greater than 101°F (38.3°C) Persistent cough, shortness of breath, congestion

Nursing Diagnosis	Expected Outcomes	Nursing Interventions
		Pain anywhere in body
		Rashes, skin breakdown, sores
		Persistent irritability, malaise
		Diarrhea (stools more than three/ day)
		Constipation for longer than 2 days
		Decreased food and fluid intake
		Headaches, increased incoordination, speech difficulties, change in level of consciousness
		White patches in mouth
		Pain with urination, incontinence, hematuria, or cloudy urine
		Dental swelling or gum pain
		Instruct in precautions to minimize contracting infections from foods
		• Avoid unpasturized milk or milk products
		• Cook all raw vegetables and fruits or wash and peel fruits
		• Cook all meals well
		• Avoid buying prepared foods such as tuna salad, egg salad, or coleslaw
		• Do not send child to bed with bottle of juice or milk
		Instruct on avoidance of child to contagious diseases
		• Avoid contact with other persons with infectious diseases
		• Request school to notify parents of outbreak of contagious diseases in classroom of child. School should receive specific teaching on importance of notifying parents of child's exposure to infections, especially chickenpox
		Instruct in avoidance in use of rectal thermometers, enemas, or suppositories
		Instruct parents to notify physician prior to dental visits
		Instruct on exposure to pets
		• Avoid touching pets' excreta (feces, urine, emeses, litter box, aquariums, bird cages)
		• Discuss with physician types of pets allowed
		• Pets should have routine health shots
		Instruct on proper hygiene of home environment
		• Hot and cold running water
		• Proper storage of foods
		• Electricity

Nursing Diagnosis	Expected Outcomes	Nursing Interventions
		• Clean bedside vaporizer daily when in use with germicidal and antifungal cleaner
		• Clean household humidifer system frequently
		• Change air conditioner filters often
		• Clean used utensils in hot soapy water and rinse well
		• Dispose of garbage frequently
		• Vacuuming should be done when child is gone several hours
		• Maintain good home hygiene especially in kitchen and bathroom
		• Do not share utensils or toothbrushes with other persons
		• Avoid exposure to blowing dust and straw.
		Inform parents of immunization precautions
		• Child should not receive live immunizations (measles, mumps, rubella, and Sabin polio)
		• Child may receive inactivated or killed vaccines but may be unable to raise an effective response
		• Annual immunization with inactivated influenza vaccine is recommended in children older than 6 months of age, and one-time administration of pneumococcal vaccine is recommended for children older than 2 years of age
		• For 1 hour direct exposure to measles and varicella, child should receive passive immunization with immune globulin and varicella zoster immunoglobulin, respectively. *Note:* Exposure to chickenpox includes 4 hours prior to outbreak of vesicles and prior to scabbing of all lesions. Varicella zoster immunoglobulin must be given within 72 hours after exposure to be effective
		• Other children in the home should receive only Salk polio, *not* Sabin polio, vaccine
		• Stress importance of receiving γ-globulin injections or infusions; instruct in correct technique of administration if performed in home
		Instruct in importance of personal hygiene of child
		• Daily bath or shower
		• Use liquid soap instead of bar soap

Nursing Diagnosis	Expected Outcomes	Nursing Interventions
		• Inspect skin for infection, rash, or skin breakdown
		• Apply lubricating cream (nonalcohol base) to dry, irritated skin and lip balm or petroleum jelly to dry lips
		• Apply No. 15 (or stronger) waterproof sunscreen for sun exposure longer than 30 minutes
		• Instruct in good oral hygiene: brush teeth after meals with fluoride toothpaste and soft toothbrush and rinse mouth with baking soda mouthwash (1 heaping teaspoon of baking soda to 1 qt. of water).
		• Inspect oral mucosa for sores or *Candida*
		• Clean rectal area gently but well after toileting
		• Wash hands well after toileting, before eating, after playing with pets, or working or playing in dirt.
		Instruct parents to provide for child's safety (e.g., safe toys and activities).
		Instruct in proper care of central line catheter.
		Instruct parents in postural drainage technique to be started daily with pulmonary congestion (should be avoided if platelet count is less than 20,000 cu mm).
2. Potential for alteration in nutrition: less than body requirements related to increased demand with infection	Child maintains appropriate weight.	Instruct in
		• Providing diet high in protein and calories
		• Obtaining daily or weekly weight
		• Providing frequent small meals
		• Making meals a pleasant experience
		• Providing mouth care prior to eating if child has oral candidiasis
		• Providing bland, cool, low acidic foods and liquids with oral soreness
		• Allowing child to suggest favorite foods
		• Reporting diarrhea, nausea, or oral sores immediately to prevent dehydration and malnutrition
		• Providing daily vitamin with iron
		• Consulting nutritionist for additional suggestions and supplemental preparations
		• Providing financial support to obtain groceries
		Instruct parents in procedure for home nasogastric or gastrostomy feedings or total parenteral nutrition

Nursing Diagnosis	Expected Outcomes	Nursing Interventions
3. Potential for activity intolerance related to frequent infections especially pulmonary infections	Child participates in activities to level of tolerance	Assess degree of activity intolerance Identify source of activity intolerance Encourage regular and frequent rest periods Provide activities, games, and toys appropriate for age and physical activities Provide occupational, physical, and speech therapy in home and school Arrange daily schedule for tolerance level
4. Disturbance in self-concept related to special precautions and frequency of hospitalizations	Child verbalizes fears and concerns about disorders	Encourage child to express concerns and feelings about disease and treatment. Explain disorders and treatment at child's level of understanding. Explain disorder, treatment, and special precautions to school personnel. Involve child in decision making of activities. Promote independence and avoid overprotection.
5. Potential for ineffective family coping related to special needs of child, feelings of guilt, and anticipatory grief	Parents and family members verbalize fears and concerns	Encourage expression of fears and concerns of all family members Introduce family to another with child with similar diagnosis. Provide genetic counseling if appropriate Provide resource and organizational support Provide respite care Encourage parents to spend quality time with other children

Appendix 11-H

The Child with Acquired Immunodeficiency Syndrome (AIDS)

Nursing Diagnosis	Expected Outcomes	Nursing Interventions
1. Potential for infection related to transmission of HIV to others	Parents (home care nurse) take precautions to eliminate exposure to themselves and others	Instruct parents/caregivers to • Reinforce casual contact will not spread HIV • Wear gloves when handling blood specimens, blood-soiled items, body fluids, secretions and excretions, and objects contaminated with these fluids • If any surface is contaminated with the child's blood, wear gloves and clean area with paper towel and bleach preparation (1 cup bleach to 1 gallon of water) • Wash hands for 30 seconds after caring for child and removing gloves • Wear gown when clothing is likely to be soiled by body fluids and body secretions or excretions; if clothes become soiled, remove immediately, place in plastic bag, and launder immediately • Place soiled linen, clothing, and contaminated gown in plastic bag and secure tightly until washing. Launder separately in 1:10 bleach solution and routine detergent • Dispose in toilet: blood, any body fluids and solutions contaminated with blood, toilet paper, and soiled tissues • Close toilet lid before flushing • Place disposable contaminated material in a securely tied plastic bag (double bag) and then dispose of promptly

Nursing Diagnosis	Expected Outcomes	Nursing Interventions
		• Avoid sharing utensils and dishes
		• Clean blood spills or blood secretions or excretions with gloves, paper towel, and bleach solution
		• Wear mask when patient has tuberculosis, when suctioning the child, or when caregiver has respiratory infection
		• Use only disposable diapers and wear gloves when changing diapers
		• Do not share thermometers, toothbrush, or other items that may be contaminated with blood
		• Clean toilet facilities frequently and when soiled
		• Soiled dressings should be changed with gloves and disposed in plastic bag and securely tied
		• Discard needles and syringes in puncture-resistant, leakproof container filled with full-strength bleach. Keep out of reach of young children. Bring container when full to the hospital for disposal
		• Encourage children to sleep in separate beds
		• Report potential transmission to other family members immediately
		• If blood or contaminated secretions or excretions get into eye, immediately rinse open eye for 15 minutes with lukewarm water and immediately report incident.
		• Modify central line catheter teaching to include use of gloves in dressing change, maintenance of line, and obtaining blood specimens
2. Knowledge deficit related to AIDS	Parents and older children verbalize understanding of disease, transmission, and treatment	Assess prior knowledge, attitudes, and fears related to AIDS Assess HIV infection in other family members Assess ability of parents to provide appropriate care to child Instruct in AIDS and the effect on the immune system Instruct in importance of prophylactic antibiotics and antifungal medications, schedule, and route of administration Inform on purpose (risk and benefits) of investigational therapies
3. Potential for disturbance in self-concept related to AIDS	Child verbalizes fears and concerns Parents demonstrate awareness of developmental and emotional needs of child	Provide simple and honest information at age-appropriate level Encourage discussion of fears and concerns

Nursing Diagnosis	Expected Outcomes	Nursing Interventions
		Assist child in understanding of reaction of others and suggest appropriate responses Continue to set limits and discipline Enable child to participate in family activities to level of tolerance

4. Potential for ineffective family coping related to social isolation, feelings of guilt, and anticipatory grief	Family members verbalize sources of stress and assist in problem solving
	Family members verbalize awareness of support services and legal rights
	Parents demonstrate ability to assist family members cope with stress and grief
		Encourage expression of feelings and concerns
		Inform parents of their right of confidentiality and participation in research information regarding care and procedures; oppose discrimination due to child's diagnosis
		Obtain permission before sharing diagnosis with others (e.g., school)
		Inform parents of legal rights related to the education of their child
		Provide family with support information
		
		  • Support groups available
		  • Family telephone network
		  • Organizations and AIDS hotline
		
		Provide financial counseling
		Provide respite care
		Discuss the special needs of siblings and normal reactions of siblings when a brother or sister is ill. Provide special time for siblings. Provide simple and honest explanations. Assist siblings to understand the reactions of others and suggest appropriate responses
		Provide psychological support (child psychologist, family therapist) for coping needs
		Provide anticipatory counseling prior to death and bereavement counseling after death
		Initiate hospice referral with consent of family

Chapter 12

Care of the Terminally Ill Child

Belinda B. Martin

It is often stated that there is nothing more difficult for a parent to face than the untimely death of a child. When the death is due to a catastrophic disease the process usually follows a long and difficult path, which includes the stages of diagnosis, treatment, the terminal phase, and the grief and bereavement period. Increased attention has recently been directed by health care providers toward providing optimum support to families of terminally ill children during these most difficult times. One way to assist these families is to offer the option of caring for the child at home with the support of a home care team. The nurse, the most significant member of this team, plays a key role in establishing home care as a viable option by participating in planning prior to hospital discharge. This helps the home care nurse to become familiar with the needs of the child and family in an effort to ensure continuity of care in the home setting.

Studies in the past decade have shown that families who elect to care for a child at home during the terminal phase have reported many positive experiences (Martinson et al. 1983; Lauer and Camitta 1980). These benefits include improved satisfaction of the child, return of control to the parents, reunification of the family in their own environment, and the ability of the siblings to participate in the care of the sick child and feel part of the family unit again (Martinson 1979).

HOSPICE SERVICES

The concept of hospice care has developed in response to advances in technology and its application to terminally ill children and their families (Exhibit 12-1). Hospice care, usually provided in the home setting, is the implementation of a philosophy that places the primary focus on comfort rather than cure. The hospice care plan is designed with emphasis on pain and symptom control management. Hospice standards require an interdisciplinary approach to home care. They also require a 24-hour availability of the home care nurse. This is necessary to provide optimal support, particularly when sudden changes in condition or death of the child occur. The hospice program must allow the parents the choice of continuing aggressive treatment and be prepared to accept the child who appears to be life threatened even though the prognosis is not clearly defined.

Hospice care is one example of the dramatic developments of the home care industry. An increasing number of patient care needs can now be met at home through the provision of home care services. These services may include the support of an interdisciplinary home team as well as the provision of appropriate medical supplies and equipment. If home care is the option selected, the home care team must assist the family in determining the most appropriate

Exhibit 12-1 Hospice Services

- Medically directed interdisciplinary team
- 24-hour availability of nursing care
- Experts in pain and symptom management
- Trained volunteers
- Bereavement follow-up services

methods of care to support the child in the final stages of life.

Hospice programs have traditionally limited enrollment to patients with a prognosis of less than 6 months who have refused further aggressive treatment. These two limitations must be eliminated when caring for pediatric patients. This provides terminally ill children and their families with the benefits of hospice support even when they elect to continue aggressive treatment or the prognosis is not clear. This gives parents the right to hospice support when the child's condition is high risk while providing the necessary assurance that they will be allowed to try any intervention they believe is necessary to save the life of their child. The freedom to make these decisions is critical to the parent's future mental health.

DISCHARGE PLANNING

Discharge planning for the terminally ill child is critical. It requires a thorough assessment of patient and family needs and the availability of community resources. Several factors should be determined prior to meeting with the family to discuss the option of home care. These include location of the family residence, type of reimbursement available to the family for home care services, including intermittent or extended care, and the type and expertise of home care services available in the community where the family lives. These determinations will prevent offering the family options that may not be financially feasible.

Hospice services will usually be the program of choice when selecting from the home care options available to parents with a terminally ill child. This is primarily because of the expertise in symptom management and the 24-hour availability of staff. However, it is important to examine the skills of the hospice caregivers who

would be assigned to a particular family to determine if they would be comfortable and skilled enough to meet the needs of the child and family. Under certain circumstances, a home health care team may be more appropriate than the local hospice provider in meeting the needs of the family. These circumstances may include language barriers, a hospice provider's discomfort with caring for children, or the child's complex clinical needs. If the home care team is selected, it is essential that a member of the team or the hospital team accept 24-hour call so that the family has support on a continuous basis. It is also important to provide psychosocial support to the family through the hospital and/or the home care providers.

Flexibility regarding the frequency of home team involvement is another important issue to consider. Most children have an irregular pattern of "good" and "bad" days. Family members who expect a child to die may witness improvement and stabilization. Emotional reactions can be erratic owing to frequent and constant changes in the child's condition. Planning on an hour-to-hour basis is often difficult; planning days or weeks at a time is virtually impossible. Therefore, it is critical that the support team members be flexible: they must make themselves available as needs arise, and they must also be able to "pull back" on the good or stable days to allow the family as much normal, uninterrupted time as possible.

Once the resources required for home care support have been determined, it is necessary to meet with the parents to discuss the option of taking their child home. Most parents are extremely anxious, and this anxiety can be significantly reduced through an informative conference. Home care should be introduced (Exhibit 12-2) as an *alternative* to hospitalization, and the family needs to understand that rehospitalization is always an option.

The family also needs to understand that the home care team works under the direction of the family's physician in the same way as the hospital team. In addition, the family needs to know that no out-of-pocket costs are experienced as a result of home care services unless it is discussed in advance and the expense is authorized by the family. This will alleviate the concern of many families regarding their ability to afford needed

Exhibit 12-2 Introductory Concepts of Home Care

- Alternative to hospitalization
- Rehospitalization always an option
- Staff members act as "consultants" to parents
- Staff members are an *addition* to hospital team, not *replacement*
- Patient's physician directs care
- Support available 24 hours a day, 7 days a week
- Cost covered by third-party payer
- Flexibility to meet family needs
- Focus on *comfort* of child
- Visit by appointment, never unannounced

Exhibit 12-3 Hospice Components

- Focus on comfort and pain and symptom management
- Patient is the family; addresses physical, psychological, and spiritual needs
- Attempt to allow family to regain control
- Goal is to achieve maximum quality of life
- Patient may continue with aggressive treatment
- Prognosis not limited to 6 months

services without causing them the embarrassment of asking.

Home care always needs to be presented as another option of care. This eliminates the idea of abandonment often introduced by a physician's statement that "there is nothing more we can do for your child so we are sending you home." It is far more supportive to suggest to parents that even though there may not be a treatment available that will arrest the child's disease the health care team can offer them support in the care of their child at home if so desired.

It is often hard for the parents to accept the idea of new persons becoming involved in the care of their child or entering their home. They may feel incompetent when they accept the idea of a home team becoming involved in their child's care. The parents need to be assured that the home team is offered as a support service available if and when needed by them. It is a "consultation" service, designed to intervene only when requested and as necessary to reassure them that they are doing the best possible job. The parents also need to be reassured that the home team is respectful of their need for control in caring for their child at home.

After the parents have been presented with all of the options available to them, it is helpful to allow them some private time to think about and discuss alternatives among themselves. The ill child should be included in this discussion in a manner appropriate for his or her age (Jackson 1975).

If a hospice program will be available to the family as the option for home support, it is

extremely important how the hospice concept is introduced to the family in order to correctly place the emphasis on living rather than dying (Exhibit 12-3). All too often well-intentioned staff members ask the parents if they would like to take their child home to die. It is far more appropriate to determine if they would like to take their child home in an effort to maximize the quality of their lives and determine later if it will be appropriate to plan for the death to occur at home. This approach will eliminate the unnecessary anxiety produced by forcing consideration of managing the death at home before the issue needs to be discussed.

PATIENT AND FAMILY ASSESSMENT

Once the requirement for home care support has been established, it is necessary to determine the care needs of the child and identify the primary caretaker in the home. Whenever possible parents should be encouraged to share this role. The responsibilities of the primary caregiver(s) need to be determined, and these must include nonclinical areas such as care of other siblings, employment, and self-care, along with the care needs of the sick child. All of these factors need to be placed within a 24-hour time frame to determine the reasonableness of the ability of the parents to manage at home and to identify the amount of supplemental support needed to make the plan manageable for the family.

For example, a plan for a single parent with three children under age 5 and a child who requires frequent suctioning around the clock would not be viable without supplemental care. This care may be provided through a friend, relative, or hospice volunteer or combination of all three. It is the responsibility of the discharge planner to make these determinations in an attempt to send a parent home with a reasonable plan for management that would prevent future problems, such as overwhelming fatigue, neglect of the siblings, or the parent's feeling of failure should the need for readmission of the child arise.

The care conference should also be used to determine the family's fears and concerns regarding caring for their child at home. The most common concerns are usually related to breathing or bleeding problems, unmanageable pain, or that the child will suffer an unpleasant death. It is helpful to discuss with the family prior to discharge the symptoms that may occur. These potential symptoms can be determined by the physician in relation to the child's specific disease. This information can be extremely helpful in reducing the family's anxieties regarding their ability to cope at home.

The family will need to be constantly reassured that the major focus of the home care team is the child's comfort and that measures can be quickly initiated to maintain optimal symptom management whenever necessary. Interventions focused on maintaining the child's comfort should be determined when symptoms are discussed. This planning should include the availability of the proper type and amount of resources in the home needed to control the symptoms that may occur. A "care package" of items such as an antiemetic, nose packing, and the stronger drug of choice for pain may be prepared and sent home at the time of discharge. The family can be instructed to place the "care package" in a safe place out of the reach of children. When the parent encounters a new or increased symptom, it can be reported to the physician or home care nurse, who can refer the parent to the "care package." This will enable parents to provide the needed symptom control without unnecessary delays.

SELECTION OF THE HOME CARE TEAM

Certain criteria should be considered when selecting a team to provide support to the family at home. A hospice team with a nurse who has pediatric expertise would seem to be the first choice. However, there are other factors to con-

Exhibit 12-4 Criteria for Selection of Home Care Team

- Use of other support systems
- Language
- Expertise in pediatric pain management
- Distance from home—30 minutes response time including who takes call and how far away they are
- Psychosocial skills in death and dying
- 24-hour availability to respond
- Philosophy of care—willingness to permit aggressive therapy and longer, more questionable prognosis
- Support staff—volunteers, medical director if home consultation seems appropriate and hospital physician not available
- Financial—accept Medicaid or Children with Special Health Care Needs reimbursement, hospice funds, awareness of family's stress related to expenses
- Physical, occupational, speech therapists to enhance quality of life
- Awareness/relationship of community resources—American Cancer Society, Make-A-Wish, mental health clinics, cultural related systems

sider when selecting the home team. Exhibit 12-4 outlines criteria to be considered when selecting a home care team.

Financial coverage for home care is a major concern for families of children with catastrophic diseases. Many of these children have been receiving complex medical care for a long period of time, and most families' financial resources are drained. The discharge planner must act as the family advocate with the third-party payer. A family may be insured by a company who contracts for all home care services from one provider. This provider may not have the specialists (e.g. pediatricians, hospice) required to meet the needs of a particular child. The discharge planner must be responsible for assessing these skills and negotiating with the third-party payer to ensure maximum quality care.

COMFORT CARE

One major role of the health care team is to help the family focus on keeping the child comfortable. Current technology makes it possible to implement almost any kind of intervention in the home setting. Families often become confused and unsure about how aggressive they should be in their child's care, particularly in the area of nutrition. Members of the health care team, particularly the physician, need to help the family focus on the philosophical and psychosocial issues related to interventions. If a child is decreasingly able to ingest food or fluid, the idea of total parenteral nutrition or intravenous feedings may be considered as options (see Chapter 7). The options that are selected need to focus on maintaining comfort and quality of life without prolonging the dying stage.

Fear of the child suffering is probably the most common and serious concern of parents as well as the ill child and other family members. Measures are now available to assess and control pain far more effectively than in the past. Families need to be reassured that pain management is a constant concern of the health care team, which will always be available to intervene to maintain the maximum comfort possible.

One major factor in successful pain management is a thorough and explicit assessment of the child's pain. This must include an assessment tool that is appropriate for the child's cognitive level. Visual analogue scales can be easily adopted for children who have numerical ability. The nurse or parent can draw a line with numbers equally spaced including one to five. The nurse explains to the child that one is no hurt and five is the worst hurt and asks the child to select the number for the current amount of pain. The Eland Color Tool, shown in Appendix 12-A, is an excellent assessment tool that describes location and intensity of pain (Eland 1985). It can be useful in children as young as 3 years of age. Once a tool is selected, the same tool must be used after any intervention to determine the degree of success.

Once the type and intensity of pain has been determined, a pain management plan can be designed. Research has determined that intervention must often use an integrated or multimodal approach (National Institutes of Health 1986). The most common component of the multimodal approach is the use of analgesic medications with progression from nonnarcotic drugs such as aspirin or acetaminophen to narcotics such as methadone or morphine. These drugs can be delivered through a variety of routes, including oral, nasogastric tube, intravenous, subcutaneous, epidural, or intrathecal.

The oral method can include liquid or tablet forms that may be swallowed or absorbed sublingually or through the buccal membranes (Pitorak and Kraus 1987). If oral medications are not an option, the child must be carefully assessed to determine which route will be most efficient and easily managed at home. Tubes that may already be in place, such as nasogastric tubes, are another simple option. If a central line is in place, continuous intravenous infusions may be the choice. If there is no central line, continuous subcutaneous infusion may be the best method (Coyle et al. 1986). Epidural or intrathecal catheter methods may also be considered when other systems are not an option (Moulin and Coyle 1986). In addition, there are a variety of portable infusion pumps available for home use and excellent protocols available for continuous infusion of drugs (Burlich 1988).

Medications used for control of chronic pain need to be administered on a "round the clock" basis for maximal pain control. Parents need to be instructed to record the intervention and related pain rating on a pain flow chart (Meinhart and McCaffery 1983). An example of such a flow chart is given in Appendix 12-B.

Options other than analgesic medications should be considered in the integrated approach to pain management. One of these options is the use of drugs to decrease the pain caused by the inflammatory process. These include corticosteroids or the nonsteroidal anti-inflammatory drugs (Appendix 12-C).

Nonpharmacological interventions may also be an effective approach to pain management. These include modalities such as acupuncture, biofeedback, transcutaneous electrical nerve stimulation, hypnosis, and physical therapy. Some interventions that can be easily initiated in the home include distraction techniques such as music, stories, television programs, visitors, or guided imagery. Guided imagery, relaxation exercises, and self-hypnosis are also effective in reducing the degree of pain (see Chapter 19).

In addition to managing symptoms related to pain, other symptoms must also be monitored in order to maintain maximum comfort and quality of life. Symptom management is most effectively performed by the design of a detailed care plan addressing the needs of each child and family. An example of this type of care plan is described in Exhibit 12-5.

Exhibit 12-5 Generalized Care Plan for Symptom Management

Symptom	Goal/Objective	Intervention
1. Pain	Pain free Activity to tolerance Decrease anxiety Maximum level of independence	Assessment for location/intensity Administration of medication Assessment of interventions Use of behavioral interventions Consult with physician
2. Dyspnea/respiratory distress	Nonanxious breathing pattern	Assess etiology. Use medication related to cause (morphine, scopolamine). Position patient with head of bed elevated. Use oxygen. Consider transfusions.
3. Wet respirations (near death)	Quiet breathing Decrease family anxiety	Instruct family in process. Give medication to decrease secretions (scopolamine patch). Provide gentle suctioning if required to prevent choking. Position to decrease noise.
4. Nausea/vomiting	Control to level of comfort to patient	Reassure family that child is comfortable. Use prescribed medications. Give small portions, dry foods; rest after eating. Provide mouth care.
5. Anorexia	Acceptance of family as part of dying process	Instruct family in ''slowing down'' process of dying, allow them to offer favorite foods but encourage not to pressure child. Provide oral hygiene.
6. Constipation	Maintenance of normal bowel pattern Prevention of impaction	Make diet interventions as permitted by child's ability to eat. Initiate bowel program when using narcotics. Use least invasive measures if medication is ineffective—suppositories to enema to digital (caution when platelet levels are decreased)
7. Seizures	Prevention of seizures Protect the patient Decrease family's anxiety	Assess for etiology. Obtain/administer prescribed drug if indicated. Instruct parent in management, detection. Implement plan for home management whenever possible.
8. Infection	Maximize patient comfort	Discuss options with physician, team. Present options to family with goals of comfort as primary focus. Use support measures for related symptoms such as fever, anxiety, respiratory symptoms.

Exhibit 12-5 continued

Symptom	Goal/Objective	Intervention
9. Skin breakdown	Maximize patient comfort	Position as comfortable. Use egg-crate or alternating-pressure mattress. Treat as family desires with minimal interruption to patient. Consult with an enterostomal therapist for appropriate interventions.
10. Bleeding	Prevention when appropriate Maximum patient comfort	Discuss platelet transfusion option with physician and family. Apply ice pack over area or pressure if appropriate. Use packing (Gelfoam or gauze). Have towels or blue pad available. Use oral hygiene for bleeding gums.
11. Fever	Maximize patient comfort with minimal intrusion	Reassure family regarding comfort of patient. Initiate cooling measures. Use medication as indicated. Instruct family in use of cooling measures, control of environment/ temperature.
12. Eye dryness	Maximize patient comfort	Use artificial tears. Instruct family in care. Keep area clean and moist.
13. Decreased level of life	Maximize quality of activity	Provide continual assessment of level of function. Maximize pain control. Use physical or occupational therapist for evaluation to obtain maximal function. Obtain equipment to assist: reclining wheelchair, bars in bathroom, ramps. Instruct family in transfer.
14. Insomnia	Improved rest pattern	Decrease anxiety about being alone, impending death. Encourage daytime activity to tolerance, range of motion exercises, body massage. Provide maximal pain and symptom control. Give prescribed medication as needed. Use night light, soft music.
15. Anxiety	Reduce to minimum	Instruct parents in potential causes for anxiety. Obtain/maintain maximum pain/ symptom control. Encourage to ventilate. Use psychosocial treatments to intervene. Provide reassurance of constant support.

continues

Exhibit 12-5 continued

Symptom	Goal/Objective	Intervention
16. Family coping	Decrease anxiety Family verbalizes understanding of impending death process Family understands function of home team intervention, 24-hour availability Family feels in control Appropriate use of coping mechanisms Prevention of sense of being overwhelmed, exhaustion	Instruct in physiological process of impending death. Instruct in function of home team; reinforce focus on comfort and 24-hour availability. Listen to family members; meet their needs; act as consultant. Provide information. Do not force response. Allow family members to use coping mechanisms (denial, anger) and help direct in appropriate expression. Offer ministerial support. Encourage psychosocial intervention from social worker, psychologist. Encourage acceptance of outside support from church, neighbors, etc. Use hospice volunteers.

Symptom management is the key to the success of home care. If the child is comfortable, the family usually remains cohesive and functional. Once the child becomes symptomatic, the family becomes distressed and coping becomes difficult. The home care nurse needs to be readily available to assist the family on the management of any symptoms that may occur. Interventions need to be determined through consultation with the primary physician and the hospital team. In some situations, admission to the hospital may be an option and should be offered to the family when indicated. Readmission may be appropriate for a brief period to determine appropriate measures for symptom control followed by discharge and resumption of home care.

FUNERAL ARRANGEMENTS

Families whose children have died have reported that funeral arrangements, whenever possible, should be made prior to the child's death. Although it is extremely difficult for families to face this issue prior to death, parents are able to plan together and include the child when appropriate. Parents experience numbness and shock after the death, and it is almost impossible for them to accomplish this kind of planning.

Families that plan to have a child home until death need to decide if an autopsy will be performed. This may be at the family's request or the request of the physician. The family needs to discuss this with the physician and be given time to think about the decision. If an autopsy will be performed, the body will need to be transported to the appropriate facility. It is helpful if these arrangements are made prior to the death of the child.

THE DEATH EVENT

Parents whose children have died have also expressed how frightening the impending death can be. They have stated that preparing them by describing possible symptoms that might cause death has been most helpful. They also have stated that it was tremendously reassuring to know that help from the home care nurse was always available. The home care nurse needs to assist the family in planning where the death will occur. Many families have elected to keep children who remain in symptom control at home. Others have readmitted their child for more treatment or symptom control, and death occurs during this admission. Many times the child will determine if he or she wants to be in the hospital or at home. These decisions can also be considered tentative, allowing the parents and child the freedom to vacillate according to the condition of the child and coping skills of the family.

GRIEF AND BEREAVEMENT

The grieving process for the family actually begins at the time the child is diagnosed and continues indefinitely. Anticipatory grieving prior to the death creates feelings of sadness, anxiety, and anger; a need to deny and/or seek information; and a need to seek emotional support. The intensity of these feelings is related to the medical status of the sick child. Remember that the process of denial, anger, guilt, shock, bargaining, and acceptance are fluid stages. Family members will move back and forth among these stages. Members of the health care team must be able to discern where family members are in their coping cycle to provide support to them (Rando 1984; Wass and Corr 1984).

After the death of the child, the family will experience intense feelings that can be categorized into three stages. The first stage can be described as a period of numbness and disbelief. The next stage is one of intense grief, which includes feelings of yearning, helplessness, anger, behavioral changes, physical symptoms, and a search for meaning. The third stage is a period of reorganization, which can be measured by criteria such as renewed bursts of energy, greater ease in making decisions, and a return to regular eating and sleeping patterns (Wass and Corr 1984).

Professionals need to be aware of the intensity and length of grief and ensure continued support to families. This support can be supplied through measures such as home bereavement visits, and local support groups made up of other families who have suffered similar losses. Professionals also need to be aware of signs of pathological grief and facilitate referral to mental health therapy resources when indicated.

REFERENCES

Burlich, R. *Guidelines for Subcutaneous Infusion of Morphine.* (Poster session) Second International Conference on Cancer Pain: July 14–17, 1988. New York.

Coyle, N.; Mauskop, A.; Maggard, J.; and Foley, K.M. "Continuous Subcutaneous Infusions of Opiates in Cancer Patients with Pain." *Oncology Nursing Forum* 13(1986):53–57.

Eland, J.M. "The Child Who is Hurting." *Seminars in Oncology Nursing* 1(1985):116–122.

Jackson, P.L. "The Child's Developing Concept of Death: Implications for Nursing Care of the Terminally Ill Child." *Nursing Forum* 14(1975):204–215.

Lauer, M.E., and Camitta, B.M. "Home Care for Dying Children: A Nursing Model." *Journal of Pediatrics* 97(1980):1032–1035.

Martinson, I.M. "Caring for the Dying Child." *Nursing Clinics of North America* 14(1979):467–474.

Martinson, I.M.; Armstrong, G.D.; Geis, D.P.; Anglim, M.A.; Gronseth, E.C.; MacInnis, H.; Kersey, J.H.; and Nesbit, M.E. "Home Care for Children Dying of Cancer." *Pediatrics* 62(1983):106–113.

Meinhart, N., and McCaffery, M. *Pain: A Nursing Approach to Assessment and Analysis.* E. Norwalk, Conn.: Appleton-Century-Crofts, 1983.

Moulin, D.E., and Coyle, N. "Spinal Opioid Analgesics and Local Anesthetics in the Management of Chronic Cancer Pain." *Journal of Pain and Symptom Management.* 1(1986):79–86.

National Institutes of Health Consensus Development Conference Statement. "The Integrated Approach to the Management of Pain." (syllabus) 6, no. 3(1986):1–18.

Pitorak, E.F., and Kraus, J.C. "Pain Control with Sublingual Morphine: The Advantages for Hospice Care." *American Journal of Hospice Care* 4, no. 2 (March/April 1987):39–41.

Rando, T. *Grief, Dying and Death.* Champaign, Ill.: Research Press Co., 1984.

Wass, H., and Corr, C., eds. *Childhood and Death.* Vol 5. New York: Hemisphere Publishing, 1984.

Appendix 12-A

Eland Color Tool

Name of Nurse _____ Date _____

INTERVIEW PROTOCOL

Ask the child, "What kind of things have hurt you before?" If the child does not reply, ask the child, "Has anyone ever stuck your finger for blood? What did it feel like?" After discussing several things that have hurt the child in the past, ask the child, "Of all the things that have ever hurt you, what has been the worst?"

1. Present eight crayons to the child in a random order.
2. Ask the child, "Of these colors, which color is like . . . ?" (the event identified by the child as hurting the most).
3. Place the crayon away from the other crayons (represents severe pain).
4. Ask the child, "Which color is like a hurt but not quite as much as . . . ?" (event identified by the child as hurting the most).

5. Place the crayon with the crayon chosen to represent severe pain.
6. Ask the child, "Which color is like something that hurts just a little?"
7. Place the crayon with the others.
8. Ask the child, "Which color is like no hurt at all?"
9. Show the four crayon choices to the child in order from their worst hurt color to the no hurt color.
10. Ask the child to show on the body outline where they hurt using the crayon for worst, middle, little, or no hurt. Then ask if the hurt is "right now" or "from earlier in the day." Ask why the area hurts.
11. Record the colors identified by the child for:
    Worst pain color _____
    Middle pain color _____
    Little pain color _____
    No hurt color _____

Source: Reprinted from *Seminars in Oncology Nursing,* Vol. 1, No. 2, pp. 116–122, with permission of Grune & Stratton, Inc., © May 1985.

Appendix 12-B

Flow Sheet—Pain

Patient _____ Date _____

Pain rating scale used* _____

Purpose: To evaluate the safety and effectiveness of the analgesic(s).

Analgesic(s) ordered: _____

Time	Pain rating	Analgesic	R	P	BP	Level of arousal	Other[†]	Plan & comments

*Pain rating: A number of different scales may be used. Indicate which scale is used and use the same one each time. Two common examples:

- 0 to 10 with 0 being no pain and 10 being as bad as it can be.
- Melzack's scale: 0 = no pain; 1 = mild; 2 = discomforting; 3 = distressing; 4 = horrible; 5 = excruciating

†Possibilities for other columns: bowel function, activities, nausea and vomiting, other pain relief measures. Identify the side effects of greatest concern to patient, family, physician, nurses, etc.

Source: Reprinted from *Pain: A Nursing Approach to Assessment and Analysis* by N.T. Meinhart and M. McCaffery, p. 361, with permission of Appleton & Lange, © 1983.

Appendix 12-C

Medications Commonly Used for Symptom Control

Fever

- Acetaminophen (Tylenol)

Nausea/Vomiting

- Diphenhydramine (Benadryl)
- Promethazine (Phenergan)
- Metoclopramide (Reglan)
- Chlorpromazine (Thorazine)
- Trimethobenzamide (Tigan)

Seizures

- Phenytoin (Dilantin)
- Phenobarbital

Increased Intracranial Pressure

- Dexamethasone (Decadron)
- Prednisone

Constipation

- Docusate sodium (Colace, Peri-Colace)
- Bisacodyl (Dulcolax)
- Glycerine suppositories (if not platelet risk)
- Senna concentrate (Senokot)

Restlessness/Sleep

- Diphenhydramine (Benadryl)
- Chloral hydrate
- Phenobarbital
- Diazepam (Valium)
- Hydroxyzine (Vistaril)

Oral Hygiene/Sores

- Hydrogen peroxide
- Nystatin (Mycostatin)
- Lidocaine 2% viscous (Xylocaine)
- Dyclonine (Dyclone)
- Nystatin, lidocaine, diphenhydramine 1:1:1

Mood Elevators

- Diazepam (Valium)
- Alprazolam (Xanex)

Skin Care

- Povidone-iodine (Betadine)

Pain Control (Analgesics)

- Acetaminophen (Tylenol)
- Acetaminophen with Codeine
- Hydromorphone (Dilaudid)
- Dolophine (Methadone)
- Morphine sulfate (elixir, rectal, long acting, sublingual, intravenous/subcutaneous)

Pain Control (Nonsteroidal Anti-inflammatory Drugs)

- Choline magnesium trisalicylate (Trilisate)
- Indomethacin (Indocin)
- Naproxen (Naprosyn)
- Piroxicam (Feldene)
- Ibuprofen (Motrin)

Dry Eyes

- Methylcellulose

Part III

Developmental Issues in the Home

Chapter 13

Cognitive Development

Joanne K.H. Howard

The pediatric home care nurse has an important role in providing explanations and instructions to children and/or adolescents about their nursing and medical care. Having an understanding of the cognitive developmental level of these patients makes it possible to present information more closely suited to their needs. In this chapter, terms and principles of Piaget's cognitive developmental theory are presented (Piaget 1952). Piaget's stages of cognitive development (sensorimotor, preoperational, concrete operations, formal operations) are discussed for five age groups (infants, toddlers, preschoolers, school-aged children, adolescents). In addition, concepts of illness causation and conceptions of internal body parts and functions are discussed for children or adolescents in the preoperational, concrete operations, and formal operations stages. Finally, criticisms of Piagetian theory are discussed.

TERMS AND PRINCIPLES OF PIAGETIAN THEORY

The focus of Piaget's cognitive developmental theory is the understanding of the growth of knowledge, particularly the characteristics or quality of children and adolescents' knowledge. The growth of knowledge is viewed as a process along with psychological growth.

Piaget viewed children as active constructionists of their knowledge. Through interactions with the environment, children gain knowledge. Meaning is not in the objects of the knower's experiences nor in the knower alone but is derived from interaction of the knower with the object. This interaction is a process and is biased in the sense that it is dependent on the knower's interpretation (Miller 1983).

Intelligence consists of two functions: organization and adaption. Organization and adaption are called functional invariants because they function in the same manner throughout all development. Organization refers to the person's integration of schemas that form the basis of one's underlying mental or cognitive structures. Specifically, schemas represent thoughts and patterns of behavior used in interaction with the environment (Miller 1983). Adaptation refers to the dynamic process in which the person interacts with the environment and includes two processes: assimilation and accommodation.

Assimilation is the taking in of new information and adding it to existing knowledge. For example, the child sees that a table is brown and adds it to his or her preexisting knowledge of other brown objects. Assimilation guarantees order (Ausubel et al. 1980). *Accommodation* is the taking in of new information that requires that preexisting knowledge be altered in some way. For example, the child learns that the table is brown because it is made from wood. The child must accommodate this new information by altering his or her understanding of all brown objects such that some brown objects may be brown because they are made from wood or some may be brown for other reasons. Accommodation leads to new schemas and guarantees adaptation (Ausubel et al. 1980). Equilibration is the self-regulating process or motivating force for assimilation and accommodation. When both assimilation and accommodation are in balance, equilibrium exists. The equilibrium state can refer to a moment-by-moment equilibrium, a final level of achievement at a given stage, or to the entire course of cognitive development (Miller 1983).

Cognitive development includes four factors: (1) physical maturation; (2) experience with the environment; (3) social experience; and (4) equilibration. Physical maturation refers to central nervous system maturation and provides, in part, for the children's interaction with the environment. Experience with the environment refers to the child's physical manipulation of objects as well as his or her reflections of these actions or objects. Social experience refers to the child's cultural and educational experiences and includes the experience of play. Equilibration, as discussed previously, serves as a force in the processes of assimilation and accommodation in which the other three factors have a role.

Piaget identified four stages of cognitive development that characterize changes in the mental or cognitive structures of children and adolescents: the sensorimotor stage, the preoperational stage, concrete operations, and formal operations. The stages are universal, have an invariant sequence, reflect primarily qualitative changes, and cover the life span. Each stage is derived from the prior stage, transforms the prior stage, and serves as preparation for a more advanced stage (Miller 1983). The rate of progression through the stages may vary, but the sequence and formal characteristics of the stages do not vary. Piaget did not attend to the transitional mechanisms from one stage to another.

In summary, children and adolescents are active knowers of their world and, through interaction with the environment, construct knowledge. This interaction is dependent on the child's physical maturation and includes the experience of acting on objects and reflecting on one's actions with those objects. Through this interaction, the child gains knowledge (assimilation) and changes the form of what is known (accommodation). These processes lead to a balanced state or equilibrium. Throughout life, these changes in the form of what is known are typified by stages that are universal and do not vary in sequence. Therefore, children's cognitive development does not merely reflect varying and limited abilities from those abilities seen in adults but entirely distinctive characteristics.

A summary of the Piagetian stages of cognitive development for various age groups is presented in Table 13-1.

INFANTS

Infants between birth and 12 months of age are in the sensorimotor stage. Four substages of the sensorimotor stage characterize the infants' cognitive development. As the name of the stage implies, infants begin to know their world through use of their senses and motor activities. During the first year, infants develop primitive concepts of space, time, causality, and intentionality (Ausubel et al. 1980).

Substage 1: Reflexes

Infants from birth to 1 month of age are in the first substage of the sensorimotor stage. Through reflexive activity stimulated by needs (e.g., hunger), infants begin to assimilate perceptual information about the world. A reflex according to Piaget is a hereditary reaction and not acquired through experience (Gruber and Voneche 1977). Reflexive activities include vision, hearing, sucking, and grasping. Repetition and rhythmicity of these experiences serve as a basis of cognitive predictability (Maier 1979). Infants do not have the notion of objects existing apart from themselves and are only able to respond to an aspect of an object that is associated with a need (e.g., mother's breast for feeding). Causality is not known by infants in the first substage since they do not have an understanding of objects apart from themselves and no notion of time between two events.

Substage 2: Primary Circular Reactions

Infants between 1 and 4 months of age are in the second substage of the sensorimotor stage. During this substage, the infant's reflexive activity begins to be replaced with voluntary activity. Circular reactions refer to the infant's

Table 13-1 Summary of Piagetian Stages for Various Age Groups

Age Group	Stage	Characteristics
Infants (0–1½ years)	Sensorimotor (substages 1–4)	Begins to know world through the use of senses and motor activities; primitive concepts of space, time, casuality, and intentionality develop.
Toddlers (1–2 years)	Sensorimotor (substages 5–6)	Learns about characteristics of objects and interrelationships among objects through trial and error; onset of the ability to mentally represent objects.
Preschoolers (2–4 years)	Preoperational (symbolic substage)	Internally represents the world in their mind as they have seen it; egocentric view; dominated by perceptions; transductive reasoning
School-aged children (5–7 years)	Preoperational (intuitive substage)	Develops qualitative identity; understanding of seriation begins; decreased egocentricity somewhat
School-aged children (7–11 years)	Concrete operations	Reasons logically with objects or events based in reality; capable of mental operations, including transitivity, seriation, classification, conservation
Preadolescents and adolescents (11+years)	Formal operations	Capable of abstract thought, hypotheticodeductive reasoning

repetition of an activity that was discovered by chance. Primary circular reactions refer to activities that are focused on the infant's body, rather than on objects. Actions are repeated for the mere pleasure of the activity. For example, the infant may repetitively bring the hand toward the mouth for sucking. Thus, activities that were noted as separate events during the first substage (e.g. sucking, grasping) become coordinated in the infant's activities during the second substage. This coordination of activities represents the beginning notions of causality with two events in a sequential relationship. Pseudoimitation also emerges in which the infant repeats an action the adult has just performed that mimicked the infant's initial action.

Substage 3: Secondary Circular Reactions

Infants between 4 and 8 months of age are in the third substage of the sensorimotor stage. During this substage infants perceive themselves as acting on things. Infants have a greater understanding of objects as separate from themselves and try to recover an object as long as it remains in their visual field. Again, the infant repetitively performs actions that have been discovered by chance for the mere pleasure of the activity. However, the actions are centered on the objects, rather than on the infant's body. Infants

try to make fascinating environmental events occur again and again (e.g. swinging a mobile). The causes of all events are still viewed as related to the infant's action. Pure imitation emerges at this substage. Only behaviors that infants can see or hear themselves produce are imitated (Caron and Caron 1982).

Substage 4: Coordination of Secondary Schemata

Infants between 8 and 12 months of age are in the fourth substage of the sensorimotor stage. During this substage the infant intentionally coordinates schema (thoughts and patterns of behavior) developed within prior substages as the means to produce a desired goal. In addition, the infant's acquired schema can be applied to novel situations. An example of infants' ability to apply acquired schema to novel situations is their imitation. Now infants can imitate the behaviors of others that they have not heard or seen themselves perform.

Object permanence, which is the understanding that an object exists despite not being present in one's visual field, develops within this substage. With the development of object permanence, infants are able to remove barriers when trying to accomplish a task. For example, the infant will attempt to search for a toy when it is placed under a blanket. The infant recognizes that the self is separate from objects. However, the infant's view of objects existing in space separate from himself or herself is still tied to action schemas (Caron and Caron 1982). Infants cannot understand that objects exist in space with no relationship to themselves. For example, a toy is placed under a blanket, removed, and then placed under a pillow while the infant observes. The infant will search for the toy under the object in which the toy was placed when initially taken from the infant (e.g., the blanket). This search error is referred to as place error (Caron and Caron 1982).

TODDLERS

Toddlers between the ages of 1 and 2 years are in the sensorimotor stage. Two substages of the sensorimotor stage characterize toddlers' cognitive development. The onset of the toddler's ability to mentally represent objects marks the end of the sensorimotor stage.

Substage 5: Tertiary Circular Reactions

Toddlers between 12 and 18 months of age are in the fifth substage of the sensorimotor stage. During this substage the toddler experiments in a trial-and-error fashion to discover multiple means to achieve a goal. These behaviors are seen in the toddler's ritualistic play. Through these repetitive trials, the toddler learns about the characteristics of objects and interrelationships among objects. Objects are viewed as distinct from the self. Place error as seen in substage 4 no longer occurs. Toddlers search for an object in the last place in which it was seen hidden. Toddlers also recognize that they, as well as others or objects, can be causes of events and they may be recipients of causes. Toddlers imitate both animate and inanimate objects.

Substage 6: Invention of New Means through Mental Combination

Toddlers between 18 and 24 months of age are in the sixth substage of the sensorimotor stage. During this substage toddlers are capable of determining a cause after observing an effect or predicting an effect when observing a cause

within the limits of their prior experiences without actually acting out the scenario. The toddler internally represents schemas that are used in these mental tasks. The beginning of symbolic representation has its roots in the sixth substage. This is evident in the toddler's use of pretense or make-believe in play. Toddlers also demonstrate deferred imitation, which is the imitation of actions that they have not seen performed in the past. In the final substage of the sensorimotor stage, toddlers recognize that objects exist apart from themselves and exist even when they are not observable. Thus, toddlers will search for objects that they have not seen.

PRESCHOOLERS

Preschoolers between the ages of 2 and 4 years are in the symbolic substage of the next stage of Piaget's cognitive developmental theory, the preoperational stage. During the symbolic substage, preschoolers use signs and symbols such as words and images to represent objects that may not be present. Thus, preschoolers are capable of internally representing the world in the mind as they have seen it. The preschoolers' view of the world is egocentric and is dominated by their experiences. Preschoolers believe that others view the world in the same manner as they do. This egocentrism is evident in preschoolers' language and play. Rosen (1985) cites qualities of the preschooler's language that reflect egocentrism: "The child does not bother to construct sentences which will provide the information which the listener needs for comprehension. He uses pronouns without explanatory referents, he leaves out necessary causal connections, and he does not offer logical proof of his assertions."

The mental representations or preconcepts that preschoolers have are dominated by their perceptions of an object or event and thus are very literal and concrete. In addition, preschoolers are able to focus on only one characteristic of an object or event at one time (referred to as "centration"), which leads to preconcepts that are fairly global. An example of centration is a preschooler's ability to see her mommy as only a mommy and not as a wife to her father. Preschoolers also judge persons on the basis of one characteristic. The child who receives a shot from a nurse may view that nurse as mean because the child has associated the nurse with a painful event.

The preschoolers' mental representations, as stated previously, are near copies of their experiences. Therefore, the preschooler's understanding of an experience is only in the direction in which the events occurred. Preschoolers cannot understand reversibility and therefore cannot retrace their steps from the end to the beginning of an event. Preschoolers who are ill may not understand that their health can return.

The preschoolers' thinking is also static in the sense that they cannot understand transformations. The preschooler who observes water being poured from a short, squatty glass to a tall, thin glass believes that the tall, thin glass contains more water. The preschooler focuses on the change in status, rather than the process.

Transductive reasoning, rather than inductive or deductive reasoning, is used by preschoolers. The preschoolers' thinking proceeds from particular to particular. Two events that occur closely in time are thought to be related. For example, the preschooler who yells at a younger brother just prior to the brother's accident may think that his yelling caused the accident.

Preschoolers are unable to delineate between physical or mechanical causes and psychological or moral ones. Preschoolers often believe that humans or supernatural beings make things happen or events occur by magic. Along with these beliefs, preschoolers believe that anything that moves is alive. Animism or ''life'' is attributed to things such as the clouds and the sun.

SCHOOL-AGED CHILDREN

Two stages constitute the cognitive development of children of school age. Young school-aged children (younger than 7 years of age) are in the intuitive substage of the preoperational stage. Older children (older than 7 years of age) are in the stage of concrete operations. By the time of preadolescence these children have developed a conceptual system that is both logical and coherent.

Preoperational Stage: Intuitive Substage

School-aged children between 5 and 7 years of age are in the intuitive substage of the preoperational stage. Children in the intuitive sub-

stage are still governed by their perceptions. Increases in young children's social experience serve to decrease their egocentricity by providing other points of view. Young children observe objects for their many different characteristics such as color, shape, and size. However, the young school-aged child is only able to reason on the basis of one characteristic at a time.

Two abilities that are qualitative and develop in children in the intuitive substage are identities and functions (Rosen 1985). The child who observes water being poured from a short, squatty glass to a tall, thin glass recognizes that the water in the tall glass is the same water that was previously in the short glass. This is evidence of qualitative identity. Young school-aged children also develop a logic of functions evident in their understanding that a change in one variable may be related to a change in another variable. For example, the child observes a scarf being pulled through a ring. The child recognizes that the scarf on the right side of the ring (though longer on that side after being pulled through the ring somewhat) is still the same scarf that was used prior to the action. However, the child cannot recognize that the length of the scarf has remained the same.

An understanding of seriation or ordering of events begins in the intuitive substage. The young school-aged child may be able to recognize two events in a series when they are in consecutive order. For example, the child understands her third birthday follows her second birthday but does not understand her third birthday also comes after her first birthday.

Concrete Operations

Children between the ages of 7 and 11 years are in the stage of concrete operations. Piaget believed that this stage represented the first stage of rational thinking in the child.

Piaget borrowed the terms or language of mathematics and logic to describe the cognitive structures of the child in concrete operations. His model is referred to as the logicomathematical model and consists of nine groupings. Groupings are cognitive structures that are logically organized. Each grouping contains multiple sets of elements (e.g., objects, actions, ideas). Four rules apply to the relationships among these elements when an operation (an internalized mental

Table 13-2 Rules for Relationships among Two Elements

Rule	Definition
Closure	Any operation combining two elements in the set must result in an element within the set.
Associativity	The combination of elements within the set must hold irrespective of the order in which they are treated.
Identity	There must be one element only that in combination with any other element leaves it unchanged.
Inverse	For each element in the set there must be another that in combination with it results in the identity element.

Source: Piaget's Theory: A Psychological Critique by G. Brown and C. Desforges, p. 33, Routledge and Kegan Paul, © 1979.

action) is performed on two of the elements. These four rules include the rule of closure, the rule of associativity, the identity rule, and the inverse or reversibility rule. Definitions for these four rules are given in Table 13-2.

As the name of the stage implies, Piaget believed that children in concrete operations perform operations or internalized mental actions on the objects of their experiences. Children are able to reason logically with those objects or events based in reality. Children in the stage of concrete operations are not able to reason logically on abstract concepts or hypotheses.

The many operations or mental actions children develop in concrete operations serve to order and relate their experiences into an organized whole (Maler 1979). These operations emerge gradually. Four of the operations include transitivity, seriation, classification, and conservation. *Transitivity* means that children understand that A-B = B-C when A is longer than B by the same amount as B is longer than C (Pulaski 1980). *Seriation* means that children can order objects according to magnitudinal dimensions such as length, weight, and color. Reversibility of thought is an inherent aspect of the operation of seriation. The child is able to think in both directions from point A to point B or from point B to point A. Transitivity has been found to be more difficult than seriation (Murray and

Youniss 1960: Achenbach and Weisz 1975; Kingma 1983).

With the operation of classification, the child is able to recognize that the class does not change despite recognition of a subclass. For example, the child is shown six yellow beads and four white ones and is asked about the number of yellow beads. The child responds appropriately. Then the child is asked about the number of total beads. Again, the child responds appropriately. The child's response indicates that he can perceive the existence of a subclass and still recognize the total class appropriately.

Decentration is evident in the emergence of the operation of conservation. The child is able to understand that an object may change in its perceptual characteristics without a change in the actual quantity of the object. Prior to concrete operations, the preoperational child was able to center on only one characteristic of an object at a time, and, thus, when the object changed in appearance, the child believed the object had also changed in quantity. Conservation of number occurs initially followed by conservation of substance, area, weight, and volume.

With the use of these various concrete operations, school-aged children are able to classify their knowledge, order it hierarchically or sequentially, and allow for transformations in their thinking. They use these operations to conduct trial-and-error experiments on the objects of their experiences. They try to determine which means create which ends and try to relate themselves to the outcome. This is referred to as deductive logic.

Along with the logicomathematical operations, Piaget also identified infralogical operations. These operations deal with continuous wholes, rather than discrete objects. An example of a continuous whole is a block of space. With infralogical operations, the integrity of the whole is not maintained when a part is removed from it. Piaget's work on space and geometry is the basis of the infralogical operations.

The ability of school-aged children to take more characteristics of objects within their experience into account is also related to their ability to take other viewpoints into account. Their social experience leads to this loss of egocentrism. They are able to separate their view from others and coordinate multiple viewpoints.

Within these social experiences there is strict adherence to rules. The child in concrete operations believes that justice is accomplished when the punishment equals the misdeed.

Piaget stated that true causality does not appear until the child is 7 or 8 years of age (Piaget 1951). True causality may be defined as a physical explanation for a natural phenomenon. Children in concrete operations explain causes less in terms of themselves, can understand intermediary steps in causality, can order the events, and can understand the reversible nature of cause and effect.

PREADOLESCENTS AND ADOLESCENTS

Preadolescents at 11 or 12 years of age enter the final stage of Piaget's cognitive developmental theory—formal operations. While the child in concrete operations is capable of mental operations with objects or experiences in the real world, the preadolescent or adolescent in formal operations is capable of thinking about the real world as well as the world of possibilities. The adolescent's thinking extends beyond the present to what is possible in the future. Adolescents use hypotheticodeductive reasoning, which means that they take into account all of the variables within a situation, form hypotheses about their interrelationships, and test each of them to derive multiple alternative solutions to a given problem. Exploration of all possible combinations of variables is referred to as combinatorial analysis. Within this problem-solving process, one variable may be held constant or neutralized while the others are examined. Prior to this stage, the child in concrete operations was only capable of negating a variable in order to not consider it within a problem-solving situation. Through the process of integrating variables, adolescents form theories. In the early stage of formal operations, these theories are simplistic and lack originality (Billingham 1983).

Along with reflecting or thinking about the content within a given problem-solving situation, the adolescent is capable of examining the problem-solving process used within the specific situation. The adolescent recognizes that a solution may be valid when it is logically derived from assumptions regardless of its factual truth.

Meta-thought refers to the adolescents' thinking about their thinking.

With the development of the ability to conjecture and create, adolescents form ideals of themselves, others within their immediate experiences, and society. Adolescents are egocentric to the extent that they sometimes cannot distinguish between their ideals and those of the world. They often give unlimited power to their views. During this time of idealism and introspection, adolescents become very critical of their appearance and behavior and think the world is focused on them as much as they are on themselves. From mentally testing their ideals often in the context of peer groups, adolescents lose their egocentrism. Toward late adolescence, they gain perspective over their ability of abstract thought, so that insight and problem solving can be accomplished with objectivity. Adolescents can then take many perspectives into account, differentiate their own from others, and derive a solution to the problem.

A fifth stage has been postulated by some researchers for cognitive development beyond formal operations. Problem solving or novel thought has been suggested as the foci for a stage beyond formal operations (Riegel 1973; Arlin 1975; Langford 1975).

CONCEPTIONS OF ILLNESS CAUSATION

Studies that have been conducted to examine children and adolescents' conceptions of illness causation have focused on the subjects' cognitive developmental level or chronological age as a function of their conceptions. Sequences for the conceptions of illness causation have been described, along with particular causes of illness named by children and/or adolescents in different cognitive developmental stages or age groups. These conceptions of illness causation are discussed for children or adolescents in three stages of Piaget's cognitive developmental theory: preoperational, concrete operations, and formal operations.

Preoperational Stage

Bibace and Walsh (1980) identified two themes of illness causation for children in the preoperational stage. These themes are phenomenism and contagion, with the former theme being the most cognitively immature one. Prior to the use of these themes to explain the cause of illness, children name irrelevant or incomprehensible causes (Redpath and Rogers 1984). Children whose explanations for illness causation are phenomenistic attribute illness to an external concrete phenomenon (often a sensory phenomenon within their immediate experience) that may exist with the illness but is not related spatially or temporally. For example, children may name the sun as the cause of a cold (Bibace and Walsh 1980). Explanations are derived from the child's own experience, focus on a specific detail of the experience as the cause, and do not specify a causal link. The theme contagion refers to the child's belief that the cause of illness is in objects or persons nearby but not touching the child or with an event that occurs just prior to the illness onset. The causal event is often more closely related to the actual illness than causal events given by children who have a phenomenistic explanation. The causal event also does not represent just a single experience. For example, the child may answer, "You catch it, that's all," when asked about how a person gets a cold (Bibace and Walsh 1980).

In conjunction with these themes by Bibace and Walsh, Blos (1978) found that preschoolchildren attributed illness to contiguous temporal and spatial cues. Potter and Roberts (1984) studied 112 healthy 5- to 9-year-old children. They found that children within the preoperational stage viewed themselves as significantly more vulnerable to contagion than children in concrete operations.

Concrete Operations Stage

Two themes for illness causation identified by Bibace and Walsh (1980) for children in concrete operations are contamination and internalization. Contamination refers to the cause of illness as another person, object, or external action. The child either touches the contaminated object or person or is involved in an action and becomes contaminated. The child does not differentiate between the mind and body, and, therefore, a harmful action by the child can result in illness. For example, the child may attribute a cold to the fact that he took off his jacket outdoors (Bibace and Walsh 1980). There is a qualitative shift from the theme contagion to the

theme contamination. The cause as defined in the latter theme is located at the surface of the body.

Numerous studies with school-aged children that serve to confirm the theme of contamination for illness causation have found that the children attribute illness to their actions; as punishment specifically for their actions, such as violating a rule; to human agents; and to factors within the environment (Richter 1943; Brazelton et al. 1953; Schechter 1961; Lynn et al. 1962; Palmer and Lewis 1976; Perrin and Gerrity 1981; Wood 1983; Gratz and Piliavin 1984). These studies have been conducted with healthy children, children with either acute or chronic illness, or hospitalized children.

Other findings from studies with school-aged children are in conflict with the attribution of punishment for the cause of illness. Instead, causes of illness named included chance and natural phenomenon (Gofman et al. 1957; Brodie 1974; Williams 1979).

Internalization, another theme of illness causation for children in concrete operations, refers to the child's recognition that the illness is located inside the body while the cause may be external. Swallowing or inhaling are two common processes of internalization. For example, the child may attribute a cold in the winter to breathing in too much cold air (Bibace and Walsh 1980). A cause of illness named by school-aged children that is related to this theme is germs or microorganisms (Nagy 1951; Palmer and Lewis 1976; Perrin and Gerrity 1981).

These two themes for concrete operations represent the child's distinction between internal and external events, although the child focuses on real, concrete external events as the cause of illness. The child is still confused about the function of internal organs with the illness experience.

Formal Operations Stage

The themes physiological and psychophysiological have been identified by Bibace and Walsh (1980) for persons in formal operations. The theme physiological refers to the malfunctioning or nonfunctioning of an internal organ or system as the cause of illness. A step-by-step sequence may be given as an explanation for the events culminating in illness. Both the host and causal agent are recognized as factors leading to the illness onset. The cause may be an external event. Multiple causes may be named, or causes may have a cumulative effect. Others have reported that children at 11 or 12 years of age name multiple causes for illnesses (Nagy 1951; Perrin and Gerrity 1981).

The theme psychophysiological represents a more mature cognitive explanation for illness causation. The cause of illness is described as a combination of physiological and psychological factors. The relation between thoughts and feelings and body functioning are recognized by persons who explain illness causation within the psychophysiological theme.

CONCEPTIONS OF INTERNAL BODY PARTS AND FUNCTIONS

Children and adolescents' understanding of internal body parts and functions is discussed for three stages of Piaget's cognitive developmental theory: preoperational, concrete operations, and formal operations. For the clinician working with ill children, it is important to remember that accurate understanding of body parts does not necessarily mean that the child understands the illness and its effects on body functioning.

Preoperational Stage

When asked to name body parts, young children often include nonorgans such as foods, blood, feces, and urine or noninternal body parts such as skin and the belly button (Tait and Ascher 1955; Gellert 1962; Porter 1974; Smith 1977; Williams 1979; Crider 1981). Gellert (1962) and Williams (1979) noted that young children conceive of the interior of the body as containing those substances that go in and come from it. Schilder and Wechsler (1935) suggested that the child can only be certain that the body contains those substances that have gone into it, such as food.

Crider (1981) has developed a sequence for the levels of conceptualization for children's conceptions of internal body parts. At the first level, which may represent children in the preoperational stage, children focus on global and observable activities of the body such as breathing without any understanding of its purpose or connection with a specific body part. The

child may label specific body parts differentiated by their spatial locations without any understanding of their purpose or function.

Concrete Operations Stage

The child in early concrete operations can name several body parts, which often include bones, the brain, the heart, blood, and blood vessels (Gellert 1962; Williams 1979). Later in concrete operations, the child may also include the intestines, stomach, muscles, liver, and lungs (Williams 1979). Systems that are frequently mentioned include the musculoskeletal and cardiovascular systems (Gellert 1962; Porter 1974; Smith 1977).

According to Crider (1981), the child at 6 or 7 years of age identifies a global function that is a perceived activity or state (i.e., working, playing) for every body part named. Next, the child more specifically labels a particular attribute (i.e., shape, substance, motion) of the body part, and this attribute is related to activities. For example, the child states that the heart pumps so that he can move around (Crider 1981). At the next level of conceptualization, the child conceives of the organ as a container in which things are displaced from it. For example, blood is pumped through the body by the heart (Crider 1981). Followed by this understanding, the child conceptualizes organ functions as having coordinated and reversible properties. The child understands that blood comes into the heart and also leaves from it. Finally, the child recognizes that a transformation of body substances takes place as a function of the organ. These transformations may have animistic or moral qualities. For example, the lungs are viewed as something that changes good air, which is inhaled, to bad air, which is exhaled (Crider 1981).

Formal Operations Stage

Persons in formal operations name body organs that represent their understanding of the coordinated and reversible functions of the organs, along with the organ's ability to transform substances at the cellular level (Crider 1981). Other body parts that are named include nerves, kidneys, and reproductive organs (Porter 1974; Crider 1981). Adolescents can also relate one organ's function to another organ's function and can hierarchically arrange organ functions from a cellular or systems' perspective (Gellert 1962).

CRITICISMS OF PIAGETIAN THEORY

Three major criticisms of Piagetian theory should be kept in mind when applying his theory to practice. Piaget has been criticized for his harsh standards and conservatism used to evaluate the child's cognitive level. Piaget has been particularly concerned with false-positive results that overestimate the child's ability (Miller 1983). Thus, the age levels given for the stages should be applied with caution. Children's cognitive levels may be more advanced than their age indicates according to the age parameters given for the stages.

The issue of regression is also not addressed in depth by Piaget. He does not offer an explanation for the child's use of formerly acquired mental operations when the environment is overwhelming. Piaget attributes the use of these operations to the lack of more efficient operations that will develop later.

Cross-cultural studies have provided insight regarding individual differences that are not explained by Piaget. Although the qualitative aspects of Piaget's theory have been verified, the rate of development has been found to be influenced by cultural factors (Dasen 1972). Marked individual differences have been found among different ethnic groups where physical and social environments, childrearing practices, and health conditions are relatively homogeneous (Dasen 1972).

REFERENCES

Achenbach, T.M., and Weisz, J.R. "A Longitudinal Study of Development Synchrony between Conceptual Identity, Seriation, and Transitivity of Color, Number and Length." *Child Development* 46(1975):840–848.

Arlin, P.K. "Cognitive Development in Adulthood: A Fifth Stage?" *Developmental Psychology* 11(1975):602–606.

Ausubel, D.P.; Sullivan, E.V.; and Ives, S.W. *Theory and Problems of Child Development.* 3d ed. New York: Grune & Stratton, 1980.

Bibace, R, and Walsh, M.E. "Development of Children's Concepts of Illness." *Pediatrics* 66(1980):912–917.

Billingham, K.A. *Developmental Psychology for the Health Care Profession. Part 1-Prenatal through Adolescent Development.* Boulder, Colo.: Westview Press, 1983.

Blos, P. "Children Think about Illness: Their Concepts and Beliefs." In *Psychologic Aspects of Pediatric Care,* edited by E. Gellert. New York: Grune & Stratton, 1978.

Brazelton, T.B.; Holder, R.; and Talbot, B. "Emotional Aspects of Rheumatic Fever in Children." *Journal of Pediatrics* 43(1953):339–358.

Brodie, B. "Views of Healthy Children toward Illness." *American Journal of Public Health* 64(1974):1156–1159.

Caron, A.J., and Caron, R.F. "Cognitive Development in Early Infancy." In *Review of Human Development,* edited by T.M. Field, A. Huston, H.C. Quay, L. Troll, and G.E. Finely. New York: John Wiley & Sons, 1982.

Crider, C. "Children's Conceptions of the Body Interior." In *Children's Conceptions of Health, Illness, and Bodily Functions,* edited by R. Bibace and M.E. Walsh. San Francisco: Jossey-Bass, 1981.

Dasen, P.R. "Cross-cultural Piagetian Research: A Summary." *Journal of Cross-Cultural Psychology* 3(1972):23–39.

Gellert, E. "Children's Conceptions of the Content and Functions of the Human Body." *Genetic Psychology Monographs* 65(1962):293–405.

Gofman, H.; Buckman, W.; and Schade, G.H. "The Child's Emotional Response to Hospitalization." *American Journal of Diseases of Children* 93(1957): 157–164.

Gratz, R., and Piliavin, J. "What Makes Kids Sick: Children's Belief about the Causative Factors of Illness." *Children's Health Care* 12(1984):156–162.

Gruber, H.E., and Voneche, J.J., eds. *The Essential Piaget.* New York: Basic Books, 1977.

Kingma, J. "Seriation, Correspondence, and Transitivity." *Journal of Educational Psychology* 75(1983):763–771.

Langford, P.E. "The Development of the Concept of Development." *Human Development* 18(1975):321–332.

Lynn, D.B.; Glaser, H.H.; and Harrison, S.G. "Comprehensive Medical Care for Handicapped Children: III. Concepts of Illness in Children with Rheumatic Fever." *American Journal of Diseases of Children* 103(1962): 42–50.

Maier, H.W. *Three Theories of Child Development.* 3d ed. New York: Harper & Row, 1979.

Miller, S.A. "Cognitive Development: A Piagetian Perspective." In *Strategies and Techniques of Child Study,* edited by R. Vasta. New York: Academic Press, 1983.

Murray, J.P., and Youniss, J. "Achievement of Inferential Transitivity and its Relation to Serial Ordering." *Child Development* 39(1960):1259–1268.

Nagy, M.H. Children's ideas of the origin of illness. *Health Education Journal* 9(1951):6–12.

Palmer, B.B., and Lewis, C.E. "Development of Health Attitudes and Behaviors." *The Journal of School Health* 46(1976):401–402.

Perrin, E.C., and Gerrity, P.S. "There's a Demon In Your Belly: Children's Understanding of Illness." *Pediatrics* 67(1981):841–849.

Piaget, J. *The Child's Conception of Physical Causality.* New York: Humanities Press, 1951.

Piaget, J. *The Origin of Intelligence in Children*. New York: International Universities Press, 1952.

Porter, C.S. "Grade School Children's Perceptions of Their Internal Body Parts." *Nursing Research* 23(1974): 384–391.

Potter, P.C., and Roberts, M.C. "Children's Perceptions of Chronic Illness: The Roles of Disease Symptoms, Cognitive Development, and Information." *Journal of Pediatric Psychology* 9(1984):13-27.

Pulaski, M.A.S. *Understanding Piaget*. New York: Harper & Row, 1980.

Redpath, C.C., and Rogers, C.S. Healthy Young Children's Concepts of Hospitals, Medical Personnel, Operations, and Illness. *Journal of Pediatric Psychology* 9(1984): 29–40.

Richter, H. "Emotional Disturbances of Constant Pattern Following Nonspecific Respiratory Infection." *Journal of Pediatrics* 23(1943):315–325.

Riegel, K.F. "Dialectical Operations: The Final Period of Cognitive Development." *Human Development* 16(1973): 346–370.

Rosen, H. *Piagetian Dimensions of Clinical Relevance*. New York: Columbia University Press, 1985.

Schecter, M. "The Orthopedically Handicapped Child." *Archives of General Psychiatry* 9(1961):247–253.

Schilder, P., and Wechsler, D. "Short Communication. What Do Children Know about the Interior of the Body?" *International Journal of Psychoanalysis* 16(1935): 355–360.

Smith, E.C. "Are You Really Communicating?" *American Journal of Nursing* 77(1977):1966–1968.

Tait, C.D., Jr., and Ascher, R.C. "Inside-of-the-Body Test. A Preliminary Report." *Psychosomatic Medicine* 27(1955): 139–148.

Williams, P.D. "Children's Concepts of Illness and Internal Body Parts." *Maternal Child Nursing Journal* 8(1979): 115–123.

Wood, S.P. "School-aged Children's Perceptions of the Causes of Illness." *Pediatric Nursing* 9(1983):101–104.

Chapter 14

Motor Development

Joanne K.H. Howard

In this chapter, normal motor development is described for five age groups: infants, toddlers, preschoolers, school-aged children, and adolescents. The understanding of normal motor development can aid the home care nurse in assessing the pediatric patient's motor skills and in instituting appropriate interventions based on the patient's motor abilities. Further assessment is necessary when children or adolescents do not demonstrate motor skills appropriate for their developmental level.

Principles that govern motor development are initially discussed, followed by a short summary of central nervous system maturation. Motor development is discussed in terms of gross motor and fine motor development for the five age groups. Gross motor development includes patterns of posture and locomotion, and fine motor development refers to the development of prehension (i.e., grasping or manipulation of objects) (Di Leo 1977). Infant reflexes are discussed prior to the description of gross and fine motor development in infants. In addition, self-care skills of each age group are presented.

PRINCIPLES OF MOTOR DEVELOPMENT

Several principles have been identified that govern motor development. The first principle is that motor development is dependent on central nervous system maturation. This principle is significant when considering the child's readiness

for a particular motor task. For example, when beginning toilet training with a child, the child's central nervous system must be sufficiently mature for the child to recognize physiological cues necessary for bowel and bladder control.

The second principle is that motor development progresses in an orderly sequence. The rate may vary with the individual, but the sequence does not vary. The differences in children's rates for achievement of developmental milestones are evident in a study by Neligan and Prudham (1969), who studied the age (in months) at which more than 3,000 children were able to sit unsupported and walk. They recorded the number of months in which 3, 10, 25, 50, 75, 90, and 97 percent of the subjects achieved the skill. The number of months for between 50 and 97 percent of the subjects was nearly twice the number of months for between 3 and 50 percent of the subjects.

The third principle of motor development is that development progresses in a cephalocaudal (i.e., head to toe) direction. The child generally gains control of the head and neck prior to upper trunk control and, later, lower body control.

The fourth principle, the proximodistal principle, is that motor development generally progresses from the central part of the body to the periphery. The child gains relatively more control over the trunk prior to control over the extremities. This principle has been challenged by Loria (1980), who studied reaching and prehensile skills of 12 normal infants at 30 weeks of age. She found that proximal ability (i.e., visually guided reaching) was not related to distal ability (i.e., prehensile skills) in the infants, and she suggested that there may be two different motor control systems that govern proximal and distal abilities.

Differentiation is the fifth principle of motor development. Development proceeds from simple to complex or from general to specific. For example, children are able to wave their arms before they are able to have fine motor control with their fingers.

CENTRAL NERVOUS SYSTEM MATURATION

At birth, the newborn's motor activity is primarily reflexive. The cerebral cortex is half its adult thickness. As the child ages, motor activity is governed more and more by the cerebral cortex. Myelinization facilitates the conduction velocity of the axons of nerve fibers. Myelinization of sensory pathways occurs first and is almost entirely completed at birth. Myelinization of motor pathways follows that of sensory pathways. Myelinization ends with myelinization of the cerebral cortex and thalamus (Lowrey 1986).

INFANTS

Reflexes

Infant reflexes that are discussed here include oral reflexes, eye reflexes, general reflexes, and reflexes involving the extremities (Table 14-1).

Oral Reflexes

Oral reflexes that are present in the full-term infant include swallowing, gag, cough, yawn, sucking, rooting, and extrusion. The swallowing, gag, cough, and yawn reflexes are present throughout a normal lifetime. An intact glossopharyngeal (ninth cranial) nerve is responsible for the gag reflex when stimulation of the posterior pharynx is elicited by food or a foreign object. The cough reflex is evoked by irritating substances to the mucous membranes of the upper respiratory tract. In response to decreased oxygen, the yawn reflex occurs and leads to an increase in inspiration. To elicit a sucking reflex, one need only put a finger in the infant's mouth. Vigorous sucking should occur. The sucking reflex may persist through 7 months. The rooting reflex is elicited by brushing or stroking the infant's cheek near the mouth. The infant will turn the head to the side that is stroked and begin to suck. This reflex may be difficult to elicit at times other than feeding times. The rooting reflex should disappear by 3 or 4 months of age but may continue until the child is 1 year old (Whaley and Wong 1979). The extrusion reflex is present until approximately 4 months of age and consists of the tongue being forced outward when it is touched or depressed.

Eye Reflexes

Reflexes that involve the eyes and are present in full-term infants include the blink reflex, pupillary reflex, and doll's eye reflex. The third (oculomotor), fourth (trochlear), and fifth (abducens) nerves are responsible for the blink reflex, which continues throughout a lifetime and can be elicited by many stimuli. A blink reflex occurs with a bright light (visuopalpebral reflex), sharp noise (cochleopalpebral reflex), painful touch (cutaneous-palpebral reflex), tapping the bridge of the nose (nasopalpebral reflex), stroking the eyelashes (ciliary reflex), or approaching or touching the cornea (corneal reflex) (Illingsworth 1983). The pupillary reflex consists of pupillary constriction when a light shines toward the eye. A bright light should not be used to test this reflex since it may evoke a blink reflex. The length of light exposure may have to be prolonged with some full-term infants to elicit the reflex (Illingsworth 1983). This reflex also persists throughout a lifetime. The doll's eyes reflex is tested by moving the infant's head slowly to the right or left. During the first 10 days of life when the reflex is present and prior to the development of fixation, the infant's eyes do not move when the head is turned (Illingsworth 1983).

General Reflexes

Reflexes that involve both upper and lower extremities that are present in full-term infants include the Moro, startle, Perez, tonic neck (asymmetrical and symmetrical), and tonic labyrinth reflexes.

Moro Reflex. The Moro reflex (Figure 14-1) is a vestibular reflex present in the child until 3 to 4 months of age. To test this reflex, the infant's head should be at midline. The infant is held at a

Table 14-1 Summary of Infant Reflexes

Reflex	Elicitation	Response	Duration of Reflex
Oral			
Swallowing	Substance in mouth	Swallow	Birth → Lifetime
Gag	Stimulation of posterior pharynx with food or foreign object	Gag	Birth → Lifetime
Cough	Stimulation of mucous membranes of upper respiratory tract by irritating substances	Cough	Day 1 → Lifetime
Yawn	Decreased oxygen intake	Yawn	Birth → Lifetime
Sucking	Finger in infant's mouth	Suck	Birth → 7 months
Rooting	Brushing or stroking of infant's cheek near mouth	Head turns to side that is stroked, and infant begins to suck.	Birth → 3 or 4 months or 1 year
Extrusion	Tongue touched or depressed	Tongue is forced outward	Birth → 4 months
Eye			
Blink	Bright light, sharp noise, tapping bridge of nose, painful touch, stroking eyelashes, touching cornea	Blink	Birth → Lifetime
Pupillary	Bright light	Pupil constricts.	Birth → Lifetime
Doll's eye	Infant's head moved slowly to right or left	Eyes do not move when head is turned.	Birth → Fixation
General			
Moro	Head at midline; infant held at 45° angle; head dropped back somewhat	Arms abduct and extend; hands open with fingers curved; then adduction of arms occurs.	Birth → 3 or 4 months
Startle	Loud noise, sternum tapped	Adduction of arms; elbows flexed; hands closed	Birth → 4 months
Perez	In suspended position, pressure is applied along spine from sacrum to neck.	Flexion of both arms and legs, lifting of the pelvis, and extension of the neck	Birth → 4 or 6 months
Tonic neck			
Asymmetric	In supine position, head is turned to one side.	Arm on the side to which the head is turned extends; other arm flexes.	Birth → 3 or 4 months
Symmetrical	Child's head is raised.	Arms extend and legs flex.	3 or 4 months → crawl
Reflexes involving the extremities			
Palmar grasp	Head is midline; object is placed in ulnar side of palm.	Fingers flex around object; muscles tense from wrist to shoulder when object is moved upward in hand.	Birth → 3 or 4 months
Plantar grasp	Stimulation of sole of foot behind toes.	Flexion of toes	Birth → 8 months
Babinski	Stroking of outer edge of sole of foot from heel upward.	Big toe dorsiflexes; other toes fan out.	Few days after birth → 1 year
Walking	In upright position, soles of feet are pressed against a surface.	Reciprocal flexion and extension of legs	Birth → 5 or 6 weeks
Placing	Anterior side of tibia is brushed against a table.	Lifts leg to "place" it on the table	Birth (except breech delivery) → 6 weeks
Crossed extension	One leg is held extended while pressure is applied to sole of foot.	Other leg attempts to push away stimulating force.	Birth → 1 month

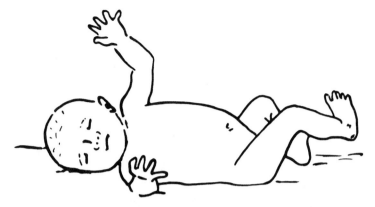

Figure 14-1 Moro reflex. *Source:* Reprinted from *High-Risk Neonatal Care* by N.S. Streeter, p. 367, Aspen Publishers, Inc., © 1986.

45° angle, and then the head is allowed to suddenly drop back somewhat. With this movement, the infant's arms become abducted and extended, the hands open although the fingers may be curved inward, and then adduction of the arms occur. Crying often occurs with this reflex.

Startle Reflex. When a loud noise occurs or the infant's sternum is tapped, the startle reflex is elicited. Abduction of the arms occur with the elbows flexed and hands closed. The reflex generally disappears by 4 months of age.

Perez Reflex. The Perez reflex is present in infants until 4 to 6 months of age. To evoke this reflex, the infant is held in a suspended prone position and pressure is applied along the spine from the sacrum to the neck. The reflex consists of the infant's flexion of both arms and legs as well as lifting of the pelvis and extension of the neck. Crying as well as urinating often occurs with this reflex.

Tonic Neck Reflexes. Both the asymmetrical (Figure 14-2) and symmetrical tonic neck reflexes are discussed. The asymmetrical neck reflex is present in infants until 3 or 4 months of age. When the infant is placed in a supine position and the head is turned to one side, the arm on the side to which the head is turned extends while the arm on the other side flexes. The legs follow the movement of the arms for their respective sides of the body but may have a reduced response. The symmetrical tonic neck reflex emerges after the disappearance of the asymmetrical tonic neck reflex. It occurs with extension or raising of the child's head. The arms

Figure 14-2 Asymmetrical tonic neck reflex. *Source:* Reprinted from *High-Risk Neonatal Care* by N.S. Streeter, p. 367, Aspen Publishers, Inc., © 1986.

extend and the legs flex. This reflex disappears when the child begins to crawl.

Righting Reflexes. The righting reflexes include the neck righting reflex, the labyrinth righting reflex, and the body righting reflex. These reflexes are responsible for the child's ability to roll from back to stomach and stomach to back, to get on the hands and knees and sit up, and to maintain normal posturing of the head, trunk, and limbs during motor activities (Illingsworth 1983). The neck righting reflex consists of the infant (in a supine position) moving the shoulders, trunk, and pelvis toward the side to which the head is turned. The reflex is strongest at 3 months of age and disappears by 10 months of age. The labyrinth and body righting reflexes do not occur during the neonatal period. The labyrinth reflex occurs at 1 to 2 months of age

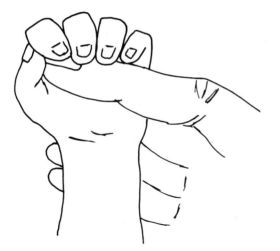

Figure 14-3 Palmar grasp. *Source:* Reprinted from *High-Risk Neonatal Care* by N.S. Streeter, p. 367, Aspen Publishers, Inc., © 1986.

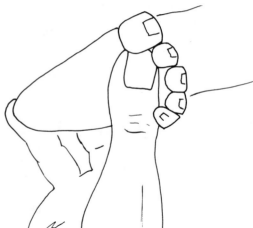

Figure 14-4 Plantar grasp. *Source:* Reprinted from *High-Risk Neonatal Care* by N.S. Streeter, p. 369, Aspen Publishers, Inc., © 1986.

and is strongest at 10 months of age. Initially, the reflex allows for the young child to lift the head while in a prone position, and later it allows the child to maintain normal head position in space while supine. The body righting reflex does not occur until 7 to 12 months of age after the neck-righting reflex disappears. This reflex enables the child to rotate one part of the body before another, which are activities that are important when the child attempts to sit or stand.

Reflexes Involving the Extremities

One reflex that involves the upper extremities is the palmar grasp reflex. Reflexes that involve the lower extremities include the plantar grasp, Babinski, walking, placing, crossed extension, withdrawal, anal, hip, heel, and leg-straightening reflexes.

Palmar Grasp Reflex. Illingsworth (1983) identified two components of the palmar grasp reflex: (1) the reflex and (2) the response to traction. With the infant's head in midline, the reflex is evoked by putting an object into the ulnar side of the palm of the hand. The fingers flex around the object when the palm is stimulated (the reflex) (Figure 14-3). Following the grasp, the infant continues to tense the muscles from the wrist to the shoulder when the object in the palm is moved upward in the hand (the

response to traction). The palmar grasp reflex disappears around 3 to 4 months of age.

Plantar Grasp Reflex. Stimulation of the sole of the foot behind the toes causes the plantar grasp reflex (Figure 14-4). This reflex consists of flexion of the toes and disappears around 8 months of age.

Babinski Reflex. The Babinski reflex is initially present a few days after birth and exists until the child walks (usually around 1 year of age). The reflex is evoked by stroking the outer edge of the sole of the foot from the heel upward. In response, the infant's big toe dorsiflexes and the other toes fan out or hyperextend.

Walking Reflex. The walking reflex is present in the infant until 5 or 6 weeks of age. When the infant is held in an upright position with the soles of the feet pressing against a surface, the infant reciprocally flexes and extends the legs. The legs may cross, and there is no movement of the trunk or arms (Figure 14-5).

Placing Reflex. The placing reflex is present at birth in full-term infants weighing over 1,800 g (Illingsworth 1983). It may not be present in infants who are born breech (Chow et al. 1979). The reflex disappears around 6 weeks of age (Chow et al. 1979). The placing reflex consists of the child lifting the leg up to "place" it

Figure 14-5 Supporting reaction and stepping. *Source:* Reprinted from *High-Risk Neonatal Care* by N.S. Streeter, p. 368, Aspen Publishers, Inc., © 1986.

on the table in response to the anterior side of the tibia being brushed against the table. Placing of the arm on the table may also be elicited by brushing the ulnar side of the arm against the table.

Crossed Extension Reflex. The crossed extension reflex is present only during the first month of life. The reflex occurs when one leg is held extended while pressure is applied to the sole. The leg that is not extended appears to push away the stimulating force by flexing, adducting, and extending.

Withdrawal Reflex. The withdrawal reflex is shown by the infant's quick flexion of the leg when it has been stimulated by a noxious agent such as a pinprick. This response may also occur in the upper extremities.

Anal Reflex. The anal reflex is present in infants at birth. The response is elicited when the infant is lying in a supine position with both legs vertical and the perianal area is touched. The anus contracts with stimulation.

Hip Reflex. The hip reflex is evident with flexion of one leg at the hip in the infant. The other leg flexes in response.

Heel Reflex. The heel reflex is elicited by tapping the heel or applying pressure on the sole of the foot. When this is done, the limb extends.

Leg-Straightening Reflex. The leg-straightening reflex is elicited by pressing the sole of the foot on a hard surface. The infant straightens the legs and body in response.

Gross Motor Development

During infancy, dramatic changes occur rapidly in the infant's gross motor abilities. The newborn's motor activity is primarily reflexive. By the end of the first year, voluntary control of movement has advanced to the point that the child can stand upright and walk.

One Month Old

During the first month of life, reflexive activity dominates the newborn's motor activity. Flexor patterns are evident with the newborn's posture. Development of slight head control is a predominant factor in gross motor development. In a prone position, the neonate can turn the head to the side and can lift the head off its resting surface momentarily. The knees are tucked under the abdomen with the hips and/or pelvis held high. In the supine position, the newborn's shoulders and hips are externally rotated and the elbows and knees are flexed. The asymmetrical tonic neck reflex is seen when the infant's head is turned to one side. When the 1-month-old infant is pulled to a sitting position there is almost complete head lag and the back is rounded. The walking reflex occurs when the infant is held standing with the feet against a hard surface.

Two Months Old

The 2-month-old infant has increasingly greater head control by being able to hold the head in midline with the rest of the body. While prone, the infant can lift the chin off the resting surface so that the infant's face is at a 45° angle from the surface. Extensor tone generally increases as flexor tone decreases. The infant's hips are extended slightly more than the hips of the 1-month-old infant. When the child is held in a sitting position, the back is less rounded and the head is held in midline, although it bobs forward. The asymmetrical neck reflex is present when the infant is in the supine position.

Three Months Old

At 3 months of age, the infant is able to hold the head up for longer periods of time. Upper body control is beginning to develop. In the prone position, the infant can bear weight on the forearms, raising the chin and shoulders so that the face is between a 45° and a 90° angle from the resting surface. The infant's pelvis is flat against the resting surface with the hips straight and the knees bent. The asymmetrical tonic reflex disappears, and symmetrical posture dominates. The child is able to bring the hands to midline owing to the disappearance of the asymmetrical tonic reflex. Reflexive rolling due to the neck righting reflex may occur when the infant is in the supine position. When the infant is pulled to a sitting position, there is only slight (if any) head lag, although the head may bob forward when the infant is held sitting. The infant may bear weight momentarily when held standing.

Four Months Old

The 4-month-old infant does not yet have complete head control under all conditions. When the infant is moved or rocked, the head still wobbles. However, when the infant is held in a sitting position, the head is held steady, enabling the infant to examine the environment. The lumbar region remains as the only curved area of the back. When the infant is prone, the infant is able to raise the face at a 90° angle from the resting surface. Another skill which the 4-month-old infant is able to do is roll from a prone (stomach) to a supine (back) position.

Five Months Old

Head control in all positions is evident with the 5-month-old infant. There is no head lag when the child is pulled to a sitting position and the infant can hold the head erect and steady. In the prone position, the infant is able to bear weight on the forearms with both elbows extended raising the upper trunk. Patterns of extension and flexion are diminishing. When lying on the back (supine), the infant may extend the legs high in the air, as well as bring the feet to the mouth. When held in a standing position, the infant can bear most weight with the legs somewhat flexed while maintaining shoulder positioning.

Six Months Old

During the sixth month of life, the child gains further control of the upper trunk. In the prone position, the child is able to raise the chest and abdomen off the resting surface, bearing weight on the hands. The infant is also able to roll from a supine (back) to a prone (stomach) position. The child anticipates being pulled to sit by lifting the head. The infant is able to sit unassisted with the trunk erect when in a chair. When sitting on the floor, the infant leans forward on the hands for support. Six-month-old children can bear almost all of their weight on their legs and will bounce when held in a standing position.

Seven Months Old

Until 7 months of age, the infant's gross motor development has primarily been centered on head and upper body control. Further gains are made in these areas as well as gains in lower body control during the seventh month. The infant can now sit without support for short periods of time and puts the hands closer to the sides of the body for balance. In the prone position, the infant is able to bear weight on one hand at a time. Lower body control is evident when the child begins to crawl (moving with the abdomen parallel to the floor). Children do not involve their legs in their first attempts with crawling, but instead they slide forward using their arms to pull themselves along. Some children may also go backward with their first attempts to crawl. Later, the legs are used with the arm movements. When the child begins to crawl, the symmetrical tonic neck reflex disappears. While held standing, children bounce and make walking movements while supporting all of their weight. These walking movements are the first stage in walking.

Eight Months Old

The 8-month-old child is able to sit steadily without support. In addition, the child can lean forward reaching for objects while maintaining postural control. The labyrinth righting reflex is responsible for the child's ability to maintain the head in a normal position in space. The child continues to crawl. Bearing all of their weight on their legs, children may stand by holding onto a table or a crib rail. When standing, the child's trunk is slightly forward and the hips are flexed.

Nine Months Old

Further gains are made in locomotion during the ninth month. Creeping (moving on the hands and knees with the abdomen parallel to the floor) develops following the child's crawling. The child's posture when first beginning to creep consists of bent-elbow posturing with the feet drawn under the hips. The child who creeps well moves contralateral extremities. The 9-month-old child is able to sit unassisted for long periods of time. When sitting, the hips are flexed and the legs are extended. Maneuverability from one position to another also is evident in the 9-month-old child. The child is able to sit up from a supine position by rolling onto the stomach, bending the legs, and pushing upward. The child is also able to go from a sitting to a prone position without difficulty.

Ten Month Old

The child continues to creep during the tenth month. Holle (1976) cites five advantages of the child's increasing mobility: (1) the child has practice holding the head up; (2) eye fixation develops with the eyes becoming used to moving to extreme positions; (3) the arm muscles are trained; (4) the leg pattern becomes more advanced; and (5) the child gains body balance with the cross pattern movement. Ten-month-old children are able to pull themselves to a standing position and cruise along furniture, holding on with both of their hands.

Eleven Months Old

The child's capability in upright posturing continues to develop within the 11th month. The child is able to maintain balance momentarily without assistance. The child also cruises using only one hand to hold onto the furniture. Walking with assistance (both hands held) is possible. In addition, 11-month-old children are able to pivot while in a sitting position so that they can pick up objects anywhere in near proximity.

Twelve Months Old

The most dramatic achievement near or shortly after the child's first birthday is the child's first independent steps. The child is now able to stand independently and walk several steps without assistance. The child's stance is very wide, providing a wide base of support. The child's feet are turned outward with the knees flexed (Cratty 1979). The child's hands are held at shoulder level or above for balance. Initially, the child's arm movements are not reciprocal and the steps are not regular (Cratty 1979). The 1-year-old child is also able to stoop and pick up objects from the floor and climb into a small chair to sit. Creeping is still evident when the child goes up stairs.

Fine Motor Development

Fine motor development in infancy proceeds from the newborn's grasp reflex to the 1-year-old child's ability to use a superior forefinger grasp and pick up small objects deftly. Hohlstein (1982) cites three major phases of the development of prehension in infancy. In phase one, infants do not use their hands in specialized movements. The infant's fingers are extended and abducted when the infant attempts to grasp an object. When the object is grasped, the fingers are flexed and adducted. Infants during this phase are beginning to develop shoulder stability and cannot always maintain postural control when upright. In the second phase, infants have shoulder stability as well as stability in the elbow joints. Infants use more precise hand movements in grasping objects. Before phase three, infants develop stability at the shoulder, elbow, wrist, and carpometacarpal joints. Infants in phase three are able to use the fingers in highly specialized movements.

Preference for various types of fine motor activities may vary among infants at a given stage in development. Kopp (1974) studied the fine motor abilities of 26 full-term and 10 preterm infants at 32 to 36 weeks of age (age corrected for the preterm infants). The infants were classified as having coordinated or clumsy movements based on clinical judgment, developmental norms, and Halverson's (1932) study of grasping. The clumsy group spent almost half the observed time in visual exploration of objects, while the coordinated group spent only one-third of the time in visual exploration and over one-half the time in manipulation of the objects. Kopp (1974) concluded that the "most important developmental issue is not what type of object interaction is used by infants but rather that the preferred style does not distract the infant from attending to relevant events occurring in his environment.[11]

One Month Old

The newborn's hands are usually closed or fisted. The palmar grasp reflex is evident. With the grasp reflex, the infant's thumb and fingers are flexed and adducted.

Two Months Old

The hands of the 2-month-old infant are often open, although the grasp reflex is still present. The child may have swiping movements toward objects without any grasp of them.

Three Months Old

The 3-month-old infant's hands are more loosely open (Illingsworth 1983). Hand regard is present. The palmar grasp reflex begins to disappear and will be replaced by ulnar and radial grasps over many months. The infant does not reach for an object before eye contact is made and cannot hold an object unless it is placed in the hand.

Four Months Old

The infant is able to hold objects indefinitely but cannot retrieve them when dropped. The 4-month-old infant is yet unable to pick up or grasp objects despite attempts of reaching for them. The infant is able to bring the hands together in midline for play as well as bring the fingers to the mouth.

Five Months Old

The child is now able to secure objects voluntarily using a primitive squeeze grasp or raking movement. The child pulls or "corrals" the object toward the body and then holds it there "squeezing" it against the other hand or the body. The infant often brings objects to the mouth with both hands.

Six Months Old

The 6-month-old infant uses a palmar or squeeze grasp. The thumb is extended and the child grasps the object with the other four digits holding the object against the heel of the palm. The child "scoops" up the objects in this fashion. In addition, 6-month-old children enjoy grabbing and playing with their feet.

Seven Months Old

The grasp of the 7-month-old infant changes to an emphasis on the radial, rather than ulnar, side of the hand. The child uses a radial-palmar or whole-hand grasp in which the fingers are curled downward over the object like a paw and the thumb is slightly adducted when the object is held against the palm. The child is able to transfer objects from hand to hand, holding onto one when another is offered.

Eight Months Old

The 8-month-old infant uses an inferior scissors grasp or a superior palm grasp. The radial side of the palm is placed over the object, the fingers press downward on the object, and the thumb opposes the first two fingers. The object is still held against the palm of the hand, rather than by the fingers alone.

Nine Months Old

The grasp of the 9-month-old infant is referred to as an inferior forefinger or a radial-digital grasp. The grasp is similar to the superior palm grasp except the last three digits of the hand move more medially than downward, thus moving toward an eventual fingertip grasp in months to come (Halverson 1932).

Ten Months Old

The inferior pincer grasp, which consists of grasping an object with the thumb and index finger, develops during the infant's 10th month. The infant's thumb presses the object against the first joint of the index finger. The child also begins to voluntarily release objects.

Eleven Months Old

The 11-month-old infant enjoys putting objects in and taking them from containers. These actions involve both grasping and releasing. A neat pincer or forefinger grasp develops. A small object can be held by the infant's fingertips of the thumb and index finger. The child must rest the hand on the surface where the object is lying to use this grasp. Slight extension of the wrist occurs with this grasp. In addition, the child is able to release an object with slight force forward.

Twelve Months Old

The superior forefinger grasp is evident in the 12-month-old child. The grasp is similar to the one that precedes it, except that the child does not need to rest the hand on the surface where the object is lying in order to grasp the object. The child's wrist is extended and deviated to the ulnar side (Erhardt 1974). The child can release large objects well but has difficulty releasing smaller objects smoothly.

Self-care Skills

The infant's self-care skills center around feeding activities. Prior to 4 months of age, the extrusion reflex is present, which makes feeding solid foods somewhat difficult. After this reflex has disappeared, solids can be introduced into the infant's diet with greater ease. The 6-month-old infant is able to use a bottle or cup with handles to drink. By 7 months of age, the child can chew solids. Children at 7 months of age are able to feed themselves larger food items such as crackers or cookies. Once the inferior pincer grasp begins to develop (at approximately 10 months of age), children are able to feed themselves a multitude of different kinds of finger foods. By 1 year of age, children are able to deftly feed themselves small bites of food.

TODDLERS

Toddlers include children who are between 12 and 36 months of age (1 and 3 years). Gross motor activity in the toddler is characterized by greater stability in walking, as well as the ability to climb and descend stairs. The toddler's fine motor activity is characterized by the child's ability to handle small objects in play.

Gross Motor Development

In the beginning of toddlerhood, the child's walk is characterized by widely spaced feet with the toes turned outward, the arms elevated, and no rotation of the back or hips. By 18 months of age, the child develops a hurried walk that resembles running. At 21 months of age, the child is able to run.

The child's ability to master stairs changes dramatically during the first year of the toddler years. Before 15 months of age, the child creeps up stairs. At 15 months of age, the child is able to walk up stairs with one hand held and creep down stairs. At 18 months of age, the child can walk down the stairs with one hand held. By 21 months of age, the toddler is able to walk up or down stairs by holding the rail.

When attempting to jump in play, the young toddler keeps one foot in contact with the ground. When playing with a ball, the 15-month-old toddler is able to hurl the ball, the 18-month-old toddler attempts to kick the ball by walking into it or stepping on it, and the 21-month-old toddler can kick the ball.

The 2-year-old child's feet when walking are less widely spaced than the younger child's, and the child's arms are down at the sides. Children put the heel of one foot in front of the toes of the other when walking and visually watch their steps (Cratty 1979). The child's steps are approximately one-half the length of the adult's step. In the second year, the child is able to walk sideways, on tiptoes, and occasionally backward (Cratty 1979). The 2-year-old child can run but cannot start and stop abruptly. At 30 months of age the child is able to alternate feet going up stairs. In terms of balance, the toddler can stand on one foot briefly (1 second) without holding on.

In jumping activities, the 2-year-old toddler jumps with both feet off the floor at the same time and can jump from a bottom step to the ground (Knobloch et al. 1980). The arms are retracted when jumping.

When playing with a ball, the 2-year-old toddler is able to throw a ball either forward or backward, although there is little weight shift. The 2½ year-old child can throw a small ball 4 to 5 feet (Cratty 1979). The larger the ball, the less distance the child can throw it (Wellman 1935). Between the second and third year of age, the child is also able to pedal a tricycle.

Fine Motor Development

Prior to the child's first birthday, the child plays with small cubes or objects by collecting them in piles. Soon after the first year, the child is able to stack two 1-inch cubes and insert a large object through a container that has an appropriately matched hole for the object. By 15 months of age, the child can stack three cubes; at 18 months of age, the child can stack four cubes; and by 21 months of age, the child can stack six cubes. The child at 18 months of age is also able to turn two to three pages of a picture book and can put small objects of various shapes into a container with appropriately matched holes for the objects.

During the second year the child's fine motor skills become further refined. At 24 months of age, the child is able to build a tower of seven cubes, thread a shoelace through a large hole (such as safety pin size), and insert small and large objects swiftly into containers with appropriately matched holes. At 30 months of age, the child can turn single pages in a book, build a tower of nine cubes, and drop small objects such as raisins in a bottle using a neat superior forefinger grasp.

With writing or drawing, young toddlers (18 months of age) hold their crayon with a suppinate grasp (holding the crayon in their fist) (Rosenbloom and Horton 1971). The child scribbles in circular, undefined patterns. Nearing the end of the toddler years (30 months of age), the child holds the crayon in a pronate manner (Rosenbloom and Horton 1971). The child holds the distal part of the crayon with the index finger straight and along the top of the crayon. The 2-year-old child can draw single lines.

Self-care Skills

During the toddler years, the child gains some skills necessary for independent feeding. The superior forefinger grasp is developed in 1-year-old children, which enables children to finger feed themselves with small bites of food. The young toddler also begins to use a spoon. When first attempting to use a spoon, the arm is pronated. The child does not have good control over the spoon, such that it may easily tip, spilling the food before reaching the mouth. During the second year, the child gains further control with a spoon, but spills are still common. During the young toddler's years, the child also develops the ability to use a cup. Initially the child can hold a cup by the handles but may tip the cup when trying to drink from it. The child is then able to drink well from the cup but may drop it when trying to release it onto the table. By the second year, the child can control a cup well and release it appropriately.

The toddler also develops skills in dressing. The young toddler helps in dressing by holding out a foot to have a shoe put on or by holding out the arms to have them put through the sleeves of a shirt. The young toddler can take off shoes, hats, mittens, and socks as well as unzip clothing (Coley 1978). During the second year, the child helps in dressing by pushing down or pulling off clothes and removing the shoes. Children are also able to put their arms through large sleeve holes and button a large front button (Coley 1978).

A major self-care skill that is initiated within the toddler years is bowel and bladder control, much to the relief of the parents or caregivers. A number of physiological as well as psychological cues for toilet training readiness must be evident before toilet training is attempted. Physiological cues include voluntary control of the anal and urethral sphincters (Whaley and Wong 1979), an awareness of the characteristics of the sensations before elimination (Scipien et al. 1975), an awareness of the discomfort when incontinent (Scipien et al. 1975), the ability to hold a specific amount of urine in the bladder up to 2 hours (Whaley and Wong 1979), the ability to walk in order to go to and leave the toilet (Brazelton 1962), and the ability to sit down, get up, and maintain balance (Brazelton 1962). Psychological cues include the ability to understand simple directions (Chow et al. 1979), the ability to communicate a desire, the absence of a terribly negative period (Brazelton 1962), and the wish to please the caregiver(s) and behave like others (Brazelton 1962).

Toilet training is most often begun between 18 and 30 months of age depending on the readiness of the child and caregiver. Brazelton (1962) studied the toilet training efforts of 1,170 children in a 10-year period. Eighty percent of the children achieved bowel and bladder control simultaneously, 12 percent achieved bowel control before bladder control, and 8 percent achieved bladder control before bowel control. The mean age for first achievement (bladder, bowel, or bladder and bowel control) was 27.7 months. No significant differences were found between boys and girls. Daytime control was achieved on the average at 28.5 months of age. Night-time control was achieved on the average at 33.3 months of age. The girls achieved night-time control about 2½ months before the boys. For urinary night-time control, the bladder must be able to retain 300 to 350 mL of urine. Brazelton (1962) found that 40 percent of the children were bedwetting at age 4 and 30 percent were still bedwetting at age 5.

PRESCHOOLERS

Preschoolers include children between 36 and 60 months of age (3 to 5 years). Increasing balance and coordination are apparent in the preschooler's gross motor activity. Preschoolers further develop fine motor skills necessary with intricate movements of the hands during writing.

Gross Motor Development

Children at 3 years of age have increasing balance and do not visually watch their steps. Bayley (1935) found that 50 percent of the 3-year-old children tested could walk 10 feet on a 1-inch wide line without falling from the line. The 3-year-old child is also able to walk heel to toe for 10 feet and balance with one foot off the ground for 3 to 4 seconds (Bayley 1935). The child between 3 and 4 years of age is able to descend stairs with alternating steps (Knobloch et al. 1980). At 4 years of age, the child can walk on a circular line (Wellman 1935). At 5 years of age, the child can maintain balance between 3 and 5 seconds standing on one foot with the arms folded (Cratty 1979).

In running activities, the preschooler gains both coordination and speed. By 5 years of age, the child demonstrates smooth reciprocal arm movements and can run reasonably fast (11.5 feet/second) (Cratty 1979).

The ability to skip is not fully attained during the preschool years. The 4- or 5-year-old child skips on one foot while walking on the other foot.

The child's ability to jump develops further in the preschool years. The 3-year-old child can broadjump 8 to 10 inches (Cratty 1979). By 5 years of age, the child can broadjump 2 to 3 feet with a two-foot take-off (Cratty 1979).

The child's ability to hop changes during the preschool years. The 3-year-old child is able to hop on one foot one to three steps without accuracy of rhythm or distance; the 4-year-old child can hop four to six steps on one foot; and the 5-year-old child can hop eight to ten steps (Cratty 1979).

When throwing a ball, the 3-year-old child throws overhand, rotating the body but not shifting weight (Cratty 1979). The child can throw a ball about 6 or 7 feet (Wellman 1935). The 4-year-old child demonstrates reasonable weight shift when throwing a ball. When catching a ball, the 3-year-old child holds the arms straight with the elbows stiff (Cratty 1979). The 4-year-old child opens the hands in an attempt to catch a ball, although the elbows are kept stiff (Cratty 1979). During the child's fifth year, the arms are held at the side of the body, allowing for some "give" when catching a ball (Wellman 1935). The 5-year-old child can catch a large ball about 75 percent of the time when it is bounced to the child from 15 feet (Cratty 1979).

Fine Motor Development

The 3-year-old child can build a tower of ten cubes. By the later preschool years, the child is able to construct complex structures with cubes and blocks. The child during the preschool years is also able to drop small objects into a container (such as a piggybank) with reasonable speed.

Fine motor skills become further evident in the preschooler's writing and drawing behaviors. Between 4 and 6 years of age, the child develops the dynamic tripod finger posture (Wynn-Parry 1966), which consists of the child's ability to use the thumb, index, and middle fingers as a tripod in holding a crayon or pencil with the fourth and fifth fingers providing added stability (Rosenbloom and Horton 1971). The writing utensil is held in the posture as most adults hold a writing utensil. This finger posture allows for highly coordinated writing movements.

The 3-year-old child is able to copy a cross, and by 4 or 5 years of age the child is able to copy a square and circle. Cutting with scissors is attempted by the preschooler but is not a refined skill until the early school-aged years.

Figures appear in the drawings of preschoolers. The 3-year-old child may draw two figures together; crude drawings of human figures and objects appear in the 4-year-old child's drawings; and more refined human figures and objects appear in the 5-year-old child's drawings (Cratty 1979). The 5-year-old child may also draw recognizable letters.

Another fine motor skill that the 5-year-old child can demonstrate with slow speed is finger opposition. The child touches each finger in turn to the thumb.

Self-care Skills

During meals, the preschooler learns to distinguish between finger foods and foods requiring a spoon. The child at 5 years of age is able to hold a spoon with the fingers when either liquid or solid foods are eaten. The child is also able to use a fork. Initially, the fork is held in the fist and then by the fingers.

With dressing activities, the 3-year-old child can manage to remove pants or a skirt by pulling them down but requires help with pulling a shirt over the head to remove it. The child can open front or side buttons or zippers. When putting on clothes, the 3-year-old child needs help in distinguishing the front from the back of clothes and may need help putting on clothes. The child can manipulate buttons and close snaps and may attempt to put on a shoe, although it may be on the wrong foot. By the fifth year of age, the child can dress independently with simple clothing. The child can put on and tie shoes, pull clothing on, put a belt through loops, button front and side buttons, and close a front or back zipper (Coley 1978).

Self-care skills in bathing develop in the following order during the preschool years: (1) the child can dry the hands; (2) the child can wash the hands; (3) the child can dry the body with help; (4) the child can wash the body including the face; and (5) the child can dry the body. Preschoolers are also able to brush their teeth independently.

As described previously, toilet training occurs within the toddler and preschool years. Three-year-old children will attempt to wipe themselves following toileting without success. By 5 years of age, children can wipe themselves following toileting, flush the toilet, and wash and dry their hands.

SCHOOL-AGED CHILDREN

School-aged children are between 6 and 11 years of age. Greater speed, strength, versatility, and accuracy become evident in the school-aged child's gross motor activities (Ausubel et al. 1980). School-aged children develop the fine motor skills necessary for cursive writing.

Gross Motor Development

Throughout much of the literature for gross motor skills of school-aged children, boys' performances exceed those of girls (Ausubel et al. 1980). Sex differences are postulated to occur, in part, due to socialization.

The school-aged child runs with more coordinated and reciprocal arm and leg movements. Running speed increases about one foot per second during each of these years (Cratty 1979). The young school-aged child is also able to skip with both feet.

Balance improves in both static and dynamic activities. The 6-year-old child can walk on a 2-inch beam (dynamic), and the 7-year-old child can maintain balance when immobile and both eyes are closed (static) (Cratty 1979). The early school-aged child is also able to hop rhythmically in place from one foot to the other, as well as hop into small squares on one foot (Cratty 1979). The child is also able to ride a bicycle.

The 7-year-old child can jump 7 inches vertically using arm action with the jump (Cratty 1979). By 7 years of age, the child can also jump rope and do jumping jacks. By 9 years of age, girls can vertically jump 8½ inches and boys can vertically jump 10 inches (Cratty 1979). Boys and girls can jump approximately 20 inches in the standing broadjump (Cratty 1979).

Increases in eye–hand coordination are evident when these children throw and catch balls. In the early years, the child has reasonable throwing skill by shifting the weight and stepping with the opposite foot from that of the throwing arm. Distances improve for boys by 11 to 23 feet between 9 and 10 years of age (Cratty 1979). For girls, distances improve between 10 and 11 years of age by 7 or 8 feet (Cratty 1979). The young school-aged child can catch a ball when it is thrown waist high from 15 feet (Cratty 1979).

Fine Motor Development

Sex differences tend to be small in fine motor skills of school-aged children (Ausubel et al. 1980). While the 5-year-old child can do the finger opposition task slowly, the 7- to 8-year-old child can do the task quickly (Cratty 1979). The child is also able to use scissors.

The school-aged child's writing and drawing abilities increase. Hand preference is established by 6 years of age (Ausubel et al. 1980). The 6-year-old child can draw a triangle; the 7-year-old child can draw a diamond; and the older school-aged child can draw three-dimensional figures. Cursive writing is usually not possible before the child is 8 or 9 years of age.

Self-care Skills

At 6 to 8 years the child gains the ability to use a knife in both spreading and cutting food. Few spills occur when eating. With dressing, the 6-year-old child gains the skills to button back buttons or snap back snaps (Coley 1978). Thus, the child has all of the abilities to be independent in dressing.

Personal hygiene skills are evident in the self-care activities of school-aged children. The child can anticipate appropriate times to wash hands, brush teeth, and bathe and/or shower and can carry out these tasks independently.

ADOLESCENTS

Adolescents include persons between 12 and 18 years of age. Sex differences in gross motor activities become apparent in adolescence, with adolescent males excelling beyond adolescent females in most activities. Increases in speed and accuracy occur in the fine motor development of adolescents.

Gross and Fine Motor Development

Until the preadolescent years (10 or 11 years of age), the growth rate for males and females is fairly equal. The growth spurt for females begins at between 10 and 14 years of age and ends near 17 years of age. Females grow between 2 and 7.9 inches during these years (Whaley and Wong 1979). The growth spurt for males begins at between 12 and 16 years of age and ends near 20 or 21 years of age. Males gain between 4 and 12 inches in height (Whaley and Wong 1979). The growth spurt begins with the growth of the extremities and neck, followed by the growth of the hips, chest, shoulders, and trunk. The head circumference also increases during the pubertal growth spurt. Awkwardness may temporarily

develop owing to these rapid skeletal changes. In general, girls are smaller than boys, have arms and legs that are proportionately shorter, have a larger trunk, and have a broader pelvis (Carpenter 1938).

The relationship between gross motor performance and age, anatomical growth, and physiological maturity has been studied. Gross motor performance in adolescent males was positively related to age, anatomical growth, and physiological maturity (Atkinson 1924; Espenshade 1940). Increases in motor performance were found to cease between 17 and 18 years of age for adolescent boys (Espenshade 1940). Gross motor performance in adolescent females was only slightly positively related to height (Atkinson 1925). A slightly negative relationship between weight and gross motor performance was found for adolescent females (Atkinson 1925). The relationship among physiological maturity and gross motor performance in adolescent females was task specific (Atkinson 1925). Increases in motor performance for female adolescents were found to cease between 13 and 16 years of age (Espenshade 1940).

In addition to skeletal changes, muscle mass increases during adolescence, particularly in male adolescents. Muscular individuals generally excel in gross motor activities (Tanner 1964). Strength was found to be positively related to gross motor skill in adolescent males but only slightly related to gross motor skill in adolescent females (Bliss 1927). The most rapid increases in strength for adolescents occur between 13 and 16 years of age for adolescent males and between 12 and 14 years of age for adolescent females (McCloy 1935). Dimock (1935) found that adolescent males' increases in strength were slightly related to their physiological maturity. Strength was most marked after the first year after the postpubescent stage.

Cardiac and pulmonary changes occur that lead to the adolescents' increased endurance during physical activity. Overall, male adolescents' greater muscle mass and capacity to carry oxygen as well as their superior height, weight, limb length, and shoulder breadth leads to better performances in gross motor activities compared with female adolescents (Ausubel 1954).

Literature attending to fine motor skills in adolescence is primarily concerned with coordi-

Table 14-2 Summary of Gross Motor, Fine Motor, and Self-care Skills for Five Age Groups

Age Group	Gross Motor Skill	Fine Motor Skill	Self-care Skill
Infants			
1 month	Pulled to sit: slight head control	Palmar grasp reflex is evident.	
2 months	Prone: lifts head so face is at 45° angle from resting surface	Makes swiping movements towards objects	
3 months	Prone: supports self on forearms	Hands are more loosely open.	
4 months	Rolls stomach to back	Hands are brought together in midline.	
5 months	Head control is evident in all positions.	Primitive squeeze grasp or raking movement	
6 months	Rolls back to stomach	Scoops objects; palmar or squeeze grasp	Drinks from cup with handles; holds bottle
7 months	Sits without support; crawls	Transfers objects; radial-palmar or whole-hand grasp	Chews solids; feeds self large food items
8 months	Stands holding onto furniture	Inferior scissors grasp or superior palm grasp	
9 months	Creeps	Inferior forefinger or radial-digital grasp	
10 months	Cruises along furniture	Voluntarily releases objects; inferior pincer grasp	Feeds self small bites of food
11 months	Walks with both hands held	Neat pincer or forefinger grasp	
12 months	Walks independently	Superior forefinger grasp	
Toddlers	Walks sideways and backward	Stacks two to nine cubes	Uses spoon
	Runs	Turns pages in book	Drinks from small cup
	Climbs and descends stairs	Scribbles	Pushes down or pulls off simple pieces of clothing
			Gains bowel and bladder control
Preschoolers	Rides tricycle	Builds complex structures with cubes	Uses fork
	Balances on one foot	Copies cross, square, and circle	Dresses independently with simple clothing by age five
	Alternates feet when descending stairs	Can perform finger opposition task slowly	Brushes teeth
School-aged Children	Skips	Has dynamic tripod finger posture*	Uses knife
	Rides bicycle	Uses cursive writing	Dresses independently
	Running speed increases.	Copies triangle, diamond, and draws three-dimensional figures	Bathes/showers independently
	Distance in throwing a ball increases.	Uses scissors	
Adolescents	Increases in strength and endurance	Increases in speed and accuracy	Independent in eating, dressing, and personal hygiene activities

Rehabilitation of the Hand, 2nd ed., by C.B. Wynn-Parry, p. 26, Butterworth Publishers, © 1966.

nation and reaction time tasks. The speed and accuracy of these tasks increases with age during adolescence (Goodgold-Edwards 1984). Gross motor ability was not found to be highly related to fine motor ability in adolescence (Espershade 1940). (Table 14-2 is a summary of gross motor, fine motor, and self-care skills of children and adolescents within each age group.)

REFERENCES

Atkinson, R.K. "A Motor Efficiency Study of Eight Thousand New York City High School Boys." *American Physical Education Review* 29(1924):56–59.

Atkinson, R.K. "A Study of Athletic Ability of High School Girls." *American Physical Education Review* 30(1925): 389–399.

Ausubel, D.P. *Theory and Problems of Adolescent Development*. New York: Grune & Stratton, 1954.

Ausubel, D.P.; Sullivan, E.V.; and Ives, S.W. *Theory and Problems in Child Development*. 3d ed. New York: Grune & Stratton, 1980.

Bayley, N.A. "The Development of Motor Abilities during the First Three Years." *Monographs in Social Research and Child Development* 1(1935):1–26.

Bliss, J.G. "A Study of Progression Based on Age, Sex, and Individual Differences in Strength and Skill. *American Physical Education Review* 32(1927):11–21.

Brazelton, T.B. "A Child-oriented Approach to Toilet Training." *Pediatrics* 29(1962):121–128.

Carpenter, A. "Strength, Power and 'Femininity' as Factors Influencing the Athletic Performance of College Women." *Research Quarterly American Physical Education Association* 9(1938):120–127.

Chow, M.P.; Durand, B.A.; Feldman, M.N.; and Mills, M.A. *Handbook of Pediatric Primary Care*. New York: John Wiley & Sons, Inc., 1979.

Coley, I.L. *Pediatric Assessment of Self-care Activities*. St. Louis: C.V. Mosby Co., 1978.

Cratty, B.J. *Perceptual and Motor Development in Infants and Children*, 2d ed. Englewood Cliffs, N.J.: Prentice-Hall, Inc., 1979.

Di Leo, J.H. *Child Development: Analysis and Synthesis*. New York: Brunner/Mazel, 1977.

Dimock, H. "A Research in Adolescence: I. Pubescence and Physical Growth." *Child Development* 6(1935):176–195.

Erhardt, R.P. "Sequential Levels in Development of Prehension." *American Journal of Occupational Therapy* 28(1974):592–596.

Espenshade, A. "Motor Performance in Adolescence Including the Study of Relationships with Measure of Physical Growth and Maturity." *Monographs of the Society for Research for Child Development* 5(1940):1–126.

Goodgold-Edwards, S.A. "Motor Learning as it Relates to the Development of Skilled Motor Behavior: A Review of the Literature." *Physical and Occupational Therapy in Pediatrics* 4(1984):5–18.

Halverson, H.M. "An Experimental Study of Prehension in Infants by Means of Systematic Cinema Records." *Genetic Psychology Monographs* 10(1932):107–284.

Hohlstein, R.R. "The Development of Prehension in Normal Infants." *American Journal of Occupational Therapy* 36(1982):170–176.

Holle, B. *Motor Development in Children: Normal and Retarded*. Oxford: Blackwell Scientific Publishers, 1976.

Illingsworth, R.S. *The Development of the Infant and Young Child*. 8th ed. Edinburgh: Churchill Livingstone, 1983.

Knobloch, H.; Stevens, F.; and Malone,A.F. *Manual of Developmental Diagnoses*. Hagerstown, Md.: Harper & Row, 1980.

Kopp, C.B. "Fine Motor Abilities of Infants." *Developmental Medicine and Child Neurology* 16(1974).

Loria, C. "Relationship of Proximal and Distal Function in Motor Development." *Physical Therapy* 60(1980): 167–172.

Lowrey, G.H. *Growth and Development of Children*. 8th ed. Chicago: Year Book Medical Publishers, 1986.

McCloy, C.H. "The Influence of Chronological Age on Motor Performance." *Research Quarterly American Physical Educational Association* 6(1935):61–64.

Neligan, G., and Prudham, D. "Norms for Four Standard Developmental Milestones by Sex, Social Class and Place in the Family." *Developmental Medicine and Child Neurology* 11(1969):413–422.

Rosenbloom, L., and Horton, M.E. "The Maturation of Fine Prehension in Young Children." *Developmental Medicine and Child Neurology* 13(1971):3–8.

Scipien, G.M.; Barnard, M.U.; Chard, M.A.; Howe, J.; and Phillips, P.J. *Comprehensive Pediatric Nursing*. New York: McGraw-Hill Book Co., 1975.

Tanner, J.M. *Physique of the Olympic Athlete*. London: Allen & Unwin, 1964.

Wellman, B.L. Motor Achievements of Preschool Children. *Child Education* 13(1935):311–316.

Whaley, L.F., and Wong, D.L. *Nursing Care of Infants and Children*. St. Louis: C.V. Mosby Co., 1979.

Wynn-Parry, C.B. *Rehabilitation of the Hand*. 2d ed. London: Butterworth, 1966.

Chapter 15

Communication Interventions

Mary Lou Fragomeni-Nuttall
Nancy Williams

This chapter provides information on the sequence of communication development and suggestions for treating the child who has disordered communication. Emphasis is placed on determining the most functional means of communication and the most functional means of facilitating the normal developmental sequence of language. The early skills needed for communication are explained to help determine the initial phase of intervention.

Children hospitalized for extended periods experience both motor and communicative developmental delays. These children, being cared for in the home, vary in age, medical etiology, and extent of intervention requirements. There is one factor that is evident in children who demonstrate delays in communicative development: a breakdown in the ability to express wants, needs, and thoughts. The information presented here can be used to give caregivers the means to increase the child's ability to participate with the environment and to reduce the frustration of those desperately trying to understand.

Communication is a process of developing and refining the rudimentary skills of hearing and vocalizing into listening and verbalizing. This process involves receptive and expressive skills that integrate with other thinking skills. Receptive skills are exemplified by hearing and seeing, complemented then by the expressive skills of gesturing and talking. Understanding of motor and sensory input from the environment, which leads to the ability to manipulate and adapt, is the cognitive process that integrates thought into expression and reception. In a normal child, this sequence can be viewed by developmental guidelines. For the child who demonstrates language delays, the correlation to chronological age may vary but the sequence of skills should progress in a manner similar to normal development.

When a child's ability to communicate is impaired, a referral to a certified speech/language pathologist (SLP) is recommended. The SLP is qualified to assess the child's ability to comprehend and express language and to recommend appropriate measures to enhance communication. The following guidelines should be used when considering a referral to an SLP:

1. The child has never received a complete speech/language assessment by a certified SLP.
2. The child and/or family demonstrate frustration in the communicative process.
3. Little or no progress has been demonstrated with the present recommendations.
4. The child has achieved all previous recommendations and the course for further facilitation of communication is unclear.

NORMAL DEVELOPMENT

The natural process of sequenced changes in communication that occur in normal children also occur in children demonstrating delays. These delays may change the timing of the acquired skills, but the sequence is normally not altered. Disordered language differs in that the sequence of development is disrupted by sensory or motor difficulties. It is important to focus on each child's skill level and needs rather than to correlate their abilities to other children at their chronological age.

Periodic plateaus commonly occur in language development. Each child develops at a different rate. When a child remains at one level for a period of time, it may be because gains are being made in other developmental areas. Each child, whether normal or with communication deficits, progresses at an individual pace. Therefore, children may not demonstrate skills exactly parallel to those on normal development charts.

Communication is often associated with a means of requesting a desired activity or object. This is one of the many roles of language in normal communication. Other functions are to obtain information, indicate notice of an event or object, display displeasure, gain relief from an undesirable situation, and acknowledge the presence of others as well as bringing them into contact.

Language development is outlined in Exhibit 15-1 to assist the home care nurse in reviewing the progression of language skills and should be used as a guideline, recalling that each child is unique in his or her strengths and rate of development.

Precursors

Precursors to learning verbal or gestural communication involve a variety of skills that allow a child to interact with the environment. From birth through the first years of life, a child uses many skills to play, communicate, investigate, and relate to his or her surroundings. These skills are necessary for initiating the communication process for the younger child learning language or for the older child who needs to redevelop these skills in order to be retrained in techniques of communication. It is these skills that give the child a desire and interest to communicate.

The importance of language precursors may be understood more clearly with examples. Without the understanding that a particular behavior may achieve a desired end result, the language learner may never use communications (means) to achieve a result (end). This failure to develop functional communication would be hindered by the lack of other precursors as well. Without initiation skills, the language learner would not repeat new gestures or words. The failure to comprehend the functional use of objects would not allow for more complex conceptualization in order to relate to others about the objects in the child's daily life. The precursors are needed sensorimotor skills that occur prior to more sophisticated language development.

The following skills can be observed or stimulated and, if absent, should be taught as the most basic skills in communication. Some age ranges have been included, but, as with all developmental ranges, these are approximate. The sequencing of activities within each area is the expected developmental ordering. Many of the skills overlap into various areas, and as retraining commences the early items common to several areas should be emphasized.

The most concrete skills of the seven precursors that are presented is *object permanence*. The concept that objects exist even when out of sight for periods of time is basic to communication development and to cognitive awareness. In normal development the following sequence exists:

1. Visual tracking observed—1–4 months
2. Visual search of where object disappears—1–4 months
3. Finds partially covered object—4–8 months
4. Finds completely covered object—8–12 months

Objects that can encourage looking, tracking, and finding include brightly colored noisemakers and toys. The use of toys with both visual and audible significance provides at least one mode of input for visually or hearing impaired children. If a child is not visually or hearing impaired, the toy can be limited to either sound (hidden bell) or visual input (flashing light) to make tracking or finding more difficult. At later stages, toys can be hidden under cups, scarves, or blankets. If needed, have the child watch you hide the toy (or hide it in the same place) and let the child discover it independently.

Exhibit 15-1 Developmental Communication Scale

1–2 Months

- Cries, random vocal play
- "Animal-like" sounds
- Stops activity when regarding a face
- Eyes follow movement
- Alerting
- Startle response to loud sounds
- Makes rudimentary head turn
- Opens eyes to voice

3–4 Months

- Cooing one-syllable vowel-like sounds
- Cries less
- Beginning vocal-social response (talks back)
- Inspects own hand
- Facial brightening/smiling in response to talking
- Regularly localizes speaker with eyes
- Frightened by angry voices
- Recognizes and responds to name
- Usually stops crying when someone talks to him or her
- Laughs, repeats own vocalizations
- Babbling, strings of syllable-like vocalizations
- Moods of pleasure up to 30 minutes

5–6 Months

- Vocalizes spontaneously to self
- Tries to imitate inflection
- More consonants when babbling
- Babbles back, belly laughs
- Imitates social play by smiling and vocalizing
- Talks to mirror image
- Looks and vocalizes to own name
- Appears to recognize words such as "daddy," "bye-bye," "mama"
- Stops or withdraws in response to "no" about 50 percent of the time

7–8 Months

- Has defined syllables—ma, da, mi, my
- Attention more concentrated; looks for toy that disappears
- Repeats oral-motor sounds—cough, raspberry, tongue-click
- More adult-like babbling for fun
- Uses defined two-syllable utterances—"mama," "choo-choo," "dada"
- Regularly stops activity when name called
- Will sustain interest in pictures if they are named

9–10 Months

- Signals emphasis and emotions by vocalizing distinct intonation patterns
- Vocalizes to gain attention
- Combines words with gestures—"no-no" with head shake, "bye-bye" with wave

Exhibit 15-1 continued

- May repeat same word for many meanings
- Understands commands with gestures

11–12 Months

- More gibberish
- Imitates inflections, gestures, and speech rhythms
- Jargon with occasional meaningful word
- Practices words that are known; produces more sounds specific to the child's language
- Aware of expressive function of language—may repeat "damn, damn"
- Babbles short sentences
- Uses appropriate intonation patterns
- Two to three words used meaningfully
- Follows one-step command without gesture
- Appears to understand simple questions—"where's the ball?"
- Shows more intense attention and response to speech over prolonged periods
- Demonstrates understanding by responding with appropriate gestures to several kinds of verbal requests

13–18 Months

- Names one object on request
- Names one black/white picture on request
- Appears to understand some new words each week
- Points to more than one body part
- Identifies more than one picture in a book
- Responds to action verb request
- Brings object from another room on request
- Identifies two or more objects from a group of familiar objects

19–24 Months

- Uses one- and two-word gestures
- Puts two words together
- Names at least three familiar objects or pictures
- Has vocabulary of 10–15 words by age 2
- Identifies several pictures
- Understands possessor–possession relationships (mama's shoe)
- Follows a number of simple requests

25–36 Months

- Points to smaller body parts: chin, elbow
- Points to pictures showing action
- Points to objects described by use
- Understands most common verbs
- Responds to two related actions (run fast)
- Likes to listen to simple stories
- Uses words "on" and "in"

37–48 Months

- Responds to primary seriation of categorization—"put them in order."
- Follows simple commands with two objects
- Follows "in, on, under, beside" when asked to do so
- Names item when cued by function—"what do you sit on?"
- Uses more adult-like language

The second precursor is an awareness of *cause and effect*. This is the recognition that specific actions give specific results and is observed at the early development of initiating communications. The expected progression is as follows:

1. Focuses on interesting objects: 0–1 month
2. Watches hands: 1–4 months
3. Indicates desire for the recurrence of an event by touching an adult's hands: 4–8 months
4. Pushes away an interfering hand: 8–12 months
5. Requests the activation of an object following its demonstration: 12–18 months
6. Activates a mechanical object: 18–24 months

The third skill is *means/end*. This precursor can be observed in motor responses that bring about a desired occurrence. Acting out of the thought process can be seen. The progression of this expected skill is as follows:

1. Reaching and grasping: 1–8 months
2. Releases one object to grasp another: 8–12 months
3. Uses props to get desired object: 12–18 months
4. Uses a mallet to pound in pegs: 18–24 months

A child reaching to make a mobile swing demonstrates the early use of means/end. This purposeful movement brings about the desired change. A more active child may pull a toy by its string or hit the pegs on a toy bench to cause a specific occurrence. The child then demonstrates greater manipulation over the environment.

Imitation, the fourth language precursor, is the most important skill in learning to communicate. It is manifested in verbal or gestural fashion, possibly both. By following another's lead, communication often begins. The following developmental levels are expected:

1. Mutual imitation: 1–4 months
2. A skill within the child's repertoire is imitated: 4–8 months
3. Child imitates new behavior: 8–12 months
4. Child imitates unfamiliar and subtle gestures: 18–24 months

Activities that encourage imitation range from sound or melody imitation to mirroring the "so big" gesture. Pat-a-cake and peek-a-boo, at the appropriate developmental level, give appropriate redundancy to early imitation.

Expecting an event to recur describes the fifth precursor, *anticipation*. Recognition that a certain environment surrounds the occurrence involves memory of details, as well as a response that prepares a person for the next event. The sequence of skills that develop is shown below:

1. Sucks before external excitement: 1–4 months
2. Looks for an object dropped in front of him or her: 4–8 months
3. Holds hands out to catch a ball: 12–18 months

During feeding, a child may suck just at the sight of the bottle. Repeated play with a familiar toy can bring about an anticipation response. Often, when daily events occur routinely, this response will be seen before a favored activity.

Relating to objects for purposeful use in the environment is the sixth precursor to language. The child demonstrates more purposeful control of surroundings as his or her experience expands. His or her interest and need to communicate also grow. The order of development for functional relating is as follows:

1. Mouth, holds object: 1–4 months
2. Waves, visually inspects, hits, stabs objects: 8–12 months
3. Demonstrates object function: 12–18 months
4. Labels objects: 18–24 months

When a child puts a spoon in his or her mouth during feeding, purposeful use of the object is shown. All activities of daily living (washing, brushing teeth, putting on shoes) provide excellent opportunities for the use of objects as tools.

The seventh and final precursor to language development is *construction of objects in space*. Spatial relations develop as a motor and visualization skill. Recognizing that objects can combine in "novel" ways is a complex skill that progresses as follows:

1. Focuses on single object: 1–4 months
2. Glances between two objects: 4–8 months

Exhibit 15-2 Types of Stimulation

Auditory

- Bell
- Clicker
- Hemi-synchronized music
- Television (never longer than 30 to 60 minutes so as not to become background noise)
- Recording of family or friend
- Loud clapping

Visual

- Light on/off, flashlight
- Sunlight
- Pictures of family, pets, friend
- Mobile (moving)
- Tinsel
- Black and white drawing of face

Taste

Place on tongue for taste only. Precautions should be taken to use only small amounts and that no substance should be left in the child's mouth. Cleaning the mouth before and after these presentations can be included as part of the stimulation program.

- Lemon
- Candy stick
- Catsup
- Chicken soup
- Ice/popsicle
- Salty breadsticks

Tactile

- Rough/smooth (washcloth)
- Wet
- Warm/cool (water, ice)
- Shaving brush
- Cotton
- Lotion (vanilla scented)

Olfactory

Pleasant or familiar odors

- Vanilla
- Cinnamon
- Nutmeg
- Perfume (family's)
- Fruit
- Chicken soup

Alerting odors

- Ammonia
- Onion
- Garlic

3. Localizes to sound: 4–12 months
4. Stacks two blocks, rings on stick: 18–24 months

The home care nurse or caretaker can observe how the child interacts with the environment and can facilitate increased interactions by providing the child with different opportunities. In the following section, a similar idea, to that discussed previously, of stimulating the senses with specific items is recommended. Once it is determined that a certain object achieves a response through a specific sense, try to combine it with another object so that learning is occurring. An example of this combination might be a simple mobile that attracts the child visually when it moves. Bells can then be added so the child associates the sounds to the mobile. Then, when the child hears the bells, he or she will look for the mobile moving.

SENSORY STIMULATION

Multisensory stimulation may be indicated for the child who is severely impaired or comatose. Some specialists believe that the comatose patient may develop increased responsiveness and increased quality of life and may even regain consciousness if given consistent and persistent stimulation (Smith 1983).

Stimulation is more effective when done at the same time of the day and in the same sequence. As these activities are used, it may become apparent that they stimulate early levels of language precursors. Family participation, using this treatment modality, should be encouraged.

Sensory stimulation can be provided through auditory, visual, tactile, taste, and olfactory senses. The variety of the presentations can change from session to session. Rarely should a presentation last longer than 10 seconds, and the whole sequence may take only 20 minutes. It may be completed in two sessions. Suggestions for each modality are provided in Exhibit 15-2.

The goal of sensory stimulation is to bring about increased awareness to the environment. This change in awareness may be observed as greater intensity in responses, more variety of responses, or an improved level of consciousness. Examples of cause/effect toys are listed in Exhibit 15-3.

Exhibit 15-3 Cause/Effect Toys

1. Objects that make noise or move by manipulation: music boxes, toy radios, or squeeze toys
2. Objects that stimulate reach: mobile; tactile materials that are suspended (tissue paper streamers, aluminum foil, yarn)
3. Objects that stimulate grasp: cloth-covered blocks that make noise, nerf balls, squeeze bulb, squeeze animals, or visual tracking rattle
4. Objects that stimulate finger movement: finger-paints, sand and water play, nontoxic clay, push button jack-in-the-box, touch me books, or finger play rattles

AUGMENTATIVE COMMUNICATIONS

Verbal communication may not be a sufficient or viable mode of expression for some children and adolescents. It is then necessary to determine how to augment existing skills and provide improved communication potential. The augmentative device may consist of a system of eye blinks for communicating yes/no responses, a simple alphabet board for spelling out words, or the use of a laser beam connected to a headband that makes a computer "talk." Establishing the need and motivation to express one's thoughts is, however, the important first step in providing an appropriate system of augmentative communication.

A child who has not developed an expressive communication system requires a different strategy from the child who has lost the means of communication. The first child must establish the precursors of language and then a system that works within his or her abilities. The child who loses the means of communication may not lose the precursors but now needs a new means of self-expression. Both of these children must be provided with stimulation that will develop language intent.

The second step in developing augmentative communication is determining the best response available to the child. Motor abilities may be a significant factor; therefore, a consultation is recommended with occupational and physical therapists. Considerations when establishing the best possible communication system are (1) need for communication, (2) cognitive skills, (3) motor abilities, (4) visuoperceptual abilities, and (5) psycholinguistic abilities.

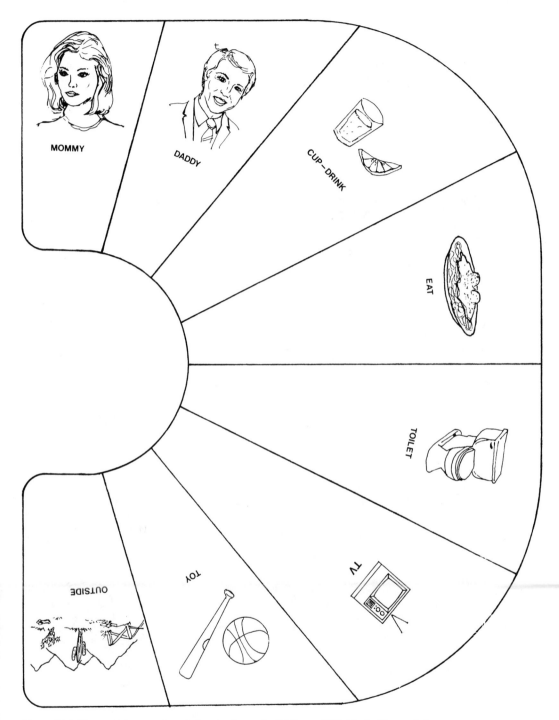

Figure 15-1 Illustrated language board. *Source:* Steven A. Williams, 1987. Used with permission.

Once a response mode has been determined and a method of operation developed, the actual use of the augmentative system requires training. When selecting vocabulary be sure to consider the persons, foods, toys, and other objects or needs the child may have. Concentrate on what the child regularly attempts to communicate. When an evaluation is not available, use the above suggestions and consider an illustrated/language board (Figure 15-1) and/or sign

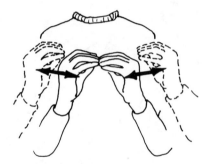

MORE
Holding hands in flat O-shape with palms and tops facing lap together once or twice.

HAPPY
Brush up and out twice with an open B on chest.

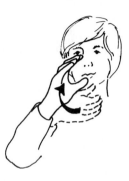

DRINK
With a C hand on mouth as if drinking.

EAT
Repeating several times, place tips of right flat O on lips.

SAD
With both five shape and palms up and slightly curved fingers, hold hands in front of face and drop slowly.

TOILET
Shake right T from left to right.

DADDY
Place thumb of right five hand on forehead.

MOMMY
Place thumb of right five hand on chin.

Figure 15-2 Examples of sign language. *Source:* Steven A. Williams, 1987. Used with permission.

language (Figure 15-2). The communication board can be simple using the provided example placed on poster board. More sophisticated language boards with more space between pictures or additional elements appropriate for the child's skills may be used. Be sure the pictures are large enough for the child to see, placed where the child can reach them, and closely represent what they are to symbolize. It is also important that the child's posture is stabilized for the best support of fine motor skills for sign language.

Vocabulary selection for a communication board or sign language requires input from those persons who regularly interact with the child. Consideration should be given to the following factors when selecting vocabulary: include items that are important to the user, can be used in a variety of contexts, can be demonstrated easily, have potential usefulness, and are within the child's experiences. Nouns, verbs, pronouns, emotions, and attributes can be used if they are commensurate to the child's language skills.

Visuoperceptual skills, posture, and ambulation potential are important factors in the physical construction of the communication board. Consider the child's vision when determining the size of the board. It may be more appropriate to use photographs of both objects and persons when photographs are available. The designed portability of the board and the arrangement of the pictures should both consider the child's posture and ambulation potential.

REFERENCE

Smith, R. "Treatment of Communication Disorders." In *Rehabilitation of the Head-injured Adult*, edited by M. Rosenthal, E. Griffith, M. Bond, and J. Miller. Philadelphia: F.A. Davis, 1983.

Chapter 16

Physical Therapy and Occupational Therapy Interventions

Nancy J. Harris
Jill K. Martindale

The major roles of physical and occupational therapists are evaluation of sensorimotor functioning and implementation of therapeutic interventions. These therapists use specific treatment techniques to minimize the effects of sensorimotor impairment and provide the child with more normal sensorimotor experiences in order to maximize independence and normal development. These specialties often overlap in pediatrics, not only in educational training but also in evaluation and treatment techniques used. In this chapter the disciplines of physical and occupational therapy are combined when appropriate and separate specialty areas are also described. Those aspects of a home therapy program that are most often expected of pediatric home care nurses when therapists are not available are included. Strongest emphasis has been placed on increasing one's awareness of the needs of the sensory- and motor-impaired child and how to respect those needs in all aspects of the child's daily routine, including handling, positioning, activities of daily living (ADLs), mobility and use of adaptive equipment. Guidelines are included that indicate when referral to a therapist is appropriate, noting which pediatric therapist(s) could best address the particular referral condition or problem (Table 16-1). Range of motion (ROM) techniques have also been included in Appendix 16-A.

REFERRAL TO A THERAPIST

An evaluation from a therapist can be helpful in determining the appropriateness, type, frequency, and duration of treatment required. The child's diagnosis, medical history, degree of impairment, intelligence, age, developmental readiness, and motivation are several factors that may affect the outcome of treatment.

Which therapy disciplines would most likely be involved in evaluations and treatment when the specific conditions or problems are identified are indicated in Table 16-1. Those conditions or problems that are appropriate to refer to a pediatric physical or occupational therapist are listed in Table 16-2. A physician's referral may be required depending on local, state, or agency practice regulations.

MANAGEMENT STRATEGIES FOR THE PEDIATRIC HOME CARE PATIENT

Based on the therapist's assessment, a number of therapeutic interventions for managing abnormal muscle tone, sensory deficits, posture and mobility, range of motion, and self-help skills may be appropriate. Some of the important management strategies that the home care nurse would be required to implement follow.

Table 16-1 Commonly used Therapy Services per Condition or Problem

Condition/Problem	Occupational Therapy	Physical Therapy	Speech Pathology
Congenital/genetic abnormalities	X	X	X
Perinatal high-risk factors	X	X	X
Neurological impairments	X	X	X
Orthopedic conditions	X	X	
Trauma/abuse	X	X	X
Minimal cerebral dysfunction/learning disabilities	X		X
Cardiopulmonary disorders	X	X	X
Metabolic/endocrine disorders	X	X	X
Neuromuscular disorders	X	X	X
Sensory impairments	X	X	
Burns	X	X	
Mental retardation	X	X	X
Emotional problems	X		
Developmental delays	X	X	X
Spinal trauma	X	X	
Feeding disorders	X		X
Cognitive delays	X		X
Language/communication delays/disorders	X		X
Perceptual disorders	X		
Fine motor difficulties/delays	X		
Gross motor difficulties/delays	X	X	
Dressing difficulties	X		
Bathing difficulties	X	X	
Grooming difficulties	X		
Toiletry difficulties	X	X	
Ambulation difficulties		X	

Table 16-2 Appropriate Referral Conditions

Condition/Problem	Occupational Therapy	Physical Therapy
Loss of range of motion	X	X
Skin breakdowns due to equipment, splints, positions, decreased mobility, etc.	X	X
Significant change in muscle tone	X	X
Development of, or significant increase in, asymmetry of posture or movement (e.g., scoliosis)		X
Equipment changes needed due to growth, wear and tear, surgery, changing tone, social appropriateness, etc.	X	X
Mastery of skill or therapy goal	X	X
Difficulty implementing therapy plans	X	X
Changing eating habits, needs, or behaviors (e.g., transitions from liquids to purees to solids; increased gagging; coughing or vomiting during feeding; significant weight loss; increase in time needed to feed; decrease in quantity of food taken)	X	
Loss of sensation	X	
Significant behavioral response to therapeutic programs or routines	X	X
Changing activities of daily living needs (e.g., puberty, increase or decrease in functional ability, age appropriateness)	X	
Change in mobility		X
Increase in deformity	X	X
Need for environmental adaptation	X	X
Change in caregiver's ability to manage home program	X	X

Table 16-3 Do's and Don'ts for Handling the Child with Abnormal Muscle Tone

Type of Muscle Tone	Do's	Don'ts
High Tone: Hypertonicity or spasticity may be present in any or all parts of the body, including lips, face, and tongue. Spasticity is manifested by resistance to passive movement. Tone is strongly influenced by mood, stress, general health condition, and position. The caregiver's handling of the patient with high tone is crucial to the management of this tone and the effectiveness of any nursing care plan. Spasticity is often found in patterns of flexion or extension synergies.	Range of motion should be included as a daily routine and can be incorporated into dressing, diapering, bathing, playtime, and positioning activities. Support the joint you are moving and hold the body part at the point of resistance in order to achieve maximal range possible. At this point you may feel a relaxation of tone and can then move the point to its fullest range. This may be more easily facilitated during water play (bath or pool) and at times of the child's greatest relaxation. (Refer to Appendix 16-A for further ROM details.)	Range of motion should not be done quickly or in a stressed or negative atmosphere. Try not to stimulate the spastic muscle groups by your hand placement. Do not neglect rotational movements and proximal joints (pelvis, scapula, neck, and spine). It is also important to include areas of skin contact and/or creases such as the axilla, groin, and palm of the hand.
	Synergies need to be "broken." The client with flexor spasticity needs to be positioned more "open," and likewise the extensor synergy requires more containment. Key points of control are usually at the thumb, scapula, neck, trunk, hips, and ankles. Carrying and positioning strategies can be incorporated with the neonate through the adult. Tone can be managed in most activities and needs to be considered carefully during feeding and toileting as well. Improved attention and social interaction can also be gained with control of muscle tone.	Do not position and carry the child in ways that reinforce the synergies of spastic flexion or extension. For example, the child with increased extension should not be positioned supine or carried with legs scissored. Do not allow abnormal movement patterns. They will become stronger with "practice" and become even more difficult to inhibit.
Low Tone: Hypotonicity is characterized by a lack of stability and, often, hypermobility of the joints. This patient usually has trouble working against gravity, and hence positioning supports and facilitating dynamic motor activity are primary goals.	Give enough support so that the child does not fatigue completely while trying to maintain a position. The child will not be able to attend or interact with the environment if primary effort is used for seeking stability. Support in alignment and symmetry of body with particular attention to optimizing eye–hand interactions and preventing deformities. See Figure 16-1A.	While it is important to provide adequate support, do not oversupport to the point where the child does not have to actively "work" to improve stability. Do not allow asymmetrical positioning with poor postural alignment. A soft, flexible support such as a beanbag chair is contraindicated and only reinforces the child's tendency to "sink" into gravity. Positioning and handling should not reinforce joint hypermobility. Lying supine with arms out to the sides and legs spread is to be avoided. "W" sitting (Figure 16-1B) and transfers in and out of sitting by spreading legs to sides should be redirected.

Table 16-3 continued

Type of Muscle Tone	Do's	Don'ts
	Care of head/neck positioning during feeding is crucial to encourage oral-motor control and to prevent aspiration (Figures 16-1C and 16-1D). Provide proximal support to achieve distal functioning. Controlled weight-bearing can be a method to improve muscle tone and stability (Figure 16-1F). Working in more upright positions such as standing and kneeling (devices can be used to assist) is often more successful than prone lying.	"Bird-feeding" with the child's head tipped back and neck extended is not only poor positioning but also extremely dangerous (Figure 16-1E). Do not place play/work materials at a level such that the child has no way to stabilize the upper extremities.
Athetoid/Mixed Tone: Fluctuating tone is characterized by an increase of mobility over a lack of stability. Mobility is often involuntary and uncontrolled. This child often knows where and how he or she wants to do something but has a great deal of difficulty executing coordinated purposeful activity. In efforts to achieve stability, the athetoid child often fixates distally. Over time, this can produce joint deformities.	Follow the general guidelines for increasing stability and providing adequate support as described for the child with low muscle tone. However, you must also incorporate the suggestions for decreasing excess tone as described above for the child with high tone. Remember that increased effort and frustration will increase tone and incoordination for the athetoid child. Provide proximal stability as well as light resistance to distal movements to improve efficiency of movement. The use of weighted wrist or ankle cuffs, utensils, or bilateral holding often helps. Keep work surfaces in close proximity to the child. Particular attention, as it relates to safety must be given to this child, especially during feeding and transferring. Remember that the child's muscle tone and control can change rapidly.	Again, follow previously outlined suggestions so as to not reinforce either the poor stability of the child with low tone or movement limitations of the child with high tone. Do not allow the child to use extraneous movements to the point at which he or she becomes fatigued, frustrated, and even less stable. In addition, do not restrict the child to the point at which he or she is frustrated or is constantly "fighting" or working against physical restraints.

Abnormal Muscle Tone

Abnormal muscle tone adversely affects all aspects of a child's development and subsequently his or her health care maintenance. It is characterized by either high tone or low tone. One may find that there is both high and low tone present or that tone may fluctuate. Management of tone during all activities must be incorporated into the nursing care plans. Intervention strategies for managing each type of abnormal tone are discussed in Table 16-3. Figure 16-1 should help clarify these strategies.

Sensory Deficits

Sensory stimuli is a crucial component of learning. Inability to perceive incoming sensory information or process internal sensory cues can greatly diminish the efficiency of the "feedback loop" of learning (Figure 16-2).

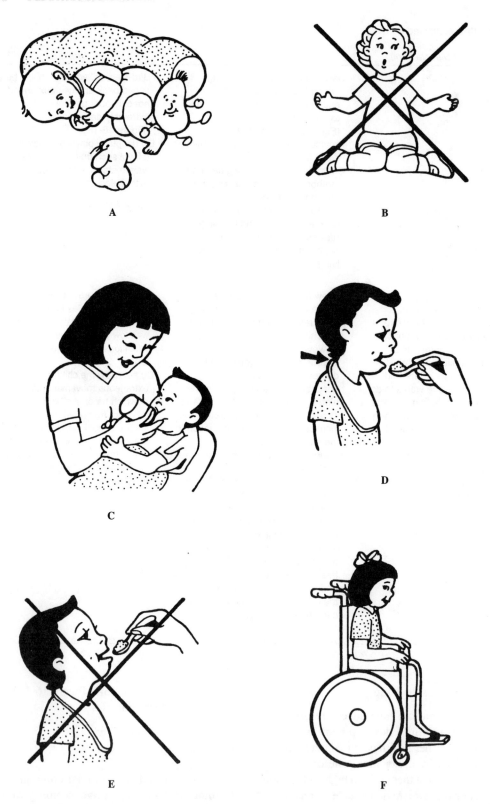

Figure 16-1 A. Assisted side-lying with midline flexion tuck. **B.** "W"-sitting. **C.** Infant feeding position with cheek support. **D.** Correct feeding presentation with head and neck in slight forward flexion. **E.** "Bird feeding": Head and neck hyperextension. **F.** Proper body alignment in sitting. *Source:* Reprinted with permission of Therapy Skill Builders, Tucson, Arizona.

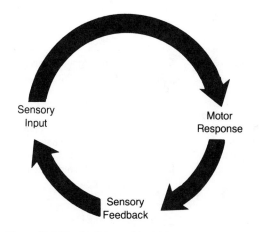

Figure 16-2 Feedback loop of learning.

Sensory perception includes vision, hearing, taste, smell, touch and pressure, gravity and movement, position and direction, pain and temperature, vibration, discrimination, and localization. Determining which of the senses or perceptual-cognitive areas have been impaired is not always clear-cut and may require thorough evaluation. Children who have had a neurological insult may manifest motor, learning, or behavioral problems. Decreased sensory functioning may cause, or compound, the observable deficit behavior. General guidelines to consider when working with a child with sensory deficits are shown in Table 16-4. The most common problems seen with the child receiving home care are included. It should be remembered that each person processes and perceives sensory information differently. It is a very subjective experience, and tolerance levels must be respected. The amount, type, and duration of stimulation tolerated can vary daily depending on mood, health, fatigue, and emotional conditions.

Auditory and visually impaired children have special needs. The materials and resources available to address those needs are extensive. Most states have specialized programs designed to specifically serve these special needs.

Posture and Mobility

The developmental areas of posture and mobility are most often associated with ambulatory patients; however, they are much broader. They encompass the multihandicapped nonambulatory child as well as the child who is developing postural control and mobility in lower positions such as prone, quadruped, and sitting. Posture is not only concerned with standing position, but also alignment in all antigravity positions and in prone, supine, and side-lying positions. Mobility includes any means of changing position (e.g., rolling, creeping/crawling, knee walking, ambulation). In the home care population it also includes transfers, movement in bed, and wheelchair mobility.

Posture and mobility are greatly affected by abnormal muscle tone. Specific orthopedic and neuromuscular conditions such as arthrogryposis, osteogenesis imperfecta, congenital hip dislocation, muscular dystrophy, cerebral palsy, and Guillain-Barré-syndrome have an obvious effect on the child's development of normal postural alignment and mobility. The development of hip dislocations, asymmetry, and spinal curvatures, such as scoliosis and kyphosis, are of great concern. Many children have problems in these areas because of imbalances in muscle tone and strength and the tendency to assume preferred, but usually not optimal, positions that reinforce abnormal patterns.

The affect on posture and mobility due to limitations in the child's cardiopulmonary capacity as in cystic fibrosis, congenital heart defects, and bronchopulmonary dysplasia cannot be neglected. The child with limited energy and endurance or who relies on equipment, such as supplemental oxygen or ventilators, will also have greater difficulty in achieving antigravity postures and developing mobility. Interventions for achieving posture and mobility goals are provided in Table 16-5.

Self-help Skills

Performance of self-help skills or ADLs is often affected in the child who is ill or has a sensory, motor, cognitive, or perceptual impairment. ADLs are the basic skills essential to every-day living. They include dressing, eating, toileting, bathing, and grooming. ADLs for the older patient may also include homemaking and functional skills for living more independently (e.g., money management, shopping, cooking, cleaning, child care, banking, leisure and social skills, and handling emergencies).

Table 16-4 Do's and Don'ts for Handling the Child with Sensory Deficits

Sensory Problem/Condition	Do's	Don'ts
1. Hypo/hypersensitivity to touch	Verbally prepare the child before touching him or her. Use firm pressure. Limit the amount of stimuli presented at a time and give the child time to adapt before changing it. Allow the child to use another sensation or another body part. Try to incorporate it into a whole body image. Pair verbal descriptions with sensory stimulation.	Don't tickle or use light feathery strokes. Avoid going against the direction of hair growth. Don't overstimulate. Don't surprise the child. Don't restrict use of compensation skills during concept formation tasks. Don't ignore the impaired body part.
2. Proprioception/kinesthesia: impairments in the perception of joint position and direction of movement can influence a child's body concept and his or her accuracy and quality of movements in space.	Provide weight bearing in proper body alignment. Work against resistance to provide increased stimulation to joint receptors. Increase graded, bilateral activities (e.g., playing catch with various sized and weighted balls, wheelbarrow walking).	Don't allow the child to only use the body parts or side of the body that he or she can perceive. Don't overdo resisted input to joints. Pain reception at joints may also be impaired. Don't encourage rapid movements.
3. Visual perception: visual perception can include ocular motor skills; depth perception; figure–ground, spatial, and position perceptions; form constancy; visual discrimination; and memory and sequencing skills.	Place materials in child's visual fields. However, it is very important to encourage and provide opportunities to explore beyond the visual fields. Minimize the confusion. Avoid "busyness" of visual presentations. Give the child alternative sensory modes to learn from. Move, touch, or talk to the child through the activity. Work on form constantly and object permanency first. Directionality, laterality, position and spatial concepts develop first on oneself, then with oneself in relationship to each other, and, last, in two dimensions (on paper). Use functional, experiential tasks that are repeated and familiar (e.g., eating, dressing, bathing).	Don't allow the child to ignore deficit sides. Don't assume the child sees things the same way you do even if visual acuity is reported to be normal. Don't work on higher level visuoperceptual skills until basic concepts are mastered.
4. Vestibular movement and gravity: movement and changes in position are an integral part in early development. The formation of body concept, motor planning, body in space, cause-and-effect concepts, spatial relationships, and ocular motor skills and the development of balance and equilibrium are dependent on experiencing movement and the effect of gravity.	For the child with limited movement experiences, introduce passive movement slowly and gradually. Observe for any signs of stress or discomfort including nausea or increased muscle tone. Begin with slow, rhythmical rocking and provide postural security or support throughout the experience. Gradually change planes and direction of movement and know that responses to linear and rotary movements may be very different. Whenever possible, allow this stimulation to be self-directed.	Don't overstimulate. Don't ignore signs of stress or discomfort. Don't allow excess tone or movement in abnormal postures.

Table 16-4 continued

Sensory Problem/Condition	Do's	Don'ts
5. Smell and taste: these are often overlooked sensations, especially for the child receiving nonoral feedings.	Identify, describe, and present smells and tastes (avoiding swallowing for the nonoral feeder) that are familiar in the home environment. Pair them with other sensations to round out concept formation. Allow choices.	Don't forget the importance of these sensations. Teach appropriate safety responses of certain smells or tastes to avoid. Never force unpleasant foods/ smells.

ADLs are a narrow specialty area within the broader confines of occupational therapy. The occupational therapist can help by (1) recommending or developing adaptive equipment to facilitate the caregiver or the child in the task at hand; (2) recommending ways to modify the task or the position of the child; (3) guiding the amount, type, and timing of assistance needed during the activity; and (4) determine the readiness (or lack of readiness) to move to the next step toward maximizing the child's independence. An occupational therapist can show the caregiver how to integrate range of motion, flexibility, exercise, activity, or language programs into the daily routine of self-help skills. Some guidance on interventions for some of the most common problems in the areas of feeding, dressing, bathing, and toileting are provided in Tables 16-6 and 16-7.

It may not be necessary to only consult an occupational therapist to perform these functions. The reader should be aware that a speech therapist specializing in feeding techniques or a physical therapist familiar with bathing equipment and programs may be available.

Feeding

The following guidelines should be considered during meal times. Make it a relaxed, social time with the family; allow for imitation; allow exploration of foods as age or stage makes appropriate; give the child choices; don't rush; keep the stress level down and try to make eating a pleasant experience. The child who is tube fed should be included at the family table and some form of oral stimulation paired with the tube feeding if possible. Feeding should always occur with the infant or child in proper position. Gen-

erally the head is slightly forward, the body is upright with the pelvis tilted forward (or semi-reclined for infants) and in good alignment, the feet are supported and the arms and shoulders are slightly forward. Avoid extremes of flexion and extension postures with the neuromuscularly involved child. These positions may make the control of breathing, chewing/sucking, and swallowing more difficult.

Suggestions for each of the basic problem areas are given in Table 16-6. If the problems persist, consult a physician and seek out a feeding therapist.

Bathing and Toileting

Bathing is a necessary activity of daily living that can be fun as well as therapeutic. Toileting is a skill that one hopes to teach the special needs child. There are special concerns to be addressed for both the caregiver and the child with neuromuscular impairments during bathing and toileting. Some of these concerns and helpful suggestions are discussed in Table 16-7.

Dressing

Some general guidelines should be followed to ease the dressing process. These guidelines apply whether the child is dressing himself or herself or being assisted. The guidelines are as follows:

- Start instruction early and establish a routine and sequence for dressing and undressing.
- The child will begin to anticipate and assist and should be given time to react.
- Undressing is learned before dressing.

Table 16-5 Do's and Don'ts for Posture and Mobility Goals

Goal	Do's	Don'ts
1. Improved head control	Position prone on forearms on wedge or over roll. Position propped kneeling or propped side-sitting over a support. Use fully supported standing as in a prone board. Work on midline positioning.	Don't allow the child to "hang" over the wedge/roll or on the shoulder girdle in sitting or when propping in prone. Watch for fatigue. Don't inadvertently develop or reinforce a preference for head turning to one side.
2. Increased eye–hand coordination and bilateral arm usage	Side-lying promotes bilateral upper extremity use and visual awareness. Provide upper extremity weight bearing in prone and propped kneeling. Leave a "window" space between the arms and the trunk. Provide a work surface in sitting and standing. Place materials to promote neck flexion and visual gaze toward hands. Provide scapular support to avoid retraction of upper extremities.	Avoid supine since this position increases upper extremity retraction. Don't always position side-lying on one side. Don't allow the upper extremities to be positioned in internal rotation and adduction with weight bearing on the radial (thumb) side of the hand.
3. Improved alignment and symmetry	Use towel rolls, foam rolls, etc. to provide trunk support in sitting. External supports such as "H"-strap harnesses and butterfly chest supports can be used. Use corner or saddle-chairs combined with a tray. Use standing devices (e.g., prone boards, standers) to achieve proper standing position.	Don't allow asymmetry or lateral trunk flexion when sitting. Don't oversupport to the point where the child does not actively "work" to maintain balance and posture. Do not work in unsupported standing if alignment is poor. Do not allow the child to ignore or favor the more involved side.
4. Increased postural extension and sitting balance	Position sitting on a firm flat surface. Try short-sitting (stool, bench, booster seat, elevated corner chair) or straddle-sitting (bench, roll, saddle-seat, push-trike). Use an elevated work surface for upper extremity supporting. Provide assistance, as needed, to balance upright in ring, half-ring, tailor and side-sitting.	Don't position in unsupported floor-sitting with legs in front of body if significant postural rounding occurs or if balance is precarious. Don't sit the child on a soft, cushioned or prefabricated molded seat. Avoid "W"-sitting. Don't allow the child to always assume a habitual sitting position.
5. Increased weight bearing and stability	Use kneeling at a support as an alternative to standing. Position in standing using a prone board, flexi-stand, or similar standing device. Use footrests in sitting or a seat low enough for feet to securely rest on.	Don't allow feet to hang unsupported in sitting. Do not use a "Johnny Jump-Up" and infant walkers unless recommended by a therapist.
6. Improved lower extremity and trunk mobility	Incorporate a variety of sitting positions (tailor, ring, half-ring, side-sitting). Encourage rotating between sitting and kneeling, sitting and quadruped to change position.	

Table 16-5 continued

Goal	Do's	Don'ts
	Place toys to the side to encourage weight-shift and trunk rotation with reach. Play in side-lying and practice turning from supine to each side. In supine, elevate pelvis with a wedge or pillow to encourage lifting legs to bring hands and feet together. Practice riding a "push-trike." In diapering/dressing incorporate mobility exercises such as alternate flexion and extension of legs ("bicycling" legs), abduction of flexed lower extremities, rotation of pelvis and trunk.	Don't allow transfers in and out of sitting by spreading the legs to the sides and doing the "splits." Discourage abnormal patterns of movement such as scooting in supine or sitting or "bunny-hopping" on hands and knees.

- Use clothes that are a little too large.
- Elastic-waisted pants and scoop-necked shirts are easier to don and doff.
- Velcro can be used to replace most fasteners.
- Hemiplegics should dress the affected limb first and undress it second.
- Elastic thread can be used for sewing on cuff buttons of the affected arm side.

There are a multitude of adaptive devices for dressing. These include trouser pulls, stocking aids, long-handled shoe horns, elastic or zippered laces, button hooks, zipper pulls, and dressing sticks. Choosing aids should be done carefully: using the wrong device could make it harder for the child instead of easier.

Before dressing or undressing the spastic child, consider the child's best positions and your best hand placements for the most con-trolled movements and tone management. Side-lying is often a more neutral position. Lying prone over your lap may work well for the smaller child with extensor spasticity. Symmetrically supported sitting maintains hips, neck, and shoulders in slight forward flexion and allows the child to participate more actively.

Patience is the key to a smooth dressing process. Remember, it takes longer to allow the child to do it for himself or herself than to do it for them. Allow yourself the needed time!

BEHAVIORAL CUES AND MANAGEMENT STRATEGIES FOR INFANTS

The following tables are based on the neurobehavioral research of Dr. T. Brazelton and Dr. Heidelise Als, who have developed the Neonatal Behavioral Assessment Scale (NBAS) and the Assessment of Premature Infant Behavior

Table 16-6 Suggestions and Equipment for Common Feeding Problems

Problems	Suggestions to Assist	Equipment to Try
1. Taking too long to take too little may indicate poor suck control.	Try providing jaw stability by placing a finger under the chin. Support the cheeks during sucking. Try putting an extra hole in the nipple, but watch that the fluid does not flow too quickly, causing the infant more distress.	Try different size, shape, and firmness of nipples. A natural nipple may help facilitate tongue elevation while a round nipple may encourage more tongue curl and sucking.

continues

Table 16-6 continued

Problems	Suggestions to Assist	Equipment to Try
2. The infant or child pulls away or withdraws from stimulation around the mouth and face or shows a lack of awareness when food is presented. This may indicate a hyper/ hyposensitivity to touch in and around the mouth.	Let the child self-direct. Encourage hand-to-mouth play. Make meal time fun—get creative and "open the hanger and let the airplane in." Use a washcloth and napkin frequently and firmly. Explore temperature and textures of food.	Try different size, shape, and firmness in nipples. Feed in an infant seat or high chair to minimize extraneous sensory stimulation and to provide stability and containment.
3. Poor lip closure around the nipple or spoon may be indicated by excessive dripping and loss of food.	Cold can facilitate puckering, but watch for adverse reactions. Offer cheek support. Try thicker foods and liquids. Place food on spoon in the mouth and wait for the upper lip to draw it off. Place formula or food on lips and encourage tongue play or lip drawing in to remove it. *Never use honey to stimulate this with an infant.*	Various infant pacifier shapes, sizes, and circumferential mouthpieces can be tried to help stimulate lip closure away from meal time. Proper seating and positioning with head in slight forward flexion Short durable straws Cups with spouts
4. Hyperactive gag reflex may make food presentation, swallowing textures, or keeping foods down a problem.	Present small amounts of food at a time. Present the spoon to the forward portion of the child's mouth and gradually "walk" it midway back and apply a firm pressure to stimulate tongue retraction. Reduce stress or changes in routines. Check food preferences and give the child a choice. Consider food allergies and structural or neurological indications with your physician.	Nipples of various size, shape, length, firmness, and flow speed Coated spoon Flatter or rounded spoons may make a difference.
5. Reflux that occurs closer to the next feeding (as the present/previous feeding) should be of concern.	Add cereal to the formula or food. Sometimes heavier food stays down better. Feed smaller amounts more frequently. Discuss with the physician any need or indications for metoclopramide (Reglan) or nutritional supplements.	"Danny sling" for maintaining prone lying after feeding on a bed with the head elevated to a 30° angle
6. The transition from liquids to purees and solids may be difficult. Increases in gagging, spitting-up, avoidance behaviors, and oral-motor incoordination may be observed.	Gradually add yogurts, custards, applesauce, mashed fruits, etc. to drinks. Change from a bottle or cup to a bowl and spoon in the thickened liquids. Ask child to remove purees from your fingers or toy. Make eating fun. Proceed to mashed, semisolids keeping lumps "together" (cottage cheese) vs. floating in liquid (soup). Allow finger play exploration of foods.	Try various-shaped cups, spoons, and bowls for specific sensorimotor problems or deficits and to encourage self-feeding and self-image/socialization. There are many items to choose from in the many books and catalogs available (see Appendix A).

Table 16-6 continued

Problems	Suggestions to Assist	Equipment to Try
	Combine liked and disliked foods. Let child hold and mouth solid foods and do assisted teaching of biting. Watch carefully.	
7. The transition to cup drinking is normally awkward. However, the child with special needs may require assistance and take longer to develop smooth, coordinated skills with minimal dripping and spills.	Start with thicker liquids. Use yogurt, applesauce, cereal, or pureed foods. Provide jaw stability. Assist with lower lip seal as needed.	Try cups with lids, preferably without spouts. Start with somewhat flexible plastic cups (nonbreakable). "Cut out cups" prevent excess neck and trunk extension and allow the caregiver to monitor the fluid flow.
8. One-handed eating	Depending on the age and ability of the child, this may require more or less manual assistance or adaptive equipment.	A damp cloth or piece of rubber matting can be placed under the plate to prevent sliding. Use suction bowls. A universal cuff or foam built-up handles can be used for those patients with decreased grasping ability. A rocker knife can be used for one-handed cutting. Bowls or plates with a lip can be used for ease of scooping food onto the spoon/fork. Food guards used with standard plates serve the same purpose.
9. Decreased motor control of the mouth and face, as well as the trunk and limbs, may interfere with effective independent feeding.	Position well. Stabilize proximally. Allow elbows on the table or lap tray. Decrease the distance the food has to travel. Add weighted resistance to limbs or utensils.	Try previously stated suggestions but concentrate on stability. Weighted utensils and wrist cuffs may decrease extraneous movements. Teflon-coated utensils help prevent injuries. The "C.P. Feeder" device minimizes motions necessary for self-feeding. Swivel spoons may help keep the food on the spoon. Two-handed drinking cup with a lid, preferably nonspout lids. Straw drinking with the cup in a cup holder decreases spilling.
10. The child with a cleft palate needs special feeding considerations.	Feed this child in an upright position. Assist manually with closing the lips together. Regulate fluid flow. Let the infant/child be in charge of the rate of feedings as well as his or her readiness for strained, pureed, or lumpy foods. Present spoon foods in small amounts. Some foods may "escape" through the nose. Don't overreact. Clean the infant and resume feeding when the child has recovered.	Mead-Johnson cleft palate set is a soft, longer nipple with a squeeze bottle. Try cross-cutting a nipple to increase flow rate but don't "drown" the child. Do not use the lamb's nipple. It is usually much too big and awkward.

Table 16-7 Bathing and Toileting Concerns and Suggestions

Concerns	Suggestions
1. Making the bathtub area safe is of great importance. Most of these suggestions can be done easily. Special grab bars and seats are available for children with neuromuscular problems through catalogues, drugstores, or medical supply companies.	Use nonskid mats or strips in and around the bathtub and floor to decrease chances of slipping. Faucet covers can be purchased or made to protect the child from accidental bumps. Use safety rails and grab bars, transfer benches, tub seats, foam pads, shower chairs, bath pillows, etc. as needed. Do not make the water too hot or cold. Besides any skin or thermoregulation changes that may occur, muscle tone is greatly affected by temperature and may make management of the child more difficult. Tub toys should be chosen carefully. Watch for mouthing of toys or soaps. Don't *ever* leave the child alone in the bathtub. Monitor the water level as well. Use "no tears" shampoos and soaps. Use soap on a rope or wash mitts with soap holder pockets, or place soap in a nylon stocking that has one end tied to a fixed point so that soap does not get lost in the bathtub area.
2. Lifting, carrying, transferring, and/or holding a child for bath care can be a physical strain on the caregiver. Always follow good principles of body mechanics. Making the transition into and out of the water smoothly is important for both you and the child.	Keep the child "collected." Use special bath seats as needed. They can help maintain a good seating posture to control tone and still leave a hand free for washing. They may also raise the child, reducing the amount of leaning or bending over into the tub. An extended shower hose can ease washing and rinsing care. Use a short stool to sit on during bath time. Use transfer aids for bath time (e.g., hydraulic or pump lifts and chairs, transfer benches). Control the child's tone. Keep the child close to your body. Do not lean over with the load! Bend your knees and let your legs do the work. Half-kneeling may be a more comfortable transition position for you while transferring the child in and out of the tub. Prepare the environment and the child. Have everything where you want it and within reach.
3. Sensory stimulation can affect autonomic functions, behavior, and motor tone and control. The hypertonic child may become more spastic, or the hypotonic child may become more flaccid.	Keep the water temperature moderate. Try keeping the infant/child wrapped in towel or a T-shirt during the transition into the water. These can be removed and replaced as tolerated/needed during bath time. Have towels ready that are large enough for wrapping the child up. Rubbing the towel over the body may be too much stimulation—rub your hands over the towel-wrapped body. This also helps maintain body warmth. Change to a dry towel to avoid chilling.
4. There are several programs available for toilet training special populations. Whatever method is used for bowel and bladder care, the toilet area must be a safe environment as well. Please consult an enterostomal nurse for specialized bowel and bladder concerns.	Safety rails may be fastened or placed over the standard toilet. Make sure the feet are supported. Child-sized commodes with attachable positioning aids, safety bar, foot rests, and head supports are available. Get assistance from occupational and physical therapists regarding the amount and types of support needed. Deflection shields are available for toilet seats or urinals and can be used for boys who will not be standing up.

Table 16-8 Identifying Approach and Self-regulation Behaviors and Avoidance and Stress Behaviors

	Approach Behaviors	*Avoidance Behaviors*
Physiological	Maintained heart rate (140–160 beats per minute, premature), (100–120 beats per minute, term) Sustained well-coordinated respiration Maintain "pink" color	Changes in heart rate Changes in respiratory rate Fluctuations in muscle tone Decreased oxygenation Seizures Hiccuping Yawning Sneezing Coughing Gagging, gasping Sighing Spitting up Bowel movement training
Motor	Hands-to-mouth maneuvers Hands-to-face Hand clasp Foot clasp Finger fold Grasping Tucking Leg/foot bracing Mouthing Suck search Sucking Hand holding Smooth, well-modulated posture tone and movements	Facial grimaces Arching/opisthotonus Finger/toe splay Prolonged tremor, twitches Arm/leg extension: "saluting," "sitting on air," "airplane" Flaccidity or "tuning out" Hypertonicity Frantic, diffuse activity Tongue thrustings Hands over face High guard arm position Hypertonic fetal tuck
State	Clear, robust sleep states Rhythmic, robust crying Able to self-quiet, self-console Focused alertness with intent Animated facial expressions Frowning Cheek softening "Ooh" face Attentional smiling Smooth transitions between states	Diffuse sleep or awake states accompanied by whimpering and twitching Eye floating Averting gaze Closed eyes while awake and reacting Strained fussing Crying Staring Strained alertness, glassy-eyed Irritability and diffuse arousal

(APIB). All caregivers working with sick or fragile infants must be able to recognize when a child is displaying approach and self-regulation or avoidance and stress behaviors and understand appropriate interventions. Caregivers must effectively control the environment and the amount and type of stimulation these infants receive. Appropriate responses to the infant's behavioral cues make all interactions easier and enhance growth and development. Parent teaching in this area is invaluable.

Interrelating systems that have been defined by Brazelton and Als are physiological (autonomic), motor, and state. The ability to achieve and maintain attentional-interactive and self-regulatory behaviors demonstrates the presence or absence of integration between these systems.

Physiological control, the most basic and vital area of concern, refers to the functioning of the autonomic nervous system, including the ability to maintain heart rate, respirations, temperature, and color. The development of motor control is characterized by the infant's ability to maintain a posture (initially flexion) or to move in and out of it with smooth actions. This control takes time to develop, especially for the premature infant, and is greatly influenced by adult interactions. State control is an infant's ability to achieve and main-

Exhibit 16-1 Strategies and Suggestions for Caregivers to Assist with Infant Stress Reduction

Reduce or Eliminate Stimulation

- Turn the light down/off.
- Put the infant down (decrease touch and movement).
- Stop rocking.
- Turn off music or play rhythmical or soothing music quietly as tolerated.
- Leave a blank wall or side of crib for the infant to turn and "escape" to.
- Decrease/eliminate mobiles, mirrors, toys from infant's direct view until infant is ready.

Provide Containment and Postural Stability

- Swaddle
- Position toward a flexor tuck and midline orientation; "nesting"—use assist toward flexion and getting hands together near the face.
- Give the hands something to grasp.
- Use a pacifier or fingers to suck on.
- Perform gentle manual assist of limbs in a contained range to prevent flailing, diffuse movements—do not restrain forcibly!
- Perform slow and gentle rhythmical tapping, stroking, or rocking to tolerance.
- Hold and carry infant securely. Contact on the infant's frontal surface is often soothing.
- Give the feet something to brace against.
- Approach and remove contact gradually, giving the infant time to adjust.
- Prepare infant by increasing, decreasing, or substituting your tactile pressures (e.g., with a toy or blanket roll).

tain various levels of sleep and wakefulness with smooth transitions between states.

It is very difficult for an infant to reach and maintain an alert state with the ability to interact or attend to the environment if the child cannot regulate his or her physiological, motor, or state systems. Normal growth and development rely on the integration of these systems. Table 16-8 describes the approach and self-regulation behaviors that indicate maturation of these systems, as well as the avoidance and stress behaviors that indicate the need for an intervention or reduction in stimuli. When an infant is showing signs of stress, particularly physiological stress, it is important that the caregiver stop what is being done and let the infant recover! Assist with the recovery if necessary. Intervention strategies

and suggestions for caregivers are discussed in Exhibit 16-1.

EQUIPMENT ISSUES

There are many types of therapeutic equipment available for home care. The pediatric physical and occupational therapist will be valuable in determining what equipment will best meet the child's needs and will help facilitate the most normal development possible. Equipment resources are listed in Appendix 16-B.

It is advisable to use caution when dealing with suppliers of therapeutic equipment. Many vendors are experienced in working with the pediatric population, but others have had little or no exposure. General guidelines to follow in choosing a vendor include the following:

- Does the vendor specialize in rehabilitation equipment, and do they have a salesperson who primarily services the pediatric clientele?
- Does the vendor prefer to involve the child's therapist in choosing and fitting the equipment?
- Does the vendor have the capacity to individually modify the equipment?

A therapist's input and consultation should be sought before using the following:

- Positioning wedges
- Rolls and bolsters
- Side-lyers (cushions that support side-lying)
- Positioning chairs such as corner chairs, tumble forms seats, "bucket"-type seats, saddle-chairs
- Therapy balls
- Bean bag chairs

A therapist should always be involved with choosing certain types of equipment to ensure correct fit, features, and adaptations, such as

- Prone boards and standing devices
- Wheelchairs
- Transportation–positioning chairs

If a wheelchair or positioning chair is selected without consulting a therapist, the prescriptive guide shown in Figure 16-3 will assist in choos-

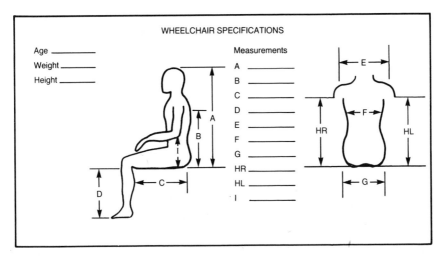

Figure 16-3 Guide for choosing the best wheelchair fit.

ing the most appropriate chair and obtaining the best fit. *Remember:* a lap belt is *always* necessary, not only for safety purposes but also to maintain correct sitting positions.

Positioning adaptations will be needed if you answer "no" to any of these questions:

1. Can the child hold his or her head upright for extended periods of time?
2. Can the child sit upright with good symmetrical posture? If no, consider a tray, lateral trunk supports, an "H"-strap harness, a butterfly chest support, a firm seat and back cushion, or combinations of the above.
3. Do the child's lower extremities maintain neutral alignment? If no, consider using an abductor to control adduction and internal rotation and lateral thigh supports to control excess abduction and external rota-

tion. Often the two are used in conjunction to optimally position the lower extremities.

4. Do the child's feet remain on the footrests? If no, consider some type of Velcro straps, heel–toe loop device, or ankle strap to ensure foot placement on footrests.
5. Does the child easily maintain sitting without sliding forward or moving into extensor patterns? If no, look at seats where the degree of hip flexion can be adjusted, chairs with varying degrees of inclination, a wedge-shaped seat cushion, or a lap/hip belt rather than a seat/waist belt.

A word of caution: The more supports and devices used, the more difficult it is to free the child in a medical emergency. Try to use "quick-release" strapping/attachments if at all possible.

Range of Motion

Range of motion (ROM) is the extent to which a particular joint is capable of being moved. Not everyone is capable of moving a joint through the same ROM. A person's range is affected by many factors, such as genetic make-up and developmental pattern, the presence or absence of disease processes, and the amount and type of physical activity in which he or she normally engages.

A ROM program is designed to meet each patient's needs and capabilities. The purpose is to preserve present joint range thus preventing deformity and further loss of motion. ROM is often a form of passive mobilization, but it can and should be incorporated when possible into an active exercise program.

The following is a list of ''points to remember'' used in range of motion:

1. When doing ROM, use good body mechanics to conserve your energy and avoid unnecessary strain.
2. Move slowly, smoothly, and rhythmically.
3. Repeat each motion approximately three times, moving through as full a range as possible.
4. Use a firm but comfortable grip. If spasticity is present, try to keep your hands on the surface of the extremity you want to facilitate (e.g., when trying to straighten the patient's elbow, try not to place your hands on the muscles that bend the elbow).
5. When moving an extremity, try to stabilize all proximal joints so as to make the patient feel secure and comfortable.
6. Generally, side-lying is the best position for doing ROM, since there will be less interference from postural reflexes in this position. Have the patient lie with his or her back toward you, head bent forward, and hips and knees in flexion.
7. Move from proximal to distal when doing each extremity since you will be less likely to forget any motions.
8. When noting ROM limitations, it is sometimes useful to compare the right and left sides. This is particularly true if the patient has more involvement on one side than the other.
9. Talk to the patient when doing ROM so that the child can be an active participant. Explain what you are doing when appropriate.

Definition of Terms

- *abduction*—lateral movement away from midline
- *adduction*—movement toward midline
- *active*—patient performs motion independently, no assistance given
- *active-assistive*—patient performs motion with assistance
- *DIP joint*—distal interphalangeal joint, last joint of finger

- *distal*—farthest from the body (e.g., hand)
- *dorsiflexion*—bending foot toward body
- *eversion*—turning the foot outward toward the little toe
- *extension*—movement bringing a limb into or toward a straight condition
- *flexion*—condition of being bent
- *inversion*—turning the foot inward toward the big toe
- *MP joint*—metacarpophalangeal joint of the hand ("knuckle")
- *opposition*—movement of thumb toward little finger
- *passive*—client does not actively move extremity
- *PIP joint*—proximal interphalangeal joint of finger (middle joint of finger)
- *plantarflexion*—pointing foot down
- *pronation*—turning hand so that palm faces downward
- *proximal*—nearest to the body (e.g., shoulder)
- *supination*—turning hand so that palm faces upward

The illustrations in Figures 16-A1 through 16-A56 show each movement involved in ROM. These pictures are included to help you learn the individual motions and optimal hand placement. Remember, you will *usually* have the patient with abnormal tone in side-lying and that the motions will be performed in that position, rather than as pictured.

Stretches

When stretching a spastic muscle, move it to the point where you meet resistance. Hold the extremity at this point until you feel it relax or "give." You can then continue the motion through the pain-free range. On reaching the end of the range, hold for several seconds to give a sustained stretch. Do not give a quick stretch since this will only increase spasticity.

A contracture is also a condition of muscle tightness, but it is caused by actual bony change in the joint and shortening of the connective tissue structures around the joint. Therefore, it is difficult to stretch out a contracture. Remember, stretching should be done just to the end of the *pain-free* range.

1. Hamstring stretch: reach for toes in long-sitting position, keeping knees straight.
2. Hip flexor stretch:
   a. Bend both knees to chest. Hold one knee up and slowly straighten the other leg down to the floor. Hold in extended position for several seconds.
   b. Lie in prone position.
3. Adductors:
   a. Hold one leg straight and push the other leg out to the side, keeping it straight.
   b. With legs bent and feet resting on floor, spread knees apart.
4. Heel cord stretch:
   a. With leg straight, place your hand so that the patient's heel is in your palm and the ball of the foot rests against your forearm. Slowly press the foot up toward the body by leaning against the foot with your arm. Make sure to keep the knee straight while stretching the heel cord.
   b. If the patient is able to stand independently, he or she can stand facing a wall and support himself or herself on extended arms. By leaning forward on his or her arms, keeping flat on the floor and body straight, the patient can actively stretch the heel cords.

Hip and Knee Flexion and Extension

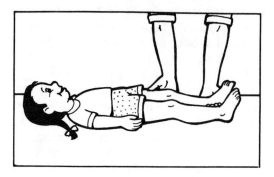

Figure 16-A1 Support under the child's knee and foot.

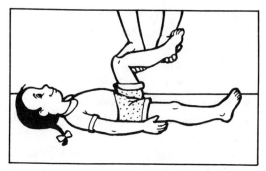

Figure 16-A2 Bend the knee toward the chest and return to a straight position. Stabilize opposite leg so it does not simultaneously lift.

Hip Abduction and Adduction

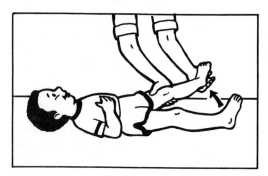

Figure 16-A3 Maintaining your support under the child's knee and foot, hold the leg in neutral rotation and move it away from midline. For the child with higher tone do this in side-lying by lifting the leg up rather than in supine as pictured. Make sure to stabilize the other leg so it does not move along with the leg you are moving. If this occurs, effectiveness of the exercise decreases.

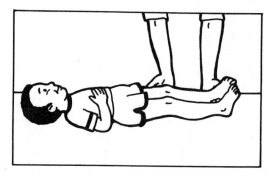

Figure 16-A4 Return to midline position.

Hip and External and Internal Rotation

Figure 16-A5 Another way to abduct the hips is to bend both legs up and apply gentle pressure to spread legs apart.

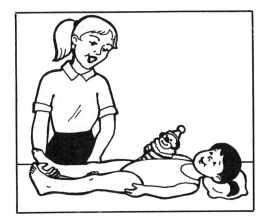

Figure 16-A6 Support under child's knee and foot.

Figure 16-A7 Bend knee toward chest to a right (90°) angle.

Figure 16-A8 Externally rotate the leg at the hip by moving knee away from midline and foot toward the opposite leg.

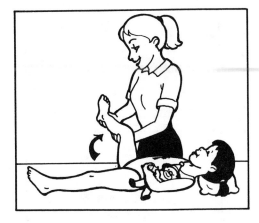

Figure 16-A9 Internally rotate by moving the foot away from midline and knee toward the opposite leg. With internal rotation it is important to only move within the easily available range. This is contraindicated in children who have hip subluxation/dislocation problems.

Straight-leg Raising

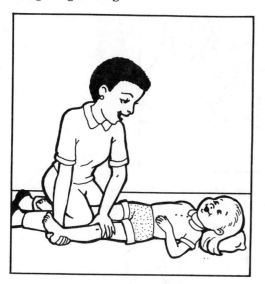

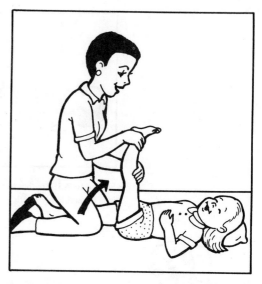

Figure 16-A10 Support over the knee and under the foot, being careful not to hyperextend knee. Again, remember to stabilize opposite leg so it does not simultaneously lift.

Figure 16-A11 Lift leg up toward chest while keeping the knee straight. Stop when you meet resistance or when you reach a 90° angle.

Ankle Dorsiflexion and Plantarflexion

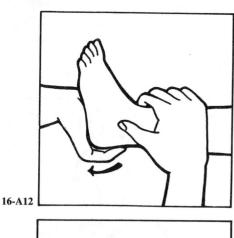

16-A12

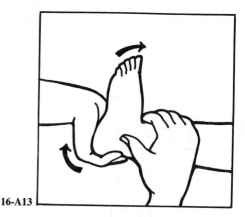

16-A13

16-A14

Figure 16-A12 Use your fingers to securely grasp the child's heel.

Figure 16-A13 Dorsiflex the ankle by pulling the heel toward you while the heel of your hand pushes the foot up and back toward the child. Make sure to maintain straight alignment by not allowing the foot to turn in or out.

Figure 16-A14 Plantarflex the ankle by pushing down on the forefoot (toes toward the floor) and bringing heel up toward leg.

Ankle Inversion and Eversion

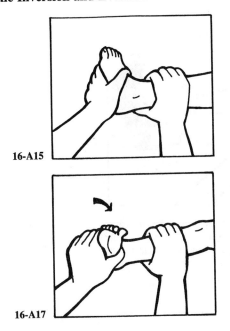

16-A15

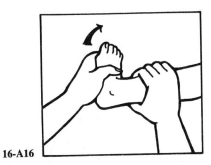

16-A16

Figure 16-A15 Hold the foot above and below the ankle in neutral alignment.

Figure 16-A16 While stabilizing above and below the ankle, evert the foot by moving it away from the midline.

Figure 16-A17 While stabilizing above and below the ankle invert the foot by moving it toward the midline.

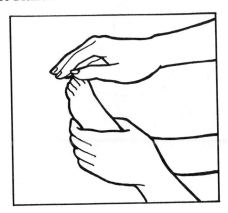

16-A17

Toe Flexion and Extension

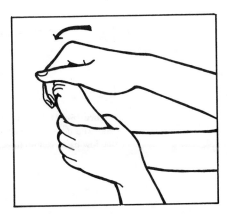

Figure 16-A18 Hold foot with one hand.

Figure 16-A19 Flex toes and then return to neutral starting position.

Shoulder Flexion and Extension

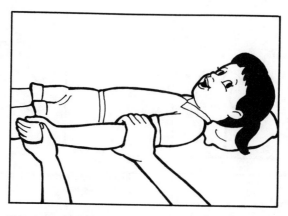

Figure 16-A20 Support at elbow and wrist with arm in neutral ("thumb-up") position. With high tone and/or decreased shoulder mobility it will be more important to support the shoulder blade from behind with one hand while you move the arm and the humerus with the other (not pictured).

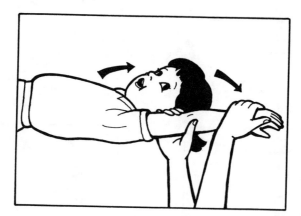

Figure 16-A21 Maintain your support and lift the arm overhead until you meet resistance or see the child compensate by arching the low back. Return to starting position.

Shoulder Abduction and Adduction

Figure 16-A22 Use same supporting position as described in Figure 16-A20.

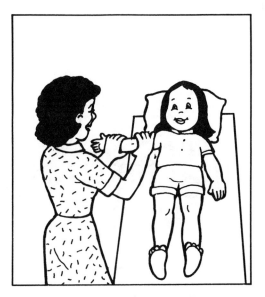

Figure 16-A23 Maintain your support and move the arm to the side away from the body, keeping it on the surface.

Figure 16-A24 Continue moving arm overhead until you meet resistance, feel very taut tendons in the axilla (armpit), or see compensation by arching the low back. Return to starting position.

Shoulder Horizontal Adduction and Abduction

Figure 16-A25 Support arm at elbow and wrist.

Figure 16-A26 Move arm away from body to shoulder height.

Figure 16-A27 and 16-A28 Horizontally abduct shoulder by bringing arm across the body, being careful not to overstretch arm at shoulder joint.

◄**Figure 16-A29** Horizontally abduct shoulder by returning the arm to neutral position and bringing it back across the body and then down alongside.

Shoulder Hyperextension

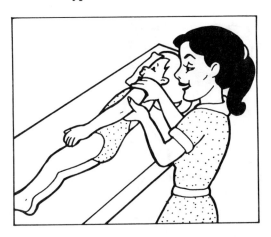 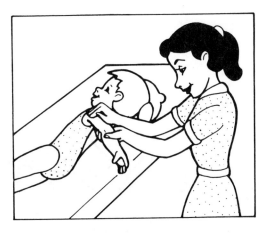

Figure 16-A30 In side-lying, support in front of shoulder with your hand over the joint and your other hand on the arm above the elbow. This will help you feel the movement and protect the shoulder from dislocation.

Figure 16-A31 Maintain this support position and bring arm behind body, keeping it in neutral alignment and not allowing internal or external rotation.

Shoulder External and Internal Rotation

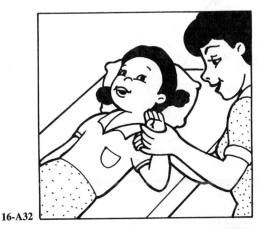

16-A32

16-A33

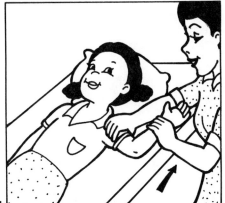

16-A34

Figure 16-A32 Position arm out to side at right angle to body. Support at front of shoulder joint and at wrist.

Figure 16-A33 Externally rotate by bringing back of hand toward the surface. Stop when you meet resistance. Return to starting position.

Figure 16-A34 Internally rotate by bringing palm of hand toward the surface. Stop when you meet resistance or when shoulder lifts off surface. Return to starting position.

Elbow Flexion and Extension

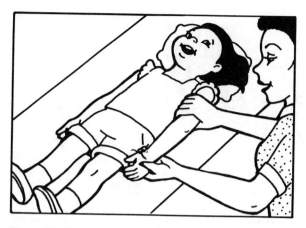

Figure 16-A35 Support arm in neutral ("thumb-up") position above elbow and at wrist.

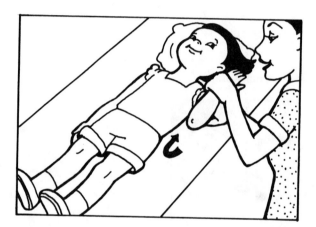

Figure 16-A36 Flex elbow by bringing hand toward shoulder. Extend by returning to neutral starting position.

Forearm Pronation and Supination

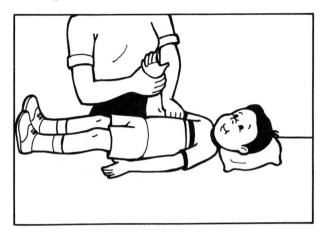

Figure 16-A37 Start with elbow bent to 90°, stabilizing upper arm and holding wrist.

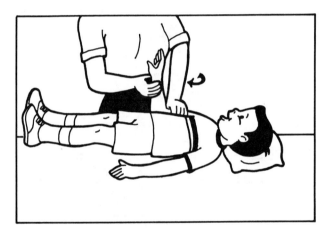

Figure 16-A38 Pronate by turning forearm so palm is down. Return to neutral.

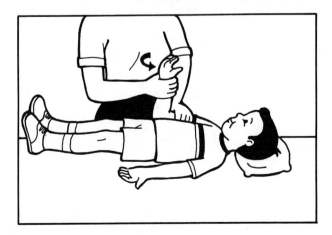

Figure 16-A39 Supinate by turning forearm so palm is up. Return to neutral.

Wrist Flexion (Palmar Flexion) and Extension (Dorsiflexion)

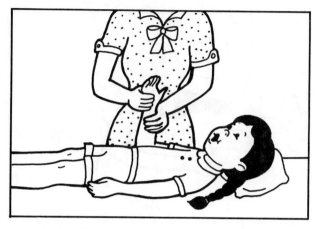

Figure 16-A40 With elbow bent, stabilize above and below the wrist.

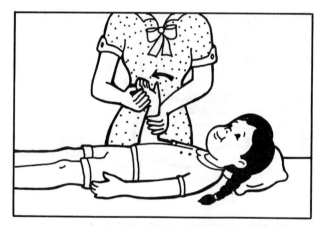

Figure 16-A41 Extend wrist by moving hand back; finger curl may increase due to natural tenodesis action of the hand.

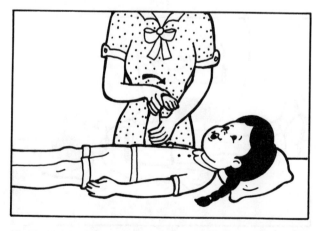

Figure 16-A42 Flex wrist by moving hand forward; fingers may extend.

Wrist Radial and Ulnar Deviation

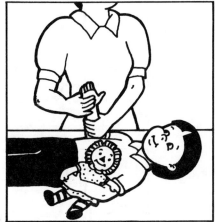

16-A43

16-A44

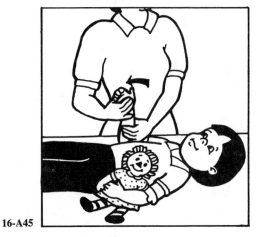

16-A45

Figure 16-A43 With elbow bent, stabilize above and below wrist.

Figure 16-A44 Radially deviate by moving hand sideways in the direction of thumb.

Figure 16-A45 Ulnarly deviate by moving hand sideways in the direction of the little finger.

Finger Flexion and Extension

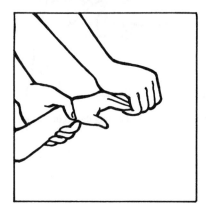

Figure 16-A46 Flex fingers by bending them into hand. Wrist position can be in neutral or slight extension.

Figure 16-A47 Extend fingers by bringing them out into a straightened position. Wrist position can be in neutral or slight flexion.

Finger Abduction and Adduction

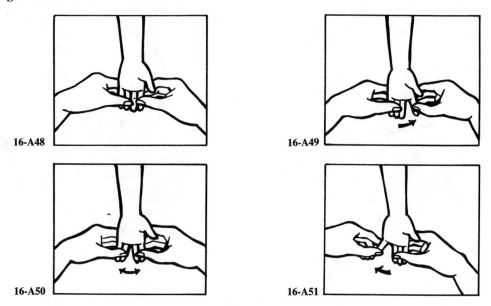

16-A48   16-A49

16-A50   16-A51

Figure 16-A48 through 16-A51 Abduct by spreading the fingers apart moving them away from the middle finger. Adduction is returning to neutral. Remember to move the middle finger side to side in both directions.

Thumb Flexion and Extension

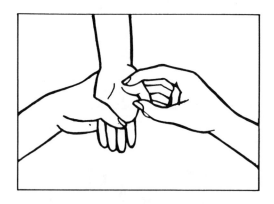

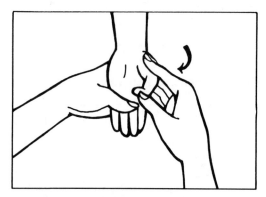

Figure 16-A52 Hold hand comfortably. If child has a subluxed or unstable thumb joint, give additional support at base of thumb to keep the bones in alignment before bending or straightening.

Figure 16-A53 Flex by bending thumb into palm, making sure both joints bend.

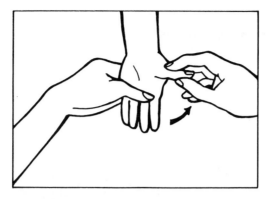

Figure 16-A54 Extend by straightening thumb. Do not hyperextend and allow the base of the thumb to sublux.

Thumb Abduction and Opposition

Figure 16-A55 Abduct thumb by moving it perpendicularly in from the index finger, not to the side, which is extension. You should form the letter "L" with the thumb in the air.

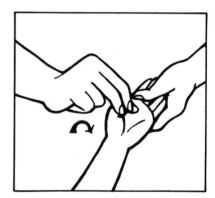

Figure 16-A56 Opposition is moving the thumb from the abducted position across the palm toward the base of the little finger.

Appendix 16-B

Equipment Resources

Self-help Aids

Comfortably Yours, 52 West Hunter Avenue, Maywood, NJ 07607

Enrichments Catalog for Better Living, P.O. Box 579, Hinsdale, IL 60521

Fashion Ease, Division of M & M Health Care Apparel Co., 1541 60th Street, Brooklyn, NY 11219

Fred Sammons, Inc., P.O. Box 32, Brookfield, IL 60513-0032

Special Clothes, P.O. Box 4220, Alexandria, VA 22303

Pediatric Rehabilitation Therapy Equipment

Achievement Products for Children, P.O. Box 547, Mineola, NY 11501

Community Playthings, Rifton, NY 12471

Danmar Products, 2390 Winewood, Ann Arbor, MI 48103

G.E.R. Devices, Inc., "Danny Sling," 14 Fairfield Street, Lowell, MA 01851

Kaye Products, Inc., 1010 E. Pettigrew Street, Durham, NC 27701-4299

J.A. Preston Corp., 60 Page Road, Clifton, NJ 07012

Ways and Means, The Capability Collection, 2800 Citrin Drive, Romulus, MI 48174

Educational/Institutional Materials

Constructive Playthings, 1227 E. 119th Street, Granview, MO 64030

Developmental Learning Materials, P.O. Box 4000, One D.L.M. Park, Allen, TX 75002

Discovery Toys, 400 Ellinwood Way, Suite 300, Pleasant Hill, CA 94523

Lakeshore Curriculum Materials Co., 2695 E. Dominguez Street, P.O. Box 6261, Carson, GA 90749

Therapy Skin Builders, 3830 E. Bellevue, P.O. Box 42050, Tucson, AZ 85733

Chapter 17

Educational Options

Deborah Klein Walker

Educational status is a key issue for children and adolescents receiving home care services. Education may not receive a high priority because of the many other medical, health, and family concerns associated with home care. Therefore, special care should be taken to ensure the child's education is not forgotten or delayed. Educational programs can be designed to meet a child's needs based on a specific functional status, developmental level, and age. The goal for all children receiving home care services is to enable them to do as much as other children their age or prepare them for when they will be able to do so. Outside of the family, children spend more time in preschool or school programs than in any other setting. Therefore, all children should have positive educational experiences to help them learn and become socially competent.

State special education statutes enacted in the 1970s, combined with PL 94-142, the Education of All Handicapped Children Act of 1975, help ensure that most children with special health care needs will have an appropriate educational experience. These statutes and their accompanying regulations propelled many school systems into the delivery of services previously considered clearly outside their responsibility. Many of these services—administering medications and complicated medical treatment regimens; providing physical, occupational, and speech therapy; transporting children from home to school and between school facilities; altering school buildings to accommodate children with serious physical and other health impairments; and revising classroom curricula and routines to meet an individual child's special health and learning needs—are available today to facilitate the education of children receiving home care services.

In this chapter the steps required to design and implement an appropriate educational program for the child receiving home care are reviewed (Exhibit 17-1). Also included is a discussion of current educational options for children with chronic illnesses and/or children dependent on medical procedures. Specific questions addressed are presented below:

- Is the child eligible for special education?
- Where is the educational program provided?
- If the program is at school, who provides the needed medical/health care?
- If the needed medical/health care is provided at school, who pays for it?

SPECIAL EDUCATION ENTITLEMENTS

The Education for All Handicapped Children Act of 1975 became effective nationwide on October 1, 1977. This act and its amendments provide for a ''free appropriate public education'' for each handicapped child with full protection for the procedural rights of children receiving special educational services and their parents. State special education requirements may impose additional requirements on local school districts, but the federal law establishes basic requirements.

Many children with special health care needs are now receiving services through special education entitlements. Children with complex medical problems receiving home care treatments following extensive hospital stays are the newest group of children to be served by this powerful civil rights legislation. The general specifications of these entitlements are outlined in this section. The great variation in state and local programs requires that persons become acquainted with specific state laws and local practices when planning and implementing educational programs. This can be accomplished by contacting any number of local, state, or regional parent centers (TAPP Project Regional Centers*).

Eligibility

The Education for All Handicapped Children Act of 1975 covers a wide range of disabilities to be served in special education. The handicaps included are "mentally retarded, hard of hearing, deaf, speech impaired, visually handicapped, seriously emotionally disturbed, orthopedically impaired, or other health impaired children, or children with specific learning disabilities, who, by reason thereof, require special education or related services." Children with normal cognitive functioning and a chronic illness (especially one with complex medical requirements) are usually categorized as having an orthopedic impairment, another health

---

*TAPP Project Regional Centers are funded by the Department of Education and are a major source for determining information about education rights and procedures. These centers have responsibility for the coordination of parent centers in all the states. The four regional centers are the New Hampshire Parent Information Center in Concord, New Hampshire; the Pacer Center in Minneapolis, Minnesota; the Washington State PAVE in Tacoma, Washington; and the Parents Educating Parents Center of the Georgia Association for Retarded Citizens in College Park, Georgia. All are given technical assistance about children with special health care needs by the Federation for Children with Special Needs in Boston, Massachusetts.

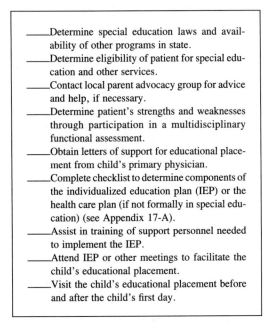

Exhibit 17-1 Checklist of Steps in Obtaining Educational Services for Pediatric Home Care Patients

_____Determine special education laws and availability of other programs in state.
_____Determine eligibility of patient for special education and other services.
_____Contact local parent advocacy group for advice and help, if necessary.
_____Determine patient's strengths and weaknesses through participation in a multidisciplinary functional assessment.
_____Obtain letters of support for educational placement from child's primary physician.
_____Complete checklist to determine components of the individualized education plan (IEP) or the health care plan (if not formally in special education) (see Appendix 17-A).
_____Assist in training of support personnel needed to implement the IEP.
_____Attend IEP or other meetings to facilitate the child's educational placement.
_____Visit the child's educational placement before and after the child's first day.

---

impairment, or a multiple handicapping condition. The determination of eligibility often hinges on interpretation of the definition of "other health impaired." Federal regulations include "chronic or acute health problems such as heart condition, tuberculosis, rheumatic fever, nephritis, asthma, sickle cell anemia, hemophilia, epilepsy, lead poisoning, leukemia or diabetes, _which adversely affects a child's educational performance_" (Federal Register 1977).

This "adverse effect test" means that to be eligible the child's condition must be serious enough to impede his or her success in a regular classroom setting (Comptroller General 1981). Unfortunately, there is no uniform definition and little advice to state or local educational authorities on how to define the functional capabilities that make a child eligible for special educational services. This lack of clarity has resulted in variation in how states and local school systems determine what chronic illnesses and conditions are serious enough to impede progress in a regular program. Because these chronic conditions are basically "medical or physical," many states require that a physician determine the extent to which the condition interferes with learning.

Ages for Services

The federal statute provides services for all children aged 3 to 21. However, if state codes exclude children from service, the state is not required to comply with the federal law. Many states exclude traditionally "non-school-age" children in the 3- to 5-year-old range and youths in the 18- to 21-year-old range from their programs.

Strong federal support for special programs for young children was demonstrated through the 1986 amendment to federal law PL 94-142. This amendment, PL 99-457, establishes a new discretionary program to help each state plan, design, and implement a comprehensive, coordinated, interdisciplinary program of early intervention services for disabled infants and toddlers and their families. Handicapped infants and toddlers may be defined by states as those with substantial developmental delays or at substantial risk of delay. Third and fourth year funding associated with PL 99-457 is contingent on states adopting policies that create a system leading to early intervention for all eligible children. This helps ensure that many more young children with special health care needs will be served in the future.

Procedures for Services

The strongest provision of the education law requires an appropriate educational program for each child. This program should be designed based on assessment of the child's needs following a multidisciplinary evaluation. If public schools cannot provide the program, private schooling or individual instruction must be supplied by the school system at public expense.

A fair assessment of the child's abilities and needs is required prior to placing the child in an educational program. The school must notify the parents of the assessment procedures and obtain their written consent. Likewise, the parent may request an assessment at any time and the school must respond within a specified time. All assessments must be made by qualified personnel in a manner consistent with the child's race, cultural background, language spoken, and disability.

The parents should attend a meeting with key personnel involved in the assessment to help write the child's individualized education plan (IEP). All issues or concerns about the child's needs in various educational settings should be addressed. All services and supports required to help the child function in the appropriate educational setting should be included in the IEP. A checklist of items for consideration in developing individualized education plans for students with physical disabilities or special health needs is located in Appendix 17-A. The IEP is the key to receiving appropriate services and planning for the child's future. Federal law requires that it be reviewed annually and reassessed based on a new multidisciplinary assessment every 3 years. An IEP document can be obtained from the department of education office in any state.

Due process procedures and safeguards are a strong component of the special education statutes. They may vary slightly from state to state, but the basic protections include written notice to parents requesting consent to conduct an assessment, specified time periods for the assessment and IEP development, specified annual reviews of the IEP, access to records, confidentiality of all personally identifiable information, the ability to request additional assessments (including an independent assessment) before the IEP is completed, and the right to a fair and impartial hearing within a specified amount of time if the parent disagrees with the IEP recommendation.

Educational Placements

All children served under the law are entitled to an education in the "least restrictive environment" or with their nonhandicapped peers to the maximum extent possible. The child's level of service depends on individual learning needs and the supports needed to facilitate the child's learning. The levels of service are listed in Figure 17-1.

Determination of placement is dependent on a wide variety of issues, including the type and severity of the child's condition, the presence of mental retardation or a clear learning disability, local practice and tradition, the availability of health and related services in a particular setting, and providers and parents' preferences. The needs of each particular child should be assessed and the least restrictive placement offered to the child and the family.

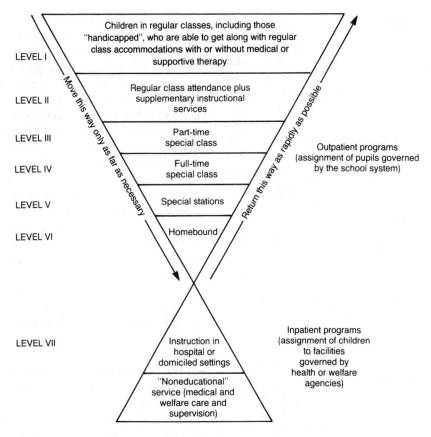

Figure 17-1 The Cascade System. *Source:* "Special Education as Developmental Capital" by E.N. Deno, *Exceptional Children*, Vol. 37, No. 3, p. 235. Copyright 1970 by The Council for Exceptional Children. Reprinted with permission.

Schools usually place children with physical disabilities (e.g., cerebral palsy, muscular dystrophy, spina bifida) and children requiring medical support systems (e.g., respirators, oxygen, dialysis) in some type of special education classroom. This placement frequently includes time in a regular classroom setting for those children who are cognitively capable. Practitioners argue that the vast majority of children with chronic illnesses (e.g., asthma, cancer, diabetes, cystic fibrosis, epilepsy, hemophilia, leukemia, congenital heart disease, kidney problems) will benefit most by primary placement in a regular classroom, but no accurate data are available concerning the efficacy of various placements for these children.

A key planning concern is that children with a chronic illness or physical disability may need classes in the home or hospital. Many children receiving home care will need homebound instruction. Most states require a 2-week waiting period before homebound instruction can begin. Children affected by this waiting period lose valuable instruction time as they change over from their regular or special classrooms to homebound instruction.

A 1981 survey found wide variation among states in the minimum number of days a student must be absent before becoming eligible for home and hospital instruction (Baird et al. 1984). Some states (Montana and South Carolina) reported no minimum requirement, while others (Indiana, Texas, and Washington) mentioned 4 weeks as the minimum length of absence necessary. These absence requirements generally referred to consecutive days missed and were not flexible enough to include frequent absences of shorter duration. Less than 2 percent of all children in special education placements nationwide are in homebound or hospital placements (Office of Special Education and Rehabilitative Services 1985).

Homebound instruction should be oriented toward facilitating the child's return to a more integrated educational placement in a school facility. The homebound teacher or tutor and the child's classroom teacher should coordinate a smooth transition to provide continuity and maximize the child's learning potential. Communication between the home or hospital teacher and the classroom teachers can be enhanced by the use of advanced technology such as radio, television, and computer links. If the homebound instruction is relatively permanent, an IEP should be written. Parents and providers who know that a particular child may need homebound instruction in the future should insist on its inclusion in the child's IEP.

Related Services

A wide variety of management issues surface for special care children in schools. Close and ongoing communication between school personnel and the medical care system (usually the child's primary care physician) is required to ascertain how the child's status will affect his or her education. Questions in a variety of domains must be addressed to help the child function in school. These domains, outlined in the checklist in Appendix 17-A, include supportive therapies, specially tailored career and vocational counseling, personal and family counseling, transportation, modification of class scheduling and classroom environment, administration of medications and special medical regimens, and curriculum adaptations. Required services can be provided to the child in special education under the "related services" provision. Federal regulations list the following services, which may be defined as a necessary part of the child's IEP by the evaluation team:

> transportation and such developmental corrective and other supportive services as are required to assist a handicapped child to benefit from special education . . . speech pathology and occupational therapy, recreation, early identification and assessment of disabilities, counseling services for diagnostic evaluation purposes . . . school health services, social work, services in school and parent counseling and training (Federal Register 1977).

The additional cost of providing these "related" services and concerns about the appropriateness of educational institutions providing health services has caused some controversy. Many of the services made available through the special education statute cannot be obtained through other public or private sources. Specialized programs for chronically ill children in the public and private sector might provide some of these related services to children and their families; however, many parents can only gain access to these services through the provisions of the special education statute. The arrangements made between health, education, and social service agencies to implement services required by PL 99-457 for the very young child may provide greater access to related services for parents of children with special health care needs.

The real dilemma surrounding the "related services" component of PL 94-142 occurs when the chronically ill child needs only "related services" and not special education program placement. The status of children with normal intelligence who are in need of related services is ambiguous under current state and federal special education codes. Although these children will probably require home care at some point, there is no nationwide standard for placement of these children as special education students.

Many of the needs of children with special health care requirements, including those with complex medical problems, could be met using school health program resources. However, local school health policies and state school health codes vary greatly and there is no federal statute or set of health codes that govern health programs in schools.

Several recent court cases interpreting the intent of PL 94-142 in delivering health services have delineated the range of acceptable burden for local school systems. In a 1984 landmark case, *Tatro v. Irving Independent School District*, the Supreme Court determined that public schools were required to provide clean intermittent catheterization as a related service. The court stated that related services included school health services provided by a school nurse or other qualified person and excluded medical services performed by a licensed physician. The school must provide the health service if the child is in special education and requires a service that can be delivered by providers designated by the courts.

Local school systems have struggled in their attempts to apply the Tatro case to other nursing procedures and situations. The federal district court ruled in *Detsel v. Board of Education of the Auburn Enlarged City School District*, 1986, that constant respirator assistance was a "medical service" and not a "health service" and was therefore not included in the related services clause of the special education laws. Court decisions to date have established that schools are not legally obligated to provide services that require expenditures of inordinate amounts of time, skill, or money. Children dependent on expensive medical regimens will require financing from sources other than education if they are to benefit from the educational program provided, regardless of their eligibility for special education.

CURRENT SCHOOL PRACTICES FOR CHILDREN WITH SPECIAL HEALTH CARE NEEDS

Is the Child Eligible for Special Education?

The child's eligibility for special education depends on several factors:

- Age in relationship to the state's education mandates
- Type of physical disability or health impairment and the child's mental function
- State and local educational system definitions of "other health impaired"
- Local practice concerning the allocation of "related services"

The real dilemma centers on children who do not need special classroom instruction but do need special health and other related services or children who require homebound instruction. Most children with a special health need fit one of these categories. School systems manage these cases using one of three basic methods:

1. They are deemed eligible for special education. This leads to development of an IEP that includes specific health and related services and a contingency plan for homebound and hospital instruction.
2. They are not considered eligible for special education but receive virtually the same services under Section 504 of the 1974 Rehabilitation Act.
3. They receive only the school health and other services available to children not eligible for special education.

Where Is the Educational Program of Children Provided?

The physical location for schooling will depend on the child's condition and the services needed to support the child in the educational program. The child may be in a normal classroom setting, a more separate class in a regular school, a separate school, or at home. The goal is to facilitate learning in the least restrictive environment. Therefore, homebound instruction should be viewed as a temporary placement and all efforts should be made to place the child in a more normalized setting. Many technology-dependent children in and out of home placements are in special classes or schools. A few with normal intelligence and no emotional concerns are in regular classrooms.

If the Program Is at School, Who Provides Needed Medical/Health Services?

The child's health needs can be met in a number of ways. The best method will vary based on the child's problem and available resources. Care can be delivered by (1) the school nurse or another nurse in the community, (2) a trained health aide or other personnel such as a teacher, (3) the child, or (4) the parent.

If the Needed Medical/Health Care Is Provided at School, Who Pays for It?

The source of payment for the medical/health care varies based on the complexity and expense of the health procedure, the child's eligibility for special education, and the child's insurance coverage. If the child is in special education and the health procedure is not complex or time consuming (e.g., catheterization vs. full respiratory monitoring), then the school provides the personnel. The school would also pay the costs of training all personnel (e.g. classroom teacher, bus driver) in emergency procedures necessary for maintaining the child's life in case of accidents. If the procedure is complex and considered a "medical service" (constant respirator assistance) rather than a "health service" (e.g., catheterization), then the child's insurance would pay the costs of providing the personnel assisting the child in school.

REFERENCES

Baird, S.; Ashcroft, S.; Dy, E.B. "Survey of Educational Provision for Chronically Ill Children." *Peabody Journal of Education* 61 (1984):75–90.

Comptroller General. *Unanswered Questions on Educating Handicapped Children in Local Public Schools.* Washington, D.C.: General Accounting Office, 1981.

Education for All Handicapped Children Act of 1974, Public Law 94-142. November 29, 1975, Section 602.

"Education of Handicapped Children: Implementation of Part b of the Education for All Handicapped Children Act." *Federal Register* 42, no. 163 (1977): section 121a.13.

"Federal Regulations for the Education for All Handicapped Children Act of 1975." *Federal Register* 42, no. 163 (1977): section 121a.5.

Office of Special Education and Rehabilitative Services. *Department of Education Annual Reports to Congress,* 1979 through 1985. Washington, D.C.: U.S. Department of Education.

Appendix 17-A

Checklist of Items for Consideration in Developing Individualized Education Plans (IEPs) for Students with Physical Disabilities or Special Health Needs

The following checklist contains items often identified by parents and professionals as important components of appropriate educational plans. Not all items will be important to all students; some students may have needs that are not reflected here. We invite your comments and suggestions for additions that can be included in future revisions.

TRANSPORTATION

[   ] Regular bus   [   ] Special Assistance
[   ] Van   [   ] To and from home to vehicle
[   ] Wheelchair car   [   ] To and from school to vehicle
[   ] Special equipment   [   ] Aide
[   ] Seat belt   [   ] Positioning
[   ] Car seat   [   ] Other _____
[   ] Other _____
NOTES: _____
_____

ACCESSIBILITY

[   ] Use of elevators   [   ] Vocational areas
[   ] Bathrooms   [   ] Auditorium (stage)
[   ] Classrooms   [   ] Administrative offices
[   ] Gym   [   ] Locker location
[   ] Cafeteria   [   ] Other _____
NOTES: _____
_____

THERAPIES

[   ] Occupational Therapy   [   ] Other _____
[   ] Physical therapy   [   ] Other _____
[   ] Speech therapy   [   ] Other _____
NOTES: _____
_____

SELF-HELP SKILLS
[   ] Eating
[   ] Dressing
[   ] Toileting
[   ] Student needs:
    [   ] Assistance
    [   ] Training

[   ] Grooming:
    [   ] Bathing/washing
    [   ] Tooth brushing
    [   ] Other _____

NOTES: _____

CURRICULUM
[   ] Materials to be modified:
    [   ] Taped
    [   ] Written in large print
    [   ] Computer software
    [   ] Other _____
[   ] Timelines set
[   ] Responsibility assigned

[   ] Methods to be adapted:
    [   ] Timelines for completing
        tasks/assignments/tests
    [   ] Written *and* spoken
    [   ] Use of computer

NOTES: _____

CLASSWORK
[   ] Backup tutoring:
    [   ] Regularly scheduled
    [   ] As needed

[   ] Make-up assistance:
    [   ] Regularly scheduled
    [   ] As needed

NOTES: _____

PHYSICAL EDUCATION
[   ] Regular program
[   ] Modified regular program
[   ] Adaptive physical
    education program
[   ] Other _____

[   ] Special equipment
[   ] Special staff
[   ] Other _____

NOTES: _____

ENRICHMENT CLASSES/ACTIVITIES
[   ] Art
[   ] Music
[   ] Computer
[   ] Other _____

[   ] Modifications needed:
    [   ] Special equipment
    [   ] Special staff
    [   ] Other

NOTES: _____

EQUIPMENT NEEDED
[   ] Typewriter
[   ] Computer
[   ] Special grip pencils

[   ] Communication devices
[   ] Extra set of books for home
[   ] Other _____

NOTES: _____

MEDICATIONS

[   ] Who administers:
    [   ] Student
    [   ] Nurse
    [   ] Teacher
    [   ] Backup person
[   ] Side effects, implications for:
    [   ] Regular school schedule
    [   ] Test schedule
    [   ] Special events/activities

[   ] Storage
[   ] Recordkeeping, logs
[   ] Instructions on self-administering for student

NOTES: _____

_____

SPECIAL HEALTH NEEDS AT SCHOOL

[   ] Regular basis
[   ] As needed
[   ] Use of bathroom as needed
[   ] Other _____

[   ] Specify:
    [   ] Who
    [   ] What
    [   ] Backup person

NOTES: _____

_____

SPECIAL SUPPLIES OR EQUIPMENT

[   ] Storage
[   ] Whose responsibility
    Other considerations: _____

[   ] At school only
[   ] Shared between home and school

NOTES: _____

_____

BACKUP MEDICAL SUPPORT

List specific health-related emergencies that may occur: _____

_____

_____

_____

Who to contact _____
Where to go _____
What to do in an emergency _____

_____

NOTES: _____

_____

MOBILITY

[   ] Need for assistance
[   ] Regular method/person
[   ] Backup person
[   ] Use of elevator
[   ] Other _____

[   ] Proximity considerations for developing schedule
[   ] Classrooms
[   ] Lunchrooms
[   ] Gym
[   ] Other

NOTES: _____

_____

POSITIONING

[　] Wheelchair
[　] Car
[　] Classroom
[　] Gym
[　] Lunch
[　] Other _____

[　] Aids:
　　[　] Prone board
　　[　] Back supports
　　[　] Other _____
　　[　] When _____

NOTES: _____
_____

STAMINA

[　] Scheduling concerns
[　] Length of day
[　] Effect on testing,
　　　especially timed ones
[　] Breaks/rest periods:
　　[　] As needed
　　[　] Regularly scheduled

[　] Identifiable signs of fatigue
[　] Whose responsibility
[　] Whose authority
[　] Role of student

NOTES: _____
_____

FIRE SAFETY

[　] Plan
[　] Who is responsible
[　] Backup person

NOTES: _____
_____

FIELD TRIPS

[　] Early notification
[　] Transportation

[　] Aide
[　] Other _____

NOTES: _____
_____

COUNSELING SERVICES

[　] School
[　] Career/vocational
[　] Personal

[　] Family
[　] Other _____
_____

EXTRACURRICULAR ACTIVITIES/PROGRAMS (This is a Section 504 issue)

[　] Special learning opportunities:
　　[　] Driver's education
　　[　] Work experience
　　[　] Job placement programs
　　[　] Other _____
[　] Extended day programs
[　] Clubs

[　] Sports programs
[　] Social events
[　] Transportation
[　] Aide
[　] Accessibility

NOTES: _____
_____

HOME/HOSPITAL TUTORING
[   ] Needed now
[   ] Possibly needed later
[   ] Outline plan (even if tentative)
NOTES: _____
_____
_____

Source: Reprinted with permission from "Collaboration among Parents and Health Professionals (CAPP) Project" by Betsy Anderson, Federation for Children with Special Needs, Boston, Massachusetts.

Part IV

Family Considerations

Chapter 18

The Parents' Perspective on Pediatric Home Care

Karen A. Shannon

The home care professional needs to understand the emotional impacts on families considering home care as an alternative to long-term institutionalization. The initial reaction of parents who discover their child will require long-term medical care is discussed in this chapter along with the stages of emotional acceptance experienced by primary caregivers in establishing effective home care. The transition from the hospital to the home and the integration of the child into the community are addressed, as well as the parents' search for effective emotional support and the need for long-term follow up.

Development of specialized home care for the technology-dependent child has created new options in health care delivery. Parents must now consider the possibility of caring for the technology-dependent child in the home. They must ask themselves if home care is the correct choice for their child, their family, and themselves. This question can only be answered affirmatively when parents and professionals can develop a relationship of support and trust based on open communication and partnership.

EXPECTATIONS OF A PARENT

"Congratulations, you are going to have a baby." These are thrilling words when a couple's dreams center around starting a family. The excited couple begins to make plans for their child's future.

What happens when those dreams are shattered and the couples' dream child is born less than perfect? No parent can prepare for the tragedy of a premature delivery with complications or the devastating news that their child has a genetic or congenital birth defect. Parents will react with shock and disbelief when the phone rings and the community hospital informs them their child has been involved in a severe accident.

In either instance parents are faced with the devastating knowledge that their child may never lead a normal life. The pain and suffering that results from the realization that their child may not lead a full and productive life is overwhelming. Parents are told, "Your child is alive, but he has some problems. We are not sure of all the long range implications, but you must now understand that you are the parent of a disabled child." It is equally devastating to be informed that their child will require the assistance of an occupational therapist, a physical therapist, a speech therapist, and an educational therapist and will require constant medical support.

These children form a new population created by the medical miracles of the 1980s. They are known as technology-dependent children. Technology is now replacing what nature has omitted or damaged in accidents. The child may require a ventilator, an infusion pump, or sophisticated medical management. Parents of these technology-dependent children must accept that the assistance of these high-technology devices provides a new umbilical cord, a medical life line required to sustain life. This assistance may only be required for a few months or years, but parents must face the realization that it could be for a lifetime. This realization often includes awareness that without technological support the child faces certain death.

The initial feelings of shock, panic, and anger quickly lead to feelings of guilt, despair, and loneliness. Parents begin to search for answers to why and how this happened to their child. They begin the search for someone or something that can make their child normal. This search never stops, but parents eventually reach the acceptance stage and begin to plan for the child's future. In this phase the parents begin to cope with limitations, make adjustments in their life style, and develop new skills for survival.

THE GRIEVING PROCESS

It is important for parents and families to realize that while the grieving process is normal and the stages predictable, it can be long and involved. Some feelings and emotions may persist longer than others, some may be missing altogether, and some may reappear after acceptance has been reached. It is important to be able to talk about those feelings and to be able to show emotion.

THE FAMILY

Tremendous strength and determination will be required of families that accept the challenge of caring for a technology-dependent child at home. Many changes in life style will result from the uncertainties caused by having the technology-dependent child in the home. Families, with the support of a committed resource team, will be able to develop the necessary survival skills and realize the ultimate reward—the chance to see their child reach his or her maximum potential in a secure and loving environment.

The family and the team have an ongoing responsibility to never give up the dream for a better tomorrow. The search for improved methods of delivering treatment and care, and the

means to gain access to the services and support required to use this new technology, is never-ending. This is especially important in a society where technological advances are made on what seems to be a daily basis, and the methods of gaining access to this technology are changing at the same pace.

One of the parent's first actions will be to search for the reason their child is disabled. Was it hereditary or did something happen during the pregnancy that altered the normal course of development? Did something happen during the birth process? Was a warning signal missed? Could this have been prevented? Was the intervention and treatment given correctly? Were the best procedures available used for my child? These questions must be explored when making plans to have another child or when resolving the experience of having a child involved in an accident. The searching continues as the parents gather information about the child's condition from physicians, nurses, and therapists. It is not unusual to find a parent researching the disease/ disability by reading all available books or articles on the subject. In time, parents may become experts through the knowledge gained from printed information and professionals.

The family will continue to seek support from the medical profession and may change physicians in their search for one who will help them find answers. This is especially true if the child's diagnosis is not easily identified or if little is known about the disease or disability. The family will continue to follow advancements in the medical field in the hope that an innovative therapy, a different medication, or a new surgical technique will help their child achieve a higher level of normalcy. Trust and rapport in the physician–parent relationship is often the key in helping parents develop the confidence they need to handle the situation. As times goes on, this relationship will grow to include a nurse or team of nurses. Nurses are the vital link in maintaining perspective and control of the situation.

THE EXTENDED FAMILY

The parents who decide to take their child home from the hospital must accept the fact that they will need to welcome many visitors. These visitors will make up what is known as the extended family. The extended family, mostly medical professionals, is an important part of the family's internal support network. The intrusion of these professionals requires that the question of respect for family privacy be addressed in the early stages of home care planning. Families will question how they can maintain privacy when bringing their child home means bringing home a support team. Proper development of communication skills through team meetings, written communication ledgers, or the use of identified and outlined tasks and responsibilities can assist in eliminating this type of question. Families can maintain whatever degree of privacy is required as long as communication, negotiation, and compromise are used to gain mutual understanding of needs and concerns.

The ground rules must be understood before entering into this new system of health care delivery. Without ground rules a misunderstanding or internal power struggle can easily destroy not only the team but also the child's chances for survival. Major ground rules established by the team should include establishing team communication networks and ensuring mutual respect for professional expertise. This process may require several months. If it requires an extended period of time, it is likely that an important element is missing from the support/training network. If so, a thorough assessment of the interworking of the team must take place to discover the missing element. Successful communications and interaction will result when the missing medical or rehabilitative element is found.

Parents must develop the skills they need to provide their child with quality, cost-effective care. They must develop these skills in order to identify needed nursing and support services, as well as required medical equipment and supplies. Comparing services and cost is a continuing activity. In addition, the search for funding to support medical costs often requires significant activity over long periods. Families are often forced to turn to church or community groups for assistance when their insurance or state health care funding can no longer provide assistance. This ongoing activity must be accepted and supported by the entire support team.

Support from friends and extended family members will be sought as the family sorts their emotions and searches for acceptance of their child by others. There are few role models available to new parents because there have been few attempts to integrate medically dependent or disabled children into families or society until this decade. As the parents continue to be successful in coordinating their child's care, they will continue to "fine tune" their own coping, stress management, and organization skills. Families are now able to truly understand the advantages of home care. When they first take the child home, crisis management is the way of life, and new home care parents repeatedly ask the question "Are we making the right decision for our child, our family, and ourselves?" The emotional stress can be overwhelming. Physically and emotionally exhausted parents are constantly required to make decisions affecting the life of their child and the well-being of their family. Developing coping skills, taking time out to reenergize, seeing a child reach a difficult milestone, and learning how to truly laugh again as a family help parents know they have made the right decision. Parents who reach this point will be able once again to function in a near-normal fashion.

The team, to reach the ultimate goal, must work together to ensure that the child's maximum developmental potential is reached and maintained. They must provide the family with the skills and support needed to be independent and self-sufficient in a world of dependency. They must recognize that a partnership is required if success is achieved for the child, family, or team.

Chapter 19

Stress Tolerance

Linda M. Gaudet
Gail M. Powers

Serious illness in a child or adolescent is a significant and unusual family stressor. An understanding of the vast array of stressors that impact the family with a seriously ill child is essential for the professional working with these families. In this chapter stress and coping in families with chronic pediatric illness are addressed, with the focus placed on the child receiving home nursing care. The term *child* refers to both children and adolescents throughout the chapter.

Family stressors are those life events or occurrences of sufficient magnitude to bring about change in the family system (Hill 1949). Baker (1969) defines a system as a set of units or elements that are actively interrelated and operate in some sense as a bounded unit. If this definition is considered within a family context, it is apparent that an understanding of family interactions and boundaries is vital to the successful provision of services to the ill child and his or her family, particularly in the home setting. In addition, the importance of establishing an initial positive rapport with the family system cannot be overstated. Therefore, the family system is examined in more detail in order to provide the nurse with a family framework rather than the more limited focus on the patient.

FAMILY SYSTEMS DEVELOPMENT

From a developmental perspective, family systems can be thought of as having a life of their own. In a manner similar to the way in which the individual child develops, family systems pass through predictable life stages (childbearing, latency, adolescence, launching) evolving new methods of taking care of themselves and coping with the demands of the external world (Carter and McGoldrick 1980). The concept of normative developmental tasks versus crises is important when considering the family system. All families can expect to experience normative developmental crises such as adolescence, the "empty nest" syndrome, and the mid-life crisis. However, when a nonnormative event such as serious pediatric illness compounds these normal developmental crises, families are faced with the task of coping with an overwhelming degree of stress. Other factors to consider that may affect family functioning are the life stage of the family (as noted above), the family structure (single parent, two parent, extended family, blended family), the family's emotional history, and the degree of pressure or support from the outside world.

Family interactions can be viewed on two levels: (1) the interactions within the family and (2) those between the family and the environment. The nurse entering the family system by working in the home setting must assess both the family's internal structure and where the family is in relation to its environment. An excellent means of making such an assessment is by examining boundaries. The clarity and flexibility of family boundaries, which are determined by the establishment of family rules and responsibilities, is a useful parameter for evaluating family functioning.

Boundaries within the family structure may be examined in terms of being open or closed. Open boundaries provide good communication and interaction between family members. Closed boundaries imply little or no communication and interaction. The nurse can intervene with the family whose closed boundaries are interfering with optimal home care of the child by assisting the family in realigning its structure. In the case of a family where the parents' reactions to their child's chronic illness has been to withdraw from each other, the simple task of assigning more parental responsibility and power in terms of both health care and family issues is often very effective. The parental unit, whether single parent or dual parent, must maintain the position of head of the family hierarchy. Nurses can reinforce this role (thus empowering parents), while mindful that although their clinical knowledge is critical to the family, the parents are the real experts on their child.

Boundaries can also be considered in terms of open or closed interactions between the family and its environment. Maintaining a balance between openness to the environment and shelter from it is a crucial aspect of family functioning. As a representative of both the health care team and society, the nurse has a unique opportunity to assist the family in developing a sense of openness and trust in relation to its environment. By clearly defining roles and expectations, in addition to conveying a willingness to advocate for the family, the nurse can enhance the family's sense of openness and trust.

FAMILY STRESSORS

Family stressors are many and varied. The family with a chronically ill child is often characterized by strained family relationships. One often finds an overinvolved relationship between the primary caregiver and the ill child, resulting in other family members feeling left out and sibling competition increasing for parental time and attention. In addition, some scapegoating may be present in which parents blame each other for a current crisis or for the genetic responsibility for the child's condition. Another source of family stress involves the modifications the family must make in activities and goals that affect decisions concerning leisure time, career, and having additional children. Other family stressors include increased tasks and time commitments, social isolation, coordination of medical care, and the necessary grieving process for the loss of a normal childhood. And last, but certainly not least, is the overwhelming financial burden that the family may find that affects almost every area of life.

Indicators of family stress may be parental and sibling somatic complaints, parental medical noncompliance, parental depression, sibling depression or acting out, sibling school problems, and marital dysfunction. Marital tension may, in fact, result in one parent moving out of the home, either temporarily or permanently.

Within the family unit, stressors more specific to the chronically ill child may be frequent hospitalizations, school absences, separations from peers and family members, isolation from normal childhood activities and experiences, painful medical procedures, and, particularly for the adolescent, enforced dependency and loss of autonomy. Knowledge of the developmental tasks of childhood and adolescence is vital in order for the nurse to properly assess delays or regressions and their subsequent relation to stress.

The nurse is in a primary position to recognize the indicators of stress for the ill child. Such indicators may be medical noncompliance, developmental regression, depression (may be "masked depression" in the form of acting out behavior), self-consciousness, self-isolation, anxiety, helplessness, and school problems.

These family stressors are fairly common to all families experiencing chronic pediatric illness. The family who has the additional stress of caring for the child dependent on medical technology within the home setting must also contend with the constant disruption of normal family life and a lack of privacy due to the presence of health care professionals. Professionals in the home setting, who strive to provide optimum care for the patient and family, must be aware of stressors and alert to possible reactions to them. They must also strive to keep the focus of treatment on the child within the total family context.

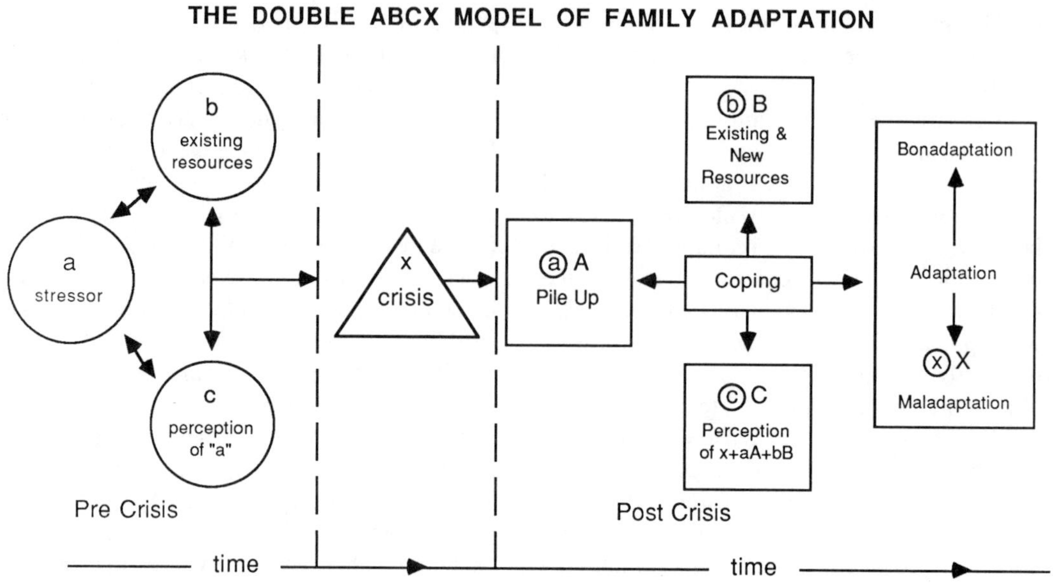

THE DOUBLE ABCX MODEL OF FAMILY ADAPTATION

Figure 19-1 The Double ABCX Model of Family Adaptation. *Source:* Reprinted with permission from *Systematic Assessment of Family Stress, Resources, and Coping* by H.I. McCubbin and J. Patterson, Family Social Science, © 1981.

FAMILY COPING

Given the tremendous degree of stress that a family with a chronically ill child experiences, the question remains, "How can we as professionals better assist these families in the coping process?" In answer to this question, the coping process has been conceptualized by McCubbin and Patterson (1981) in an effort to find why some families grow and thrive in the face of multiple stressors and others grow weaker and possibly dissolve. Their Double ABCX Model of Family Adaptation presented in Figure 19-1 looks at family efforts over time to adapt to multiple stressors through the use of family resources and perceptual factors in an attempt to achieve family balance or bonadaptation.

Normally when a family experiences a stressful event (a), the family draws on its resources (b), and its members have a perception of the event (c), each of which interact and result in stress. The stress may become a crisis (x) if the family is unable to use resources (b) and define the situation adequately (c).

In families experiencing pediatric chronic illness, however, not only are there normative stressors but often a pileup of stressors (A) as well. Coping for these families involves both their existing and new resources (B), in conjunction with their perceptions of the crisis (C),

resulting in an adaptation (X). This adaptation may be a bonadaptation or a maladaptation.

Family stressors (A) have previously been examined. The three remaining components of the model will now be examined in relation to the family with a chronically ill child.

Resources (B)

Often it is the social worker and/or discharge planner who is looking at resources, both existing and new, in order to assist the family in coping with a chronically ill child during hospitalization. However, in the case of the pediatric nurse providing home care, it is the nurse who has most frequent contact with the family and therefore may become involved in assessing family resources and/or connecting the family with community resources. Nursing staff can provide an invaluable service to the family by making community resource referrals available to them. Appendix A contains an extensive list of such resources and provides the nurse with the means for obtaining an excellent foundation in this area.

Perception (C)

The family's perception of the crisis (diagnosis of the illness or subsequent crises) is criti-

Exhibit 19-1 Tips on Reframing the Crisis

The meaning that any event has depends on the "frame" in which it is perceived. Professionals can assist parents in changing the "frame" or meaning of a pediatric health crisis by

- Paying attention to the positive value of the family's behavior and views
- Identifying the family's strengths and resources
- Encouraging new skills and opportunities for emotional and developmental growth
- Challenging generalizations, resistance, comparisons, and incomplete or inaccurate information
- Asking reframing questions, such as "Compared with what?", "What would happen if?", and "What is the worst thing that could happen?"
- Reframing the perceived problem within the family's frame of reference and as an opportunity for growth

cal in determining the kind of adaptation the family makes. If the family views the situation as hopeless, a maladaptation may occur, resulting in a dysfunctional family. If, on the other hand, the situation is viewed as a challenge, a bonadaptation, resulting in a functional family, is more likely. McCubbin and Patterson (1981) have found that the family's efforts to redefine a situation as a challenge, or as an opportunity for growth, appear to play an important role in facilitating family coping and eventually adaptation.

Several authors have suggested that parental attitudes have a strong influence on how well children with chronic illness adjust to their situation (Freeman 1968; Garrard and Richmond 1963; Mattson 1972). It would appear, therefore, that the nurse working in the home setting could play an important role by reframing the situation for the family in a positive context whenever possible (Exhibit 19-1). Consider the following example: Nurse M. is working with the Smith family and observes the family becoming more and more helpless in its attitude concerning their child's illness and care. The family's perception of the problem could be reframed by the nurse noting the behavioral indicators of family strengths and new gains made. Nurse M. might also relay to the family observations made of the ill child's strengths and note opportunities for emotional and developmental growth.

Adaptation (X)

Before successful family adaptation can take place, parents must be able to face their problems with a minimum of stress in order that their energies can be mobilized to meet the many tasks ahead of them. Families who do not adapt well to their child's chronic illness often view themselves as victims, powerless to fight the "system" or perhaps even supernatural forces.

Families who adapt well, on the other hand, often view themselves as activists. Many of these families become involved in efforts to "normalize" the child's life, to initiate aggressive searches of services for the child, and in some cases to bring about societal changes supportive of families with handicapped or chronically ill children. In meeting the challenges that their stressful situation imposes, these families make a bonadaptation, resulting in helping themselves and others.

It would appear useful, then, for nurses working with these families to assess, as early as possible, which families are dysfunctional as well as those that are at risk for becoming dysfunctional. One means of assessing parental coping patterns has been developed by McCubbin and colleagues (1983) and is entitled Coping Health Inventory for Parents (CHIP). The CHIP was developed to record what parents find helpful or not helpful to them in the management of family life when their child has a medical condition requiring continued care. The parent records how helpful each of 45 coping behaviors is to him or her on a scale ranging from not helpful to extremely helpful (see Appendix 19-A). The CHIP assists parents in examining the need to balance the demands of caring for the ill child with their needs to (1) invest in themselves as individuals, (2) attend to the family unit, and (3) understand the medical situation.

The CHIP can easily and conveniently be used in the home setting. It is an excellent tool for determining differences in coping between mothers and fathers when administered to each parent separately, thus allowing the nurse to assist parents in better understanding each others' response to their child's illness. The reliability and validity of the CHIP has been noted by other researchers as well (Gaudet and Powers 1986; Powers et al. 1986; McCubbin and Patterson 1981).

INTERVENTIONS

Individual Therapy

The pediatric patient can benefit by numerous forms of psychotherapy. Forms of therapy that can be used by nurses are relaxation training, imagery, and hypnosis (Hilgard and LeBaron 1984; Mills and Crowley 1986). These modalities can be extremely effective for pain management and as coping techniques.

Relaxation Therapy

The child can be taught progressive deep muscle relaxation according to his or her age and cognitive development. With the younger child or one with limited cognitive development, the nurse would begin by having the child close his or her eyes. The child would then be asked to take two deep breaths and very slowly let all the air out. The next step would be to pretend he or she had two lemons, one in each hand; to squeeze those lemons as hard as possible; and then very slowly to let go of the lemons. Next the child is asked to pretend he or she is a very old person who is all wrinkled: "Wrinkle up your nose and face as hard as you can. Hold it for a minute, and now pretend those wrinkles just magically fall off your face, and your face is relaxed and smooth." The last step is to have the child squeeze his or her toes as tightly as possible. Then, "Pretend those toes magically turn into soft, white fluffy marshmallows. Your marshmallows are beginning to melt into a white creamy puddle. And as those marshmallows just melt away, all your pain and tightness in your body will melt along with them, slowly leaving your body." The older child with a higher cognitive level can be taken through additional muscle groups beginning with the head and progressing down to the feet, requesting that he or she first tighten and then relax his or her muscles.

Imagery

Imagery is a powerful tool when time is a consideration and immediate results are desired. The child is asked to close his or her eyes and picture an object that is perceived as particularly pleasant. The nurse can help the child focus on the object by describing it in terms of all the child's senses—sight, hearing, smell, taste, and touch. The very young child responds well to visualizing food, such as an ice cream cone. "Close your eyes and imagine a delicious ice cream cone. The cone holding the ice cream is dark brown and kind of bumpy. Your ice cream could be a dark brown chocolate, a pretty pink strawberry, or perhaps a cool white vanilla. I know that whatever flavor you choose, it will be your own very special flavor. Now just imagine that cold ice cream first touching your lips and tongue and then very slowly sliding down your throat. And now you can begin to bite into that crunchy cone. You might even hear the noise your cone makes as you slowly crunch every delicious bite. And when you are finished with your special cone, taking all the time you need, you may open your eyes, knowing you can bring your cone back in your mind any time you want and continue to taste, feel, and see your special treat."

The older child can be taken on a guided visual trip to a place that is very special to him. The first step is to gather information about the child's favorite places and experiences, either actual or desired. For instance, if the child describes having had pleasant experiences at the beach (or would like to), the following guided imagery might be developed: "Close your eyes and allow yourself to become very relaxed. Take two deep breaths and let go of your air very slowly. Now picture yourself standing on a cliff high over a beach. As you come closer to the edge of the cliff, you notice some stairs going down to the beach and the ocean beyond. You walk over to those stairs going down to the beach and the ocean beyond. You very carefully begin to walk down the steps. When you reach the bottom of the stairs, you decide to take off your shoes and allow your bare feet to feel the sand warmed by the sun. You begin walking across the sand toward the ocean, and suddenly a huge wave seems to come up out of nowhere. As the wave approaches the shore, you run up to it and catch the last part of it as it now gently rolls up to the shore's edge and in between your toes. The water is very cold, but it feels so good on your feet. As the water begins to go back out toward the ocean, you squish your toes even further into the wet sand and allow yourself to experience that cool, moist feeling. At the same time you notice that the sun is warming your back and there is a cool mist on your face from the ocean spray. You may want to walk along the beach for a while, or perhaps you would like to sit down along the water's edge for a few moments, just allowing yourself to experience the beach and the ocean. When you are ready, you can walk back across the beach over to the stairs and slowly climb back up the cliff. Very slowly you may open your eyes and begin to stretch your arms, knowing that you may go back to your special place any time you wish.'' These types of guided imagery are very effective for both the younger and older child when attempting to divert the child's attention from pain or medical procedures.

Hypnosis

Hypnosis is another excellent therapeutic tool when working with the pediatric patient. The nurse can assist the child in accessing his or her inner resources, thus giving the child more control over his or her body and illness. For nurses desiring training in medical hypnosis, there are seminars available for beginning through advanced training (see Appendix A).

Play Therapy

Play therapy is one of the most effective and versatile means of working with the pediatric patient. An excellent reference for play therapy has been written by Oaklander (1978), who conceptualizes the play therapy process as a way in which the therapist can open doors and windows to the child's inner world. The therapy provides a means for the child to express feelings, arrive at closure, make choices, and lighten burdens. Various projective techniques are used, including drawing, storytelling, puppetry, and roleplaying.

Drawing Technique. The nurse could ask the child to first draw his or her pain, second, draw the pain looking all better, and third, draw how the first picture could become the second picture. This process allows the child to develop some awareness of feelings and coping methods in relation to pain. The same procedure could be used with the child's actual illness or disability rather than pain. Another excellent drawing technique, which is quite simple yet effective, is to ask the child to draw a feeling, such as anger. By allowing the child to use any color or artistic means (pencil, pen, crayon, or marker), the opportunity is provided for the development of awareness and emotional catharsis. The nurse

need not interpret the drawing; the child can simply be asked to talk about the picture. The technique works equally well with preschoolers to adolescents.

Puppetry. Hand puppets are an excellent means of providing a nonthreatening way for the child and nurse to communicate. Children up through 12 years of age (and often beyond) will express thoughts and feelings through puppets that they might never do in a more direct manner. Animal hand puppets work well, and it is useful to have one with a happy face and one with a sad face. Puppets dressed as nurses and physicians are also very useful. The nurse and child can take turns using various hand puppets (stuffed animals and plastic figures will also work well), each responding spontaneously to the other.

An important point to remember is that the nurse need not purchase special play equipment (other than crayons, markers, and paper). The nurse also has the advantage of working in the child's home setting and may have a wealth of play material belonging to the child and his or her siblings. The nurse need only bring imagination and creativity, while using the child's own play resources. An example would be to use the child's play figures or animals and take a fantasy trip to the hospital. The nurse and child could experience the preparation and trip there, and once they arrived they could go through admitting, getting settled, and an explanation of routines and procedures. An excellent source of further information on play materials and ideas is the Child Life Worker located in many hospital pediatric units.

Storytelling. Storytelling is an activity that most children are certain to enjoy. The nurse can assist the child in coping with illness by presenting a story that has a positive outcome. In the case of a terminal illness, positive ways can be provided in which both the child and the family are coping and assure the child that everyone will be all right. The knowledge that his or her family will be very sad but that they will feel better someday can be very reassuring to a child (this would be an excellent time to have the child draw the picture "sad").

Roleplaying. Roleplaying is a fun and very useful way to allow the child to practice coping techniques and ways of relating to other individuals. For example, the nurse could take the role of a parent, allowing the child to practice expressing his or her feelings and concerns to parents.

When using play therapy there are two very important points to remember. The first is to always be mindful of the child's cognitive and developmental level of functioning. The second is take the child's lead, allowing his or her needs and actions to serve as a guide. With these two points in mind, the nurse can then provide an experience that is both useful and mutually enjoyable for the child and nurse.

Behavior Therapy

Behavior therapy can be a useful technique for nurses involved in compliance issues with pediatric patients. The nurse providing home care has the advantage of observing the child in a natural setting. Ideally, there will be a mental health professional available to assist in developing a behavior program. The focus would be on behavior rather than emotional or dynamic issues and would be aimed at providing concrete, direct, and rapid relief of the problem at hand (Gillmore 1986; Rimm and Masters 1979). The clinician typically would conceive of a hierarchy of reinforcers from primary (e.g., food) to social behavior. The appropriate reinforcer would function either to increase or decrease behavior. It would be helpful to write down the program, either in chart form or as a contractual agreement. The child, family, and nurse would then be reasonably clear as to expectations and consequences, leaving little room for misunderstandings.

Family Therapy

Based on the systems perspective developed earlier in this chapter, it would appear that the most effective and efficient approach to treatment of the emotional and behavioral components of illness would be a family systems approach; therefore, the treatment of choice would be family therapy. A key difference in working with most families and those with chronic pediatric illness, however, is their reason for requiring family therapy. Rather than the existence of long-standing psychopathological processes, the family therapists would typically find myriad logistical difficulties (arranging home life around the care of the ill child) and prolonged developmental transitions (into school, adolescence, and adult life) that have left family structures rigid and obsolete (Mitchell and Rizzo 1985). Reactive versus proactive patterns are often found as a result of families dealing with repeated crises. These families, therefore, appear to respond more positively to treatment that is short term and oriented to problem solving and managing resources.

One short-term problem-solving approach used by the family therapist is in-home family therapy. The approach is based on the premise that the difficulty encountered in the family setting cannot be duplicated in an artificial setting. In the case of the pediatric patient receiving home care, it would seem more practical to observe the difficulties the family may encounter with other systems (such as nurses and other ancillary health care providers) and intervene appropriately in the family's natural setting. In addition, requiring a family with a chronically ill child to meet in an office setting is often difficult to achieve. Other advantages of in-home therapy are the increased likelihood of full compliance of all family members in the therapy process and the flexibility of hours necessary to meet the family's needs.

In addition to applying the problem-solving approach, which is primarily focused on the here and now, it can be extremely helpful to ascertain the transgenerational history of illness, loss, and crisis in the family; or in other words, "What is the family's illness belief system?" (Rowland 1984). Some of the important areas that should be covered in the initial family session are (1) the family's understanding of the disease, including its progression and outcome; (2) the family's experience with crisis and how it was handled; and (3) the family's experience with and willingness to work with health care systems.

Family therapy is an essential component of services for families experiencing chronic pediatric illness. It is important to recognize, however, that current funding often does not provide for family therapy. Until increased funding becomes a reality, a good resource for families would be family counseling centers that offer sliding fee scales. Some insurance plans also cover the cost of family therapy up to 80 percent.

Group Therapy

Group therapy is the gathering together of individuals with similar situations for the purpose of some type of therapeutic intervention. Increasingly, health care professionals have become aware of the many benefits of group therapy. The benefits of group therapy that are not available in a one-to-one approach are (1) sharing of emotions, such as fear, anxiety, anger, and loneliness with a peer group, (2) gaining insight and a feeling of support without necessarily participating overtly, (3) allowing group members the valuable experience of helping each other therapeutically, and (4) sharing and receiving information vital to medical management and coping. The group modality is also important when working within a systems perspective, providing valuable interactional information.

Parent Groups

The primary interactional components of a parent group are education, support, self-help, and therapy. The group may deal primarily with one component or any combination of components. It is up to the group leader or leaders (it is helpful to have a co-leader to assist with the group process) to evaluate the needs and desires of the group and choose the appropriate components.

The parent of a chronically ill child has many conflicting emotions to deal with on a personal level, yet the everyday needs and demands of the ill child are more often than not put above his or her own needs. The group is a place where parents can concentrate on their own needs, explore and clarify their emotions, and "let go" if necessary. The parent who can tend to his or her own needs in such a way is more likely to direct increased energy into the care of his or her child in a focused manner.

Children's Groups

The primary goals of a group for children with chronic illness are (1) the opportunity to normalize their situation and (2) the opportunity to openly express emotions with other children who are experiencing similar problems. If possible the group should be divided into two sections—children aged 6 to 11 and adolescents— thus allowing the adolescents to deal with their specific issues of independence, autonomy, dating, sexuality, marriage, and genetics as they pertain to their illness. The opportunity for both children and adolescents to deal openly with their feelings in a neutral, supportive environment can often result in their readiness to help their parents in managing home care and lessen the need for acting out behavior in the home.

Sibling Groups

Siblings of children with chronic illness may have many different feelings about the patient, his or her illness, and the attention he or she receives. Sympathy, resentment, loneliness, misunderstanding concerning the illness, and a fear for their own health are typical feelings for siblings of the chronically ill child. The group setting for siblings can provide an opportunity to normalize the family situation and an opportunity to have their own time and attention, which is typically focused on the ill child.

Staff Groups

Personnel working with chronically ill children often receive little support or preparation for coping with the emotional demands of working with this group (Littlehales and Teyber 1981). Somehow we have developed the mistaken notion that to acknowledge feelings of fear, grief, sadness, and helplessness is incompatible with being competent, efficient, and effective.

A staff support group can provide for opportunities to share common experiences, problem solve, and deal with feelings by ventilating, clarifying, and validating. The three major areas that would most likely be addressed in such a group are (1) patient care issues, (2) emotional needs of both the patient and the provider, and (3) interactions with the social system in which care is being provided (the family in the case of home care). The combined stress of dealing with these three areas often leads to exhaustion, more commonly referred to as "burnout." The group process is an excellent preventative measure to deal with this common problem.

Respite Care

Respite care is included as an intervention with the awareness that if it is not provided for the family, it is very possible that other forms of intervention may be jeopardized. Respite care may be defined as the temporary relief of obligations and stress. Parents require occasional respite from the stress of caring for a chronically ill child in the home. An opportunity for parents to get away and attend to themselves and their marriage is essential for personal and marital health maintenance.

The ill child is also in need of occasional respite from his or her normal environment. For the mobile child, recreational camps and field trips with children with similar conditions can be an invaluable experience.

Genetic Counseling

Technology in the genetics field has been rapidly expanding; however, the developing social and psychological services for families with genetic disorders and birth defects are lagging. A genetic diagnosis can be potentially devastating, since it affects families over their life span and is multigenerational. Genetic misinformation can be used as a weapon of attack, blame, and criticism within a troubled family (McCollum 1975). Accurate and properly transmitted genetic information, on the other hand, can be relieving.

Families require a specialized setting that provides the dual components of information and assistance. Large medical centers usually have genetic clinics with both geneticists and social workers available. The local March of Dimes is also a good resource and can provide families with information from the Birth Defect Information System in the form of a computer printout. Examples of diseases in which genetic counseling would be important are cystic fibrosis and hemophilia. In the case of hemophilia, female siblings have special concerns about being carriers; therefore, a special effort should be made to provide counseling to them as they approach childbearing age.

The Parent as Case Manager

Encouraging the parent to become his or her child's case manager can be extremely effective in fostering a parental sense of control, usefulness, and reduced anxiety. It also is a very efficient means of coordinating an often vast array of services. A formal record-keeping system can become a parent's lifeline to mastery of the "system" rather than becoming overwhelmed by it. The parent should be encouraged to keep a record of all clinic visits (including treatments and medications given), home records of the child's health (symptoms, fevers, side effects; noting incident, date, time, and duration), conferences with medical staff, and a log of all phone and written contacts (Exhibit 19-2).

In addition, the parent may find it helpful to prepare a background sheet for the child, including developmental milestones, health and medical history, and primary contacts with service providers. If the parent keeps a supply of these

Exhibit 19-2 Contact Log Sheet

Person Contacted _____ Date _____

Organization _____ Telephone _____

Address _____

_____

Question/Information _____

_____

_____

_____

Outcome _____

_____

Follow-up—What do I do next?

    Short Term: _____

_____

    Long Term: _____

_____

sheets available, there will be considerable time and effort saved when initiating a new service contact.

There are some specific methods the parent can implement in the home to ensure the smooth delivery of home nursing care. An equipment and supply inventory list is useful for identifying the quantity of supplies on hand and the need for reordering. Written nursing schedules should be required to be in place in the home at least 2 weeks ahead of time to allow for efficient planning and elimination of nursing coverage gaps. A bedside notebook containing sections on medical management, communication between nurses and the family, and a log for nurses to sign in and out would also be useful.

The parent using the above examples of case management becomes the child's "front line" case manager, assisted by a backup system of professionals for guidance and support. Some families will wish to assume responsibility for their child's case management as soon as possible, and others will prefer to rely on professional case management that allows for increasing parental responsibility on a gradual basis. Some excellent resources are available to assist parents in case management and coping with their child's chronic illness (Goldfarb et al. 1986; Gittler and Colton 1986; Kaufman and Lichtenstein, no date).

Coordination of Services

One of the biggest stressors many families find themselves facing is the lack of coordination of services. The parent attempting to take on the case management of a child often faces this immediate and sometimes overwhelming stressor. Therefore, coordination of services has been included here as a most important intervention.

Any discussion of coordination of services would be incomplete without mentioning the landmark Vanderbilt Study, officially titled "Public Policies Affecting Chronically Ill Children and Their Families" (Hobbs and Perrin 1985). This study has heightened awareness at a national level of (1) the need to coordinate services for the chronically ill child and his or her family and (2) the need for some type of national policy and federal funding. Vanderbilt University sponsored state conferences that have been conducted across the country and have served as the impetus for many state and local programs.

Examples of local efforts to coordinate services and provide direction and support for families are Children's Chronic Care Services in Southern Arizona (providing information and referral, case management, and parent therapy groups) and SKIP (Sick Kids [Need] Involved People), which assists children dependent on medical technology. SKIP has developed into a national organization with many local chapters (see Appendix A). Many additional efforts such as these are needed in order to assist families in dealing with the lack of coordination of services.

CASE STUDY: THE TAYLOR FAMILY

After examining various interventions designed to assist families coping with chronic pediatric illness, it may be useful now to examine a case study. We will look at what actually happened with this family and then examine what might have been done differently using some of the interventions previously mentioned.

The Taylors anxiously awaited the birth of their first child, full of hopes and dreams typical of a young expectant couple. Those dreams appeared to become reality when Mrs. Taylor delivered a seemingly healthy infant girl. However, the Taylors began having serious concerns about their daughter when the child, Jackie, was 6 months old and not developing normally. After completing a series of tests with several doctors, the Taylors received the devastating news that their daughter had an inherited enzyme deficiency that would eventually attack every part of her body. They were informed that Jackie would have multiple problems and would die before the age of 9 years.

Initially Mr. Taylor found it very difficult to accept and deal with his only child's diagnosis of a fatal disease. There was no counseling or support group offered to the Taylors; therefore, they dealt with the shock and pain the best they knew how. Mrs. Taylor became totally involved with the demands of caring for her ill child; Mr. Taylor threw himself into his work and attempted to avoid his daughter and the reality of the home situation as much as possible.

The marital stress that followed was considerable. Mr. Taylor was unable to talk to his wife about their daughter, assist with physician appointments or other care, or support his wife in any other way. She had a need to talk; he had a need to keep it all inside. This situation continued for an entire year, until the family changed pediatricians. The new physician told Mrs. Taylor that she was on the verge of both physical and emotional exhaustion. He also informed her that he would not take her daughter as a patient unless Mr. Taylor came in to talk to him. In addition, the pediatrician indicated that the time had come for Mr. Taylor to come to terms with his daughter's illness. Mr. Taylor reluctantly agreed to talk with the pediatrician, and following that conversation, Mrs. Taylor described her husband as a new person. He became involved in Jackie's care and could enjoy her without dwelling on her diagnosis. He also became more supportive of his wife and they began talking about having another child.

One year later, with the help of a supportive physician and the results of an amniocentesis, their second child, Sandra, was born. The care required by both Jackie and their newborn daughter was constant and exhausting. The Taylors were able to support each other at this point; however, their sense of isolation was intense. The grandparents lived out of town and were dealing with their own pain to the extent that they were unable to give much support to the Taylors. In addition, the family had recently moved to a new city and had few acquaintances.

As far as Jackie's medical care was concerned, there was nothing the physicians could do for her other than keep her comfortable and treat her recurrent infections. Pain was a frequent and serious concern for the Taylors. Their primary goal was to provide care for Jackie in their home as long as possible while at the same time providing her with pain relief.

The final crisis in Jackie's short life lasted over 2 months. With increasing intracranial pressure came increased pain. Jackie was hospitalized at this point; however, the physicians resisted the Taylors' desire to increase her pain medication, fearing dangerous side effects. After 1 week in the hospital, the Taylors convinced the physicians to allow administration of a stronger pain medication in the home setting. The family arranged for 24-hour per day home care so that their daughter could die at home. The nurses caring for Jackie had pediatric intensive care experience and were highly efficient and supportive to the family. Jackie died peacefully and pain free at 7 years of age.

A New Alternative

The following treatment plan could have been more beneficial to this family:

As soon as the diagnosis was made, the physician would make a referral to an agency that would provide a case manager or advocate for the Taylor family. This individual would provide immediate supportive counseling and begin coordinating all necessary services. The Taylors would then be linked up with a support group consisting of families in similar situations.

The case manager would provide the Taylors with a computerized printout of all services and information pertinent to their situation and would also develop a treatment plan geared to their individual needs and desires, in this case a plan for home care. The next step would be to gather together the Taylors' closest relatives and friends (the significant others in their lives) and explain what they could expect and would need from each other, followed by an open dialogue encouraging the expression of feelings.

Once the family became somewhat stabilized, a regular system of respite care would be arranged so that the Taylors could regain some strength and refocus on their relationship (the Taylors did not have one vacation in 7 years). In addition, in-home family therapy would be available to address current issues and prevent future problems.

The nurse would play a crucial role in assisting Jackie to cope with her painful and terminal illness. She would begin teaching Jackie some age-appropriate relaxation and imagery techniques to alleviate pain as soon as possible after home care was initiated. This could be followed by helping Jackie to adjust to her terminal illness by using a variety of play therapy techniques. Among them could be roleplaying using various methods of coping, expression of feelings by using hand puppets and drawings, and storytelling involving feelings and coping techniques. The nurse could also instruct Jackie's parents in these techniques, thus providing an opportunity for mutually satisfying parent–child interaction.

In summary, a true family systems perspective would be taken, involving the patient, her family, and other significant areas of their lives. The developmental needs of both the patient and the family would be taken into account and every effort made to individualize treatment.

A natural question at this point might be "Where would the funding come for this 'ideal' treatment plan?" Components such as the support group and the case manager largely could be a volunteer effort. Private foundations and grants are a possibility, as is a national funding source as suggested by the Vanderbilt Study.

REFERENCES

Baker, F. "Review of General Systems Concepts and their Relevance for Medical Care." *Systemics* 7 (1969): 209–229.

Carter, E., and McGoldrick, M. *The Family Life Cycle.* New York: Gardner Press, 1980.

Freeman, R.D. "Emotional Reactions of Handicapped Children." In *Annual Progress in Child Psychiatry and Child Development*, edited by S. Chess and A.Thomas. New York: Brunner/Mazel, 1968.

Garrard, S.D., and Richmond, J.B. "Psychological Aspects of the Management of Chronic Disease and Handicapping Conditions in Childhood. In *The Psychological Basis of Medical Practice*, edited by H.E. Leif, V.H. Leif, and N.R. Leif. New York: Harper & Row, 1963.

Gaudet, L.M., and Powers, G.M. "Differences in Coping Patterns in Parents of Chronically Ill Children." Educational Resources Information Center (ERIC) Clearinghouse for Counseling and Personnel Services, University of Michigan (Ann Arbor), and abstracted in *Resources in Education*, July 1986. ERIC document reproduction No. ED 266-374.

Gillmore, J. "Behavior Therapy." In *Manual of Clinical Child Psychiatry*, edited by K.S. Robson. Washington, D.C.: American Psychiatric Press, 1986.

Gittler, J., and Colton, M. *Community-Based Case Management Programs for Children With Special Health Care Needs*, prepared by National Maternal and Child Health Resource Center, 1986, grant #MCJ-193790-01 U.S. Department of Health and Human Services Public Health Service, HRSA, BHCDA, Division of Maternal and Child Health.

Golfarb, L.A.; Brotherson, M.J.; Summers, J.A.; and Turnbull, A.P. *Meeting the Challenge of Disability or Chronic*

Illness—A Family Guide. Baltimore: Paul H. Brookes, 1986.

Hilgard, J.P., and LeBaron, S. *Hypnotherapy of Pain in Children with Cancer.* Los Altos, Calif.: William Kaufman, 1984.

Hill, R. *Families under Stress.* New York: Harper, 1949.

Hobbs, N., and Perrin, J. *Issues in the Care of Children with Chronic Illness.* San Francisco: Jossey-Bass, 1985.

Kaufman, J., and Lichtenstein, K.A. *The Family as Care Manager: Home Care Coordination for Medically Fragile Children*, prepared by George University Child Development Center for the Division of Maternal and Child Health under grant #MCJ-113368.

Littlehales, D.E., and Teyber, E.C. "Coping with Feelings: Seriously Ill Children, Their Families, and Hospital Staff." *Health and Social Work* 10 (1981):58–62.

Mattson, A. "Long-term Physical Illness in Childhood: A Challenge to Psychosocial Adaptation." *Pediatrics* 50 (1972):801–811.

McCollum, A.T. *The Chronically Ill Child.* New Haven, Conn.: Yale University Press, 1975.

McCubbin, H.I.; McCubbin, M.A.; Nevin, R.S.; and Cauble, E. *CHIP—Coping health inventory for parents.* Madison, Wis.: Family Stress, Coping, and Health Project, University of Wisconsin, 1983.

Mills, J.C., and Crowley, R.J. *Therapeutic Metaphors for Children and the Child Within.* NY; Brunner/Mazel, 1986.

McCubbin, H.I., and Patterson, J. *Systematic Assessment of Family Stress, Resources, and Coping.* St. Paul, Minn.: Family Social Science, 1981.

Mitchell, W., and Rizzo, S.J. The adolescent with special needs. In *Adolescents and Family Therapy*, edited by M.P. Mirkin and S.L. Koman. New York: Gardner Press, 1985.

Oaklander, V. *Windows to our Children.* Moab, Utah: Real People Press, 1978.

Powers, G.M.; Gaudet, L.M.; and Powers, S. "Coping Patterns of Parents of Chronically Ill Children." *Psychological Reports* 59 (1986):519–522.

Rimm, D.C., and Masters, J.C. *Behavior Therapy: Techniques and Empirical Findings.* New York: Academic Press, 1979.

Rowland, J.C. "Toward a Psychosocial Typology of Chronic and Life-threatening Illness." *Family Systems Medicine*, 2 (1984):245–262.

CHIP
Coping-Health Inventory
for Parents
Family Health Program
Hamilton I. McCubbin   Marilyn A. McCubbin
Robert S. Nevin   Elizabeth Cauble

PURPOSE

CHIP—The Coping-Health Inventory for Parents was developed to record what parents find helpful or not helpful to them in the management of family life when one or more of its members is ill for a brief period *or* has a medical condition which calls for continued medical care. Coping is defined as personal or collective (with other individuals, programs) efforts to manage the hardships associated with health problems in the family.

DIRECTIONS

- To complete this inventory you are asked to read the list of "Coping behaviors" below, one at a time.
- For each coping behavior you used, please record how helpful it was.
    HOW HELPFUL was this COPING BEHAVIOR to you and/or your family: Circle ONE number
    - 3 = *Extremely* Helpful
    - 2 = *Moderately* Helpful
    - 1 = *Minimally* Helpful
    - 0 = *Not* Helpful
- For each Coping Behavior you did *Not* use please record your "Reason."
    Please RECORD this by *Checking* ☑ one of the reasons:

    Chose not to use it   Not possible

    ☐   or   ☐

PLEASE BEGIN: Please read and record your decision for EACH and EVERY Coping Behavior listed below.

COMPUTER CODES: IID ☐☐☐☐   GID ☐☐☐   FAMID ☐☐☐☐

COPING BEHAVIORS

COPING BEHAVIORS	Extremely Helpful	Moderately Helpful	Minimally Helpful	Not Helpful	Chose Not To	Not Possible	F	S	M
1 Trying to maintain family stability	3	2	1	0	□	□	O		□
2 Engaging in relationships and friendships which help me to feel important and appreciated	3	2	1	0	□	□ 12	□	O	
3 Trusting my spouse (or former spouse) to help support me and my child(ren)	3	2	1	0	□	□	O	□	
4 Sleeping	3	2	1	0	□	□		O	□
5 Talking with the medical staff (nurses, social worker, etc.) when we visit the medical center	3	2	1	0	□	□		□	O
6 Believing that my child(ren) will get better*	3	2	1	0	□	□	O	□	
7 Working, outside employment	3	2	1	0	□	□	□	O	
8 Showing that I am strong	3	2	1	0	□	□	O		□
9 Purchasing gifts for myself and/or other family members	3	2	1	0	□	□	□	O	
10 Talking with other individuals/parents in my same situation	3	2	1	0	□	□		□	O
11 Taking good care of all the medical equipment at home	3	2	1	0	□	□	O		□
12 Eating	3	2	1	0	□	□		O	□
13 Getting other members of the family to help with chores and tasks at home	3	2	1	0	□	□	O	□	
14 Getting away by myself	3	2	1	0	□	□	□	O	
15 Talking with the Doctor about my concerns about my child(ren) with the medical condition*	3	2	1	0	□	□	□		O
16 Believing that the medical center/hospital has my family's best interest in mind	3	2	1	0	□	□	O	□	
17 Building close relationships with people	3	2	1	0	□	□	□	O	
18 Believing in God	3	2	1	0	□	□	O		□
19 Develop myself as a person	3	2	1	0	□	□	□	O	
20 Talking with other parents in the same type of situation and learning about their experiences	3	2	1	0	□	□		□	O
21 Doing things together as a family (involving all members of the family)	3	2	1	0	□	□	O	□	
22 Investing time and energy in my job	3	2	1	0	□	□		O	□
23 Believing that my child is getting the best medical care possible*	3	2	1	0	□	□ 34	O		□
24 Entertaining friends in our home	3	2	1	0	□	□ 35	□	O	
25 Reading about how other persons in my situation handle things	3	2	1	0	□	□		□	O
26 Doing things with family relatives	3	2	1	0	□	□	O	□	
27 Becoming more self-reliant and independent	3	2	1	0	□	□		O	□
28 Telling myself that I have many things I should be thankful for	3	2	1	0	□	□	O	□	
29 Concentrating on hobbies (art, music, jogging, etc.)	3	2	1	0	□	□	□	O	
30 Explaining our family situation to friends and neighbors so they will understand us	3	2	1	0	□	□		□	O
31 Encouraging child(ren) with medical condition to be more independent*	3	2	1	0	□	□	O	□	
32 Keeping myself in shape and well groomed	3	2	1	0	□	□		O	□
33 Involvement in social activities (parties, etc.) with friends	3	2	1	0	□	□	□	O	
34 Going out with my spouse on a regular basis	3	2	1	0	□	□	□	O	

COPING BEHAVIORS	Extremely Helpful	Moderately Helpful	Minimally Helpful	Not Helpful	I do not cope this way because: Chose Not To	Not Possible	For Computer Use Only F	S	M
35 Being sure prescribed medical treatments for child(ren) are carried out at home on a daily basis	3	2	1	0	□	□		□	○
36 Building a closer relationship with my spouse	3	2	1	0	□	□	○	□	
37 Allowing myself to get angry	3	2	1	0	□	□		○	□
38 Investing myself in my child(ren)	3	2	1	0	□	□	○		□
39 Talking to someone (not professional counselor/ doctor) about how I feel	3	2	1	0	□	□	□	○	
40 Reading more about the medical problem which concerns me	3	2	1	0	□	□		□	○
41 Talking over personal feelings and concerns with spouse	3	2	1	0	□	□	○	□	
42 Being able to get away from the home care tasks and responsibilities for some relief	3	2	1	0	□	□		○	□
43 Having my child with the medical condition seen at the clinic/hospital on a regular basis*	3	2	1	0	□	□	○	□	
44 Believing that things will always work out	3	2	1	0	□	□	○	□	
45 Doing things with my children	3	2	1	0	□	□	○		□

FAM □□58

SUP □□60

MED □□62

PLEASE Check all 45 items to be sure you have either circled a number or checked a box for each one. This is important.

*Related to the eigenvalue for statistical analysis. For more information about scoring, write to the Family Stress Coping and Health Project, 1300 Linden Drive, University of Wisconsin at Madison, Madison, WI 53706.

Source: © Hamilton I. McCubbin, 1983. Reprinted with permission from *Family Assessment Inventories for Research and Practice*, University of Wisconsin-Madison, 1987.

Chapter 20

Future Issues in Pediatric Home Care

Wendy Votroubek

Pediatric home care services have expanded within the past 5 to 10 years because of changes within the health care delivery system. Higher survival rates among children with chronic illnesses and congenital anomalies have caused hospitals to send children home who depend on medical equipment or extended nursing care. The Office of Technology Assessment has reported that on an annual basis 17,000 children depend on respirators or infusion therapy of drugs or nutrition; an additional 30,000 children need dialysis, cardiac monitoring, or treatment with high-technology equipment (Lutz 1987; U.S. Congress 1987).

Pediatric home care will continue to expand in the future. The cost savings of home care are unquestionable; home care for a ventilator-dependent child can save funding sources between $12,000 and $25,000 after 2 months of home care (Votroubek, 1987). Parents have also helped pediatric home care to expand. By requesting the option of home care as an alternative to long-term hospitalization for their technology-dependent child, parents are a major advocacy group for home care. Family interactions are a major component of the healing process when a child is cared for at home.

The future of pediatric home care depends on many factors. The issues raised from these factors will be critical to the status of pediatric home care and include alternative settings to home care, financing, the future of home care agencies, research and policy issues, and the long-term care of the population served by pediatric home care.

ALTERNATIVE SETTINGS TO HOME CARE

Caring for the child at home in the past has not always been appropriate because of acuity, cost, or family dynamics. The child and family have then needed assistance in the transition from hospital to home, or the child has needed to live in another institution for an extended or indefinite period of time. Economic forces in the future will continue to encourage home care for a medically needy and/or technology-dependent child as an alternative to long-term institutionalization. It is critical then that a variety of settings be available to the child and family that can provide alternatives to hospitalization or home care.

Alternative Programs: Professional Caregivers

Alternative settings of care must be available when the child cannot be cared for in the home. Institutions are not usually the first choice for placement for the technology-dependent or medically fragile child. They must, however, be an option when home care ceases to be feasible or is no longer the best option for the technology-dependent child, his or her family, or community and fiscal agencies (Michigan Department of Public Health 1984). Additional alternatives to be considered are pediatric nursing homes, foster homes, group homes, and programs that provide respite care training and transitional medical care between the hospital and home. The settings and methods may vary, but the goal for the child must be to be able to participate in a program that provides quality care by pediatric trained staff, allows family involvement, and includes age-appropriate stimulation and socialization.

Skilled Nursing Facilities

Skilled nursing facilities (SNFs) have been an important source of care for many elderly, chronically ill persons in the past but frequently have not had sufficient staff to provide intensive nursing care nor an environment conducive to pediatric care and child development (U.S. Congress 1987). Furthermore, many SNFs have not accepted technology-dependent children. SNFs for pediatric patients have been scarce. These institutions usually have had long waiting lists that have required the use of an intermediate-care facility. In the future, pediatric SNFs must be available because they are the least restrictive institutional setting of care.

Foster Care

Foster care has been used when families are unable to keep their medically fragile child at home. It has also been used as a transition between the hospital and home or as an extended respite for families who have been caring for their own child at home. Foster care provides adequately for the child, but it is not normally the first choice since the parents must relinquish custody of their child.

Technology-dependent children are usually harder to place in foster homes than other children. The U.S. federal government has provided matching subsidies with the states to families adopting special needs children and to families that provide foster care. Children under these programs are then automatically eligible for Medicaid, whereas normal eligibility criteria would apply if they remained with their biological parent.

The varied medical needs of some of the children placed in foster homes have resulted in programs that have used professional nurses as foster parents. Both registered nurses and licensed practical nurses are used for the "medical" foster homes and function similarly to other foster parents. The advantages to the nurse foster parent are apparent with the medically needy child. Nurses understand the underlying pathophysiology of the child's condition and are able to provide basic aspects of the child's care.

Incentives will be needed in the future to encourage foster families to care for the medically needy child in their home. Subsidies must continue to be available especially for nurses who have decided to become foster parents in lieu of other employment opportunities. In addition, nursing care must be available when the foster parents care for more than one medically needy child in the home, especially if one is a ventilator-dependent child.

Community Group Homes

The community group home has been another home care alternative. Many states regulate group homes in the same manner as foster homes. Group homes have been used in the past for developmentally disabled children and have recently begun to be used to provide alternative methods of care for the medically fragile child. However, group homes do not usually accept the technology-dependent child (U.S. Congress 1987).

Group homes are needed in the future to provide care for medically fragile children, including those who are ventilator dependent. Group homes are needed for the provision of transitional care between the hospital and home and as a respite for the family. Funding sources, especially those of the last resort, must be willing to pay for the child's care outside the traditional hospital or home setting.

Medical Day-care Programs

Medical day-care programs are another alternative to the traditional home care placement. Day-care programs provide ongoing medical care and socialization opportunities for the child while parents maintain employment. Many day-care programs also provide the family with instructions and skills necessary to care for their child at home.

Third-party reimbursement for medical day-care programs has been very poor. Most funding sources view the programs as additional care, not as a service in lieu of traditional hospital or home care. One program in Florida as been successful in getting third-party reimbursement (Pierce et al. 1987). In the future, many more opportunities for reimbursement and an increased number of available programs are needed to provide care for children whose parents are unable to provide for them 24 hours a day.

Alternative Programs: Nonprofessional Caregivers

Another alternative setting to home care is the use of nonprofessional caregivers. Although nonprofessional caregivers do not provide the same expertise as registered and licensed practical nurses, they can be used to provide respite to the child and family at a significant cost savings to the insurers.

Trained nurse's aides have been used to provide care for the medically needy, non-ventilator-dependent child. The type of children most frequently seen are those with a terminal illness, bronchopulmonary dysplasia, or developmental delay such as cerebral palsy.

Trained lay caregivers on the other hand have been used to provide ongoing home care for the clinically stable technology-dependent child. These motivated individuals, preferably relatives and/or neighbors, are designated at the time of discharge and trained in the care of the child and use of medical equipment. Their training and work is supervised by a registered nurse who is directly responsible for their actions, and their payment is generally in the same bracket as the trained nurse's aide. They are responsible for the total care required by the child.

Although this alternative can provide a cost savings to the insurers, it is not without problems. The issue of liability exists when technology-dependent children are cared for by nonprofessional caregivers. Reimbursement is another concern when nurse's aides are used. Most funding sources will pay only for skilled nursing care and will not consider payment of nurse's aides. Local funding sources may be more willing to pay for unlicensed care if decisions can be made at a local level.

As the number of children requiring a certain level of care at home increases, so will the need for alternative settings of home care and alter-

native caregivers. In the future additional programs will be necessary, the ones mentioned previously reflect those most likely to be available. As changes occur and alternatives are found, it is important to remember the child should be placed in the least restrictive environment surrounded by capable and caring adults.

LONG-TERM CARE

Long-term care is an important concern for medically needy children who require ongoing care. Because of the changing needs, as the patients reach adolescence and adulthood, home care may not be feasible. The medically needy young adult should not be expected to be dependent forever on the family as he or she ages nor should the patient be without an option for socialization with others who have similar needs.

American health policy makers and health workers have proposed the development of long-term care for the growing technology-dependent population that is based on their level of independence and medical needs. The programs include hospital-based home care programs, special apartment complexes for the disabled, and trained nurse's aides. Additional programs considered are group homes and teaching homes.

Group homes are one example of a program that could provide long-term care. The group home would house three to four semi-independent medically needy persons and one medically trained nonhandicapped person. The clients would receive assistance with their medical needs but would organize their own activities of daily living. Community involvement and assistance would be available through sheltered workshops or local employment opportunities.

Other arrangements would be necessary for those children requiring either more or less care. Group homes for those requiring continuous nursing assistance would have trained caregivers, either professional or nonprofessional, to manage the child's medical needs. This would be similar to a nursing facility but without the confines of an institution. Children with less acute needs could be housed in groups of 10 to 20. Minimal assistance would be required since these persons would be independent in most aspects of their care.

Teaching homes are an alternative that can provide intensive intervention to help the patient to achieve independence. They are residences where a small group with severe and profound handicaps live with staff members and receive ongoing training. The purpose is to teach the skills required to live independently in the community. Skills include self-care, independent living skills, and appropriate social behaviors (NICHCY 1986). Some persons stay in the teaching home for as long as 1 to 2 years and are then discharged to a community residence or similar setting. Teaching homes have been used for technology-dependent children and adults, but the concept is appropriate for easing the transition of these persons into the community.

The long-term care options for medically needy adolescents and adults often seem unobtainable because of the associated cost and the limited availability of public aid. Community programs, when feasible, are certainly less expensive than home care in a private residence. However, for those children who require continual medical supervision the options are limited and opportunities for major cost savings are almost nonexistent.

Public policy in the future must address this issue. Options for long-term care are limited, but the population is increasing in size. Because the population is not politically significant, professionals working with medically needy children, adolescents, and young adults need to be aware of their needs and advocate accordingly.

THE FUTURE OF HOME CARE AGENCIES

Competition to maintain market dominance in health care has brought new forces into ownership of home care agencies. Both freestanding and nonprofit home care agencies in the past were owned by local individuals or large corporations; within the past 5 to 10 years, hospitals, health maintenance organizations, (HMOs) and even non–health care entities have actively pursued the ownership and management of home care agencies. The ownership was accomplished in many ways: by one or more individuals with a local agency, by a franchise office of a large corporation, or by a branch office of a large company. The ownership could also be locally with a hospital or HMO or independent agency in a contractual arrangement with the hospital or HMO.

It is possible in the future that large private insurance companies and other insurers will also enter into the home health care market. Insurance companies with HMO and preferred provider components could purchase a national and/or local home care agency and/or durable medical equipment company to offer complete health care for the subscriber. This horizontal and vertical integration would provide a new source of revenue, be a less costly alternative to fixed rate payment, and provide a good management tool under prospective payment (O'Donnell 1987).

It is uncertain whether this type of expansion is feasible. It would require intense planning and reorganization. However, as reimbursement methods and technology growth continue to encourage less costly alternatives to inpatient hospitalization, it is possible the situation may change. Incentives to offer high-quality care may be lessened or disappear. Insurance companies, however, may increase their home health benefits and offer more comprehensive coverage to consumers to help provide alternatives.

THE FUTURE OF FINANCING

One of the most significant determinants in the quality of health care is its cost. Medically fragile children such as those appropriate for pediatric home care use greater amounts of health care and more costly services. This utilization pattern, combined with the inflation of health care costs, means that the lifetime maximum health insurance benefits are met early in the child's life. As benefits are exhausted and insurance companies refuse to increase them, the child's family is forced to exhaust savings, pensions, and other financial resources. The financial, emotional, and social burdens are enormous, and the gaps in financing must be addressed.

Home health care financing must be studied. Public policies in the 1980s provided new programs for funding pediatric home care including the Medicaid waiver and the Consolidated Omnibus Budget Reconciliation Act (COBRA). However, new programs will be required in the 1990s to continue financing home care for the medically needy child and reduce risk to both the family and provider. Many policy options have been outlined that address the problem of financing home health care for the medically needy child and family and include the following:

1. State-mandated high-risk pools. High risk pools provide health insurance for state residents unable to obtain adequate health insurance coverage from private insurers or HMOs due to current practices regarding certain mental or physical conditions (Leonard 1986). This option requires all insurers to establish a pool to provide comprehensive coverage at reasonable premium rates. Actual losses or profits are shared equally by the insurers participating in the pool (McManus et al. 1986). Premiums are 125 to 200 percent higher than other individual insurance policies offered in the state (Flint 1986).

2. State-financed catastrophic expense programs. These programs require the state to define a threshold catastrophic limit beyond which the state would become payor of last resort. The programs would be financed through general revenue funds and serve the uninsured as well as the underinsured who have exhausted their benefits (McManus et al. 1986).

3. State-mandated catastrophic health insurance. Coverage is available under this type of plan from individual insurers or through pooling arrangements designed to share risks and profits. Unlike the risk pooling concept, funds come from subscriber premiums with reimbursement available only after a prescribed threshold has been reached (McManus 1987).

4. Catastrophic health insurance is a very popular policy option. The likelihood, however, of children being included is questionable and depends on garnering necessary political support (McManus 1987).

POLICY AND RESEARCH RECOMMENDATIONS

The future of pediatric home care is dependent to a large extent on public policy issues and how they are implemented to provide for medically needy children. All policies should ensure family solidarity and provide care in the least restrictive environment (Caring Institute 1987).

Policy considerations for the future include long-term home care. Policy makers also will have to consider whether a classification system similar to the diagnosis related groups should be used with pediatric home care. Another consideration to be addressed is respite care. Respite care is available now, but with limited resources and limited hours of care. Respite care often can allow the parents to continue caring for their child at home. Although it raises the immediate cost of home care, it may lower the cost by insuring the family to provide ongoing care.

Research has many applications to help guide public policy planning and the future of home care. Much of the research conducted to date has centered on ventilator-dependent children. More research is needed to allow the successful expansion of home care and ensure quality care for the chronically ill child.

Issues to be addressed in the future include the following:

- Effectiveness of home care and development of appropriate outcome measures (Although some of this information is available, more information is needed on the long term effects of home care on the child and family.)

- Effects of various environments on the child and family, including home care, medical foster homes, group homes, and specialty programs

- Alternative site placement, caregiver programs, and/or long-term care for medically needy children and their families

- Efficacy of specialty home care programs for chronically ill children. Included in this are "tune ups" at home for cystic fibrosis patients, home care teaching programs for newly diagnosed diabetics, and hospice and home care programs for the terminally ill.

REFERENCES

Caring Institute. *The Crisis of Chronically Ill Children in America: Triumph of Technology—Failure of Public Policy.* Washington, D.C.: Foundation for Hospice and Home Care, March 23, 1987.

Flint S., ed. "Risk Pools for Chronically Ill Children." *Child Health Financing Report III*, no. 4 (1986):2–4.

Leonard, A. *A Guide to Health Care Coverage for the Child with a Chronic Illness of Disability.* Madison, Wis.: Center for Public Representation, 1986.

Lutz, S. "Technology Fueling Growth in Pediatric Home Care Programs." *Modern Health Care* 15(1987):60–63.

McManus, M. "Catastrophic Insurance Gains Momentum." *Child Health Financing Report* IV, no. 2(1987): 1–2.

McManus, M.; Newacheck, P.; and Matlin, N. "Catastrophic Childhood Illness." *Child Health Financing Report* III, no. 3(1986):1–2.

Michigan Department of Public Health, Division of Services to Crippled Children. *Guidelines for Homecare of Respondents, Task Force Report*, August 14, 1984.

National Information Center for Handicapped Children and Youth (NICHCY). "Community Based Living Arrangements." *News Digest*, April 1986:5.

O'Donnell, K. "Why are Many Hospitals Having Trouble with Home Healthcare?" *Health Industry Today*, February 1987:51–53.

Pierce, P.; Freedman, S.; and Reiss, J. "Prescribed Pediatric Extended Care (PPEC): A New Link in the Continuum." *Children's Health Care* 16(1987):55–59.

U.S. Congress, Office of Technology Assessment. *Technology-dependent Children: Hospital v. Home Care—A Technical Memorandum*. Washington, D.C.: U.S. Government Printing Office, May 1987.

Votroubek, W. "Cost Comparison for a Ventilator-Dependent Child." Tucson, Az: Medical Personnel Pool, 1987.

Appendix A

DIRECTORY OF RESOURCES

The following are organizations that professionals and families can use to obtain information and support. This list is not comprehensive. While providing many major sources of information, there are other national organizations that are not listed that also provide services. In addition, information and support can be obtained through local community agencies such as United Way organizations, local community agencies, church organizations, hospitals, and other community groups.

Advocacy and Financing

American Association for Continuity of Care
1101 Connecticut Avenue, N.W., Suite 700
Washington, DC 20036

Association for the Care of Children's Health
3615 Wisconsin Avenue, N.W.
Washington, DC 20016

Coordinating Center for Home and Community
 Care, Inc.
P.O. Box 613
Severn Professional Building
Millersville, MD 21108

Children's Defense Fund
122 C Street, N.W.
Washington, DC 20001

Disability Rights Center, Inc.
1346 Connecticut Avenue, N.W.
Washington, DC 20036

Health Care Case Management Division
Family Health and Habilitative Services, Inc.
5700 S.W. 34th Street, Suite 323
Gainesville, FL 32608

Federation for Children with Special Needs
312 Stuart Street
Boston, MA 02116

Health Care Financing Administration
Public Information
330 Independence Avenue, N.W., Room 4248
Washington, DC 20201

Make Today Count, Inc.
P.O. Box 303
Burlington, IA 52601
(for parents of seriously ill children)

National Association for Home Care
519 C Street, N.E.
Washington, DC 20002

National Center for Child Advocacy
P.O. Box 1182
Washington, DC 20013

National Center for Education in Maternal and
 Child Health
3520 Prospect Street, N.W.
Washington, DC 20057

National Information System for Health
  Related Services
University of South Carolina
1244 Blossom Street
Columbia, SC 29208

National Maternal and Child Health Resource
  Center
College of Law Building
The University of Iowa
Iowa City, IA 52242

Parentele
1301 E. 38th Street
Indianapolis, IN 46205
(for parents of children with handicaps)

Parents Helping Parents
47 Maro Drive
San Jose, CA 95127

Pathfinders
5000 W. 39th Street
Minneapolis, MN 55416

Sick Kids (Need) Involved People
216 Newport Drive
Severna Park, MD 21146

Vanderbilt University
Institute for Public Policy Studies
1208 18th Avenue South
Nashville, TN 37212

American Cancer Society
1599 Clifton Rd NE
Atlanta, GA 30329

Association for Brain Tumor Research
3725 Talman Avenue
Chicago, IL 60618

Cancer Information Clearinghouse
National Cancer Institute
Office of Cancer Communications
9000 Rockville Pike
Building 31, Room 10A-18
Bethesda, MD 20892

Children's Oncology Camps of America, Inc.
c/o Dr. Edward Baum, MD
2300 Children's Plaza
Chicago, IL 60614

Corporate Angels
Priscilla Blum
Westchester County Airport
Bldg #1
White Plains, NY 10604

Cancer Information Service
National Cancer Institute
9000 Rockville Pike
Building 31, Room 10A-19
Bethesda, MD 20205

Candlelighters Foundation
123 C Street, S.E.
Washington, DC 20003
(parents support for pediatric cancer)

International Association of Cancer Victims
  and Friends
7740 W. Manchester Avenue, #110
Playa Del Rey, CA 90291

Leukemia Society of America, Inc.
733 Third Avenue
New York, NY 10017

Make-A-Wish of America
2600 N. Central Avenue #936
Phoenix, AZ 85004

Ronald McDonald House Coordinator
c/o Golin Communications, Inc.
500 North Michigan Avenue
Chicago, IL 60614

Cardiac/Respiratory

American Academy of Allergy and
  Immunology
611 E. Wells Street
Milwaukee, WI 53202

American Heart Association
7320 Greenville Avenue
Dallas, TX 75231

American Lung Association
1740 Broadway
New York, NY 10019

Asthma and Allergy Foundation of America
19 W. 44th Street
New York, NY 10036

Cystic Fibrosis Association
6000 Executive Boulevard, Suite 309
Rockville, MD 20852

Mothers of Asthmatics
5316 Summit Drive
Fairfax, VA 22030

National Association for Sickle Cell Disease,
  Inc.
3460 Wilshire Boulevard, Suite 1012
Los Angeles, CA 90010

National Cystic Fibrosis Research Foundation
3379 Peachtree Road, N.E.
Atlanta, GA 30326

National Foundation for Asthma, Inc.
P.O. Box 30069
Tucson, AZ 85751

National Foundation for Sudden Infant Death,
  Inc.
1501 Broadway
New York, NY 10036

National Heart, Lung and Blood Institute
Building 31, Room 4A-21
9000 Rockville Pike
Bethesda, MD 20892

National Institute of Allergy and Infectious
  Disease
Building 31, Room 7A-32
9000 Rockville Pike
Bethesda, MD 20892

Sudden Infant Death Syndrome
3520 Prospect Street, N.W.
Washington, DC 20057

Endocrine/Diabetes

American Association of Diabetes Educators
500 North Michigan Avenue
Suite 1400
Chicago, IL 60611

American Diabetes Association
1660 Duke Street
P.O. Box 25757
Alexandria, VA 22313

Juvenile Diabetes Foundation, International
23 East 26th Street
New York, NY 10010

National American Diabetes Association
600 Fifth Avenue
New York, NY 10020

National Diabetes Information Clearinghouse
Box NDIC
Bethesda, MD 20205

Equipment and Supplies

Consumer Care Products, Inc.
6405 Paradise Lane
Sheboygan Falls, WI 53085

Toy Library Association
1800 Pickwick Avenue
Chicago, IL 60025

Toys-to-Go (trademark)
Children's Specialized Hospital
Mountainside, NJ 07091

Grief and Dying

Compassionate Friends
P.O. Box 1347
Oakbrook, IL 60521

Grief Institute
P.O. Box 623
Englewood, CA 80151

Hospice, Inc.
765 Prospect Street
New Haven, CT 06511

International Association for Near-Death
  Studies
University of Connecticut
Box U-20
Storrs, CT 06268

Shanti Project
890 Hayes Street
San Francisco, CA 94117

Society for the Right to Die
250 W. 57th Street
New York, NY 10107

Hematological Disorders

AIDS Information
U.S. Public Health Service
Hubert Humphrey Building, Room #721-H
200 Independence Avenue, S.W.
Washington, DC 20201
AIDS Hotline: 1-800-342-AIDS

AIDS Project Los Angeles, Inc.
7362 Santa Monica Blvd.
West Hollywood, CA 90046

Aplastic Anemia Foundation of America
P.O. Box 22689
Baltimore, MD 21203

Cooley's Anemia Foundation
105 E. 22nd Street
New York, NY 10017

Immune Deficiency Foundation
P.O. Box 586
Columbia, MD 21045

High Risk Infant

National Center for Clinical Infant Programs
733 15th Street, N.W.
Washington, DC 20005

International Council for Infant Survival
P.O. Box 3841
Davenport, IA 52808

Parents of Premature and High Risk Infants,
    International Inc.
33 West 42nd Street
New York, NY 10036

Premature Incorporated
10200 Old Katy Road, Suite 100
Houston, TX 77048

Learning Disabilities

Association for Children with Learning
    Disabilities
4156 Library Road
Pittsburgh, PA 15234

California Association for Neurologically
    Handicapped Children
645 Odin Drive
Pleasant Hill, CA 94523

Neuro-Developmental Treatment Association
P.O. Box 70
Oak Park, IL 60303

Mental/Neurological Disabilities

Administration on Developmental Disabilities
U.S. Department of Health and Human
    Services

Room 348F.5 HHH Building
200 Independence Avenue, S.W.
Washington, DC 20201

American Association on Mental Deficiency
5201 Connecticut Avenue, N.W.
Washington, DC 20015

Association for Retarded Citizens—National
    Headquarters
P.O. Box 6109
2501 Avenue J
Arlington, TX 76011

Council for Exceptional Children
    (Developmentally Delayed)
1411 Jefferson Davis Highway, Suite 900,
    Jefferson Plaza
Arlington, VA 22202

Developmental Disabilities Office
U.S. Department of Health and Human
    Services
200 Independence Avenue, S.W., Room 338E
Washington, DC 20201

Joseph P. Kennedy, Jr., Foundation
Suite 205
1701 K. Street, S.W.
Washington, DC 20006

National Aid to Retarded Citizens
2709 East Street
Arlington, TX 76011

National Association for Retarded Citizens
420 Lexington Avenue
New York, NY 10017

National Association for Retarded Citizens
209 Avenue E East
Arlington, TX 76011

National Center on the Rights of the Mentally
    Impaired
1600 20th Street, N.W.
Washington, DC 20009

National Head Injury Foundation, Inc.
P.O. Box 567
Framingham, MA 01701

National Institute of Neurological and
    Communicative Disorders and Strokes
Office of Scientific and Health Reports
Building 31, Room 8A-06
9000 Rockville Pike
Bethesda, MD 20892

Parents of Down Syndrome Children
11507 Yates Street
Silver Spring, MD 20902

President's Committee on Mental Retardation
Washington, DC 20201

Metabolic

The Oley Foundation for Home Parenteral and
Enteral Nutrition
214 Hun Memorial
Albany Medical Center
Albany, NY 12208

United Ostomy Association
1111 Wilshire Blvd.
Los Angeles, CA 90017

Miscellaneous Resources

American Burn Association
New York Hospital—Cornell Medical Center
525 E. 68th Street, Room F-758
New York, NY 10021

Arthritis Foundation
1314 Spring Street, N.W.
Atlanta, GA 30309

Arthritis Information Clearinghouse
P.O. Box 9782
Arlington, VA 22209

Epilepsy Foundation of America
4351 Garden City Drive
Landover, MD 20785

National Epilepsy League
6 N. Michigan Avenue
Chicago, IL 60602

National Genetics Foundation
555 West 57th Street
New York, NY 10019

National Kidney Foundation
116 E. 27th Street
New York, NY 10016

National Organization for Rare Disorders
P.O. Box 8923
New Fairfield, CT 06812

Tay-Sachs Prevention Program
Room 408
1015 Walnut Street
Philadelphia, PA 19107

Physical Disabilities

Association for the Care of Children in
Hospitals
3615 Wisconsin Avenue
Washington, DC 20016

Association for the Care of Children's Health
3615 Wisconsin Avenue
Washington, DC 200

Centers for Disease Control
Office of Public Inquiries
Birth Defects Branch
1600 Clifton Road, N.E.
Atlanta, GA 30330

Clearinghouse on the Handicapped
Office of Special Education and Rehabilitation
Services
Department of Education
Switzer Building, Room 3119-S
Washington, DC 20202

Closer Look
P.O. Box 1492
Washington, DC 20013
(resource for parents of children with
handicaps)

Coordinating Council for Handicapped
Children
407 S. Dearborn Street
Chicago, IL 60605

Federation for Children with Special Needs
312 Stuart Street, 2nd Floor
Boston, MA 02116

March of Dimes Birth Defects Foundation
1275 Mamaroneck Avenue
White Plains, NY 10605

Muscular Dystrophy Association of America,
Inc.
810 Seventh Street
New York, NY 10019

National Easter Seal Society
2023 W. Ogden Avenue
Chicago, IL 60612

National Information Center for the
Handicapped
Box 1492
Washington, DC 20013

National Center for Law and the Handicapped
University of Notre Dame
P.O. Box 477
South Bend, IN 46656

National Injury Information
5401 Westbard Avenue, Room 625
Washington, DC 20207

National Information Center for Handicapped
Children and Youth
P.O. Box 1492
Washington, DC 20013

National Office of Muscular Dystrophy
Association
810 Seventh Avenue
New York, NY 10019

National Paraplegia Foundation
333 N. Michigan Avenue
Chicago, IL 60601

National Rehabilitation Information Center
The Catholic University of America
4407 8th Street, N.E.
Washington, DC 20017

National Society for Crippled Children and
Adults
11 S. LaSalle
Chicago, IL 60603

National Spinal Cord Injury Foundation
369 Elliot Street
Newton Upper Falls, MA 02164

Office for Handicapped Individuals
330 Independence Avenue, S.W.
Washington, DC 20201

President's Committee on Employment of the
Handicapped
1111 20th Street, N.W.
6th Floor
Washington, DC 20036

Rehabilitation Services Administration Office
of Special Education and Rehabilitative
Services
Switzen Building
330 C. Street, S.W.
Washington, DC 20202

Spina Bifida Association of America
343 S. Dearborn Street
Chicago, IL 60604

United Cerebral Palsy
66 E. 34th Street
New York, NY 10016

Sensory

Alexander Graham Bell Association for the
Deaf
3417 Volta Place, N.W.
Washington, DC 20007

American Council of the Blind
Suite 506
1211 Connecticut Avenue, N.W.
Washington, DC 20036

American Foundation for the Blind
15 W. 16th Street
New York, NY 10011

American Speech and Hearing Association
10801 Rockville Pike
Rockville, MD 20852

Association for the Visually Handicapped
1839 Frankfort Avenue
Louisville, KY 40206

International Association of Parents of the
Deaf
814 Thayer Avenue
Silver Spring, MD 20910

The National Association for Hearing and
Speech Action
6110 Executive Boulevard
Suite 1000
Rockville, MD 20852

National Association for the Visually
Handicapped
305 East 24th Street, Room 17-C
New York, NY 10010

National Information Center on Deafness
Gallaudet University
7th and Florida Avenue, N.E.
Washington, DC 20002

National Library Service for the Blind and
Physically Handicapped
The Library of Congress
Washington, DC 20442

National Society for Autistic Children
169 Tampa Avenue
Albany, NY 12208

Index

Page numbers in *italics* refer to exhibits, figures, and tables in, or footnotes to, the text.

About the Editors

Patricia A. McCoy, RN, MS, MBA, attended Madison General Hospital School of Nursing in Madison, Wisconsin. She received her BSN and MS in Nursing from the University of Wisconsin in Madison. The MBA was awarded from Fairleigh Dickenson University in Rutherford, New Jersey. She has several years of clinical and management experience in pediatric and neonatal intensive care systems. In addition, she provided clinical expertise for pediatric home care programs in Madison, Wisconsin, and Tucson, Arizona. She has published for *Caring Magazine* and has been a featured lecturer on discharge planning for the pediatric ventilator-dependent patient.

Ms. McCoy is currently the Director of Quality Assurance at the 20 Tactical Fighter Wing Hospital of RAF Upper Heyford, England. In addition, she is a Visiting Fellow in Nursing Management and Quality Assurance for the International Management Center, England. As a consultant, she is lecturing throughout the United Kingdom on health care management, nursing management, and quality assurance. She has published several articles regarding these subjects in Great Britain.

Wendy Votroubek, RN, MPH, received her nursing degrees from Long Beach City College and California State University at Long Beach. The MPH was awarded from the University of North Carolina at Chapel Hill with a specialty in maternal and child health. She has lectured numerous times on pediatric home care on a national, state, and local level. She has also published an article in *Caring Magazine* on discharge planning for the ventilator-dependent child. She has many years of experience in pediatric home care, including direct patient care and management.

Ms. Votroubek is currently the Pediatric Pulmonary Clinical Nurse Specialist for the Arizona Health Sciences Center in Tucson, Arizona. She was working for Medical Personnel Pool, Inc. as the Pediatric Home Care Supervisor when editing this book. She has developed standards of care for pediatric home care, a diabetic home care program for newly diagnosed juvenile diabetics, and a cystic fibrosis home care program for patients with cystic fibrosis. She was a member of the American Thoracic Society, Pediatric Pulmonary Section Task force to develop standards for home care for children with chronic respiratory conditions.